What the Rest
Think of the West

What the Rest Think of the West

Since 600 AD

———

Selected and with commentary by

Laura Nader

中

UNIVERSITY OF CALIFORNIA PRESS

University of California Press, one of the most distinguished university presses in the United States, enriches lives around the world by advancing scholarship in the humanities, social sciences, and natural sciences. Its activities are supported by the UC Press Foundation and by philanthropic contributions from individuals and institutions. For more information, visit www.ucpress.edu.

University of California Press
Oakland, California

Library of Congress Cataloging-in-Publication Data

What the rest think of the West : since 600 AD / selected and with commentary by Laura Nader.
    p.   cm.
Includes bibliographical references and index.
ISBN 978-0-520-28577-4 (cloth : alk. paper)
ISBN 978-0-520-28578-1 (pbk. : alk. paper)
ISBN 978-0-520-96116-6 (ebook)
1. Civilization, Western—Public opinion.   2. United States—Civiliza-
tion—Foreign public opinion.   3. United States—History—Foreign public
opinion.   4. Public opinion—Middle East.   5. Public opinion—
China.   6. Public opinion—India.   7. Public opinion—Japan.   I. Nader,
Laura, editor.
  CB245.W513   2015
  909′.09821—dc23

                                          2015001144

24   23   22   21   20   19   18   17   16   15
10   9   8   7   6   5   4   3   2   1

In memory of my brother Shafeek Nader—visionary

CONTENTS

Euro-American observations of Asian, African, Oceanic, and New World societies have had a privileged place in the anthropological canon. Class readings rarely include outsider observations on the United States, for example. Even non-Western anthropology students in Western universities rarely conduct fieldwork in the West, and anthropologists of countries such as Brazil, Mexico, and India overwhelmingly prefer to study their own people. This pattern holds in allied disciplines, leaving the impression that non-Western observers have had little to say about the West. Yet civilizations and their arcs are not simple, nor are they easily crammed into short time frames. We might take a longer and broader view by studying the work of non-Western scholars and travelers commenting on what they define as "West." Call them the Rest. Thus the motivation for this book.

As a collection, the readings initially constituted a syllabus for a graduate seminar that I taught in the late 1980s called Orientalism, Occidentalism, and Control. The seminar was conceived partly in response to Edward Said's *Orientalism,* a treatise about European writing about the Orient. For Said, European representations of the Orient as lesser made an extraordinarily powerful mode of control. In his book, Said noted that Occidentalism was not comparable to Orientalism because of evident power differentials; he was writing in the context of what he describes as Western encroachment and European settler colonization in Palestine, followed by Israeli-Arab wars. Yet power differentials are no reason to ignore Occidentalism or occidentalisms.

Over many centuries power differentials change, as implied in the title of Stewart Gordon's "When Asia Was the World" (2008) and as recognized in contemporary reporting on the current rise of China and India and the challenge they pose to Western hegemony. I was moved to extend Said's time dimension, to take a broader historical approach that would include powerful configurations from past centuries, even in the face of power differentials.

The seminar eventually morphed into the graduate seminar "Occidentalism and Control," as well as forming the core of an undergraduate course, "Comparative Society." Thus, first and foremost, the selections here reflect centuries of the Rest—writers of various languages, traditions, religions, and ethnicities—describing and creating representations of their corresponding West from 600 AD to 2012. For a general audience, this collection is meant to be a corrective both to the popular view of "civilizations" as monolithic units and to oversimplified local relativism—which is not to deny local knowledge or core states self-described as civilizations. If nothing else, history is by definition dynamic and malleable. Relating only the dominant perspectives of each time period obscures and rigidifies history. Ironically, the Rest's comments on the West's excessive materialism have recently come full circle, as described in "How India Became America" (Akash Kapur in the *New York Times*, March 9, 2012). Gandhi was already writing about such issues as early as 1909 (see Gandhi's writings in these selections).

The selections included here also commonly imply *translations* of representations—something I had no control over. Some translations were worth waiting for, such as Rifa'ah Al-Tahtawi's study on Paris, first published in 1836 and not translated into English until 2004, or Ahmed Faris Al-Shidyaq, whose prolific early-nineteenth-century Arabic writings on parts of the Mediterranean and Europe appeared in English only in 2013. Much, of course, can also be lost in translation, especially when the work deals with sensitive contemporary issues. And some references written about European Americans, such as *The Japan That Can Say No* (1991), were never intended for translation, causing uproar when translated without permission.

Another hurdle for the project was identified by students. Many of those who wrote about a "West" were travelers, merchants, missionaries, musicians, diplomats, poets, even cartoonists, among others; they were also all elites. Their descriptions could not have represented people from working or lower feudal classes because they had to be literate in order to record their observations, and in many cases they were highly literate.

Students also asked why only four "civilizations" were to be included in the book? Why leave out Africa and indigenous people elsewhere? For example, they argued, I could include observations from Aztec, Mayan, or Incan civilizations. And what about the "lesser civilizations" in Southeast Asia, for example? Good point. The overall strategy implied by my choices was to reflect major contemporary power configurations. Euro-American exceptionalism generally assumes the West's lasting presence and positional superiority, even though China and India are on the rise. This had to be addressed: other "civilizations" still exist today and they also consider themselves exceptional! As for other voices, there are indeed many writers from Africa and the Americas who have published perceptive accounts of "the West," and they might be productively brought together, just not in this volume. In addition, some civilizations collapsed, their records were destroyed, or their demise came early. It is difficult to assemble this type of material.

A final comment on the selection process. Due to space considerations, the pieces included here are excerpts, not complete works. They are meant to entice the reader to know more from these observers, many of whom have published books. The texts are not interpretations or summaries of writings. They are written by Christian, Islamic, Hindu, Buddhist, and secular authors. Beyond the immediate practical issues of length, as with any selection, there are personal biases. Mine include the belief that looking in the mirror—seeing ourselves as others see us—is a catalyst for discovery, as well as the felt need to reduce hubris in a world that is increasingly one world, to see Samuel Huntington's "clash of civilizations" (1996) as—in Said's words—a clash of ignorance. And although I am aware that those who suffer from hubris and provincialism are the least likely to seek out such readings, there are many who do seek discovery—of others, of themselves, and of *Homo sapiens* writ large. Having witnessed colleagues express surprise that "the Other is *not* mute," and never has been, and having enjoyed responses from audiences of all ages and professions to some of the startling observations that follow, I am encouraged to finally share the work with my contemporary literates—that they may engage with very different past worldviews (that are not so past) in order to understand the contemporary world.

ACKNOWLEDGMENTS

A project that develops over decades has a number of institutions and people to acknowledge. Initial support for this work came from a seed grant from the Committee on Research at the University of California, Berkeley, followed by several small grants from the Center for Middle Eastern Studies, also at UC Berkeley, in 1991 and 2001. In October 1991, I had a several-weeks visit at the Library of Congress in Washington, D.C. Prosser Gifford made arrangements for me to meet with area librarians, who informed me of relevant collections and of specific authors, namely George Atyieh, Hisao Matsumoto, Chi Wang, and Allen Thrasher. Colleagues have also been helpful at key moments: Andrew Gunder Frank, Sandra Naddaff, Talal Asad, Edward Said, Ashraf Ghani, Nikkie Keddie, Lawrence Cohen, Gerald Berreman, Linda Hess, Liu Xin, Ellen Hertz, Junko Habu, and Beth Berry. Also key were students specializing in one or another of the areas covered in the selections: Ayfer Bartu, Mayssun Sukarieh, Monica Eppinger, Dina Omar, Chris Hebdon, Yalda Asmatey, Melissa Macauley, Tim Fuson, Roberto Gonzalez, and countless other students who since 1990 have participated in my seminars. In particular, Ayfer Bartu, Alana Sheldon, and Hallie Wells were involved at different stages in the process of completing the manuscript, and Aurora Feeney-Kleinfeldt, in helping with the final details. Tarek Milleron, always careful with detail, helped edit the materials, and Bill Nelson was the mapmaker. Suzanne Calpestri and Kathleen Gallager in the Anthropology Library were helpful beyond the call of duty, and Kathleen Van Sickle was always ready to rescue when the need arose. At the University of California Press I especially thank Reed Malcolm for his critical interest and professional support, as well as his assistant, Stacy Eisenstark, for her attention to the details of publication. All in all, the work was collaborative, which includes the anonymous reviewers as well as Erik Harms for their penetrating comments and wise advice. However, most gratitude goes to authors who from 600 AD to the present shared their observations with a long line of interested readers.

Introduction

Comparative Consciousness

The volume of European and American writings about the rest of the world is vast and widely read. By contrast, most people educated in Western universities are largely ignorant of the body of literature written by other peoples about both Europeans and Americans. Americans were less ethnocentric after World War II than now, when exceptionalism and cultural entitlement penetrate politics. This is so even though Euro-Americans are involved in unilateral interventions in the Islamic world—in Afghanistan, Iraq, Yemen, Somalia, Libya, Western Africa—all part of the War on Terror, and despite our current foreign trade policy that focuses on Asia, and in particular on China. In our current moment, the historical anthropological perspective adds to a salutary decentering of popular narratives. The readings in this book speak to Orientalism, Eurocentrism, American exceptionalism, and cosmopolitanism, and open up our thinking about intercultural communication.

Even before I became an anthropologist, my fascination with the gaze on the Other was always marred by the absence of a return gaze, whether I was looking at *National Geographic* or some other magazine. To look without being looked at was somehow unnatural or maybe even deceitful—or so it seemed in some unconscious awareness. That unexamined awareness was only a sleeping observation until I came across Carleton Coon's *General Reader in Anthropology* (1948) while in graduate school. In his volume, Coon included observations that travelers had about Western peoples as well as Euro-American observations about the Other. Yet for the most part my consciousness would slip back into dormancy, only to reappear now and then. For example, when I carried out my first fieldwork among the Zapotec peoples of southern Mexico, Zapotec friends would accompany me to

Oaxaca City for their first visit and participate in life in the local restaurants and hotels. They commented on the dirtiness as they moved about the city and, in a manner totally unself-conscious, asked how to use tableware. For them it was first contact. For me it was a rare chance to see first contact. When, decades later, a Zapotec elder and his wife visited Berkeley, they would comment daily on what they saw as different—for example, noticing the lack of sociability among couples dining together, or delighting over the bathtub, a thing they had previously only heard about.

Among anthropologists the issue of comparative consciousness or reciprocal viewing was addressed in the 1970s, but only partially. Anthropologists began to speak about many voices, or multivocality, and separated the anthropologist's voice from the many voices speaking to and about him or her. Non-Western anthropologists began to speak about and to Western anthropologists. Yet the gaze was not truly reciprocal. Too few anthropologists (or anybody else, for that matter) were studying the West or even Third World locales other than their own. Once in a while an intellectual would revolt, as in *Los Hijos de Jones,* by a Mexican economist, an imagined study of an American Park Avenue family as a way to comment on Oscar Lewis's *The Children of Sánchez,* a study some Mexican intellectuals thought was outrageous or just disrespectful.

One might have expected to find greater sensitivity in feminist literature, or some reflective critical awareness to surface as Western women gazed upon the Other, but they looked for no return gaze. In studies of Middle Eastern women, I thought a return gaze might be noticed, especially after I attended a conference on family and kinship in the Middle East, during which a researcher reported that an Egyptian religious figure on television regularly used Euro-American observations about Western women to persuade Muslim women of their comparative advantages over the West. For example, the cleric said that European women were disrespected by their menfolk in arenas as disparate as sexuality, naming after marriage, inheritance, and equal pay. The gaze might be returned, but feminist scholars simply do not acknowledge, let alone incorporate, that gaze in a comparison of what we regularly find in the Western popular media.

For some years I worked on an idea stimulated by that conference encounter and the many previous encounters of mirrored images. For each cultural observation I would ask, "As compared to what?" The result was "Orientalism, Occidentalism, and the Control of Women" (1989), an article in which I sought to discover the means by which women both of the "Orient" and of the "Occident" (reflecting two different patriarchies) were controlled through the exercise of male dogmas in each society, both pointing a finger at the other without looking in the mirror. These two civilizations, one Islamic and one Western, have carried on a conversation about the status of women, though it has not been analyzed as control over women in *both* civilizations. Reviewers of my paper were clearly uncomfortable with a return gaze, as they were in spades when Edward Said's *Orientalism* (1978) appeared. In my case, a variety of pretenses disallowed publication in the United States: it was written in nonacademic style, it was a defense of Islamic women, it was wrong, and so forth. The article was immediately accepted for publication by an enlightened editor in Belgium, where earlier pointed criticisms were not made by the journal editor or peer reviewers. In response to the article after publication, many acknowledged it in their own articles, and some European journals reprinted it. A comparative consciousness is probably a universal characteristic of human thinking, but the comparison is often implicit. In a procedure thought to be more scientific, we focus on the object of study, forgetting about the eye that sees and the subjectivity embedded in knowledge production.

The need for exchange is clear. A comparative consciousness is necessary for understanding, for writing good science, for avoiding international misunderstanding, for fostering mutual respect, indeed for cultivating all that is required if we are to live together peaceably on this planet with our differences. As noted earlier, "Orientalism, Occidentalism, and Control" was the seminar I led about five extant civilizations—Chinese, Japanese, Indian, Islamic, and the youngest of all, Western civilization—and how they speak about one another—as in, *They have technology but no civilization,* or *They have spirituality but no development.* Peoples from these civilizations all see their worlds in the present rather than as buried in some past era. A contemporary stance was all the more imperative because Euro-Americans regularly recognize the other four as past civilizations or as passé (in need of development), though China is the largest mass of humanity and one of the oldest continuous civilizations.

A word about the anthropological use of the term *civilization* is necessary at this point. A. L. Kroeber (1947), when he was the dean of American anthropology, spoke of the beginnings of human civilization starting with the fossil record. Thus, for Kroeber, to be *Homo sapiens* is to be civilized. He also noted that civilization advances because it tends by nature to be cumulative. But, he asked, will the admission of a mere swelling of bulk satisfy those who wish to believe in progress? noting that it is pleasant to believe that one's time and ways are superior. Later, University of Chicago archaeologist Robert Braidwood (1957) clarified the meaning of the term in a manner that did not presuppose superiority over other means of human organization such as hunting and gathering or subsistence agriculture. For Braidwood and other anthropologists, a "civilization" (the term not implying superiority) is characterized by writing, a well-developed division of labor as a result of the production of surplus that enabled the development of specialization and specialists, and the practice of arts and sciences. It is in the simultaneous presence of those components that the essence of mirrored complexities among civilizations is configured. Although "civilizations" may appear to some people as independent entities, they are not. Diffusion and borrowing have always been commonplace worldwide, critical to cumulative development and innovation—configurations of cultural growth as Kroeber (1947) put it. Recognizing the diffusion of ideas and material techniques means that there are no strict boundaries between Chinese science, Indian science, and Islamic science, or between these and European science, for that matter. Eric Wolf, in *Europe and the People without History* (1982), reminded us, "The more ethnohistory we know, the more clearly 'their' history and 'our' history emerge as part of the same history" (19). Contrary to Huntington's clash of civilizations, humans have been borrowing from each other since the beginning. According to Kroeber and others, however, all specialized divisions of labor so characteristic of large configurations inevitably take on an impersonal character (Kroeber 1947, 282). Literacy, for example, is related to conditions of alienation, but Kroeber was not a unidirectionalist. He noted that reversals in history have resulted from collapse of large states and the extinction of material cultures. Freud wrote about "civilization and its discontents," and Durkheim highlighted the problem of social order with attention to anomie. Any thoughtful analysis of "civilization" must attend to its critical failures as well as its triumphs. In this respect, the Middle East is a prime example, and subject matter for interested archaeologists and historians.

In thinking about how to organize the materials for this reader, I came to avoid binding it to a strict time line, because interaction appeared at different times, as readers will readily acknowledge. Although four periods of human contact seemed possible (first contact, colonial period, postcolonial, and contemporary), not all of the civilizations experienced Western colonization. China and Japan did not. Islamic and Hindu entities were heavily colonized, and all experienced periods of Western militarism and imperialism. Both China and Japan were parties to "unequal treaties" in the nineteenth century.

Although clear linguistic terms indicate that the sun rises in the East and sets in the West, and although most societies have a term for "West," it is not always obvious what reference to the West or Westerners means in the case of each locale. For the Chinese Buddhist Kuanzang (or Hiuen Tsiang), West was India and places beyond. For Al-Tahtawi, it meant traveling through the Mediterranean Sea to Marseille and then Paris. For some nineteenth-century Chinese travelers, West was the United States. For the twentieth-century Turkish sisters Zeyneb and Melek Hanoum, traveling west meant traveling to Europe.

So what is meant by *West*? For the Arab Ibn Fadlan in 921–922, the term might have meant going north and west across the Caspian Sea into southern Russia and meeting up with the Vikings. Clearly, for contemporary peoples *West* is not always meant to indicate geographic location. For Rudyard Kipling in 1889, the truism "East is East and West is West and never the twain shall meet" referred to both different physiognomies and different configurations of Occidental and Asiatic civilizations. With European colonizations, *West* came to mean what we now know as Euro-American. Europeans, at least since de Tocqueville's two-volume study

Democracy in America (2003 [1836]), have considered the United States "the extreme West." Even Californians refer to East Asia and the West Indies. Undoubtedly *the West* as a cultural term reflected not so much ideas about places and geography as a construction of European origin years in the making, as Stuart Hall argues in "The West and the Rest: Discourse and Power" (1996). For Hall the West is a historical construct, and its meanings change over time, as N. Keddie (1972) also observes in "Is There a Middle East?" Levant, Orient, Near East, Far East, Middle East . . . The definitions of such terms change with different periods. One of the outcomes of such regional distinctions has been to study an area as bounded, cut off from the rest of the world. Nothing could be further from reality, as J. Abu-Lughod (1989) points out in her description of trade routes prior to European hegemony.

The authors of the pieces included here represent a variety of people from places we may for present purposes call East (or various subparts of the East): missionaries, travelers, explorers, musicians, diplomats, political figures, corporate executives, cartoonists, academic intellectuals, and just plain folks. Although most are members of elite groups, they all have some things in common: they are all literate and are commenting on a West or Westerners. Sometimes what they see is exotic, sometimes barbaric or threatening, worthy of emulation, or all of those things. Their writing has had an impact in their home countries, often lasting centuries. Sometimes, as with Mirza Abu Taleb Khan, they see complementarity rather than equality between men and women. Khan analyzes how the social circumstances of Europe and Asia logically led to different norms regarding the customs of women in different countries—an illustration of the types of findings noted by outside observers.

Although all of the authors traveled West and commented on people and places, their purposes vary widely, depending on whether they represent a constituency— for example, a government, trading partners, a colonial liberation movement, a student mission, an exile group—or are simply writing a personal commentary or intellectually professing, and depending on whether this is their first contact or not, and whether the piece is a response to happenings in their own culture or the one they are observing. Widely influential in their home countries in their time, these writings will at least make visible to readers many aspects of life that today are too often invisible to those who view the world through a lens of exceptionalism or simplified conceptions of difference—stereotyping. Reading these selections heightens a sensitivity, a curiosity, an awareness of being one player among many worldwide, and of being seen differently depending on who is observing. Europeans see Americans as egalitarian but racist, and the Chinese comment on American inequality. Different conclusions result from different travelers' observations, as with Ibn Fadlan on cleanliness and modesty among the Vikings, or "the negro problem" that caught the attention of Chinese visitors to the United States. The same variation is true in commentaries on the family, women, the treatment of the elderly, Western dinner parties, culinary habits, modes of dress, bragging, and hypocrisy. What most travelers do agree on, however, is the primacy of technology in the West—in all its variety from wondrous to menacing. Whereas Rifaʿah Al-Tahtawi discussed the technological and scientific advancements of the French in the first half of the nineteenth century, Mohandas Gandhi, writing at the beginning of the twentieth century, regrets materialism in all its forms. In contrast, the authors of *The Japan That Can Say No* use Japan's technological advancement as a sign of social and cultural parity with the West. When it is the reader's society that is being observed and written about, the descriptions are a reminder that the powerful in this era might not always be so. Western colonialism flourished at one point, then morphed or subsided.

Some of these writings reflect their authors' prejudices or have been adjudged misrepresentations. Awareness of underlying general assumptions includes self-reflexive emphasis as well as antagonisms. "We are all human" is a phrase often uttered by Middle Easterners in Western contexts. The very titles of some of their books are informative: *India Speaks to America* (1966), *The Japanese Discovery of Europe* (1969), *The Crusades through Arab Eyes* (1984), *Land without Ghosts* (1989), or *The Japan That Can Say No* (1989). Vine Deloria Jr.'s title, writing from the point of view of Native Americans, sums it up bluntly: *We Talk, You Listen* (1970). In his inaugural address at St. Andrews, John Stuart Mill put it this way: "Without knowing the language of a people, we never really know their thoughts, their feelings, and their type of character: and unless we do possess this knowledge, of some other people than ourselves, we remain, to the hour of our death, with our intellects only half expanded."

World historian Stewart Gordon (2008) observes that "the Asian world noticed and commented on itself—a self-consciousness not yet typical of Europe" (188). He outlines configurations that might explain this missing trait—trading communities, institutions that made it easy for men to move long distances for employment positions, the religious calling for priests and religious teachers. But above all, trade mattered—and the absence of states with strict boundaries, I might add. Sharp contrasts between Orientalism and Occidentalism are an anachronism from the nineteenth century, but nevertheless reflect a formulaic linguistic distinction still influencing thinking people. The most perceptive authors are those who see themselves in the mirror. When Zeyneb Hanoum went to Europe, she reported on "a double sensation, the one of coming face to face with the reality, and the other, the effort of driving from my mind the remembrance of what I expected to find" (Hanoum 1913:237). Zeyneb argued that her position as an outsider to European culture made it possible for her to understand the condition of European women; she felt that she was too close to Turkish women to comment on them (215).

Subjectivity and objectivity are related types of reasoning on a spectrum. Mirza Abu Taleb Khan maintains a balance between objectivity and subjectivity in his analysis of both the vices and virtues of the English. In such writings as Khan's, objectivity and subjectivity exist concurrently, the author often using them as analytical devices, inserting critical commentary between objective, neutral descriptions of their observations. Objectivity and subjectivity intermingle when the writer uses metaphors to describe things new to him or her as related to things familiar: railways are iron roads, parliaments are fish markets, and for the early Japanese traveler in the United States, presidents are elected by auction. The observer's understanding of the world shapes his or her views of the unfamiliar. Al-Jabarti is often referred to as the greatest Arab historian because he was objective and maintained neutrality. He wrote like an eyewitness, covering events of Napoleon's invasion of Egypt. But then, Al-Jabarti was not a traveler. He was at home in Egypt, anchored in the there-and-then of actions around him.

In *What the Rest Think of the West,* Occidentalism is not a mirror image to Orientalism. No such academic hegemony comes from the East. On the other hand, the travelers' reports strengthen the dynamic aspects of cultural interactions and the historical perspectives as they persist or change, not by passive responses from the Rest to the West but rather with agency, both personal and cultural. If Gandhi's writings are different from the others, it is because he is not writing about another place as he experiences it, but is giving an opinion on that civilization for India after contemplating his experiences. His is a challenge to the positional superiority of the imperialistic West based on material wealth.

What the accounts in this volume do describe is a sense of the relationship between two groups from one observer's point of view. Biases and stereotypes in the accounts remind us that there is an element of distortion in *all* representations. As long as one thinks of truth as a faithful correspondence between representation and reality, one may find these selections maddening or easily dismissed. But Said would argue that one cannot think of truth outside of history, and thus reading these selections enables one to take a critical perspective through a variety of lenses. Rather than one Occidentalism, we have multiple occidentalisms, moving us closer to context and history, and to understanding that actions often bear on prior actions and that there is no encounter in which power steps aside.

While perusing these occidentalisms, readers may grasp that the specifics of particular circumstances matter a good deal. Generalizations and stereotypes are part and parcel of human interactions, but we can keep their limits in mind. This collection might therefore be thought of as a means to a kind of self-discovery. To understand new things, we have to describe them in words we already know, to look in terms of other things we already understand, and these encounters may in turn inspire us to reconsider what we think we know. As the Scottish poet Robert Burns put it, "O would some Power the small gift give us / to see ourselves as others see us!" His challenge was to know ourselves better by a look in the mirror.

REFERENCES

Abu-Lughod, Janet. 1989. *Before European Hegemony.* Cambridge: Oxford University Press.

Braidwood, Robert J. 1957. *Prehistoric Men.* Chicago: Chicago Natural History Museum.

Burns, Robert. 1786. "To a Louse, on Seeing One on a Lady's Bonnet at Church."

Coon, Carleton. 1948. *A Reader in Cultural Anthropology.* Huntington, NY: R. E. Krieger.

Deloria Jr., Vine. 1970. *We Talk, You Listen.* New York: Delta Press.

De Tocqueville, Alexis. 2003 [1836]. *Democracy in America.* New York: Penguin Classics.

Gordon, Stewart. 2009. *When Asia Was the World: Traveling Merchants, Scholars, Warriors, and Monks Who Created the "Riches of the East."* Boston: Da Capo Press.

Hall, Stuart. 1996. "The West and the Rest: Discourse and Power." In *Modernity: An Introduction to Modern Societies.* Stuart Hall, David Held, Don Hubert, and Kenneth Thompson, eds. New York: Wiley-Blackwell. Pp. 184–228.

Keddie, Nikki. 1972. *Sayyid Jamal Ad-Din "Al-Afghani": A Political Biography.* Berkeley: University of California Press.

Kipling, Rudyard. 1889. "The Ballad of East and West." *Pioneer.* December 2, 1889.

Kroeber, A. L. 1947. *Configurations of Culture Growth.* Berkeley: University of California Press.

Lewis, Oscar. 1961. *The Children of Sánchez: Autobiography of a Mexican Family.* New York: Random House.

Nader, Laura. 1989. "Orientalism, Occidentalism and the Control of Women." *Cultural Dynamics,* Vol. 2, No. 3, pp. 323–355.

Urquidi, Victor L. 1969. *Los Hijos de Jones.* Austin: Instituto de Estudios Latinoamericanos, Universidad de Texas.

Wolf, Eric R. 1982. *Europe and the People without History.* Berkeley: University of California Press.

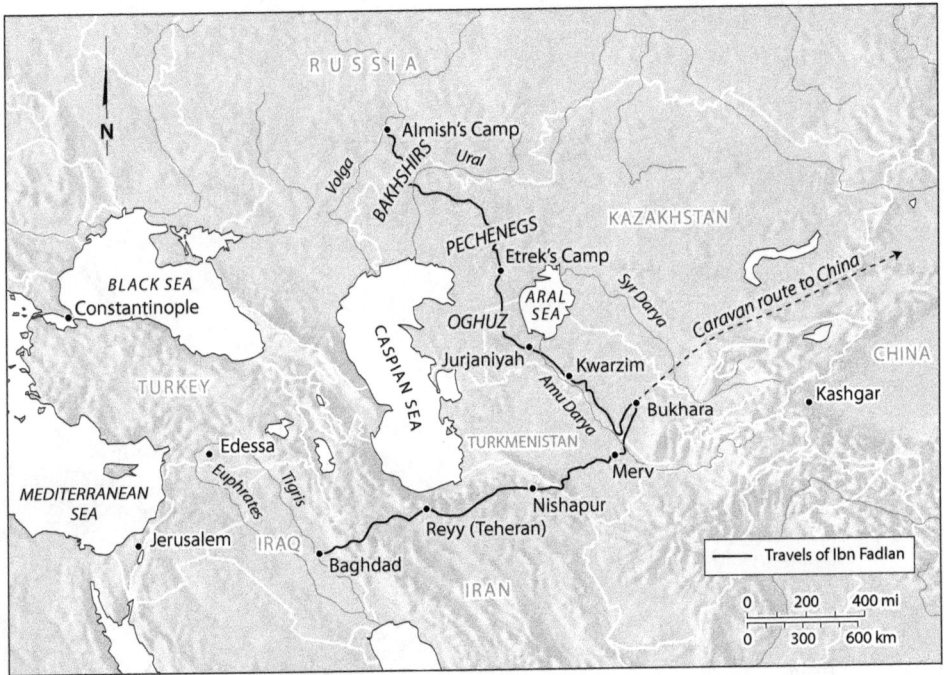

MAP 1. Travels of Ibn Fadlan.

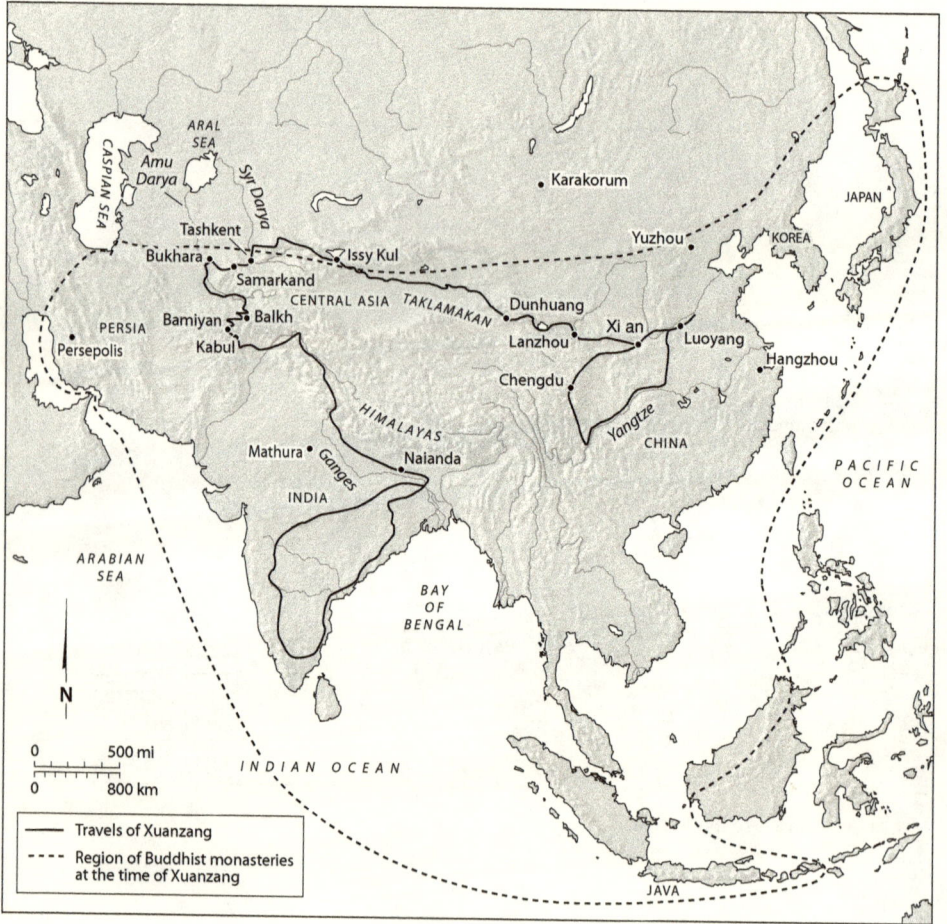

MAP 2. Travels of Xuanzang.

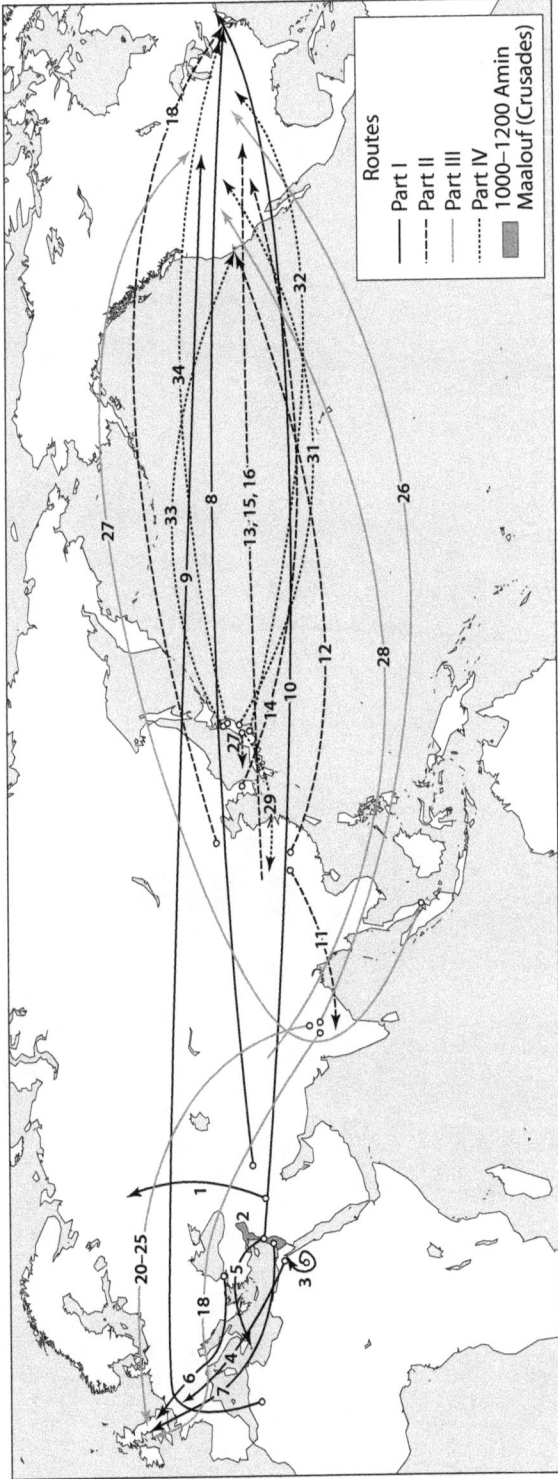

MAP 3. The rest in their West: observers and observed, 629–2013.

Routes	
——	Part I
– – –	Part II
⋯⋯⋯	Part III
〰〰	Part IV
▓	1000–1200 Amin Maalouf (Crusades)

1 fl. 922 Ibn Fadlan
2 1000–1200 Amin Maalouf
3 1798 Abd Al-Rahman Al-Jabarti
4 1836 Rifa'ah Al-Tahtawi
5 fl. 1850 Faris Al-Shidyaq
6 1913 Zeyneb Hanoum
7 1978 Edward Said
8 2006 Mahmoud Ahmadinejad
9 2007 Khalil Bendib

10 2012 Mayssoun Sukarieh
11 629 Hiuen Tsiang
12 1882–85 Huang Zunxian
13 1903 Liang Qichao
14 1934 No-Yong Park
15 1943–44 Fei Xiaotong
16 1953 Francis L.K. Hsu
17 1987 Zhao Fusan (no route)
18 2008 Gao Xiqing

19 2008 Xinhuanet (no route)
20 1799–1803 Mirza Abu Taleb Khan
21 1832 Raja Rammohun Roy
22 1870 Keshub Chunder Sen
23 1901 Dadabhai Naoroji
24 1909 M.K. Gandhi
25 1954 N.C. Chaudhuri
26 1966 B.N. Chakravarty
27 2006 Arun Bala

28 2013 Akbar Ahmed
29 838–47 Ennin
30 1798 Honda Toshiaki (no route)
31 1860 Masao Miyoshi
32 1893 Fukuzawa Yukichi
33 1961 Yuzuru Katagiri
34 1990 Shintaro Ishihara

PART ONE

Middle Eastern Travelers and Their Observations

The Rus

Ahmad Ibn Fadlan, c. 922

From the eighth to tenth centuries AD, the Varangians, as Norsemen from Sweden and the Isle of Gotland were called, found portages between riverine routes that linked Scandinavia to Constantinople via the Dnieper River and Black Sea, and to Baghdad's hinterlands via the Volga River and Caspian Sea. By 830 AD, the Varangians had established themselves as the ruling class among the Slavic settlements from the southern Baltic coast to Kiev in a new polity known as the Rus. From these areas of settlement, Rus nobility ranged on voyages of trade and plunder, selling furs, wax, and slaves captured in northern Europe to heavily populated areas.

It was such trading raiders from the Rus that Ibn Fadlan met along the Volga in 922. Ahmad Ibn Fadlan chronicled the voyage of an embassy sent from Baghdad by the caliph Al-Muqtadir to the capital of a Finno-Ugric khanate located on the upper reaches of the Volga, a locale that had recently converted to Islam. At a time when large sections of central Asian Turkic populations were converting to Islam and being incorporated into the structure of the Islamic world, Ibn Fadlan recorded the mores and customs of the Rus through the eyes of a well-educated representative from the capital of Islamic civilization.

About Ibn Fadlan as a person we know almost nothing beyond personal and biographical details gleaned from his account of the caliph's mission to the king of the Volga Bulgars. The *Yaqut Geographic Dictionary* states that he was a scholar who started his life as the assistant chief scribe to the army general Muhammad ben Suleiman, who led wars that ranged from Egypt to China. Ibn Fadlan's interaction with peoples of the region newly annexed to the Islamic caliphates gave him many insights about the habits, customs, and laws of the Rus. This knowledge raised his position in the court of the caliph. As a confidant

Ibn Fadlan, Ahmad. 2005. "The Rus." From *Ibn Fadlan's Journey to Russia: A Tenth-Century Traveler from Baghdad to the Volga River*. Richard N. Frye, transl. Princeton, NJ: Markus Wiener. Pp. 63–71. Reprinted by permission of the publisher.

in this court, Ibn Fadlan was then sent as a teacher of Islamic laws to the Bulgars. The journey, which started in 921 and lasted for three and a half years, took him and his fellow travelers from Baghdad to Bukhara and Kawarezm, south of the Aral Sea. They spent the winter in Jurjaniya, then crossed the Ural River to reach the Bulgar capital of Kazan. Throughout the journey, Ibn Fadlan recorded his observations on the Bulgars and their interactions with local Finnic tribes.

Ibn Fadlan's *Risalah* is considered the only extant firsthand account of the Eurasian steppe that appeared between Herodotus (fifth century BC) and the Catholic missions to the Mongols (thirteenth century AD). His work has been the subject of writings by Russian, Norwegian, German, Danish, English, and Arab authors and translators. The most important translation into English was published in 1923 after the discovery of his work in a Mashhad, Iran, library. His book and geography touches on nomads and conversion, rivalries between Byzantines and Iranians, merchants in inner Asia in pre-Islamic times, and the Byzantine and Sasanian trade with northern Russia.

The *Risalah* portrays Ibn Fadlan as a man educated in the Islamic sciences, a physician and man of law, and a sometime missionary. The work itself reveals Ibn Fadlan as a keen and fair observer. For instance, after his description of the ritual sacrifice and cremation of a young maiden he includes the voice of the Rus themselves as they criticize Arab customs: "They, the Arab communities, are stupid. . . . You go and cast into the earth the people whom you both love and honor most among men. Then the earth, creeping things, and worms devour them. We, however, let them burn for an instant and accordingly he enters into paradise at once in that very hour" (Ibn Fadlan 2005:70).

Ibn Fadlan sees the Varangians as they probably cannot see themselves—people in a liminal space, perpetual traders in an expatriate setting. He describes a wild and licentious people, tattooed paganism, and—for such water-focused people—much filth. He also records profligate sexuality and the lack of jealousy—all that is the inverse of urbanity and refinement. Particularly spectacular is probably the only eyewitness account of the burial rituals of a prominent chief, which included the sacrifice of a maiden who, after funerary rites of violence, sexuality, and fire, went to her death along with the honored leader.

. . .

I saw the Rusiya when they came hither on their trading voyages and had encamped by the river Itil. I have never seen people with a more developed bodily stature than they. They are as tall as date palms, blond and ruddy, so that they do not need to wear a tunic nor a cloak; rather the men among them wear a garment that only covers half of his body and leaves one of his hands free.

Each of them has an axe, a sword, and a knife with him, and all of these whom we have mentioned never let themselves be separated from their weapons. Their swords are broad bladed, provided with rills, and of the Frankish type. Each one of them has from the tip of his nails to the neck figures, trees, and other things, tattooed in dark green.

Each of the women has fastened upon the two breasts a brooch of iron, silver, copper, or gold, in weight and value according to the wealth of her husband. Each brooch has a ring to which a knife is likewise fixed, and is hung upon the breast. Around the neck the women wear rings of gold and silver.

The man, if he possesses ten thousand *dirhams,* has a neck ring made for his wife. If he has twenty thousand in his possession, then he has two neck rings made for her. And so his wife receives another neck ring with the addition of each ten thousand *dirhams.* Accordingly it often happens that there are a number of neck rings upon the neck of one of them. They consider as the most highly prized ornaments the green glass beads made out of clay, which are formed on the polishing stone. They bargain for these beads, and buy a bead for a *dirham* a piece, and string them into necklaces for their women.

They are the dirtiest creatures of God. They have no shame in voiding their bowels and bladder, nor do they wash themselves when polluted by emission of semen, nor do they wash their hands after eating. They are then like asses who have gone astray.

They come from their own country, moor their boats on the strand of the Itil, which is a great river, and build on its banks large houses out of wood. In a house like this ten or twenty people, more or less, live together. Each of them has a couch whereupon he sits, and with them are fair maidens who are destined for sale to the merchants, and they may have intercourse with their girl while their comrades look on. At times a crowd of them may come together, and one does this in the presence of the others. It also happens that a merchant, who comes into the house to buy a girl from one of them, may find him in the very act of having intercourse with her, and he [the Rus] will not let her be until he has fulfilled his intention.

As a matter of duty they wash daily their faces and heads in a manner so dirty, and so unclean, as could possibly be imagined. Thus it is carried out. A slave girl brings each morning early a large vessel with water, and gives the vessel to her master, and he washes his hands and face and the hair of his head. He washes it and combs it with a comb into the bucket, then blows his nose and spits into the bucket. He holds back nothing impure, but rather lets it go into the water.

After he has done what was necessary, the girl takes the same vessel to the one who is nearest, and he does just as his neighbor had done. She carries the vessel from one to another, until all in the house have had a turn at it, and each of them has blown his nose, spat into, and washed his face and hair in the vessel.

When their boats come to this anchorage, each one of them goes ashore with bread, meat, onions, milk, and mead, and betakes himself to a tall wooden pole set upright, that has a face like a man. Around it are small images and behind these are long, tall poles driven into the earth. And he comes to the great image and prostrates himself before it. Then he says: "O my lord, I have come from a far country and have with me so many slave girls for such a price, and so many sable pelts," until he has enumerated all the goods which he has brought for sale. Then he continues: "I have brought this offering to Thee." Then he lays down what he had brought before the wooden image and continues: "I wish that Thou shouldst provide me with a merchant who has many *dinars* and *dirhams,* and who would buy from me at the price I desire, and will raise no objection to me to aught what I may say." Then he departs.

If he has difficulties in his trading, and the days of his stay are prolonged, then he makes a second and a third offering. Should difficulties again arise over what he hopes to attain, he then brings a gift to each of these little figures, and begs them to intercede, saying: "These are the wives, daughters, and sons of our lord." And so he continues to approach each image, one after the other, and to beg them and implore them to intercede, and prays before them in abasement.

His dealings often go on more easily, and he sells everything he has brought with them. Then he says: "My lord has fulfilled my desire. I must repay Him." He gathers a number of sheep and oxen, slaughters them, gives away a part of the meat as alms, and brings the remainder and casts it before that great wooden image and before the little wooden images which stand around it. He hangs the heads of the cattle, or those of the sheep, on the poles, which are erected in the earth. In the night the dogs come and devour all, and he who has made this sacrifice says: "Verily my lord is content with me, and he has eaten up my gift."

If one of them falls ill, they erect a tent for him at a distance from themselves, and leave him there. They put beside him a little bread and water, do not approach him, and do not speak to him. Indeed what is still more, they do not visit him at all during all the days of his illness, especially if he is weak or if he is a slave. When he has recovered and gets up, he comes back to them. If, however, he dies, they cremate him. If he is a slave they let him be, and then the dogs and carrion fowl devour him. If they catch a thief or a robber, they lead him to a thick tree, throw a trusty rope around his neck and hang him to the tree, and he remains hanging until with the wind and the rain he falls to pieces.

They told me that they carry out many ceremonies when their chiefs die, the least whereof is the cremation, and it interested me to find out more about it. Finally the news was brought to me that a prominent man among them had died. They laid him in a grave, and covered it with a roof for ten days until they were through with the cutting out and sewing together of his garments. Thus it is; if [the dead] is poor they make a boat and place him in it and burn the boat. If he is a rich man, they gather his possessions together and divide them in three parts. One third remains for his family; with the second third they cut out garments for him, and with third part they brew mead for themselves, which they drink on the day when his slave girl kills herself and is cremated with her master. They drink the mead to insensibility, day and night. It often happens that one of them dies with his beaker in his hand.

When a high chief dies, his family says to his slave girls and servants: "Which one of you wishes to die with him?" Then one of them answers: "I." When he [or she] has said this he is bound. He can in no way be allowed to withdraw his word. If he wishes it, it is not permitted. For the most part, this self-sacrifice is made by the maidens.

When the above-mentioned man had died, his relatives said to his slave girls: "Who will die with him?" Thereupon one of them answered: "I." Then the relations of the deceased charged two girls to watch her and go with her wherever she went. Indeed they even washed her feet with their own hands. The relatives of the deceased then began to occupy themselves with the preparations for the funeral ceremonies, to have the garments cut out for him, and to prepare whatever was necessary. The slave girl meanwhile drank all day long and sang joyfully, and enjoyed herself in view of the future.

When the day had come on which he and the maiden should be cremated, I put in an appearance at the river where his bark lay. I saw that this already had been hauled up on land. There were four props set up for the boat, of birch and other wood, and around the boat had been built a large structure like a large scaffold of wood. Then they hauled the ship further up, until it was placed inside this structure.

The people then began to move hither and thither, and to speak words that I did not understand, while he was still lying in his grave, out of which they had not taken him. Then they brought a couch, placed it on the ship, and covered it with draperies of Byzantine brocade, and also with pillows of Byzantine brocade.

Thereupon an old woman came, whom they call the angel of death, and spread the draperies mentioned over the couch. She had held the oversight over the sewing of the garments of the deceased and their completion. This old woman kills the girl. I saw that she was an old giantess, fat and grim to behold.

When they came to his grave, they removed the earth from the timbers and raised the timbers, drew him forth in the same garment in which he had died, and I saw how he had turned black from the cold earth. I also noted that they had put in his grave mead, fruits, and a kind of mandolin. They now took all of these out of the grave. Naught had changed in the deceased apart from the color of his skin. They then dressed him in stockings, trousers, boots, [and] a tunic and cape of brocade with gold buttons. They put a cap of brocade and sable pelts upon him and carried him into the tent that had been erected on the boat. Here they placed him upon the quilts, propped him up with cushions, brought mead, fruits, and flowers, and laid these beside him. They also brought bread, meat, and onions, and strewed them before him. Then they brought a dog, cleft it in two halves, and laid it in the boat. Thereupon they brought all his weapons and laid them by his side. Then they took two horses, drove them until they perspired, then cleft both of them in twain with a sword and laid their flesh in the boat. Then they brought two cows, cut them in two likewise and laid them in the boat. Then they brought a cock and a hen, killed them and threw both into the ship. The maiden who wished to be put to death went here and there, and entered each of the tents where the head of each tent had intercourse with her saying: "Say to thy lord, I have done this out of love of thee."

On Friday in the afternoon they brought the maiden to a structure, which they had erected like a doorframe. She put both her feet on the palms of the men, and was lifted up onto this doorframe, and said her piece. Then they let her down again. Thereupon they put her up a second time. She repeated what she had done the first time, and then they let her down, and let her go up a third time. Again she did as she had done on the first two occasions. Then they gave her a hen. She cut off its head and cast it away. They took the hen and laid it in the boat. Thereupon I asked the interpreter what her actions meant. He said: "When they raised her up the first time, she said: 'Behold, I see my father and mother'; the second time she said: 'There I see all my deceased relatives sitting'; the third time she said: 'There I behold my lord sitting in paradise, and paradise is fair and green, and around him are men and servants. He calls me; bring me to him.'"

Then they led her to the boat. She took off the two armlets that she wore and gave them to the old woman whom they call the angel of death, who was to kill her. Then the slave girl took off two anklets that she had and gave them to the two maidens who had waited on her, and who were the daughters of the old woman known as the angel of death.

Then the people lifted her onto the boat, but did not yet let her go into the tent. Hereupon came men with shields and staves and gave her a bowl of mead, whereupon she sang and drank it. The interpreter said to me: "With this she is bidding goodbye to her friends." Then she was given another beaker. She took it and sang for a long time, while the old woman was urging her to finish the goblet, and to go into the tent where her lord lay.

I saw then how disturbed she was. She wished to go into the tent, but put her head between the tent and the side of the boat. Then the old woman took her by the head, made her go into the tent, and also entered with her.

Whereupon the men began to beat their shields with the staves so that her shrieks would not be heard, and the other maidens become terrified. Then six men went into the tent, and all had intercourse with the girl. Then they placed her beside her dead lord; two men seized her by the feet and two by the hands. Then the old woman placed a rope in which a bight had been made, and gave it to two of the men to pull at the two ends. Then the old woman came to her with a broad-bladed dagger and began to jab it into her ribs and pull it out again, and the two men strangled her until she was dead.

After they had laid the maiden they had killed beside her master, wood for kindling the fire was prepared. The closest relative of the deceased approached, and took a piece of wood, kindled it and then walked backwards to the boat, keeping his face turned toward the spectators, holding the burning brand in one hand, and placing his other on his anus. He was naked and walked backwards until he reached the boat and set fire to the wood that had been prepared beneath the boat. Then the people came with kindling and other firewood, each having a brand burning at the end, and laid this stick in the pile of wood. Fire then spread through the wood and spread to the kindling, the boat, the man, the maiden, and every-thing that was in the boat. A strong and violent wind sprang up through which the flames were fanned and greatly enhanced.

A man of the Rusiya was standing beside me and I heard him talking to the interpreter, and I asked what the Rus had said to him. The interpreter answered that he said: "They, the Arab communities, are stupid." So I asked: "Why?" He said: "You go and cast into the earth the people whom you both love and honor most among men. Then the earth, creeping things, and worms devour them. We, how-ever, let them burn for an instant, and accordingly he enters into paradise at once in that very hour," and he burst into immoderate laughter.

He said: "His Lord sent the wind for love of him, so that he may be snatched away in the course of an hour." In fact an hour had not passed when boat, wood, maiden, and lord had turned to ashes and dust of ashes. Then they built on the site of the boat that they had hauled up out of the stream something like a rounded mound. In the middle of this they erected a great beam of birch wood, and wrote upon it the name of the man and the name of the king of the Rus, whereupon they departed.

One of the customs of the king of the Rusiya is that with him in his palace he has four hundred men from among his most valiant and trusted men. They die when he dies and are killed for his sake. Each one has a slave girl who waits on him, washes his head, and prepares for him what he eats and drinks. He has another slave girl with whom he has intercourse. These four hundred sit under his throne, which is a large throne, studded with precious gems. Forty slave girls, who are intended for his bed, sit by him on his throne. He may have sexual intercourse with one of them in the presence of the companions whom we have mentioned. He does not come down from the throne. Whenever he wants to answer a call to nature, he does it in a basin. When he wishes to ride they bring him his horse to the throne, and he mounts it from the throne. When he wishes to dismount he brings the horse so that he dismounts from it onto the throne. He has a viceroy who leads his armies, attacks the foe, and represents him before his people.

REFERENCES

Hraundal, Thorir Jonsson. 2013. "The Rus in Arabic Sources: Cultural Contacts and Iden-tity." Unpublished doctoral dissertation, University of Bergen, Bergen, Norway.

McKeithen, James E. 1979. "The Risalah of Ibn Fadlan: An Annotated Translation with Introduction." *Dissertation Abstracts International* (40[10A], 5437), 25 (UMI No. AAG8008223).

2

From The Crusades through Arab Eyes

Amin Maalouf, 1984

Amin Maalouf portrays the Crusades based on the testimonies of Arab historians and chroniclers who left us their observations of the Frankish invasions—among them Ibn Jubayr (1144–1217), Ibn al-Qalanisi (1073–1160), Ibn al-Athir (1160–1233), Kamal al-Din Ibn al-Adim (1192–1262), Abu-Shama (1203–1267), Bahā' al-Din Ibn Shaddad (1145–1234), 'Imad al-Din al-Asfhani (1125–1201), Sibt Ibn al-Jawzi (1186–1256), Jamal al-Din Ibn Wasil (1207–1298), and Abul' Fida' (1273–1331). A Lebanese Christian, Maalouf narrates, in the 1980s, events of the eleventh, twelfth, and thirteenth centuries. Maalouf sought to write what might be called a true-life model of the Crusades "from a hitherto neglected point of view." Thus, he covers two centuries that "shaped the West and the Arab world alike, and that affect relations between them even today" (Maalouf 2006:foreword). Maalouf weaves what is an often fragmentary history into a continuous account that covers two centuries of Frankish invasions.

Too many European narratives that tell the story of the Crusades objectify the Muslims. Maalouf's project revives a Muslim voice and perspective that enrich history by providing points of view based on Arab sources. The region, whose richness and complexity derived in no small part from decentralized political and economic systems and a multiplicity of religious ideologies and institutions, was a vibrant part of the world system before European hegemony. The Islamic world comprised far-flung city-states connected to one another by land routes, sea lanes, kinship, and ideas. Strings of city-states were loosely affiliated with the political patronage of metropolises like Baghdad or Cairo, and a city's elite was often associated with a particular school of Islam. The region was packed with native Christians, Muslims, Jews, Arabs, Turks, Egyptians, Armenians, Syrians, Palestinians, Greeks, and highly specialized trades and craftsmen. Unlike their invaders, the defenders saw the initial

Maalouf, Amin. 2006. *The Crusades through Arab Eyes*. Jon Rothschild, transl. London: Saqi Books. Pp. 3–6, 17, 18, 37–38, 50–52, 66, 77–81, 128–132, 177, 198–200. It is printed here with the permission of the publisher.

European attacks in the late eleventh century as projections of Byzantine power, the latest in a series of skirmishes going back several centuries. But war meant something different for the Crusaders. More than economic or political conquest, it was religious ideology that motivated their action; they did not respond to ransoms, gifts, or overtures of alliance as Byzantines and their neighbors expected. Europeans were converts to Christianity, invaders from a politically and ethnically fragmented western Europe who blindly faced *one enemy*. The threat was to them foreign and unfamiliar.

European account after account of the Franj invasion indicates a fundamental belief on the part of the Crusaders that the people they were conquering were barbaric and savage, and thus the rules and laws of civility did not apply. "In Ma'arra our troops boiled pagan adults in cooking pots; they impaled children on spits and devoured them grilled" (39). Maalouf shows how the Franj instilled their imperial presence and attempted to wipe out entire populations, along with their heritage and their history. The conquered described this manner of attack and the Franj's habitual conduct and ways of living—the way they practiced medicine, their notions of science, their notions of justice, their use of powerful physical force—as highly uncivilized. Europeans' brutality and their unforgiving destruction of Muslim cities and people starkly contrasts with the more lenient and even generous treatment of the European invaders by the great Kurdish leader Saladin and others, who despite their brutality thought the Crusaders were capable of becoming equals through the civilizing influence of Arab society.

Maalouf does not hide the weaknesses of the Muslim world and is careful to point out the quantitative exaggerations of some of the witnesses. Yet, while the Europeans denounced Muslims as infidels and barbarians, the Muslims viewed the invading Europeans as "beasts superior in courage and fighting ardor but in nothing else, just as animals are superior in strength and aggression" (39). The Muslims had their own ideas about what constituted "civilization." Before the Crusaders came, Muslims, Christians, and Jews lived in peace in Jerusalem. Rather than favoring existing Christians, European Christians in their slaughters made no distinction between Muslims, Christians, Jews, or other peoples indigenous to the places they invaded, the birthplaces of these three world religions. In his epilogue Maalouf points out that a sense of persecution and suspicion of the West has been a lasting effect of the Crusades on the Arab world, one that continues into the present.

Amin Maalouf was born in Beirut in 1949. He studied sociology and economics at Saint Joseph French University in Beirut, where he worked as the director of the Lebanese daily *Annahar*. With the eruption of the 1975 civil war, Maalouf moved as a refugee to Paris, where he still lives.

• • •

THE FRANJ ARRIVE

In that year, news began to trickle in about the appearance of Franj troops, coming down from the Sea of Marmara in an innumerable multitude. People took fright. This information was confirmed by King Kilij Arslan, whose territory was closest to these Franj.

The King Kilij Arslan whom Ibn al-Qalānisi mentions here was not yet seventeen when the invaders arrived. The first Muslim leader to be informed of their approach, this young Turkish sultan with the slightly slanting eyes would be the first to inflict a defeat upon them—but also the first to be routed by the formidable knights.

In July 1096 Kilij Arslan learned that an enormous throng of Franj was en route to Constantinople. He immediately feared the worst. Naturally, he had no idea as to the real aims of these people, but in his view nothing good could come of their arrival in the Orient.

The sultanate under his rule covered much of Asia Minor, a territory the Turks had only recently taken from the Greeks. Kilij Arslan's father, Süleymān, was the first Turk to secure possession of this land, which many centuries later would come to be called Turkey. In Nicaea, the capital of this young Muslim state, Byzantine churches were still more numerous than Muslim mosques. Although the city's garrison was made up of Turkish cavalry, the majority of the population was Greek, and Kilij Arslan had few illusions about his subjects' true sentiments: as far as they were concerned, he would never be other than a barbarian chieftain. The only sovereign they recognized—the man whose name, spoken in a low whisper, was murmured in all their prayers—was the basileus Alexius Comnenus, "Emperor of the Romans." Alexius was in fact the emperor of the Greeks, who proclaimed themselves the inheritors of the Roman empire. The Arabs, indeed, recognized them as such, for in the eleventh century—as in the twentieth—they designated the Greeks by the term Rūm, or "Romans." The domain conquered from the Greek empire by Kilij Arslan's father was even called the Sultanate of the Rūm.

Alexius was one of the most prestigious figures of the Orient at the time. Kilij Arslan was genuinely fascinated by this short-statured quinquagenarian, always decked in gold and in rich blue robes, with his carefully tended beard, elegant manners, and eyes sparkling with malice. Alexius reigned in Constantinople, fabled Byzantium, situated less than three days' march from Nicaea. This proximity aroused conflicting emotions in the mind of the young sultan. Like all nomadic warriors, he dreamed of conquest and pillage, and was not displeased to find the legendary riches of Byzantium so close at hand. At the same time he felt threatened: he knew that Alexius had never abandoned his dream of retaking Nicaea, not only because the city had always been Greek, but also and more importantly because the presence of Turkish warriors such a short distance from Constantinople represented a permanent threat to the security of the empire.

Although the Byzantine army, torn by years of internal crisis, would have been unable to undertake a war of reconquest on its own, it was no secret that Alexius could always seek the aid of foreign auxiliaries. The Byzantines had never hesitated to resort to the services of Western knights. Many Franj, from heavily armored mercenaries to pilgrims en route to Palestine, had visited the Orient, and by 1096 they were by no means unknown to the Muslims. Some twenty years earlier—Kilij Arslan had not yet been born, but the older emirs in his army had told him the story—one of these fair-haired adventurers, a man named Roussel of Bailleul, had succeeded in founding an autonomous state in Asia Minor and had even marched on Constantinople. The panicky Byzantines had had no choice but to appeal to Kilij Arslan's father, who could hardly believe his ears when a special envoy from the basileus implored him to rush to their aid. The Turkish cavalry converged on Constantinople and managed to defeat Roussel; Süleymān received handsome compensation in the form of gold, horses, and land.

The Byzantines had been suspicious of the Franj ever since, but the imperial armies, short of experienced soldiers, had no choice but to recruit mercenaries, and not only Franj: many Turkish warriors also fought under the banners of the Christian empire. It was precisely from his congeners enrolled in the Byzantine army that Kilij Arslan learned, in July 1096, that thousands of Franj were approaching Constantinople. He was perplexed by the picture painted by his informants. These Occidentals bore scant resemblance to the mercenaries to whom the Turks were accustomed. Although their number included several hundred knights and a significant number of foot-soldiers, there were also thousands of women, children, and old people in rags. They had the air of some wretched tribe evicted from their lands by an invader. It was also reported that they all wore strips of cloth in the shape of a cross, sewn onto the backs of their garments.

The young sultan, who doubtless found it difficult to assess the danger, asked his agents to be especially vigilant and to keep him informed of the exploits of these new invaders. He had the fortifications of his capital inspected as a precaution. The walls of Nicaea, more than a *farsakh* (six thousand meters) in length, were topped by 240 turrets. South-west of the city, the placid waters of the Ascanian Lake offered excellent natural protection.

Nevertheless by early August the serious nature of the threat had become clear. Escorted by Byzantine ships, the Franj crossed the Bosporus and, despite a blazing summer sun, advanced along the coast. Wherever they passed, they were heard to proclaim that they had come to exterminate the Muslims, although they were also seen to plunder many a Greek church on their way. Their chief was said to be a hermit by the name of Peter. Informants estimated that there were several tens of thousands of them in all, but no one would hazard a guess as to where they were headed. It seemed that Basileus Alexius had decided to settle them in Civitot, a camp that had earlier been equipped for other mercenaries, less than a day's march from Nicaea.

The sultan's palace was awash with agitation. While the Turkish cavalry stood ready to mount their chargers at a moment's notice, there was a constant flow of spies and scouts, reporting the smallest movements of the Franj. It transpired that every morning hordes several thousand strong left camp to forage the surrounding countryside: farms were plundered or set alight before the rabble returned to Civitot, where their various clans squabbled over the spoils of their raids. None of this was surprising to the sultan's soldiers, and their master saw no reason for particular concern. The routine continued for an entire month.

One day, however, toward the middle of September, there was a sudden change in the behavior of the Franj. Probably because they were unable to squeeze anything more out of the immediate neighborhood, they had reportedly set out in the direction of Nicaea. They passed through several villages, all of them Christian, and commandeered the harvests, which had just been gathered, mercilessly massacring those peasants who tried to resist. Young children were even said to have been burned alive.

Kilij Arslan found himself taken unawares. By the time the news of these events reached him, the attackers were already at the walls of his capital, and before sunset the citizens could see the smoke rising from the first fires. The sultan quickly dispatched a cavalry patrol to confront the Franj. Hopelessly outnumbered, the Turks were cut to pieces. A few bloodied survivors limped back into Nicaea. Sensing that his prestige was threatened, Kilij Arslan would have liked to join the battle immediately, but the emirs of his army dissuaded him. It would soon be night, and the Franj were already hastily falling back to their camp. Revenge would have to wait.

But not for long. Apparently emboldened by their success, the Occidentals decided to try again two weeks later. This time the son of Süleymān was alerted in time, and he followed their advance step by step. A Frankish company, including some knights but consisting mainly of thousands of tattered pillagers, set out apparently for Nicaea. But then, circling around the town, they turned east and took the fortress of Xerigordon by surprise.

The young sultan decided to act. At the head of his men, he rode briskly towards the small stronghold, where the drunken Franj, celebrating their victory, had no way of knowing that their fate was already sealed, for Xerigordon was a trap. As the soldiers of Kilij Arslan well knew (but the inexperienced foreigners had yet to discover), its water supplies lay outside and rather far from the walls. The Turks quickly sealed off access to the water. Now they had only to take up positions around the fortress and sit and wait. Thirst would do the fighting in their stead.

[. . .]

As Ibn al-Qalānisi was later to write: *The Franj cut the Turkish army to pieces. They killed, pillaged, and took many prisoners, who were sold into slavery.*

During his flight, Kilij Arslan met a group of cavalry coming from Syria to fight at his side. They were too late, he told them ruefully. The Franj were too numerous and too powerful, and nothing more could be done to stop them. Joining deed to word, and determined to stand aside and let the storm pass, the defeated sultan disappeared into the immensity of the Anatolian plateau. He was to wait four years to take his revenge.

Nature alone seemed still to resist the invader. The aridity of the soil, the tiny mountain pathways, and the scorching summer heat on the shadowless roads slowed the advance of the Franj. After Dorylaeum, it took them a hundred days to cross Anatolia, whereas in normal times a month should have sufficed. In the meantime, news of the Turkish debacle spread throughout the Middle East. *When this event, so shameful for Islam, became known,* noted the Damascene chronicler, *there was real panic. Dread and anxiety swelled to enormous proportions.*

Rumors circulated constantly about the imminent arrival of redoubtable knights. At the end of July there was talk that they were approaching the village of al-Balana, in the far north of Syria. Thousands of cavalry gathered to meet them, but it was a false alarm: there was no sign of the Franj on the horizon. The most optimistic souls wondered whether the invaders had perhaps turned back. Ibn al-Qalānisi echoed that hope in one of those astrological parables of which his contemporaries were so enamored: *That summer a comet appeared in the western sky; it ascended for twenty days, then disappeared without a trace.* But these illusions were soon dispelled. The news became increasingly detailed. From mid-September onwards, the advance of the Franj could be followed from village to village.

On 21 October 1097 shouts rang out from the peak of the citadel of Antioch, then Syria's largest city: "They are here!" A few lay-abouts hurried to the ramparts to gawk, but they could see nothing more than a vague cloud of dust far in the distance, at the end of the broad plain, near Lake Antioch. The Franj were still a day's march away, perhaps more, and there was every indication that they would want to stop to rest for a while after their long journey. Nevertheless, prudence demanded that the five heavy city gates be closed immediately.

In the souks the morning clamor was stilled, as merchants and customers alike stood immobile. Women whispered, and some prayed. The city was in the grip of fear.

[...]

THE CANNIBALS OF MA'ARRA

I know not whether my native land be a grazing ground for wild beasts or yet my home!

This cry of grief by an anonymous poet of Ma'arra was no mere figure of speech. Sadly, we must take his words literally, and ask with him: what monstrous thing came to pass in the Syrian city of Ma'arra late in that year of 1098?

Until the arrival of the Franj, the people of Ma'arra lived untroubled lives, shielded by their circular city walls. Their vineyards and their fields of olives and figs afforded them modest prosperity. The city's affairs were administered by worthy local notables devoid of any great ambition, under the nominal suzerainty of Ridwān of Aleppo. Ma'arra's main claim to fame was that it was the home town of one of the great figures of Arab literature, Abu'l-'Alā' al-Ma'arri, who had died in 1057. This blind poet, a free-thinker, had dared to attack the mores of his age, flouting its taboos. Indeed, it required a certain audacity to write lines like these:

> The inhabitants of the earth are of two sorts:
> Those with brains, but no religion,
> And those with religion, but no brains.

Forty years after his death, a fanaticism come from afar descended on this city and seemed to prove this son of Ma'arra right, not only in his irreligion, but also in his legendary pessimism:

> Fate smashes us as though we were made of glass,
> And never are our shards put together again.

His city was to be reduced to a heap of ruins, and the poet's oft-expressed mistrust of his compatriots would find its cruelest vindication.

During the first few months of 1098 the inhabitants of Ma'arra uneasily followed the battle of Antioch, which was taking place three days' march north-west of them. After their victory, the Franj raided several neighboring villages, and although Ma'arra was spared, several of its families decided to abandon the town for more secure residences in Aleppo, Homs, and Hama. Their fears proved justified when, towards the end of November, thousands of Frankish warriors arrived and surrounded the city. Although some citizens managed to flee despite the siege, most were trapped. Ma'arra had no army, only an urban militia, which several hundred young men lacking any military experience hastily joined. For two weeks they courageously resisted the redoubtable knights, going so far as to hurl packed beehives down on the besiegers from the city walls.

> To counter such tenacity, *Ibn al-Athīr wrote*, the Franj constructed a wooden turret as high as the ramparts. Some Muslims, fearful and demoralized, felt that a more effective defense was to barricade themselves within the city's tallest buildings. They therefore abandoned the walls, leaving the positions they had been holding undefended. Others followed their example, and another point of the surrounding wall was abandoned. Soon the entire perimeter of the town was without defenders. The Franj scaled the walls with ladders, and when the Muslims saw them atop the walls, they lost heart.

It was 11 December, a pitch-dark night, and the Franj did not yet dare to penetrate the town. The notables of Ma'arra made contact with Bohemond, the new master of Antioch, who was leading the attackers. The Frankish commander promised to spare the lives of the inhabitants if they would stop fighting and withdraw from certain buildings. Desperately placing their trust in his word, the families gathered in the houses and cellars of the city and waited all night in fear.

The Franj arrived at dawn. It was carnage. [. . .]

[. . .]

On that terrible day of July 1099, Iftikhār was ensconced in the Tower of David, an octagonal citadel whose foundations had been welded with lead. It was the strongest point of the system of defensive fortifications. He could have held out for a few more days, but he knew that the battle was lost. The Jewish quarter had been invaded, the streets were strewn with bodies, and fighting was already raging alongside the great mosque. He and his men would soon be completely surrounded. Nevertheless, he continued to fight. What else could he do? By afternoon, fighting had practically ceased in the center of the city. The white banner of the Fatimids now waved only over the Tower of David.

Suddenly the Frankish attack was halted and a messenger approached. He was carrying an offer from Saint-Gilles, who proposed that the Egyptian general and his men be allowed to leave the city alive if they would surrender the tower to him. Iftikhār hesitated. The Franj had already broken their commitments more than once, and there was no indication that Saint-Gilles would now act in good faith. On the other hand, he was described as a white-haired sexagenarian respected by all, which suggested that his word could be trusted. In any event, Iftikhār was sure that Saint-Gilles would eventually have to negotiate with the garrison, since his wooden tower had been destroyed and all his attacks repelled. Indeed, he had been dithering on the walls since morning, while his colleagues, the other Frankish commanders, were already plundering the city and arguing about who would get which houses. Carefully weighing the pros and cons, Iftikhār finally announced that he was ready to yield, provided that Saint-Gilles would promise, on his honor, to guarantee his safety and that of all his men.

The Franj kept their word, Ibn al-Athīr notes conscientiously, *and let them depart by night for the port of Ascalon, where they camped.* And then he adds: *The population of the holy city was put to the sword, and the Franj spent a week massacring Muslims. They killed more than seventy thousand people in al-Aqṣā mosque.* Ibn al-Qalānisi, who never reported figures he could not verify, says only: *Many people were killed. The Jews had gathered in their synagogue and the Franj burned them alive. They also destroyed the monuments of saints and the tomb of Abraham, may peace be upon him!*

Among the monuments sacked by the invaders was the mosque of ʿUmar, erected to the memory of the second successor of the Prophet, the caliph ʿUmar Ibn al-Khaṭṭāb, who had taken Jerusalem from the Rūm in February 638. The Arabs would later frequently invoke this event, to highlight the difference between their conduct and that of the Franj. ʿUmar had entered Jerusalem astride his famous white camel, and the Greek patriarch of the holy city came forward to meet him. The caliph first assured him that the lives and property of the city's inhabitants would be respected, and then asked the patriarch to take him to visit the Christian holy places. The time of Muslim prayer arrived while they were in the church of Qiyāma, the Holy Sepulchre, and 'Umar asked his host if he could unroll his prayer mat. The patriarch invited 'Umar to do so right where he stood but the caliph answered: if I do, the Muslims will want to appropriate this site, saying "'Umar prayed here." Then, carrying his prayer mat, he went and knelt outside. He was right, for it was on that very spot that the mosque that bore his name was constructed. The Frankish commanders, alas, lacked 'Umar's magnanimity. They celebrated their triumph with an ineffable orgy of killing, and then savagely ravaged the city they claimed to venerate.

Not even their co-religionists were spared. One of the first measures taken by the Franj was to expel from the Church of the Holy Sepulchre all the priests of Oriental rites—Greeks, Georgians, Armenians, Copts, and Syrians—who used to officiate jointly, in accordance with an old tradition respected by all previous conquerors. Dumbfounded by this degree of fanaticism, the dignitaries of the Oriental Christian communities decided to resist. They refused to tell the occupiers where they had hidden the True Cross, on which Christ died. In the minds of these men, religious devotion to the relic was compounded by patriotic pride. Indeed, were they not fellow citizens of the Nazarene? But the invaders were not impressed. They arrested the priests who had been entrusted with custody of the Cross and tortured them to make them reveal the secret. Thus did the Franj manage to forcibly deprive the Christians of the holy city wherein lay their most precious relics.

While the Occidentals were completing the massacre of a few hidden survivors and laying their hands on the riches of Jerusalem, the army raised by al-Afḍal was advancing slowly across Sinai. It reached Palestine twenty days after the tragedy. The vizier, who was personally in command, hesitated to march on the holy city directly. Although he had nearly thirty thousand men, he did not consider his position strong, for he lacked the matériel for a siege and was frightened by the determination shown by the Frankish knights. He therefore decided to camp with his troops in the environs of Ascalon and to dispatch an embassy to Jerusalem to sound out the enemy's intentions. When they reached the occupied city, the Egyptian emissaries were led to a knight with long hair and a blond beard, a big man who was introduced to them as Godfrey of Bouillon, the new master of Jerusalem. It was to him that they delivered the vizier's message, which accused the Franj of having abused his good faith and proposed to negotiate some arrangement with them if they would promise to leave Palestine. The Occidentals' response was to assemble their forces and set out without delay on the route to Ascalon.

So rapid was their advance that they arrived near the Muslim camp before the scouts had even reported their presence. With the very first engagement, *the Egyptian army gave way and fell back toward the port of Ascalon,* Ibn al-Qalānisi relates. *Al-Afḍal also withdrew. The sabers of the Franj triumphed over the Muslims. Neither foot-soldiers, nor volunteers, nor the people of the city were spared in the killing. About ten thousand souls perished, and the camp was sacked.*

It was probably several days after the Egyptian debacle that the group of refugees led by Abū Saʾad al-Ḥarawi reached Baghdad. The *qāḍī* [judge] of Damascus was not yet aware that the Franj had just won another victory, but he knew that the invaders were now masters of Jerusalem, Antioch, and Edessa, that they had beaten Kilij Arslan and Danishmend, that they had crossed all of Syria from north to south, massacring and pillaging at will and with impunity. He felt that his people and his faith had been scorned and humiliated, and he meant to raise such a great cry that the Muslims would finally awake. He would shake his brothers out of their torpor, provoke them, scandalize them.

[. . .]

TRIPOLI'S TWO THOUSAND DAYS

[. . .] [I]t was precisely the shortage of men caused by their losses that was responsible for the most lasting and spectacular achievement of the Franj in Arab lands: the construction of fortresses. To mitigate their numerical weakness they built fortresses which were so well protected that a handful of defenders could hold off a multitude of attackers. Despite the handicap of numbers, however, for many years the Franj commanded a weapon even more formidable than their fortresses, and that was the torpor of the Arab world. There is no better illustration of this state of affairs than Ibn al-Athīr's description of the extraordinary battle that unfolded before Tripoli at the beginning of April 1102.

> Saint-Gilles, may God curse his name, returned to Syria after having been crushed by Kilij Arslan. He had only three hundred men left. Fakhr al-Mulk, the lord of Tripoli, sent word to King Duqāq and to the governor of Homs: "Now is the time to finish off Saint-Gilles for ever, for he has so few troops!" Duqāq dispatched two thousand men, and the governor of Homs came in person. The troops of Tripoli joined them before the gates of the city, and together they marched into battle against Saint-Gilles. The latter threw a hundred of his soldiers against the Tripolitanians, a hundred against the Damascenes, and fifty against the troops of Homs; he kept fifty behind with him. At the mere sight of the enemy, the troops of Homs fled, and the Damascenes soon followed. Only the Tripolitanians held their ground, and when he saw this, Saint-Gilles attacked them with his two hundred other soldiers, defeating them and killing seven thousand of them.

Three hundred Franj triumphing over several thousand Muslims? But the unlikely account of the Arab historian seems to match the facts. [. . .]

[. . .]

In March 1109 everything seemed ready for a concerted attack by land and sea. The terrified Tripolitanians observed all these preparations, but did not lose hope. Had not al-Afḍal promised to send a fleet more powerful than any they had ever seen, with enough food, fighters, and matériel to hold out for a year?

The Tripolitanians had no doubt that the Genoese vessels would flee the moment the Fatimid fleet sailed into view. Let it only arrive in time!

At the beginning of the summer, Ibn al-Qalānisi says, *the Franj launched an attack on Tripoli with all their forces, driving their mobile towers toward the city walls. When the people of the city saw what violent assaults they would have to face, they lost heart, for they understood that their defeat was inevitable. Food supplies were exhausted, and the Egyptian fleet was nowhere in sight. The winds were blowing against them, for such was the will of God, who determines what things will come to pass. The Franj redoubled their efforts and took the city by storm,* on 12 July 1109. After two thousand days of resistance, the city of goldsmiths and libraries, of intrepid seamen and learned *qāḍīs,* was sacked by the warriors of the West. The hundred thousand volumes of the Dār al-'Ilm were pillaged and burned, so that "impious" books would be destroyed. According to the chronicler of Damascus, *the Franj decided that one-third of the city would go to the Genoese, the other two-thirds to the son of Saint-Gilles. All that King Baldwin desired was set aside for him.* Most of the inhabitants were sold into slavery, the rest were despoiled of their property and expelled. Many headed for the port of Tyre. Fakhr al-Mulk ended his life in the vicinity of Damascus.

And the Egyptian fleet? *It arrived in Tyre eight days after the fall of Tripoli,* Ibn al-Qalānisi relates, *when all had been lost, because of the divine punishment that had struck the inhabitants.*

The Franj selected Beirut as their second target. Lying next to the Lebanese mountains, the city was ringed by pine forests, in particular in the suburbs of Mazrat al-'Arab and Ra's al-Nabah. There the invaders would find the wood they needed to construct the instruments of siege. Beirut had none of the splendor of Tripoli, and its modest villas could not easily be compared to the Roman palaces whose marble ruins were still scattered across the grounds of ancient Berytus. But because of its port, it was a relatively prosperous city, situated on the rocky slope where, according to tradition, St. George had slain the dragon. Coveted by the Damascenes, *held negligently by the Egyptians,* Beirut finally had to confront the Franj on its own, beginning in February 1110. Its five thousand inhabitants fought with an ardor born of despair, as they destroyed the siege towers one after another. *Never before or since did the Franj face such a harsh battle,* Ibn al-Qalānisi exclaimed. The invaders were unforgiving. On 13 May, when the city was taken, they threw themselves into a blind massacre. To set an example.

The lesson was well learned. The following summer, *a certain Frankish king* (the Damascene chronicler may be forgiven for failing to recognize Sigurd, the sovereign of distant Norway) *arrived by sea with more than sixty vessels packed with fighters intent on making their pilgrimage and waging war in the lands of Islam. They headed towards Jerusalem, Baldwin joined them, and together they laid siege, by land and sea, to the port of Saida,* the ancient Phoenician city of Sidon. The walls of this city, destroyed and rebuilt more than once in the course of history, are impressive even today, their enormous blocks of stone lashed relentlessly by the Mediterranean. But the inhabitants, who had shown great courage at the beginning of the Frankish invasion, no longer had the heart to fight, since, according to Ibn al-Qalānisi, *they feared that they would suffer the same fate as Beirut. They therefore sent their qāḍī with a delegation of notables to ask Baldwin to spare their lives. He accepted their request.* The city capitulated on 4 December 1110. This time there was no massacre, but a massive exodus to Tyre and Damascus, which were already bulging with refugees.

In the space of eighteen months three of the most renowned cities of the Arab world—Tripoli, Beirut, and Saida—had been taken and sacked, their inhabitants massacred or deported, their emirs, qāḍīs, and experts on religious law killed or forced into exile, their mosques profaned. Could any power now prevent the Franj from pressing on to Tyre, Aleppo, Damascus, Cairo, Mosul, or—why not?—even Baghdad? Did any will to resist remain? Among the Muslim leaders, probably not. But among the population of the most seriously threatened cities, the relentless holy war waged for the past thirteen years by the pilgrim-fighters of the West was beginning to have its effect: the idea of *jihād,* which had long been no more than a slogan used to enliven official speeches, was being reasserted. Groups of refugees, poets, and even men of religion were now preaching it anew.

It was one of these religious figures—'Abdu Faḍl Ibn al-Khashāb, a qāḍī of Aleppo, small of stature but loud of voice—who resolved, by sheer tenacity and strength of character, to waken the sleeping giant of the Arab world. His first public initiative was to rekindle, twelve years on, the scandal that al-Harawi had aroused in the streets of Baghdad. This time, however, there would be a genuine riot.

[...]

AN EMIR AMONG BARBARIANS

[...] [I]n 1138, 'Unar had sent his friend the chronicler Usāmah Ibn Munqidh to Jerusalem to explore the possibility of Franco-Damascene collaboration against the master of Aleppo. Well received by the Franj, Usāmah had worked out the principles of an accord. Once embassies were established, the chronicler returned to the holy city at the beginning of 1140, carrying detailed proposals with him: the Frankish army would force Zangī to withdraw from the vicinity of Damascus; the forces of the two states would unite in the event of any fresh danger; Mu'īn al-Dīn would pay twenty thousand dinars to defray military expenses; finally, a joint expedition would be mounted, under 'Unar's command, to occupy the fortress of Baniyās, which had recently fallen into the hands of one of Zangī's vassals, and to restore it to the king of Jerusalem. As a demonstration of good faith, the

Damascenes would send the Franj hostages selected from the families of major city dignitaries.

In practice, all this amounted to living under a Frankish protectorate, but the population of the Syrian metropolis was resigned to it. Frightened by the *atabeg*'s brutal methods, they unanimously approved the treaty negotiated by 'Unar, whose policy proved undeniably effective. Fearing that he would be caught in a pincer movement, Zangī withdrew to Baalbek, which he entrusted as a fiefdom to a reliable man, Ayyūb, father of Saladin. He then headed north with his army, promising Ayyūb that he would soon return to avenge this setback. After the departure of the *atabeg*, 'Unar occupied Baniyās and handed it over to the Franj, in accordance with the terms of the treaty. He then made an official visit to the Kingdom of Jerusalem.

Usāmah, who had become the leading Damascene specialist on Frankish affairs, went with him. Fortunately for us, this emir-chronicler did more than simply participate in diplomatic negotiations. He had an inquisitive mind and was a keen observer who left us unforgettable testimony about mores and daily life during the time of the Franj.

> When I was visiting Jerusalem, I used to go to al-Aqṣā mosque, where my Templar friends were staying. Along one side of the building was a small oratory in which the Franj had set up a church. The Templars placed this spot at my disposal that I might say my prayers. One day I entered, said *Allāhu akbar*, and was about to begin my prayer, when a man, a Franj, threw himself upon me, grabbed me, and turned me toward the east, saying, "Thus do we pray." The Templars rushed forward and led him away. I then set myself to prayer once more, but this same man, seizing upon a moment of inattention, threw himself upon me yet again, turned my face to the east, and repeated once more, "Thus do we pray." Once again the Templars intervened, led him away, and apologized to me, saying, "He is a foreigner. He has just arrived from the land of the Franj and he has never seen anyone pray without turning to face east." I answered that I had prayed enough and left, stunned by the behavior of this demon who had been so enraged at seeing me pray while facing the direction of Mecca.

If the emir Usāmah did not hesitate to call the Templars "my friends," it was because he believed that their barbarian mores were gradually being refined by contact with the Orient. *Among the Franj*, he explains, *we find some people who have come to settle among us and who have cultivated the society of the Muslims. They are far superior to those who have freshly joined them in the territories they now occupy.* He considered the incident in al-Aqṣā mosque "an instance of the vulgarity of the Franj." And he mentioned others as well, gathered during his frequent visits to the Kingdom of Jerusalem.

> I happened to be in Tiberias one day when the Franj were celebrating one of their holidays. The knights had come out of the city to engage in a jousting tournament.

They brought with them two decrepit old women whom they stood at one end of the field; at the other end was a pig, hung suspended over a rock. The knights then organized a foot-race between the two old women. Each one advanced, escorted by a group of knights who obstructed her path. The old women stumbled, fell, and picked themselves up at almost every step, amid loud bursts of laughter from the spectators. Finally, one of the old women, the first to finish, took the pig as the prize for her victory.

An emir as well-educated and refined as Usāmah was unable to appreciate this burlesque Gallic humor. But his condescending pout shriveled into a grimace of outright disgust when he witnessed what the Franj called justice.

In Nablus, *he relates,* I had the opportunity to witness a curious spectacle. Two men had to meet each other in individual combat. The cause of the fight was this: some brigands among the Muslims had invaded a neighboring village, and a farmer was suspected of having acted as their guide. He ran away, but was soon forced to return, for King Fulk had imprisoned his children. "Treat me fairly," the farmer had asked him, "and allow me to compete against my accuser." The king then told the lord who had been granted this village as a fiefdom, "Bring the man's adversary here." The lord had selected a smith who worked in the village, telling him, "It is you who will fight this duel." The possessor of the fiefdom wanted to make sure that none of his peasants would be killed, for fear that his crops would suffer. I looked at this smith. He was a strong young man, but was constantly asking for something to drink, whether he was walking or sitting. As for the accused, he was a courageous old man who stood snapping his fingers in a gesture of defiance. The viscount, governor of Nablus, approached, gave each man a lance and shield, and had the spectators form a circle around them.

The struggle was joined. The old man forced the smith back, pressed him towards the crowd, and then returned to the center of the arena. There was an exchange of blows so violent that the rivals seemed to form a single column of blood. The fight dragged on, despite the exhortations of the viscount, who was anxious to hasten its conclusion. "Faster," he shouted at them. The old man was finally exhausted, and the smith, taking advantage of his experience in handling the hammer, dealt him a blow that knocked the old man down and caused him to lose his lance. He then leapt upon him and tried to dig his fingers into his eyes, but he could not manage it, for there was too much blood. The smith then rose and finished off his opponent with a thrust of his lance. A rope was immediately wound around the neck of the corpse, which was dragged to a gallows and hanged. In this example you may see what justice is among the Franj!

The emir's indignation was quite genuine, for justice was a serious business among the Arabs in the twelfth century. The judges, or *qāḍīs*, were highly respected men who were obliged to adhere to a meticulous procedure fixed by the Koran, before rendering their verdict: first came indictment, then plea, then testimony. The "judgment of God" to which the Occidentals often resorted seemed a macabre farce to the Arabs. The duel described by the chronicler was only one of the forms of trial by ordeal. The test of fire was another. There was also the water torture, which Usāmah described with horror.

> A large cask had been set up and filled with water. The young man who was the object of suspicion was pinioned, suspended from a rope by his shoulder-blades, and plunged into the cask. If he was innocent, they said, he would sink into the water, and they would pull him out by the rope. If he was guilty, it would be impossible for him to sink into the water. When he was thrown into the cask, the unfortunate man made every effort to descend to the bottom, but he could not manage it, and thus had to submit to the rigors of their law, may God's curse be upon them! He was then blinded by a red-hot silver awl.

The Syrian emir's opinion of the "barbarians" was hardly modified when he discussed their science. In the twelfth century the Franj lagged far behind the Arabs in all scientific and technical fields. But it was in medicine that the gap between the developed East and the primitive West was greatest. Usāmah observed the difference.

> One day, *he relates,* the Frankish governor of Munaytra, in the Lebanese mountains, wrote to my uncle the sultan, emir of Shayzar, asking him to send a physician to treat several urgent cases. My uncle selected one of our Christian doctors, a man named Thābit. He was gone for just a few days, and then returned home. We were all very curious to know how he had been able to cure the patients so quickly, and we besieged him with questions. Thābit answered: "They brought before me a knight who had an abscess on his leg and a woman suffering from consumption. I made a plaster for the knight, and the swelling opened and improved. For the woman I pre-scribed a diet to revive her constitution." But a Frankish doctor then arrived and objected, "This man does not know how to care for them." And, addressing the knight, he asked him, "Which do you prefer, to live with one leg or die with two?" When the patient answered that he preferred to live with just one leg, the physician ordered, "Bring me a strong knight with a well-sharpened battleaxe." The knight and the axe soon arrived. The Frankish doctor placed the man's leg on a chopping block, telling the new arrival, "Strike a sharp blow to cut cleanly." Before my very eyes, the man struck an initial blow, but then, since the leg was still attached, he struck a sec-ond time. The marrow of the leg spurted out and the wounded man died that very instant. As for the woman, the Frankish doctor examined her and said, "She has a demon in her head who has fallen in love with her. Cut her hair." They cut her hair. The woman then began to eat their food again, with its garlic and mustard, which aggravated the consumption. Their doctor affirmed, "The devil himself must have entered her head." Then, grasping a razor, he cut an incision in the shape of a cross, exposed the bone of the skull, and rubbed it with salt. The woman died on the spot. I then asked, "Have you any further need of me?" They said no, and I returned home, having learned much that I had never known about the medicine of the Franj.

Scandalized as he was by the ignorance of the Occidentals, Usāmah was even more deeply shocked by their morals: "The Franj," he wrote, "have no sense of honor. If one of them is walking in the street with his wife and encounters another man, that man will take his wife's hand and draw her aside and speak to her, while the husband stands waiting for them to finish their conversation. If it lasts too long, he will leave her with her interlocutor and go off!" The emir was troubled: "Imagine this contradiction! These people possess neither jealousy nor honor, whereas they are so courageous. Courage, however, comes only from one's sense of honor and from contempt for that which is evil!"

The more he learned of their ways, the more wretched did Usāmah consider the Occidentals to be. He admired nothing about them except their martial qualities. One may thus readily understand that when one of the "friends" he had made among them, a knight in King Fulk's army, proposed to take Usāmah's young son to Europe to initiate him in the rules of chivalry, the emir politely declined the invitation, muttering under his breath that he would prefer that his son go "to prison rather than to the land of the Franj." Fraternization with these foreigners had its limits. Besides, the famous collaboration between Damascus and Jerusalem, which had afforded Usāmah the unexpected opportunity to get to know the Occidentals better, soon appeared as a brief interlude. A spectacular event would now rekindle all-out war against the occupier: on Saturday 23 September 1144 the city of Edessa, capital of the oldest of the four Frankish states of the Middle East, fell into the hands of the atabeg 'Imād al-Dīn Zangī.

If the fall of Jerusalem in July 1099 marked the climax of the Frankish invasion, and the fall of Tyre in July 1124 the completion of the phase of occupation, the reconquest of Edessa has gone down in history as the capstan of the Arab riposte to the invaders and the beginning of the long march to victory.

[. . .]

THE TEARS OF SALADIN

[. . .] It is true that the greatness of Saladin lay also in his modesty.

One day when Salāh al-Dīn was tired and was trying to rest, one of his *mamlūks* came to him and handed him a paper to sign. "I am exhausted," said the sultan, "come back in an hour." But the man insisted. He fairly stuck the page in Salāh al-Dīn's face, saying, "Let the master sign!" The sultan replied, "But I have no inkwell here." He was seated at the entrance to his tent, and the *mamlūk* remarked that there was an inkwell inside. "There is an inkwell, at the back of the tent," he cried, which meant, in effect, that he was ordering Salāh al-Dīn to go and get the inkwell himself, no less. The sultan turned, saw the inkwell, and said, "By God, you're right." He reached back, bracing himself with his left hand, and grasped the inkwell in his right. Then he signed the paper.

This incident, related by Bahā' al-Dīn, Saladin's personal secretary and biographer, is a striking illustration of what made him so different from the monarchs of his time, indeed of all times: he was able to remain humble with the humble [. . .]
[. . .]

So it was that on Friday 2 October 1187, or 27 Rajab 583 by the Muslim calendar, the very day on which Muslims celebrate the Prophet's nocturnal journey to Jerusalem, Saladin solemnly entered the holy city. His emirs and soldiers had strict orders: no Christian, whether Frankish or Oriental, was to be touched. And indeed, there was neither massacre nor plunder. Some fanatics demanded that the Church of the Holy Sepulchre be destroyed in retaliation for the excesses committed by the Franj, but Saladin silenced them. On the contrary, he strengthened the guard at the Christian places of worship and announced that the Franj themselves would be allowed to come on pilgrimage whenever they liked. The Frankish cross attached to the Dome of the Rock mosque was removed, of course. And al-Aqṣā mosque, which had been turned into a church, became a Muslim place of worship again, after its walls had been sprinkled with rose water.

Most of the Franj remained in the city as Saladin, surrounded by a mass of companions, went from sanctuary to sanctuary weeping, praying, and prostrating himself. The rich made sure to sell their houses, businesses, or furniture before going into exile, the buyers generally being Orthodox or Jacobite Christians who planned to stay on. Other property was later sold to Jewish families settled in the holy city by Saladin.

As for Balian, he sought to raise the money needed to buy back the freedom of the poorest citizens. In itself, the ransom was not excessive, although for a prince it regularly ran to several tens of thousands of dinars, sometimes even a hundred thousand or more. But for ordinary people, something like twenty dinars per family represented a year or two's income. Thousands of unfortunates had gathered at the gates of the city to beg for coins. Al-'Ādil, who was as sensitive as his brother, asked Saladin's permission to free a thousand poor prisoners without payment of any ransom. When he heard this, the Frankish patriarch asked the same for seven hundred others, and Balian for another five hundred. They were all freed. Then, on his own initiative, the sultan announced that all old people would be allowed to leave without paying anything and that imprisoned men with young children would also be released. When it came to Frankish widows and orphans, he not only exempted them from any payment, but also offered them gifts before allowing them to leave.

Saladin's treasurers despaired. If the least fortunate were to be set free for nothing, they argued, at least the ransom for the rich should be raised. The anger of these worthy servants of the state knew no bounds when the patriarch of Jerusalem drove out of the city accompanied by numerous chariots filled with gold, carpets, and all sorts of the most precious goods. 'Imād al-Dīn al-Asfahānī was scandalized:

I said to the sultan: "This patriarch is carrying off riches worth at least two hundred thousand dinars. We gave them permission to take their personal property with them, but not the treasures of the churches and convents. You must not let them do it!" But Salāh al-Dīn answered: "We must apply the letter of the accords we have signed, so that no one will be able to accuse the believers of having violated their treaties. On the contrary, Christians everywhere will remember the kindness we have bestowed upon them."

The patriarch paid his ten dinars just like everyone else, and was even provided with an escort to make sure that he reached Tyre without incident.

Saladin had conquered Jerusalem not to amass gold, and still less to seek vengeance. His prime objective, as he himself explained, was to do his duty before his God and his faith. His victory was to have liberated the holy city from the yoke of the invaders—without a bloodbath, destruction, or hatred. His reward was to be able to bow down and pray in places where no Muslim would have been able to pray had it not been for him. On Friday 9 October, a week after the victory, an official ceremony was organized in al-Aqṣā mosque. Many religious leaders competed for the honor of delivering the sermon on this memorable occasion. In the end, it was the *qāḍī* of Damascus Muḥī al-Dīn Ibn al-Zaki, the successor of Abū Saʿad al-Ḥarawi, who was designated by the sultan to mount the pulpit, garbed in a superb black robe. Although his voice was clear and powerful, a slight tremor betrayed his emotion as he spoke: "Glory to God who has bestowed this victory upon Islam and who has returned this city to the fold after a century of perdition! Honor to this army, which He has chosen to complete the reconquest! And may salvation be upon you, Ṣalāḥ al-Dīn Yūsuf, son of Ayyūb, you who have restored the spurned dignity of this nation!"

REFERENCE

Jaggi, Maya. 2002. "A Son of the Road" (Profile of Amin Maalouf). In *The Guardian Online*, 15 November 2002. http://www.theguardian.com/music/2002/nov/16/classicalmusicandopera.fiction (accessed 14 January 2015).

3

From Napoleon in Egypt

Abd Al-Rahman Al-Jabarti, 1798

Born into a wealthy family of *ulama,* or Islamic scholars, Abd Al-Rahman Al-Jabarti (1753–1825) was trained as a religious man at the University of Al-Azhar in Cairo. He studied medicine at the university, but he is best known for his histories of Egypt, particularly his chronicle of events in Egypt under Napoleonic occupation.

The French invasion of Egypt lasted three years—1798 to 1801—and constituted a watershed encounter between two civilizations. When Napoleon conquered Cairo and other main ports and cities of Egypt, his goal was not to replace the already well established civilization—or so he said. The French expressed no explicit concern for converting the population to Christianity, changing the present culture, or uprooting civilians (though all of these outcomes did happen to some degree). In a letter addressed to the people of Egypt, Napoleon stated, "O ye Qadis, Shaykhs and Imams; O ye Shurbajiyya and men of circumstance, tell your nation that the French are also faithful Muslims, and in confirmation of this they invaded Rome and destroyed there the Papal See, which was always exhorting the Christians to make war with Islam" (Al-Jabarti 1975:26). This address was followed by five articles delimiting a new state of affairs for the newly occupied territory. With these five edicts, Napoleon stated the new modes of conduct that villages must abide by lest they invite attack. More important, he outlined the regulations of indirect rule (27). The French claimed that they were occupying Egypt only to remove its tyrannical rulers for the benefit of the people (and specifically to protect and expand Egypt's trade routes). The violent acts of the French, as well as their appropriation of resources, were mostly normalized under French law and tax systems, or carried out ostensibly to protect Egyptian and French security.

Al-Jabarti, Abd al-Rahman. 1975. *Napoleon in Egypt: Al-Jabarti's Chronicle of the French Occupation, 1798.* Shmuel Moreh, transl. Princeton, NJ: Markus Wiener. Pp. 96–118 (footnotes omitted). Reprinted with the permission of the publisher.

The invaders left the world copious records in French of their conquest of Ottoman Egypt, records that scholars have mined for histories of the two nations. The most impressive document to come out of the French colonization was a multivolume description of Egypt, the handiwork of scholars whom Napoleon had recruited for his conquest and colonization. These documents reveal the invaders' perceptions of Egypt and the subsequent French occupation.

Al-Jabarti wrote altogether contrasting versions of these cataclysmic years. His first work, *Tarik Muddat al Faransis Fi Misr* (History of the French Presence in Egypt), covers six months of the invasion and records his immediate reaction to the conquest. The second is *Muzhir al-Taqdis bi Dhahab Dawlat al-Faransis* (The Demonstration of Piety in the Demise of French Society), in which he expresses his rejection of all manifestations of the invasion. But his principal work, *Aja 'ib al-Athar fi al-Tarajim wa al-Akhbar* (Wondrous Seeds of Men and Their Deeds), chronicles the history of Egypt from 1688 to 1821 and was banned under Muhammad Ali's rule, as Al-Jabarti was critical of his modernization project. In 1870 the ban on its publication was lifted, and in 1879–80 the entire work was published. This chronicle, which is generally known in English simply as *Al-Jabarti's History of Egypt*, became a world-famous historical text partly by virtue of its eyewitness accounts of Napoleon's invasion and Muhammad Ali's seizure of power.

Al-Jabarti's historiography of Ottoman Egypt (1688–1821 AD) is monumental, a work of genius, according to historians in- and outside the Muslim world. One historian has described him as "one of the greatest historians of the Muslim world of all times, and by far the greatest historian of the Arab world in modern times" (Ayalon 1960:218). Another scholar, C. E. Bosworth, comments that when Al-Jabarti writes about the Frankish archaeologists, he expresses "his sense of wonder that people were prepared to expend so much time, labor, and money on transporting these relics . . . to Europe, and that people in Europe were prepared to pay even vaster sums for these objects" (Bosworth 1977:231). Bosworth concludes from this that Al-Jabarti's "judgment is thus a neutral and impartial one and shows that the mind of a very great scholar was able to comprehend and to reproduce in a fair way activities which were . . . well-nigh inexplicable" in his own culture (231).

In *Al-Jabarti's Chronicle of the French Occupation* (Al-Jabarti 1975; transl. Moreh), the first six months of the three-year French occupation established the central themes of the Franco-Egyptian encounter: efforts to win cooperation of the *ulema* (body of religious figures) in governing Egypt, the burden of French atrocities, the defeat of the Mamluk army, and Egyptian reactions to the French expeditions' research institute. Though critical of the foreign-born Mamluk military elite, Al-Jabarti is most contemptuous of Bonaparte's attempt to pass himself off as a liberator of Egypt from Mamluk oppression. He dismisses French revolutionary ideals: "Their term 'liberty' means that they are not slaves like the Mamluks" (28), he writes, dismissing the French claim that "[all people] 'are equal in the eyes of God' the Almighty" as "a lie and stupidity" (30). Al-Jabarti is appalled at the way the French treat the dead, notes their lack of modesty especially when relieving themselves in public, and views their habit of promiscuous sex as part of the episodic chaos and human depravity of the occupation. Although they are the wronged party in this invasion, the Egyptians are nowhere valorized by Al-Jabarti. In describing the utter disunity and haphazard opportunism of Copts, Greeks, Shami Christians, Bedouins, Jews, nobles, townsfolk, and peasants, and the orgy of looting that many took part in, he hardly depicts Egyptians in a sympathetic light. He sees the French as manipulating the situation while blasphemously claiming to be the true defenders of Islam against Mamluk misrule and pretending to be friends of all Egyptians, especially those willing to accept such as may be offered at the point of a bayonet—in the most consequential confrontation between Christendom and Islam since the Crusades.

Al-Jabarti makes astute observations on the structure of the French Republic in a somewhat humorous analysis of the occupiers' systems of rank and their notions of equality and liberty in comparison to those of Egyptians. He also analyzes the emperor himself, starting from the very meaning of his name and moving on to his spoken rhetoric of divine right, which Al-Jabarti does not hesitate to strategically and logically debunk. Al-Jabarti recounts how this friendly, almost fatherly figure failed to free Egyptians from oppression, having simply changed the faces of the oppressors from Mamluks to French. Egyptians faced many indignities under this regime change, including the imposition of heavy taxation, the loss of property and goods, and the destruction of their mosques. Al-Jabarti returns the one-sided gaze of imperial history. He initiates a dialogue with the French military. Napoleon Bonaparte landed at Alexandria in 1798, but his justifications for the invasion of Egypt sound eerily like those of both the British government and American president George W. Bush for the invasion of Iraq.

· · ·

THE MONTH OF JUMĀDĀ AL-ŪLĀ

[. . .]

When the French became insistent in their demands, deciding inexorably that those Shaykhs should be brought to them, the Shaykhs spoke with the French asking them what their intentions were and how those accused were to be treated. The interpreter replied that they were to be imprisoned and detained and would be severely reprimanded so that others might learn from this example. The Shaykhs replied "This would be an ugly deed and most improper, for indeed it is appropriate that the 'ulamā' be venerated and that they be treated with reverence and honor." However, the French did not heed them for they had already made up their minds and would not listen to their exhortation since their decision had already been made. In reply to this they cried out "If their imprisonment is unavoidable then let them be imprisoned with men of their own class." At this point Satan's gang agreed and detained them somewhere in al-Bakrī's house. Moreover some double-dealer, and I believe him to be one of those accursed Shāmī Christians, informed about Ibrāhīm Efendi, the secretary in charge of the spices (kātib al-bahār), that he had gathered a number of those rogues on the day of the riot and given them swords, guns, instruments of war, and cudgels. In addition he told the French that he had hidden several Mamlūks in his house as well as a number of important people. He had provided the fighters stationed at the wall with a well-known cannon-piece which he had brought out from his own house and other accusations without any basis and calumnies out of all proportion. The French thereupon ordered that he be brought in and dispatched him to the house of the Aghā where he was imprisoned.

After the riots, when the French had gained the upper hand over the people, they were seized with fear and put on the *cocarde* (*warda*) which they had formerly rejected and disdained, pinning it on their breasts, their shoulders, and their headgear. Then the Aghā and rulers ordered the people to desist from this, warning them not to make them or wear them. Furthermore, they said "When you were asked to wear it you haughtily disdained it; however now, after you have openly revealed your enmity and made it public you show affection and loyalty!" So they removed the *cocarde*. They had also hung the colored *bandieras* upon houses and caravanserai.

On Sunday the eighteenth Shaykh al-Sādāt and the other Shaykhs went to the house of the Ṣārī 'Askar and tried to intercede for the prisoners, these being the five above-mentioned Shaykhs and the secretary in charge of the spices as well as the rest of the common Muslim prisoners who were imprisoned in the Aghā's house, and that of the Qā'im Maqām and the Citadel. The interpreter conveyed their intercession to him and he replied with a hand gesture meaning, be patient. On this they left. When the Shaykh al-Sādāt got up to leave he exclaimed "No intercession was heeded and no request fulfilled!"

On that day, they proclaimed safe-conduct in the market places calling upon the people not to disturb one another. At the same time arrests continued day and night as did also the sudden raids and looting (by the French) behaving as enemy against enemy. As for all the goods which were looted from Christians and found in al-Jawwāniyya, they were returned in their entirety to their owners. However, of the property stolen from the Muslims none was returned at all.

And on that day 'Umar al-Qulluqjī (the Guard) mediated on behalf of the Maghribīs of al-Faḥḥāmīn quarter and gathered a great number of them as well as some others and presented them to the Ṣārī 'Askar who picked out the young men and the strong among them. Then he gave them swords and weapons and made them an independent body of soldiers with the above-mentioned 'Umar al-Qulluqjī at their head. Thus they went out of the Ṣārī 'Askar's house with the Shāmī drum (*ṭabl al-Shāmī*) before them according to the custom of the Maghribī soldiers. They went toward the north, since some of the villages had staged a revolt against the French soldiers at the time of the insurrection and fought them. The rebels had also fired at two boats bearing a number of French soldiers and fought them. But when the Maghribīs arrived, they subdued the riot. They razed the village of 'Ashma and killed its head who was called Ibn Sha'īr, plundering his house and furnishings, stealing his goods and livestock. And these all were in great quantities. Then they brought forth his brothers and children and killed them all except one young child whom they appointed *shaykh* (village head) in lieu of his father.

Then, the Maghribī soldiers were quartered at Bāb Sa'āda in Cairo where the authorities assigned to them some Frenchmen to come every day and train them in their methods of war and their way of giving commands. The trainees would stand in a row, their guns in their hands and their instructor in front of them. He would give them commands using the disgusting words of their own language. For example, when he said: "*Hardabūsh!*" (*Garde à vous*) they would raise their rifles, holding them in their clasped hands from their lower parts. Then the instructor would exclaim: "*Harsh!*" (*Marche*) and they would lower their arms, and so on.

On that day Barthélemy the European set out for Siryāqūs with a number of soldiers pursuing those who had fled eastward but he was unable to reach them. He collected *tafrīda* (appointed tax) and *kulaf* (impost for the upkeep of the military) from the villages, acting tyrannically in levying and collecting them and after some days returned to Cairo.

On Wednesday Shaykh Muḥammad al-Mahdī, the Secretary of the Dīwān, took up the case of Ibrāhīm Efendī, the secretary in charge of the spices, subtly bringing the matter to the Ṣārī 'Askar's attention with the help of the Vizier who was known by the name of Ruznāmjī. Consequently the Ṣārī 'Askar transferred Ibrāhīm Efendī from the Aghā's house to his own residence and demanded a statement of what belonged to the Mamlūks from the register of the spices.

On Thursday the word spread that Imperial ships had arrived at the port of Alexandria bearing a Qāḍī 'Askar and such other tales which were without basis.

On that day French boats, about forty in number set out to the north with French soldiers.

On Friday night on the twenty-fourth of the month a camel-rider arrived from Shām with letters, among which were a *firmān* bearing the Imperial cipher (*ṭurra sulṭāniyya*) and a letter from Aḥmad Pasha, another from Bakr Pasha to his Muṣṭafā Bey and a letter from Ibrāhīm Bey directed to the Shaykhs. All these letters were written in Arabic. Their contents after the impressive introductions were Qur'ānic verses, *ḥadith,* and traditions pertaining to *jihād* (holy war), curses upon the French nation and degrading statements about them, mentioning the corruption of their faith, their lies and deceit. The rest of the letters were in the same vein. So Muṣṭafā Bey took these letters and delivered them to the Ṣārī 'Askar who denounced them, saying "This is a forgery invented by Ibrāhīm the Mamlūk in order to stir up enmity and hatred between us and yourselves. As for Aḥmad Pasha he is merely a meddler and was never a Wālī in Shām or Egypt, for the Wālī of Shām is Ibrāhīm Pasha. As for the Wālī of Egypt he is 'Abd Allāh ibn al-'Aḍm who is at present Wālī of Shām; for I am best informed in this matter. He is to come to Egypt in a few days in the capacity of Wālī. Then we will live with him just as the Mamlūks lived with the Wālīs." Enclosed in these letters there was a note announcing the death of Muḥammad Pasha the Grand Vizier and of some other high Ottoman officials who had mixed with the French but the manner in which they died was not known. And it is said that the Grand Vizier was banished to Sāqiz and was killed there. But only God knows the truth of these matters.

During these days the meetings of the Dīwān stopped. The French concentrated on setting up barricades at several parts and constructing buildings on the hills surrounding the city in which they placed cannons and bombs. They also demolished several places in al-Jīza, fortifying the sites extraordinarily well. They did likewise in the old city of Cairo, in the surroundings of Shubrā, and in Inbāba. Several mosques were demolished, among others the mosque near the Dikka bridge and the Mosque of al-Maqs, known nowadays as the Mosque of Awlād ibn 'Anān, which is situated on the Nāṣirī canal near Bāb al-Baḥr. They cut down many trees, including the palms of the gardens, such as those in the fields of al-Ma'diyya opposite Awlād ibn 'Anān and the fields of Miṣbāḥ in the Sākit mosque district. They also demolished the Mosque of Kāzrūnī in al-Rawḍa and cut down the trees of al-Jīza which were at [Jāmi'] Abū Hubayra. They dug a great number of trenches and the like, and (cut down) the palms of al-Ḥillī, Būlāq, and so on. They demolished the houses and pulled down the palaces. They destroyed the windows and the gates and they burnt all the beams so that destruction proliferated in all these places and the owl hooted in them and the raven croaked.

On Saturday night a group of French soldiers appeared at the house of al-Bakrī at midnight and asked for the imprisoned Shaykhs to be brought to the Ṣārī 'Askar so that he might speak with them. On going out of the house, they found a great number of soldiers waiting for them outside who arrested them. Al-Jawsaqī lagged behind and then raised his voice, calling out "Hey, this is treachery!" Then one of the soldiers punched him and threw him on the ground on his face. They dragged the Shaykhs along the ground among them towards the Mosque of al-Azbak. Then they stripped them and tied their hands behind their backs and went with them up to the Citadel and put them in jail until the next forenoon. Then they took them out and made them descend through Bāb al-Jabal behind the Citadel where they shot them dead. They thereupon buried them in the ravine at the *Mizrāq* (a place where soldiers train in throwing javelins) at the foot of the Citadel and covered them with earth. However, most of the people did not know what had happened to them for days.

And on the morning of that day some of the Shaykhs rode to the Katkhudā 'l-Pasha thinking that they were still alive. So he rode with them to the Ṣārī 'Askar and the Shaykhs spoke with him about this matter. The Ṣārī 'Askar said to them through the interpreter "The Ṣārī 'Askar says to you that you should be patient, this is not the right time." So they got up and left him. The latter also rose and went about his affairs. Then all the other Shaykhs arrived but did not find him so they went back.

On Tuesday several French soldiers came to al-Azhar quarter near the mosque and stood there. People suspected evil from them and stampeded. They shut the shops and vied with one another in fleeing. Their opinions differed concerning these soldiers and all related versions according to their own conjectures, thoughts, and twisted imaginations.

Then one of the Shaykhs went and informed the Ṣārī ʿAskar of what was happening so they sent someone ordering them to leave. So they left. The people then returned and opened their shops, while the Wālī, the Aghā, and Barthélemy passed [through the quarter] proclaiming safe-conduct. So the situation calmed down. It was said that one of the French officers had come to visit the guard (qulluq) who resided near the shrine of al-Ḥusaynī and sat with him for a while. Those soldiers were his corps and they stood there waiting for him. They may also have done so to frighten the people and intimidate them, fearing that a riot would break out, when the word spread that the Shaykhs had been killed.

On that day they wrote notices and posted them in the market-places proclaiming an amnesty, warning against stirring up riots and stating that the Muslims who had been killed were an equal compensation for the French who had been killed.

And on that day the French started a count of immovable property (amlāk), registering it and demanding a stated imposition on it. However, no one opposed this or uttered a single word.

On that day the French removed the gates from the by-streets and small quarters which had no outlet to others. These were the places which had previously been left alone and their inhabitants had been spared since they had settled with the French before the event, by bribing the guards and mediators. The by-streets of the Ḥusayniyya quarter were treated in the same manner. After the event had passed the French changed their minds about leaving those gates in place, and went about removing them and bringing them to where gates were collected in al-Azbakiyya at Raṣīf al-Khashshāb. There they smashed some of these gates and cut their beams to pieces, and transported others of them on carts to where they were setting up barricades in various parts of the city. Others were sold as firewood and the metal parts were also sold.

On Wednesday night a gang fell upon the gate of Ṭaylūn and destroyed it, passing from there to the market itself, smashing the lamps. They broke into three stores and stole the goods of the Maghribī merchants which were in them, killing the guard and then leaving.

On the Thursday the Shaykhs went to the Ṣārī ʿAskar and interceded on behalf of the son of al-Jawsaqī the Shaykh of the blind men's guild who was being detained at the house of al-Bakrī. Their intercession was accepted by the Ṣārī ʿAskar and he was freed.

THE MONTH OF JUMĀDĀ AL-THĀNĪ

This month began on Saturday. On that day the French sent a number of notices throughout the country and posted up some in the market-places and alleys written by the French through the mouth of the Shaykhs, its contents being as follows:

"A copy of advice from all the *'ulamā'* of Islam in Cairo.

"We seek refuge in God from all civil strife, be it in open or in secret. Before God we declare that we dissociate ourselves from all those people who spread evil upon the earth. We inform all the inhabitants of Cairo that disturbances have occurred in the city perpetrated by ruffians and evil people who stirred up malice between the subjects and the French soldiers after they had been friends and companions together. As a consequence, a number of Muslims were killed and some houses were looted. However, the kindness of God mysteriously came and the strife was suppressed by virtue of our intercession with General Bonaparte and this calamity ended. For he is a man of perfect wisdom who is compassionate and sympathetic towards the Muslims and filled with love for the poor and the miserable. And were it not for him the soldiers would have burnt the whole city, looted all the property, and killed the entire population of Cairo. Therefore you should not stir up civil discord nor obey the commands of the wicked abettors of disorder nor heed the words of the hypocrites. Follow not the wicked ones and do not be off with those who perish, who are foolish and too incompetent to foresee the consequences; so that you may save your birthplaces and be at rest with regard to your families and religion. For verily God, glory be to Him, 'giveth His kingdom to whom He pleaseth' and 'ordained what He pleaseth.' Thus we inform you that everyone who was involved in stirring up this civil discord, was killed to the last man. And thus God delivered the country and mankind from them. And our advice to you is that you should not throw yourselves into perdition by your own hands but busy yourselves with your own livelihoods, fulfil the obligations of your religion, and pay the taxes (*kharāj*) imposed upon you. For 'Religion compels us to give you proper advice.' And let it be done with that."

On this letter were the signatures of al-Bakrī, al-Sharqāwī, al-Amīr, al-Ṣāwī, al-Fayyūmī, al-Mahdī, al-'Arīshī, al-Sirsī, Muṣṭafā al-Damanhūrī, Muḥammad al-Dawākhilī, and Yūsuf al-Shubrakhītī.

On that day the French ordered the remainder of those living by the Birkat al-Azbakiyya and its surroundings to pack and move from their houses so that their (the French) compatriots who were scattered about would come together and live in one single quarter. This was as a result of the fear of the Muslims which had gripped them and to such an extent that no Frenchman would go unarmed. He who had no arms would take a stick or a whip or the like. This happened after they had already felt safe with the Muslims and had ceased to bear arms at all and had played and joked with them. For example, when a Muslim would stroll at night alone and pass a group of Frenchmen they would joke with him and vice versa. However, after this incident (rebellion) occurred both sects felt mutually repelled and each was on his guard toward the other. The Muslims also desisted from going to the markets from sunset to sunrise.

On the fifth of that month the authorities released Ibrāhīm Efendī the secretary of the spices who went to his house.

On the eighth, they executed four Coptic Christians among them two carpenters who, it was said, had got drunk in a wine shop, and had roamed in their drunkenness breaking into some shops and stealing some things. It was also said that they had done this several times until the Copts finally got angry.

On that day they also wrote a number of notices and sent some copies to the country and posted up others in the quarters and markets, also written through (the mouth of) the Shaykhs. However the text of this notice exceeded the former. It was worded as follows:

"A copy of advice from the ʿulamāʾ of Islam in Cairo.

"We inform you, O inhabitants of cities and capitals of provinces, you the Faithful. And you, O inhabitants of the countryside, both bedouin and peasants. We inform you that Ibrāhīm Bey and Murād Bey and the rest of the Mamlūk faction sent letters and proclamations to all the provinces of Egypt in order to stir up civil discord among the people and they claimed that these letters were sent by His Majesty the Sultan and by some of his Viziers. But this claim is false and slanderous and the reason was that they were extremely grieved and distressed and that they were most infuriated by the ʿulamāʿ of Cairo and its inhabitants since they did not agree to leave Egypt with them or to abandon their families and birthplaces. So they were intent upon causing civil discord and evil between the subjects and the French army in order to ruin the country and bring about the total destruction of its subjects. The cause of all this being the great distress that befell the Mamlūk faction at the loss of their rule and of their being deprived of the kingdom of Egypt. Had they been right in their claim that these letters were sent by the Sultan of Sultans, he would have dispatched them openly by appointed Aghās from his court. Therefore we say to you that the French, unlike the rest of the European people, always have had affection for the Muslims, and their creed, and have hated the unbelievers and their nature. Indeed they are dear friends to His Lordship the Sultan, backing him as allies and faithful to his companionship and always ready to help him. The French love his friends and hate his enemies. For this reason there is great animosity between the French and the Muscovites since the latter are inimical to Islam and its followers who profess the Unity of God to the extent that the Muscovites wish to conquer Islāmbūl and in addition plan all manner of subterfuges and perverted intrigues in order to take all the Ottoman Muslim countries. But this will not happen because of the alliance with the French and their love for and backing of the Ottoman Empire. They (the Muscovites) are determined to take over the Aya Ṣofya and all the other mosques and turn them into churches wherein they can practice their corrupt rites and detestable religion of the Muscovites. Meanwhile the French nation is helping His Majesty the Sultan to conquer their country, with God's will not leaving one of them alive. So we advise you, O provinces of Egypt. Do not stir up civil discord or evil acts among people, do not oppose the French soldiers in any manner; for if you do, harm, destruction, and misfortune shall befall you. Do not heed the words of the abettors of disorder, 'and obey not the bidding of those who commit excess, who act disorderly on the earth and reform not,' 'and speedily have to repent of what ye have done.' What you have to do is but to pay the taxes (kharāj) imposed upon you, to all the tax-farmers (multazims), that you may dwell in your birthplaces safely and be secure and at rest with regard to your families and property. For indeed His Excellency Bonaparte the grand Ṣārī ʿAskar, Commander of the Armies (Amīr al-Juyūsh), agreed with us that he will not contest anyone in his practice of Islam, nor will he oppose us with regard to the laws which God has decreed upon us. What is more he will remove all the injustice from among the people and restrict himself only to collecting taxes. He will eliminate the financial injustices which the tyrants have invented. Do not set your hopes on Ibrāhīm or Murād but return to your Lord, the King of the Kingdom and Creator of His slaves. For His Prophet and most honored Messenger said 'Strife is fast asleep, may God curse anyone who would awaken it among the nations.' Benedictions and peace upon him. And that is the end."

Thus the letter terminated bearing the signatures of the aforementioned Shaykhs, written by the secretary of the Dīwān, Shaykh Muḥammad al-Mahdī.

On the thirteenth of the month they killed two people at Bāb Zuwayla, one of them a Jew. However, the reason for their execution was not ascertained.

On that day they removed objects placed in trust belonging to the daughter of Ibrāhīm Bey and her husband from the house of the father-in-law (nasīb) of Ibrāhīm Katkhudā Manāw who was formerly Katkhudā Mustaḥfiẓān. These objects were boxes containing gold-work, jewels, gold and silver vessels, household effects and clothing in great quantities.

On the fifteenth a group of French soldiers passed by the Gate of Zuwayla at night and broke into some of the shops belonging to the sugar makers and they robbed them of their sugar and the loss was theirs.

On that day it was pointed out that someone had two cases in trust for Ayyūb Bey the Daftardār so they looked for him and ordered him to present them, which he did after denying several times that they were in his possession. Inside these cases they found jeweled weapons, strings of pearl beads, jeweled daggers, and the like.

On the twentieth they printed a number of notices which they posted up in the market-places, the content being: "On Friday the twenty-first we intend to fly a vessel (ballon) over al-Azbakiyya Pond by means of a device belonging to the French people." As was their custom, the people made a great fuss about it. When the day came the people and many of the French gathered in the afternoon to see this wondrous event and I was among them. I saw a cloth in the form of a large tent upon an erected pole. The cloth was colored in white, red, and blue. The pole upon which the cloth was suspended was set upon something like the cylindrical form of a sieve in the midst of which there was a bowl out of which came a wick immersed in certain oils. This bowl hung from intercrossing iron wires running from it to the cylinder. The cylinder itself was bound with pulleys and ropes which were held by people standing on the roofs of near-by houses. About an hour after the ʿaṣr they lit this wick and its smoke rose into the cloth and filled it. The cloth swelled and became like a ball. The smoke sought to rise to its center but it did not find any exit, so it drew the apparatus aloft with itself. Meanwhile the people pulled it with ropes until it rose from the ground. They cut the ropes and it soared into the air, moving with the wind. Then it began to sail with the wind for a very little while and then its bowl fell with the wick, the cloth following suit. The French were embarrassed at its fall. Their claim that this apparatus is like a vessel in which people sit and travel to other countries in order to discover news and other falsifications did not appear to be true. On the contrary, it turned out that it is like kites which household servants (farrāsh) build for festivals and happy occasions.

That same night at the time of the ʿishāʾ (evening prayer) the French gave a display of fireworks, fire-crackers, and rockets in al-Azbakiyya. It seemed that that day and night was one of their festivals because the Ṣārī ʿAskar invited the Shaykhs and notables among the merchants and all of them put on new garments. On that night the French passed through the markets very frequently and the dogs barked at them. So they threw poisoned bread to the dogs; the dogs ate it with the result that a great number of them died.

The next day people found the bodies of the dogs in the market-places dead. So the French hired some people to drag the corpses to the dump.

On the twenty-fifth a number of soldiers set out for Murād Bey and also toward Kardāsa because of the bedouin. They also went to Suez and al-Ṣāliḥiyya. They took the camels of the water-carriers together with their waterskins and their donkeys. As a result the water supply dwindled and its price went up so that a skin of water cost ten niṣf fiḍḍas if at all obtainable.

On that day they succeeded in uncovering several caches in various places in which there were chests, goods, arms, china and copper vessels in tremendous amounts, and the like. It was said that those who were in Kardāsa were bedouin known as ʿArab al-Ghazw nomads from Banī ʿAlī, wandering during the year in the countryside and districts stealing and snatching whatever they came upon. It was also said that they were Maghribīs whom Murād Bey had brought by means of ʿAlī Pasha al-Ṭarābulsī, from parts of the Maghrib.

And so this month passed with its major and minor events which are impossible to record because of their great number.

Among these events was that in the Ghayṭ al-Nūbī adjacent to al-Azbakiyya they (the French) constructed some buildings with compartments and places for amuse-

ment and licentiousness including all kinds of depravities and unrestricted entertainment, among them drinks and spirits, female singers and European dancers and
the like. One of their notables was in charge of it. On the day of its opening he held
a banquet to which he invited the notables of the French and some of those of the
Muslims and the Shaykhs. That night they set off a display of firecrackers, rockets
with firing and illuminations (*shunnuk*). The French appointed attendants, cooks,
and cupbearers. At its gate sat a man who would take from every person entering
ninety *niṣf* (*fiḍḍas*) and give him in return a piece of paper which would serve as a
certificate allowing him to come and go on that day. And when someone would
come to this place and occupy himself with food, drink, fornication, and gambling
according to his heart's desire he would pay for each of these services according to
what it cost. If he took a private compartment which would be his alone he had to
pay rent for each month that he held it. He would then receive a key and furnish it
as he wished. This service was not restricted to the French only but was available to
anyone who wanted it, whether he be European, Muslim, Copt, Greek, or Jew.

Among these events also was the demolition of the courtyard of the Nilometer
(*qāʿat al-miqyās*) in al-Rawḍa and the mosque of Abū Hubayra in al-Jīza. The
French levelled the hill near al-Laymūn bridge and built towers and artillery points
on it. They did the same to the hill which is at the al-Nāṣirī canal adjacent to the
Maghribī and they filled in the part of the canal which was adjacent to it with earth.
They tore down the Dikka bridge and filled in the area where it had stood with the
debris of the adjacent mosque which they had demolished as well as that of houses
surrounding it which they had also destroyed. They filled in the part near the
bridge, making it level with the pavement at its banks continuing to the bridge. In
the same way they demolished the buildings opposite the Ṣārī ʿAskar's house and
constructed in their place a wide square. They filled in the part of Birkat al-Azbakiyya which was opposite this square so that the bridge became level with the pavement. They also demolished the dwellings opposite this square on the other side
and turned the area into a walled-up road running along the filled-in portion of the
Nāṣirī canal, adjacent to the Maghribī which connects with Būlāq. They also
demolished a great part of the house of ʿAlī Katkhudā al-Ṭawīl near his dwelling.
And they also filled in the part of the pond which was opposite it and also pulled
down the houses opposite. They filled in the mouth of the canal of al-Raṭlī pond
and cut down the trees of the garden of the secretary of the spices which is opposite
the bridge of al-Raṭlī pond and cut the trees of the bridge, also demolishing its wall
which is adjacent to al-Ḥājib bridge and from the other side they demolished the
wall of the garden opposite it and cut down its trees and they made it into a road
connecting with the mosque of Ẓāhir Baybars in the direction of al-ʿĀdiliyya. They
pulled down the minaret of the mosque turning it into a tower, and flattened its
walls as they wished and set upon it cannons and machines of war. And so it came
about that the pedestrian who comes from the direction of Qubbat al-Naṣr and

al-'Ādiliyya on his way to al-Azbakiyya, passes by way of the above-mentioned al-Ẓ āhirī mosque to al-Ḥājib bridge then to the bridge of al-Raṭlī pond on to its filled-in canal until he reaches the road known as al-Shaykh Shu'ayb near the pottery factory. If he wishes to go to al-Azbakiyya he goes to the right towards Bāb al-Ḥadīd. If he wants al-'Adawī quarter and al-Sha'riyya Gate he has to go to the left. And they leveled these roads by evening the high places with the lower. They cut through part of the hill which was an obstacle to the road which is near the canal. They demolished the wall of al-Junayna and cut down some of its trees which are adjacent to Bāb al-Ḥadīd. They also pulled down the walls and buildings which intervene between Bāb al-Ḥadīd and the public square which is just outside the mosque of al-Maqs which is used as a place for selling millstones. All this in order to connect this road with al-Azbakiyya. They built fortifications, towers, and buildings on Tall al-'Aqārib in al-Nāṣirīyya. They demolished several of the Amīr's houses and they took the rubble and marble to the buildings on the hills and other places.

To the administrators of affairs (managers), the astronomers, scholars, and scientists in mathematics, geometry, astronomy, engraving and drawing, and also to the painters, scribes, and writers they assigned al-Nāṣirīyya quarter and all the houses in it, such as the house of Qāsim Bey, the Amīr of the Pilgrimage known as Abū Sayf, and the house of Ḥasan Kāshif Jarkas which he founded and built to perfection, having spent upon it fantastic sums of money amounting to more than a hundred thousand dinārs. When he had completed plastering and furnishing it, the French came and he fled with the others and left all that it contained, not having enjoyed it for even a whole month. The administrators, astronomers, and some of the physicians lived in this house in which they placed a great number of their books and with a keeper taking care of them and arranging them. And the students among them would gather two hours before noon every day in an open space opposite the shelves of books, sitting on chairs arranged in parallel rows before a wide long board. Whoever wishes to look up something in a book asks for whatever volumes he wants and the librarian brings them to him. Then he thumbs through the pages, looking through the book, and writes. All the while they are quiet and no one disturbs his neighbor. When some Muslims would come to look around they would not prevent them from entering. Indeed they would bring them all kinds of printed books in which there were all sorts of illustrations and *cartes* (*kartāt*) of the countries and regions, animals, birds, plants, histories of the ancients, campaigns of the nations, tales of the prophets including pictures of them, of their miracles and wondrous deeds, the events of their respective peoples and such things which baffle the mind. I have gone to them many times and they have shown me all these various things and among the things I saw there was a large book containing the Biography of the Prophet, upon whom be mercy and peace. In this volume they draw his noble picture according to the extent of their knowledge and judgment about him. He is depicted standing upon his feet looking toward Heaven as if menacing all creation. In his right hand is the sword and in his left the Book and around him are his Companions, may God be pleased with them, also with swords in their hands. In another page there are pictures of the Rightly Guided Caliphs. On another page a picture of the Midnight Journey of Muḥammad and al-Burāq and he, upon whom be mercy and peace, is riding upon al-Burāq from the Rock of Jerusalem. Also there is a picture of Jerusalem and the Holy Places of Mekka and Medīna and of the four Imāms, Founders of the Schools, and the other Caliphs and Sultans and an image of Islāmbūl including her Great Mosques like Aya Ṣofya and the Mosque of Sultan Muḥammad. In another picture the manner in which the Prophet's Birthday is celebrated and all the types of people who participate in it (are shown); also (there are) pictures of the Mosque of Sultan Sulaymān and the manner in which the Friday prayers are conducted in it, and the Mosque of Abū Ayyūb al-Anṣārī and the manner in which prayers for the dead are performed in it, and pictures of the countries, the coasts, the seas, the Pyramids, the ancient temples of Upper Egypt including the pictures, figures, and inscriptions which are drawn upon them. Also there are pictures of the species of animals, birds, plants and herbage which are peculiar to each land. The glorious Qur'ān is translated into their language! Also many other Islamic books. I saw in their possession the *Kitāb al-Shifā* of Qāḍī ʿIyāḍ, which they call *al-Shifā al-Sharīf* and *al-Burda* by Abū Ṣīrī, many verses of which they know by heart and which they translated into French. I saw some of them who know chapters of the Qur'ān by heart. They have a great interest in the sciences, mainly in mathematics and the knowledge of languages, and make great efforts to learn the Arabic language and the colloquial. In this they strive day and night. And they have books especially devoted to all types of languages, their declensions and conjugations as well as their etymologies. They possess extraordinary astronomical instruments of perfect construction and instruments for measuring altitudes of wondrous, amazing, and precious construction. And they have telescopes for looking at the stars and measuring their scopes, sizes, heights, conjunctions, and oppositions, and the clepsydras and clocks with gradings and minutes and seconds, all of wondrous form and very precious, and the like.

In a similar manner they assigned the house of Ibrāhim Katkhudā al-Sinnārī and the house of the former Katkhudā Zayn al-Fiqār and neighboring houses to the studious and knowledgeable ones. They called this *al-Madāris* (the Schools) and provided it with funds and copious allowances and generous provisions of food and drink. They provided them with a place in the house of the above-mentioned Ḥasan Kāshif and built in it neat and well-designed stoves and ovens, and instruments for distilling, vaporizing, and extracting liquids and ointments belonging to medicine and sublimated simple salts, the salts extracted from burnt herbs, and so forth. In this place there are wondrous retorts of copper for distillation, and vessels and long-necked bottles made of glass of various forms and shapes, by means of which acidic liquids and solvents are extracted. All this is carried out with perfect skill and wondrous invention and the like.

On that day the news arrived of the death of Ḥāliḥ Bey, Amīr al-Ḥajj. He had set out for Jerusalem with the Maḥmal of the Pilgrimage, placed it there and then returned to Gaza where he became ill with fever for several days and died.

THE MONTH OF RAJAB

Rajab started on a Sunday. On the third of this month Shaykh al-Sādāt celebrated the birthday of Sayyida Zaynab at the bridges of Sibā'. The Ṣārī ʿAskar Bonaparte was invited. He came to the house in which the Shaykh dwelt on the eve of the celebration and that was the house of Ayyūb Jāwish. He had supper with his people of distinction and after that returned home, riding.

On that day the French executed one of the soldiers called Muṣṭafā Kāshif, one of the *mamlūks* of Ḥusayn Bey who is known as Shuft. He had escaped together with the other escapers and had come back without permission and had hidden in the house of Shaykh Sulaymān al-Fayyūmi. The Shaykh Sulaymān handed him over to Muṣṭafā the Aghā Mustaḥfiẓān in order that he might obtain safe-conduct for him. When the latter informed the French of his presence they ordered his execution. So they killed him and then cut off his head with which they roved through the town, proclaiming "This is the punishment of those who re-enter Cairo without the permission of the French."

On Thursday the fifth of the month the Ṣārī ʿAskar of the Qalyūb district came to Cairo with Sulaymān al-Shawārbī who was the Shaykh of the district. When they arrived they took the Shaykh to the Citadel and imprisoned him there. It was said that the French had stumbled upon a letter of his which he had sent to Siryāqūs at the time of the revolt, inciting people of this area to revolt and ordering them to make ready for the time of the call if he found that the French were losing in Cairo. They punished him because of this letter and imprisoned four of the troopers (*Ajnād*) at the same time too.

On that day they invented a cannon which fired at noontime every day, because among the French the hours of day and night start from noon.

On Wednesday the tenth of the month the criers announced that anyone who wished to purchase a horse or a donkey should present himself on the twelfth of the month in Būlāq and buy from the French whichever ones he wished. To this effect they prepared notices which they posted up in the market-places and alleys. These were printed with the emblem, the sign and cipher (of the French Republic), as was their custom, and its contents were as follows:

"Let it be known to all people of Egypt that on Friday the 12th of Rajab at two o'clock a great number of horses, shall be sold by the French Republic in Būlāq. For this purpose we have granted permission to anyone who wishes to buy horses to do so as he pleases."

On Monday, the sixteenth of the month Ṣārī ʿAskar Bonaparte set out for Suez taking with him Sayyid Aḥmad al-Maḥrūqī and Ibrāhīm Efendi the secretary of the spices in addition to his counsellors (managers—*mudabbirūn*), some engineers, painters, Jirkis al-Jawharī, and Antoun (al-Ṭūn) Abū Ṭāqiya the Copt, and others. He also took a number of soldiers, cavalry and infantry, some cannons, wagons, litters borne by two camels, a number of camels bearing the ammunition, water, and provisions (*qūmānya*—It. *comania*).

On that day they started once again to arrange the Dīwān as formerly but with a new system. They appointed sixty members, Shaykhs of the Theologians, Shaykhs of guilds, Copts, and the French. To this effect they wrote notices, some copies of which were sent to the notables others being posted up in the markets as usual. Those who were appointed to the Dīwān received these notices directed to them personally. It is appropriate to present the main part of the roll written concerning this matter, in the name and in the words of the Ṣārī ʿAskar, because of its falsifications and weak-minded deceit and its audacious presumption in claiming Mahdīhood or Prophethood, and proving these claims by their antithesis. The contents are as follows:

"In the name of God the Merciful the Compassionate.

"From Bonaparte the Commander of the French Armies directed to all the inhabitants of Egypt of all ranks:

"We hereby inform you that some senseless and empty-headed people who do not foresee the consequences of their actions have recently instigated civil discord and spread evil among the inhabitants of Cairo. As a result God destroyed them for their deeds and malicious intentions. However the Creator, who is Praised and Exalted, commanded me to be compassionate and merciful with His servants. I have acted in accordance with His command and have become merciful and compassionate towards you. Nevertheless, I was seized with anger and intense grief because of the civil discord which was stirred up among you. For this reason, two months ago I abolished the Dīwān which I had set up for you for the good order of the country and the improvement of your condition. And now we intend to reinstitute the Dīwān as it was, for your good behavior and actions during the above-mentioned period have made us forget the sins of the evil ones and those who stirred up the civil strife which occurred formerly. O ʿulamāʾ, Sharīfs, and Imāms, inform your people and your communities that he who is inimical to me and who opposes me does so only because of an error of the mind and corruption of thoughts. Verily he shall find no refuge or deliverance to save him from me in this world, neither shall he escape the hands of God for he opposes the destiny of God who is Praised and Exalted. Indeed the sensible man knows that our acts are His will and divine decree and he who doubts this is stupid and devoid of perception. Also tell your people that since the beginning of time God has decreed the destruction of the enemies of Islam and the breaking of the crosses by my hand. Moreover He decreed from eternity that I shall come from the West to the Land of Egypt for the purpose of destroying those who have acted tyrannically in it and to carry out the tasks which He set upon me. And no sensible man will doubt that all this is by virtue of God's decree and will. Also tell your people that the many verses of the glorious Qur'ān announce the occurrence of events which have occurred and indicate others which are to occur in the future. Indeed the words of God in His book are truth and righteousness which are inevitable in their realization. Once these facts settle in your minds and become firm in your ears then let your nation return to good intentions and loyalty. Indeed there are some of them who refrain from cursing me and showing me enmity out of fear of my weapons and great power and they do not know that God sees the secret thoughts, He 'knoweth the deceitful of eye, and what men's breasts conceal.' And those who bear such secret thoughts oppose the decisions of God and they are hypocrites, and the curse and affliction of God shall surely befall them for God knoweth the secret things. Know ye also that it is in my power to expose what is in the heart of every one of you, for I know the nature of man and what is concealed in his heart at the very moment that I look upon him even though I do not state or utter what he is hiding. However, a time and a day will come in which you will see for yourselves that whatever I have executed and decreed is indeed a divine decree and irrefutable. For no human effort, no matter how devoted, will prevent me from carrying out God's will which He has decreed and fulfilled by my hand. Happy are they who hasten in unity and ardor to me with good intentions and purity of heart and that is all."

After this came the rest of the commands and the names of the people who were appointed to carry them out. He then referred to the General and Permanent Dīwāns and the choosing of fourteen members by ballot for the Permanent Dīwān and fourteen for the General Dīwān together with the French directors and managers and other people. He also mentioned the assignment of monthly salaries to the members of the Permanent Dīwān and so on.

On the eighteenth of this month they [the French] wandered among the mills and chose from each one a horse or accepted a financial arrangement instead. And that is to say when they had set up the horse market in Būlāq, the millers had bought a great number and every Frenchman who sold his horse made a mark on its ear. Afterwards they would go through the mills and take instead of their own horses whatever (horses) they found suitable or felt like.

On the twenty-fourth Sayyid Aḥmad al-Maḥrūqī and the chief secretary of the spices arrived from Suez, that being because the Ṣārī 'Askar intended to go to the district of Bilbays and they asked his permission to return to Cairo which he granted. So they went back with fifty soldiers whom he had sent to take them to Cairo. Bonaparte went meanwhile to the Sharqiyya. This group brought news (when they arrived in Cairo) that when the inhabitants of Suez heard of the arrival of the soldiers they fled and abandoned Suez, some going to al-Ṭūr and others with the bedouin. The approaching troops looted whatever they found of the belongings of those who had fled, such as coffee beans, household effects, and the like. They destroyed the houses and smashed their wooden parts and water jars. And when the Ṣārī ʿAskar arrived accompanied by the merchants, they informed him of this affair and told him that these doings were improper. So he retrieved some of the booty from the troops and promised to get back the rest or pay the price of the goods when they reached Cairo and that for this purpose they should write a list of the looted property, all empty talk. Indeed when he departed from that place, the soldiers grabbed the property which he had got back in addition to what they had not managed to steal before. Also two boats were found coming to Suez containing a quantity of coffee beans, one of which sank. Then some French got together and boarded small boats and made for the sunken ship in a diving-bell (?) (ghāṭis) and extracted it (the cargo) by means of instruments which they had constructed.

During the period of his stay at Suez Bonaparte began to ride about examining the area in all directions of the shore and the land night and day. He took with him as food three roasted chickens wrapped in paper and he had no cook, or valet to make his bed or servant to pitch his tent.

On Saturday several French soldiers arrived from Bilbays with about thirty bedouin bound with ropes. They also took prisoner several of their children, male and female, and entered Cairo with them, conducting them with a procession with drummers preceding them. They also brought three loads of merchandise and some camels which had been stolen from the merchants when they were returning from the Ḥajj.

On Sunday night at the end of the month of Rajab the Ṣārī ʿAskar reached Cairo from Bilbays bringing with him some bedouin, together with ʿAbd al-Raḥ mān Abāẓa the brother of Sulaymān Abāẓa Shaykh of the ʿAyāyda and others as hostages. They attacked Abū Zaʾbal and al-Munayyir and plundered them. They took the riding beasts and cattle there and brought them to Cairo, their owners, men, women, and children, following them.

On that day they also executed Sulaymān al-Shawārbī, the Shaykh of the bedouin and Shaykh of Qalyūb, in addition to three others who were said to be from the bedouin of the Sharqiyya. They brought them down from the Citadel to al-Rumayla through (with the help of) the Aghā and cut off their heads. Then they carried off the body and head of al-Shawārbī in a chest and his slaves (atbāʿ) took him and went with him to his village, Qalyūb.

This month ended with the general and particular events that occurred, as for example that a number of soldiers climbed and broke into some houses at night, robbing belongings and killing some people in the houses and alleys for nothing. And it happened on the night of the twenty-seventh that a group (of Frenchmen) came upon the house of Shaykh Muḥammad ibn al-Jawharī which is in al-Azbakiyya near Bāb al-Hawā. They broke and removed the window of the reception room which looks down upon the pond, entered by it, and ascended to the top of the house where there were three women servants and a girl servant and the porter. Shaykh Muḥammad, the landlord mentioned above, had moved with his womenfolk to another house and had left some furnishings in this house in addition to these people. He would visit it now and then and sometimes go to the other one. When they got into the upper part of the house those women woke up and screamed. So they struck them and killed them. But the girl hid in a corner. Meanwhile they wrought havoc in the house and took whatever they wanted and descended. Then the porter and his son woke up also and hid. When morning dawned and the word spread the Ṣārī ʿAskar was absent. So the Shaykhs of the Dīwān rode to the Qāʾim Maqām and spoke to him of this incident. The Qāʾim Maqām showed an interest in investigating who had done such a thing.

Other events of the month included the aggressive behavior of the guards and their severe insistence that the lamps in the roads be lit. When they passed at night and found a lamp which had gone out because of the wind or because of its oil running due to the thickness of the wick and the like, they would nail up the shop or house where this had happened, and would not remove the nails until the owner had made an arrangement and paid whatever they felt like demanding. Sometimes they would deliberately smash the lamp for this purpose. It happened that it rained at night and a number of lamps were extinguished in Mirjūshi market because these lamps are placed in boxes of wicker palm-branches upon which paper was stuck. So the paper got wet and the water reached the wick and put it out. So they nailed up all those places whose lamps went out and when the owners woke up they made an arrangement in order to have the nails removed. This happened in a number of streets with the result that on that day they collected a great quantity of money. They did the same even in the alleys and cul-de-sacs until people had no other occupation but to mind their lamps and to check them, especially during the long nights of the winter.

And judgment belongeth to God alone, He is the One, the Conquering!

REFERENCES

Al-Jabarti, Abd al-Rahman. 1998. *Muzhir al-Taqdis bi-Dhahab Dawlat al-Faransis*. Cairo: Al-ʿArabi lil-Nashr wa-al-Tawziʾ.

Al-Jabarti, Abd Al-Rahman, Thomas Phillip, and Guido Schwald. 1994. *Abd Al-Rahmann Al-Jabarti's History of Egypt*. Stuttgart, Germany: Franz Steiner.

Ayalon, David. 1960. "The Historian al-Jabarti and His Background." *Bulletin of the School of Oriental and African Studies*, Vol. 23, No. 2.

Bosworth, C. E. 1977. "Al-Jabarti and the Frankish Archaeologists." *International Journal of the Middle East Studies*, Vol. 8, No. 2 (April).

Holt, P. M. 1962. "Al-Jabarti's Introduction to the History of the Ottoman Egypt," *Bulletin of the School of Oriental and African Studies, University of London*, Vol. 25, Nos. 1–3.

4

An Imam in Paris

Rifaʿah Al-Tahtawi, 1836

Rifaʿah Al-Tahtawi lived from 1801 to 1873. Born an only child just as the last French soldiers were leaving Egypt in defeat, he was from a noble and wealthy family of sharifs, several being judges, scholars, and specialists in Arabic grammar and poetry, a family whose members could be found in the region of Upper Egypt. With the introduction of Mohammed Ali's land reforms, Al-Tahtawi's family lands were expropriated and the family was reduced to poverty. In 1817 Rifaʿah enrolled at Al-Azhar University, where he received a classical education in the Islamic sciences and Arabic language. His teachers included such eminent scholars as Hasan Al-Attar, a man known as notoriously reformist with wide interests beyond the religious sciences and Arabic language. Al-Attar instilled in Al-Tahtawi a love of learning and a passion for poetry, and aroused his interest in medicine, history, geography, astronomy, and the new European sciences, to which he had been introduced during the French occupation of Egypt. It was through Al-Attar that Al-Tahtawi was included in the student mission to France dispatched by Mohammed Ali to Paris twenty-five years after Napoleon's occupying forces were expelled from Egypt.

From 1826 to 1831 Al-Tahtawi served as the imam of this educational mission, a contingent. The students learned French, developed skills in translation, and learned various technical fields—in order to know the West beyond its capacity as occupier. Al-Tahtawi thought that Islamic society could advance not by blindly copying Europe, but rather by borrowing those things that could benefit the Muslims' native societies and by rediscovering the wealth of Islamic culture and sciences. As Al-Tahtawi was quick to emphasize, the French "acknowledge that we were their teachers in all sciences . . . credit goes to the precursor" (Al-Tahtawi

Al-Tahtawi, Rifaʿa Rafiʿ. 2011. *An Imam in Paris: Account of a Stay in France by an Egyptian Cleric (1826–1831)*. Daniel L. Newman, transl. and intro. London: Saqi Books. Pp. 152–154, 166–171, 173–174, 177–180, 218–219, 222, 230–231, 233–234, 241, 248, 274, 328, 331, 339 (footnotes omitted). It is printed here with the permission of the publisher.

2011:105). Thus his "scientific mission" was to observe and record the culture and habits of the French (73), in part to uncover and reveal the ways of the French in their own environment, as that would help to dispel some of the mystery around Napoleon's invasion of Egypt in 1798, and in part, as it turned out, to trace what the French had derived from Islamic science.

In his first few weeks in Marseilles in 1826, Al-Tahtawi conveys two clear impressions: wealth and rootlessness. He perceives wealth—or more precisely, excess—in French cultural practices and material culture, from table customs to the interiors of homes and cafés. The café, glittering with mirrors and bustling with waiters, serves as the locus of everyday spectacle. At table, the French take one dish after another, with a separate plate for each person and specific utensils for different dishes. French homes have carpets, but also feature chairs and raised beds. Al-Tahtawi meets a man of Egyptian descent in Marseille whom a French woman "had taken away" from Egypt when he was small. The man knows little of his own background: only the name of his native village, his parents' names, and three childhood tenets of Islam. All of these signify much to Al-Tahtawi. He is able to piece together the man's kinship affiliations, the significance of his forefathers, and the Egyptian locales where the man's relatives are concentrated. He shows by the man's example what it means to raise people without a history.

Al-Tahtawi's writing reveals a deep sense of appreciation for French culture and society, though, as his translator notes, the idea "of combining eulogy and (often fierce) criticism has its roots in classical Arabic literature" (252–253). He compares certain qualities about the French as being closer to Arab than to Turkish culture, such as the concept of honor in France, and describes the French love of freedom as something inherently shared by Arabs. Impressed by the organization of French society and the pursuit of scientific knowledge in France, he generalizes that the French are people like anyone else, people who have achieved through the pursuit of learning and justice, all things Muslims had pursued long before the European ascent to power. Again, self-recognition is possible by the use of comparison—a look in the mirror.

The mirror effect is rarely present in Western descriptions of the East; its exclusion becomes a means for Westerners to distance themselves from other peoples. Investigating the possibility of mirror images between East and West brings integration. Al-Tahtawi constantly compares the West with the East. He compares the Egyptian city of Alexandria to "Frankish cities" even before he sees one (126. 131), juxtaposing their architecture (216), their methods of teaching (274), their clothing (223), their restaurants (220), and just about everything else. At one point, he reverses Orientalist scholarship by calling Montesquieu the Ibn Khaldun of Europe. He compares and contrasts various properties of coffeehouses in Marseilles and Egypt (151, 152), then he notices his own reflection in the mirrors covering the walls (153) and himself becomes situated in the scene. To better communicate with his Egyptian audience, Al-Tahtawi draws a good deal on various poets and what they have to say on a given issue: "Such is the division [of arts and sciences] drawn up by Frankish scholars. However, in our country there is very often no difference between sciences and arts. . . . Prose is the language used in the [French] sciences, history, trade, correspondence, speeches and so on. As a result of the vastness of the Arabic language, there are many scientific books that have been written in verse; in French, on the other hand, scientific books are never written in verse." Al-Tahtawi goes on to muse over which modes of writing are more "natural," and reflects on the untranslatability of the eloquence and rhetorical devices of one language into that of another language. One who delights in understanding, he delivers much of his insight with humor (261).

In 2001, on the bicentenary of Al-Tahtawi's birth, the Egyptian Supreme Cultural Council organized a symposium in which more than fifty participants from Egypt and Europe presented research on the work of this modernist who mediated Western scientific and educational resources and methods in Egypt. Al-Tahtawi's book *Takhlis al-Ibriz Bariz* (The Extraction of Gold in a Summary of Paris) was published in 1836 in Arabic.

. . .

FROM OUR DEPARTURE FROM MARSEILLES TO THE ARRIVAL IN PARIS AND ON THE ITINERARY BETWEEN THE TWO CITIES

[. . .]

The first time we went out to visit the town, we passed superb shops, whose shop windows consisted of these mirrors, and which were filled with beautiful women. This was at noon time. The women of this country are used to revealing their face, head, the throat as well as what lies beneath it, the nape of the neck and what lies beneath it, and their arms almost up to the shoulders. It is also the custom that the shopping is strictly for women, whereas labor is the preserve of men. And so, we took pleasure in looking at them [the women] in these shops, coffee houses, etc., and at what went on inside them.

The first wonderful thing on which our gazes rested was a magnificent coffee house. We went in and saw that it was extraordinary both in terms of appearance and arrangement. The owner was a woman who sat at a large raised desk. In front of her, there were inkwells, pens and a list. The coffee was actually made in a room far away from the patrons, and young waiters moved between the public sitting area and the coffee room. The room where people sit is fitted with chairs upholstered with flower-print fabrics, and the tables are made out of superior mahogany wood. Each table is covered with a black or colored marble slab. In this type of coffee house they sell all types of beverages and pastries. When one of the customers orders something from a waiter, he submits it to the owner, who orders that it be brought to him. She writes it down in her ledger and tears off a small piece of paper on which the price is put. The waiter gives this to the customer when the latter wishes to pay. Normally, when someone wants to drink coffee, it is brought together with sugar, so that the customer can mix it in his coffee where it dissolves before drinking. We did all this in accordance with their custom. Their coffee-cups are quite large—on the whole about the size of four cups used in Egypt. In fact, it is a goblet, rather than a cup. In these types of coffee houses, there are daily newspapers for patrons to read.

When I entered this coffee house and sat down there, it felt like being in a huge bazaar because of the huge numbers of people there. When a group of people appeared both inside and outside, their faces appeared on all sides in the mirrors, and one could see the multiplicity of people walking around, sitting and standing. One thus got the impression that this coffee house was a street, and I realized that it was an enclosed coffee house only because I saw our multiple images [reflected] in the mirrors. I became aware that all of this was due to the peculiar properties of the glass. In our country, the mirror usually duplicates the image of one person, as someone said on the subject:

> I veil the view of the mirror from him
> for fear it should double before my eyes
> I suffer what is my unique suffering
> but what if two stars should reveal themselves?

Because of the great number and size of mirrors on the walls in Frankish dwellings, they tend to multiply a single image from all sides and corners.

The period of our stay in Marseilles after quarantine was spent studying the individual sounds, i.e. the spelling of the French language.

In the city of Marseilles, there are many Christians from Egypt and Syria, who accompanied the French during their retreat from Egypt. All of them wear French clothes. It is rare to find a Muslim among those who left with the French: some of them have died, whereas others have converted to Christianity—may God protect us from that! This is especially true for the Georgian and Circassian Mamlūks and women who were taken by the French when they were still very young. I came across an old woman who had remained with her religion. Among those who converted to Christianity, there was a certain ʿAbd al-ʾĀl, of whom it is said that the French had made him Agha of the Janissaries during their time [in Egypt]. When they left, he followed them, and remained a Muslim for about 15 years, after which he converted to Christianity—may God protect us from that!—because of his marriage to a Christian woman. Shortly afterwards, he died. However, I saw two of his sons and one daughter, who came to Egypt and who were all Christians. One of them is currently a teacher at the School of Abū Zaʾbal.

[...]

ON THE TOPOGRAPHY OF PARIS; ITS
GEOGRAPHICAL LOCATION, SOIL,
CLIMATE AND SURROUNDING AREA

[...]

The changing nature of the air and of the weather in Paris is a strange thing; it may vary in the course of a single day, or from one day to the next. For instance, one morning it may be so wonderfully bright and clear that nobody would expect it to change, but then, in less than half an hour, the brightness can disappear completely and give way to heavy showers. It can be 24 degrees one day, whereas the following day temperatures barely reach 12 degrees. Hence, one is seldom safe from changes in the weather in this country. The temperament of the weather, in fact, is like that of its people, as will be discussed later.

Naturally, one must protect oneself against the dangers of these changes, even though the Paris air is on the whole good and salubrious. While its heat does not generally attain Cairo levels, one never gets used to it. Perhaps this is because of the transition from extreme cold to extreme heat. Although it is possible to bear the cold without much fatigue, it is not possible for people to work except if they warm themselves by fire. This is why in all coffee houses, hotels, factories and shops fireplaces have been built in the ground in order to make fire. They are built in such a way that the smoke from the [burning] wood does not permeate the room. In fact, these fireplaces are connected to the outside, with the air drawing out the smoke, which is thus driven from the interior of the house. In some rooms, they have a kind of oven, which is fitted with an iron door and to which one connects a tinplated pipe. This pipe is stuck into an opening leading to the outside. People then put wood in the oven and close the door of the furnace; the smoke rises towards the pipe and from there to the outside. As the oven and pipe become hot, they heat rooms, reception halls, etc. They have another, equally strange thing, called a "Russian chimney." Usually, the chimney or oven, which the French refer to as *poêle* (*bwāl*)—"stove"—is beautifully decorated on the outside, and extremely clean.

A fireplace always has marble sides, the middle part being made out of iron. Because of the beautiful craftsmanship, the French consider it an object of ornamentation for their houses. In winter, people sit around it, and one of the greatest honors one can extend to a guest is to invite him to sit close by the fire in winter, which is hardly surprising. We pray God to save us from the heat of Gehenna. How capable is the one who said:

> Fire is the fruit of winter. He who wants
> to eat fruit in winter must be able to bear the heat.

In short, heating is part of the everyday provisions of the French in winter as they need it to protect themselves from the cold. By way of protection against the rain they use shields, i.e. umbrellas, which we call *shamsiyyāt* ("parasols"), i.e. sun shields. The French call this thing a *parapluie*. When it is hot, women walk around with parasols, but the men can never do this.

The soil of this city is fertile, rich and productive. How can it be otherwise as none of the many houses is without a large garden with trees, vegetation, etc.? Most foreign plants are found in this city since the French take a keen interest in creating a natural environment for foreign plants and animals in their country. For instance, the palm tree grows only in hot regions; however, the French have tried numerous ways to plant at least one species of them, which, though it does not produce fruit, serves as a sample for their study of botany. It is common knowledge in our country that the palm tree can be found only in Islamic countries. Nevertheless, at the time of the discovery of America, they found palm trees, which, so it seems, could not be transplanted to our country. To this one should add the words by the learned scholar al-Qazwīnī in his book entitled ʿAjāʾib al-makhlūqāt wa gharāʾib al-mawjūdāt ("The Wonders of Creation and the Marvels of Existing Things"): *"the palm tree is a blessed, wondrous tree; one of its wonderful properties is the fact that it grows only in Islamic countries."* The palm tree that is found in non-Islamic lands is perhaps a special species that may correspond to the name "palm tree" used by botanists, whereas that which is restricted to Muslim lands is, because of the favorable climate in these regions, the date palm. This is something one should reflect on.

Near Paris there is a source of cold mineral water. The city is traversed by two rivers; the biggest and most famous is the Seine (al-Sīn); the other is that of the Gobelins (Ghūblān). Some of the chemists among the Franks have stated that the waters that are least mixed with foreign substances are those of the Nile of Egypt, the Ganges (al-Kank) in the Hind and the Seine in Paris. It is because of this that the medical profession claims that the water has properties that are beneficial for human health. Their water is far better than that of other rivers for the tasty preparation and cooking of vegetables, the dissolution of soap, for washing, etc.

Within Paris, there are three islands in the river Seine, one of which is called the île de la Cité (jazīrat al-Sīta), which marks the location of ancient Paris. The word cité in fact means "city," and so it would be like saying "the island of the city." How different this is from the Nile and Roda Island (al-Rawḍa), and from the Nilometer; there is no comparison between a promenade there [and one in Paris] except for the fact that Cairo is traversed by al-Khalīj and Paris by the Seine. However, the latter divides the whole of Paris into two parts. Heavily laden ships sail on it, and it has nice clean quays along its banks. Nevertheless, it is not pleasant to walk along it. What a difference there is between the water of the Nile and that of the Seine in terms of taste, and other things. If the water of the Nile were filtered before usage, as is the custom with the water of the Seine, it would be one of the greatest medicines. I would also say that there is a huge difference in taste between the water of the Seine and that drawn from wells, brooks and irrigation canals in Upper Egypt.

In short, there is a big difference in soil, water, fruit—except perhaps for the peaches—and the climate between Egypt and Paris. And if it were not for the Parisians' sagacity, skill, excellent organization and their commitment to the interests of their country, their city would be worth nothing at all. Take, for instance, the Seine; on warm days it is a pleasant excursion site, but in winter its temperatures drop to 8 degrees below zero with the result that carriages can trundle around on it. Or look at the trees of this city; they are in leaf in the hot season, but in the cold season they are bald and ugly to look at and resemble wooden poles. However, this is the case in all cold countries. In this respect, somebody once said:

> Why, so I asked the branch, are you naked in winter
> while in spring you appear fully attired?
> It said that spring had announced its advent
> and I doffed my clothing for the bringer of this glad tiding

Also consider the weather in this city; in winter and on most warm days, the sky is always dark. If one goes for a walk, the first hour may be nice, while the next one is made miserable as the previously enjoyed pleasure is chased by thunder and lightning and torrential rains. The people there are not bothered by this. On other days, one may quote the words by somebody who described a violently cold day as *"a day on which one's wine freezes, and the embers go out; whose departure makes heavy things light, and whose onslaught makes light things heavy."* The French frequently visit the places of entertainment on winter nights, without making any effort to protect themselves from the damaging effects of the cold night air. We pray to God the Almighty for protection against the bitter cold.

If only Cairo were maintained and amply provided with the means of civilization, it would surely be the queen of cities, the pinnacle of the cities of the world, and thus live up to the widespread colloquial saying of its people that Cairo is "the mother of the world" (*umm al-dunyā*). I praised it during my stay in Paris in a poem, which also included a eulogy of our ruler—may the glory of his rule last forever. Amen.

While Cairo remains devoid of the inconveniences of the cold of Paris, it also lacks the things that are necessary in times of heat, such as means to help refresh the air. For instance, it is easy for the Parisians to sprinkle water on a vast open area in the hot season. They construct a large vat fitted with wheels, with horses pulling this vehicle. This vat has several skillfully made spouts, from which the water is expelled with great force and speed. The wheels do not cease to turn when the spouts are open, so a vast plot of land is sprinkled in about one quarter of an hour, something for which a group of men would need more than an hour. But they also have other devices at their disposal. Our Cairo should have things like this because of its overwhelming heat.

One of the strange things about the river Seine is that there are large boats on it, which contain the best-constructed baths in the whole of Paris. Each bathing establishment has at least 100 bathrooms. However, we shall have occasion to talk of this later.

[. . .]

ON THE PEOPLE OF PARIS

[...] [T]he masses in this country are not like some herd of animals as in most barbarous countries. All the sciences, arts and crafts—even the lowly ones—are recorded in books, so it is imperative for each craftsman to know how to read and write in order to perfect his professional skills. Every craftsman wants to create something for his craft that nobody before him has thought of, or perfect that which others have invented. Apart from a desire to increase their gain, it is vanity that pushes them in this, the glory ensuing from a reputation and the desire to leave a lasting memory. [...]

The character traits of the French include curiosity, the passion for all things new, as well as the love of change and alternation in all things, especially when it comes to clothing. Indeed, this is never stable among them. To this day, not a single fashion has stuck with them. This does not mean they completely change their outfit, rather that they vary their wardrobe. For instance, they never give up wearing a hat (*burnayṭa*) in favor of a turban; instead, they will sometimes wear one type of hat and then, after a while, another, with a different shape, color, etc.

Other features of their character are dexterity and agility. Indeed, one can see a respectable personage running down the street like a small child. One also finds fickleness and frivolity in their nature; people there go from happiness to sadness and vice versa, from seriousness to jesting and vice versa, so that in the space of one day they can do several contradictory things. While this is true for unimportant matters, it is not the case for important issues; their political opinions do not change. Each person remains faithful to his ideology and opinions and supports them for the entire duration of his life.

[...]

Another characteristic peculiar to the French is the money they spend on personal pleasures, [on gratifying their] diabolic urges, and on entertainment and games; here, they exceed all bounds.

The men are slaves to the women here, and under their command, irrespective of whether they are pretty or not. One of them once said that amongst the savages women are destined to be slaughtered, in Eastern countries they are like furniture, whereas the Franks treat them like spoilt children. As the poet said:

> Be disobedient to women, for this is rightly guided obedience
> The man who hands women his halter will not prevail
> They prevent him from developing many of his virtues
> even if he were to strive towards knowledge for a thousand years!

The Franks do not have a bad opinion of their women, despite their many faults. If one among them—even a notable—is convinced of immoral behavior by his wife, he leaves her completely, and dissociates himself from her for the remainder of his life; yet, the others do not learn a lesson from this. It is indeed necessary to protect oneself against women. [...]

[...]

Another of their vices is the small measure of chastity displayed by many of their women, as we have stated before, and the absence of jealousy by their men with regard to things that arouse jealousy among Muslims. A French cynic stated: *"Do not be misled by the refusal of a woman whom you asked to satisfy a desire, and do not infer from this that she is chaste, but rather that she is experienced."* How could it be otherwise, as among them adultery is part of the [human] faults and vices rather than a mortal sin, particularly in the case of unmarried people? It is as if their women bear out the following words by a wise man: *"Do not be misled by a woman, and do not trust in money, even if there is an abundance of it."* Another one said that women are traps set by Satan. [...]

In short, this city, like all the great cities of France and Europe, is filled with a great deal of immorality, heresies, and human error, despite the fact that Paris is one of the intellectual capitals of the entire world, and a center for foreign sciences—the "Athens" of the French. Previously, I have already compared Paris to some extent with Athens, i.e. the city of the Greek philosophers. Then I read words to this effect by a French author, who said: *"Of all men, the Parisians are those who most resemble the inhabitants of Athens; to be more precise, they are the Athenians of our day. They have the mind of the Romans, and the character of the Greeks."*

We have already stated that the French are among those whose decision about whether something is good or bad is based solely on reason. I should like to add here that they reject anything that transcends the rational. They believe that things inexorably take their natural course; that religions appeared merely to guide man to do good things, and to eschew the opposite; that the civilization of countries, the striving of people and their progress in breeding and refinement will replace religions, after which in civilized countries political issues will take over the role of religious laws.

Another of their bad customs is their claim that the intellect of their philosophers and physicists is greater and more perceptive than that of prophets. They have a great many abominable customs. Some among them even deny fate and divine decree, even though there is a maxim stating that *"the wise man is he who believes in fate and acts with resolution in all things."* At the same time, man should not attribute all things to fate or advance it as an excuse or pretext before something has happened. According to a popular saying, *"to leave many things to fate is a sign of weakness."* Another person once said: *"If a dispute breaks out, then silence is preferable to words; if war breaks out, then organization is better than trusting in fate."* Others among them believe that God the Almighty created humankind, imposed a wonderful order upon it, completed it and has not ceased to observe it through one of His qualities called "Providence," which relates to all possible things, i.e. it prevents any imbalance from disturbing the order of Creation. We shall have occasion to talk about some of their doctrines in another section of the present book.

The people of Paris have a white skin, infused with a red tint. It is rare to find a native Parisian with a brown skin. This is because they do not customarily allow marriages between a White man and a Negro woman—or vice versa—in order to protect themselves against the mixing of their color. [. . .]

[. . .]

ON THE HOUSING OF THE PEOPLE OF
PARIS AND RELATED MATTERS

[. . .]

In winter, all the rich people of Paris live in the city itself. As we have already mentioned when talking about the climate in the Paris region, each house has fireplaces, and fires are lit in every hall and room. During periods of heat, the well-off live in the country, since the air is more wholesome in the castles in the country than in the center of Paris. Other people go to other towns in France or to neighboring countries in order to breathe the air of foreign lands, to discover [other] countries and to get to know the customs of the peoples. This happens especially at the time of the year they call "the work-free period" or "leisure period," i.e. the holidays.

Even women travel, either alone or accompanied by a man with whom they have entered into an agreement regarding the journey and whose expenses they pay for along the way. Indeed, women also have a passion for knowledge, for discovering the secrets of beings and learning more about them. Is it perhaps not so that some of them come from Europe to Egypt to see its wonders like the pyramids, the temples, etc.? They are like men in every respect. To be sure, there are even some women of wealth and high status who give themselves to a foreigner without being married. And when they become pregnant and fear a scandal, they journey to another country supposedly to travel around or for some other reason in order to give birth to the child, who is then entrusted to a nanny for a special fee and raised in a foreign land. However, this sort of thing does not happen frequently. To put it differently, not every lightning cloud sheds its rain in abundance. Among French women there are those with great virtue and others who display quite the contrary. The latter are in the majority since the hearts of most people in France, whether male or female, are in thrall to the art of love. Their amorous passion is an aim in itself since they do not believe that they serve any other purpose. At the same time, a relationship may develop between a young man and a young girl which then leads to marriage.

One must praise the French for the cleanliness of their houses, which are devoid of all dirt, even though this pales into oblivion next to the cleanliness of the houses of the Dutch, who surpass all nations in their attachment to exterior cleanliness, just as in ancient times the people of Egypt were known to be the cleanest people in the world. However, their descendants, the Copts, did not follow their example. As Paris is clean, it is also free of venomous vermin, even insects. One never hears of a person who has been stung by a scorpion. The commitment on the part of the French to keeping their houses and clothes clean is truly wondrous. Their houses are always bright because of the many windows, which are placed with such magnificent engineering skill that they allow light and air both inside and outside the houses. The window panes are always made out of glass so that even when they are closed the light is never blocked out.

Both the rich and the poor always have curtains in front of the windows. Often the people of Paris also have curtains over their beds, which resemble a kind of mosquito net.

ON THE FOOD OF THE PEOPLE OF PARIS AND THEIR EATING AND DRINKING HABITS

You should know that wheat is the staple food of the people of Paris. In most cases this comes in small grains, except when it has been imported from abroad. They grind it in wind and water mills, and bake it into bread at the baker's. The bread is sold in special shops, and everyone has a daily ration which they buy from the baker. This way of doing things saves time and money, since everybody is occupied with their own activities, and to make the bread at home would add to their workload. The market supervisor instructs the bakers to have enough bread for the city every day. In reality, there is never a shortage of bread in Paris, nor of any other foodstuffs for that matter. The people of this city also eat meat, legumes, vegetables, dairy produce, eggs and things of this kind. In general, their meals consist of numerous dishes, even among the poor.

[...]

The total annual food and drink consumption of the people of this city is approximately as follows: they spend more than 35 million francs on bread, about 10 million francs on [cooking] fat and 5,000 francs on eggs. In terms of meat, they go through about 81,430 bulls, 13,000 cows, 470,000 sheep and goats and 100,000 wild boar and pigs. One of the strange things in Paris is their ingenuity when it comes to preserving perishable foodstuffs. For instance, thanks to a special technique, milk can be kept for a period of five years without its undergoing any changes. Meat remains tender for ten years, while fruit is stored so that it can be found out of season. Despite their expertise with regard to food and pastry, etc., their food lacks flavor and, with the exception of peaches, the fruit in this city has no real sweetness.

As for their wine houses, they are innumerable. There is not a single district that is not teeming with those places. It is only the lowliest of people who gather there, the riff-raff with their women. They are given to a great deal of shouting when they leave those places and say things to the effect of "Drink, drink." Yet, despite their state of drunkenness, they generally do not cause any real harm. One day, it happened that as I was walking along a street in Paris a drunk shouted at me, "Hey, you Turk!," and grabbed me by my clothes. I was near a confectionery shop, so I entered with him and sat him down on a chair. I then jokingly said to the proprietor of the shop, "Would you like to buy this man for some sweets or candied nuts?" To which the owner replied, "Here things are not like in your country where you can dispose of the human species at your will." My only retort to this was that I said, "In his current state, this drunken person is not part of the human race." All of this took place while the man was sitting down on his chair, oblivious to everything that was going on around him. I left him in that shop and went on my way.

[...]

ON THE ENTERTAINMENTS OF PARIS

[...]

There are two types of balls: public balls, where everybody is allowed to enter—for instance, dances in coffee houses or parks—and private balls, where a group of people are invited to dance, sing and enjoy themselves, which is a bit like a wedding in Egypt.

Balls always include men and women. The hall itself is brightly lit, with chairs so that guests can sit down. However, it is mainly the women that sit down, and no man will ever sit down before all women have found a place; if a woman joins a company and there is no seat available, then one of the men will get up and offer her his seat. Conversely, a woman does not get up to give up her seat. In social gatherings, a female is always treated with greater regard than a man. So, when somebody enters the house of his friend, he must first greet the lady of the house before the master. And regardless of his rank, he comes after his wife or the ladies of the house.

[...]

Everyone in France loves dancing, which is considered something distinguished and elegant, instead of morally depraved. By the same token, it never departs from the rules of decency, whereas in Egypt the dance is one of the specialities of women since it arouses desires. Conversely, in Paris, it is a special kind of jump, which is entirely devoid of even the slightest whiff of debauchery. Every man can invite a woman to dance with him, and when the dance is over, another one may invite her for the second one and so on, irrespective of whether the man knows the lady or not. The women are pleased if many men want to dance with them. They do not content themselves with one or two; rather, they like to be seen dancing with many men as they weary of being attached to one and the same thing. [...]

Sometimes, a special dance is performed, during which the man puts his arm around the waist of his partner, while holding her hand most of the time. In short, touching the upper part of the body of a woman, irrespective of who she is, is not considered indecent by these Christians. The more a man talks with women and praises them, the more he is considered a man of good breeding. It is also the mistress of the house who greets the people gathered.

[...]

ON HYGIENE IN THE CITY OF PARIS

[...]

There are many different types of bathhouses in Paris. But while they are indeed cleaner than Egyptian baths, the latter are more beneficial, more perfected and generally better. Paris bathhouses have several small rooms, each of which contains a copper bath where there is room for only one person. Although some rooms have two baths, Europeans do not use a communal bath as we do in Egypt. Their way of doing things is more decent since people cannot see each other's private parts. In the bathrooms there is even a curtain between the two baths so that the person in one bath cannot see his companion in the other. When entering these small baths one does not experience the same pleasure as one gets in an Egyptian bath. People do not sweat since the heat is restricted to the bathtub, and does not fill the room. Nevertheless, it is possible to order a steam bath, which they prepare for you, and for which a special price is charged.

In the bathhouse there are two rows of cabins, one for men and one for women. In addition to the fixed baths, there are also portable baths; if somebody wants to take a bath in his house or if he is ill, etc., the bath is brought to him in a cart shaped like a barrel, half of which contains the cold water, the other half the hot water. The people from the bathhouse also bring a cauldron, which they place in the person's house and fill with hot water for the person to use to wash himself. When he is finished, the bath is taken back to the bathhouse.

There exists a type of bath in which only part of the body is submerged and which the French call a *demi-bain*. It is used in the treatment of certain diseases. There are many bathhouses in Paris, of which about 30 are famous.

As for the physical exercises for the benefit of the body, there are schools where they teach the science of swimming. There are three of those on the river Seine. In other schools, people are taught to make the body agile and to enable it to perform extraordinary feats like acrobatics, wrestling, etc.

ON THE INTEREST IN MEDICAL SCIENCES IN PARIS

[...]

The medical sciences, which are also called *'ilm al-ḥikma*, comprise the science of healing, surgery, anatomy, the art of physiology *(al-fisiyūlūjiyā)* for ascertaining a man's state of health based on his condition (i.e. diagnostics), hygiene, veterinary medicine and others.

There are a great many doctors in Paris, to the extent that there are several physicians in each district. What is more, the streets are so full of doctors that if a man is afflicted with an ailment in the street, he will immediately find one. The position of the sick in relation to the doctor varies. There are patients who request the doctor to visit them at home, the latter charging a specific fee for each house call. Other sick people go to see the doctor at his home, in which case the doctor has fixed hours during which he stays at home in order to receive people. Still other sick people go to a house called a "house of health" (*maison de santé*), which is destined for people who pay a fixed sum for their food, drink, accommodation, doctor's care, service, etc.

[. . .]

ON CHARITY IN THE CITY OF PARIS

[. . .]

From all of this, it becomes apparent that while in Paris more is done for charitable works than anywhere else, it is primarily aimed at the collective [that is, society as a whole] or the kingdom. The situation is quite different when it concerns individual people. It is possible to see a man in the street who does not go to subsidized hospitals or such places and who collapses in the middle of the road because of hunger. Or you can sometimes see people brushing beggars off and sending them away empty-handed, claiming that there is never an excuse for begging—if the beggar is able to work, he does not need to beg, and if he is not, then he belongs in a hostel or somewhere like that. It must be said that in most cases their beggars are master tricksters when it comes to obtaining money. They even go as far as to pretend to be mutilated or the like, in order to arouse people's pity.

[. . .]

ON EARNINGS IN THE CITY OF PARIS AND THE ENTREPRENEURIAL SKILLS THERE

[. . .]

One of the reasons for the wealth of the French is that they know how to save and manage their expenses, to the extent that they have recorded it and turned it into a science which is a branch of the administration of affairs of the kingdom. They are highly ingenious in finding ways of acquiring wealth, such as not clinging to things that entail expenditure. [. . .]

[. . .]

ON THE ORGANIZATION OF INSTRUCTION IN
READING AND WRITING, ETC., WHICH WE RECEIVED
AT THE BEGINNING

One of the educational habits of the people of Paris is to teach a person to read by means of books with large characters so that their shapes become embedded in his mind. These books contain the letters of the alphabet in their order, followed by a number of words exemplifying nouns and verbs. It is by this method that people learn how to write; one memorizes these words and pronounces them in the way that they should be pronounced so that people learn to speak really well from a very early age. Afterwards, you find a number of sentences that are easy to understand and that are suitable for young children. Here are some sentences from the book we used: *"This is a horse with three legs; birds have only two legs, but they have wings with which they fly; as for the fish, it swims in the water,"* etc. These are of course the kinds of things that are known to the speaker. This method is, in fact, similar to the [Arab] grammarians' *"the sky is over us, and the earth is below us,"* which is an example of something that does not contain new information. However, this differs from the way in which they explain composition: *"Speech is the assembled expression that conveys a complete self-contained meaning through composition."* [...]

  [...]

ON THE DIVISION OF THE SCIENCES AND ARTS
ACCORDING TO THE FRANKS

The Franks have divided human knowledge into two parts: the sciences and the arts. The former are achievements that have been empirically proven. Art, on the other hand, denotes skills, i.e. knowledge of the techniques for certain things in accordance with specified rules.

The sciences are subdivided into mathematical branches and non-mathematical branches. The latter are, in turn, split into natural and theological sciences. The mathematical sciences are made up of arithmetic, geometry and algebra. The natural sciences are composed of natural history, physics and chemistry. Natural history is taken to refer to botany, mineralogy, and zoology. These three branches are called "the classes of production": i.e. the botanical class, the mineral class and the animal class.

As for theology, it is also referred to as "metaphysics."

The arts are subdivided into intellectual arts and applied arts. The former are closest to the sciences and include, for instance, the science of eloquence and rhetoric, grammar, logic, poetry, drawing, sculpture and music. All of these are intellectual arts because they require scientific rules. Conversely, the applied arts are the crafts.

Such is the division drawn up by Frankish scholars. However, in our country there is very often no difference between sciences and arts; a distinction is made based only on whether an art is an independent science or serves as a tool for another.

[. . .]

ON THE ART OF WRITING

[. . .]

This is the science of elegant expressions, or the science of making the expression appropriate to what is required by the circumstances. Its general aim is to enable a person to enunciate his inner thoughts in pure and eloquent speech. Viewed from this angle, this science is not peculiar to the Arabic tongue, but can be found in any other language. In European languages, it is referred to as "rhetoric" ('ilm al-rīthūrīqī). But as this science is more complete and more perfected in Arabic than in other languages, especially the art of style ornaments and tropes (badī '), and as it is poorly developed in European languages, it may seem that it is one of the specialities of Arabic. The eloquence of the style of the Qur'ān, which was sent down to man as an inimitable creation, is exclusive to Arabic.

Something that is considered to be eloquent in one language may in another be wholly devoid of elegance, or even repulsive. Conversely, an expression may be eloquent in two or more languages. For instance, if you wish to express the fact that a man is courageous by comparing him to a lion, as in *"Zayd is a lion,"* then this is acceptable in languages other than Arabic. However, if you wish to express the beauty of a person by comparing him to the sun or [by referring to] the redness of his cheeks by saying that they are ablaze, this is considered beautiful in Arabic but not at all so in the language of the Franks. [. . .]

REFERENCES

Gran, Peter. 2002. "Tahtawi in Paris." *Al-Ahram Weekly Online,* No. 568 (10–16 January). http://weekly.ahram.org.eg/2002/568/cu1.htm (accessed 17 January 2015).

Radhi, al-Mustaqeem Mahmod. 2005. "The West in the Travel Journal of an Imam in Paris." Pauline Fan, transl. *Ide,* October–December 2005.

5

On the Music of the Maltese and of Others

Ahmed Faris Al-Shidyaq, c. 1850

Ahmed Faris Al-Shidyaq was born in the Levant in 1805 or 1806 and died in 1887 in Turkey. Al-Shidyaq is considered the founding father of modern Arabic literature, and an irreverent thinker. He was born as Faris in Lebanon to a Christian Maronite family that suffered oppression. Members of this literary family worked as secretaries for the governor of Mount Lebanon. Following a conflict with the governor that cost the life of Faris's paternal grandfather, the family moved to Beirut, where Faris and his brother attended Warraq school, after which the two worked together as copyists. In 1820 his brother converted to Protestantism and was excommunicated and imprisoned by the Maronite church. Eventually Faris's grandfather, father, and brother died as "martyrs for freedom of thought and inclination," to use his own words. After the death of his brother, Faris left the country an exile and returned only for a brief visit a decade later. Although a steadfast skeptic, Al-Shidyaq converted to Islam and was known as a Christian Muslim. He founded the first Arabic-language newspaper, *al-Jawa'ib* in Istanbul in 1861. His two books relating his travels in Europe were published in Tunis in 1863.

Al-Shidyaq is primarily known for his masterpiece *Al-Saq ala-l-Saq Fi Ma Huwa al-Fariaq* (The Thigh over the Thigh: On Who is Hariyaq), a foundational and irreverent text of Arabic linguistic and literary modernity, written and published in Arabic in Paris in 1855. In spite of his literary fame, Al-Shidyaq was silenced in Lebanon for his attack on secularism, his anticlerical positions, his profoundly subversive ideas, and his biting satire and irony. Although *Al-Saq* was initially censored in Lebanon, it was finally translated and published in Paris in 1991, and in English in 2013 with a useful foreword by Rebecca C. Johnson.

Cachia, Pierre. 1973. "A 19th Century Arab's Observations on European Music." *Ethnomusicology,* Vol. 17, No. 1, pp. 42–51 (all but one footnote omitted). Reprinted with the permission of the Society for Ethnomusicology, Indiana University.

Al-Shidyaq is the ultimate freewheeling comparativist, examining Arabs alongside their non-Arab peers, "leaving no society safe from his satirizing gaze" (Johnson 2013:xxiii). He satirizes emirs, Maronite priests, Protestant missionaries, and Orientalist scholars alike.

In the following selection Al-Shidyaq points out differences that he observed between European and Arab music, noting that each culture has its own distinctive music and that one has to be accustomed to the music to appreciate it. Despite his admiration for European elaboration of musical instruments, he concludes that he himself has yet to develop an appreciation: "On the whole, the Franks have made some departures in this art which do not agree with our taste" (Cachia 1973:46). He observes that the introduction of sheet music in Europe enabled music to be performed by anyone, so that musicians were no longer dependent on memory as in the past. The contrast emphasizes cultural differences between literate and preliterate peoples; a written form of music introduces a radical change in musical conception, which Al-Shidyaq believes impoverishes music. His thoughts on the effects of writing music down lead him to conclude not only that French music lacks spontaneity but also that the capacity for learned improvisation and citation seems to have been lost. Al-Shidyaq's observation that literacy changes the musician's relationship to his music's past bears on the contemporary music scene. Once a musical expression is fixed, it changes the dynamic between musicians and music and between musicians and their audience.

Admitting he is no music expert, Al-Shidyaq believes he is nonetheless qualified to comment on European music because he can "distinguish what is sound therein from what is unsound" (Cachia 1973:42) and because the response to music is essentially a response to the sounds, not to the words that are sung. His main critique of nineteenth-century European music is its failure to produce any deep sentimental feelings. Its strength, he believes, is its ability to move one to "zeal and enthusiasm," to spur one to action, to instill military valor, "making the lives of cowards cheap to them," and to fill the listener with courage and hope. Arab music, on the other hand, is concerned "entirely with tenderness and love."

These notes on European music are unabashedly biased and refreshingly frank. But Al-Shidyaq points out that his less-than-enthusiastic response to European music is not unique to Arabs, as Europeans have a similar response to his own preferred music. "I have met some Franks," he writes, "who responded emotionally to Egyptian music . . . at first they used to recoil from it and say that it was saddening" (49). Both Egyptian and European children had their own melodies to put them to sleep, and it is these sounds that each group became accustomed to; anything else would initially sound strange. Al-Shidyaq's awareness that aesthetic tastes are acquired and learned minimizes the harshness of his argument, making his approach more palatable, yet throughout he assumes the natural superiority of his own culture's music-making. For example, he notes that European musicians cannot produce semitones or quartertones. Besides, he writes, for all their instruments, the Europeans have no lute or reed flute.

. . .

Before I venture on to this difficult ground, I must beg of those who associate with the masters of the Art permission thus to foist myself amongst them although I am not reckoned one of them; I have nevertheless learnt enough about it to be able to distinguish what is sound therein from what is unsound. This therefore I say:

A philosopher has said: "The Art of Music is a redundancy of *mantiq* [either "speech" or, by a derivation parallel to that of the Greek from *logos*, "logic"] which the mind exteriorizes by sound since it cannot exteriorize it by analogy."[1]

Those who take the word *mantiq* here in its technical sense [of "logic"] interpret this [dictum] as meaning that the foundations of this art are mental. This follows from the fact that the Ancients used to transmit it by hearing and taste. The hearer registered what he heard in his imagination or memory without seeing any signs of it. Similarly, the disciple learnt it from his master by registration in his memory and imitation, and by virtue of the faculty [i.e., special gift] which established these refrains in his imagination. This is why in acquiring this art reliance used to be placed on the faculty of taste.

Now, however, the Franks have brought the modulations and rhythms of sound within reach of the sense of sight, using for them conventional graphic representations and symbols in the same way that letters are used for ideas. The learning of the Art, therefore, no longer depends upon memory and great application as it used to in the past. Those of them [i.e., the Franks] who know how to produce notes when they see these signs can play any piece of music even without previous knowledge of it; even if twenty of them were to assemble with such graphic signs before them, you would find them all following them as one.

This interpretation [of the philosopher's definition in terms of formal logic] may be refuted on the ground that if music were a redundancy of Logic it would be practiced uniformly even as logic is one in its canons. Yet people differ widely therein: the melodies favored by the Arabs do not move others—nay, the Arabs themselves differ from one another, the Egyptians being unmoved by Syrian melodies—and European melodies leave them all unmoved.

The word *mantiq* may, however, be taken in its linguistic meaning [of "speech"]. This indeed is what is intended here, for we find the following [confirmatory] passage in the commentary written by the king of cultured men Ibn Nubātah on the *Risālah* of Ibn Zaydūn: "Musical notes are redundancies of speech which, because the tongue is incapable of uttering them, nature brings out as melodies, in a reiterating sound, not an intermittent one; once they are exteriorised, the spirit becomes enamoured of them, and the heart yearns for them." What is intended by "in a reiterating sound, not an intermittent one" is that the sound is prolonged and modulated, but not interrupted as it is in the pronunciation of letters of the alphabet.

Now if the art of Music is a redundancy of speech as here interpreted, it ought to follow that each nation has musical attainments peculiar to it, for each language has beauties and [powers of] expression which are not to be found in any other. But this is not how things turn out in fact. Thus the languages of China and of India have adornments which are not to be found in any other, yet their music is free of such adornments. As for Frankish melodies, they move only such among us as have become accustomed to them.

These melodies of theirs [i.e., of the Franks] fall into four categories. The first, which is the best, is what is sung in places of entertainments, thus corresponding to our *muwashshaḥāt*. In this, the voice is prolonged and made to quaver, it is lowered and raised, it is made thin or broad or tremulous. It is in this category that rousing, inciting and threatening [motifs] are to be found. The second resembles chanting in churches, and is almost devoid of tremolo. The third is that which is sung in grief and great sorrow; for this they use a delicate kind of singing, resembling heart to heart communication; whoever hears it understands what is intended even if he is ignorant of the language—it is as when you see someone on the verge of tears: you know intuitively that he is about to weep, even though you may not know why. The fourth is used in humorous songs and dialogues. In this there is seldom any quavering, but much use of the *coup de glotte*. Its effect derives from the fact that they combine it with many things including comical gestures: they laugh while singing, they titter, they weep, they yawn, they sneeze, they imitate the clucking of hens, the twittering of birds, and other things.

Alternate singing, which is very effective, is used in all these categories, but it is commonest in the fourth; peculiar to this last category is the coining of vocables.

Just as they have a comical kind of singing, so they have a kind of dancing that will make even a bereaved mother titter.

As for the Arabs, they say that [of the various kinds of musical compositions known to them] *raṣd* moves deeply, *sīkāh* causes joy, *ṣabā* and *biyāt* stir up sorrow, *ḥijāzī* revives and makes one tender, and so on.

The two [i.e., Frankish and Arab music] differ on a number of counts.

One is that the Franks have no "free" music unbound by those graphic signs of theirs to which any verse may be sung, so that if you suggest to one of them that he should sing a couple of lines extempore, as is done among us with [classical monorhyme] odes and with [the post-classical, multi-rhymed fixed metrical compositions known as] *mawāliyyā*, he cannot do so. This is strange considering their excellence in this art, for singing in this fashion is natural, and was in use among them before these graphic signs and symbols came into being. I wonder how they sang before Guido d'Arezzo rose to prominence in Italy.

The second difference is that if, [say,] ten of their singers assemble in order to sing a stanzaic poem, some will tackle one part of it in one mode, the others another part in a different mode; if, for example, the song is in [the mode called] *raṣd*, one will sing part of it in this mode in a loud voice, another will sing a part in the mode called *nawā* in a delicate voice, yet another a part in the octave higher in a high voice, so that the listener hears it in different modes. This they call "harmony," meaning the blending of voices in singing. This way of singing has advantages and disadvantages. The advantages reside in the fact that the listener hears at one and the same time one poem in different modes by different voices, which is as if he heard one poem in all the different meters of prosody. The disadvantages are in fact that one's hearing cannot fully register all the points of emission of these various sounds. In my opinion, this kind of music is more felicitously rendered by instruments than by human voices.

The third is that the singing of the Franks, like their recitations, can move one not only to tenderness, passion, or zest for dancing, but also to zeal and enthusiasm. Songs which inspire zeal and enthusiasm are those which mention fighting, revenge, or the defense of truth; when the coward hears them, especially [if accompanied] by military instruments, his life becomes cheap to him. As for Arab singing, it is concerned entirely with tenderness and love. Truly appropriate to it are the two meanings of the word *ṭarab* [commonly used to designate the reaction to music], which is a lightness affecting man as a result of either joy or sorrow. When one of us hears either vocal or instrumental music, love penetrates his heart so that his affection becomes apparent and his soul yearns as a friend yearns for his intimate, until in the end gladness turns to sadness; it is no wonder then that sighs rush out and tears gush out, for it is when joys abound and their moon is round that by the moonlessness of grief they are penetrated, and with sorrow impregnated, until one is submerged in a sea of rapture and set ablaze with the fire of passion. This is why it has been said that the verbs *ṭarraba* and *shajā* [both used for "to stir" either to joy or to sadness] are opposites.

The fourth is that the voices of the Franks remain consistent only in the *raṣd*. True, one finds in their instruments [means of producing] the principal modes pertaining to all the notes; indeed all their semitones and quartertones are there except for two modes which have no semitones. Yet they [i.e., the performers] remain consistent only in the first mode [i.e., the *raṣd*]. I have heard from them the *rahāwī*, *būsalīk*, and *iṣfahāni* modes, but never any of the others. Indeed I have heard some of our own songs performed on their instruments, and they were all in the *raṣd*. Long, by God, have I strained my ears that I might hear our own notes from them, but to no avail, so that I was seized with perplexity. On the one hand, I could see that their instruments were both numerous and skillfully made, and I considered that all sciences had come into their hands and all arts were theirs alone, and that in this art they had attained wonders which—as already indicated—had passed out of our reach. On the other hand, I find that their attainments are exclusively in the *raṣd* mode. True, this mode is the first of the principal modes, and in Egypt and Tunis more songs are sung in this mode than in any other; all the same, the excellence of the *ṣabā*, the *biyāt* and the *ḥijāzī* is not to be denied.

On second thoughts, however, it is not surprising that they should have missed some accomplishments in this art as they have missed some in others. An example [of accomplishments that they have failed to attain] in other fields is the multiplicity of our prosodic meters. Another is certain rhetorical embellishments such as rhyming in prose: [of the various forms of *belles-lettres*] they practice only poetry, which in literary compositions is the equivalent of free music in singing, for rhymed prose is superior to poetry. Yet another is their inability to pronounce the guttural letters.

I did once inquire about this of one of their artists. I said, "The principal modes exist alike with you and with us, and so do the semitones; what remains to be discussed is the way they are in fact used. Now when we use, say, a semitone, [we use it] with its own mode; you however use it with a different mode, so that to us it appears to be dissonant. How is the true way to be known?" His reply was merely that with them this art had been based on geometric [sic] principles which cannot be flouted; so that it is incorrect for any mode to be used except with a different one.

For all that, and in spite of my fondness for their melodies, I have often heard from them gross dissonances. I was once induced by the descriptions of those who praised her to listen to a singer whose reputation was such that she had sung in the presence of the Czar of Russia. When I heard her I was indeed stirred by the sweetness of her voice and the extent to which she could prolong her breath in singing; yet insofar as my perception goes, I did hear dissonances from her.

If it were established that the melodies to which the Greeks sing their hymns in their churches to-day are similar to those which were sung in the days of the Greek philosophers, this would be a further indication of the deficiency of Frankish melodies, for the notes of the Greeks are close to ours.

The fifth difference is that their instrumentalists—with the exception of the violinists—are not good at producing semitones or quartertones unless those are graphically represented to them. As for their flute, it has several holes in addition to the seven [with which the Arabs are familiar], and every pair of holes has a [metal] cover [key] so arranged that when one nostril [opening] is stopped the other provides an outlet. However, the skill involved in ensuring that they are stopped or used approximates to the skill we require in altering the movements of the fingers. These semi- and quartertones are similar to *rawm* or *ishmām* in grammar.

On the whole, the Franks have made some departures in this art which do not agree with our taste, and others in which they cannot be emulated. From the details given above, you will know that their songs of zeal and enthusiasm are unknown among us, and that our "free" music is unknown among them. One strange fact is that for all the abundance of their instruments and implements, they have no lute—many as its virtues are—and no flute made of reed, for their flute fulfils the function of our reed-pipe. Yet most learned men assert that music derives origins from the sound of the wind in the reeds, though others say it comes from the twittering of birds, others from the murmur of water, and yet others that it is derived from the sounds made by Tubal-cain's hammers, that the first to establish the principles of this art was Jubal in 1800 B.C. [Gen. 4:21–22], and that the flute was invented in 1506 and is [to be] attributed to Higgins.

Apropos the blacksmith's [i.e., Tubal-cain's] hammers, it is related in the commentary on al-Ḥarīrī's *Assemblies,* in the biographical note on al-Khalīl, that the first to work out the principles of prosody and to regulate Arab poetry thereby was al-Khalīl ibn Aḥmad Abū 'Abd ar-Raḥmān al-Farāhīdī al-Azdī. The way it came about was that he was passing by the fullers' bazaar in Baṣrah and heard the fuller's instrument, that is to say the mallet, make different sounds: from one building he heard *toc*, from another *toc-toc*, from yet another *to-to-toc, to-to-toc*. This set him wondering, and he exclaimed: "By God, I shall build on this basis an obscure science!" And he founded prosody, which deals with the rules of verse.

The most moving of Frankish instruments is the concertina. It is a form of organ, a kind of bellows which can be opened out and compressed; it is an invention of Wheatstone's.

It is well-known that the more delicate a person's nature becomes and the more gentle his character, the readier he is to compete on the race-course of musical response and the more eager to breathe in the fragrance of its effluvia; for he who is enamored of brilliant notions and witty speech no sooner hears a melody than he visualizes, in association with it, such beauty as makes him wander with passion like a madman, before the dullard is even aware that it is music. This is the more so when the singing is expressive and the occasion felicitous. In the learned al-Ṣafadī's commentary on the *Lāmiyyat al-'Ajam* we find: "He who is not moved by the lute and its chords, or by spring and the flowers it affords, is of so corrupt a disposition that he tests the skill of a physician." Plato said, "Let him who grieves listen to pleasant sounds, for when the spirit grieves its light is dimmed, but when it hears what stirs it and gives it joy it brightens up again." And Isḥāq ibn Ibrāhīm al-Mawṣilī said: "The worst music or poetry is the mediocre, for the highest stirs and the lowest excites laughter and wonder, but the mediocre neither stirs nor makes one laugh."

It would be manifestly wrong to say that it was because of my ignorance of the language that I was not stirred by these [Frankish] melodies, for the response to music is essentially a response to the sounds, and not to the words that are sung.

In music as in other things, the Maltese waver: they are neither like the Franks nor like the Arabs. Their villagers have but a few songs, and when they sing they strain their voices excessively, so that they shock the ear. They resemble the Franks in that they confine themselves to the *raṣd*, and the Arabs in that when a number of them assemble to sing they use sounds which belong to one mode only, also in that one of them stands up to recite and the others respond. Their notables learn Italian melodies.

Most blind people in Malta make a livelihood by playing musical instruments. Whenever someone returns from a trip, or has a baby, or gets married, or has a child baptized, or is promoted, or makes a very profitable deal, they hasten to congratulate him. Nothing that happens in the country escapes them. It is related that the daughter of one of the notables committed adultery, but managed to conceal her pregnancy from her family and went away for a while until she was delivered of her child. When she returned to her home, however, a band of them came to play before the house. The father asked them why, and they gave him the news of his daughter's confinement; it was then that he understood why she had been away.

It seems to me that the music that used to be sung in the days of the Caliphs was closer to that of the inhabitants of the Maghrib to-day than to that of the Arabs of the East.

The word with which the North Africans intersperse their singing *ad libitum* is *dī-dī*, even as the Egyptians and Syrians use *yā layl* and the Turks *amān*.

The *Qāmūs* says: "There was at first no *ḥudā'* [caravan song, said to have been the first form of Arab music]. Then a bedouin beat his young slave and bit his fingers, so that as he walked the lad kept saying, "*dī-dī*," intending "*yā yadī*" [Oh, my hand!]. Then the camels stepped out to [the rhythm of] his cries, so he [i.e., his master] said, "Keep on at it!" and bestowed a robe upon him. That is the origin of the *ḥudā'*."

The names given to musical notes by the North Africans are different from the names in use among us. They claim that they learnt this art from the Andalusians. The Tunisians have a more sedate style [than that of other North Africans].

It seems that [the short song called] *mawālī* is a monopoly of Egyptians and Syrians, as are the vertical flute and the psaltery.

The common tendency [among performers] is for anyone who has sung a piece well to think that there is no one with a perceptive ear that has not heard him. If however he does not sing well, he will make some sort of excuse for himself by clearing his throat or coughing, putting the blame for his shortcoming on some mishap. This happens when the singer is not a professional; the trained one is seldom exposed to such failings, because the voice is like an instrument: the more practiced it is, the more polish it has.

Just as Egyptian singing is more stirring and of higher quality than the singing of all other Arabs, so is the singing of Italians better than that of other Franks. This is because their language abounds in vowel sounds, so that like ours it is well-suited to singing and to prosody; also because their voices are emitted from the chest. The English language, on the other hand, is so full of quiescent consonants that it can be adapted to the kind of singing that calls for prolongations and modulations only by the distortion of words and by flouting the rules of pronunciation; what does come out well is the comic song. Besides, their voices always come out of their throats; their singers seem to sing while choked with morsels of food.

The Franks all say that Arab singing comes out of the nostrils. Even if this were to be admitted, it would not be incompatible with the rousing of aesthetic responses and emotions, for the French language cannot be spoken without nasalization, yet it is the most musical of all Frankish languages, and often produces an emotional response even in those who hear it for the first time in their life.

I have met some Franks who responded emotionally to Egyptian music, but only after a long sojourn in Egypt: at first they used to recoil from it and say that it was saddening. It is no secret that habit affects all things, pronunciation and melody above all. One need observe no more than that our children and those of the Franks alike are put to sleep with song, and thus become used to [a particular style of] it from an early age; once it has commingled with their constitution, anything different sounds strange. In fact the Maltese put their children to sleep with songs which resemble nothing as much as they do the lamentations of our wailing-women. Indeed were it not for habit, the Franks with all their skill would not be incapable of uttering our gutturals—just as it is habit that has given their women their rights in wholesale fashion, and denied our women theirs.

NOTES

For a bibliography of Arabic works on Shidyaq, see Anīs al-Maqdisī 1963:181. In European languages, references to him are made in Fleet et al. 2008; Brockelmann 2012; Cremona 1955; Abu-Lughod 1963; Hourani 1962; Cachia 1962, 1963, 1966. The martyrdom of Asʿad al-Shidyaq is said to be the basis of Khalil Gibran's story "Yūḥannā al-Majnūn" in ʿArāʾis al-Murūj, translated by H. M. Nahmad as *Nymphs of the Valley* (Gibran 1948).

1. I have not been able to trace this quotation to its source, but this is presumably Greek, since it is on a Greek foundation that Arab musical theory was elaborated; Greek musical theorists translated into Arabic by the 10th Century included Aristoxenos, Euclid, Ptolemy and Nicomachos—see H. G. Farmer, *History of Arabian Music*, London, Luzac, 1929, esp. p. 152. [. . .]

REFERENCE

Johnson, Rebecca C. 2013. "Foreword." In Ahmad Faris al-Shidyaq. *Leg over Leg, Volume One*, ix–xxxi. Humphrey Davies, ed. and transl. New York: New York University Press.

6

From A Turkish Woman's Impressions

Zeyneb Hanoum, 1913

When *A Turkish Woman's Impressions,* by Zeyneb Hanoum and edited by Grace Ellison, was published in 1913, it immediately received reviews in the *New York Times* ("A Turkish View," May 4, 1913) and the *Times Literary Supplement* (March 13, 1913). Since 1913 there have been no scholarly reviews of the book and few scholars have analyzed Hanoum's work or that of editor Grace Ellison. The *New York Times* article was subtitled "Europe as Seen by a Woman Who Has Escaped from Turkey." The *TLS* headlined its double review "Veiled Women." Both reviews were substantive, and the *TLS* noted, "It is decidedly healthy for us to see the tables turned against our self-complacency by the candid criticism of a Turkish lady," and ended, "Morbid people can often see others very clearly and much of her criticism hits the mark." Hanoum's book was not reprinted until 2005.

By the beginning of the twentieth century, the Ottoman Empire was in significant decline due to constant warring with rising European powers and Russia throughout the nineteenth century. Despite a failing economy and weakening military, Western education was flooding into the region. Zeyneb Hanoum (the penname for Hadidje Zennour/Hadice Zenur) and her sister Melek Hanoum (the penname for Nourye Neyr-el-Nissa/Nurye-iNisa) were the daughters of Nuri Bey—a progressive senior bureaucrat in Abdulhamid II's government—and the granddaughters of French nobleman the Marquis de Blosset de Chateauneuf, who served as a military officer for the sultan, fell in love with a Circassian woman, converted to Islam, and changed his name to Reshid Bey. Zeyneb and Melek received a liberal Western, multilingual education in Turkey. As they reached adulthood, marriage was arranged for Zeyneb. She rejected it.

In 1904 Zeyneb, an admirer of French author Pierre Loti, contacted Loti to thank him for his semi-autobiographical *Aziyade* (1879). Upon finding out that Loti (the penname for

Hanoum, Zeyneb. 1913. *Selections from a Turkish Woman's Impressions.* Grace Ellison, ed. London: Seeley, Service & Co. Ltd. Pp. ix–x, 53–55, 65–72, 155–159, 164–167, 194–196, 212–216, 238, 246.

Louis Marie Julien Vaiud), a French naval officer, was restationed in Istanbul, Zeyneb got him to agree to write a new romance about women in Turkey. His fictional *Les Desenchantées,* based on clandestine meetings with the sisters, was published in 1906. Turkish reviewers criticized the book as imaginary and unfair. One story holds that fear of consequences they would face for unauthorized contact with a foreigner caused the sisters to leave Turkey. Their escape caused a scandal at the time and created a sensation in Europe. In Fontainebleau in 1906, the sisters met Grace Ellison, a successful young British feminist and journalist, who herself had visited Turkey several times and would later publish *An Englishwoman in a Turkish Harem* (1915). Ellison befriended and corresponded with the sisters and later gathered their letters as *A Turkish Woman's European Impressions.*

The Hanoum sisters returned to Istanbul six years after leaving Turkey. Zeyneb wrote on a wide range of topics, from the veil to her ideas about freedom and democracy. Her letters to Ellison imply that the reason for the sisters' departure was the political climate in Turkey. Before arriving, Zeyneb had idealized Europe. Over six years, however, her positive expectations changed to disenchantment and disillusionment. She confronts this head on when she writes of feeling a double sensation: "the one of coming face to face with the reality, and the other, the effort of driving from my mind the remembrance of what I expected to find" (Hanoum 1913:238). Perhaps her disappointment says more about her personal myth of Europe than it does about Europe itself, as she moves from criticizing the Ottoman government and the treatment of elite women to extolling her newfound "freedom" in the West. As she travels, the tone of her letters changes to match her growing disenchantment with the very mood that led her and her sister to leave Constantinople and Turkey for a "free" life in Europe. She begins to express her longing to return to Turkey, insisting on the qualities of Turkish life that are better than the European, among them "the old experience of calm" (155). In her acute observations Zeyneb shows us a Europe largely veiled to itself but revealed to us through her insights.

In the first days after her arrival in France, reporters assailed her with personal questions. Zeyneb resisted, and her account of these confrontations exposes us to the fallacy of salacious journalism and the French culture of public confession. Toward the end of her European stay, she confronted a Paris editor for encouraging the public airing of dirty laundry, giving center space to horrible crimes and scandals about government officials. What Zeyneb characterizes as the confusion of spectacle for truth in the Western press disappoints her. For her the press figures not as a truth-revealing agency with liberating effects, but a gossip-mongering stimulus that obfuscates some of the well-known facts: "How horrible it is to find in the daily papers the names of people mercilessly branded." (209–210). And she asks the insightful question: "But where are the few *intellectuelles*?"

Zeyneb repeatedly contrasts the bustle of European cities with the calm of the harem life she left in Turkey. Some of her impressions are negative, as in her sense of relief upon leaving Paris with its "chattering, irritating, inquisitive, demonstrative and obliging women," (155) while others are positive, as in her observations about the purposeful noise of London and the aristocratic movement of Venice (223). A most striking contrast for Zeyneb is the lack of hospitality and generosity of spirit extended in the West generally (227). Where is "Christian charity"? she asks (53), as she critiques the practice of Christianity, comparing it to her knowledge of Christ's teachings gleaned from her elite Turkish education.

Zeyneb realized that European women—whom she had thought of as more liberated because they did not have to wear a veil, watch the world from behind lattice screens, or live most of their lives in a harem—were actually restricted and socially confined in their own way, a product of their cultural environment. Although British women could inhabit public space in ways that their Turkish counterparts could not, public freedom did not necessarily translate into gender equality or liberation. In fact, Zeyneb observed British women trying to make themselves as dull and inoffensive as possible by choosing to discuss uncontroversial subjects. Most interesting is the distinction she draws between European men and women. Her travels led her to claim that men from Turkey and England were alike, whereas the women in the two countries were different. This disaggregation of gender and culture foreshadows contemporary feminist theory as a framework for thinking comparatively about gender. Zeyneb writes: "In every country there are women—though they may be a mere handful—who are above class, above nationality, and dare to be themselves. These are the people I appreciate the most" (216).

Zeyneb returned to Turkey in 1912, never married, and died in 1963.

. . .

BEWILDERING EUROPE

[. . .]

FONTAINEBLEAU, Oct. 1906.

You ask me to give you my first impression of France (wrote Zeyneb), but it is not so much an impression of France, as the impression of being free, that I am going to write. What I would like to describe to you is the sensation of intense joy I felt as I stood for the first time before a window wide open that had neither lattice-work nor iron bars.

It was at Nice. We had just arrived from our terrible journey. We had gone from hotel to hotel, but no one would give us shelter even for a few hours. Was that Christian charity, to refuse a room because I was thought to be dying? I cannot understand this sentiment. A friend explained that a death in an hotel would keep other people away. Why should the Christians be so frightened of death?

I was too ill at the moment to take in our awful situation, and quite indifferent to the prospect of dying on the street. Useless it was, however, our going to any more hotels; it was waste of time and waste of breath, and I had none of either to spare. No one advised us, and no one seemed to care to help us, until, by the merest chance, my sister remembered our friends in Belgrade had given us a doctor's address. We determined to find him if we possibly could. In half an hour's time we found our doctor, who sent us at once to a sanatorium. There they could not say, "You are too ill to come in," seeing illness was a qualification for admittance. But I shall not linger on those first moments in Europe: they were sad beyond words.

It must have been early when I awoke the next morning, to find the sun forcing its way through the white curtains, and flooding the whole room with gold. Ill as I was, the scene was so beautiful that I got out of bed and opened wide the window, and what was my surprise to find that there was no lattice-work between me and the blue sky, and the orange trees, and the hills of Nice covered with cypress and olives? The sanatorium garden was just one mass of flowers, and their sweet perfume filled the room. With my eyes I drank in the scene before me, the hills, and the sea, and the sky that never seemed to end.

A short while after, my sister came in. She also from her window had been watching at the same time as I. But no explanation was necessary. For the first time in our lives we could look freely into space—no veil, no iron bars. It was worth the price we had paid, just to have the joy of being before that open window. I sign myself in Turkish terms of affection.—Your carnation and your mouse,

ZEYNEB.

THE ALPS AND ARTIFICIALITY

TERRITET, Dec. 1906.

I wonder if you know what life is like in a big *caravanserai* on the shores of Lake Leman in December. This *hotel* is filled from the ground to the sixth floor, and from east to west with people of all ages, who have a horror of being where they ought to be—that is to say, in their own homes—and who have come to the Swiss mountains with but one idea—that of enjoying themselves. What can be the matter with their homes, that they are all so anxious to get away?

I have been more than a month in this place, and cannot get used to it. After the calm of the Forest of Fontainebleau and the quiet little house where, for the first time, we tasted the joys of real rest, this existence seems to me strange and even unpleasant. Indeed, it makes me tired even to think of the life these people lead and their expense of muscular force to no purpose.

But the doctor wished me to come here, and I, who long above everything else to be strong, am hoping the pure air will cure me.

On the terrace which overlooks the lake I usually take my walks, but when I have taken about a hundred steps I have to sit down and rest. Certainly I would be no Alpinist.

One thing to which I never seem to accustom myself is my hat. It is always falling off. Sometimes, too, I forget that I am wearing a hat and lean back in my chair; and what an absurd fashion—to lunch in a hat! Still, hats seem to play a very important rôle in Western life. Guess how many I possess at present—twenty.

I cannot tell whom I have to thank, since the parcels come anonymously, but several kind friends, hearing of our escape, have had the thoughtfulness and the same original idea of providing us with hats. Hardly a day passes but someone sends us a hat; it is curious, but charming all the same. Do they think we are too shy to order hats for ourselves, and are still wandering about Switzerland in our *tcharchafs* [a cloak and veil worn by Turkish women when walking out of doors]?

. . .

Every morning the people here row on the lake, or play tennis—tennis being one of their favorite forms of amusement. I watch them with interest, yet even were I able I should not indulge in this unfeminine sport.

Women rush about the court, from left to right, up and down, forwards and backwards. Their hair is all out of curl, often it comes down; and they wear unbecoming flat shoes and men's shirts and collars and ties.

The ball comes scarcely over the net, a woman rushes forward, her leg is bared to the sight of all; by almost throwing herself on the ground, she hits it back over the net, and then her favorite man (not her husband, I may mention), with whom she waltzes and rows and climbs, chooses this moment to take a snapshot of her most hideous attitude. What an unpleasant idea to think a man should possess such a souvenir!

And yet after tennis these people do not rest—on they go, walking and climbing; and what is the use of it all?—they only come back and eat four persons' share of lunch.

At meal-time, the conversation is tennis and climbing, and climbing and tennis; and again I say, I cannot understand why they employ all this muscular force to no higher end than to give themselves an unnatural appetite.

A friend of my father's, who is staying here, tells me the wonderful climbing he has accomplished. He explains to me that he has faced death over and over again, and only by the extraordinary pluck of his guide has his life been spared.

"And did you at last reach your friend?" I asked.

"What friend?"

"Was it not to rescue some friend that you faced death?"

"No," he said, "for pleasure."

"For pleasure," I repeated, and he burst out laughing.

He spoke of this as if it were something of which to be proud, "and his oft-repeated encounters with death," he said, "only whetted his appetite for more." Was life then of so little value to this man that he could risk it so easily?

Naturally in trying to explain this curious existence I compare it with our life in the harem, and the more I think the more am I astonished. What I should like to ask these people, if I dared, is, are they really satisfied with their lot, or are they only pretending to be happy, as we in Turkey pretended to be happy? Are they not tired of flirting and enjoying themselves so uselessly?

We in Turkey used to envy the women of the West. We, who were denied the rights of taking part in charitable works, imagined that the European women not only dared to think, but carry their schemes into action for the betterment of their fellow-creatures.

But are these women here an exception? Do they think, or do they not? I wonder myself whether they have not found life so empty that they are endeavoring to crush out their better selves by using up their physical energy. How is it possible, I ask myself, that, after all this exercise, they have strength enough to dance till midnight. Life to me at present is all out of focus; in time perhaps I shall see it in its proper proportions.

We go down sometimes to see the dancing. Since I have been here, I perfectly understand why you never find time to go to balls, if dancing in your country is anything like it is here. When we were children of twelve, before we were veiled, we were invited to dances given in Constantinople. I have danced with young attachés at the British Embassy, yet, child though I was, I saw nothing clever in their performance.

All the people at this dance are grown up, not one is under twenty—some are old gentlemen of fifty—yet they romp like children all through the evening till deep into the night, using up their energy and killing time, as if their life depended on the rapidity with which they hopped round the room without sitting down or feeling ill.

The waltz is to my mind senseless enough, but the lancers? "The ring of roses" the little English girls play is more dignified.

It seems to me that women must forfeit a little of the respect that men owe to them when they have romped with them at lancers.

To-night, I have found out, dancing here is after all an excuse for flirting. In a very short while couples who were quite unacquainted with one another become very intimate. "Oh! I could not wish for a better death than to die waltzing," I heard one young woman say to her partner. His wishes were the same. Surely the air of Switzerland does not engender ambition!

One gentleman came and asked me if I could dance. I said, "Yes, I can *dance*," laying particular emphasis on the word *dance*. But I do not think he understood.

"Will you dance with me?" he asked.

"No," I replied, "I *dance* by myself." He stared at me as if I were mad—probably he took me for a professional dancer.

• • •

When you come to stay with us at Nice, after we have had enough of this pure air to justify our leaving Switzerland and these commonplace and unsympathetic people, and we are in our own villa again and free to do as we will, then we will teach you Turkish dances, and you will no longer be surprised at my criticisms.

Dancing with us is a fine art. In the Imperial Harem more attention is paid to the teaching of dancing than to any other learning. When the Sultan is worn out with cares of state and the thousand and one other worries for which his autocratic rule is responsible, his dancing girls are called into his presence, and there with veils and graceful movements they soothe his tired nerves till he almost forgets the atrocities which have been committed in his name.

A Turkish woman who dances well is seen to very great advantage; a dancing woman may become a favorite, a Sultana, a Sultan's mother, the queen of the Imperial Harem.

I can assure you a Western woman is not seen at her best when she dances the lancers.—Your affectionate

ZEYNEB.

DREAMS AND REALITIES

HENDAYE, July 1907.

What a relief! What a heart-felt relief to leave Paris! Paris with its noise and clamour and perpetual and useless movement! Paris which is so different from what I expected!

We have had in Paris what you English people call a "season," and I shall require many months of complete rest, to get over the effects of that awful modern whirlwind.

What an exhausting life! What unnecessary labor! And what a contrast to our calm harem existence away yonder. I think—yes, I almost think I have had enough of the West now, and want to return to the East, just to get back the old experience of calm.

Picture to yourself the number of new faces we have seen in six weeks. What a collection of women—chattering, irritating, inquisitive, demonstrative, and obliging women, who invite you again and again, and when you do go to their receptions you get nothing for your trouble but crowding and pushing.

All the men and women in Paris are of uncertain years. The pale girl who serves the tea might be of any age from fifteen to thirty, and the men with the well-trimmed fingers and timid manners are certainly not sixty, but they might be anything up to forty.

But where are the few *intellectuelles?* Lost between the lace and the teacups. They look almost ashamed of being seen there at all. They have real knowledge, and to meet them is like opening the chapter of a valuable Encyclopedia; but hardly has one taken in the discovery, when one is pushed along to find the conclusion of the chapter somewhere in the crowd, if indeed it can be found.

As you know, since our arrival from Nice we have not had one free evening. The *Grandes Dames* of France wanted to get a closer view of two Turkish women, and they have all been charming to us, especially the elder ones.

Yes, charming is the word which best applies to all these society ladies, young and old, and is not *to be charming* the modern ideal of civilization? These women are all physically the model of a big Paris dressmaker, and morally what society allows them to be—some one quite inoffensive. But it is not their fault that they have all been formed on the same pattern, and that those who have originality hide it under the same exterior as the others, fearful lest such a blemish should even be suspected!

But really, am I not a little pedantic? How can I dare to come to such a conclusion after a visit which lasts barely a quarter of an hour?

At luncheon and dinner the favorite topics of conversation are the pieces played at the theaters or the newest books. Marriage, too, is always an interesting subject, and everyone seems eager to get married in spite of the thousand and one living examples there are to warn others of what it really is. This supreme trust in a benign Fate amuses me. Every bride-elect imagines it is she who will be the one exception to the general rule. Turkish women do not look forward to matrimony with the same confidence.

Divorce has a morbid fascination for the men and women here: so have other people's misfortunes. And as soon as a man or woman is down—a woman particularly—everyone delights in giving his or her contribution to the moral kicking.

I must own, too, I cannot become enthusiastic about Mdlle. Cecile Sorel's clothes nor the grace of a certain Russian dancer. What I would like to talk about would be some subject which could help us two peoples to understand each other better, but such subjects are carefully avoided as tiresome.

Do you remember how anxious we were to hear Strauss's *Salome* discussed, and what it was in all this work which interested these Paris Society ladies?— nothing more nor less than whether it was Trohohanova or Zambelli who was to dance the part of Salome.

That was a disappointment for me! All my life I looked forward to being in a town where music was given the place of honor, for in Constantinople, as you know, there is music for everyone except the Turkish woman.

I had no particular desire to see the monuments of Paris, and now I have visited them my affection for them is only lukewarm. The Philistine I am! I wish I dared tell the Parisians what I really thought of them and their beautiful Paris! I had come above all things to educate myself in music, and now I find that they, with their unbounded opportunities, have shamefully failed to avail themselves of what to me, as a Turkish woman, is the great chance of a lifetime.

[...]

A BULL-FIGHT

Guess, my dear, where I have been this afternoon. Guess, guess! I, a Turkish woman, have been to a bull-fight! There were many English people present. They are, I am told, the *habitués* of the place, and they come away, like the Spaniards, almost intoxicated by the spectacle.

This is an excitement which does not in the least appeal to me. Surely one must be either prehistoric or decadent to get into this unwholesome condition of the Spaniards. Is the sight of a bull which is being killed, and perhaps the death of a toreador, "*such a delightful show,*" to quote the exact words of my American neighbor? He shouted with frenzy whilst my sister and two Poles, unable to bear the sight of the horses' obtruding intestines, had to be led out of the place in an almost fainting condition.

As for myself, I admit to having admired two things, the suppleness of the men and the brilliant appearance of the bull-ring. The women of course lent a picturesque note to the *ensemble* with their sparkling jewels, their faces radiant as those of the men, their dark eyes dancing with excitement, and their handsome gowns and their graceful mantillas. But shall I ever forget the hideous sight of the poor horse staggering out of the ring, nor the roars of the wounded bull? It was a spectacle awful to look upon. What a strange performance for a Turkish woman, used to the quiet of our harem life!

Perhaps, however, for those to whom life has brought no emotion or sorrow, no joy or love, those who have never seen the wholesale butchery to which we, alas! had almost become accustomed—perhaps to these people this horrible sight is a necessity. Spanish writers have told me they have done their best work after a bull-fight, and before taking any important step in life they needed this stimulus to carry them safely through. I can assure you, however, I heaved a sigh of relief when the performance was over, and not for untold gold would I ever go to see it again.

After leaving the scene I have described to you, we followed the crowd to a little garden planted with trees, which is situated in the Calle Mayor and stretches along the side of the stream till it meets the Bidassoa. This is the spot where, on cool evenings, men and maidens meet to dance the Fandango. Basque men with red caps are seated in the middle to supply the music. On the sandy earth, which is the ballroom, the couples dance, in and out of the gnarled trees, to the rhythm of dance music, that is strange and passionate and at the same time almost languishing.

The music played was more Arabian than anything I have yet heard in the West, but unfortunately the modern note too was creeping into these delightful measures. The Basques with their red caps, bronzed faces, white teeth, and fine manly figures, the women with their passionate and supple movements and decorated mantillas, and the almost antique frame of Fontarabia, proud of its past, hopeful for its future, were all so new and so different to me.

But it is dark now, the dancing has ceased, the crowd has dispersed. How good it is to be out at this hour of the evening. I, who am free (or think I am), delight in the fact there are no Turkish policemen to question me as to what I am doing.

. . .

But alas! alas! I spoke of my freedom a little too soon. Even in this quiet city can I not pass unobserved?

"Have you anything to declare?" a Custom House officer asks me.

"Yes," I replied, "my hatred of your Western 'Customs,' and my delight at being alive."—Your affectionate friend,

ZEYNEB.

AND IS THIS REALLY FREEDOM?

[. . .]

But, my dear, why have you never told me that the Ladies' Gallery is a harem? A harem with its latticed windows! The harem of the Government! No wonder the women cried through the windows of that harem that they wanted to be free! I felt inclined to shout out too. "Is it in Free England that you dare to have a harem? How inconsistent are you English! You send your women out unprotected all over the world, and here in the workshop where your laws are made, you cover them with a symbol of protection."

The performance which I saw through the harem windows was boring enough. The humbler members of the House had little respect for their superiors, seeing they sat in their presence with their hats on, and this I am told was the habit of a very ill-bred man. Still perhaps this attitude does not astonish me since on all sides I hear complaints of the Government. It is a bad sign for a country, my dear. Are you following in Turkey's footsteps? Hatred of the Government and prison an honor! Poor England!

I was very anxious to see the notorious Mr. Lloyd George. Since I have been in London his name is on everyone's lips. I have heard very little good of him except from the ruffians at the street corner meeting, and yet like our Hamid he seems to be all-powerful. For a long time, I could not distinguish him in the crowd below, although my companion spared no pains in pointing him out. I was looking for some one with a commanding presence, some one with an eagle eye and a wicked face like our Sultan, some one before whom a whole nation was justified in trembling. But I still wonder whether I am thinking of the right man when I think of Mr. Lloyd George.

There is not much excitement in your House of Commons, is there? I prefer the Chamber of Deputies, even though some one fired at M. Briand the day I went there. There at least they are men of action. Here some members were so weary of law-making, that they crossed their legs, folded their arms, and went to sleep whilst their colleagues opposite were speaking. I thought it would have been more polite to have gone out and taken tea, as the other members seemed to be doing all the time. It would have given them strength to listen to the tiresome debate.

To me, perhaps, the speaking would have been less unbearable if the harem windows had not deadened the sound, which, please notice, is my polite Turkish way of saying, they all spoke so indistinctly.

The bell began to ring again. The members of Parliament all walked towards the harem to this curious direction, "Eyes to the right and nose to the left."[1] And at last my friend took me away.

[...]

THE CLASH OF CREEDS

[...]

I have had the pleasure, since I have been here, of seeing two diplomatists with whose voices I was familiar for many years in Constantinople. My father highly esteemed them both; they often came to see him. When they had drunk their coffee, sometimes my father sent for us to come and play and sing to them, and from behind a curtain they courteously thanked us for our performance.

Although I had so often heard their voices I never had an opportunity of seeing a photo of either of them, and I can't tell whether I was agreeably surprised or not. Have you ever tried putting a body to a voice?

. . .

What a magnificent city London is! If you English are not proud of it, you ought to be. It is not only grand and magnificent but has an aristocratic look that despises mere ornament.

Here in London I have a feeling of security, which I have had nowhere else in the world. It is the only capital in Europe I have so far seen that gives me a sense of orderliness not dependent on authority. It seems to me as if English character were expressed even in the houses of the people. You can tell at a glance what kind of people dwell in the house you are entering. How different is Paris! What a delight to have no concierge, those petty potentates who, as it were, keep the key of your daily life, and remedy there is none.

For the first time since I left Turkey I have had here the sensation of real home life. As you know, we have no flats in Turkey, and have room to move about freely—room for your delightful English furniture, which to me is the most comfortable in the whole world.

Like ours, the houses here are made for use, and their wide doors and broad passages seem to extend a welcome to you which French houses hardly ever do. In France you smell economy before you even reach the door-mat.

You who are in Turkey can now understand what I have suffered from this narrowness of French domestic life. You can imagine my surprise when, the morning after my arrival here, a big tray was sent into my room with a heavy meal of eggs, bacon, fish, toast, marmalade, and what not. I thought I must have looked ill and as if I needed extra feeding, and I explained to my hostess that my white skin was not a sign of anemia but my Oriental complexion: all the eggs and bacon in the world would not change the color of my skin. She was not aware that the Mahometan never eats pork, and like so many others, seemed to forget that bacon, like pork, came from a forbidden source.

I do not find London noisy, but what noise there is one feels is serving a purpose. Life seems so serious; everyone is busy crowding into twelve hours the work of twenty-four. We Turks take no heed of the passing hours.

The Englishmen remind me of the Turks. They have the same grave demeanor, the same appearance of indifference to our sex, the same look of stubborn determination, and, like the Turk, every Englishman is a Sultan in his own house. Like the Turk, too, he is sincere and faithful in his friendships, but Englishmen have two qualities that the Turks do not possess. They are extremely good business men, and in social relations are extremely prudent, although it is difficult to say where prudence ends and hypocrisy begins.

But if Englishmen remind me of Turks, I can find nothing in common between English and Turkish women. They are in direct contrast to one another in everything. Perhaps it is this marked contrast that balances our friendship. A Turkish woman's life is as mysterious as an Englishwoman's life is an open book, which all can read who care. Before I met the suffragettes, I knew only sporting and society women. They were all passionately absorbed in their own amuse-ments, which as you know do not in the least appeal to me. I suppose we Turkish women who have so much time to devote to culture become unreasonably exacting. But everywhere I have been—in England, Germany, France, Italy, and Spain—I have found how little and how uselessly the women read, and how society plays havoc with their taste for good books.

Englishwomen are pretty, but are deficient in charm. They have no particular desire and make no effort to please. You know the charm of the Turkish woman. The Englishwoman is pig-headed, undiplomatic, brutally sincere, but a good and faithful friend. The Turkish woman—well, you must fill that in yourself! I am too near to focus her.

But now that I have seen the women of most countries, you may want to know which I most admire.

Well, I will tell you frankly, the Turkish woman. An ordinary person would answer, "Of course," but you are not an ordinary person, so I shall at once give you my reasons. It is not because I am a Turkish woman myself, but because, in spite of the slavery of their existence, Turkish women have managed to keep their minds free from prejudice. With them it is not what people think they ought to think, but what they think themselves. Nowhere else in Europe have I found women with such courage in thinking.

In every country there are women—though they may be a mere handful—who are above class, above nationality, and dare to be themselves. These are the people I appreciate the most. These are the people I shall always wish to know, for to them the whole world is kin.—Your affectionate friend,

ZEYNEB.

THE END OF THE DREAM

[. . .]

But I expected in France the same good honest Turks I knew in our Eastern villages, and it was from the Eastern simplicity and loyalty that I drew my conclusions about the people of the West. You know now what they are! And do not for a moment imagine that I am the only one to make this mistake: nine out of ten of my compatriots, men and women, would have the same expectation of them. Until they have come to the West to see for themselves and had some of the experiences that we have had, they will never appreciate the calm, leisurely people of our country.

How dangerous it is to urge those Orientals forward, only to reduce them in a few years to the same state of stupidity as the poor degenerate peoples of the West, fed on unhealthy literature and poisoned with alcohol.

You are right: it is in the West that I have learned to appreciate my country. Here I have studied its origin, its history (and I still know only too little of it), but I shall take away with me very serious knowledge about Turkey.

[. . .]

[T]he letter came from Turkey, and the Turkish stamp almost frightened me: for a long time I had not the courage to open it. When at last I slowly cut the envelope of that letter, I found it contained the cutting of a newspaper which announced the death of the dear old uncle whom more than anyone I was longing to see again.

Outside the conquerors were crying out, even louder than before, "More Turkish losses, more Turkish losses." I folded up the letter and put it back in its envelope with a heart too bitter for tears.

. . .

What did it all mean? What was the warning that fate was sending to me in this cruel manner? *Désenchantée* I left Turkey, *désenchantée* I have left Europe. Is that rôle to be mine till the end of my days?—Your affectionate friend,

ZEYNEB.

NOTE

1. I leave my friend's spelling unchanged.

REFERENCES

Ellison, Grace. 1915. *An Englishwoman in a Turkish Harem*. Cambridge University Press.

Loti, Pierre. 1989 [1906]. "Les Désenchantées" in *Pierre de l'Acádemie française*. Claude Gagnière, ed. Paris: Omnibus.

———. 2008 [1879]. *Aziyadé: Suivi de Fantôme d'Orient*. Claire Laboygues, ed. Clermont-Ferrand, France: Èditions Paleo.

7

From Orientalism

Edward Said, 1978

Edward Said was born a secular Christian in Jerusalem, Palestine, in 1935. In 1947–1948 his family fled to Egypt, where he was enrolled in British schools before leaving for the United States to complete his secondary education and earn degrees at Princeton and Harvard. To say he is the product of the strong historical currents that have defined his variegated life is to understate the complex life composition of this professor of comparative literature. His book *Orientalism* (1978) integrated his Middle Eastern roots with his education in Western schools, and as a critique of Western education this seminal book consolidated his voice.

In *Orientalism* Said describes the processes through which Western academics invented the idea of the Orient. Focusing primarily on French and British intellectuals, Said demonstrates the "enormously systematic discipline by which European culture was able to manage—and even produce—the Orient politically, sociologically, militarily, ideologically, scientifically and imaginatively during the post-Enlightenment period" (Said 1978:3). He argues that Western intellectuals' constructions of the Orient did not reflect empirical realities; rather their depictions were imagined—prerequisites for gaining power over the Orient by means of a plethora of images constructed by scholars, historians, and artists. And although the military used such imaginings, European intellectuals and artists were complicit in efforts to subjugate the East. In his introduction, Said describes in particular a "subtle and persistent Eurocentric prejudice against Arab-Islamic peoples and their culture" (8), and illustrates how misinformation, repeated often enough, can become accepted as solid academic work. Said further refined this theme in his 1994 book, *Culture and Imperialism,* in which he describes the Western cultural imagination that inspired Europeans to extend their rule across the globe while justifying their right and obligation to dominate other peoples.

Edward Said's work has become so much a part of Euro-American academic thought that many assume his Western education makes him an insider critic. Others argue that his work reflects his outsider Arab-Islamic heritage. Ferial Ghazoul (1993 [1992]) asserts that Said unmasked prejudice disguised as intellectual thought. Although Said was trained mostly in the West as a literary critic in Western institutions of learning, "Western discourse . . . has remained, in both its public and specialized forms, indifferent, if not downright hostile to Said's roots. It is not surprising that the suppressed part of himself will find opportunities to break forth" (157).

I have also written that Said fits the "oppositional strain," or the role of the *skeptic* or *doubter*—all words that might refer to an Eastern tradition both subjective and objective, and that recognizes that the Other is never mute (Nader 2010, 2013). Anything but ethnocentric, he is a cosmopolitan who incorporated into his work high English and American culture, as well as his own high Arab culture of literature and politics, poetry and novels. Said's message was not that Orientalist scholars purposely "misrepresented" the Middle East in a vacuum, but that the Western political-intellectual culture that surrounded such representations linked logically to imperialism. Listening to contemporary news reports on the Middle East, for example, reminds one of Said's observation that in other situations such reporting might openly be called racist. Any interaction between culturally distinct groups of people has a power dimension. In his afterword to the 1995 edition of *Orientalism,* Said provides a rich commentary on his "reading back into the book that I wrote what others have said, in addition to what I myself wrote after." As a critical scholar, Said pursues the idea that the development and maintenance of cultures requires the construction of opposites, of "others." In his 2003 edition, however, published shortly before his death that year, Said concludes that "rubrics like 'America,' 'the West,' or 'Islam' . . . invent collective identities for large numbers of individuals who are actually quite diverse . . . and [these rubrics] must be opposed" (xxviii). This is to be accomplished by critical thought—humanism.

· · ·

INTRODUCTION

I

On a visit to Beirut during the terrible civil war of 1975–1976 a French journalist wrote regretfully of the gutted downtown area that "it had once seemed to belong to . . . the Orient of Chateaubriand and Nerval."[1] He was right about the place, of course, especially so far as a European was concerned. The Orient was almost a European invention, and had been since antiquity a place of romance, exotic beings, haunting memories and landscapes, remarkable experiences. Now it was disappearing; in a sense it had happened, its time was over. Perhaps it seemed irrelevant that Orientals themselves had something at stake in the process, that even in the time of Chateaubriand and Nerval Orientals had lived there, and that now it was they who were suffering; the main thing for the European visitor was a European representation of the Orient and its contemporary fate, both of which had a privileged communal significance for the journalist and his French readers.

Americans will not feel quite the same about the Orient, which for them is much more likely to be associated very differently with the Far East (China and Japan, mainly). Unlike the Americans, the French and the British—less so the Germans, Russians, Spanish, Portuguese, Italians, and Swiss—have had a long tradition of what I shall be calling *Orientalism,* a way of coming to terms with the Orient that is based on the Orient's special place in European Western experience. The Orient is not only adjacent to Europe; it is also the place of Europe's greatest and richest and oldest colonies, the source of its civilizations and languages, its cultural contestant, and one of its deepest and most recurring images of the Other. In addition, the Orient has helped to define Europe (or the West) as its contrasting image, idea, personality, experience. Yet none of this Orient is merely imaginative. The Orient is an integral part of European *material* civilization and culture. Orientalism expresses and represents that part culturally and even ideologically as a mode of discourse with supporting institutions, vocabulary, scholarship, imagery, doctrines, even colonial bureaucracies and colonial styles. In contrast, the American understanding of the Orient will seem considerably less dense, although our recent Japanese, Korean, and Indochinese adventures ought now to be creating a more sober, more realistic "Oriental" awareness. Moreover, the vastly expanded American political and economic role in the Near East (the Middle East) makes great claims on our understanding of that Orient.

It will be clear to the reader (and will become clearer still throughout the many pages that follow) that by Orientalism I mean several things, all of them, in my opinion, interdependent. The most readily accepted designation for Orientalism is an academic one, and indeed the label still serves in a number of academic institutions. Anyone who teaches, writes about, or researches the Orient—and this applies whether the person is an anthropologist, sociologist, historian, or philologist—either in its specific or its general aspects, is an Orientalist, and what he or she does is Orientalism. Compared with *Oriental studies* or *area studies,* it is true that the term *Orientalism* is less preferred by specialists today, both because it is too vague and general and because it connotes the high-handed executive attitude of nineteenth-century and early-twentieth-century European colonialism. Nevertheless books are written and congresses held with "the Orient" as their main focus, with the Orientalist in his new or old guise as their main authority. The point is that even if it does not survive as it once did, Orientalism lives on academically through its doctrines and theses about the Orient and the Oriental.

Related to this academic tradition, whose fortunes, transmigrations, specializations, and transmissions are in part the subject of this study, is a more general meaning for Orientalism. Orientalism is a style of thought based upon an ontological and epistemological distinction made between "the Orient" and (most of the time) "the Occident." Thus a very large mass of writers, among whom are poets, novelists, philosophers, political theorists, economists, and imperial administrators, have accepted the basic distinction between East and West as the starting point for elaborate theories, epics, novels, social descriptions, and political accounts concerning the Orient, its people, customs, "mind," destiny, and so on. *This* Orientalism can accommodate Aeschylus, say, and Victor Hugo, Dante and Karl Marx. A little later in this introduction I shall deal with the methodological problems one encounters in so broadly construed a "field" as this.

The interchange between the academic and the more or less imaginative meanings of Orientalism is a constant one, and since the late eighteenth century there has been a considerable, quite disciplined—perhaps even regulated—traffic between the two. Here I come to the third meaning of Orientalism, which is something more historically and materially defined than either of the other two. Taking the late eighteenth century as a very roughly defined starting point Orientalism can be discussed and analyzed as the corporate institution for dealing with the Orient—dealing with it by making statements about it, authorizing views of it, describing it, by teaching it, settling it, ruling over it: in short, Orientalism as a Western style for dominating, restructuring, and having authority over the Orient. I have found it useful here to employ Michel Foucault's notion of a discourse, as described by him in *The Archaeology of Knowledge* and in *Discipline and Punish,* to identify Orientalism. My contention is that without examining Orientalism as a discourse one cannot possibly understand the enormously systematic discipline by which European culture was able to manage—and even produce—the Orient politically, sociologically, militarily, ideologically, scientifically, and imaginatively during the post-Enlightenment period. Moreover, so authoritative a position did Orientalism have that I believe no one writing, thinking, or acting on the Orient could do so without taking account of the limitations on thought and action imposed by Orientalism. In brief, because of Orientalism the Orient was not (and is not) a free subject of thought or action. This is not to say that Orientalism unilaterally determines what can be said about the Orient, but that it is the whole network of interests inevitably brought to bear on (and therefore always involved in) any occasion when that peculiar entity "the Orient" is in question. How this happens is what this book tries to demonstrate. It also tries to show that European culture gained in strength and identity by setting itself off against the Orient as a sort of surrogate and even underground self.

Historically and culturally there is a quantitative as well as a qualitative difference between the Franco-British involvement in the Orient and—until the period of American ascendancy after World War II—the involvement of every other European and Atlantic power. To speak of Orientalism therefore is to speak mainly, although not exclusively, of a British and French cultural enterprise, a project whose dimensions take in such disparate realms as the imagination itself, the whole of India and the Levant, the Biblical texts and the Biblical lands, the spice trade, colonial armies and a long tradition of colonial administrators, a formidable scholarly corpus, innumerable Oriental "experts" and "hands," an Oriental professorate, a complex array of "Oriental" ideas (Oriental despotism, Oriental splendor, cruelty, sensuality), many Eastern sects, philosophies, and wisdoms domesticated for local European use—the list can be extended more or less indefinitely. My point is that Orientalism derives from a particular closeness experienced between Britain and France and the Orient, which until the early nineteenth century had really meant only India and the Bible lands. From the beginning of the nineteenth century until the end of World War II France and Britain dominated the Orient and Orientalism; since World War II America has dominated the Orient, and approaches it as France and Britain once did. Out of that closeness, whose dynamic is enormously productive even if it always demonstrates the comparatively greater strength of the Occident (British, French, or American), comes the large body of texts I call Orientalist.

It should be said at once that even with the generous number of books and authors that I examine, there is a much larger number that I simply have had to leave out. My argument, however, depends neither upon an exhaustive catalogue of texts dealing with the Orient nor upon a clearly delimited set of texts, authors, and ideas that together make up the Orientalist canon. I have depended instead upon a different methodological alternative—whose backbone in a sense is the set of historical generalizations I have so far been making in this Introduction—and it is these I want now to discuss in more analytical detail.

II

I have begun with the assumption that the Orient is not an inert fact of nature. It is not merely *there*, just as the Occident itself is not just *there* either. We must take seriously Vico's great observation that men make their own history, that what they can know is what they have made, and extend it to geography: as both geographical and cultural entities—to say nothing of historical entities—such locales, regions, geographical sectors as "Orient" and "Occident" are man-made. Therefore as much as the West itself, the Orient is an idea that has a history and a tradition of thought, imagery, and vocabulary that have given it reality and presence in and for the West. The two geographical entities thus support and to an extent reflect each other.

Having said that, one must go on to state a number of reasonable qualifications. In the first place, it would be wrong to conclude that the Orient was *essentially* an idea, or a creation with no corresponding reality. When Disraeli said in his novel *Tancred* that the East was a career, he meant that to be interested in the East was something bright young Westerners would find to be an all-consuming passion; he should not be interpreted as saying that the East was *only* a career for Westerners. There were—and are—cultures and nations whose location is in the East, and their lives, histories, and customs have a brute reality obviously greater than anything that could be said about them in the West. About that fact this study of Orientalism has very little to contribute, except to acknowledge it tacitly. But the phenomenon of Orientalism as I study it here deals principally, not with a correspondence between Orientalism and Orient, but with the internal consistency of Orientalism and its ideas about the Orient (the East as career) despite or beyond any correspondence, or lack thereof, with a "real" Orient. My point is that Disraeli's statement about the East refers mainly to that created consistency, that regular constellation of ideas as the pre-eminent thing about the Orient, and not to its mere being, as Wallace Stevens's phrase has it.

A second qualification is that ideas, cultures, and histories cannot seriously be understood or studied without their force, or more precisely their configurations of power, also being studied. To believe that the Orient was created—or, as I call it, "Orientalized"—and to believe that such things happen simply as a necessity of the imagination, is to be disingenuous. The relationship between Occident and Orient is a relationship of power, of domination, of varying degrees of a complex hegemony, and is quite accurately indicated in the title of K. M. Panikkar's classic *Asia and Western Dominance*.[2] The Orient was Orientalized not only because it was discovered to be "Oriental" in all those ways considered commonplace by an average nineteenth-century European, but also because it *could be*—that is, submitted to being—*made* Oriental. There is very little consent to be found, for example, in the fact that Flaubert's encounter with an Egyptian courtesan produced a widely influential model of the Oriental woman; she never spoke of herself, she never represented her emotions, presence, or history. *He* spoke for and represented her. He was foreign, comparatively wealthy, male, and these were historical facts of domination that allowed him not only to possess Kuchuk Hanem physically but to speak for her and tell his readers in what way she was "typically Oriental." My argument is that Flaubert's situation of strength in relation to Kuchuk Hanem was not an isolated instance. It fairly stands for the pattern of relative strength between East and West, and the discourse about the Orient that it enabled.

This brings us to a third qualification. One ought never to assume that the structure of Orientalism is nothing more than a structure of lies or of myths which, were the truth about them to be told, would simply blow away. I myself believe that Orientalism is more particularly valuable as a sign of European-Atlantic power over the Orient than it is as a veridic discourse about the Orient (which is what, in its academic or scholarly form, it claims to be). Nevertheless, what we must respect and try to grasp is the sheer knitted-together strength of Orientalist discourse, its very close ties to the enabling socio-economic and political institutions, and its redoubtable durability. After all, any system of ideas that can remain unchanged as teachable wisdom (in academies, books, congresses, universities, foreign-service institutes) from the period of Ernest Renan in the late 1840s until the present in the United States must be something more formidable than a mere collection of lies. Orientalism, therefore, is not an airy European fantasy about the Orient, but a created body of theory and practice in which, for many generations, there has been a considerable material investment. Continued investment made Orientalism, as a system of knowledge about the Orient, an accepted grid for filtering through the Orient into Western consciousness, just as that same investment multiplied— indeed, made truly productive—the statements proliferating out from Orientalism into the general culture.

Gramsci has made the useful analytic distinction between civil and political society in which the former is made up of voluntary (or at least rational and non-coercive) affiliations like schools, families, and unions, the latter of state institutions (the army, the police, the central bureaucracy) whose role in the polity is direct domination. Culture, of course, is to be found operating within civil society, where the influence of ideas, of institutions, and of other persons works not through domination but by what Gramsci calls consent. In any society not totalitarian, then, certain cultural forms predominate over others, just as certain ideas are more influential than others; the form of this cultural leadership is what Gramsci has identified as *hegemony*, an indispensable concept for any understanding of cultural life in the industrial West. It is hegemony, or rather the result of cultural hegemony at work, that gives Orientalism the durability and the strength I have been speaking about so far. Orientalism is never far from what Denys Hay has called the idea of Europe,[3] a collective notion identifying "us" Europeans as against all "those" non-Europeans, and indeed it can be argued that the major component in European culture is precisely what made that culture hegemonic both in and outside Europe: the idea of European identity as a superior one in comparison with all the non-European peoples and cultures. There is in addition the hegemony of European ideas about the Orient, themselves reiterating European superiority over Oriental backwardness, usually overriding the possibility that a more independent, or more skeptical, thinker might have had different views on the matter.

In a quite constant way, Orientalism depends for its strategy on this flexible *positional* superiority, which puts the Westerner in a whole series of possible relationships with the Orient without ever losing him the relative upper hand. And why should it have been otherwise, especially during the period of extraordinary European ascendancy from the late Renaissance to the present? The scientist, the scholar, the missionary, the trader, or the soldier was in, or thought about, the

Orient because he *could be there,* or could think about it, with very little resistance on the Orient's part. Under the general heading of knowledge of the Orient, and within the umbrella of Western hegemony over the Orient during the period from the end of the eighteenth century, there emerged a complex Orient suitable for study in the academy, for display in the museum, for reconstruction in the colonial office, for theoretical illustration in anthropological, biological, linguistic, racial, and historical theses about mankind and the universe, for instances of economic and sociological theories of development, revolution, cultural personality, national or religious character. Additionally, the imaginative examination of things Oriental was based more or less exclusively upon a sovereign Western consciousness out of whose unchallenged centrality an Oriental world emerged, first according to general ideas about who or what was an Oriental, then according to a detailed logic governed not simply by empirical reality but by a battery of desires, repressions, investments, and projections. If we can point to great Orientalist works of genuine scholarship like Silvestre de Sacy's *Chrestomathie arabe* or Edward William Lane's *Account of the Manners and Customs of the Modern Egyptians,* we need also to note that Renan's and Gobineau's racial ideas came out of the same impulse, as did a great many Victorian pornographic novels (see the analysis by Steven Marcus of "The Lustful Turk"[4]).

And yet, one must repeatedly ask oneself whether what matters in Orientalism is the general group of ideas overriding the mass of material—about which who could deny that they were shot through with doctrines of European superiority, various kinds of racism, imperialism, and the like, dogmatic views of "the Oriental" as a kind of ideal and unchanging abstraction?—or the much more varied work produced by almost uncountable individual writers, whom one would take up as individual instances of authors dealing with the Orient. In a sense the two alternatives, general and particular, are really two perspectives on the same material: in both instances one would have to deal with pioneers in the field like William Jones, with great artists like Nerval or Flaubert. And why would it not be possible to employ both perspectives together, or one after the other? Isn't there an obvious danger of distortion (of precisely the kind that academic Orientalism has always been prone to) if either too general or too specific a level of description is maintained systematically?

My two fears are distortion and inaccuracy, or rather the kind of inaccuracy produced by too dogmatic a generality and too positivistic a localized focus. In trying to deal with these problems I have tried to deal with three main aspects of my own contemporary reality that seem to me to point the way out of the methodological or perspectival difficulties I have been discussing, difficulties that might force one, in the first instance, into writing a coarse polemic on so unacceptably general a level of description as not to be worth the effort, or in the second instance, into writing so detailed and atomistic a series of analyses as to lose all track of the general lines of force informing the field, giving it its special cogency. How then to recognize individuality and to reconcile it with its intelligent, and by no means passive or merely dictatorial, general and hegemonic context?

[...]

THE LATEST PHASE

Since World War II, and more noticeably after each of the Arab-Israeli wars, the Arab Muslim has become a figure in American popular culture, even as in the academic world, in the policy planner's world, and in the world of business very serious attention is being paid the Arab. This symbolizes a major change in the international configuration of forces. France and Britain no longer occupy center stage in world politics; the American imperium has displaced them. A vast web of interests now links all parts of the former colonial world to the United States, just as a proliferation of academic subspecialties divides (and yet connects) all the former philological and European-based disciplines like Orientalism. The area specialist, as he is now called, lays claims to regional expertise, which is put at the service of government or business or both. The massive, quasi-material knowledge stored in the annals of modern European Orientalism—as recorded, for example, in Jules Mohl's nineteenth-century logbook of the field—has been dissolved and released into new forms. A wide variety of hybrid representations of the Orient now roam the culture. Japan, Indochina, China, India, Pakistan: their representations have had, and continue to have, wide repercussions, and they have been discussed in many places for obvious reasons. Islam and the Arabs have their own representations, too, and we shall treat them here as they occur in that fragmentary—yet powerfully and ideologically coherent—persistence, a far less frequently discussed one, into which, in the United States, traditional European Orientalism disbursed itself.

1. *Popular images and social science representations.* Here are a few examples of how the Arab is often represented today. Note how readily "the Arab" seems to accommodate the transformations and reductions—all of a simply tendentious kind—into which he is continually being forced. The costume for Princeton's tenth-reunion class in 1967 had been planned before the June War. The motif—for it would be wrong to describe the costume as more than crudely suggestive—was to have been Arab: robes, headgear, sandals. Immediately after the war, when it had become clear that the Arab motif was an embarrassment, a change in the reunion plans was decreed. Wearing the costume as had been originally planned, the class was now to walk in procession, hands above heads in a gesture of abject defeat. This was what the Arab had become. From a faintly outlined stereotype as a camel-riding nomad to an accepted caricature as the embodiment of incompetence and easy defeat: that was all the scope given the Arab.

Yet after the 1973 war the Arab appeared everywhere as something more menacing. Cartoons depicting an Arab sheik standing behind a gasoline pump turned
up consistently. These Arabs, however, were clearly "Semitic": their sharply hooked
noses, the evil mustachioed leer on their faces, were obvious reminders (to a
largely non-Semitic population) that "Semites" were at the bottom of all "our"
troubles, which in this case was principally a gasoline shortage. The transference
of a popular anti-Semitic animus from a Jewish to an Arab target was made
smoothly, since the figure was essentially the same.

Thus if the Arab occupies space enough for attention, it is as a negative value.
He is seen as the disrupter of Israel's and the West's existence, or in another view of
the same thing, as a surmountable obstacle to Israel's creation in 1948. Insofar as
this Arab has any history, it is part of the history given him (or taken from him: the
difference is slight) by the Orientalist tradition, and later, the Zionist tradition.
Palestine was seen—by Lamartine and the early Zionists—as an empty desert
waiting to burst into bloom; such inhabitants as it had were supposed to be incon-
sequential nomads possessing no real claim on the land and therefore no cultural
or national reality. Thus the Arab is conceived of now as a shadow that dogs the
Jew. In that shadow—because Arabs and Jews are Oriental Semites—can be placed
whatever traditional, latent mistrust a Westerner feels towards the Oriental. For
the Jew of pre-Nazi Europe has bifurcated: what we have now is a Jewish hero,
constructed out of a reconstructed cult of the adventurer-pioneer-Orientalist
(Burton, Lane, Renan), and his creeping, mysteriously fearsome shadow, the Arab
Oriental. Isolated from everything except the past created for him by Orientalist
polemic, the Arab is chained to a destiny that fixes him and dooms him to a series
of reactions periodically chastised by what Barbara Tuchman gives the theological
name "Israel's terrible swift sword."

Aside from his anti-Zionism, the Arab is an oil supplier. This is another negative characteristic, since most accounts of Arab oil equate the oil boycott of 1973–
1974 (which principally benefited Western oil companies and a small ruling Arab
elite) with the absence of any Arab moral qualifications for owning such vast oil
reserves. Without the usual euphemisms, the question most often being asked is
why such people as the Arabs are entitled to keep the developed (free, democratic,
moral) world threatened. From such questions comes the frequent suggestion that
the Arab oil fields be invaded by the marines.

In the films and television the Arab is associated either with lechery or blood-
thirsty dishonesty. He appears as an oversexed degenerate, capable, it is true, of
cleverly devious intrigues, but essentially sadistic, treacherous, low. Slave trader,
camel driver, moneychanger, colorful scoundrel: these are some traditional Arab
roles in the cinema. The Arab leader (of marauders, pirates, "native" insurgents)
can often be seen snarling at the captured Western hero and the blond girl (both of
them steeped in wholesomeness), "My men are going to kill you, but—they like

to amuse themselves before." He leers suggestively as he speaks: this is a current debasement of Valentino's Sheik. In newsreels or news-photos, the Arab is always shown in large numbers. No individuality, no personal characteristics or experiences. Most of the pictures represent mass rage and misery, or irrational (hence hopelessly eccentric) gestures. Lurking behind all of these images is the menace of *jihad*. Consequence: a fear that the Muslims (or Arabs) will take over the world.

Books and articles are regularly published on Islam and the Arabs that represent absolutely no change over the virulent anti-Islamic polemics of the Middle Ages and the Renaissance. For no other ethnic or religious group is it true that virtually anything can be written or said about it, without challenge or demurral. The 1975 course guide put out by the Columbia College undergraduates said about the Arabic course that every other word in the language had to do with violence, and that the Arab mind as "reflected" in the language was unremittingly bombastic. A recent article by Emmett Tyrrell in *Harper's* magazine was even more slanderous and racist, arguing that Arabs are basically murderers and that violence and deceit are carried in the Arab genes.[5] A survey entitled *The Arabs in American Textbooks* reveals the most astonishing misinformation, or rather the most callous representations of an ethnic-religious group. One book asserts that "few people of this [Arab] area even know that there is a better way to live," and then goes on to ask disarmingly, "What links the people of the Middle East together?" The answer, given unhesitatingly, is, "The last link is the Arab's hostility—hatred—toward the Jews and the nation of Israel." Along with such material goes this about Islam, in another book: "The Moslem religion, called Islam, began in the seventh century. It was started by a wealthy businessman of Arabia, called Mohammed. He claimed that he was a prophet. He found followers among other Arabs. He told them that they were picked to rule the world." This bit of knowledge is followed by another, equally accurate: "Shortly after Mohammed's death, his teachings were recorded in a book called the Koran. It became the holy book of Islam."[6]

These crude ideas are supported, not contradicted, by the academic whose business is the study of the Arab Near East. (It is worth noting incidentally that the Princeton event I referred to above took place in a university that prides itself on its department of Near Eastern Studies founded in 1927, the oldest such department in the country.) Take as an instance the report produced in 1967 by Morroe Berger, a professor of sociology and Near Eastern studies at Princeton, at the behest of the Department of Health, Education, and Welfare; he was then president of the Middle East Studies Association (MESA), the professional association of scholars concerned with all aspects of the Near East, "primarily since the rise of Islam and from the viewpoint of the social science and humanistic disciplines,"[7] and founded in 1967. He called his paper "Middle Eastern and North African Studies: Developments and Needs," and had it published in the second issue of the

MESA Bulletin. After surveying the strategic, economic, and political importance of the region to the United States, and after endorsing the various United States government and private foundation projects to support programs in universities—the National Defense Education Act of 1958 (a directly Sputnik-inspired initiative), the establishing of links between the Social Science Research Council and Middle Eastern studies, and so on—Berger came to the following conclusions:

> The modern Middle East and North Africa is not a center of great cultural achievement, nor is it likely to become one in the near future. The study of the region or its languages, therefore, does not constitute its own reward so far as modern culture is concerned.
>
> ... Our region is not a center of great political power nor does it have the potential to become one.... The Middle East (less so North Africa) has been receding in immediate political importance to the U.S. (and even in "headline" or "nuisance" value) relative to Africa, Latin America and the Far East.
>
> ... The contemporary Middle East, thus, has only in small degree the kinds of traits that seem to be important in attracting scholarly attention. This does not diminish the validity and intellectual value of studying the area or affect the quality of work scholars do on it. It does, however, put limits, of which we should be aware, on the field's capacity for growth in the numbers who study and teach.[8]

As a prophecy, of course, this is fairly lamentable; what makes it even more unfortunate is that Berger was commissioned not only because he was an expert on the modern Near East but also—as is clear from the report's conclusion—because he was expected to be in a good position to predict its future, and the future of policy. His failure to see that the Middle East was of great political significance, and potentially of great political power, was no chance aberration of judgment, I think. Both of Berger's main mistakes derive from the first and last paragraphs, whose genealogy is the history of Orientalism as we have been studying it. In what Berger has to say about the absence of great cultural achievement, and in what he concludes about future study—that the Middle East does not attract scholarly attention because of its intrinsic weaknesses—we have an almost exact duplication of the canonical Orientalist opinion that the Semites never produced a great culture and that, as Renan frequently said, the Semitic world was too impoverished ever to attract universal attention. Moreover, in making such time-honored judgments and in being totally blind to what is before his eyes—after all, Berger was not writing fifty years ago, but during a period when the United States was already importing about 10 percent of its oil from the Middle East and when its strategic and economic investments in the area were unimaginably huge—Berger was ensuring the centrality of his own position as Orientalist. For what he says, in effect, is that without people such as him the Middle East would be neglected; and that without his mediating, interpretative role the place would not be understood, partly because what little there is to understand is fairly peculiar, and partly because only the Orientalist can interpret the Orient, the Orient being radically incapable of interpreting itself.

The fact that Berger was not so much a classical Orientalist when he wrote (he wasn't and isn't) as he was a professional sociologist does not minimize the extent of his indebtedness to Orientalism and its ideas. Among those ideas is the specially legitimated antipathy towards and downgrading of the material forming the main basis of his study. So strong is this in Berger that it obscures the actualities before his eyes. And more impressively still, it makes it unnecessary for him to ask himself why, if the Middle East "is not a center of great cultural achievement," he should recommend that anyone devote his life, as he has, to the study of its culture. Scholars—more than, say, doctors—study what they like and what interests them; only an exaggerated sense of cultural duty drives a scholar to the study of what he does not think well of. Yet it is just such a sense of duty Orientalism has fostered, because for generations the culture at large put the Orientalist at the barricades, where in his professional work he confronted the East—its barbarities, its eccentricities, its unruliness—and held it at bay on behalf of the West.

I mention Berger as an instance of the academic attitude towards the Islamic Orient, as an instance of how a learned perspective can support the caricatures propagated in the popular culture. Yet Berger stands also for the most current transformation overtaking Orientalism: its conversion from a fundamentally philological discipline and a vaguely general apprehension of the Orient into a social science specialty. No longer does an Orientalist try first to master the esoteric languages of the Orient; he begins instead as a trained social scientist and "applies" his science to the Orient, or anywhere else. This is the specifically American contribution to the history of Orientalism, and it can be dated roughly from the period immediately following World War II, when the United States found itself in the position recently vacated by Britain and France. The American experience of the Orient prior to that exceptional moment was limited. Cultural isolates like Melville were interested in it; cynics like Mark Twain visited and wrote about it; the American Transcendentalists saw affinities between Indian thought and their own; a few theologians and Biblical students studied the Biblical Oriental languages; there were occasional diplomatic and military encounters with Barbary pirates and the like, the odd naval expedition to the Far Orient, and of course the ubiquitous missionary to the Orient. But there was no deeply invested tradition of Orientalism, and consequently in the United States knowledge of the Orient never passed through the refining and reticulating and reconstructing processes, whose beginning was in philological study, that it went through in Europe. Furthermore, the imaginative investment was never made either, perhaps because the American frontier, the one that counted, was the westward one. Immediately after World War II, then, the Orient became, not a broad catholic issue as it had been for centuries in Europe, but an administrative one, a matter for policy. Enter the social scientist and the new expert, on whose somewhat narrower shoulders was to fall the mantle of Orientalism. In their turn, as we shall see, they made such changes in it that it became scarcely recognizable. In any event, the new Orientalist took over the attitudes of cultural hostility and kept them.

One of the striking aspects of the new American social-science attention to the Orient is its singular avoidance of literature. You can read through reams of expert writing on the modern Near East and never encounter a single reference to literature. What seem to matter far more to the regional expert are "facts," of which a literary text is perhaps a disturber. The net effect of this remarkable omission in modern American awareness of the Arab or Islamic Orient is to keep the region and its people conceptually emasculated, reduced to "attitudes," "trends," statistics: in short, dehumanized. Since an Arab poet or novelist—and there are many— writes of his experiences, of his values, of his humanity (however strange that may be), he effectively disrupts the various patterns (images, clichés, abstractions) by which the Orient is represented. A literary text speaks more or less directly of a living reality. Its force is not that it is Arab, or French, or English; its force is in the power and vitality of words that, to mix in Flaubert's metaphor from *La Tentation de Saint Antoine,* tip the idols out of the Orientalists' arms and make them drop those great paralytic children—which are their ideas of the Orient—that attempt to pass for the Orient.

The absence of literature and the relatively weak position of philology in contemporary American studies of the Near East are illustrations of a new eccentricity in Orientalism, where indeed my use of the word itself is anomalous. For there is very little in what academic experts on the Near East do now that resembles traditional Orientalism of the sort that ended with Gibb and Massignon; the main things that are reproduced are, as I said, a certain cultural hostility and a sense based not so much on philology as on "expertise." Genealogically speaking, modern American Orientalism derives from such things as the army language schools established during and after the war, sudden government and corporate interest in the non-Western world during the postwar period, Cold War competition with the Soviet Union, and a residual missionary attitude towards Orientals who are considered ripe for reform and re-education. The nonphilological study of esoteric Oriental languages is useful for obvious rudimentary strategic reasons; but it is also useful for giving a cachet of authority, almost a mystique, to the "expert" who appears able to deal with hopelessly obscure material with firsthand skill.

In the social-science order of things, language study is a mere tool for higher aims, certainly not for reading literary texts. In 1958, for example, the Middle East Institute—a quasi-governmental body founded to oversee and sponsor research interest in the Middle East—produced a *Report on Current Research.* The contribution "Present State of Arabic Studies in the United States" (done, interestingly enough, by a professor of Hebrew) is prefaced by an epigraph announcing that "no longer is knowledge of foreign languages, for instance, the sole province of the scholars in the humanities. It is a working tool of the engineer, the economist, the social scientist, and many other specialists." The whole report stresses the importance of Arabic to oil-company executives, technicians, and military personnel. But the report's main talking point is this trio of sentences: "Russian universities are now producing fluent Arabic speakers. Russia has realized the importance of appealing to men through their minds, by using their own language. The United States need wait no longer in developing its foreign language program."[9] Thus Oriental languages are part of some policy objective—as to a certain extent they have always been—or part of a sustained propaganda effort. In both these aims the study of Oriental languages becomes the instrument carrying out Harold Lasswell's theses about propaganda, in which what counts is not what people are or think but what they can be made to be and think.

> The propagandist outlook in fact combines respect for individuality with indifference to formal democracy. The respect for individuality arises from the dependence of large scale operations upon the support of the mass and upon experience with the variability of human preferences. . . . This regard for men in the mass rests upon no democratic dogmatisms about men being the best judges of their own interests. The modern propagandist, like the modern psychologist, recognizes that men are often poor judges of their own interests, flitting from one alternative to the next without solid reason or clinging timorously to the fragments of some mossy rock of ages. Calculating the prospect of securing a permanent change in habits and values involves much more than the estimation of the preferences of men in general. It means taking account of the tissue of relations in which men are webbed, searching for signs of preference which may reflect no deliberation and directing a program towards a solution which fits in fact. . . . With respect to those adjustments which do require mass action the task of the propagandist is that of inventing goal symbols which serve the double function of facilitating adoption and adaptation. The symbols must induce acceptance spontaneously. . . . It follows that the management ideal is control of a situation not by imposition but by divination. . . . The propagandist takes it for granted that the world is completely caused but that it is only partly predictable. . . .[10]

The acquired foreign language is therefore made part of a subtle assault upon populations, just as the study of a foreign region like the Orient is turned into a program for control by divination.

Yet such programs must always have a liberal veneer, and usually this is left to scholars, men of good will, enthusiasts to attend to. The idea encouraged is that in studying Orientals, Muslims, or Arabs "we" can get to know another people, their way of life and thought, and so on. To this end it is always better to let them speak for themselves, to represent themselves (even though underlying this fiction stands Marx's phrase—with which Lasswell is in agreement—for Louis Napoleon:

"They cannot represent themselves; they must be represented"). But only up to a point, and in a special way. In 1973, during the anxious days of the October Arab-Israeli War, the *New York Times Magazine* commissioned two articles, one representing the Israeli and one the Arab side of the conflict. The Israeli side was presented by an Israeli lawyer; the Arab side, by an American former ambassador to an Arab country who had no formal training in Oriental studies. Lest we jump immediately to the simple conclusion that the Arabs were believed incapable of representing themselves, we would do well to remember that both Arabs and Jews in this instance were Semites (in the broad cultural designation I have been discussing) and that both *were being made to be* represented for a Western audience. It is worthwhile here to remember this passage from Proust, in which the sudden appearance of a Jew into an aristocratic salon is described as follows:

> The Rumanians, the Egyptians, the Turks may hate the Jews. But in a French drawing-room the differences between those people are not so apparent, and an Israelite making his entry as though he were emerging from the heart of the desert, his body crouching like a hyaena's, his neck thrust obliquely forward, spreading himself in proud "salaams," completely satisfies a certain taste for the oriental [*un goût pour l'orientalisme*].[11]

NOTES

1. Thierry Desjardins, *Le Martyre du Liban* (Paris: Plon, 1976), p. 14.

2. K. M. Panikkar, *Asia and Western Dominance* (London: George Allen & Unwin, 1959).

3. Denys Hay, *Europe: The Emergence of an Idea,* 2nd ed. (Edinburgh: Edinburgh University Press, 1968).

4. Steven Marcus, *The Other Victorians: A Study of Sexuality and Pornography in Mid-Nineteenth Century England* (1966; reprint ed., New York: Bantam Books, 1967), pp. 200–219.

5. R. Emmett Tyrell, Jr., "Chimera in the Middle East," *Harper's*, November 1976, pp. 35–38.

6. Cited in Ayad al-Qazzaz, Ruth Afiyo, et al., *The Arabs in American Textbooks,* California State Board of Education, June 1975, pp. 10, 15.

7. "Statement of Purpose," *MESA Bulletin,* Vol. 1, No. 1 (May 1967): 33.

8. Morroe Berger, "Middle Eastern and North African Studies: Developments and Needs," *MESA Bulletin,* Vol. 1, No. 2 (November 1967): 16.

9. Menachem Mansoor, "Present State of Arabic Studies in the United States," in *Report on Current Research 1958,* ed. Kathleen H. Brown (Washington, DC: Middle East Institute, 1958), pp. 55–56.

10. Harold Lasswell, "Propaganda," in *Encyclopedia of the Social Sciences* (1934), 12:527. I owe this reference to Professor Noam Chomsky.

11. Marcel Proust, *The Guermantes Way,* transl. C. K. Scott Moncrieff (1925; reprint ed., New York: Vintage Books, 1970), p. 135.

REFERENCES

Kennedy, Valerie. 2000. *Edward Said: A Critical Introduction.* Malden, MA: Wiley-Blackwell.

Ghazoul, Ferial J. 1993 [1992]. "The Resonance of the Arab-Islamic Heritage in the Work of Edward Said." In *Edward Said: A Critical Reader*. Michael Sprinker, ed. Oxford: Blackwell.

McCarthy, Conor. 2010. *The Cambridge Introduction to Edward Said*. Cambridge: Cambridge University Press.

Musallam, Basim. 1979. "Review Essay: Power and Knowledge." *MERIP Reports*, Vol. 9, No. 6, pp. 19–26.

Nader, Laura. 2010. "Side-by-Side: The Other Is Not Mute." In *Edward Said: A Legacy of Emancipation and Representation*. Adel Iskandar and Haken Rustom, eds. Berkeley: University of California Press.

———. 2013. *Culture and Dignity: Dialogues between the Middle East and the West*. Hoboken, NJ: Wiley-Blackwell.

Rubin, Andrew N., ed. 2005. *Humanism, Freedom, and the Critic: Edward W. Said and After*. Washington, DC: Georgetown University Press, 2005.

Said, Edward. 1994. *Culture and Imperialism*. New York: Vintage Books.

———. 1995. *Orientalism*. With new afterword. New York: Penguin Books.

———. 2003. *Orientalism*. With new preface. New York: Penguin Books.

8

The President of Iran's Letter to the President of the United States

Mahmoud Ahmadinejad, 2006

Mahmoud Ahmadinejad was born in 1956 in Aradan, in north-central Iran, where his father worked as a blacksmith. When he was a year old his family moved about eighty-two miles northwest, to Teheran. Thus Mahmoud Ahmadinejad grew up in a country still reeling from a U.S.-aided coup to install the pro-Western Shah Mohammed Reza Pahlavi as head of state, during a period when many Iranians resented Western incursion into Iran's politics. As a young student Mahmoud Ahmadinejad excelled in school, entered Iran University of Science and Technology in 1975, and in 1979 graduated with an undergraduate degree in engineering. At the university he became politically active. He produced anti-shah materials pointing to the 1979 revolution against the shah. In Iraq's war against Iran he was a volunteer militiaman working with the Iranian Revolutionary Guard.

His educational interests included pursuance of an MA in engineering at Iran University of Science and Technology, and in 1989 he joined its faculty, married another university professor, and held government posts including governor of a province and advisor to the ministry of culture and higher education. He received his doctorate in transportation engineering in 1997 and remained in his teaching position at the university.

In 2003 he was appointed mayor of Teheran, a position in which he could make good use of his political skills to repeal moderate reforms in favor of new cultural restrictions favored by Iran's religious leadership. In 2005 he ran for Iran's presidency. Promoting himself as a man of the people, he adopted a populist program of ending poverty, corruption, and social injustices. With his presidential landslide he soon became an international figure, especially after taking a hard line on Iran's right to develop nuclear arms, leading to Iran's collision with the United States as well as with the United Nations Security Council (UNSC). His

Ahmadinejad, Mahmoud. 2006. "La lettre de Mahmoud Ahmadinejad à George W. Bush." *Le Monde*, May 9. http://www.lemonde.fr/proche-orient/article/2006/05/09/la-lettre-de-mahmoud-ahmadine-jad-a-george-w-bush_769886_3218.html.

comments on Israel further enlarged his presence, though he claimed he had been misin-
terpreted and his comments exaggerated. Then came sanctions, inflation, and unfulfilled
campaign promises. His presidential tenure came to an end in 2013. A "simple man" with
"simple tastes," who scored 132nd out of 400,000 competitors in the national university
entrance exams, as president of Iran he was a controversial figure both nationally and internationally whose relations with developed countries were not good but were strong with
developing countries—a maverick.

In 2007 Columbia University president Lee C. Bollinger faced the problem of how to
introduce Ahmadinejad at a campus speaking engagement to which Bollinger himself had
not invited the former Iranian president, but for which he would be held to account. Bollinger introduced him in a ten-minute verbal assault that violated the most basic expectations of civility. Bollinger called Ahmadinejad a petty and cruel dictator, thereby missing an
opportunity both as an educator and as a host. He might have provided some history of the
reasons Iran has had grievances against the United States since the removal of Mohammad
Mossadegh in 1953, or mentioned the Iran-Contra affair and the taking of American hostages. In addition, he might have mentioned the American support of Iraq's war on Iran,
which cost the country more than a million lives, and the U.S. government's threatened
embargo on trade with Iran, as the president of a great university might have done.
Ahmadinejad's response to these verbal attacks was different according to Middle Eastern
traditions of hospitality; in his country a host customarily does not treat a guest in such an
insulting manner. "In Iran," Ahmadinejad told his Columbia audience, "tradition requires
when we invite a person to be a speaker, we actually respect our students enough to allow
them to make their own judgment, and don't think it necessary, before the speech is given
even, to come in with a series of complaints to provide vaccination to the students and
faculty" (Cooper 2007). The civilized and the barbarian as public presentations.

The following letter to President George W. Bush is Ahmadinejad's comment on Western hypocrisy.

. . .

Mr. George Bush, President of the United States of America,

For some time now I have been thinking, how one can justify the undeniable
contradictions that exist in the international arena—which are being constantly
debated, especially in political forums and amongst university students. Many
questions remain unanswered. These have prompted me to discuss some of the
contradictions and questions, in the hopes that it might bring about an opportunity to redress them.

Can one be a follower of Jesus Christ (PBUH [peace be upon him]), the great
Messenger of God,

Feel obliged to respect human rights,

Present liberalism as a civilization model,

Announce one's opposition to the proliferation of nuclear weapons and
WMDs,

Make War and Terror his slogan, And finally,

Work towards the establishment of a unified international community—a community which Christ and the virtuous of the Earth will one day govern, But at the same time,

Have countries attacked;

The lives, reputations and possessions of people destroyed and on the slight chance of the . . . of a . . . criminals in a village city, or convoy for example the entire village, city or convey set ablaze. Or because of the possibility of the existence of WMDs in one country, it is occupied, around one hundred thousand people killed, its water sources, agriculture and industry destroyed, close to 180,000 foreign troops put on the ground, sanctity of private homes of citizens broken, and the country pushed back perhaps fifty years. At what price? Hundreds of billions of dollars spent from the treasury of one country and certain other countries and tens of thousands of young men and women—as occupation troops—put in harm's way, taken away from family and love ones, their hands stained with the blood of others, subjected to so much psychological pressure that everyday some commit suicide an[d] those returning home suffer depression, become sickly and grapple with all sorts of aliments; while some are killed and their bodies handed of their families.

On the pretext of the existence of WMDs, this great tragedy came to engulf both the peoples of the occupied and the occupying country. Later it was revealed that no WMDs existed to begin with.

Of course Saddam was a murderous dictator. But the war was not waged to topple him, the announced goal of the war was to find and destroy weapons of mass destruction. He was toppled along the way towards another goal, nevertheless the people of the region are happy about it. I point out that throughout the many years of the . . . war on Iran Saddam was supported by the West.

Mr. President,

You might know that I am a teacher. My students ask me how can these actions be reconciled with the values outlined at the beginning of this letter and duty to the tradition of Jesus Christ (PBUH), the Messenger of peace and forgiveness.

There are prisoners in Guantanamo Bay that have not been tried, have no legal representation, their families cannot see them and are obviously kept in a strange land outside their own country. There is no international monitoring of their conditions and fate. No one knows whether they are prisoners, POWs, accused or criminals.

European investigators have confirmed the existence of secret prisons in Europe too. I could not correlate the abduction of a person, and him or her being kept in secret prisons, with the provisions of any judicial system. For that matter, I fail to understand how such actions correspond to the values outlined in the beginning of this letter, i.e. the teachings of Jesus Christ (PBUH), human rights and liberal values.

Young people, university students and ordinary people have many questions about the phenomenon of Israel. I am sure you are familiar with some of them.

Throughout history many countries have been occupied, but I think the establishment of a new country with a new people, is a new phenomenon that is exclusive to our times.

Students are saying that sixty years ago such a country did not exist. The show old documents and globes and say try as we have, we have not been able to find a country named Israel.

I tell them to study the history of WWI and II. One of my students told me that during WWII, which more than tens of millions of people perished in, news about the war, was quickly disseminated by the warring parties. Each touted their victories and the most recent battlefront defeat of the other party. After the war, they claimed that six million Jews had been killed. Six million people that were surely related to at least two million families.

Again let us assume that these events are true. Does that logically translate into the establishment of the state of Israel in the Middle East or support for such a state? How can this phenomenon be rationalized or explained?

Mr. President,

I am sure you know how—and at what cost—Israel was established: Many thousands were killed in the process.

Millions of indigenous people were made refugees.

Hundreds of thousands of hectares of farmland, olive plantations, towns and villages were destroyed.

This tragedy is not exclusive to the time of establishment; unfortunately it has been ongoing for sixty years now.

A regime has been established which does not show mercy even to kids, destroys houses while the occupants are still in them, announces beforehand its list and plans to assassinate Palestinian figures and keeps thousands of Palestinians in prison. Such a phenomenon is unique—or at the very least extremely rare—in recent memory.

Another big question asked by people is why is this regime being supported? Is support for this regime in line with the teachings of Jesus Christ (PBUH) or Moses (PBUH) or liberal values? Or are we to understand that allowing the original inhabitants of these lands—inside and outside Palestine—whether they are Christian, Muslim or Jew, to determine their fate, runs contrary to principles of democracy, human rights and the teachings of prophets? If not, why is there so much opposition to a referendum?

The newly elected Palestinian administration recently took office. All independent observers have confirmed that this government represents the electorate. Unbelievingly, they have put the elected government under pressure and have advised it to recognize the Israeli regime, abandon the struggle and follow the programs of the previous government.

If the current Palestinian government had run on the above platform, would the Palestinian people have voted for it? Again, can such position taken in opposition to the Palestinian government be reconciled with the values outlined earlier? The people are also saying why are all UNSC resolutions in condemnation of Israel vetoed?

Mr. President,

As you are well aware, I live amongst the people and am in constant contact with them—many people from around the Middle East manage to contact me as well. They do not have faith in these dubious policies either. There is evidence that the people of the region are becoming increasingly angry with such policies.

It is not my intention to pose to[o] many questions, but I need to refer to other points as well.

Why is it that any technological and scientific achievement reached in the Middle East regions is translated into and portrayed as a threat to the Zionist regime? Is not scientific R&D [research and development] one of the basic rights of nations?

You are familiar with history. Aside from the Middle Ages, in what other point in history has scientific and technical progress been a crime? Can the possibility of scientific achievements being utilized for military purposes be reason enough to oppose science and technology altogether? If such a supposition is true, then all scientific disciplines, including physics, chemistry, mathematics, medicine, engineering, etc., must be opposed.

Lies were told in the Iraqi matter. What was the result? I have no doubt that telling lies is reprehensible in any culture, and you do not like to be lied to.

Mr. President,

Don't Latin Americans have the right to ask, why their elected governments are being opposed and coup leaders supported? Or, why must they constantly be threatened and live in fear?

The people of Africa are hardworking, creative and talented. They can play an important and valuable role in providing for the needs of humanity and contribute to its material and spiritual progress. Poverty and hardship in large parts of Africa are preventing this from happening. Don't they have the right to ask why their enormous wealth—including minerals—is being looted, despite the fact that they need it more than others?

Again, do such actions correspond to the teachings of Christ and the tenets of human rights?

The brave and faithful people of Iran too have many questions and grievances, including: the coup d'état of 1953 and the subsequent toppling of the legal government of the day, opposition to the Islamic revolution, transformation of an Embassy into a headquarters supporting the activities of those opposing the Islamic Republic (many thousands of pages of documents corroborates this claim), support for Saddam in the war waged against Iran, the shooting down of the Iranian passenger plane, freezing the assets of the Iranian nation, increasing threats, anger and displeasure vis-à-vis the scientific and nuclear progress of the Iranian nation (just when all Iranians are jubilant and collaborating their country's progress), and many other grievances that I will not refer to in this letter.

Mr. President,

September Eleven was a horrendous incident. The killing of innocents is deplorable and appalling in any part of the world. Our government immediately declared its disgust with the perpetrators and offered its condolences to the bereaved and expressed its sympathies.

All governments have a duty to protect the lives, property and good standing of their citizens. Reportedly your government employs extensive security, protection and intelligence systems—and even hunts its opponents abroad. September eleven was not a simple operation. Could it be planned and executed without coordination with intelligence and security services—or their extensive infiltration? Of course this is just an educated guess. Why have the various aspects of the attacks been kept secret? Why are we not told who botched their responsibilities? And, why aren't those responsible and the guilty parties identified and put on trial?

All governments have a duty to provide security and peace of mind for their citizens. For some years now, the people of your country and neighbors of world trouble spots do not have peace of mind. After 9.11, instead of healing and tending to the emotional wounds of the survivors and the American people—who had been immensely traumatized by the attacks—some Western media only intensified the climates of fear and insecurity—some constantly talked about the possibility of new terror attacks and kept the people in fear. Is that service to the American people? Is it possible to calculate the damages incurred from fear and panic?

American citizen[s] lived in constant fear of fresh attacks that could come at any moment and in any place. They felt insecure in the streets, in their place of work and at home. Who would be happy with this situation? Why was the media, instead of conveying a feeling of security and providing peace of mind, giving rise to a feeling of insecurity?

Some believe that the hype paved the way—and was the justification—for an attack on Afghanistan. Again I need to refer to the role of media. In media charters, correct dissemination of information and honest reporting of a story are established tenets. I express my deep regret about the disregard shown by certain Western media for these principles. The main pretext for an attack on Iraq was the existence of WMDs. This was repeated incessantly—for the public to, finally, believe—and the ground set for an attack on Iraq.

Will the truth not be lost in a contrived and deceptive climate? Again, if the truth is allowed to be lost, how can that be reconciled with the earlier mentioned values? Is the truth known to the Almighty lost as well?

Mr. President,

In countries around the world, citizens provide for the expenses of governments so that their governments in turn are able to serve them.

The question here is what has the hundreds of billions of dollars, spent every year to pay for the Iraqi campaign, produced for the citizens?

As your Excellency is aware, in some states of your country, people are living in poverty. Many thousands are homeless and unemployment is a huge problem. Of course these problems exist—to a larger or lesser extent—in other countries as well. With these conditions in mind, can the gargantuan expenses of the campaign—paid from the public treasury—be explained and be consistent with the aforementioned principles?

What has been said, are some of the grievances of the people around the world, in our region and in your country. But my main contention—which I am hoping you will agree to some of it—is: Those in power have specific time in office, and do not rule indefinitely, but their names will be recorded in history and will be constantly judged in the immediate and distant futures.

The people will scrutinize our presidencies.

Did we manage to bring peace, security and prosperity for the people or insecurity and unemployment? Did we intend to establish justice, or just supported especial interest groups, and by forcing many people to live in poverty and hardship, made a few people rich and powerful—thus trading the approval of the people and the Almighty with theirs? Did we defend the rights of the underprivileged or ignore them? Did we defend the rights of all people around the world or imposed wars on them, interfered illegally in their affairs, established hellish prisons and incarcerated some of them? Did we bring the world peace and security or raised the specter of intimidation and threats? Did we tell the truth to our nation and others around the world or presented an inverted version of it? Were we on the side of people or the occupiers and oppressors? Did our administration set out to promote rational behavior, logic, ethics, peace, fulfilling obligations, justice, service to the people, prosperity, progress and respect for human dignity or the force of guns. Intimidation, insecurity, disregard for the people, delaying the progress and excellence of other nations, and trample on people's rights? And finally, they will judge us on whether we remained true to our oath of office—to serve the people, which is our main task, and the traditions of the prophets—or not?

Mr. President,

How much longer can the world tolerate this situation? Where will this trend lead the world to? How long must the people of the world pay for the incorrect decisions of some rulers? How much longer will the specter of insecurity—raised from the stockpiles of weapons of mass destruction—hunt the people of the world? How much longer will the blood of the innocent men, women and children be spilled on the streets, and people's houses destroyed over their heads? Are you pleased with the current condition of the world? Do you think present policies can continue?

If billions of dollars spent on security, military campaigns and troop movement were instead spent on investment and assistance for poor countries, promotion of health, combating different diseases, education and improvement of mental and physical fitness, assistance to the victims of natural disasters, creation of employment opportunities and production, development projects and poverty alleviation, establishment of peace, mediation between disputing states and distinguishing the flames of racial, ethnic and other conflicts where would the world be today? Would not your government and people be justifiably proud? Would not your administration's political and economic standing have been stronger? And I am most sorry to say, would there have been an ever increasing global hatred of the American governments?

Mr. President, it is not my intention to distress anyone.

If prophets Abraham, Isaac, Jacob, Ishmael, Joseph or Jesus Christ (PBUH) were with us today, how would they have judged such behavior? Will we be given a role to play in the promised world, where justice will become universal and Jesus Christ (PBUH) will be present? Will they even accept us?

My basic question is this: Is there no better way to interact with the rest of the world? Today there are hundreds of millions of Christians, hundreds of millions of Moslems [sic] and millions of people who follow the teachings of Moses (PBUH). All divine religions share and respect on[e] word and that is monotheism or belief in a single God and no other in the world.

The holy Koran stresses this common word and calls on a[ll] followers of divine religions and says: [3.64] Say: O followers of the Book! Come to an equitable proposition between us and you that we shall not serve any but Allah and (that) we shall not associate aught. With Him and (that) some of us shall not take others for lords besides Allah, but if they turn back, then say: Bear witness that we are Muslims. (The Family of Imran).

Mr. President,

According to divine verses, we have all been called upon to worship one God and follow the teachings of divine prophets. To worship a God which is above all powers in the world and can do all He pleases. The Lord which knows that which is hidden and visible, the past and the future, knows what goes on in the Hearts of His servants and records their deeds. The Lord who is the possessor of the heavens and the earth and all universe is His court planning for the universe is done by His hands, and gives His servants the glad tidings of mercy and forgiveness of sins. He is the companion of the oppressed and the enemy of oppressors. He is the Compassionate, the Merciful. He is the recourse of the faithful and guides them towards the light from darkness. He is witness to the actions of His servants, He calls on servants to be faithful and do good deeds, and asks them to stay on the path of righteousness and remain steadfast. Calls on servants to heed His prophets and He is a witness to their deeds. A bad ending belongs only to those who have chosen the life of this world and disobey Him and oppress His servants. And a good and eternal paradise belong[s] to those servants who fear His majesty and do not follow their lascivious selves.

We believe a return to the teachings of the divine prophets is the only road leading to salvations. I have been told that Your Excellency follows the teachings of Jesus (PBUH), and believes in the divine promise of the rule of the righteous on Earth.

We also believe that Jesus Christ (PBUH) was one of the great prophets of the Almighty. He has been repeatedly praised in the Koran. Jesus (PBUH) has been quoted in Koran as well; [19.36] And surely Allah is my Lord and your Lord, therefore serves Him; this is the right path, Marium.

Service to and obedience of the Almighty is the credo of all divine messengers.

The God of all people in Europe, Asia, Africa, America, the Pacific and the rest of the world is one. He is the Almighty who wants to guide and give dignity to all His servants. He has given greatness to Humans.

We again read in the Holy Book: The Almighty God sent His prophets with miracles and clear signs to guide the people and show them divine signs and puri[f]y them from sins and pollutions. And He sent the Book and the balance so that the people display justice and avoid the rebellious.

All of the above verses can be seen, one way or the other, in the Good Book as well.

Divine prophets have promised: The day will come when all humans will congregate before the court of the Almighty, so that their deeds are examined. The good will be directed towards H[e]aven and evildoers will meet divine retribution. I trust both of us believe in such a day, but it will not be easy to calculate the actions of rulers, because we must be answerable to our nations and all others whose lives have been directly or indirectly affected by our actions.

All prophets speak of peace and tranquility for man—based on monotheism, justice and respect for human dignity.

Do you not think that if all of us come to believe in and abide by these principles, that is, monotheism, worship of God, justice, respect for the dignity of man, belief in the Last Day, we can overcome the present problems of the world—that are the result of disobedience to the Almighty and the teachings of prophets—and improve our performance?

Do you not think that belief in these principles promotes and guarantees peace, friendship and justice?

Do you not think that the aforementioned written or unwritten principles are universally respected?

Will you not accept this invitation? That is, a genuine return to the teachings of prophets, to monotheism and justice, to preserve human dignity and obedience to the Almighty and His prophets?

Mr. President,

History tells us that repressive and cruel governments do not survive. God has entrusted the fate of man to them. The Almighty has not left the universe and humanity to their own devices. Many things have happened contrary to the wishes and plans of governments. These tell us that there is a higher power at work and all events are determined by Him.

Can one deny the signs of change in the world today? Is this situation of the world today comparable to that of ten years ago? Changes happen fast and come at a furious pace.

The people of the world are not happy with the status quo and pay little heed to the promises and comments made by a number of influential world leaders. Many people around the world feel insecure and oppose the spreading of insecurity and war and do not approve of and accept dubious policies.

The people are protesting the increasing gap between the haves and the have-nots and the rich and poor countries.

The people are disgusted with increasing corruption.

The people of many countries are angry about the attacks on their cultural foundations and the disintegration of families. They are equally dismayed with the fading of care and compassion. The people of the world have no faith in international organizations, because their rights are not advocated by these organizations.

Liberalism and Western style democracy have not been able to help realize the ideals of humanity. Today these two concepts have failed. Those with insight can already hear the sounds of the shattering and fall of the ideology and thoughts of the liberal democratic systems.

We increasingly see that people around the world are flocking towards a main focal point—that is the Almighty God. Undoubtedly through faith in God and the teachings of the prophets, the people will conquer their problems. My question for you is: Do you not want to join them?

Mr. President,

Whether we like it or not, the world is gravitating towards faith in the Almighty and justice and the will of God will prevail over all things.

Vasalam Ala Man Ataba'al hoda
Mahmood Ahmadi-Najad
President of the Islamic Republic of Iran

REFERENCES

Cooper, Helene. 2007. "Ahmadinejad, at Columbia, Parries and Puzzles." *New York Times,* September 25. http://www.nytimes.com/2007/09/25/world/americas/25iht-ahmedine-jad.1.7626558.html?pagewanted=all&_r=0 (accessed January 19, 2015).

Naji, Kasra. 2008. *Ahmadinejad: The Secret History of Iran's Radical Leader.* Berkeley: University of California Press.

9

Democracy Cartoons

Khalil Bendib, 2007

Khalil Bendib was born to a war refugee family in Paris after his parents escaped certain death at the hands of French vigilantes in Constantine, Algeria. The first-ever native radiologist in Algeria, his father had found himself on a list of local notables to be executed as retaliation for the assassination of Constantine's French police chief, but he was alerted by a police captain who happened to be a patient of his.

Algeria's war of independence would promptly catch up with the Bendibs in their Parisian exile, and, six months after Khalil was born, they abruptly departed again, this time for Rabat, Morocco. Barely able to draw, at age four Khalil Bendib found himself obsessively sketching Algerian soldiers in Rabat saluting the banned flag of Algeria—in retrospect, his first (proto–)political cartoons.

Upon Algeria's independence in 1962, the Bendibs returned to their country, and this is where Khalil Bendib spent his formative years, until age twenty, when he landed in Berkeley, California, as a foreign student. The Mediterranean climate, hills, and sea views he found in Berkeley, where he eventually settled, reminded him of his native Algiers, and the cosmopolitan atmosphere made him feel that this would be an ideal place to become an artist.

After one year studying English, Bendib went to the University of Southern California in Los Angeles for a master's degree in Geology. Gradually he moved from geology to earn his master's in East Asian languages and cultures instead. Japanese culture had always attracted him for its stunning visual aesthetic, an influence that critics have noted in his artistic work.

Bendib, Khalil. 2003. "Democracy: Arab Style/American Style" and "Public Broadcasting, USA-Style." In *It Became Necessary to Destroy the Planet in Order to Save It!* High Point, NC: Plan Nine. Pp. 10 and 158. http://www.bendib.com/democracy/Democracy-Arab-US-style.jpg and http://www.bendib.com/media/Public-broadcasting.jpg (accessed June 1, 2014). Copyright © Khalil Bendib, www.bendib.com; all rights reserved.

In 1987 Bendib worked as an editorial cartoonist with the Gannett newspapers at their California flagship newspaper, the *San Bernardino Sun,* where he spent eight years and won numerous small awards for his work. In 1994, his first public monument—a nine-foot bronze sculpture—was dedicated in Santa Ana to honor Palestinian American peace activist and community leader Alex Odeh, who had been assassinated in October 1985 and whom Bendib had known well.

The project was a turning point in Bendib's life, as it allowed him to become an integral part of Southern California's Arab American community and to befriend such community leaders as Casey Kasem and Don Bustany, among others. His later public sculptures include two monuments, one in upstate New York and one in Minneapolis, memorializing the 1948 Deir Yassine massacre in Palestine.

After resigning from his position at the *San Bernardino Sun* in 1995 because of the paper's excessive political censorship, Bendib completed one more public monument in Diamond Bar, a suburb of Los Angeles, and headed up to Berkeley, where he had long wanted to return.

Despite the decline of the newspaper industry over the past two decades, Bendib's cartoons have enjoyed increased popularity and demand thanks to his propensity to speak his mind and to the Internet's magical powers of diffusion. Bendib has received commissions from organizations such as Oxfam, Greenpeace, Global Exchange, the California Faculty Association, Code Pink, and United Farm Workers, to name a few. He has published a number of collections of his cartoons in major newspapers such as the *New York Times* and *USA Today.* In 2011 he coauthored a graphic novel titled *Zahra's Paradise,* about the 2009 Green Revolution in Tehran. A *New York Times* best seller, this book has been translated into sixteen languages to date. Bendib has just now been commissioned by Metropolitan to produce a graphic novel on the subject of whistleblowers and the national security state.

Bendib is the coproducer of Pacifica Radio's *Voices of the Middle East and North Africa,* a weekly show that airs every Wednesday at 2 P.M. throughout Northern California.

10

Empire as Everyday Life, Everyday Life as Imperialism

Mayssoun Sukarieh, 2012

After growing up during the Lebanese civil war, and being homeschooled by family members when schools were closed, Mayssoun Sukarieh graduated from the American University in Beirut. In 2009 Sukarieh earned her PhD from the University of California, Berkeley.

Sukarieh's essay "Empire as Everyday Life, Everyday Life as Imperialism" exposes the personal terror and mistreatment she went through upon arriving in the United States two weeks after September 11. She had traveled from Beirut to present a paper at the Oral History Association at Columbia University, but was stopped at John F. Kennedy Airport in New York City, detained, questioned, and put on a plane back to Beirut. She describes never before having felt so "terrorized and terrified" (Sukarieh 2012:1).

Throughout her time in the United States, as a graduate student and then as a researcher, Sukarieh continued to document the blatant arrogance and ignorance that weaves through U.S. culture and politics, especially regarding Arabs and Muslims. As she documents in her PhD dissertation, "Winning Hearts and Minds: Education, Culture, and Control," Americans act as though they know everything about Arabs, yet at the same time they have become missionaries for the American Dream, which many Arabs who come to the United States try to realize. Sukarieh's research extends from Washington, D.C., to the Arab Gulf, and then to Jordan.

It is useful to contrast Sukarieh's writings with that of Rana Kabbani's powerful book of essays, *A Letter to Christendom* (1989), which deals with the question of assimilation or confrontation with European culture when one becomes a "Westernized Muslim." Like Sukarieh's personal story, Kabbani's deals with anti-Muslim humiliations in the Western

Mayssoun, Sukarieh, 2012. "Empire as Everyday Life, Everyday Life as Imperialism." Unpublished manuscript. Printed with the permission of the author.

world. However, Sukarieh zeroes in on the American empire as an ethnographer trained to examine imperial controlling processes.

As she reflects upon her experiences, Sukarieh recognizes not only that Americans lack understanding of Arab culture but also that "what we [Arabs] lack is a project that protects us from this production of knowledge about us that is part and parcel of colonizing us" (Sukarieh 2012:13). As she examines what she terms deceptive American business practices, she writes that programs devised for Arab "terrorist youth" are tested on poor "youth at risk" in the United States beforehand. If Americans did not control the rhetoric about the Arab world, there might be a better understanding of the commonalities between the two cultures, and the prevention of both Arabs and disadvantaged Americans falling victim to what Sukarieh sees as the control of youth.

Sukarieh has been a visiting assistant professor in the Department of Anthropology and the Center for Arab and Middle Eastern Studies at the American University of Beirut, and later held a postdoctoral teaching and research post in the Department of Anthropology at the American University in Cairo. Her studies primarily focus on youth, elites, and cultures of neoliberal development in the Middle East. Her work has appeared in *Political Legal Anthropology (PoLAR)*, *Sociology*, the *Journal of International Labor Studies*, and the *Journal of Youth Studies* and on websites such as the *Electronic Intifada*, the Center for Research on Globalization, *Middle East Report*, and the Middle East Research and Information Project. She is at present a postdoctoral fellow at the Cogut Center for the Humanities at Brown University.

· · ·

The minute the plane lands in Washington, D.C., in 2006, my heart starts to beat rapidly. "I will be picked randomly," I tell the passenger sitting next to me. "Don't worry," she says; "you're flying domestically, so there won't be any problems." I hope not. Freaking out in airports is a habit I developed in 2001, on September 28, when I was arrested and put on a plane back to Lebanon from JFK Airport in New York City.

That time, I was traveling to attend the Oral History Association annual conference to present a paper entitled "Silencing of Memory among Palestinian Refugees in Lebanon." U.S. policies toward Middle Eastern travelers was not clear at that time, only two weeks after 9/11, and I was assured by the head of the society at the time, Mary Clark from the Oral History Center at Columbia University, that there wouldn't be any trouble for me to come to the United States despite my Lebanese background. It is ironic that my first encounter with terror was in New York City at the hands of the U.S. government. I remember being singled out with a few other travelers and taken aside to be investigated. The invitation I had from the OHA could not save me. I was denied entry into the United States and put in a cell until the next day, when I was escorted by police to a plane and sent back home.

I have never felt as terrorized and terrified in my life as that night at JFK, despite having grown up during the Lebanese civil war. Neither the infighting among groups in our neighborhood nor the heavy Israeli shelling of Lebanon in 1982 could rival the fear of being alone in that room, not knowing what my fate would be, not even understanding why I was denied entry to what I still thought of as a democratic state. All of a sudden I became representative of the terrorists who committed 9/11, or a spokesperson for the Muslim world that was accused in its totality of the terrorist attacks. All of a sudden I was the representative of "the other" who is perceived as a terrorist because terrorism is supposedly inherent in Muslim culture; it runs in the blood of Muslims; it is inherent in their genes and not a result of American foreign policies in the region. All of a sudden I was the "terrorist" who hates America just because America is better, and America is free-dom, liberty, and democracy. All of a sudden I was an Arab, and no matter what my political views or opinion about 9/11 were, I was an enemy who would be stopped at airports on every single visit, even when flying domestically.

Since then I have always expected the worst at airports, so that when I landed at Dulles International in Washington, D.C., in 2006, I was thinking of my night at JFK in 2001. We form a line as we leave the plane and enter Dulles; airport officials are starting to pick those people who look "different"—Asians, Arabs, Latinos . . . My heart is starting to beat even more; I get to the counter, and the officer sends me to the special-treatment lane. I start to cry . . . I have so much rage inside and I am not used to hiding how I feel, but the stories of torture in U.S. prisons used to make me think a million times before reacting . . . I used to just cry silently, cry over the state of a world that looks like nothing more than a big bundle of oppres-sion and injustice, cry in particular over a messed-up situation in my part of the world. This time I bite my pride and just accept. Two women search my bag, emp-tying it item by item. I feel invaded, not only in my privacy but also in my pride. During these searches I always think of the contradictions of this culture, a culture that is so concerned about privacy but that never respects it. After the bag search I am asked to collect my items and pack them up again before being searched myself. This is the ultimate invasion, of my body and soul. "Hold your hands up . . . You can lower them now . . . Separate your feet, turn around . . . Raise your head . . . Lower your head . . ." they order while searching me. I am crying silently and full of anger. My getting visibly anxious always makes the security officers think I am hiding something, and so they search me even more. I try to tell two other officers that I am crying because I feel humiliated. "It's random," one of them says, "and we need to preserve security." "How is this random and how come I am always picked 'randomly' on every single flight in the U.S.?" I say, crying.

After being detained for a while, I am released. The officers who body-search me are always immigrants or white, but they are definitely poor. What makes them accept this, what are they getting from the system that makes them try to protect it, what from corporate America is at stake for them? I think of the reasons that make these women totally believe in the system, believe that I am a threat just because of my nationality. Maybe it is their job, but most of them do their job very well even when no one is watching them. It must be the rhetoric of "us versus them" that has infected the whole nation and has made them believe I am "the other" and therefore a threat.

It is February 2006. I am now in Washington D.C., in the "Belly of the Beast" as it is called in the global south. D.C. makes visitors realize how imperialism has penetrated the fabric of American culture, how it has infected the imagination of its inhabitants to the extent that it has become habitual and institutionalized; it defines their characters. D.C. makes visitors realize that empire as a way of life has blocked other ways of understanding the reality that Americans encounter and the situations they face.

After being released from the airport, I took a taxi to N Street, where I had previously arranged to rent a room in an apartment. Looking for a room to share in D.C. was itself an experience. I came close to getting an apartment many times, until I was asked where I am from; the mere fact of my background was enough for the landlord to apologize for the sudden unavailability of the room. It happened quite a few times before I decided to look for a non-American to stay with in D.C. I ended up with a Moroccan who had been working in the fast-food industry for a while. Nour's apartment was filled with appliances, some that he needed and others he did not. One could barely find room to set foot in the living room. When I inquired about his reasons for keeping all these, Nour, who didn't know how he fell into the habit of consuming, said, "Having friends who are always buying makes it hard for one to resist. I used to spend all what I get from my cheap labor work into consuming; it became like an illness. It is only this year, when I went to Morocco and came back, that I decided to stop buying. I am planning to go back home in a year or two, and I won't need any of these back home. In America, even if you do not have a big home you use whatever space you have to keep things you might never use, or only use for a bit."

The first instruction I got from Nour was not to cross O Street because it marks the boundary of a dangerous neighborhood. N Street is kind of a border between corporate D.C., which extends to H Street, and the nongentrified area of the city, which starts with O Street. I did not need to go up O Street anyway, because most of the places I intended to visit—the corporate headquarters, the offices, and the meeting spots in restaurants and cafés—didn't go farther than H Street. Out of curiosity I ventured once to O Street. There is a total absence of high heels and ties, the corporate look one finds from N Street down, an absence of fancy cafés and restaurants designed for those experts, an absence of development, and an absence of the feeling of being in the capital of an empire. O Street and the surrounding neighborhood seem as if they could be anywhere outside of the United States in the so-called Third World countries—broken pavement, sidewalks in disrepair, tired faces, poverty, shabbiness. O Street should be what corporate America and its elites try to develop; so what makes them go to Iraq and Afghanistan and other parts of the world? I never dreamt to see poverty in the heart of empire. How effective Hollywood is, and the American dream! However, walking up O Street, all I could think of was the idea that this is a more dangerous area than the corporate area down on N Street. How come the poor, who do not have control over their own lives on O Street and up, are more dangerous than those experts who are redesigning the world, helping to further its plunder, and fabricating lies for the empire? And what makes a fast-food worker from Morocco—my roommate— abide by the perception that O Street, the "poor people street," is dangerous, while N Street and above is safe? But then again, is it any wonder? Aren't the oppressed and the occupied accused of being terrorists? And is not academia more focused on justice than on injustice, on studying the poor and not the rich—and even when we study wealth, is it not in relation to poverty?

I had come to Washington, D.C., to conduct field research for my PhD dissertation. Mine was a multisite ethnographic study of how culture was used by the Bush administration in the post-9/11 period to secure the consent of the Arab world to American economic, political, and military leadership in the region, and more generally, how culture is harnessed to power in the current conjectural political and economic phase of neoliberalism. I wanted to analyze the core infrastructure and dominant ideologies of U.S. cultural intervention projects in the Arab region by tracing how ideas, institutions, programs, and relationships are constructed in the heart of the U.S. empire in Washington, D.C.; extended out to centers of U.S. and regional power in key Arab cities and states; and from there, introduced into local, on-the-ground practices and initiatives throughout the entire Middle East and North Africa. By now, a fairly extensive literature on the structure of U.S. imperialism in the post– World War II era in Europe, and elsewhere around the globe, has documented the deep involvement of innumerable cultural and educational institutions, as well as dense networks of private, public, and voluntary organizations, in spreading American cultural ideals overseas in the service of U.S. foreign policy interests (which, in turn, are strongly shaped by the interests of American economic and political elites).

In my dissertation I argue that the U.S. cultural intervention project in the Arab world run by the Bush administration in the post-9/11 period represents a continuation of these cultural fronts. Not only are the same strategies and rhetoric previously used to extend U.S. power in Western Europe, Latin America, and elsewhere being used in the current battle of ideas in the Middle East, but often the same institutions and programs are involved in the Middle East; for example, the National Endowment of Democracy, the International Republican Institute, Freedom House, the Center for Education Development, and well-known think tanks such as Rand and Brookings, to name but a few.

I was worried about securing interviews in D.C. Studying elites is not as easy as studying the poor. First of all, I thought, these people work all the time and they won't have time for me. But second and more important, coming from a part of the world where we think the United States is coherent, unassailable, and strong, I thought these people would be suspicious of me. Do we not see it in the movies—how all departments coordinate and work together, and how they know about everything that happens inside and outside the United States?

"We have to start from the basics of democracy," says David, my first interviewee, a director of one of the so-called NGOs (nongovernmental organizations) based in D.C. that operate in the Middle East. He was responding to my question about what Americans mean when they say they want to teach Arabs and Muslims about democracy. It was April 2006 in downtown D.C. I had come to research the American project of "winning the hearts and minds of Muslim/Arab youth" (I used the terms *Muslim* and *Arab* interchangeably in my interviews, since the Americans involved in this project seemed to think that every Arab is a Muslim). David used to work with the U.S. State Department before moving to "an NGO that provided 'capacity building services' for the Arab/Muslim world." Traveling in the Arab world for the State Department, David claims, gave him expertise in the region. It is a phenomenon I have found prevalent among Americans: they visit a country for two months and consider themselves experts in that country for the rest of their lives. David spoke with confidence and trust in his knowledge of the whole Muslim world, a world that he believes does not read and is mostly illiterate. Whenever I challenged his claims, the answer was always ready: "I traveled in Morocco and Saudi Arabia as a state department staff, and people do not read! I mean sometimes they read the Quran but nothing else." A few visits to Morocco and Saudi Arabia for work seem to have endowed David with an expertise on the whole region, dubbed now the Greater Middle East. David is not alone in this—I frequently met with NGO staff whose only qualifications to work on the "Middle East" were visits through the Peace Corps and other such organizations. Is this how the empire makes its experts? And how are these "experts" supposed to rule over an extremely complicated region? How are they supposed to control the people? Or even to teach them the so-called skills of democracy? The empire is not as smart as I thought; it started to seem naïve and ignorant. But how is it then still so powerful?

I met David during his lunch break in one of the K Street cafés. K is the street of international political organizations. It is the street where elites devise policies for the world from behind their desks in fancy offices. It is common to see elites from different organizations meeting over lunch to discuss their work. I had met an interviewee from the World Bank a week before, at a K Street café. The street has a special feeling. People look alike: They are all in formal attire. It is a shiny street with shiny shoes, shiny hair, and shiny faces. They even walk the same, speak in the same tones, use the same words and expressions, and even their body language is similar. I used to call it the "trik truk" street, referring to the sound of men and women walking down the street in their noisy heels, especially during lunch breaks when they invade the cafés and restaurants, or later in the afternoon as they are leaving work. They look like standardized products coming out of a factory, I used to think. Where is the individualism that capitalism promises to provide? They almost have the same identity, regardless of their color, ethnicity, nationality, or gender. They are products of the same schools and training programs. Where is the individual identity, and where the freedom to be themselves? Where is the diversity, that new buzzword in our democratic world?

While interviewing David, I could not help but overhear what those sitting next to me were talking about: projects on governance, the war on terror, visits to different places in the world . . . There is a lot of arrogance in the way these elites talk. It seems quite normal for them to be heading, overlooking, organizing, or coordinating projects that stretch from Latin America to the so-called Middle East. They all talk in a similar tone, which I have come to label "the corporate voice": confident, assertive and loud, hiding the speakers' insecurities. After a few weeks in D.C., I started to feel that I was in a spy hub, some sort of informal spy network where these young elites, through their work in NGOs and "international organizations," collect data and create projects to manage people overseas. What is that if not spying? But let's call it "data collection," as we call the hands of American empire nongovernmental organizations.

I had met David at a panel held by the Center for the Study of Islam and Democracy at which the president of the National Endowment for Democracy, Carl Greshman, was speaking about the achievements of their endowment programs in the region and the challenges ahead. Greshman talked about the need to shift from democracy promotion programs to a promotion of moderate Islam against radical Islam. I talked to David during the discussion session after Greshman's hour-long colonial talk, in which all present seemed to agree with his call for changing the culture of radicalism and spreading a culture of moderation. Refreshments and drinks were offered after the speech. David, like almost all the other audience members, filled his plate with food. It always seems during such events that people have never seen food in their lives, or maybe that they are on the brink of starvation and are trying to stock up on as much food as they can. There is something amazing about that culture, all built on profit. Any time something is free, you need to get the most you can, even if you don't need all of it, even if it might cause you problems—like a stomachache, in this situation. Immediate profit—taking advantage as much as you can. It is capitalism as inscribed in the DNA of Americans. It is capitalism as lived in everyday life and as manifested in the details of daily interactions between Americans.

Later, during our interview at the café on K Street, I asked David what he meant by "the basics of democracy." He explained, "Like listening to each other, arguing, conducting a dialogue, accepting difference, and trying to understand that others have a different point of view." After four months in D.C., I had developed an immunity to being angered by every sweeping generalization my interviewees would tell me. Calmly, I asked David to elaborate on his view. He said, "Well, imagine ten Muslim men are meeting to discuss a topic—Muslim *men* not women, because Muslim women are not allowed to talk"—he laughs. "They start to shout . . . shout . . . shout, and the one with the louder voice will impose his opinion. So what we are trying to do is to teach them how to sit and discuss, converse, talk and listen to each other. You have to start from this, from the individual. Democracy can't be achieved overnight, it has a long way to go, and there is a lot we have to do. It is a long way ahead." My heart was broken thinking of the difficult task awaiting Americans in the Arab/Muslim world! Haram! What a task to have to teach Arabs/ Muslims to be democratic—it is even harder than teaching Americans not to think of themselves as exceptional!

I tried suggesting to David that some Arabs do speak and listen to each other: "But I am an 'Arab woman,' according to your definition, and I am here in D.C. talking to you, listening to what you have to say. Before coming to the U.S., I used to discuss issues with my friends and family in Lebanon, to old people, to young people, and we listened to each other." David tells me that the reason I know how to listen is that I was educated at Berkeley. I tell him that I came to Berkeley only to do my graduate studies, and that I knew how to talk and listen to others before coming to America. "Yes," he tells me, "but you were at the American University of Beirut as an undergraduate." David, like most of my interviewees in D.C., has interrogated me before we started the interview about my educational background, and he knows most of my CV. I assure David that I learned how to talk and listen to others as a child, from my family, friends, neighborhood, and Arab-language public school, before being exposed to Americans and their system of education and democracy. I tell David my memories of long discussions and debates we used to have in my home, with friends of my parents, relatives, neighbors, and colleagues of different political backgrounds—Communists, Nasserites, Baathists all together . . . I tell David that my father and his friends used to argue passionately over politics, but the next day they used to meet again, open political discussions, and then again disagree and argue together, but they always stayed friends with different visions of the Arab world. David responds, "Well, you grew up in Lebanon, and Lebanon is not like other Middle Eastern countries; it is Westernized; it is different from other Muslim countries, and more open to ideas." He tells me he has been to Morocco and Saudi Arabia and assures me that they lack the culture of democracy, the basic skills of democracy. But Saudi Arabia is an American protectorate—this is what we say in the Arab world, that it is owned by ARAMCO (the Saudi Arabian Oil Company)—so why did you not teach the Saudis how to argue and dialogue? David had no answer. Thinking I was joking, he laughed, and I laughed along to ease the tension and continue the interview. I guess David was not listening to what I was trying to tell him. Why would he anyway? I am just an "Arab" who does not understand, and I am just a woman who has no voice. I am not supposed to know, I was not taught to know. He knows, and all I can do is listen to what he has to say. After all, is he not the expert on the Arab world and on Muslim culture? Did he not go for a few visits to Saudi Arabia, and one to Morocco?

Being exposed to such sweeping stereotypes became part of my experience in D.C. From time to time, after I revealed that I am from the so-called Middle East, I was asked why I was not veiled. From time to time I was asked about the conditions of women in the region, especially while riding the bus, when people would pick up on my accent as I talked on my cell phone. It always starts with "Where are you from? You have an accent." Then come sweeping claims about the region, and about me as a representative of that region and its women ("How come you aren't veiled? How did your parents allow you to come by yourself to the U.S.?"), and the immediate labeling of me as a Muslim based on the mere fact that I am from the Middle East, as if Christ was not born in Palestine! My reactions finally became either sarcasm or a feeling of sadness about the state of the world. In fact, these shocking remarks—"You have a Muslim accent," for example—helped me better understand the relation between culture and power, and the way American elites perpetuate certain perceptions about constructed enemies—in this case Muslims—in order to spread ignorance and wage wars. My confrontations with these stereotypes helped me understand the production of ignorance in the United States in the service of power. They helped me understand how ignorance, like knowledge, is situated, and how both are produced in the interests of power. Situated ignorance is manifested for the service of empire in the United States, and it is then packaged and exported to other nations of the world, including my own.

Hearing the rhetoric of America's democracy promotion project on TV or reading this rhetoric in the news did not prepare me for hearing American elites say it directly to my face: "Arab culture is backward. Arab culture is terrorist. Arab culture is incompatible with globalization. There is a reason why the Arabs are left behind; it is their culture. Arab women are oppressed! What we are doing is to try to empower them. Arab youth are marginalized and we want to promote their inclusion"—inclusion *in what* is left to everybody's imagination. "There's a need to change the Arab curriculum because it is this curriculum that teaches youth to be terrorists! There is a gap between the Arab world and the West. The Arab World lacks democracy." How to process these sweeping statements? One might expect the speakers to refine their words when talking directly to an "Arab." To my shock, this was not the case. What makes these elites totally blind to my presence, to my feelings as an "Arab woman" upon hearing such statements? How could they speak so forcefully and with such confidence about a world that many of them have never been to, or have visited only briefly, or at most have read a book or two about? How can one speak of a heterogeneous culture in such homogenized terms?

Who assigned Americans the role of saviors of "Arab women" and youth, and modernizers of Arab culture? What makes Americans believe they are the know-it-all people? Is it their feeling of being exceptional that makes them think that whatever they have—or think they have—is demanded everywhere else in the world? Or leads them to think they don't need to read much about other parts of the world in order to act upon them? Or endows them with a native expertise about the whole world?

It seems the seventeenth-century Puritan John Winthrop's phrase "we shall be as a city upon a hill" is still alive and has not lost its power. It seems that, like my interviewee David, every other American views themselves as agents of God's will and purpose. They have become missionaries of the American Dream to those who are not following the American Way. If such "underdeveloped" people refuse to open their minds to the idea of development, they are agents of evil and must be dealt with by force. Is that not the case with Muslims, who now need to be educated in what Henry Lewis Morgan, the father of American anthropology, called "rights of property, and rights of citizenship, which are common to ourselves"?[1] Listening to David's statements, I thought that the nation's calling has perhaps been changed from being a "city on a hill" to being an active crusader in reforming the world to conform with the American Dream—after all, is America not "the World's best Hope," as Thomas Jefferson remarked in his first inaugural address?

My outrage at what the American empire was inflicting on Iraq and other parts of the world made the experience of interviewing the democracy promoters of D.C. personally exhausting. I used to cry after each interview, as I came to understand just how multipronged the U.S. project in the Arab world was, how intricate and sophisticated their war in our part of the world was, only part of which involved the dropping of bombs: war on culture, war on minds, war on consciousness. Each time I finished an interview in Washington, I used to walk in the streets and cry. Who gave you the right to go to different places of the world and redesign them however you see fit? How can you do that? What is it in your culture that makes you do this without question or reflection? What is it in your culture that allows you to talk to me about my culture with all sorts of stereotypes without even thinking that I might disagree? Many of the Americans in D.C. working on changing Arab culture and integrating the Arab world into the global economy are young, in their twenties and early thirties. What gives such young people this authoritative voice? How can a twenty-something-year-old be so sure of his ability to change another people's culture after just one visit to the place where they live? What makes a thirty-year-old an expert in changing the curriculum of the Arab world? Do they truly believe in what they are saying? Or is it that they need jobs? Where does interest end and ideology begin in such cases? Why is work in NGOs appealing to the youth (besides the missionary aspect)—could the attraction be about alienation? Alienation from this individualistic culture, its consumption habits, its loneliness, its meaninglessness? Are the elites trying to outsource these problems of the American population by sending them abroad? Alienation, exceptionalism, and the missionary attitude are what come across in conversations with these American youth, and they are part of the way empire is lived and experienced in the everyday.

Throughout my stay in Washington, D.C., my feelings and reactions to such sweeping statements fluctuated from a sense of pity for the ignorance of the American elites I was meeting, to outrage when recognizing that imperial culture seems to be inscribed in their DNA. Thinking of the production of knowledge about the Arab World, the hegemonic media presentations about the region, and the presentations of its inhabitants in Hollywood movies, books, cartoons, and so on, I would somehow exempt them from any responsibility for their beliefs and say *haram!*— Poor them! They do not know. Slowly I started to see them as victims of the dominant media and dominant perceptions of the so-called Middle East, created for the service of empire. Slowly I started to see them as victims of the same dominant idea, the American Dream, that people in the global south are victims of. At other times, when news was bad from the "region" and when I heard them bragging about the democracy they enjoyed in the United States, their agency, and the choices they have as opposed to the lack of choice we in the Arab world suffer from, my feelings of pity for them vanished and were replaced by anger at their failure to act to stop the atrocities their government was inflicting on different parts of the world. Aren't they telling me they live in a democracy? Aren't they are the ones bragging about the choices they can make since they live in a democracy? So they should be held responsible for what their government is doing! But then, I tried to convince myself that even these illusions were part of what citizens of the empire are made to believe: they are sold the illusion of living in a democracy, of having choices and ... I would go back to my feelings of pity—*haram!* They think they have a choice ... But again, hearing the news, I would think, They do not even need to know anything to be against the killings of others, against wars, against death, destruction, and occupation, and I would become outraged at the deafening silence of the inhabitants of the capital of the American empire. It does not take much knowledge for them to be empathetic, to be humane, to dissent. But then again, I would try to stay humane myself by considering that they are made to think that the people of the Arab World, those Muslims, are savages and terrorists, so why am I asking them to be humane in the way they look at subhumans? Why am I asking them to empathize with others they are made to be scared of? But then, I tried to get myself out of this circle, of giving excuses to the hands of empire, by thinking that it is not the duty of the occupied to try to humanize the occupier. After all, it is all about interests, and these people are thriving and earning their living from projects of empire. Why am I fooling myself into thinking that if they knew better they would act? Sometimes knowledge is a recipe for inaction, is it not?

Along with feelings of outrage, I also felt a sense of envy as I saw up close the dense networks of NGOs, think tanks, government offices, and corporations in the heart of Washington that worked together to promote America's democracy project in the rest of the world. K Street, after all, is the "lobby street." I longed to see such a common project of collaboration and shared vision in the global south—but one geared to the politics of liberation, not colonization. I longed for "those who are seeking another world" to have our own Massachusetts Avenue, which is where in D.C. most of the democracy-promoting organizations are located: brown bag sessions over lunch, reports from researchers just coming in from the field, conferences about the state of America's interests in faraway places. These sessions made me long for a project in the global south that I could be part of: promoting institutions that work to produce knowledge not about faraway places we would like to colonize but about our own part of the world, to try to understand it better and appreciate it more. It was then that I realized that what we lack in the Arab world is not the lags and gaps that Americans speak of when talking about our culture. What we lack is a project that protects us from this production of knowledge about us that is part and parcel of colonizing us. What we lack is a project that puts the minds of our young to good use and protects us from paralyzing and destructive outside interference. This feeling of sadness and envy was exacerbated when I saw the large numbers of young Arabs in D.C. who have been attracted to the United States to work in its institutions. I envied Americans' ability to pull in brains from all over the world to work on their project. Why is it that these scholars, researchers orphaned from projects in their own world, are pushed one way or another to come work in the United States even if that means the subordination of their own people?

ON THE SAME PROJECTS BEING CARRIED OUT IN AMERICA

If American involvement in the Arab/Muslim world is to bring the Arab/Muslim world into the global economy and protect the United States and the international community from the terrorism of Muslim youth, why are the same winning-hearts-and-minds projects of contemporary American foreign policy being implemented among youth within the United States? In fact, many of America's democracy promotion programs now being projected onto the Arab World were first developed, tested, and used on domestic populations before they were exported abroad. Instead of controlling "terrorist youth," as they do in the Arab World, in the United States such projects are aimed at controlling "youth at risk." Supposedly these projects have been specifically designed for young Arabs, yet they turn out to be a generic cookie-cutter model made "Arab" by surface dressings of multiculturalism. The same textbooks and curriculum materials are literally translated into

Arabic and have Arab examples substituted where American examples existed before. Talk about multiculturalism becoming a hegemonic culture in D.C., aiming to serve the interests of elites!

Americans are using the same subordinating tactics on their own population—there is nothing that the Americans are implementing on Arab youth that they haven't implemented in the United States, particularly among the marginalized youth of the ghettos and the South. In this sense, D.C. is not a center where Americans are designing projects to subdue the Arab world; this is not a case of Americans versus Arabs, but of corporate America against the marginalized, or those who are affected by its projects whether in the United States or in the Arab world or anywhere in the global south. Projects involving youth traveled with American imperialism to open the market first to Latin America, then to Eastern Europe, and are now invading the so-called Greater Middle East. Realizing, for example, that the Center for Educational Development or the Center for Civic Education implements the same projects in the United States as it does abroad shifts one's understanding of what is being done.

Once I realized this, the "us" of my questions started to include the marginalized of this country itself. It was no longer America versus the Arab World, but instead the elites against the marginalized. It was then that the "us" in my questions went beyond the "us" in a certain geographic area called the Arab world to include different spaces of the world, even in this heart of the U.S. empire known as D.C. It certainly made life more complicated, since I could no longer point the finger and say, "You Americans, stop messing with the Arab World!" The finger is pointed instead to the gated communities of elites around the globe whose interests have become entangled in this globalizing world. My anger toward these elites and these institutions was put in a different perspective when I started to learn more about these NGOs, think tanks, and corporations. My question "How they could do this to us?" turned into "How they could do this to their young people here too?" I learned that all of these organizations that got involved in parts of the Arab world have also worked with young poor Americans, the marginalized and oppressed of this part of the world. This made me question the notion of democracy in the United States. If programs meant to colonize other parts of the world through ideological and cultural control are implemented in the United States, then how can U.S. elites claim that they live in a democracy? Is not an informed citizenry an important factor in any democracy? If the marginalized are exposed to programs of cultural control, and if the whole citizenry is subject to round-the-clock misinformation through the media and other means, how can America be a democracy, and what is it they sell to the world then? How can one sell to the world what one does not own?

Even though these programs are used on the Arab world today, as they are used or have been used on non-elite youth in the United States (inner-city youth, youth of color, youth from the working and poor classes), one key difference is that in the United States, the youth are taught to be patriotic Americans. With that, they are taught what it means to be an American in the world, the unreflective notion of the United States' role in the world, of its right to have power—in short, they are taught American exceptionalism. They accept that there is nothing out of the ordinary in the fact that America sends its young people around the world to proselytize—that is, to spread democracy it does not have, to plunder the world, and to wage wars to reform the world. All this is accepted by the American masses, even if they themselves are subject to the injustices of a system that seeks to control them as it is controlling youth in other parts of the world. Hence most of the ground-level workers often come from non-elite backgrounds and have been put through these programs themselves in one form or another, becoming true believers of the American mission abroad.

When I talked to people in D.C., the elites and heads of programs knew what they were doing, but with some other people it was hard to tell whether they were just ignorant or whether not knowing was part of marketing their work in the Middle East. Ignorance is a manufactured tool the American elites use to market their programs abroad for their own people. I am reminded of Henry Fairlie's definition of "the establishment": "not those people who hold and exercise power as such. It is the people who create and sustain the climate of assumption and opinion within which power is exercised by those who hold it by election or appointment."[2] Those elites who are the leaders of the economic and political system are also the makers of the way of life for those who will sustain the system. They order the priorities and relationships in terms of a system, they integrate the parts of the system into a whole. After all, the free market is not a collection of entrepreneurs but a network of capitalists that can only be understood as a system.

THE MAN IN THE STREET

He was lying face down on the sidewalk, seemingly unconscious or semiconscious, by a crosswalk on K Street, with all of its cars and pedestrians rushing by. A man in his sixties maybe, with worn-out clothes and an old black hat. I saw him out of the corner of my eye from the other side of the street, six lanes of traffic away, and I expected at first that one of the many people walking right next to him would stop to check to see if he was alright. But nobody stopped. They stood right over him as they waited for the light to change, talking on their cell phones and not even looking at him, as if he were not there—men and women, old and young alike, office workers emerging from their offices in the early evening rush hour. The light turned green and the office workers started to cross the street, literally stepping over the man on the sidewalk without pause. I crossed the street in the opposite direction to check on him, and when I got close, I saw the blood that had run from the man's mouth into a crack in the sidewalk—blood that had run for so long it had already darkened and congealed. He had been lying here for a while. I touched the man on the shoulder—he was breathing but was barely conscious—called 9–1–1, and waited with him until an ambulance came to take him to a hospital emergency room.

It was one of the scariest scenes I have ever witnessed, one that stays with me always and captures the essence of Washington culture for me. What makes people here so indifferent to those around them? What makes them so indifferent to an injured and prostrate man? What makes them forget to put themselves in the shoes of others and to go about their daily routine without stopping to ask? What turns them into machines? What makes them lose their humanity? Speaking with an American friend about what I saw, I was told, "People get scared of being sued if they try to help and something happens to him, so they stay away." But why not call for help without touching him? Where is the culture of volunteerism that Americans are trying to spread to the Arab world, which our culture supposedly lacks? Not even during times of war have I ever seen such a thing: for then, people volunteer to help even under the falling bombs.

Upset by the scene I had witnessed on K Street, I wrote to my brother in Beirut, cursing this D.C. culture of inhumanity. I got an email back telling me that soon this won't be a scene you see only in D.C. or other American cities. It is slowly creeping into cities all over the world: it is the culture of capitalism, under which production and profit rule, where we do not get involved in anything that won't bring us gain. I got scared of what will befall us when we are all fully integrated in global capitalism: we will all become individuated, cold, lonely, lacking sympathy and empathy. Who told these young American experts in Washington that the rest of us want to be integrated into the global economy? It was then that I became so scared of the spread of American corporate culture and ideals to our part of the world, of the integration of the Arab world into global capitalism, and of the loss of a sense of humanity that seems to have been imposed on the streets of the heart of American empire.

ON HOPE FROM A SELF-DEFEATING EMPIRE

If I have learned anything from my fieldwork in D.C., it is that the ignorance production about the United States that its elites have constructed has helped sustain the empire, but will also lead to its own demise. It seems the empire will be defeated by its own internal contradictions, by its elites' projects. The ignorance production machine that has been turned on in order to wage wars beyond U.S. borders and to make American citizens complicit in the elites' projects is turning against these elites; it produced ignorant workers for the empire, orientalized workers who adopted the perception of other cultures, and this empire is hard to dismantle.

Knowing the colonized is one of the keys to colonizing them. If Americans are blinded by the misinformation they have been fed, and if the American mindset is distorted by the ignorance production machine, then the empire is falling—or so I used to think. By the end of my D.C. fieldwork, the empire as a system was not as strong as I used to think it was, but was instead subject to collapse caused not only by the growing resistance to empire but also by forces of its own making: its misinformation system and, more important, the culture of capitalism based on self-interest, individualism, and profit. By the end of my D.C. fieldwork, I realized that the empire is also sustained by the rest of the world's ignorance of the United States—a system that is strong and that works—and by our being victims of the American Dream. Being in D.C. gave me hope that if we only break the fear, things will change—not only for us, but also for Americans.

NOTES

1. Henry Lewis Morgan, *League of the Ho-Dé-No-Sau-Nee or Iroquois* (New York: Dodd, Mead, 1922), 115.

2. Fairlie quoted in William Appleman Williams, *Empire as a Way of Life* (New York: Ig Publishing, 2007), 17.

REFERENCES

Kabbani, Rana. 1989. *A Letter to Christendom*. London: Virago Press.

Sukarieh, Mayssoun. 2009. "Winning Hearts and Minds: Education, Culture, and Control." Ph.D. dissertation, University of California, Berkeley.

Sukarieh, Mayssoun, and Stuart Tannock. 2014. *Youth Rising? The Politics of Youth in the Global Economy*. London: Routledge.

PART TWO

Chinese Travelers and Their Observations

11

From Buddhist Records of the Western World

Xuanzang (Hiuen Tsiang), 629

Xuanzang, or Hiuen Tsiang (603–664), was a famous Chinese Buddhist, a monk-scholar and traveler who, perhaps more than any other known figure, represented the interaction between China and India in the Tang period (618–907). Born in Luoyang, a province in central China, Tsiang was the youngest of four children of a conservative Confucianist father. Tsiang descended from a family of scholars; a great grandfather was an imperial college professor. Tsiang's father instructed all his children in orthodox Confucianism, but Tsiang was a particularly gifted and eager student. Despite his Confucian upbringing, at an early age Tsiang showed interest in becoming a Buddhist monk, following in the steps of his eldest brother. Tsiang was ordained a monk in 622 at the age of nineteen. Intrigued by the inconsistencies in Chinese Buddhist texts, Tsiang decided to travel to India, the birthplace of Buddhism—but only after he had mastered Sanskrit and other Indian languages.

Tsiang's journey through Central Asia to India started in 627, albeit without the permission of the emperor, who had banned foreign travel because of a war between the Tang Dynasty and Eastern Turks. Once in India Tsiang traveled extensively, recorded his impressions and observations, and studied grammar, logic, and mathematics. In 645 he returned to China, where he translated almost 1,330 Buddhist scriptures into Chinese and founded the Faxiang School to teach Buddhism and other forms of knowledge acquired during his nearly two-decade-long trip.

Tsiang's book *Journey to the West in the Great Tang Dynasty* was written in 646 at the request of the emperor. Much later the book became one of the primary sources for the

Hiuen Tsiang 1906. *Buddhist Records of the Western World*. Samuel Beal, transl. London: Kegan Paul, Trench, Trübner & Co. Pp. 69–90 (some notes omitted).

study of medieval Central Asia and India, and was first translated into French by Stanislas Julien in 1857. The English translation of the book from which the following excerpt was taken was done in 1884 by Samuel Beal.

In his notes from his seventh-century pilgrimage to India, Tsiang makes systematic observations about social structures (political, educational, religious, and military) and cultural elements (such as notions of time and space). He writes of a well-regulated civilization, one with a standard educational system represented by different schools of thought among intellectuals. He also describes, without noting any apparent contradiction between them, the coexistence of two powerful scriptural traditions, the Vedas and Buddhism.

Hiuen Tsiang seems a tolerant observer. Although the Indians have "no sort of chopstick" and eat with their fingers, he regards them as clean. Although their clothing is "not cut or fashioned" and not colored or embellished, he does not consider them poor or drab. He is willing to draw similarities in dress and behavior to people in his home country, and models civilization from a position of thoughtful inquiry and respect. Tsiang's work was incorporated into other scholarly works, and his achievement has become one of the most used storylines of Chinese popular culture. Not only has the story of *Journey to the West* lived on in the novel by that name, a classic of Chinese literature, but for the past fourteen hundred years it has also been the stock of folk-opera performance, entertaining villagers throughout China. For millions of illiterate villagers, Hiuen Tsiang's account has formed a collective imagination of a civilized but wondrous Other.

Italicized parentheticals are the translator's insertions.

. . .

THREE COUNTRIES, VIZ., (1) LAN-PO, (2) NA-KIE LO-HO, AND (3) KIEN-T'O-LO

Names of India

On examination, we find that the names of India (T'ien-chu) are various and perplexing as to their authority. It was anciently called Shin-tu, also Hien-tau; but now, according to the right pronunciation, it is called In-tu. The people of In-tu call their country by different names according to their district. Each country has diverse customs. Aiming at a general name which is the best sounding, we will call the country In-tu. In Chinese this name signifies the Moon. The moon has many names, of which this is one. For as it is said that all living things ceaselessly revolve in the wheel (*of transmigration*) through the long night of ignorance, without a guiding star, their case is like (*the world*), the sun gone down; as then the torch affords its connecting light, though there be the shining of the stars, how different from the bright (*cool*) moon; just so the bright connected light of holy men and sages, guiding the world as the shining of the moon, have made this country eminent, and so it is called In-tu.

The families of India are divided into castes, the Brâhmaṇs particularly (*are noted*) on account of their purity and nobility. Tradition has so hallowed the name of this tribe that there is no question as to difference of place, but the people generally speak of India as the country of the Brâhmaṇs (Po-lo-men).

Extent of India, Climate, &c.

The countries embraced under this term of India are generally spoken of as the five Indies. In circuit this country is about 90,000 *li*; on three sides it is bordered by the great sea; on the north it is backed by the Snowy Mountains. The north part is broad, the southern part is narrow. Its shape is like the half-moon. The entire land is divided into seventy countries or so. The seasons are particularly hot; the land is well watered[1] and humid. The north is a continuation of mountains and hills, the ground being dry and salt. On the east there are valleys and plains, which being well watered and cultivated, are fruitful and productive. The southern district is wooded and herbaceous; the western parts are stony and barren. Such is the general account of this country.

Measures of Length

To give a brief account of matters. In point of measurements, there is first of all the *yôjana* (*yu-shen-na*); this from the time of the holy kings of old has been regarded as a day's march for an army. The old accounts say it is equal to 40 *li*; according to the common reckoning in India it is 30 *li*, but in the sacred books (*of Buddha*) the *yôjana* is only 16 *li*.

In the subdivision of distances, a *yôjana* is equal to eight *krôśas* (*keu-lu-she*); a *krôśa* is the distance that the lowing of a cow can be heard; a *krôśa* is divided into 500 bows (*dhanus*); a bow is divided into four cubits (*hastas*); a cubit is divided into 24 fingers (*aṅgulis*); a finger is divided into seven barleycorns (*yavas*); and so on to a louse (*yúka*), a nit (*likshâ*), a dust grain, a cow's hair, a sheep's hair, a hare's down, copper-water,[2] and so on for seven divisions, till we come to a small grain of dust; this is divided sevenfold till we come to an excessively small grain of dust (*aṇu*); this cannot be divided further without arriving at nothingness, and so it is called the infinitely small (*paramâṇu*).

Astronomy, the Calendar, &c.

Although the revolution of the *Yin* and *Yang* principles and the successive mansions of the sun and moon be called by names different from ours, yet the seasons are the same; the names of the months are derived from the position (*of the moon in respect*) of the asterisms.

The shortest portion of time is called a *t'sa-na* (kshana); 120 *kshaṇas* make a *ta-t'sa-na* (takshaṇa); 60 of these make a *la-fo* (lava); 30 of these make a *mau-hu-li-to* (muhûrta); five of these make "a period of time" (*kâla*); six of these make a day and night (*ahôrâtra*),[3] but commonly the day and night are divided into eight kalâs.[4]

The period from the new moon till full moon is called the white division (Śukla-paksha) of the month; the period from the full moon till the disappearance (*of the light*) is called the dark portion (Kṛǐshṇa-paksha). The dark portion comprises fourteen or fifteen days, because the month is sometimes long and sometimes short. The preceding dark portion and the following light portion together form a month; six months form a "march" (*hing, s. ayaṇa*). The sun when it moves within (*the equator*) is said to be on its northward march; when it moves without (*the equator*) it is on its southern march. These two periods form a year (*vatsara*).

The year, again, is divided into six seasons. From the 16th day of the 1st month till the 15th day of the 3d month is the season of gradual heat; from the 16th day of the 3d month till the 15th day of the 5th month is called the season of full heat; from the 16th day of the 5th month till the 15th day of the 7th month is called the rainy season; from the 16th day of the 7th month till the 15th day of the 9th month is called the season of growth (*vegetation*); from the 16th day of the 9th month to the 15th day of the 11th month is called the season of gradual cold; from the 16th day of the 11th month to the 15th day of the 1st month is called the season of great (*full*) cold.[5]

According to the holy doctrine of Tathâgata, the year is divided into three seasons. From the 16th day of the 1st month till the 15th day of the 5th month is called the hot season; from the 16th day of the 5th month till the 15th day of the 9th month is called the wet season; from the 16th day of the 9th month to the 15th day of the 1st month is called the cold season. Again, there are four seasons, called spring, summer, autumn, winter. The three spring months are called *Chi-ta-lo* (Chaître) month, *Feï-she-kie* (Vaiśâka) month, *She-se-ch'a* (Jyêshṭha); these correspond with the time from the 16th day of the 1st month to the 15th of the 4th month. The three summer months are called *'An-sha-cha* (Âshâḍha) month, *Chi-lo-fa-na* (Śrâvaṇa) month, *Po-ta-lo-pa-to* (Bhâdrapada) month; these correspond to the time between the 16th day of the 4th month to the 15th day of the 7th month. The three autumn months are called *'An-shi-fo-ku-che* (Âśvayuja) month, *Kia-li-ta-ka* (Kârttika) month, *Wi-kia-chi-lo* (Mârgaśîrsha) month; these correspond to the time between the 16th day of the 7th month to the 15th day of the 10th month. The three months of winter are called *P'o-sha* (Pushya) month, *Ma-ku* (Mâgha) month, and *P'o-li-kiu-na* (Phâlguna) month; these correspond with the time between the 16th day of the 10th month to the 15th day of the 1st month in China. In old times in India the priestly fraternity, relying on the holy teaching of Buddha, had a double[6] resting-time (*during the rains*), viz., either the former three months or the latter three months; these periods were either from the 16th day of the 5th month to the 15th day of the 8th month, or from the 16th day of the 6th month to the 15th day of the 9th month.

Translators of the *Sûtras* (*king*) and the *Vinaya* (*liu*) belonging to former generations employed the terms *Tso-hia* and *Tso-la-hia*[7] to signify the rest during the rainy season; but this was because the ignorant (*common*) people of the frontier countries did not understand the right sounds of the language of the middle country (*India*), or that they translated before they comprehended the local phrases: this was the cause of error. And for the same reason occur the mistakes about the time of Tathâgata's conception, birth, departure from his home, enlightenment, and *Nirvâṇa*, which we shall notice in the subsequent records.

Towns and Buildings

The towns and villages have inner gates;[8] the walls are wide and high; the streets and lanes are tortuous, and the roads winding. The thoroughfares are dirty and the stalls arranged on both sides of the road with appropriate signs. Butchers, fishers, dancers, executioners, and scavengers, and so on, have their abodes without the city. In coming and going these persons are bound to keep on the left side of the road till they arrive at their homes. Their houses are surrounded by low walls, and form the suburbs. The earth being soft and muddy, the walls of the towns are mostly built of brick or tiles. The towers on the walls are constructed of wood or bamboo; the houses have balconies and belvederes, which are made of wood, with a coating of lime or mortar, and covered with tiles. The different buildings have the same form as those in China: rushes, or dry branches, or tiles, or boards are used for covering them. The walls are covered with lime and mud, mixed with cow's dung for purity. At different seasons they scatter flowers about. Such are some of their different customs.

The *saṅghârâmas* are constructed with extraordinary skill. A three-storied tower[9] is erected at each of the four angles. The beams and the projecting heads are carved with great skill in different shapes. The doors, windows, and the low walls are painted profusely; the monks' cells are ornamental on the inside and plain on the outside.[10] In the very middle[11] of the building is the hall, high and wide. There are various storeyed chambers and turrets of different height and shape, without any fixed rule. The doors open towards the east; the royal throne also faces the east.

Seats, Clothing, &c.

When they sit *or rest* they all use mats;[12] the royal family and the great personages and assistant officers use mats variously ornamented, but in size they are the same. The throne of the reigning sovereign is large and high, and much adorned with precious gems: it is called the Lion-throne (*siṁhâsana*). It is covered with extremely fine drapery; the footstool is adorned with gems. The nobility use beautifully painted and enriched seats, according to their taste.

Dress, Habits, &c.

Their clothing is not cut or fashioned; they mostly affect fresh-white garments; they esteem little those of mixed color or ornamented. The men wind their garments round their middle, then gather them under the armpits, and let them fall down across the body, hanging to the right. The robes of the women fall down to the ground; they completely cover their shoulders. They wear a little knot of hair on their crowns, and let the rest of their hair fall loose. Some of the men cut off their moustaches, and have other odd customs. On their heads the people wear caps (*crowns*), with flower-wreaths and jeweled necklets. Their garments are made of *Kiau-she-ye* (kau-śêya) and of cotton. *Kiau-she-ye* is the product of the wild silkworm. They have garments also of *Ts'o-mo* (kshauma), which is a sort of hemp; garments also made of *Kien-po-lo* (kambala) which is woven from fine goat-hair; garments also made from *Ho-la-li* (karâla).[13] This stuff is made from the fine hair of a wild animal: it is seldom this can be woven, and therefore the stuff is very valuable, and it is regarded as fine clothing.

In North India, where the air is cold, they wear short and close-fitting garments, like the Hu people. The dress and ornaments worn by non-believers are varied and mixed. Some wear peacocks' feathers; some wear as ornaments necklaces made of skull bones (the *Kapâladhârinas*); some have no clothing, but go naked (*Nirgranthas*); some wear leaf or bark garments; some pull out their hair and cut off their moustaches; others have bushy whiskers and their hair braided on the top of their heads. The costume is not uniform, and the color, whether red or white, not constant.

The Shamans (Śramaṇas) have only three kinds[14] of robes, viz., the *Sang-kio-ki*, the *Ni-fo-si-na*. The cut of the three robes is not the same, but depends on the school. Some have wide or narrow borders, others have small or large flaps. The *Sang-kio-ki* covers the left shoulder and conceals the two armpits. It is worn open on the left and closed on the right. It is cut longer than the waist. The *Ni-fo-si-na* has neither girdle nor tassels. When putting it on, it is plaited in folds and worn round the loins with a cord fastening. The schools differ as to the color of this garment: both yellow and red are used.

The Kshattriyas and the Brâhmaṇs are cleanly and wholesome in their dress, and they live in a homely and frugal way. The king of the country and the great ministers wear garments and ornaments different in their character. They use flowers for decorating their hair, with gem-decked caps; they ornament themselves with bracelets and necklaces.

There are rich merchants who deal exclusively[15] in gold trinkets, and so on. They mostly go bare-footed; few wear sandals. They stain their teeth red or black; they bind up their hair and pierce their ears; they ornament[16] their noses, and have large eyes. Such is their appearance.

Cleanliness, Ablutions, &c.

They are very particular in their personal cleanliness, and allow no remissness in this particular. All wash themselves before eating; they never use that which has been left over (*from a former meal*); they do not pass the dishes. Wooden and stone vessels, when used, must be destroyed; vessels of gold, silver, copper, or iron after each meal must be rubbed and polished. After eating they cleanse their teeth with a willow stick, and wash their hands and mouth.

Until these ablutions are finished they do not touch one another. Every time they perform the functions of nature they wash their bodies and use perfumes of sandal-wood or turmeric.

When the king washes[17] they strike the drums and sing hymns to the sound of musical instruments. Before offering their religious services and petitions, they wash and bathe themselves.

Writing, Language, Books, the Vêdas, Study

The letters of their alphabet were arranged by Brahmâdêva, and their forms have been handed down from the first till now. They are forty-seven in number, and are combined so as to form words according to the object, and according to circumstances (*of time or place*): there are other forms (*inflexions*) used. This alphabet has spread in different directions and formed diverse branches, according to circumstances; therefore there have been slight modifications in the sounds of the words (*spoken language*); but in its great features there has been no change. Middle India preserves the original character of the language in its integrity. Here the pronunciation is soft and agreeable, and like the language of the Dêvas. The pronunciation of the words is clear and pure, and fit as a model for all men. The people of the frontiers have contracted several erroneous modes of pronunciation; for according to the licentious habits of the people, so also will be the corrupt nature of their language.

With respect to the records of events, each province has its own official for preserving them in writing. The record of these events in their full character is called *Ni-lo-pi-ch'a* (Nîlapita, *blue deposit*). In these records are mentioned good and evil events, with calamities and fortunate occurrences.

To educate and encourage the young, they are first taught (*led*) to study the book of twelve chapters (*Siddhavastu*).[18]

After arriving at the age of seven years and upwards, the young are instructed in the five *Vidyâs, Sâstras* of great importance.[19] The first is called the elucidation of sounds (*Śabdavidyâ.*) This treatise explains and illustrates the agreement (*concordance*) of words, and it provides an index for derivatives.

The second *vidyâ* is called *Kiau-ming* (*Śilpasthâna-vidyâ*); it treats of the arts, mechanics, explains the principles of the *Yin* and *Yang* and the calendar.

The third is called the medicinal treatise (*Chikitsâvidyâ*); it embraces formulae for protection, secret charms (*the use of*) medicinal stones, acupuncture, and mugwort.

The fourth *vidyâ* is called the *Hêtuvidyâ* (*science of causes*); its name is derived from the character of the work, which relates to the determination of the true and false, and reduces to their last terms the definition of right and wrong.

The fifth *vidyâ* is called the science of "the interior" (*Adhyâtmavidyâ*); it relates to the five vehicles,[20] their causes and consequences, and the subtle influences of these.

The Brâhmaṇs study the four *Vêda Sâstras*. The first is called *Shau* (*longevity*); it relates to the preservation of life and the regulation of the natural condition. The second is called *Sse* (*sacrifice*); it relates to the (*rules of*) sacrifice and prayer. The third is called *Ping* (*peace* or *regulation*); it relates to decorum, casting of lots, military affairs, and army regulations. The fourth is called *Shu* (*secret mysteries*); it relates to various branches of science, incantations, medicine.[21]

The teachers (*of these works*) must themselves have closely studied the deep and secret principles they contain, and penetrated to their remotest meaning. They then explain their general sense, and guide their pupils in understanding the words which are difficult. They urge them on and skillfully conduct them. They add luster to their poor knowledge, and stimulate the desponding. If they find that their pupils are satisfied with their acquirements, and so wish to escape to attend to their worldly duties, then they use means to keep them in their power. When they have finished their education, and have attained thirty years of age, then their character is formed and their knowledge ripe. When they have secured an occupation they first of all thank their master for his attention. There are some, deeply versed in antiquity, who devote themselves to elegant studies, and live apart from the world, and retain the simplicity of their character. These rise above mundane presents, and are as insensible to renown as to the contempt of the world. Their name having spread afar, the rulers appreciate them highly, but are unable to draw them to the court. The chief of the country honors them on account of their (*mental*) gifts, and the people exalt their fame and render them universal homage. This is the reason of their devoting themselves to their studies with ardor and resolution, without any sense of fatigue. They search for wisdom, relying on their own resources. Although they are possessed of large wealth, yet they will wander here and there to seek their subsistence. There are others who, whilst attaching value to letters, will yet without shame consume their fortunes in wandering about for pleasure, neglecting their duties. They squander their substance in costly food and clothing. Having no virtuous principle, and no desire to study, they are brought to disgrace, and their infamy is widely circulated.

So, according to the class they belong to, all gain knowledge of the doctrine of Tathâgata; but, as the time is distant since the holy one lived, his doctrine is presented in a changed form, and so it is understood, rightly or not, according to the intelligence of those who inquire into it.

Buddhist Schools, Books, Discussions, Discipline

The different schools are constantly at variance, and their contending utterances rise like the angry waves of the sea. The different sects have their separate masters, and in various directions aim at one end.

There are eighteen schools, each claiming pre-eminence. The partisans of the Great and Little Vehicle are content to dwell apart. There are some who give themselves up to quiet contemplation, and devote themselves, whether walking or standing still or sitting down, to the acquirement of wisdom and insight; others, on the contrary, differ from these in raising noisy contentions about their faith. According to their fraternity, they are governed by distinctive rules and regulations, which we need not name.

The *Vinaya* (*liu*), discourses (*lun*), *sûtras* (*king*), are equally Buddhist books. He who can entirely explain one class of these books is exempted from the control of the *karmadâna*. If he can explain two classes, he receives in addition the equipments of an upper seat (*room*); he who can explain three classes has allotted to him different servants to attend to and obey him; he who can explain four classes has "pure men" (*upâsakas*) allotted to him as attendants; he who can explain five classes of books is then allowed an elephant carriage; he who can explain six classes of books is allowed a surrounding escort. When a man's renown has reached to a high distinction, then at different times he convokes an assembly for discussion. He judges of the superior or inferior talent of those who take part in it; he distinguishes their good or bad points; he praises the clever and reproves the faulty; if one of the assembly distinguishes himself by refined language, subtle investigation, deep penetration, and severe logic, then he is mounted on an elephant covered with precious ornaments, and conducted by a numerous suite to the gates of the convent.

If, on the contrary, one of the members breaks down in his argument, or uses poor and inelegant phrases, or if he violates a rule in logic and adapts his words accordingly, they proceed to disfigure his face with red and white, and cover his body with dirt and dust, and then carry him off to some deserted spot or leave him in a ditch. Thus they distinguish between the meritorious and the worthless, between the wise and the foolish.

The pursuit of pleasure belongs to a worldly life, to follow knowledge to a religious life; to return to a worldly life from one of religion is considered blameworthy. If one breaks the rules of discipline, the transgressor is publicly reproved: for a slight fault a reprimand is given or a temporary banishment (*enforced silence*); for a grave fault expulsion is enforced. Those who are thus expelled for life go out to seek some dwelling-place, or, finding no place of refuge, wander about the roads; sometimes they go back to their old occupation (*resume lay life*).

Castes—Marriage

With respect to the division of families, there are four classifications. The first is called the Brâhman (*Po-lo-men*), men of pure conduct. They guard themselves in religion, live purely, and observe the most correct principles. The second is called Kshattriya (*T'sa-ti-li*), the royal caste. For ages they have been the governing class: they apply themselves to virtue (*humanity*) and kindness. The third is called Vaiśyas (*feï-she-li*), the merchant class: they engage in commercial exchange, and they follow profit at home and abroad. The fourth is called Sûdra (*Shu-t'o-lo*), the agricultural class: they labor in ploughing and tillage. In these four classes purity or impurity of caste assigns to every one his place. When they marry they rise or fall in position according to their new relationship. They do not allow promiscuous marriages between relations. A woman once married can never take another husband. Besides these there are other classes of many kinds that intermarry according to their several callings. It would be difficult to speak of these in detail.

Royal Family, Troops, Weapons

The succession of kings is confined to the Kshattriya (*T'sa-li*) caste, who by usurpation and bloodshed have from time to time raised themselves to power. Although a distinct caste, they are regarded as honorable (*or* lords).

The chief soldiers of the country are selected from the bravest of the people, and as the sons follow the profession of their fathers, they soon acquire a knowledge of the art of war. These dwell in garrison around the palace (*during peace*), but when on an expedition they march in front as an advanced guard. There are four divisions of the army, viz.—(1) the infantry, (2) the cavalry, (3) the chariots, (4) the elephants.[22] The elephants are covered with strong armor, and their tusks are provided with sharp spurs. A leader in a car gives the command, whilst two attendants on the right and left drive his chariot, which is drawn by four horses abreast. The general of the soldiers remains in his chariot; he is surrounded by a file of guards, who keep close to his chariot wheels.

The cavalry spread themselves in front to resist an attack, and in case of defeat they carry orders hither and thither. The infantry by their quick movements contribute to the defense. These men are chosen for their courage and strength. They carry a long spear and a great shield; sometimes they hold a sword or saber, and advance to the front with impetuosity. All their weapons of war are sharp and pointed. Some of them are these—spears, shields, bows, arrows, swords, sabers, battle-axes, lances, halberds, long javelins, and various kinds of slings.[23] All these they have used for ages.

Manners, Administration of Law, Ordeals

With respect to the ordinary people, although they are naturally light-minded, yet they are upright and honorable. In money matters they are without craft, and in administering justice they are considerate. They dread the retribution of another state of existence, and make light of the things of the present world. They are not deceitful or treacherous in their conduct, and are faithful to their oaths and promises. In their rules of government there is remarkable rectitude, whilst in their behavior there is much gentleness and sweetness. With respect to criminals or rebels, these are few in number, and only occasionally troublesome. When the laws are broken or the power of the ruler violated, then the matter is clearly sifted and the offenders imprisoned. There is no infliction of corporal punishment; they are simply left to live or die, and are not counted among men. When the rules of propriety or justice are violated, or when a man fails in fidelity or filial piety, then they cut his nose or his ears off, or his hands and feet, or expel him from the country or drive him out into the desert wilds. For other faults, except these, a small payment of money will redeem the punishment. In the investigation of criminal cases there is no use of rod or staff to obtain proofs (*of guilt*). In questioning an accused person, if he replies with frankness the punishment is proportioned accordingly; but if the accused obstinately denies his fault, or in despite of it attempts to excuse himself, then in searching out the truth to the bottom, when it is necessary to pass sentence, there are four kinds of ordeal used—(1) by water, (2) by force, (3) by weighing, (4) by poison.

When the ordeal is by water, then the accused is placed in a sack connected with a stone vessel and thrown into deep water. They then judge of his innocence (*truth*) or guilt in this way—if the man sinks and the stone floats he is guilty; but if the man floats and the stone sinks then he is pronounced innocent.

Secondly, by fire. They heat a plate of iron and make the accused sit on it, and again place his feet on it, and apply it to the palms of his hands; moreover, he is made to pass his tongue over it; if no scars result, he is innocent; if there are scars, his guilt is proved. In case of weak and timid persons who cannot endure such ordeal, they take a flower-bud and cast it towards the fire; if it opens, he is innocent; if the flower is burnt, he is guilty.

Ordeal by weight is this: A man and a stone are placed in a balance evenly, then they judge according to lightness or weight. If the accused is innocent, then the man weighs down the stone, which rises in the balance; if he is guilty, the man rises and the stone falls.

Ordeal by poison is this: They take a ram and make an incision in its right thigh, then mixing all sorts of poison with a portion of the food of the accused man, they place it in the incision made in the thigh (*of the animal*); if the man is guilty, then the poison takes effect and the creature dies; if he is innocent, then the poison has no effect, and he survives.

By these four methods of trial the way of crime is stopped.

Forms of Politeness

There are nine methods of showing outward respect—(1) by selecting words of a soothing character in making requests; (2) by bowing the head to show respect; (3) by raising the hands and bowing; (4) by joining the hands and bowing low; (5) by bending the knee; (6) by a prostration;[24] (7) by a prostration on hands and knees; (8) by touching the ground with the five circles; (9) by stretching the five parts of the body on the ground.

Of these nine methods the most respectful is to make one prostration on the ground and then to kneel and laud the virtues of the one addressed. When at a distance it is usual to bow low;[25] when near, then it is customary to kiss the feet and rub the ankles (*of the person addressed*).

Whenever orders are received at the hands of a superior, the person lifts the skirts of his robes and makes a prostration. The superior or honorable person who is thus reverenced must speak gently (*to the inferior*), either touching his head or patting his back, and addressing him with good words of direction or advice to show his affection.

When a Śramaṇa, or one who has entered on the religious life, has been thus respectfully addressed, he simply replies by expressing a good wish (*vow*).

Not only do they prostrate themselves to show reverence, but they also turn round towards the thing reverenced in many ways, sometimes with one turn, sometimes with three: if from some long-cherished feeling there is a call for marked reverence, then according to the desire of the person.

Medicines, Funeral Customs, &c.

Every one who falls sick fasts for seven days. During this interval many recover, but if the sickness lasts they take medicine. The character of these medicines is different, and their names also. The doctors differ in their modes of examination and treatment.

When a person dies, those who attend the funeral raise lamentable cries and weep together. They rend their garments and loosen their hair; they strike their heads and beat their breasts. There are no regulations as to dress for mourning, nor any fixed time for observing it.

There are three methods of paying the last tribute to the dead: (1) by cremation— wood being made into a pyre, the body is burnt; (2) by water—the body is thrown into deep flowing water and abandoned; (3) by desertion—the body is cast into some forest-wild, to be devoured by beasts.

When the king dies, his successor is first appointed, that he may preside at the funeral rites and fix the different points of precedence. Whilst living they give (*their rulers*) titles according to their character (*virtue*); when dead there are no posthumous titles.

In a house where there has been a death there is no eating allowed; but after the funeral they resume their usual (*habits*). There are no anniversaries (*of the death*) observed. Those who have attended a death they consider unclean; they all bathe outside the town and then enter their houses.

The old and infirm who come near to death, and those entangled in a severe sickness, who fear to linger to the end of their days, and through disgust wish to escape the troubles of life, or those who desire release from the trifling affairs of the world and its concerns (*the concerns of life*), these, after receiving a farewell meal at the hands of their relatives or friends, they place, amid the sounds of music, on a boat which they propel into the midst of the Ganges, where such persons drown themselves. They think thus to secure a birth among the Dêvas. Rarely one of these may be seen not yet dead on the borders (*of the river*).

The priests are not allowed to lament or cry for the dead; when a father or mother of a priest dies they recite their prayers, recounting (*pledging*) their obligations to them; reflecting on the past, they carefully attend to them now dead. They expect by this to increase the mysterious character of their religious merit.

Civil Administration, Revenues, &c.

As the administration of the government is founded on benign principles, the executive is simple. The families are not entered on registers, and the people are not subject to forced labor (*conscription*). The private demesnes of the crown are divided into four principal parts; the first is for carrying out the affairs of state and providing sacrificial offerings; the second is for providing subsidies for the ministers and chief officers of state; the third is for rewarding men of distinguished ability; and the fourth is for charity to religious bodies, whereby the field of merit is cultivated (*planted*). In this way the taxes on the people are light, and the personal service required of them is moderate. Each one keeps his own worldly goods in peace, and all till the ground for their subsistence. These who cultivate the royal estates pay a sixth part of the produce as tribute. The merchants who engage in commerce come and go in carrying out their transactions. The river-passages and the road-barriers are open on payment of a small toll. When the public works require it, labor is exacted but paid for. The payment is in strict proportion to the work done.

The military guard the frontiers, or go out to punish the refractory. They also mount guard at night round the palace. The soldiers are levied according to the requirements of the service; they are promised certain payments and are publicly enrolled. The governors, ministers, magistrates, and officials have each a portion of land consigned to them for their personal support.

Plants and Trees, Agriculture, Food, Drink, Cookery

The climate and the quality of the soil being different according to situation, the produce of the land is various in its character. The flowers and plants, the fruits and trees are of different kinds, and have distinct names. There is, for instance, the Amala fruit (*Ngán-mo-lo*), the Âmla fruit (*Ngán-mi-lo*), the Madhuka fruit (*Mo-tu-kia*), the Bhadra fruit (*po-ta-lo*), the Kapittha fruit (*kie-pi-ta*), the Amalâ fruit (*'O-mo-lo*), the Tinduka fruit (*Chin-tu-kia*), the Udumbara fruit (*Wu-tan-po-lo*), the Môcha fruit (*Mau-che*), the Nârîkêla fruit (*Na-li-ki-lo*), the Panasa fruit (*Pan-na-so*). It would be difficult to enumerate all the kinds of fruit; we have briefly named those most esteemed by the people. As for the date (*Tsau*), the chestnut (*Lih*), the loquat (*P'i*), and the persimmon (*Thi*), they are not known. The pear (*Li*), the wild plum (*Nai*), the peach (*T'au*), the apricot (*Hang* or *Mui*), the grape (*Po-tau*), &c., these all have been brought from the country of Kaśmîr, and are found growing on every side. Pomegranates and sweet oranges are grown everywhere.

In cultivating the land, those whose duty it is sow and reap, plough and harrow (*weed*), and plant according to the season; and after their labor they rest awhile. Among the products of the ground, rice and corn are most plentiful. With respect to edible herbs and plants, we may name ginger and mustard, melons and pump-kins, the *Heun-to* (*Kaṇḍu?*) plant, and others. Onions and garlic are little grown; and few persons eat them; if any one uses them for food, they are expelled beyond the walls of the town. The most usual food is milk, butter, cream, soft sugar, sugar-candy, the oil of the mustard-seed, and all sorts of cakes made of corn are used as food. Fish, mutton, gazelle, and deer they eat generally fresh, sometimes salted; they are forbidden to eat the flesh of the ox, the ass, the elephant, the horse, the pig, the dog, the fox, the wolf, the lion, the monkey, and all the hairy kind. Those who eat them are despised and scorned, and are universally reprobated; they live out-side the walls, and are seldom seen among men.

With respect to the different kinds of wine and liquors, there are various sorts. The juice of the grape and sugarcane, these are used by the Kshattriyas as drink; the Vaiśyas use strong fermented drinks;[26] the Śramaṇas and Brâhmaṇs drink a sort of syrup made from the grape or sugarcane, but not of the nature of fermented wine.[27]

The mixed classes and base-born differ in no way (*as to food or drink*) from the rest, except in respect of the vessels they use, which are very different both as to value and material. There is no lack of suitable things for household use. Although they have saucepans and stewpans, yet they do not know the steamer used for cooking rice. They have many vessels made of dried clay; they seldom use red cop-per vessels: they eat from one vessel, mixing all sorts of condiments together, which they take up with their fingers. They have no spoons or cups, and in short no sort of chopstick. When sick, however, they use copper drinking cups.

Commercial Transactions

Gold and silver, *teou-shih* (native copper), white jade, fire pearls,[28] are the natural products of the country; there are besides these abundance of rare gems and vari-ous kinds of precious stones of different names, which are collected from the islands of the sea. These they exchange for other goods; and in fact they always barter in their commercial transactions, for they have no gold or silver coins, pearl shells, or little pearls.[29]

The boundaries of India and the neighboring countries are herein fully described; the differences of climate and soil are briefly alluded to. Details refer-ring to these points are grouped together, and are stated succinctly; and in refer-ring to the different countries, the various customs and modes of administration are fully detailed.

NOTES

1. Has many fountains.

2. An enumeration corresponding to that in the text will be found in the *Lalita Vistara* (Foucaux, p. 142) and in the *Romantic Legend of Buddha* (p. 87). The expression copper-water may refer to the size of the small hole made in the *tamrî* or copper cup for the admission of water.

3. Three in the day, three in the night.

4. Four for the day and four for the night; each of these *kalâs* is again divided into four parts or periods (*she*).

5. These six seasons (*r̆itavas*) are respectively (1) Vasanta, including the months of Chaitra and Vaiśâkha; (2) Grîshma—Jyêshṭha and Âshâḍha; (3) Varshâs—Śrâvaṇa and Bhâdrapada; (4) S'aradâ—Âśvîna and Kârttika; (5) Hemanta—Mârgaśîrsha and Pushya; and (6) S'iśira—Mâgha and Phâlguna. In the south they are reckoned as beginning a month later.

6. I have preferred not to alter the text, and so translate the passage literally. The "double period" of rest during the rainy season was an early ordinance, found in the Vinaya. It was so arranged that those who were prevented from arriving at the appointed time might begin their "rest" a month later. If, however, we suppose the symbol *liang* to be a mistake for *yu*, then the passage will run thus: "The priestly fraternity retired into fixed dwellings during the rainy season." [. . .]

7. I cannot but think that *hia* and *la* in these phrases are intended to be phonetic equivalents for *Varsha*, and that the author is pointing out the error of those who adopted such inadequate sounds. M. Julien's explanation, however, may be the correct one [. . .].

8. Such is the meaning generally assigned to the symbols *leu yen*. I do not understand the translation given by Julien; the texts perhaps are different.

9. The phrase *chung koh* means "a storeyed room or pavilion"; so at least I understand it. M. Julien translates as though it meant a double-storeyed room, or a pavilion with two storeys. The passage literally translated is: "Angle towers rise on the four sides; there are (or they are) storeyed buildings of three stages."

10. I take *li shu* to mean "the monks" or "the religious," the dark-clad.

11. The phrase *ngau shih* may mean "the sleeping apartments," as Julien translates; but I hesitate to give it this meaning, because the monks slept in their cells, and not in a dormitory. The hall I take to be the hall for religious worship. The account here given corresponds very closely with the description of the Vihâras in Nepâl at the present day.

12. The expression here used may mean "matted beds" or "seats." It is commonly used to denote the *nishadyâ* (Pâli, *nisîdanarh*) or mats used by Buddhists.

13. The Japanese equivalents are *Ka-ra-tsi*.

14. There are only two names given in the text. The first, viz., the *Seng-kia-chi—Saṅghati* is omitted. The other two are the *Saṅkakaklhâ* and the *Nirâsana*.

15. It may also mean that the great merchants use only bracelets.

16. This may also mean "they have handsome noses."

17. Julien translates [this as] "when the king is going out"; but in my copy it is as in the text.

18. This work in twelve chapters is that called *c* (*Sih-ti-chang*) in the *Fan-i-ming-i-tsi* (book xiv. 17 a). It is called *Sih-ti-lo-su-to* by I-tsing [. . .] by mistake for *Sih-ti-po-su-to*, i.e., Siddhavastu. [. . .]

19. Or, it may be translated "the great S'âstra, or S'âstras of the five Vidyâs," in Chinese, *Ming.* [. . .]

20. The five Vehicles, *i.e.,* the five degrees of religious advance among the Buddhists: (1) The vehicle of Buddha, (2) of the Bôdhisattvas, (3) of the Pratyêka Buddha, (4) of the ordained disciple, (5) of the lay disciple.

21. The four *Vêdas*, in the order they are here spoken of, are the *Âyur Vêda*, the *Yajur Vêda*, the *Sâma Vêda*, the *Atharva Vêda*.

22. *I.e.,* the *pattakâya, aśvakâya, ratkakâya,* and *hastikâya* divisions.
23. Compare the weapons in the hands of soldiers represented in the Ajaṇṭâ frescoes. [...]
24. To kneel on all-fours. [...]
25. *K'i sang,* to bow to the ground. [...]
26. *Shun lo,* high-flavored spirits.
27. Called, therefore, "not-wine-body," *i.e.,* non-alcoholic.
28. If *fo* is a mistake for *kiang,* as it probably is, the substance would be "amber."
29. This translation differs from Julien's. The text is probably corrupt.

REFERENCES

Li, Hwui. 1911. *The Life of Hiuen-Tsiang.* Samuel Beal, transl. London: Kegan Paul, Trench, Trübner & Co.

Li, Rongxi. 1995. *A Biography of the Tripitika Master of the Great Ci'en Monastery of the Great Tang Dynasty.* Sramana Huli and Shi Yancong, transl. Berkeley, CA: Numata Center of Buddhist Translation and Research.

12

Two Poems

Huang Zunxian, 1882–1885

The Opium War of 1840–1842 taught the Chinese that they needed to know more about the West—the Far West. China's first treaty with the United States dates to 1844, when little serious written work on the United States existed in China but when the Chinese considered the American nation, along with other Western countries, to be uncivilized and barbaric. The Chinese had experienced predatory behavior by the British and other Europeans, though this occurred in the late 1860s, before Chinese visitors to the United States began to publish accounts of their voyages.

The first diplomatic mission to the United States arrived in 1868, and one Chinese official published his journal a few years later: a series of observations about the technological wonders he found, including railroads and roads. A member of this delegation, Zhang Deji, a speaker of English, published eight books on his foreign travels to Europe and the United States. While in the United States, he visited cities like New York, Boston, and Washington, DC, where he observed Congress in session and recorded his impressions of the people he observed.

In 1872, Chen Lanbin came with a number of Chinese students; they visited various parts of the United States and kept official diaries. In 1876, while the United States was hosting the American Centennial Exposition in Philadelphia, Li Gui was sent to report on it. By 1881, Car Jun was advising Chinese envoys on how to cope with Western dinner parties.

The two poems that follow were written by Huang Zunxian and published between 1882 and 1885, when he was Chinese consul-general in San Francisco. Before arriving, he viewed the United States as the most advanced nation in the world, a model for China. Disillusionment followed as he learned about the terrible violence against Chinese workers in the United States and the Chinese government's incapacity to defend its people.

Huang Zunxian. 1993 [1882–1885]. "Two Poems." In *Land without Ghosts: Chinese Impressions of America from the Mid-Nineteenth Century to the Present*. R. David Arkush and Leo O. Lee, eds. Berkeley: University of California Press. Pp. 61–70. Reprinted with the permission of the publisher.

Besides a reformer and diplomat, Huang Zunxian was a poet of high caliber. In these selections he expresses his bitterness about anti-Chinese discrimination in America, which in his view contravened the ideals of America's first president, George Washington: "Red and yellow and black and white / Were all to be treated as one" (Huang Zunxian. 1993 [1882–1885]:70). If democracy did not work in America how could it be a model for China? His analysis of the 1884 elections could have been written about twenty-first-century U.S. elections: "This party denounces the other party; / Their mouths all make the same racket." (66). Nevertheless, by 1884 the governments of both countries were negotiating reparations for Chinese who had suffered at the hands of mobs and been widely discriminated against. In 1901, the United States and other countries invaded Peking in response to the anti-foreign violence of the Boxer uprisings, events not dissimilar to what had happened to Chinese immigrants in the United States.

. . .

EXPULSION OF THE IMMIGRANTS

Alas! What crime have our people committed,
That they suffer this calamity in our nation's fortunes?
Five thousand years since the Yellow Emperor,
Our country today is exceedingly weak.
Demons and ghouls are hard to fathom;
Even worse than the woodland and monsters.
Who can say our fellow men have not met an inhuman fate,
In the end oppressed by another race?
Within the vastness of the six directions,
Where can our people find asylum?

When the Chinese first crossed the ocean,
They were the same as pioneers.
They lived in straw hovels, cramped as snail shells;
For protection gradually built bamboo fences.
Dressed in tatters, they cleared mountain forests;
Wilderness and waste turned into towns and villages.
Mountains of gold towered on high,
Which men could grab with their hands left and right.
Eureka! They return with a load full of gold,
All bragging this land is paradise.
They beckon and beg their families to come;
Legs in the rear file behind legs in the front.
Wearing short coats, they braid their queues;
Men carry bamboo rainhats, wear straw sandals.
Bartenders lead along cooks;
Some hold tailors' needles, others workmen's axes.

They clap with excitement, traveling overseas;
Everyone surnamed Wong creates confusion.

Later when the red-turbaned rebels rose up,
Lists were drawn of wanted rebels.
Pursued criminals fled to American asylums,
Gliding like snakes into their holes.
They brandished daggers in the same house;
Entered markets, knife blades clashing.
This was abetted by the law's looseness.
And daily their customs became more evil.

Gradually the natives turned jealous.
Time to time spreading false rumors,
They say these Chinese paupers
Only wish to fill their money bags.
Soon as their feet touch the ground,
All the gold leaps out of the earth.
They hang ten thousand cash on their waists,
And catch the next boat back to China.
Which of them is willing to loosen his queue,
And do some hard labor for us?
Some say the Chinese are shiftless;
They first came with bare arms.
When happy, they are like insects milling about;
Angry, like beasts, biting and fighting.
Wild, barbaric, they love to kill by nature;
For no reason, blood soaks their knives.
This land is not a hateful river;
Must it hold these man-eating crocodiles?
Others say the Chinese are a bunch of hoodlums,
By nature all filthy and unclean.
Their houses are as dirty as dogs';
Their food even worse than pigs'.
All they need is a dollar a day;
Who is as scrawny as they are?
If we allow this cheap labor of theirs,
Then all of us are finished.
We see our own brothers being injured;
Who can stand these venomous vermin?

Thus, a thousand mouths keep up their clamor,
Ten thousand eyes, glare, burning with hate.

Signing names, the Americans send up a dozen petitions;
Begging their rulers to reconsider.
Suddenly the order of exile comes down,
Though I fear this breaks our treaties.
The myriad nations all trade with each other;
So how can the Chinese be refused?
They send off a delegation to China,
To avoid the attacks of public opinion.
A dicer can sometimes throw a six after a one;
They have decided to try their luck with this gamble.
Who could have imagined such stupidity,
That we would agree to this in public, eyes closed?
With all of the iron in the six continents,
Who could have cast such a big mess?
From now on they set up a strict ban,
Establishing customs posts everywhere.
They have sealed all the gates tightly,
Door after door with guards beating alarms.
Chinese who leave are like magpies circling a tree,
Those staying like swallows nesting on curtains.
Customs interrogations extend to Chinese tourists;
Transients and even students are not spared.
The nation's laws and international relations
Are all abandoned in some high tower.

As I gaze east, the sea is boundless, vast;
More remote, huge deserts to be crossed.
The boatman cries, "I await you";
But the river guard shouts, "Don't cross!"
Those who do not carry passports
Are arrested as soon as they arrive.
Anyone with a yellow-colored face
Is beaten even if guiltless.
I sadly recollect George Washington,
Who had the makings of a great ruler.
He proclaimed that in America,
There is a broad land to the west of the desert.
All kinds of foreigners and immigrants,
Are allowed to settle in these new lands.
The yellow, white, red, and black races
Are all equal with our native people.

Not even a hundred years till today,
But they are not ashamed to eat his words.
Alas! In the five great continents,
Each race is distinct and different.
We drive off foreigners and punish barbarians,
Hate one another, call each other names.
Today is not yet the Age of Great Unity;
We only compete in cleverness and power.
The land of the red man is vast and remote;
I know you are eager to settle and open it.
The American eagle strides the heavens soaring,
With half of the globe clutched in his claw.
Although the Chinese arrived later,
Couldn't you leave them a little space?

If a nation does not care for its people,
They are like sparrows shot in a bush.
If the earth's four corners won't accept them,
Wandering in exile, where can they rest?
Heaven and earth are suddenly narrow, confining;
Men and demons chew and devour each other.
Great China and the race of Han
Have now become a joke to other races.
We are not as simple as the black slaves,
Numb and confused wherever they be.
Grave, dignified, I arrive with my dragon banners,
Knock on the custom's gate, hesitant, doubtful.
Even if we emptied the water of four oceans,
It would be hard to wash this shame clean.
Other nations may imitate this evil;
No place left to hold our drifting subjects.
In my far travels I recall Da Zhang and Shu Hai;
In my recent deeds, ashamed before Generals Wei and Huo.[1]
I ask about Sage Yu's travels, vast, limitless;
When will China's territory expand again?
(translation by J. D. Schmidt)

THE ELECTION OF 1884

Blow the horn for the Democratic Party,
Beat the drum for the Democratic Party,
Hoist the banner of the Democratic Party,

Write pamphlets for the Democratic Party.
Fellow citizens, hold your peace;
Please listen to our party's plea.
Each person voices his opinions,
Each person has his own inner feelings.
Joined together we make a nation;
A man alone is but a foot of earth.
The man we name must be supported by all;
He will be father to us all.

Beat the drum for the Republican Party,
Blow the horn for the Republican Party,
Write pamphlets for the Republican Party,
Hoist the banner of the Republican Party.
Please listen to our party's plea;
Fellow citizens, hold your peace.
Each person has his own inner feelings,
Each person voices his opinions.
A man alone is but a foot of earth;
Joined together we make a nation.
He will be father to us all;
The man we name must be supported by all.

One party brags to the other party:
Look what we will accomplish.
We will champion business and labor;
We will put protectionist policies first.
Gold must accord with the price of silver;
We should have a unified policy.
Everybody a farmer on his own land
Must have ten more bushels of wheat.
Upon this our American land
Permit no foreigners to come and trespass.
Yellow men from far away
Should be excluded from our gates.
Let them not defile our reputation;
Allow them not to snore beside our couch.
Just like Jesus breaking bread
To feed and gratify a thousand people,
As soon as our party wields power
The effect of our policies will be seen in days.

The other party castigates this party,
Saying what is the use of all these empty words.

The other party denounces this party:
Your party's leader is a scoundrel;
In youth he was a vagabond thief
Reported to have stolen neighbors' cattle;
He is said to keep a certain prostitute
And to like to dally in brothels.
He is addicted to dice, a scheming pilferer.
He looks like a devil from the underworld,
Only dressed like an ape with a cap on.
He covers up his countless vices.
Fellow citizens, can't you recognize this?
Who wants to follow one who bares his behind
To shit on the head of the Buddha?
Were his face armored with ten layers of steel
It could hardly conceal his shame.
This party denounces the other party;
Their mouths all make the same racket.

One day a circus tent is set up
To accommodate a thousand spectators.
Rows and rows of black leather benches
Crisscross the ground in tiers;
Colorful lanterns countless in number
Illuminate the ornate canopy.
A boozy rough mounts the stage
To churn and revolve his overgrown tongue.
Yellow beard curling all around,
His piercing green eyes flashing,
From his mouth comes forth a river of words,
Rolling waves that will not be stemmed.
His boisterous laugh rips through the roof;
His anger threatens to pull down the pillars.
At times the audience cheers him on,
At times it boos in disapproval.
The palms of their hands make a sound like thunder
As they beat together in rhythmic union.
At the conclusion hands are raised
To express approval for the party's decisions.

The speeches have yet to come to an end
When a parade is loosed inside the hall.
In steel helmets and coats of mail,
They march on both the right and the left.
Ornate elephants in golden braid,
White horses bridled in purple silk.
The pounding of footsteps is loud and clear;
The sight of the rifles like a forest of masts.
On their faces some wear masks,
Some hold long weapons in their arms.
Gold eyes pretending to be dreadful demigods;
Black faces painted like the king of devils.
Like Christian crusaders of long ago
Their crimson pennons wave in the wind.
All together they sing patriotic songs;
Their musical voices encircle the rafters.
Thousands and myriads of heads are moving;
Wall after wall they press forward.
The people standing at the side are asked
To see the grandeur of the party displayed.

Out of range of the crowd's eyes and ears,
The stress is on coaxing with sweet words.
Treats like green tender tea,
Wine of a crystalline emerald hue,
Gifts like black velvet woven with stripes,
And a medley of woolens of crimson color.
Even such trinkets as hairpins
Are given out to lure the women.
Candidates pay their respects to the rich and learned on high,
And below call on the lowly of the street.
With ruffians as well as common criminals,
They shake the hands of all whom they see.
They offer things deprecatingly,
Saying this little gift is from so and so.
Holding up a colored placard,
They ask the voters to remember their names:
"I know that you, Sir, have many an in-law,
I know that you, Sir, have uncles and nephews.
I therefore beseech your loyal support;
Our party will surely win the election."

They remind the voters again and again,
Please do not make any mistake.
. . . .
Alas! George Washington!
It is nearly a hundred years now
Since the flag of independence was raised
And oppressive rule was overthrown.
Red and yellow and black and white
Were all to be treated as one.

Every man was to be granted his freedom,
All the resources were to be used for their profit.
The people's intelligence was to be developed;
The wealth of the nation was to be doubled and trebled.
Such a magnificent and grand nation:
We sigh with awe at the music of its name.
Who would have guessed this presidential election
Would reveal so many strange things?
Friends are embroiled in angry strife,
Zealously disputing the nation's succession.
In serious cases riots lead to disasters;
On a smaller scale there are assassinations.
Innocent parties are commonly entangled,
And even officials dragged into jail.
Striving for fairness, it produces selfishness.
Abuses are begotten by the general interest.
Is the one chosen of virtue, after all,
Worthy of assuming high office?
How can we imagine the Age of Grand Harmony on earth?
(translation partly after Chang-fang Chen)

NOTE

1. The ancient sage emperor Yu is supposed to have traveled 230,000 Chinese miles from Zhang Hai to Shu Hai. Wei Qing and Huo Chubing were Han dynasty generals who drove off the barbarian Huns.

REFERENCE

Schmidt, J. D. 2007. *Within the Human Realm: The Poetry of Huang Zunxian, 1848–1905.* Cambridge: Cambridge University Press.

13

The Power and Threat of America

Liang Qichao, 1903

Throughout the eighteenth century, the Chinese found little they wanted from the mostly British traders whose demand for Chinese teas, porcelain, and other luxury goods grew. To pay for Chinese products, the British East India Company began to transport opium from the Indian subcontinent to southern China. Opium addiction became a central issue in China's foreign policy. The British military response to the Chinese prohibitions, ushering in what are now known as the Opium Wars (1839–1842), ended with the Treaty of Nanjing, giving British subjects open trade in coastal Chinese cities.

Relative to other Western powers' involvement in the China trade, that of American traders was insignificant and played a negligible role in the Opium Wars. U.S. interests were promoted by Christian missionaries, who began their proselytizing on the coast and who, following a Sino-American treaty, were able to move to the interior after 1858. In 1882, the United States passed the Chinese Exclusion Act, which provided for a ten-year moratorium on Chinese immigration.

China itself had been transformed from an imperial nation to an enormous war zone in the late 1800s and early 1900s. Liang Qichao, well-known for his activism, reflects on a critical moment in Chinese history when he was looking to America as a possible model for a new China, yet realizing that Chinese culture would not allow a duplicate of Western democracy.

Widely considered one of the most influential Chinese reformists of the twentieth century, early on Liang Qichao was devoted to integrating Western ideas with Chinese political thought and educational methods. After a conservative coup in China and before his trip to

Liang Qichao. 1989 [1903]. "The Power and Threat of America." In *Land without Ghosts: Chinese Impressions of America from the Mid-Nineteenth Century to the Present.* R. David Arkush and Leo O. Lee, eds. Berkeley: University of California Press. Pp. 81–95. Reprinted with the permission of the publisher.

the United States in 1898, he was exiled to Japan, where he published on behalf of Chinese reformers. Liang traveled to the United States in 1903 and spent five months there. Prophetic and critical of the conditions he encountered, his writings suggest an ominous future for Chinese-U.S. relations. He condemned the gross economic inequalities in American society, as well as the shortcomings of the Chinese—a polite way to criticize.

In one section of his account, Liang's evaluations of the Rockefeller Trust and one of President Theodore Roosevelt's speeches follow his account of a meeting with J. P. Morgan, juxtaposing the United States' admonishments and threats to China. He was impressed with Morgan's "sole motto for his success": that "the outcome of any venture depends on preparations made ahead of time." Given the threats projected by Roosevelt's audacious imperialist claims and by U.S. trusts, J. P. Morgan's advice to Liang becomes Liang's advice to China: be ready for future confrontation with an already powerful United States. In the final analysis, Liang's pleas for reform are not motivated by the prospect of alliances with the West, but by an urgent desire to defend China. His words of advice do not stand alone but are corroborated, ironically, by one of the wealthiest American businessmen, who symbolizes threat and caution at the same time.

Reflecting on the Monroe Doctrine, Liang states that the original meaning of "the Americas belong to the people of the Americas" has been "transformed into 'the Americas belong to the people of the United States.'" And who knows, he asks, whether this outlook will not evolve ultimately into "the world belongs to the United States?" (Liang Qichao 1989 [1903]:90). Although the character of J. P. Morgan (from whom he requested and received a five-minute meeting) impressed him, Liang describes the creation of the business trust as "a giant monster" whose slaying he considers unlikely: "The trust is the darling of the twentieth century, and certainly cannot be destroyed by human effort, as it is recognized by all of even the slightest learning. From now on, domestic threats will grow into international threats, and the nation that will be most severely victimized will surely be China" (89).

Liang foreshadows the tensions to come: "It is clear that we cannot look at this problem as if observing a fire from the opposite shore" (89). He describes his anxiety when listening to political speeches by Theodore Roosevelt, and questions the president's motives in talking publicly about "playing a great role on the world's stage" and "carrying out our great purpose." Liang recapitulates these anxieties with the statement, "I could not stop feeling afraid and could not fathom the intention of Roosevelt and the American people" (90).

Liang then moves into a discussion of inequalities, racism, and the savage practice of lynching blacks, about which he writes, "Such a phenomenon is unimaginable among civilized countries" (91). He concludes with the profound question, "The American Declaration of Independence says that people are all born free and equal. Are blacks alone not people?" (91).

· · ·

NEW YORK

Uncivilized people live underground, half-civilized people live on the surface, and civilized people live above the ground. Those who live on the surface usually live in one- or two-story houses.... Some houses in Peking have entrances going down several stone steps, almost as if going underground. In New York, buildings of ten to twenty stories are not rare, and the tallest reaches thirty-three stories. This can truly be called above the ground. But ordinary residential buildings in big cities in America also have one or two basements, and so are both above and below ground.

Everywhere in New York the eye confronts what look like pigeon coops, spiderwebs, and centipedes; in fact these are houses, electric wires, and trolley cars.

New York's Central Park extends from 71st Street to 123d Street [in fact, 59th to 110th], with an area about equal to the International Settlement and French Concession in Shanghai. Especially on days of rest it is crowded with carriages and people jostling together. The park is in the middle of the city; if it were changed into a commercial area, the land would sell for three or four times the annual revenue of the Chinese government. From the Chinese point of view this may be called throwing away money on useless land and regrettable. The total park area in New York is 7,000 [Chinese] acres, the largest of any city in the world; London is second with 6,500 acres. Writers on city administration all agree that for a busy metropolis not to have appropriate parks is harmful to public health and morals. Now that I have come to New York, I am convinced. One day without going to the park leaves me muddled in mind and spirit.

Every day streetcars, elevated trains, subway trains, horse carriages, automobiles, and bicycles go clitter-clatter above and below, banging and booming to left and right, rumbling and ringing in front and behind. The mind is confused and the soul is shaken. People say that those who live in New York for a long time must have sharper eyes than ordinary people or else they would have to stand at intersections all day, not daring to take a step.

POVERTY

New York is the most prosperous city in the world, and also the bleakest. Let me briefly describe New York's darker side.

Anti-Oriental agitators criticize the Chinese above all for their uncleanness. From what I have seen of New York, the Chinese are not the dirtiest. In streets where Italians and Jews live, in the summer old women and young wives, boys and girls, take stools and sit outside their doors, clogging the street. Their clothing is shabby, their appearance wretched. These areas are not accessible by streetcar and even horse-drawn carriages seldom go there. Tourists are always coming to see how they live. From the outside there is building after multistoried building, but inside each building dozens of families are tenants. Over half of the apartments have no daylight or ventilation, and gas lights burn day and night. When you enter, the foul smell assaults your nose. Altogether, in New York about 230,000 people live in such conditions.

According to statistics for 1888, on Houston and Mulberry streets (where most of the people are Italians, with some Germans, Chinese, and Jews), the death rate was 35 per thousand, and 139 per thousand for children under five. In comparison, the overall death rate for New York was 26 per thousand, so the hardship of these poor people can be imagined. These rates, it is said, are due to the lack of air and light where they live. Another statistician says there are 37,000 rented apartments in New York, in which over 1,200,000 people live. Such dwellings are not only unhealthful but also harmful to morality. According to a statistician again, of the 483 people living in one building on a certain street in New York, in one year 102 people committed crimes. So great is the influence of these conditions.

"Crimson mansions reek of wine and meat, while on the road lie frozen bones. Rich and poor but a foot apart; sorrows too hard to relate." So goes Du Fu's poem [Tang dynasty]. I have witnessed such things myself in New York. According to statistics of the socialists, 70 percent of the entire national wealth of America is in the hands of 200,000 rich people, and the remaining 30 percent belongs to 79,800,000 poor. Thus the rich people in America are truly rich, and this so-called wealthy class constitutes no more than one four-hundredths of the population. It can be compared with one hundred dollars being divided among 400 people, with one person getting seventy dollars and the remaining thirty dollars being divided among 399 people, each getting a little over seven cents. How strange, how bizarre! This kind of phenomenon is seen in all civilized countries, particularly in big cities, [but] New York and London are the most notorious. The unequal distribution of wealth has reached this extreme. I look at the slums of New York and think with a sigh that socialism cannot be avoided.

J. P. MORGAN

This afternoon I went to visit Morgan. Morgan has been called the king of trusts and the Napoleon of the business world. I had no business to discuss with him, but was led by curiosity to meet this man whose magical power is the greatest in America. All his life he has only received guests and never called on others. Even presidents and prime ministers, if they need his help in their nations' financial matters, come to consult him and do not expect him to visit them. I was also told that his appointments are limited to one to five minutes each. Even extremely important problems can be decided in this briefest span of time, so far without error. His energy and acumen are truly unrivaled. I wrote a letter two days ago expressing my wish to request a five-minute conversation. At the appointed time, I went to his Wall Street office to visit him. There were scores of visitors in his receiving room, who were led to see him one by one; no one exceeded five minutes. As I had nothing to ask of him and did not want to waste his precious time, I went in and talked with him for only three minutes. He gave me a word of advice:

The outcome of any venture depends on preparations made ahead of time; once it is started, its success or failure is already decided and can no longer be altered. This is the sole motto for his success in life, and I was deeply impressed.

THE INDUSTRIAL TRUST

In New York City at the turn of the century, a monster was created called the "trust." This monster was born in New York, but its power had spread to all of the United States and is speeding over the whole world. In essence, this monster, whose power far exceeds that of Alexander the Great or Napoleon, is the one and only sovereign of the twentieth-century world. For years I have wanted to find out its true nature; now in New York, I finally have the opportunity. . . .

The origins of the trust can be traced to the Oil Trust of 1882, which was the personal creation of [John D.] Rockefeller, known to the world as the petroleum king. Then in 1883, the Cotton Oil Trust was formed, in 1886 the Bread Trust, and in 1887 the Sugar Refining Trust. Their profits were conspicuous and startled all the world. Thenceforth the whole country became crazed about trusts, until today almost 80 percent of the capital of the entire United States is under the control of trusts. The United States today is the premier capitalist nation in the world, and American capital amounts to almost half that of the entire world. Thus somewhat less than half of the world's total capital is now in the hands of this tiny number of trust barons. Alas! How strange! How amazing! . . .

In sum, the trust is the darling of the twentieth century, and certainly cannot be destroyed by human effort, as is recognized by all of even the slightest learning. From now on, domestic trusts will grow into international trusts, and the nation that will be most severely victimized will surely be China. It is clear that we cannot look at this problem as if observing a fire from the opposite shore.

THEODORE ROOSEVELT'S SPEECH

For several days after I read this speech by President Roosevelt in the newspaper, I felt frightened . . . and could not get rid of my anxiety. [Here Liang quotes at length Roosevelt's assertions about the need for American "imperialism" particularly in the Pacific region.] What was his point in talking about "role" and "purpose" when he said, "playing a great role on the world's stage" and "carrying out our great purpose"? I hope my countrymen will ponder this.

Although these words are Roosevelt's, in fact they represent American public opinion. . . .

The general trend of world affairs is daily concentrating more and more on the Pacific, as those with even a little knowledge of world affairs will affirm. Why? Because this trend is converging on China, as those with a little knowledge of current affairs can also say. In that case, no country is in a better position to utilize the Pacific in order to hold sway over the world than China. But China is unable to become the master of the Pacific, and politely yields this position to others. How then can I bear talking about the Pacific? But that is not all I cannot bear to mention.

THEODORE ROOSEVELT

On the 17th [of May] I visited President Roosevelt at the White House. At the time, Roosevelt had just returned from touring the country, and the reception room was filled with guests. He led me to a side room, where we talked about half an hour. Our conversation was not particularly profound. . . .

In personality Roosevelt is like Kaiser Wilhelm II of Germany. Of the heads of the various countries of the world, only these two men have great ambition and talent and the aura of one who would create a new epoch. . . . Since McKinley, the Republican Party has leaned toward an imperialistic policy; Roosevelt, in particular, assumes an extremely aggressive posture and is full of ambition. There is a chapter in his book called "The Life of Struggle." All his speeches take war as the means for building up a nation; from this his character can be seen. For the next presidential election, Roosevelt already controls the majority, and will probably be reelected. If so, during the seven years of Roosevelt's presidency, America's rapid progress will be inestimable.

As everyone knows, America has for several decades considered the Monroe Doctrine an inalienable diplomatic principle. During McKinley's and Roosevelt's terms in office, however, the nature of the Monroe Doctrine underwent a considerable change, and this must be looked into if we want to understand world trends. . . .

The original meaning of the Monroe Doctrine was "the Americas belong to the people of the Americas," but this has become transformed into "the Americas belong to the people of the United States." And who knows if this will not continue to change, day after day from now on, into "the world belongs to the United States"? The pretext for all this will still be the Monroe Doctrine. Alas, how extraordinary! If you do not believe me, please read Roosevelt's speech on the Monroe Doctrine. . . .

When I read this speech, I thought and thought about his words "the Monroe Doctrine is invincible." I could not stop feeling afraid, and could not fathom the intention of Roosevelt and the American people. If the Monroe Doctrine means only that "the Americas belong to the people of the Americas," then what is the need for a navy? Even if it means "the Americas belong to the people of the United States," what is the need for such a powerful navy? If the doctrine is generally defensive and for self-preservation, then other countries will probably tolerate it;

but if it is directed against other nations, than I do not know what the purpose can be. Alas, the meaning of Roosevelt's words about being "invincible" can be imagined! Hawaii and the Philippines have been annexed; how can they be taken away without overthrowing the hegemon? I fear that there will soon be a successor to our Opium War with England, battle of Tonkin Gulf with France, and battle of Kiaochow Bay with Germany.

LYNCHING

Americans have an unofficial form of punishment known as "lynching" with which to treat blacks. Such a phenomenon is unimaginable among civilized countries. It started with a farmer named Lynch. Because he had been offended by a black, he suspended him from a tree to wait for the police officers to arrive, but the black man died before they came. So his name has been used for this ever since. Recently the common practice is burning people to death. Whenever a black has committed an offense a mob will be directly gathered and burn him without going through the courts.

Had I only been told about this and not been to America myself I would not have believed that such cruel and inhuman acts could be performed in broad daylight in the twentieth century. During the ten months I was in America I counted no less than ten-odd accounts of this strange business in the newspapers. At first I was shocked, but have become accustomed to reading about it and no longer consider it strange. Checking the statistics on it, there have been an average of 157 such private punishments each year since 1884. Hah! When Russia killed a hundred and some score Jews, the whole world considered it savage. But I do not know how to decide which is worse, America or Russia.

To be sure there is something despicable about the behavior of blacks. They would die nine times over without regret if they could possess a white woman's flesh. They often rape them at night in the forest and then kill them in order to silence them. Nine out of ten lynchings are for this, and it is certainly something to be angry about. Still, why does the government allow wanton lynchings to go unpunished even though there is a judiciary? The reason is none other than preconceived opinions about race. The American Declaration of Independence says that people are all born free and equal. Are blacks alone not people? Alas, I now understand what it is that is called "civilization" these days!

LIBRARIES

The various university libraries I have seen do not have people who retrieve books [from the stacks], but let students go and get them on their own. I was amazed. At the University of Chicago, I asked the head of the library whether or not books were lost this way. He answered that about two hundred volumes were lost every year, but hiring several people to supervise the books would cost more than this small number of books and, further, would inconvenience the students. So it is not done. In general, books are lost mostly during the two weeks before examinations because students steal them to prepare for examinations, and many of them are afterwards returned. In this can be seen the general level of public morality. Even a small thing like this is something Orientals could not come close to learning to do in a hundred years.

CHINESE FLAWS

From what has been discussed above, the weaknesses of the Chinese people can be listed as follows:

1. Our character is that of clansmen rather than citizens. Chinese social organization is based on family and clan as the unit rather than on the individual, what is called "regulating one's family before ruling the country." . . . In my opinion, though the power of self-government of the Aryans of the West was developed earlier, our Chinese system of local self-government was just as good. Why is it that they could form a nation-state and we could not? The answer is that what they developed was the city system of self-government, while we developed a clan system of self-government. . . . That Chinese can be clansmen but cannot be citizens, I came to believe more strongly after traveling in North America. . . .

2. We have a village mentality and not a national mentality. I heard Roosevelt's speech to the effect that the most urgent task for the American people is to get rid of the village mentality, by which he meant people's feelings of loyalty to their own town and state. From the point of view of history, however, America has been successful in exercising a republican form of government precisely because this local sentiment was there at the start, and so it cannot be completely faulted. But developed to excess it becomes an obstacle to nation-building. . . . We Chinese have developed it too far. How could it be just the San Francisco Chinese? It is true everywhere at home, too. . . .

3. We can accept only despotism and cannot enjoy freedom. . . . When I look at all the societies of the world, none is so disorderly as the Chinese community in San Francisco. Why? The answer is freedom. The character of the Chinese in China is not superior to those of San Francisco, but at home they are governed by officials and restrained by fathers and elder brothers. The situation of the Chinese of Southeast Asia would seem different from those in China; but England, Holland, and France rule them harshly, ordering the breakup of assemblies of more than ten people, and taking away all freedoms. This is even more severe than inside China, and so they are docile. It is those who live in North America and Australia who enjoy the same degree of freedom under law as Westerners. In towns where there are few of

them, they cannot gather into a force and their defects are not so apparent. But in San Francisco, which leads the list of the free cities with the largest group of Chinese living in the same place, we have seen what the situation is like. . . .

With such countrymen, would it be possible to practice the election system? . . . To speak frankly, I have not observed the character of Chinese at home to be superior to those in San Francisco. On the contrary, I find their level of civilization far inferior to those in San Francisco. . . . Even if there are some Chinese superior to those in San Francisco, it is just a small matter of degree; their lack of qualification for enjoying freedom is just the same. . . .

Now, freedom, constitutionalism, and republicanism mean government by the majority, but the overwhelming majority of the Chinese people are like [those in San Francisco]. If we were to adopt a democratic system of government now, it would be nothing less than committing national suicide. Freedom, constitutionalism, and republicanism would be like hempen clothes in winter or furs in summer; it is not that they are not beautiful, they are just not suitable for us. We should not be bedazzled by empty glitter now; we should not yearn for beautiful dreams. To put it in a word, the Chinese people of today can only be governed autocratically; they cannot enjoy freedom. I pray and yearn, I pray only that our country can have a Guanzi, a Shang Yang,[1] a Lycurgus, a Cromwell alive today to carry out harsh rule, and with iron and fire to forge and temper our countrymen for twenty, thirty, even fifty years. After that we can give them the books of Rousseau and tell them about the deeds of Washington.

4. We lack lofty objectives. . . . This is the fundamental weakness of us Chinese. . . . The motives of Europeans and Americans are not all the same, but in my estimation the most important are their love of beauty, concern for social honor, and the idea of the future in their religion. These three are at the root of the development of Western spiritual civilization, and are what we Chinese lack most. . . .

There are many other ways in which the Chinese character is inferior to that of Westerners; some happened to impress me so I recorded them, but others I have forgotten. Let me now list several that I noted down, in no particular order:

Westerners work only eight hours a day and rest every Sunday. Chinese stores are open every day from seven in the morning to eleven or twelve at night, but though shopkeepers sit erect there all day, day in and day out, without rest, they still fail to get as rich as the Westerners. And the work they do is not comparable to the Westerners' in quantity. Why? In any kind of work the worst thing is to be fatigued. If people work all day, all year they are bound to be bored; when they are bored they become tired, and once they are tired everything goes to waste. Resting is essential to human life. That the Chinese lack lofty goals must be due to their lack of rest.

American schools average only 140 days of study a year, and five or six hours every day. But for the same reason as before, Westerners' studies are superior to those of the Chinese.

A small Chinese shop often employs several or more than a dozen people. In a Western shop, usually there are only one or two employees. It may be estimated that one of them does the same amount of work that it takes three of us to do. It is not that the Chinese are not diligent, they are simply not intelligent.

To rest on Sunday is wonderful. After each six days, one has renewed energy. A person's clarity of spirit depends on this. The Chinese are muddle-headed. We need not adopt their Sunday worship, but we should have a program of rest every ten days.

When more than a hundred Chinese are gathered in one place, even if they are solemn and quiet, there are bound to be four kinds of noise: the most frequent is coughing, next come yawning, sneezing, and blowing the nose. During speeches I have tried to listen unobtrusively, and these four noises are constant and ceaseless. I have also listened in Western lecture halls and theaters; although thousands of people were there, I heard not a sound. In Oriental buses and trolleys there are always spittoons, and spitters are constantly making a mess. American vehicles seldom have spittoons, and even when they do they are hardly used. When Oriental vehicles are on a journey of more than two or three hours, more than half of the passengers doze off. In America, even on a full day's journey, no one tries to sleep. Thus can be seen the physical differences between Orientals and Westerners. . . .

On the sidewalks on both sides of the streets in San Francisco (vehicles go in the middle of the street), spitting and littering are not allowed, and violators are fined five dollars. On New York trolleys, spitting is prohibited and violators are fined five hundred dollars. They value cleanliness so much as to interfere and restrict freedom. Since Chinese are such messy and filthy citizens, no wonder they are despised.

When Westerners walk, their bodies are erect and their heads up. We Chinese bow at one command, stoop at a second, and prostrate ourselves at a third. The comparison should make us ashamed.

When Westerners walk their steps are always hurried; one look and you know that the city is full of people with business to do, as though they cannot get everything done. The Chinese on the other hand walk leisurely and elegantly, full of pomp and ritual—they are truly ridiculous. You can recognize a Chinese walking toward you on the street from a distance of several hundred feet, and not only from his short stature and yellow face.

Westerners walk together like a formation of geese; Chinese are like scattered ducks.

When Westerners speak, if they are addressing one person, then they speak so one person can hear; if they are addressing two people, they make two people hear; similarly with ten and with hundreds, thousands, and tens of thousands. The volume of their voices is adjusted appropriately. In China, if several people sit in a room to talk, they sound like thunder. If thousands are gathered in a lecture hall, the [speaker's] voice is like a mosquito. When Westerners converse, if A has not finished, B does not interrupt. With a group of Chinese, on the other hand, the voices are all disorderly; some famous scholars in Peking consider interrupting to be a sign of masterfulness—this is disorderliness in the extreme. Confucius said, "Without having studied the *Book of Poetry* one cannot speak; without having studied the rites, one cannot behave." My friend Xu Junmian also said, "Chinese have not learned to walk and have not learned to speak." This is no exaggeration. Though these are small matters, they reflect bigger things.

NOTES

The editors of the volume from which the foregoing text is taken, *Land without Ghosts* (Liang Qichao 1989 [1903]), collected a wide range of writings by Chinese visitors to the United States. In discussing the sources of Chinese writings on the West, the editors inform us that a "surprising number of nominally Oriental views of the West in Western languages are counterfeit" (2). Their book structures the selections into six chronological categories ranging from "Exotic America" to "Flawed America," reflecting the political and cultural situations that affected the way in which the Chinese viewed American culture.

1. Guanzi and Shang Yang were both political reformers of the first millennium BC, remembered for strengthening the power of the ruler in an autocratic, non-Confucian way.

REFERENCES

Chang, Hao. 1971. *Liang Ch'i-Ch'ao and Intellectual Transition in China.* London: Oxford University Press.

Huang, Philip. 1972. *Liang Ch'i-ch'ao and Modern Chinese Liberalism.* Seattle: University of Washington Press.

Xiao, Yang. 2002. "Liang Qichao's Political and Social Philosophy." In *Contemporary Chinese Philosophy.* Chung-ying Cheng and Nicholas Bunnin, eds. Malden, MA: Blackwell. Pp. 17–36.

14
___

American Democracy in Crisis
and The Collapse of American
Capitalism

No-Yong Park, 1934

No-Yong Park's book *An Oriental View of American Civilization* was not reviewed kindly. One reviewer in the *Annals of the American Academy of Political and Social Science* critiqued Park's technique of using comparative elements of "the good and the bad, the advantages and the disadvantages" in two civilizations, rather than "stand[ing] as the determining judge" (Price 1934:258). Park was also a widely acclaimed lecturer. His publicity referred to him as the Oriental Mark Twain, a humorist with audiences in the thousands of attendees who appreciated his insights no matter whether they were Republican or Democrat. Newspapers of the day reported that he "interacted and entertained," "told us things not generally known in this country," made "a contribution to international amity," and gave people "food for thought."

Born in Korea, No-Yong Park received his education in China and Japan before coming to the United States, where he earned a PhD at Harvard University. He authored many popular books, including *Chinaman's Chance* (1940), *Retreat of the West* (1937), and *An Oriental View of American Civilization,* from which come the following selections, written during the American depression of the 1930s.

Using the "Doctrine of the Mean," known by some as "the happy medium" and extolled by philosophers East and West, Park writes about the American people writ large: American women, families, churches, education, democracy, capitalism, journalism, President Franklin Delano Roosevelt—but not religion. Many of his comparisons are as relevant today as in 1934. His essays "American Democracy in Crisis" and "The Collapse of American Capitalism" are especially pertinent now in the wake of the Great Recession of 2008 and the contemporary political environment of a weak American democracy. As noted in Eastern traveler reports, it seems an Eastern tradition to compare what one experiences in the

Park, No-Yong. 1934. *An Oriental View of American Civilization.* Boston and New York: Hale, Cushman and Flint. Pp. 81–99.

West to one's home cultures. Park is no exception. Having lived in two other alien cultures before coming to the United States, he is both objective and subjective about this alien society and culture.

At the very start he notes "curious similarities between the Chinese political chaos and the American industrial anarchy"—the former amounting to political feudalism and the latter economic feudalism (Park 1934:91). "The capitalists in America," he adds, "have been as free as the militarists in China, and the people in the one country as much subjugated to them as in the other" (92). He is partial to Franklin Delano Roosevelt as the perfect example of the "Doctrine of the Mean"—not too much to the left or to the right extreme. In regard to American democracy he generalizes: "The retreat of democracy before the onslaught of dictatorship is a product of this turbulent age. Democracy is better suited to peaceful times, but dictatorship is more appropriate for times of crisis" (81). On the indifference of the people, which makes democracy fictional, he comments, "Americans make business their life and politics a joke," and points out that when politics becomes a playground for jokers and crooks, the people lose respect for both government and law. Park concludes that democracy is not for all people everywhere (85). All of his observations can be found in views expressed in our contemporary newsrooms, blogs, and even universities, views that challenge the possibility that the United States can simultaneously be a democracy and an empire, or whether state capitalism in China could ever lead to democracy.

. . .

AMERICAN DEMOCRACY IN CRISIS

The collapse of democracy and the rise of dictatorship is one of the most alarming developments in modern times. Russia, Italy, Germany, one after another came under the sway of some form of dictatorship. Even the United States of America has come under a semi-dictatorship. Hitler, Stalin and Mussolini appear to be prophets of a new era, the era of dictatorship. It would seem almost that democracy has seen its day and is now resigning in favor of Fascism or Hitlerism.

The retreat of democracy before the onslaught of dictatorship is a product of this turbulent age. Democracy is better suited to peaceful times, but dictatorship is more appropriate for times of crisis. It is quite natural, then, that Hitler and Mussolini should have arisen in this stormy, turbulent, present-day world of ours. The dictators will probably continue to run the whole show so long as the weather is bad and the sea is rough. But no sooner will the crisis be over than these dictators will be forgotten and buried. No one can tell when the crisis will be ended. No one can tell when this violent storm created by the World War will become calm. But one thing is sure, and that is that the storm will not last forever. The present collapse of the democratic system, therefore, cannot be regarded as a defeat, although it may be regarded as a temporary resignation. With this belief, I shall review the workings of American democracy.

American democracy is a child of the seventeenth and eighteenth century political thinkers of Europe. Milton, Sydney, Harrington, Locke, Rousseau, Montesquieu are some of the men who may be called the fathers of American democracy. So far as the *theory* of democracy goes, America has contributed nothing new but in practical politics her contribution is immeasurable. America proved that democracy is applicable in large states as well as in small states; she succeeded in creating a national government in a federal state; she introduced the presidential system in contrast to a parliamentary one; she built up the doctrine of judicial supremacy; she has made the best attempt that has been made to use the principles of checks and balances and of the separation of powers; and after all she has demonstrated that democracy is not a mere ideal but an actual working principle. The fact that the Union has been preserved for one hundred and fifty years and that the people have enjoyed freedom, liberty and prosperity unprecedented in history is a great tribute to American democracy.

The success of American democracy is due to the temperament, the wisdom, and the experience, of the American people, received in England as well as in America, and, above all, it is due to the malleable character of American democratic institutions. When an institution is so rigid as to prevent orderly changes in a peaceful way, it is bound to invite war and revolution with ruin and destruction. All of the twenty-five great dynastic changes in Chinese history were executed by war and bloodshed. By this one can easily understand the expense of an absolute monarchy or dictatorship. It is easy to put up a dictatorship, but it is very expensive to get rid of one. Democratic institutions also may be made so rigid as to tolerate no peaceful changes. But the American nation has found it possible to launch one of the greatest revolutions in world history without wasting one drop of blood. The way the American people set up a temporary semi-dictatorship is nothing short of a miracle.

The success in America, however, is no proof that it will work elsewhere. What makes a government good or bad is not so much in the form or principles of the government as in the application of it. The best government is that government which fits best into the prevailing conditions of a country, and the worst is the opposite. Democracy may be a good political principle for some people at some times, but not good for all peoples in all times. I cannot help feeling that the leaders of the Chinese revolution made a great mistake in thinking that democracy is better than monarchy or aristocracy.

Even if it is assumed that the eclipse of democracy is only a temporary phenomenon, and that democracy has accomplished much in America and elsewhere, and that it has a greater future, no one can deny that it has many shortcomings and weaknesses. The domination of the so-called democratic government by a small minority representing vested interests is one of the inherent dangers. Looking from the outside, America seems to be a truly democratic country. The executive is elected by the people, laws are made by the people, money is raised by the people and spent for them. Every citizen of mature age has the same vote, and every one has precisely the same right to run for any government position, including the office of president. But a peek into the inside will convince any man that there is not much of democracy in democracy. It is not the people who actually rule; it is a handful of irresponsible self-appointed autocrats representing the vested interests that move the wheels of the government, dictate the affairs of state, make and unmake laws, and defeat or elect the president. In reality, under a republic the people are as completely dominated by the minority as under a monarchy or a dictatorship. One difference, however, is that in the republic the people think they are controlling their leaders as the little sparrows which fly after the eagle would think the big bird is being chased away by them.

Another great danger arises from the indifference of the so-called sovereign people. When the people had no vote, they shouted and yelled for it as the child would cry out for a new toy at sight. But when the vote was given them, they forgot all about it, and fell asleep in indifference. Even those who do vote do not know how to vote intelligently. But the Americans are no exception. The same is true of all peoples in all ages. That is the reason why democracy at its best is a fiction and republicanism a delusion.

The Americans make business their life and politics a joke. No one goes to the butcher for a surgical operation. Nor does one go to the barber for a dog license. He goes to the doctor or the city hall. But when he comes to politics, the most compli-cated of all sciences, he goes to any Tom, Dick and Harry. In order to be a lawyer, or a physician, one must study law or medicine and pass an examination and get a license to practice his profession. Even the grocer must know his onions before he can sell them. But in order to be a ruler of the state, no education, no experience, no examination, no license is necessary. Will Durant hit the nail on the head when he said: "But to those who deal with our incorporated ills, and risk our hundred million lives in peace and war, and have at their beck and call all our possessions and all our liberties, no specific preparation is required; it is sufficient if they are friends of the chief, loyal to the organization, handsome, suave, hand-shakers, shoulder-slappers, or baby-kissers, taking orders quietly, and as rich in promises as a weather bureau."

Since no training, no license is required, any joker can throw his hat into the ring and may be elected by the careless people. Consequently, the jokers play the role of statesman in America in the same manner as a butcher would play the role of physician. As a matter of fact, the continued flow of the clowns into politics demoralizes the government service and exposes the ship of state to a hazardous journey. If American democracy is to be blessed with a lasting felicity, the people must prevent the jokers from monkeying with politics.

The great problem before the people in America to-day seems to be precisely the same as that stated by Plato in his "Republic": namely, the task of training philosopher statesmen. To be sure, Plato's method of training the philosopher statesmen cannot be used to-day but his idea was a noble one; it was, "philosophers must be kings and kings must be philosophers." Plato passed away without seeing his dreams come true. But the Chinese were actually practicing that ideal long before Plato's time. The civil service examination which was used from the Chow Dynasty (1125–255 B.C.) till 1905 A.D. aimed to produce philosopher statesmen, the idea which was so dear to Plato. The Chinese had the right idea about statesmanship but they erred in their method of training philosophers. Their notion of a philosopher was a man who is well versed in ancient classics and poetry. To them creed was more important than knowledge and discipline was more important than wisdom. Consequently, the civil service examination turned out to be frozen formalism and putrid classicism. Instead of creating live philosophers with their own minds, it produced dead slaves without a soul. The price of that system was stagnation for three thousand years.

The idea of the philosopher statesman is making headway in America in recent years. The "Brain Trust" of President Roosevelt is one expression of such an ideal. But the goal is very far away. The number of philosopher statesmen is very insignificant when compared to the mass of untrained clown politicians.

Most of those who come to play the game of politics come as lawyers, surgeons, journalists, undertakers or soap-box orators, and they do not intend to stay in politics long. They had better not with the scant knowledge they have in social sciences. They know they cannot make politics their life work. They know that they will have to quit in a few years' time. But they hold the great power of the state in their hands for the time being and not a few of them come under the temptation to indulge in graft and corruption while they are in power. With the growth of time corruption tends to increase. Professor Beard might say that the cases of Dougherty, Fall, Doheny and Sinclair of recent years are not comparable to the Credit Mobilier Scandal, the Whisky Ring, the Black Friday Episode, the Mulligan Letters and the Star Route Frauds of the good old days. But a glance into almost any municipal government of to-day will convince one that corruption in America is as dark as it can be painted. The remark that "government is an institution in which you squeeze, I squeeze, and he squeezes," may be as nearly true in America as in China.

Since the government is a playground of the jokers and of the crooks, the people have no respect for the government and no respect for the laws. The Americans make more laws than any other people in the world. Think of it, they make more than sixteen thousand laws every year! But they violate them more than any other people in the world. At times it seems as if they made laws just so that they could break them. The very fact that the cost of crime in America is about thirteen billions of dollars annually, and that the cases of robbery in the city of Chicago alone are twenty-four times as many in a year as in all of England and Wales, indicates the seriousness of the situation. Whatever they do, the Americans do superlatively well and even in the field of crime they make the most enviable record. We Chinese cannot laugh at America, for we have more bandits than America has. But we must give the Americans the credit of having better bandits than we.

All the cases of theft, robbery, and burglary, however shocking as they may seem, would shrink to insignificance when compared with the activities of the organized gangs who openly defy the laws and the authority of the government in broad daylight. It is estimated that there are about eight hundred adult gangs which draw an annual revenue of three billion dollars, all from the business of vice and crime. Alphonse Capone, who rightly deserves the title of "Chicago's Mussolini," was reputed to draw an annual income of fifty million dollars for himself and his gang, and over ten per cent of that sum is understood to have gone to the government officials in the form of bribery. By defiance, intimidation, murder and bribery, the gangs presided over Chicago with their majestic greatness year in and year out. But all the city officials, the Mayor, the Aldermen, Sheriff, police, down to the garbage cleaners, were all so weak, timid, corrupt and slavish that not one dared to raise a finger at the underworld king. What a big joke on democracy! At last the Federal Government stepped in and sent Capone away so that the people of Chicago have a chance to say a word during his absence.

It is undoubtedly true that much of the lawlessness has been due to the prohibition, the World War, the presence of large numbers of persons who are of foreign extraction in the United States. These form more than eighty-seven per cent of the gangs in Chicago, negroes form a little over seven per cent and native born Americans slightly more than five per cent. In the course of time the crime situation may change. But if American democracy does not make some improvement to catch up with the gangs, the government of the people, by the people, for the people may become a government of the gangs, by the gangs, for the gangs.

THE COLLAPSE OF AMERICAN CAPITALISM

There are curious similarities between the Chinese political chaos and the American industrial anarchy. The former may be described as political feudalism and the latter as economic feudalism. The political feudalism in China is the creation of armed bandits, and the economic feudalism in America has been the creation of gamblers and speculators. The collapse of the Chinese political machinery is largely due to failure in controlling the armed bandits, and the collapse of the American industrial system has been largely due to failure in controlling the profit-makers and exploiters. In the one country a handful of arrogant and unscrupulous militarists wages political wars, endless and interminable, and in the other a small group of selfish and irresponsible capitalists has staged industrial wars which have been no less deadly in their effects. In the one country, the armed militarists are kings and dictators, and in the other the selfish capitalists are armed with industrial machinery. But in both countries, the sufferers have been the innocent people.

The capitalists in America have been as free as the militarists in China, and the people in the one country as much subjected to them as in the other. There is no other country in the world where the militarists are so free to exploit the masses as in China. Nor is there any other country where the capitalists have been so free and so uncontrolled as in America. China is a country of free militarists and America has been a land of free capitalists, free to exploit, free to gamble, free to wage wars, free from all responsibilities. Nothing can explain the situation better than the gambling in stocks and other securities. Probably one of the most diabolical things in the world is this gambling in securities. Hanging may be too good a reward for most of these speculators, but they have been left practically uncontrolled to cheat, rob the people of millions and to put the entire nation into jeopardy. A movement towards control is now under way. This control must not be so rigid as to smother individual initiative, but the extent of the freedom which the capitalists have hitherto enjoyed in America is beyond the imagination of any reasonable man. There can be no economic security in America until the irresponsible blood-suckers have been brought under control, as there can be no political order in China unless the armed militarists are brought under rule.

The American capitalists have been as irresponsible as the Chinese militarists in dealing with their fellow men. The Chinese militarist drags the poor fellows into his service. He pays them while they risk their lives in the battlefield, but when the crisis is over, he is not responsible for the well-being of his men. They are scattered throughout the country and become the burden of the people. Precisely the same situation has prevailed in America. A few years ago when business conditions were good the workers were paid well. The thrifty and hard-working saved a few dollars every week for the rainy day that might overtake them. Some bought stocks, some deposited their money in banks, others bought bonds. It seemed for some time that the wage earners would all be financially independent, sooner or later. But when prosperity vanished, millions of men were thrown out into the streets. These jobless men had no means of living through the workless days. Unlike the practice in some European countries, there was no unemployment insurance to which they could look for help. The only hope they had was those savings they had accumulated. Look what became of their savings! Their stocks went to pieces. Their banks, many of them, closed their doors. Their bonds lost their values, some of them nearly one hundred per cent. These men were as helpless as they were hopeless. But their employers disclaimed responsibility for their welfare and these men thus without the means to live, became the burden of the public.

The greatness of a nation does not depend on the size of its territory, or the number of its population, or the strength of its army and navy; it rests on its ability to maintain justice—justice that will insure every man what is due to him, be it reward or punishment. There is no justice in the Chinese political chaos, nor has there been justice in the American economic anarchy. There is no justice in a state where armed men, like Chinese bandits and Japanese soldiers, are kings, nor in a country where speculators and profit-makers are left uncontrolled. In the one case, a few bandits armed with machine-guns run amuck and rob and murder innocent millions, and in the other, a few unscrupulous blood-suckers armed with industrial machinery drive the helpless people into poverty, misery and extermination. Look at the suffering millions in China, the victims of robbery, banditry, war and bloodshed. Look at the thousands of jobless American workmen, who once were proud, honest, willing, efficient workers, but who were driven into darksome slums, sheltered like pigs and fed by charity. No doubt some of them were the victims of their own sins, but most of them have been the victims of the gamblers and speculators, who deserve nothing but an electric chair and a stone overcoat. No civilized state should allow its soldiers to use the instruments of war against the innocent population, nor should it allow its speculators and the reckless producers to use the machinery of industry to enslave and slaughter mankind. Both must be drastically controlled, or else civilization itself may be ruined and destroyed.

There is another striking similarity between the American industrial condition and the Chinese political situation. The Americans have gone as far with their business as the Chinese have gone with their politics. From time immemorial the Chinese have lived democracy but their democracy has never extended beyond the walls of the little villages. Since the revolution in 1912 they have tried to extend the principle to the entire state but so far they have failed. Therefore, there is turmoil and unrest in China. Similarly, the Americans demonstrated their business genius but their success has been confined only within the walls of the individual plants, and so far they have failed to extend the system, the plan and the mechanism operating within the factory to the entire state. Therefore chaos came in American industry.

There is no question that the American business man, in general, has made a great success, individually, within his own plant. He has organized billion-dollar corporations, and systematized, standardized and improved his machines, his staff and all that has to do with efficiency within his own business. But outside of his business he has done little or nothing. He has had no plans, no system, no mechanism, not a thing to protect him and his fellow men. Hence economic society became nothing but chaos and disorder. The minute he left his office, he was out in the dark, kicked, tossed, dragged and trampled down by the surging mass of unknown forces beyond his control. His success within his own plant was compromised by his failure outside of his plant. His system and his plan, which had eliminated waste and increased production within the plant, were completely lost by his lack of plan and his inability to organize and direct the forces outside of his business. A success in individual industry, he has been a failure in national economy.

Since there has been neither a plan nor a system but only a mess of confusion and disorder, he has had no way of telling what would happen next. True, there are some business charts based on various statistics. But they are no more reliable than the prophecies of the fortune tellers. All that he has been able to do has been to clean, polish, repair or replace the machines and spur them up to the maximum speed. He has been surrounded by clouds of uncertainties and unable to see beyond the gateposts. But he has driven the wheels of industry in a hit-or-miss fashion through the eternal darkness. He has produced as fast as the machines could turn out products without knowing how far the consumers would race with him. He has kept on turning the wheels until the markets have all been flooded with his goods, with the economic equilibrium upset and the whole structure of the credit system itself broken to pieces. Then has come a crisis, a panic, a depression, to greet him at his office. He can sell no more of his goods. He shuts down his plant and his competitors do the same. Millions of workers are thrown into the streets.

In his radio address on May 7, 1933, President Roosevelt summarized the situation very beautifully in the following words:

> We found ourselves faced with more agricultural products than we could possibly consume ourselves and surpluses which other nations did not have the cash to buy from us except at prices ruinously low. We have found our factories able to turn out more goods than we could possibly consume, and at the same time we were faced with a falling export demand. We found ourselves with more facilities to transport goods and crops than there were goods and crops to be transported.
>
> All of this has been caused in large part by a complete lack of planning and a complete failure to understand the danger signals that have been flying ever since the close of the World War. The people of this country have been erroneously encouraged to believe that they could keep on increasing the output of farm and factory indefinitely and that some magicians would find ways and means for that increased output to be consumed with reasonable profit to the producer.

It seems to me that the problem of America is not one of invention or the perfection of bigger turbines, for instance, or more powerful machinery in general, but is one of control, regulation and co-ordination of the various economic forces lying outside the individual plants and industry. In the old days, when each man or household was an independent, self-sufficing economic unit, there was no necessity of control and planning, but in this machine age, when all men and all nations are dependent on one another, the question of co-ordination and regulation is a question of life and death for all. The business situation to-day is like the weather. Everybody, as Mark Twain said, talks about it but nobody does anything about it. So long as business remains like the weather, outside of human control, there will always be cold, bleak wintry nights as well as hot, sultry summer days. The great challenge to twentieth century men, therefore, seems to be the question of harnessing economic forces for the service of mankind.

Since 1929, many thoughtful men and women have been seriously considering the question of economic control and planning. The entire country was flooded with literature on the Russian experiment. Norman Thomas, exponent of Socialism, was winning an unprecedented popularity in America. Both the employed and the unemployed, the young and the old, the educated and the uneducated, street cleaners and barbers, politicians and bootleggers, all were talking about Socialism, Communism and Capitalism. While the country was literally seething with cries for economic planning and reform, Franklin D. Roosevelt walked into the White House and silenced them all. President Roosevelt not only could talk but could act, as well, and no one would listen to anybody who could do nothing but talk. Naturally, the long-winded senators and representatives had to take back seats for the moment.

REFERENCES

Park, No-Yong. 1937. *Retreat of the West*. Boston: Hale, Cushman and Flint.

———. 2011 [1940]. *Chinaman's Chance: An Autobiography*. Whitefish, MT: Literary Licensing.

Price, Maurice T. 1934. "Review of No Yong Park's *An Oriental View of American Civilization*." *Annals of the American Academy of Political and Social Science*, Vol. 175 (September): 257–258. doi: 10.1177/000271623417500156.

15

The Shallowness of Cultural Tradition

Fei Xiaotong, 1943–1944

Fei Xiaotong was a student at Yenching University in Beijing when he took a course from Robert Park, founder of the "Chicago School" of sociology. Park was a man who believed in firsthand empirical research. From China, Fei went to England, where he studied anthropology under the tutelage of Bronislaw Malinowski; he conducted his first fieldwork on peasant life in China. During World War II, the U.S. Department of State invited him to spend a year in the United States. Although it was a busy year meeting with other social scientists at the University of Chicago and elsewhere, he found time to write articles about the United States for Chinese consumption. Early on, his writings were admiring of how Americans had, for example, dealt with the war effort and the democratic manner in which wartime rationing had proceeded. But as the year moved on, his enchantment became a critique that compared Chinese culture with what he was experiencing in the United States, as seen especially in his observations on the "negro question" and the isolation of individual American households from their neighbors and larger communities. Fei's writings were popular and influential in both the United States and China, but in the late 1940s his disappointment with U.S. support of the unpopular Nationalist regime in China positioned Fei as a supporter of American democracy but a critic of American foreign policy.

In the following selection Fei writes about Americans' lack of traditional culture. On the one hand, Americans are not weighed down by tradition, which allows them to innovate more boldly than might be seen in China. But he then calls American culture a hodgepodge, and argues that tradition need not be an obstacle to innovation. Both the United States and China disregard tradition, he observes, but for the wrong reasons. When Americans try to convince Fei that they really do respect the past and tradition, their devotion

Fei Xiaotong. 1989. "The Shallowness of Cultural Tradition." In *Land without Ghosts: Chinese Impressions of America from the Mid-Nineteenth Century to the Present*. R. David Arkush and Leo O. Lee, eds. Berkeley: University of California Press. Pp. 172–181. Reprinted with the permission of the publisher.

seems self-conscious and artificial. In the end he argues for living in a world with ghosts (read: ancestors). We need history, he says, a feeling for history. "I can't get used to people who know only the present moment" (Fei Xiaotong 1989:178). What's left after that moment?

In a sense Fei was feeling the alienation that sociologist David Riesman described in his best-selling analysis of American culture, *The Lonely Crowd* (1950), and what the dystopians meant by the phrase "History is bunk." A lack of history or ancestor knowledge basically dilutes kinship and other social ties between people. Fei makes other arresting observations— "They think of the unknown as static"—and notes the standardization of hotels, furnishings, and homes.

In 1979 Fei came back to the United States for a short visit, bringing with him ten other Chinese social scientists. Finding the pace of life even more dizzying than before, he wrote about cars, gasoline, and roads as the essence of American capitalism, as well as the electronic technologies that encourage people to use the telephone instead of writing letters. Imagine if he were to visit the United States today! Fei was a prolific writer, inspirational to many, a public anthropologist, though sometimes seen as an agent of American imperialism. He was also disgraced in China during periods of anti-Americanism—a scholar wedged in between two different worlds.

. . .

THE DARING OF A YOUNG CULTURE

The one thing we Chinese can be proud of is the length of our history. It is undeniable that only we have a culture that has been handed down since ancient times and is still extant and vigorous. But we should not blind ourselves to the fact that this long history, for all its beauty, makes for a force of tradition that restricts us and makes it difficult to modernize quickly. A person reared under its tenets of caution and of following precedent cannot help feeling startled on coming to this new continent, which lacks a long history. Here people are so bold, daring, and willing to experiment that they become rushed, careless, and superficial. A young culture, like a young person, has no taboos. I really do feel alarmed, not that their youthful lack of restraint may lead them into trouble and harm—if, given free rein, they kill themselves in a fall, it will have been of their own free will. What worries me is that the fruit of our experience and prudence may dry up in the shade into a tasteless chestnut, to be thrown into the fire by others, where it will not even produce much heat.

The United States was founded less than two centuries ago. If I should attend its bicentennial celebration, I will probably be able to bring my grandchildren, for it will not take place for over thirty years! Two hundred years ago this continent was a land of red men and whites. People traveling in the wild interior carried a pistol at each side. I remember reading in a history book that just a generation before Lincoln there were still instances of Indians burning and looting villages. Now what was a savage and desolate land two centuries ago has become a booming civilization reminiscent of the classical idea of Utopia, where "doors are not locked at night nor lost articles picked up by others." Such a transformation is a rare achievement in modern times. The people who have accomplished this unprecedented performance cannot be without some special character and ability. What it is I think can be summed up in the word "boldness."

Without boldness they could not have turned their backs on their homelands and come to make their fortunes in this wilderness. Boat after boat of immigrants from all over the world converged on the new continent, each person fed up with the suffocating decay of his old country, coming to this open land in the hope of being able to develop freely. America is a hodgepodge of the cultures of the world, a melting pot of the world's peoples. But for all their differences, Americans have one thing in common: a pioneering spirit, manifested in their boldness of character. To understand America one must look at a youth of sixteen. Every cell in a sixteen-year-old's body is reproducing, growing, and not yet at maturity; but this body can already exist independently. The growing cells are synthesized into a bold and spirited confidence. How could this youth not think himself a favorite of Heaven with limitless prospects? But there has also never been a sixteen-year-old who understood clearly what kind of a world he would wake up in or what tasks awaited him. Habits not yet fixed, tradition not yet formed—this is America.

Not long after coming to Washington, I became tired of paying formal visits and one evening sought out a young anthropologist.[1] Though we had just met, there was a kind of connection between us. At the time that I had been studying the village of Kaixiangong, he too was doing fieldwork in an Asian village. Though we had never exchanged ideas, our two books were published at about the same time, our style of work was about the same, and as soon as we met we could dispense with formality. I said to him, "After spending several days with gray-haired people all day I'm restless. Let's the two of us go out and have fun and see some American sights." He thought for a moment. "We'll go to an American Chinese restaurant, and you can see what becomes of Chinese things when they come to America."

I thought, why not? Although I had had a Chinese meal in Miami, I had not had one since coming to Washington, and could in addition find out how strong "Americanization" really was. The word "Americanization" has a special significance in the United States. Americans have all come from other places, as I said; they came bringing a variety of customs and ideas about social behavior, but people with different ways of life cannot easily live together in the long run, and so they came up with this slogan of people from various places melting together in a pot to produce an American culture that is not identical with any of the originals.

The Chinese restaurant my friend and I went to had entertainment and was a little like a small nightclub. The waiters were Chinese, dressed neatly in tuxedos.

They spoke the Toisan Cantonese dialect, which is the language common among Chinese-Americans. I spoke to them in Mandarin, which did not surprise them, only they apologetically replied in English that they could not understand me. . . . It was called a Chinese restaurant but, except for the overdone and offensive Chinese decor, nothing made me feel the slightest at home. The names "chop suey" and "chow mein" on the menu, seemingly half-Chinese and half-Western, are in fact peculiar dishes and neither Chinese nor Western. "Chop suey" is shredded pork, or sometimes beef or shrimp, fried together with various vegetables. It is really a very ordinary dish, though I do not know why it has to be called by this odd name, which is neither Chinese nor English. But in any case I did not like it and tried it only once. "Chow mein" is a transliteration of *chaomian* [fried noodles], which is reasonable enough, but what is strange is that though fresh noodles are available, these are deep fried and then baked dry to serve to foreigners. In some restaurants these fried noodles are not bad, a little like the *liang mian Huang* of Suzhou snack bars.

The table setting was completely Western, with knife and fork, except that because I was a newly arrived countryman they brought me some bamboo chopsticks stamped "Made in China." What made me most uncomfortable was the glass of water. American ice water has its good points (except for Chicago's, which tastes of bleach), but to drink it with Chinese food that has been cooked in oil is all wrong. I'm amazed American stomachs can stand such an invasion of congealed grease; maybe this is the reason foreigners say Chinese food is hard to digest. In any case they cannot put down a meal without ice water.

Looking up from the table, I saw right in front of us a troupe of half-naked women doing Spanish dances. I had seen Spanish dancing once when I was in London: some of the audience there wore evening clothes, all had come to see the dancing, and they sat attentively, applauding at the end of each number. Here it was different. People were at the same time eating chow mein, joking with girl friends, and watching out of the corners of their eyes the many swinging legs. The music accompanying the Spanish dancing was jazz, which is currently popular in America. I do not claim to know much about music but cannot understand why these sounds are considered music at all. Suddenly the dancing stopped and, to the same kind of "music," a young woman whom one would guess to be Cuban came on and in a loud voice sang one of her country's folk songs. Constantly moving about on the stage and announcing the numbers with a megaphone was a man whom one knew at a glance to be a product of southern Europe.

At that moment, in that spot, various cultures of different origin came helter-skelter together and were arrayed, as though oblivious to the fact that these were Chinese waiters, Oriental embroidery, Spanish dancing, Cuban songs, jazz music, a south European face. A great number and variety of elements inextricably mixed—a merry laugh, a hearty drink, a new culture! As we came out of the restaurant my anthropologist friend asked me what I thought of it. What could I say? "Truly bold! A young culture!"

A WORLD WITHOUT GHOSTS

Accepting an invitation from the University of Chicago, I went there to work on my book "Earthbound China." After I arrived, a secretary showed me to room 502 on the fifth floor of the Social Sciences Building and asked politely if it would do for an office. When I noticed the name "Robert Park" in the brass card-holder on the door, the alert secretary hurried to say, "I was waiting until you decided before putting your name up."

"Don't change the name. I like that one," I told her. But she could hardly have understood why.

Robert Park had been my teacher. He came to Yenching University [in Peking in 1932] when I was an undergraduate there. Though I was just an ignorant student, I absolutely worshipped him—except for the old man's perverse insistence on teaching at 7 A.M. and never missing a class or even coming late, which meant I had to skip breakfast to get there on time. For better or worse, his course determined the direction my life has taken in the ten-odd years since, and to him should go the credit or the blame. The founding father of the Chicago school of sociology, he maintained that sociology should take as its subject understanding human nature. Perhaps I liked him because he wanted me to read novels and not sociology textbooks. More than reading novels, he urged going and personally experiencing different kinds of life. Ten years later I still follow this teaching. On this trip to the United States, I had hoped to go hear his classes again. But I was busy with other things, and it was half a year before I got to Chicago, and the old professor had already gone south to escape the Chicago cold. And so it happened that I was put in his office.

This arrangement, whether accidental or not, was full of meaning for me. I had been an unremarkable student in Professor Park's class, a matter for some regret, and ten years later, though still without achievements, I remained eager for a word of praise from the teacher. I was secretly happy that, sitting in the chair he had used, I would surely absorb something of his spirit, and hoped to write a book that would compensate for my earlier failure to be worthy of the pains he had taken in rising so early all those mornings to teach us. There is here a sort of historical causal connection: because of a past memory the present takes on a significance greater than anything in the current situation. My strong desire to have the name left on the door arose out of a need for concrete, living, moving history. I felt that if the nameplate, the old books lining the walls, even the air in the room were not disturbed, then, surrounded by this lingering past, perhaps in a few months I would see a draft of "Earthbound China" on the table. But if these were disturbed, all might be lost.

This, in fact, is the "tradition" of which I have written in an earlier article. Tradition need not be an obstacle to innovation. True, it has its bad side. When old people, with the various privileges and respect that have been accorded them in the past, prevent any change in the status quo, that is a bad aspect of tradition. But it is also undeniable that everything new is born out of that which is old. These ties of kinship should not be obliterated, and recognizing them gives to the connection between old and new the significance of succession and continuity. If we can develop this kind of feeling for history, I believe the world and mankind will be richer. When we go on a trip into the country, we can enjoy the scenery merely as a present phenomenon; if we have left there earlier memories worth recalling, this can bring on a pleasant nostalgia; and if this is a historical site, our feelings are further enriched because of what others did there. People do not live only in the here and now; life is not just a string of moments. We need history, for it is a wellspring of inspiration. When we take tradition in this way, that is another aspect of it.

Sometimes I think the world is very strange. We in the Orient accept tradition, but what we seize on is its bad side. The West seems to want to disregard it, with the result that the good side is lost too.

Of course, it is not entirely true that Westerners purposely disregard tradition. For the most part, they all know much more about the history of their own country than I do. Every child who goes to New York has to go gaze at the huge Statue of Liberty and then on the way back visit the church that George Washington frequented. In Washington, D.C., there are the hundred-foot-tall Washington Monument, the Lincoln Memorial, and now the Jefferson Memorial. Buildings just a few hundred years old are preserved as historical monuments. On a personal level, Americans keep diaries and write autobiographies. I have elsewhere described how on Thanksgiving the year before last my host brought out a big pile of his father's diaries. At Professor Redfield's house, Mrs. Park especially wanted me to see the pictures of Redfield ancestors in a corner of the living room.[2] On Professor Ogburn's staircase wall were neatly lined up generation after generation of ancestor portraits. Perhaps because at a dinner party I had once expressed the view that Americans lack any feeling for history, all the friends I came into contact with were particularly anxious to correct my misapprehension by showing me their concern for their ancestors. All this is true, but still I feel their regard for tradition is to a greater or lesser extent conscious, intellectual, and artificial. It is not the same as ours. The reason I feel this way is that I have found Americans do not have ghosts.

When tradition is concrete, when it is a part of life, sacred, something to be feared and loved, then it takes the form of ghosts. This is equivalent to the statement by Durkheim that God is the representation of social cohesion. As I write this, I feel in my heart that Chinese culture in its essence is rather beautiful. To be able to live in a world that has ghosts is fortunate. Here let me relate some personal experiences.

When I was a boy, because the family was in decline . . . we lived in a big old building of which at least half was closed off awaiting uncles who seldom came home, and in another part of which were dark rooms that had never seen sunlight. . . . In these dark and desolate rooms, there were more places for ghosts than for people. . . . This environment was already sufficiently frightening, but in addition not a day passed when people did not talk of ghosts to scare or amuse us children. . . . I am not exaggerating when I say that to a child like me brought up in a small town, people and ghosts were equally concrete and real. . . .

Because I grew up half in a world of ghosts, I was particularly interested in them. Gradually my fear changed to curiosity and then to attraction, to the point that I even feel a little sorry for people raised in a world without ghosts. The thing that felt most strange to me during almost a year of living in America was that no one told me any stories of ghosts. I do not want to overpraise such a world, but I will admit that children who grow up in it are more comfortable than we and do not have to live with fear in their hearts all day long. But perhaps there is a heavy price for this, a price I would be unwilling to pay.

The beginning of my gradual change in attitude toward ghosts occurred the year my grandmother died. One day not long after her death, I was sitting in the front room looking toward her bedroom. It was almost noon. Normally at that time Grandmother would go to the kitchen to see how the lunch preparations were coming along, soon after which lunch would be served. This had been a familiar sight for me, and after her death the everyday pattern was not changed. Not a table or chair or bed or mat was moved. Every day close to noon I would feel hungry. To my subconscious mind the scene was not complete without Grandmother's regular daily routine, and so that day I seemed to see her image come out of her bedroom once more and go into the kitchen.

If it was a ghost I saw, it was the first one in my life. At the time I felt nothing unusual, for the scene was so familiar and right. Only a little later when I remembered that Grandmother was dead did I feel upset—not frightened, but sad the way one feels at a loss that should not have occurred. I also seemed to realize that a beautiful scene, once it had existed, would always be. The present loss was just a matter of separation in time, and this separation I felt could be overcome. An inextinguishable revelation had struck; the universe showed a different structure. In this structure our lives do not just pass through time in such a way that a moment in time or a station in life once past is lost. Life in its creativity changes the absolute nature of time: it makes past into present—no, it melds past, present, and future into one inextinguishable, multilayered scene, a three-dimensional body. This is what ghosts are, and not only did I not fear them, I even began to yearn for them.

I cannot get used to people today who know only the present moment. To take this moment as [the sum of] existence is a delusion. Our every act contains within it all the accumulated history from the beginning of the universe right down to the present, and this every act will determine the destiny of endless future generations. If the present moment, fragmentary, abstract, false, is taken for life, this life will necessarily be shallow and base and even empty—since the moment cannot last, one might as well indulge oneself and revel, for when the instant is gone what is left?

American children hear no stories about ghosts. They spend a dime at the "drugstore" to buy a "Superman" comic book. This "Superman" is an all-knowing, resourceful, omnipotent hero who can overcome any difficulty. Let us leave aside the question of what kind of children this teaching produces; the point worth noting here is that Superman is not a ghost. Superman represents actual capabilities or future potential, while ghosts symbolize belief in and reverence for the accumulated past. As much as old Mrs. Park, trying to lessen the distance between East and West, might lead me over to the corner of the living room to look at faded photographs, it was the Redfield's little boy who showed me the heart of American culture, and it lay in Superman, not ghosts.

How could ghosts gain a foothold in American cities? People move about like the tide, unable to form permanent ties with places, to say nothing of other people. I have written elsewhere of the gap between generations. It is an objective social fact that when children grow up they no longer need parental protection, and the reflection of this in the family is children's demand for independence. Once when I was chatting at a friend's house, his daughter sat with us chain-smoking. The father happened to remark that it was senseless to smoke like that, but she paid no heed and afterwards told me that she was eighteen, it was none of the old man's business, smoking was her own affair. Eighteen is an important age for a girl; after that her parents need not support her, but neither can they tell her what to do.

I also know an old professor whose son teaches in the same university as he but lives apart from him—which might be all right, but he seldom even visits. During the war they could not get a maid and it made my heart sick to see the professor's wife, old and doddering, serving a guest coffee with shaking hands.

When I was staying at the Harvard Faculty Club, I noticed sitting at the same table every morning a white-haired old gentleman who lived upstairs and who from his looks was not long for this world. Whenever I saw him I felt outraged. He must have been a famous professor who had educated countless people and worked hard for society. Now old and failing, cast out of the world into this building, without relatives even to care for him much less give him pleasure, he might as well have been dead. One day he said softly to the waitress, "I don't know if I'll be able to make it down the stairs tomorrow." Afterwards I asked her where his home was, but she did not know the answer and only shook her head. In America, when children grow up they have their own homes, where their parents are mere guests.

Outside the family there is certainly much social intercourse, but dealings with people are always in terms of appointments. On my office desk is an appointment calendar marked in fifteen-minute intervals with a space for a person's name beside each. Apart from business there are various kinds of gatherings, but if you go to one you will find it is no more than social pleasantries: a few words with this person, a few words with that one—it is hard even to remember their names. I cannot say all Americans pass their lives like this. But I once asked a fairly close acquaintance how many friends he had whom he could drop in on at any time without a previous engagement. Counting on his fingers, he did not fill one hand. In fact, unless they have business or an engagement they spend most of their time at home, where they don't much like to be disturbed by guests. At any rate, friends warned me not to go barging in on people all the time.

With interpersonal ties like these, naturally they seldom see ghosts after death. Moreover their movements are so easy and they have contacts with so many people, that there seldom comes about the kind of relationship I had with my grandmother, living interdependently for a long time, repeating the same scenes, so that these scenes came to seem an inalterable natural order. Always being on the move dilutes the ties between people and dissolves the ghosts.

As to attachments to places, that is another thing that made me uncomfortable in America. Not the beds and mattresses, for I believe there are none more comfortable than those of the Americans, but the constant moving around that year was the cause of my discomfort. I visited many places, but when I think of them now it seems I went nowhere, for I felt no particular attachment to any place as all were alike, differing only a little in the height of the buildings. The cities are all more or less the same, at least for a traveler: you get off the train and your bags are taken by a black man who everywhere wears the same type of cap (you may not encounter this kind of man, but you will not encounter any other); you take a similar taxi to a similar hotel—no matter what hotel, if you have stayed anywhere once, you will not feel it unfamiliar. The hotel rooms are all comparable, some bigger and some smaller, but none lacking a bathroom, a cold-water tap, a Simmons mattress, and nice stationery and envelopes. Since it is the same everywhere, you can never take away a particular impression from any hotel.

Hotels are not exceptions; it is basically the same with homes in American cities. Moving house is no more difficult than changing hotels; a phone call is all it takes. Move here, move there—the houses are about the same. In New York I thought of renting a house and visited ten possibilities in succession. In the end I said to the friend who was accompanying me, "Why bother to see each one? Why not draw straws?" Moving here and there dilutes people's ties with houses.

Whenever I return to my native place, I go to see the house I lived in as a child. I have lots of questions about the tung tree and the loquat tree; the tung tree still has my name carved on it. In London, where people do not move so frequently, I still remember where I lived on Lower Station Road and Ridge Avenue [?]; while I was in the United States I heard that the old buildings there had been bombed, and it made me feel bad for several days. In America, at least for me, no house has yet produced such a feeling.

I cannot get used to the way lights illuminate all the parts of a room either. Living in such rooms gives you a false sense of confidence that this is all of the world, that there is no more to reality than what appears clearly and brightly before your eyes. I feel the attitude of Westerners toward the unknown is very different from that of Orientals. They think of the unknown as static, waiting for people to mine it like an ore—not only not frightening, but a resource for improving life in the future. They are very self-assured. We Orientals feel some measure of reverence for the unknown; our reverence for fate makes us content with our lot, makes us aware of human limitations, and keeps our eyes fixed on the humanly attainable. I cannot assert that this attitude is ultimately due to the form of the houses we live in as children, but I believe that my own early feelings of uncertainty toward the big kitchen and the back garden and my fright toward the closed-off rooms have still not dissipated, but only expanded into my view of the universe. If many people in traditional China had similar experiences, then these experiences may have determined the basic structure of our traditional attitudes toward people and things.

In a world without ghosts, life is free and easy. American eyes can gaze straight ahead. But still I think they lack something and I do not envy their lives.

NOTES

1. The young anthropologist was John Embree, whose *Suye Mura,* about a Japanese village, had been published in 1939, the same year as Fei's *Peasant Life in China,* on the Chinese village called Kaixiangong.

2. Robert Redfield, the University of Chicago anthropologist, was married to Robert Park's daughter; Margaret Park Redfield helped Fei translate *Earthbound China* into English.

REFERENCES

Arkush, R. David. 1981. *Fei Xiaotong and Sociology in Revolutionary China.* Cambridge, MA: Harvard University Press.

Riesman, David. 1950. *The Lonely Crowd: A Study of the Changing American Character.* In collaboration with Nathan Glazer and Reuel Denney. New Haven: Yale University Press.

16

From Americans and Chinese

Francis L. K. Hsu, 1953, 1970

This selection is unusually direct, simply because the author is an anthropologist, a professional observer of other societies. In his book *Americans and Chinese*, Francis Hsu (1970
[1953]) compares two cultures, one his place of birth, the other a culture "where change is
desired because it is equated with progress, and where neither the physical nor the human
scene is constant" (xiii). His book, he tells us in its preface, is the "report of a marginal man's
life experience and his reflections upon it" (xiii). While Hsu realizes that there is no simple
formula for examining cultural practices, the comparative method—which requires one to
simultaneously look in the mirror while observing the other culture—allows for the
researcher's proper perspective, thereby limiting the tendency to judge one society's reality
with another's ideal blueprint. Such an approach, he believes, obviates universal models.
Hsu is aware that consciousness might be eclipsed by self-satisfied smugness the longer he
lives in the United States, but he is more concerned with anxieties about a world out of
control. He is critical of "modernity," defined in terms of machines and efficiency, as the real
meaning of freedom.

The introduction to Hsu's *Americans and Chinese* looks at "the good and the bad" in
order to differentiate American culture from Western culture more generally. Comparison
is not merely a foil for prejudice or its opposite, self-praise, but serves the purpose of pedagogy. For Hsu, the American scene provides evidence of deep insecurity, which depends on
oneself or the nuclear family. Hsu argues that what Americans lack is the kind of anchorage
that comes from being part of something larger than the self. Such insecurity becomes a
threat to democracy. In this respect Hsu's observations resonate both with Chinese observers of the United States who preceded him and with a number of American social analysts,

Hsu, Francis L. K. 1970 [1953]. *Americans and Chinese: Purpose and Fulfillment in Great Civilizations.*
Garden City, NY: Doubleday Natural History Press. Pp. 317–332, 405–408, 434–436. Reprinted with the
permission of the publisher.

including Erich Fromm, David Riesman, or Christopher Lasch, who also speak about American loneliness and the demise of the American family, which is individuated by American capitalism. In the selection that follows, Hsu addresses the problems of old age, the generation gap, race, and sex and violence, in what is partly a summary of his overall thesis—and that of other Asian visitors to the United States—that Americans lack cohesive family units.

Francis Hsu was born in a southern Manchurian village in 1909. He died in California in 1999, having experienced wars and attended educational institutions while living in the United States. He lived in southern Manchuria during the Sino-Japanese and Russo-Japanese Wars, a time of both internal and external threats: famines, epidemics, student strikes, Western brutalities, and Japanese invasions. He left his village for Shanghai to continue his education, and eventually boarded a boat for England and Europe. His doctorate in anthropology was completed at the London School of Economics, after which he settled permanently in the United States. Most of his work focused on the emotional rather than the economic environment of "lost individuals"—his was a psychological anthropology. Although he was not without methodological critics for generalizing and describing culture as if homogenous, he nevertheless rose to the top of his profession, chairing the anthropology department at Northwestern University for many years and serving as elected president of the American Anthropological Association.

. . .

AMERICAN PROBLEMS

The United Press once reported from France that "Bernarr MacFadden parachuted from a plane at 6:03 P.M. Friday and landed on the left bank of the winding Seine River. . . . The American physical culturist was 85 [and] made the parachute jump to 'prove to everyone that I am young.'" MacFadden's fame was more than matched by the Englishman Chichester, who sailed around the world alone in his boat, *Gypsy Moth,* but even more so by the septuagenarian William Willis, who set out for the last time into the Atlantic from a New England port in a tiny eleven foot, six inch boat christened *The Little One.* After Willis perished in this voyage, *Life* magazine's feature article about him was entitled, "An Ancient Mariner Who Defied Age and the Oceans" (October 4, 1968). Willis never let his wife voyage with him and reportedly always commanded his own resources—and no one else's. MacFadden and Willis were, of course, unusual men but their activities were not, in fact, outside the American pattern of behavior as old age approached.

Old Age

At middle age, Americans turn to regimens that give them a sense of continuing youthfulness. Men undertake activities that purport to sustain physical strength and vigor; women seek the beautician and the masseuse who promise to maintain their waning glamour. For the average American, the approach of old age means the end of almost everything that gives life meaning. To the average Chinese, however, it marks the beginning of a loftier and more respected status. At the threshold of old age, the self-reliant American faces problems rarely known to his Chinese brethren. The first consequence of old age is the loss of economic independence, or at least the likelihood of a lowered standard of living. At sixty-five, although a person may still be physically and mentally sound, he finds most, if not all, doors to employment closed. Even long before reaching this age, if he has not worked on the same job continuously or does not have something special to offer, he may already have been shunned by employers. If his savings, pension, and Social Security are substantial, he can engage in charitable, religious, or communal activities. But the self-reliant American finds these poor substitutes for those social and business activities which once occupied his time and energies.

Overshadowing his economic weakness is the average American oldster's problem of social isolation. His children, whether single or married, have drifted away from him. Even if they are physically near, he has little place in their lives. He might be useful to them in an emergency, or a welcome occasional guest in their household. But if he resides with them permanently, he is likely to be an object of toleration or pity. The grown-up children have their own friends, who don't usually enjoy his company, and their own activities in which it is often impossible for him to participate. Far from being able to retain what authority he exercised in his active years, he is reduced to social oblivion. His advice, especially if it goes contrary to the inclination of the young, is unsought and unheeded.

The Chinese elder has no fear of unemployment. Long before he is physically unable to work, he is likely to have retired to live on the fruits of his children's labor. An older man who does seek employment not only is not handicapped by age, but, if equally qualified otherwise, is in fact preferred to a younger person.

The relative economic security of the Chinese elder is surpassed by his social importance. Instead of restricting their associations to persons of their own age level, Chinese men and women continually seek the counsel and company of their elders. Even in recreational activities, of which social gambling is a very important form, the old regularly join the young. Furthermore, the elders enjoy a degree of authority over the young that is unheard of in the West. When living under the same roof, the former tend to exercise full control. If sons live separately from their elders, the authoritative position of the old is somewhat modified, but not surrendered, and their advice is sought on important matters.

A recent letter from a friend brought home to me the contrast between Chinese and American attitudes toward old age. In the course of describing a vacation visit she and her family had with her grandmother, who is ninety-seven years old, she said:

Her mind is so clear that it is a lot of fun to talk with her. The thing that pleases her most is the fact that the children enjoy her company and are not afraid of her. I don't know why they should be afraid, because she is gentle and sweet, but, being a true American, I guess she thinks age is ugly.

My reaction to this letter was one of amazement. In spite of my close contact with American ways, the idea that age can inspire fear in a child, particularly one related to the aged person, remains unimaginable to me. But, as my friend implied, this is not unusual in America. Another friend told me of the following episode. A four-year-old boy, his parents, and his grandparents were dining out when an elderly couple entered the restaurant. The two were obviously bent and crippled with age. The four-year-old, mouth agape, stared at them until his sixty-three-year-old grandfather reprimanded him for doing so. Whereupon the child asked:

"What's wrong with those people, Grandpop?"

"Nothing, they are old, that's all."

"We don't have any old people where we live, do we?"

These episodes are symptomatic of the fact that, in the normal course of American life, the old and feeble do not enter the orbit of the very young. When they do, the young tend to regard them with curiosity and probably apprehension. More important, those who are advanced in years tend to decline admitting that they are old—the very word is taboo. The boy's last remark to his aging grandfather exemplifies this common attitude. Lastly, these episodes also indicate the psychological difficulties of the old: the painful self-consciousness that the American oldster experiences in his struggle to carry on and come to terms with his new situation.

None of this appears in the Chinese scene. Chinese infants grow up in their grandparents' arms, and many children share their elders' beds. Chinese oldsters do not dolefully admit they are old, they proudly announce the fact. Tombstones, inscribed with inflated ages, are often commissioned by the elderly. In Chinese families, grandparents, as originators of the parents, fill the elevated role of superparents. Just as "a son is never ashamed of his mother's lack of beauty," so no grandson finds the physical awkwardness of his grandparents distasteful.

The aspirations and expectations of the old therefore differ widely in America and in China. Undoubtedly many aged Americans accept the inevitable with grace, but nevertheless it is rare to meet an old person who does not refer to his age without a definite sense of either regret or bravado. The usual American reaction to old age is an open refusal to recognize it. Some, though financially able, refuse to retire while many of those who cease to work still go back to their offices day after day because they do not know what else to do. In an effort to provide an outlet for such persons, some companies have begun to hire them as routine clerical help. The Washington National Insurance Company of Evanston, Illinois, in 1952, employed in this capacity five men whose average age was over sixty and who formerly had held sales and executive positions at salaries up to about $18,000 a year.[1]

Other Americans who refuse to admit that they are past middle age seek to carry on through the antics of youthful exhibitionism. In this, Messrs. MacFadden and Willis, whom we met in a previous paragraph, have ample company. There are eighty-year-old grandmothers who hit the headlines by riding a motorcycle or by racing ancient autos between New York and Chicago. There are equally ancient males who achieve an evanescent fame by making a singing debut or climbing the interior steps of the Washington Monument on their hands. When the *Life* writer described the ocean-conquering Willis as an ancient mariner who defies age, he was merely giving the public what it wants. For the standard news peg for interviews with those who have become news worthy simply by reaching a ripe old age is their answer to the question of how to stay young though old. A typical response is that of a woman who, at one hundred years, attributed her long life to a "firm refusal to grow old."

The artificiality of the principal "solution" of the American old-age problem has been apparent for some time. The tenuous security of money—whether in savings, pensions, stocks and bonds, private insurance, or government benefits—disappears as economic forces chip it away bit by bit. As the index of inflation mounts, the index of security vanishes. The individual who has looked away from persons and to money for his salvation finds that he has made a losing gamble on one of the most unstable of life's rewards. In China, far more disastrous inflations than any America has ever known have periodically left the aged without individual economic resources. Within the last hundred years many currencies have been inflated out of existence, taking with them nearly all personal savings. But although this caused difficulties, it was not catastrophic, for the real security of the aged Chinese lay elsewhere. Also, the American half measures of employment in menial tasks, however worthy the aim of the employer may be, and maintaining the illusion of youth, however satisfactory it may at first appear, face two drawbacks in common. Neither course of action brings the desired happiness or sense of fulfillment, and both must be abandoned at some point.

It is for such reasons that the relatively recent science of geriatrics cannot be expected to produce significant results as long as it treats the old-age problem in America in terms of (a) more Social Security or fuller employment, (b) more thorough medical attention or more recreational facilities, or (c) maintaining the youthfulness of the aged. The need which these stopgaps cannot supply is one that is required by all humans: the feeling of belonging, of being an accepted, normal, and integral member of society, and of having some importance among his fellow human beings. As the number of Americans sixty-five years and over increases,[2] the aged find it increasingly difficult to integrate themselves into a divisive society. As the pace of normal society accelerates, the aged find it harder to keep up. Furthermore, a lengthened span of physical survival is no substitute for an abbreviated life of social worth. At the same time, since the whole approach of geriatrics is one of outsiders helping secondary citizens to be useful and happy, it cannot but be intolerable to the aged who wish to keep their self-respect, particularly when we recall that these persons have always lived by the ideal of self-reliance.

Some sociologists may take issue with the Chinese-American contrast drawn here. In particular they can point to a body of survey data in the United States since the 1950s showing that mutual aid (including physical and social care of the aged) and social activities (including visitation, joint recreational, and ceremonial activities) among kin members outside the nuclear family are not at all rare.[3] However, what these sociologists have not sufficiently taken into account and what they have certainly failed to understand is the fact that economic and social aids given the old are based on the donor's *choice*. Instead, one of these sociologists concludes that "the alienation from their families of most old people in America" is a "myth," and that this myth is "created and perpetrated by professional workers in the field of aging and by old people themselves."[4]

If alienation of the aged from their families is nothing but a myth, why do social workers and the old people themselves continue to operate on and entertain it? The sociologist's answer is that the old people who believe in neglect by children are most likely to be without children and the social workers see only the problem cases.[5] My view is that the first half of the explanation is untrue and the second half misunderstands the evidence.

In the first place, even results of attitude studies used by sociologists attacking the so-called "myth" indicate a strong desire for complete independence on the part of all parties concerned. "Young couples, when asked about accepting aid from parental families, almost universally reject this as an acceptable source of income." "Middle-aged parents are equally adamant in stating their expectation that they will never receive support from their children."[6] "These elderly people, products of the 'Protestant ethic' (or immigrants into it), *must* be independent in order to maintain their self-esteem. To many, even death is preferable to 'becoming a burden.'"[7]

It is clear that the nuclear nature of the American family is not simply a concept in the minds of old people without children or social workers who only see problem cases. Both groups do no more than express the general American orientation, which is amply confirmed by other inquiries.[8]

In the second place, Americans do not merely see the independence of the nuclear family and of the self as the desirable norm—a remote ideal. They actively live it. This is where the social workers find the data in support of their working principles. In their study of the aged in San Francisco (both healthy and sick) Clark and Anderson conclude that "a good relationship with children in old age depends, to a large extent, on the graces and autonomy of the aged parent—in short, on his ability to manage gracefully by himself. . . . The parent must remain strong and independent. If his resources fail, then conflict arises."[9]

What happens when the parent's resources fail? A visit to any institution for the aged will bear out Jules Henry's conclusion on "Human Obsolescence":

> As for the patients [in one public and two private institutions], they live out their last days in long stretches of *anxiety* and *silent reminiscing*, punctuated by outbursts of *petulance* at one another, by TV viewing, and by visits from their relatives. There is no inner peace, and *social life* is *minimal*. Meanwhile the patients *reach out* to the researcher and would engage her endlessly on conversation if she would stay. There is yearning *after communion but no real ability to achieve it*. In this we are all very much like them.[10]

Finally, it is in the United States, but not in China that the aged have become a specialized minority group with identifiable interests and formalized characteristics. In the 1953 edition of this book I wrote:

> Instead of resorting to geriatric agencies the aged in America increasingly flock to old people's homes where they can find some emotional security in relative equality, in contrast to their position in the society at large, among their aged fellows. In addition, instead of being able to relax during their last years, for the purpose of public education and legislative action in their interests, they are more and more compelled to give organizational form to the separate segment of society which they presently compose. Already the word "minority" has been applied to the aged in America.

We must note that both anticipated trends have become more evident than before. The aged form or join old people's colonies. California, Florida, and Arizona are among three of the most popular states for retirement communities. Residents of most of these colonies "voluntarily" segregate themselves from the outside world, develop clubs of their own centered entirely inside the community, and then sever connections with organizations in which they were active before. They claim a preference for their own company or allege that voluntary segregation has enabled them to enjoy "more contact with younger people" than others who did not. They patronize a whole group of magazines designed for the aged.[11] Since the early 1960s, they have been active in age associations that stand on the platform of "positive recognition to send aggressive demands for change across the age border."[12] Outstanding among these associations is the National Council of Senior Citizens, formed to fight for Medicare. It now has over two million members.

> They continue to demand respect, income, housing, and better medical care as the rights of all retired people. NCSC does not place polite requests for benefits before a benevolent society. Assuming a partner's place in the process of change, the Council argues from its members' experiences with using a retired constituent in their lives to the adjustments America must make to use a retired constituent in the culture.[13]

In other words, the older people have decided to "organize around their independence and their needs at the same time, instead of having to choose between admitting dependence in order to ask for assistance . . . or claiming independence by denying a need for assistance."[14]

The aged in the United States have voluntarily segregated themselves and become so well organized for positive demands precisely because they have no respected place in the self-reliant American culture. On the other hand, the aged in China did not have to segregate themselves and get organized (and still do not) because they automatically enjoy high esteem in the mutual dependence framework of the Chinese culture.

One can, of course, see that not all Chinese sons were filial to their parents, just as there are American cases where the old are well taken care of or never lose their status. The company of wealthy oldsters often is prized by relatives and friends; they are sought after by directors of charities and the heads of endowed institutions; their names frequently appear in the social columns. American elders who possess special talents that do not disappear with age, and those who have achieved national fame and distinction are often equally fortunate. The public concern about President Eisenhower through his many heart ailments is but one example. But the neglected oldsters in China and the pampered septuagenarians in the United States are both relative minorities among the aged in their respective societies. The many American epithets such as the "old fogey farm," the "vegetable patch," and the "freeloaders," for retirement communities and their residents,[15] are indicative of the deep-seated American attitude toward the aged.

There will be little reason for the Chinese to regard age as a problem so long as they maintain their pattern of continuity between the generations, whereby age brings not penalty but honor. And we should not forget the ancient teaching that the individual must be prepared for a fall even when at the summit of his power. Hence the proverb says:

> No human can abide in health and peace for three years
> Any more than a flower can retain its bloom for a hundred days.

Generation Gap

"Teen-agers Tell of Arson on West Side"; "Son of Victim Held as Bandit"; "Boy Attacker of Four Women Gets 2–24 Years"; "Two Boys Admit They Tried to Wreck Trains"; "Sex Orgies Involving Four Teen-age Girls"; "Boy, 16, Kills 3 Kin over Use of Car." These were familiar items of each day's newspaper when this book first saw print in 1953. Today, these are still frequent headlines. Most people would unhesitatingly term these to be instances of juvenile delinquency. But with the many student riots on famous campuses such as Columbia and California, the papers are flooded with another kind of headlines: "Black Students Call a Boycott"; "NYU Head Says

Students May Picket"; "U. of C. Students Tent-In to Protest Housing Policy"; "Pot Party at a University"; "Student Radicals Agree to Back Mexican Revolt"; and "Hippie Victim Buried in Suburban Dignity." To most of these the term juvenile delinquency is not applied. Instead we now speak of the generation gap.

Do the massive student protests, the hippie and yippie movements, the waves of dropouts and runaways—all of whom feel alienated from the adult world and the American culture—constitute new developments? I submit that they do not. Both the more recent developments and much of the more familiar juvenile delinquency are manifestations of the same generation gap. Self-reliance cannot but sharpen the demarcation between the generations. The problem of the aged is one facet of that sharpened demarcation; adolescent and youthful turbulence, dissatisfaction and disillusionment, are another.

Many causes have been attributed to adolescent crimes: physical growth leading to the ability to defy parental control, glandular disturbances, poverty, release from school, lack of legal responsibility, occupational uncertainty, confusion of values, and many more. For a time, many writers, educators, parents, and welfare workers attacked the "danger" of comic books. Fredric Wertham, a popular psychiatrist, pronounced comic books to be the "common denominator of boyhood aggression and adolescent crimes."[16] A Senate committee report on comic books stressed their "delinquency-producing effects."[17]

The various explanations appear impressive until we consider the fact that, though all of these alleged causes of youthful crimes are to be found in China, the Chinese have had no problem of adolescent criminality.[18] In truth, many of the "causes" attributed to adolescent criminality in this country are present in China to an even greater extent. All human beings are subject to the same biological changes; all reach a point where they can physically defy their parents. Furthermore, before 1949 not all Chinese youngsters of school age were in school; most of them never went to school. During the first half of the twentieth century, Chinese young men and women in urban centers suffered from worse than occupational uncertainty; most of them knew long periods of unemployment or were exploited as apprentices in blind-alley trades. Since late in the nineteenth century, youths in China, both educated and uneducated, were confronted with every confusion of values and ideas imaginable. The educated in particular were forced to wrestle with foreign "isms" coming from every direction, and most were simply caught between knowledge acquired in school and old mores still practiced at home.

Chinese youngsters in urban areas were also exposed to comic books. These were purchased or rented at a fraction of a cent per day. On many streets of Shanghai were rows of bookstands purveying such series as "Small Folks Books." Among the themes were murder, robbery, mayhem, and kidnaping. Though lacking in ultrascientific adventures, Chinese comic books contained gory accounts of the supernatural. In place of Western characters like Hopalong Cassidy, they had female vigilantes such as "The Thirteenth Sister." Both Chinese and American comics share one additional trait—crime does not pay.

Despite these seemingly basic similarities, adolescents among the two peoples behave very differently. American parents and educators consider adolescence as a period marked by numerous forms of behavior difficulties including even the tendency to criminality. The Chinese did not even have a term for adolescence, and have never been plagued by the problem of the youthful offender. Crime statistics can never tell us the full, or perhaps not even a completely accurate story, but as symptoms they are useful. For example, during the most efficient years of the Nationalist government, 1931 to 1933, when police records were fairly accurate, statistics show that Chinese males between thirteen and twenty committed less crime than all other seven-year groups under fifty-one[;] of these juvenile crimes, minor offenses predominated.[19]

In the United States, various sources indicate the preponderance among all criminals, not only of youthful male offenders (especially in the age bracket of seventeen to twenty), but also of major crimes committed by them. Furthermore, while the crime statistics in the United States also leave much to be desired, there is insistent evidence that the juvenile crime rate has been and is on the increase, dramatically outstripping the population increase at least in some categories such as assault and property offenses.[20]

The problem of narcotics addiction [...] is equally illuminating. The usual view is that juveniles fall victim to the habit because of the peddler, the foreign smuggler, the uncertainties of an "era of crisis," or poverty. But the truth is that juveniles do not simply *fall* victims to external inducements. For nearly a century China suffered from dope peddlers, foreign smugglers, and political and economic crises. Even the Japanese and Korean narcotics dens protected and promoted by powerful invaders since the middle thirties did not create a juvenile addiction problem in China.

The occurrence of juvenile delinquency or its absence is in each case part of a larger cultural context. Neither can be understood by resorting to these myopic explanations. Instead they must be examined in terms of the overriding influence exerted by a people's way of life.

There are, as detailed [earlier], very distinct differences between the social atmospheres breathed by Chinese and American children. The world of Chinese children is not divorced from their parents' world. From the first, they are in contact with the Janus-face of mankind; they have impressed upon them the importance of obedience to social conventions; they learn the distinction between what their parents say and what their elders in fact do. By adolescence, they have learned most of the ropes.

Except among the very poor or immigrants from southern and eastern Europe, American children generally lead an existence quite distinct from that of their parents. The self-reliance that is emphasized in family training undeniably encourages behavior superficially imitative of adult life. But this simulation of adult roles is a totally ineffective substitute for a real initiation into adult life, since the sole concern of the former is with the surface aspects of the latter. There is little to give the adolescent an awareness of human frailties and strengths, a realistic introduction into what are commonly called the ways of the world.[21]

This becomes difficult or impossible because the teaching of self-reliance has another and far more significant consequence: as children grow, the gulf between them and their parents progressively widens. From the first, the elders have interests and activities that they pursue while the child remains with a sitter. Having no integrated place in their parents' doings, the youngsters soon find in their playmates a society that is equally exclusive and in turn unconcerned with the world of its elders. It is therefore vain to hope, as some educators and parents presently do, that television may restore that family unity which they say has been undermined by the attractions of non-family commercial amusements. It is plain that the American family bond has not been weakened or destroyed by the lack of home entertainments, and its cohesion will not be restored by such artificial solutions.[22]

It is thus not surprising that the majority of Americans enter adolescence with a romantic concept of life. Unprepared for the imperfections of the real world, they tend to be easily disillusioned. Humanity's inconsistencies and weaknesses, especially when discovered in those whom they have idolized, confuse or shock young persons whose idealized view of life proves no guide to its true nature. These experiences come as no surprise to Chinese adolescents.

Furthermore, while Chinese parents, reflecting the pattern of mutual dependence, welcome their children's progress toward adulthood, the American pattern of self-reliance causes parents to erect barriers to their offspring's independence. The first direct presentation of this conflict occurs at school age, but when children enter adolescence the struggle becomes more pronounced. For at this point American parents see before them the threat of being completely relegated to the background. They tend, naturally enough, to react by intensifying their efforts to delay or prevent their children's full independence. In this campaign, the elders have a variety of resources at their disposal: love, money, persuasion, and personal or legal force.

This leads to a situation often unbearable to the American adolescent. Having been raised to be self-reliant, he is now resentful toward efforts to turn him back from his self-seeking activities. In addition, the highly competitive American society demands that the self-respecting individual achieve success as quickly as possible. Even the boundary of legality need not restrain him. For, like the successful and therefore respected businessman who prides himself on operating "just within the law," the adolescent reduces himself to the principle of "anything goes" so long as you don't get caught. Disillusioned by the inconsistencies of the real adult world,[23] innocent of its intricacies but pressed by the desire to achieve success in a hurry, the American adolescent finds himself in far greater difficulties than he experienced during his grade school days. His parents' concern over him now only seems authoritarian, and more of a stumbling block to his freedom than before. But, standing alone, his insecurity vis-à-vis reality seems also greater than before. He cannot retreat from this dilemma without losing his self-respect.

The result is emotional agitation. Since individuals differ widely in their temperament, intelligence, and circumstances, this emotional turbulence expresses itself in diverse ways, which include mild forms such as sulky moods, quarrelsomeness, incorrigibility, hostility to parents, and the more drastic forms of misconduct such as drag racing, joy rides in stolen autos, robbery, sex orgies, narcotics addiction, and apparently unmotivated murder.

However, we shall never unearth the root of juvenile delinquency in America as long as we regard it as a matter of youth being led astray by a few bad influences or unfortunate individual circumstances that may be locally adjusted. In the 1953 edition of this book I wrote:

> For, quite apart from those forms of misconduct usually described as crimes, there are other and sometimes more ominous phenomena which are rarely pointed out as a juvenile problem. For example, in the St. Louis, Mo., riot of June 21, 1949, when public swimming pools were opened to Negroes, *Life* magazine (July 4, 1949) reported that "teenagers made up a surprisingly large percentage of the rioters. In the Cicero, Illinois, affair of 1951, when a Negro family moved into an all-white apartment house, all Chicago newspapers reported a preponderance of youthful rioters.

What we saw in the early 1950s were minor samples of what we have since witnessed on a grander scale: riots and sit-ins on the campus, the hippie and yippie love-ins in the streets, the proliferation of the use of drugs, the drop-outs and the cop-outs, the "student power" anti-draft and anti-Vietnam demonstrations, the violence of the civil rights movement, and the bloodshed of the Chicago Democratic Convention—all of which are predominantly youth-oriented.

The reader will probably at once note that, in this brief account of disturbances involving youth, from robbery to civil rights demonstrations. I have combined the lawful and the illegal, those with lofty purposes and those that are anti-social by any definition, and those in support of racial prejudices and those that aim at bringing about justice. This I have done advisedly. For the American youth, in his search for independence, is confronted with a complex of possibilities, none of which is very close to him but all or any one of which may become urgent at any particular time. But the central thing is some action to give meaning to the needs of the self. As one youth puts it:

> One year I joined in to "ban the bomb"; another year it was stylish to demand "civil rights"; this year the call is for "peace in Vietnam." But where is the real immediacy

of any of these causes for me? It is difficult to act on an abstraction. It has taken the exclusiveness of black power for me to realize that my battle with society also must be concrete and personally direct; conviction can only be sincere when the battle is to improve your life and not your soul. As I see things now the only real issue for me at this time is draft resistance. I can meaningfully express my general outrage about the war in Vietnam by specifically resisting the immediate threat of being drafted to serve in that war. Protest without some personal investment, without putting something on the line, becomes hollow; it becomes no more than a caricature of itself.[24]

The particular goals and methods used are, then, far less important than the stresses facing the identity-seeking youth in a self-reliant way of life. These stresses cannot be pinned on a single source (such as "identity crisis"), but come from a concatenation of circumstances. On one side is [the] transitory and insecure nature of all the individual's human relationships. On the other side is his parents' increased interference (real or imagined) with his freedom and independence because they are also threatened by the same transitory and insecure nature of all their human relationships. Finally these opposing forces operate in a culture that sanctifies success for the sake of success. Under the circumstances the American youth defends himself against the instability of his human relationships by making sure of his acceptance in some group. He furthers his needs for success by attaining some position of achievement in the group that accepts him. He also has to accomplish his efforts without consistent direction other than that of the dictates of his group.

The misconduct of the Chinese adolescent is more of an individual matter; his behavior is rarely dictated by his peer group. For the one group to which he is closely attached, and consequently the one group whose rules or commands have any real meaning, is the kinship group. If he gets into trouble, he not only incurs the displeasure of his parents and kinsmen, but he receives little moral support from most persons his own age. Those who support his misconduct will surely be termed by society as "fox friends and dog comrades."[25]

The American adolescent's misconduct is likely to be the price of belonging to his own age group. Trouble with the law merely hurts his parents, whom he often intentionally disregards, but it earns him a firmer place among his own gang, and it is their rejection he fears. Under this compulsion, he is likely to do anything dictated by his gang.[26]

[...]

WORLD UNREST: COMMUNISM AND AMERICA

The present situation of America, remote as the proposition might at first appear, can be viewed as somewhat analogous to China's position when, in a consequence of external pressures, the society's internal mechanisms were confronted by problems for which they were not fashioned to deal. America, like China, for many years rejoiced in its isolation from the rest of the world. Insulated from warring Europe and chaotic Asia by two great oceans, Americans were free to shape their own destiny in their own way. The Great Wall psychology was as true of America as it was of China. Then, almost without warning, the walls crumbled, the oceans were reduced to ponds, and geographic distance no longer meant security. Neither people were able to ignore the world any longer; complete freedom of action disappeared forever. In countless ways, the world was making its presence felt in similarly numberless aspects of individual and national life.

In both societies many persons, trapped between the patterns of psychological satisfaction to which they are accustomed and the realities of the present, either despair of the future or point to the past as the only hope. In China the dream is to return to Confucianism; in the United States complete self-reliance and unbridled free enterprise are still idealized. Likewise, in both countries some make a fetish of ignoring and retreating from the troubles around them, seeking individual refuge in art, business, entertainment, or scientific inquiry, while still others dream of finding a single, simple solution, which overnight would set matters aright. This is what occurs whenever walls are breached.

Here, however, the similarity ends. We must now take into account once again the great difference in the manner of life that was led behind the protective barriers. China's way of life was static. She was the sleeping lion, and the problem was to awaken her and to substitute action for the torpor that had enfeebled her. The American condition is quite the opposite. Americanism is almost synonymous with dynamism. It is no accident that in the history of American life we see a new optimism, a new vision, an almost ecstatic carefreeness unknown to the rest of the world. The dream of unlimited expansion and unlimited progress, while first recorded in European thought, was given embodiment in the living achievements of American life. For those achievements Americans need apologize to no one, neither to those "artistic" souls here or abroad who have quailed before the specter of "materialism," nor to their own consciences.

The fact is that America is the envy of the world, in spite of the resentment and even hatred against her,[27] particularly of those millions who have been so occupied with the problems of survival that, unlike many well-fed bohemians and intellectuals, they find this misnamed materialism very appealing. The American press and the United States information agencies thought they had struck propaganda pay dirt when in 1950 (during the Korean War) the Chinese Communist mission to the United Nations General Assembly went on a buying spree in New York. But Chinese visitors to the United States have always indulged themselves in this fashion, acquiring cameras, household appliances, and autos. Among Chinese students, a description of the ideal life was to live in an American house (for its conveniences), to eat Chinese food (for its delicate satisfactions to the alimentary tract), and to marry a Japanese wife (for her obedience to the master).

Furthermore, far more than her so-called material achievements, American democracy has exercised a still greater attraction to those people who have suffered under warlords, emperors, and despots of all hues and forms. Malfunctions there may be in the American government, just as the economic plenitude of America may be purchased in part at the cost of other values, but most of mankind in its misery and subjection would show no hesitation whatsoever if they could exchange their world for the one in which Americans live.

This is one cause of the difficulties that America faces in Asia today. Until not very long ago, the world's non-Western peoples looked upon the achievements of the West with astonishment, fear, and probably envy. But Western ways were not their ways. They did not aspire to take on those ways; they also did not know how. The situation [has] changed greatly and rapidly since World War II. Those who once were overawed now know many of the means by which the West achieves its ends. Those once held in thrall by fear have since discovered cracks in the Western power and have witnessed the spectacle of Western armies being defeated by Asian forces. Those once resigned to envy of the West are now convinced that they are capable of improving their material welfare and terminating their status as inferiors.

The immediate causes of unrest vary from place to place. The goals of organized groups, their methods, and the nature of their leadership also are different. But the basic issues are everywhere the same. The few remaining colonial and semi-colonial lands are straining against the chains that have bound them, and the newly independent but economically and politically still-weak nations are straining to better themselves in the Western model. It is into the resulting struggle which America has been almost imperceptibly drawn.

The American Dilemma

America has spent billions for the economic recovery of Western Europe and continues to spend billions for its military security. This is done not out of charity or sentiment, but for strategic reasons of self-defense. This would be difficult enough if the problem were confined to Europe, but it is not. The former and present European colonies, protectorates, and spheres of influence are beset by dual pressures that often commingle and coalesce. Native liberation movements and internal tensions or simple struggles for power frequently are penetrated by Communists so that, as the chief exponent of the fight against Communism, America becomes labeled as the abettor and even the inheritor of imperialism—and with good reason. After unsuccessfully aiding the French to crush the Vietnamese independence fighters, America simply slipped into the former colonial master's shoes and Americanized the war in Vietnam. In the process she tried to keep in power first the playboy emperor Bao Dai, then the dictator Diem, and finally military men Thieu and Ky and their generals, some of whom were in the first place actually fighting on the side of the French against their own countrymen. Would the American people have tolerated as heads of their government men who had collaborated with their enemies?

[...]

I have tried to show that, for lack of a better word, Western spirituality is a consequence of the individual's detachment from the primary groups. This spirituality is responsible both for the material magnificence of Western culture and also for its recurring determination to destroy what it has created. It is this committal to the abstract which is responsible for a government of laws and a bill of rights, but it also makes it possible for the West to kill millions of men in the name of the salvation of mankind. It is the doctrine of absolute evil that enables the West to be so relentless in its attack upon social ills but, in its complement as the belief in absolute good, leads Westerners into imposing their particular brand of the good upon each other and upon other peoples of the world.

And I wish to say further that the purposelessness and insecurity of the liberated individual will not be redressed with any degree of permanence by a restoration or reaffirmation of "faith," be it political, economic, or moral. The road that begins in individualism and self-reliance travels surely and directly to the totalitarian state. Paradoxical though this seems to be, the present direction of Western society is proof enough of its validity. In pursuing self-reliance, the individualist societies undermine kinship and community ties, prevent intimacy among human beings except in the marital sphere, consciously attack all customs and traditions, and glorify instability and change. If there is no longer the unity of the primary group, there is the unity of the Communist party or the Hitler Youth Corps, or the yippie colony, or a secret society for anti-Establishment, or the Ku Klux Klan, or the crime syndicate. If direction is no longer provided by custom and tradition, there is the demagogue to point the way. If instability and change leave us without anchorage, the police state is ready to assign us a place and a number in the scheme of things. If, in sum, we do not "belong," if we are purposeless and insecure, Big Brother is ready to admit us to his society, solve our problems for us, and otherwise provide us with what we desire. He grants us the opportunity for emotional release in gigantic parades, monstrous rallies, and organized violence. He gives us the fanatical "faith" the Western spirit craves: the absolutes, the abstractions, a sense of mission and infallibility, the symbols to hate and the symbols to love. He asks but one price, and this price millions have proved themselves ready to pay: the surrender of personal freedom.

Extreme individualism thus ends by destroying the liberty it intended to defend, and Western society as a whole wrecks itself against the rocks upon which it builds. With the advent of ultimate weapons, Western men now hold the potentiality of destroying the world with them in this process. It is indeed ironic that Americans, having jointly with other Westerners broken down Japanese and Chinese doors and foisted their presence on the Asians, had to use the atom bomb on the Japanese and even now think they need anti-ballistic missiles to "protect" themselves against the Chinese. Those who believe in destruction will surely project their own belief onto others.

The Communist appeal to the West and to China is thus of two different kinds, though, in the most fundamental sense, Communism has found its source of strength in a response to what was, in each case, the basic weakness of the society. However, despite the fact that the Communists have triumphed in China while they have at least been brought to a temporary standstill in the West, I cannot but believe that in the long run the West, by way of the irrevocable polarization of its individual-centered peoples behind major or minor causes, stands in more serious danger of succumbing to Communism or some other brand of totalitarianism than does China.

The Chinese are not motivated by abstract principles. They believed themselves to be superior to others, but never saw themselves as the chosen people who alone would live while all others would perish. They do not see the world or mankind as irreparably divided between the absolutely good and the absolutely evil, the completely just and the completely unjust. The Chinese do not commit themselves to a god—be that god a religious deity, a philosopher of dialectical materialism, or a little father in Moscow or Peiping. They lack the zeal of the missionary—be that missionary a preacher of Christianity or Marxism—to carry the one message of truth to the unenlightened, much less to enforce that message upon the disinterested or unwilling. National militancy, class struggle, inevitable war, unconditional surrender—all of these are ideas that fit the Western pattern of life but which are in fact wholly alien to the Chinese. If the Chinese believe that there is sin, it is the unforgivable fault of setting son against father, group against group, and insisting that one man, class, race, religion, or nation must drive another to ruin and construct the future upon the wreckage.

Why these things are so has been the subject of this book. The Chinese have their place. They belong. They, therefore, do not give themselves irrevocably to gods or heroes, nor do they seek the infinite or attempt to control the finite. The fundamental impulse of the Chinese is to live and let live and thus preserve what they cherish most—the solidity of human relations within the primary group, and the assurance that human relations beyond it will help and not endanger it. Between the individual and the totalitarian state, protecting the freedom of the former and warding off the impositions of the latter, stands this primary group and all those institutional bulwarks of men and custom which arise out of it and are associated with it. But in the West, as every year passes, between the individual and his freedom and the state and its authority there is less of this type of protection. It is just

this bulwark of human solidarity that individualism and self-reliance have succeeded in weakening and even destroying. And it is upon these troubled ruins that
totalitarianism arises.

NOTES

1. Chicago *Daily News,* June 12, 1952.

2. In 1900 only 4.1 per cent of the population was sixty-five or older. In 1940 the figure reached 6.8
per cent. The estimated figure for 1960 is 20 per cent (according to L. A. Scheele, U.S. Surgeon-General,
in *Parade* magazine, January 27, 1952).

3. The best summary I know of these recent findings is given by Marvin B. Sussman, "Relationships
of Adult Children with Their Parents," in *Social Structure and the Family: Generational Relations,* edited
by Ethel Shanas and Gordon F. Streib (Englewood Cliffs, New Jersey, 1965), pp. 68–70.

4. Ethel Shanas, "The Unmarried Old Person in the United States: Living Arrangements and Care
in Illness, Myth and Fact," paper prepared for the International Social Science Research Seminar in
Gerontology, Markaryd, Sweden, August 1963, quoted in Margaret Blenker, "Social Work and Family
Relationships in Labor Life with Some Thoughts on Filial Maturity," Chapter 3 in *Social Structure and
the Family, Generational Relations,* p. 50.

5. Shanas and Streib, *Social Structure and the Family, Generational Relations,* p. 49.

6. Sussman, "Relationships of Adult Children with Their Parents," p. 79.

7. Margaret Clark and Barbara Gallatin Anderson, *Culture and Aging: An Anthropological Study of
Older Americans* (Springfield, Ill., 1967).

8. Helen Codere, "A Genealogical Study of Kinship," *Psychiatry,* Vol. 18, No. 1, February 1955,
pp. 65–79; and David Schneider, *American Kinship: A Cultural Account* (Englewood Cliffs, New Jersey,
1968).

9. Clark and Anderson, *Culture and Aging,* p. 275, reprinted by permission of Charles C. Thomas.

10. Jules Henry, *Culture Against Man,* © 1963 by Random House, Inc. Reprinted by permission.

11. For example, *Modern Maturity, Senior Citizen, Dynamic Maturity,* and *Harvest Years.*

12. Jennie-Keith Hill, "The Culture of Retirement" (unpublished Ph.D. dissertation, Anthropology
Dept., Northwestern University, 1968), p. 194.

13. Ibid., p. 194.

14. Ibid.

15. Some other epithets are the "elephant farm," "old people's Russian roulette," "foyers to the tomb,"
"waiting rooms for death," "public housing for well-to-do," "geriatric ghettos," "geriatric capitals," and
"sunset skyscrapers." Ibid., Appendix.

16. *Saturday Review of Literature,* May 29, 1948.

17. "Comic Books and Juvenile Delinquency," Interim Report of the Committee on the Judiciary,
Report No. 62, 1955, Washington, D.C., Government Printing Office. Later Senate hearings were held
on the role of television in juvenile delinquency: *Juvenile Delinquency, Television Programs,* Hearings
held April 6 and 7, 1955, before the Subcommittee to Investigate Juvenile Delinquency of the Committee
on the Judiciary, 1955, Washington, D.C., U.S. Government Printing Office.

18. Since World War II and the establishment of the power of the Nationalist regime, Taiwan has
reported some problems in this area. The peculiar political circumstances on that island and the lack of
information from mainland China since 1949 have made it necessary for me to deal only with China
before 1949. Where applicable I shall also draw upon my knowledge of the Chinese in Hawaii.

19. From the police files of fourteen capital cities. (*Ministry of the Interior Year Book,* 1936,
Shanghai.)

20. Some students have cautioned against "an alarmist attitude" toward juvenile crime. Thus Wolfgang, noting the lack of sharp increases of [the] juvenile crime rate in certain categories such as rape and murder while admitting sharp increases in other categories such as various forms of assault, maintains that "any overall increase in juvenile delinquency can be largely attributed to the population increase in the ages from 14 to 18." This seems to me to be a complacent view. Why should the "overall increase in juvenile delinquency" keep pace with population increase in spite of our better schools, better counseling services, better recreation facilities, better prevention and detection measures as well as unprecedented material prosperity? Isn't this an admission that all such efforts including education are useless? On the other hand, Wolfgang argues that "a certain amount of delinquency has always existed, will continue to exist, and perhaps should exist." He notes that the "attributes associated with the delinquents sound similar to descriptions of the Renaissance Man who defied the authority and static orthodoxy of the middle ages, who was aggressive, richly assertive, this-world rather than other-world centered, and was less banal, more innovative, than his medieval predecessors." (Marvin E. Wolfgang, "The Culture of Youth," Office of Juvenile Delinquency, Welfare Administration, U.S. Department of Health, Education and Welfare, 1967, reproduced in *Task Force Report: Juvenile Delinquency and Youth Crime*, President's Commission on Law Enforcement and Administration of Justice, U.S. Government Printing Office, Washington, D.C., 1967, p. 152.) Here Wolfgang sees juvenile delinquency in terms of the wider context of social change, and his view is in essential agreement with the thesis of this book. This will be dealt with when we examine Chinese weaknesses in the next chapter.

21. Some scholars see this contrast as between agricultural (or "primitive") and industrialized (or "modern") societies. The fact is that the parent-child relationship even among second and third generation Chinese in Hawaii is still close to the Chinese pattern described.

22. The unpopularity of the Vietnam War did not create the generation gap. The inconsistency between forcing youths to die for a colonial-type struggle when they have been brought up to side with the underdog has merely aggravated the gap that already existed. The ending of the Vietnam War will, therefore, not end or even reduce it.

23. This disillusionment is the single major component of the alienation described by Kenneth Keniston in his book *The Uncommitted* (New York, 1960).

24. Richard Lorber and Ernest Fladell, "The Generation Gap," *Life* magazine, May 17, 1968. Reprinted by permission.

25. Some readers may regard the activities of the Red Guards as conflicting with these observations. But [. . .] the Red Guards were instigated as a *new* political movement designed to induce youths away from their parents.

26. The dictates of the group range from the literal to the abstract. Two widely publicized killings are illustrative. On June 26, 1952, two New York City youths, aged sixteen and seventeen, after accepting a "dare" to kill someone, murdered a man they had never seen before. In their confession, they said they killed the stranger to prove they "weren't chicken." Three days before this, a twenty-nine-year-old war veteran walked into the office of the American Physical Society at Columbia University and shot and killed an eighteen-year-old stenographer, the only person present at the time. The reason? The society had repeatedly refused to publish a treatise he had written, and so he decided to murder "a lot of physicists" to secure publicity for his views. In these two crimes, one committed by youths who apparently had no previous record of delinquency, and the other by a young man with a lengthy history of psychiatric disorders, there is a common factor: the desire for recognition. To obtain or retain the esteem of others, two "normal" youths killed a stranger; seeking revenge upon those who had denied him a place of respect, who had prevented his success, an "abnormal" youth committed the same act. Whatever distinctions psychiatrists might draw between these two cases, it is plain that society's demands upon the individuals concerned were different only in the degree of their literalness.

27. We shall deal with the subject of Asian and African resentment of the United States below. Here we need to note that resentment or hatred is not incommensurate with envy.

REFERENCES

Commager, Henry S. 1970 [1953]. Introduction to Francis L. K. Hsu. *Americans and Chinese: Purpose and Fulfillment in Great Civilizations* Garden City, NY: Doubleday Natural History Press. Pp. xxi–xxviii.

Nagata, Shuichi. 1972. "Review of Americans and Chinese: Purpose and Fulfillment in Great Civilizations." *American Anthropologist,* Vol. 74, No. 4: 835–836.

Têng, Ssu-Yü, and John K. Fairbank. 1954. *China's Response to the West: A Documentary Survey, 1839–1923.* Cambridge, MA: Harvard University Press.

17

Some Thoughts on Certain Aspects of Modern Western Culture

Zhao Fusan, 1987

After relations between the United States and China were normalized under President Richard Nixon, American academics traveled to China. One sociologist friend of mine summarized his visit by noting that in China all problems were considered to be social problems, to which I responded that in the United States all problems are seen to be personal problems. In the following reading Zhao Fusan discusses the sources of social and personal problems in the two societies.

Born in Shanghai in 1926, Zhao Fusan received his BA from Saint John's University in 1946, and the following year began working for the Young Men's Christian Association in Beijing. He worked at the Institute of World Religions and the Chinese Academy of Social Sciences and served as CASS vice-president in the 1980s. From 1985 to 1989 Zhao represented China at the United Nations Educational, Scientific, and Cultural Organization (UNESCO). During the June 4, 1989, Tiananmen Square massacre he was the leader of a UNESCO delegation meeting in Paris at which all the delegates were shocked by the news of Tiananmen Square. Zhao publically said he was shocked by the Tiananmen massacre, expressed condolences to the victims, and noted that China's history would be affected by the event from that time on. Worried that he would be escorted to Beijing, Zhao decided not to return to China but went to his daughter's home in Paris. From that time on he was in exile, spending the next ten years in both Europe and the United States, where he taught at the University of Oklahoma. After retirement he moved to Belgium. Among his scholarly publications is *The History of Christianity in China* (1979), published in Chinese under the pseudonym of Yang Zhen.

In 1987, the Foreign Broadcast Information Service in Beijing published "Some Thoughts on Modern Western Culture," lectures by Zhao Fusan. These talks take the approach that

Zhao Fusan. 1987. "Some Thoughts on Certain Aspects of Modern Western Culture—Notes on Book Reading," Parts I and II. In "Renmin Ribao on Modern Western Culture," Parts I and II. *FBIS [Foreign Broadcast Information Service] Daily Report: China*, No. 067 (April 8): K28–K35, and No. 072 (April 15): K21–K29.

understanding another culture requires a long-term view because culture is never at a standstill—it develops over time. Fusan introduces one hundred–odd years of Western scholarship analyzing the "morbid state of Western culture" to supplement what the Chinese might already know. For data he uses analyses of the Western capitalist political system written not by Chinese Marxist scholars but rather by Western scholars such as John Locke, Jacques Barzun, Robert Nisbet, Robert Bellah, Daniel Bell, and Seymour Martin Lipset. Fusan compares Chinese and Western civilization as part of the discussion among alarmed Chinese academics motivated by the question, Why are some Chinese envious of and impressed with Western culture without knowing why? Endeavoring to understand why the United States is the most popular foreign destination for young Chinese, Fusan examines relations between the individual and society. The scope of his writings is inclusive and multidisciplinary.

Part I of "Renmin Ribao on Modern Western Culture" asks the question, "Is democratic theory for export?" the title of a talk given by Jacques Barzun in 1986 in which he asked, "What is the democratic theory we want to export?" Barzun's conclusion was that democracy does not have a theory, but is a general principle. The best system of mankind for liberty's sake is rule by the people. The democratic principle is related to social equality and freedom.

In his second topic, "Capitalist Society and the Way of Life Bred in It," Fusan reports that American sociologists observe that individual success is a central motivating factor in American life, achievable as long as a person works hard. This creates competition among citizens and isolates one from the rest, thereby corroding social ethics and morality. Fusan reminds us that in *American Democracy,* Alexis de Tocqueville referred to the existence of isolated individuals as running counter to democratic ideals. Drawing on Robert Bellah's work on the American middle class and the place of work and success in restricting people's concern with larger society, Fusan concludes that the "poverty in materialism" is unhealthy for society and that China must hold it in check. Of course we know that did not happen.

In Part II, Fusan pursues "the concept of the value of individualism" to illustrate that as capitalism has developed it has tended to ignore public welfare in favor of individual interests. The author takes his argument back to John Locke, whose seventeenth-century theory provides the philosophical basis for the "modern ideology of individualism," which, Fusan argues, has brought about the individual's spiritual loneliness. Fusan ponders what China's acceptance of state capitalism might hold. The questions he considers deal with "the internal contradictions of the capitalist system" and the fundamental contradiction between bureaucratic organizations and the principle of equality. As China begins to modernize, Fusan notes, it could avoid problems by learning from Western thinkers.

That was 1987. By 2014 many of the problems isolated by American sociologists years earlier were being felt not only in the United States but also in China.

. . .

RENMIN RIBAO ON MODERN
WESTERN CULTURE—PART I

For some time, academic circles have conducted many discussions about the comparison between Chinese and Western cultures. It is no doubt necessary to use the gains and losses experienced by foreign countries for reference in the course of building the socialist culture of our country. Due to my own indolence, I have not read many articles on the analysis of Western culture and often feel as if something were missing. After all, all human societies must make a thorough inquiry into the relations between man and the natural world and readjust the relations between individuals and society in order to achieve the coordinated development of society and its members, thus generating culture. The cultural scope in its broad sense is very big and includes material civilization, political systems, education, science, literature, art, philosophy, religions, morality, customs, and modes of social life. In our usual discussion about civilization, we, for the greater part, refer to the narrow sense of culture—the part of spiritual civilization which is the aspect of the relations between individuals and society. It is only in this aspect that contents are very extensive. Moreover, since culture is part of history, it is not at a standstill and solidified but continuously develops; there are unavoidably various trends in the course of development. This makes it harder for Chinese people to study Western civilization. It is therefore a very necessary long-term work to seriously study it. In the hope that China will enter the world's advanced ranks in material and spiritual civilization as soon as possible, people are envious of Western culture. It seems unnecessary to cherish such envy when they [Westerners] do not know why they cherish it. Over the past 100-odd years, Western scholars with breadth of vision regardless of whether they were Marxists or not, unceasingly analyzed the morbid state of Western culture. It is a pity that very little of this analysis has been introduced into China. The Chinese people's observation and understanding of Western capitalist culture is somewhat limited. In studying Western social culture, except for our own perceptual knowledge, we must have the aid of Western social scientists' study of the society in which they live. Our own perceptual knowledge and Western social scientists' study often supplement each other.

The culture of an era cannot be divorced from ideology or, as [it] is often called now, the concept of value. It is expressed in the mode of social life and in the political system which upholds everything. The political system is the most concentrated and obvious part, next is people's mode of life, and the concept of value is the most abstract. These are the problems in which intellectual circles at home are now quite interested. Therefore, we might as well study the analysis and appraisal of the contemporary capitalist ideological theory and ideology in three aspects—the capitalist political system, mode of life, and concept of value—by some Western scholars who are not Marxists.

"Can a Democratic Theory Be Exported?"

This was the subject of a speech recently delivered on invitation by Jacques Barzun, adviser on humanities to the president of Columbia University in the United States and professor of history and cultural studies, on 17 September 1986, at the

Morgenthau Memorial Seminar, held once a year by the Carnegie Association of Ethics and International Affairs.

At the outset of his speech, Professor Barzun said that the U.S. foreign policy had been frequently expressed in that it hoped that the other countries would adopt a U.S.-type democratic system. "However ... what on earth do we want other people to copy? What is, after all, the democratic theory we want to export? With the existence of all kinds of different democratic systems, which constitution is the best? What is the basis of its theory? Over the past 40 years, due to the marked achievements in the communist theory of Marx and Lenin, our need for theory is even more urgent. . . . The theory which competes with ours is apparently more attractive and persuasive. We have imputed all this to the fact that the other side has eloquent agents and we do not have our own theory."

Can it be said that only a small number of books and journals introduce Western democracy? According to Barzun, the question is: "Different people put forward different answers and this put us in a weak position at the very beginning. Some people will mention the 'Declaration of Independence' and the Federal Constitution and other people will mention Rousseau, Edmund Burke, or Thomas Paine. There are also two volumes of a masterpiece, 'American Democracy' by de Tocqueville, and a wonderful booklet on the British Constitution by Walter Bagehot, not to mention the literature of all southern states and the eloquent masterpieces of John Adams, Thomas Jefferson, and Abraham Lincoln. Speaking in general terms, these works can be regarded as constituting democratic theory. However, they cannot constitute a system and are inconsistent. The spokesmen for the southern states feared democracy and John Adams and Thomas Paine contradicted each other and were only partially consistent with Jefferson. The contradictions between the works of Burke and those of Rousseau are even more obvious. De Tocqueville pointed out the special conditions of the United States and showed that the U.S. system could not be transplanted. Bagehot also came to a similar conclusion on Great Britain: Only by first turning the citizens of a country into British people can we enforce a British constitution.

"It is very difficult to organize all this into a unified theory but the matter does not end here. If we read these documents, we can discover that each one of them used different vocabulary to talk about different things, such as democracy, republic, liberal government, representative government, and constitutional monarchy. In addition, we also have natural rights, citizen's rights, equality in the face of law, equal opportunity, and so on; we also have universal suffrage, rule by the majority, division of powers, two-party system, and so on; we must also not forget half a dozen subjects which are related to modern democratic procedure, like the system of primary election, deciding by citizens' votes, proportional representation system, and so on. . . . Furthermore, every theoretician gave a different explanation of the decisive wordings and there have never been any concentrated authorities in the whole of the West who can give universally acknowledged annotations."

Barzun's conclusion is: "I am sure that democracy does not have a theory but a general principle. . . . This general principle is: The best system of mankind for liberty's sake is rule by people and includes, inter alia, political and social equality." He then also expounded and proved the implication of equal opportunity, which is ambiguous.

After giving a lengthy exposition, Barzun returned to this question of "what foreign countries could copy and absorb from the U.S. political system and its complicated political procedure" and came to a conclusion, saying: "First, there is no democratic theory which can be exported but democracy is a process of historic development. Second, in the process of the historic development of democracy, many forms and measures are adopted to attain the elusive target: 'human freedom.' Third, the form of democracy currently existing is changing and the conflict between equality and freedom has reached an unprecedentedly serious stage. With freedom, the government is required to control as little as possible, and with equality, the government is required to control as much as possible. No wonder the political mechanism of the free world has met with a great pressure and its citizens are tense."[1]

Here Jacques Barzun did not deal with his views on today's Western democratic system. Arthur Schlesinger Jr., a famous American historian, pointed out: In American history, freedom and democracy have played an active part and also caused many disappointments. Some problems were not solved, some grievances not redressed, and some criminals not punished. We cannot also expect that this system can be implemented more quickly and bigger reform carried out. The U.S. political procedure "has sometimes become a pretext for delaying actions and a mask for injustice and it has been especially so in recent years. . . . People increasingly feel that in today's new world where large economic, military, and knowledge companies wield power, freedom and democracy cannot play its part. People, particularly the younger generation, have come to believe that two-party politics is merely a farce, gradually taken a skeptical attitude toward the democratic mechanism, and lost interest in the democratic procedure."[2] Two experts, Ian Mills and John Irwin of the scientific policy research group of the University of Sussex in Britain stated with extensive and detailed figures and data that the freedom which British people enjoy is determined by many social and economic conditions and that on the other hand, organs set up by the government in the name of protecting freedom have infringed upon people's freedom and power.[3]

Some people living in socialist China have not clearly understood what socialism is and criticized the lack of a fixed type of socialism. In fact, from the very beginning, Marx and Engels clearly stated that the socialist and communist theory was a general principle. Lenin pointed out that socialism was not an a priori type but was created by millions of people in the course of actions. It is common knowledge of world history and world political history that the formation of any one social system is not done in an a priori way in the mind of a certain individual but is the progress of the history of a society. A new system must be gradually perfected in the course of development and this is also political common sense. Some people have used the emergence of the "Great Cultural Revolution" [in China] to negate the socialist system but, if they read some modern world history, they will see that although France experienced 5 republics, 2 empires, and 12 constitutions after the 1789 Revolution, no man of insight will negate the bourgeois republic coming down in one continuous line from the great revolution because France experienced various historic episodes. While Western ideological circles are becoming skeptical about the authenticity and feasibility of the Western democracy system, some people think that the import of the Western state system must be an ideal for carrying out reform of the Chinese political structure, and it seems that Western scholars of insight put forward different views in anticipation of this. Even if we do not dispute whether the Western democratic system is good or bad, the American political system is first a product of the American historic conditions, and even after some 200 years, has only a "principle" but not a theory. It cannot possibly be "exported." People who vainly attempt to implement the capitalist political system in China think that they can get theoretical support from the West. If they adopt a serious attitude, they will eventually be disappointed. This illusion can only show that they lack a little bit of historic[al] knowledge as well as knowledge of political theory and that while living in the realities of the world, they do not understand the realities of Western politics. It does not seem at all strange that people who have grown up over the past 30 years when our country was closed to the outside world are liable to be lacking in such knowledge. It is not very difficult to remedy this defect and what is needed is the spirit of seeking knowledge, an objective study attitude, a scientific analytical method, and the avoidance of the formation of a cursory prejudice. It appears that we must make efforts in this respect.

Capitalist Society and the Way of Life Bred in It

How do people live in a Western capitalist society? This is determined by what people show the greatest concern for in their life. Taking the United States as an example, while studying the aims of the general American public many sociologists hold that what people pursue is often individual success, whose implication is high income, high position, and high consumption and enjoyment. This aim pursued by individuals has no connection with the aim of society and it is pursued by individuals from their own interests and with themselves as the center of everything.

Since the pursuit of individual interests is the aim of life as well as the motivating force of life, this has become a social hallmark of capitalism and is naturally considered reasonable, practical, and the best by theoreticians who uphold the capitalist system. This idea that so long as an individual works hard, he will be successful runs through theory, works, school education, and news reports. [Benjamin] Franklin (1706–1790), who came from a poor family, has been considered typical. Franklin lived in the 18th century. At that time, people held that in society, so long as everyone did their best to pursue individual interests, public interests were naturally embodied in them. This optimism reflected a social desire of the thinkers in the Enlightenment of Western Europe in the 18th century. Half a century after the founding of the United States, that is, in the 1830s, French social philosopher de Tocqueville felt sympathy for the new continent and lived in the United States, hoping to investigate whether the American democratic society could maintain a free political system or slide into another dictatorship. In his work *American Democracy* (two volumes published respectively in 1835 and 1840), he praised the American people for forging ahead to seek personal interests and, at the same time, was worried that if this society where people competed with each other, with individual interests as the motivating force, continued to develop, they would eventually lose freedom in the competitive society where the weak were the prey of the strong. He depicted the United States with the word "individualism," which had just emerged at that time and held that although individualism was milder than egotism and laid some stress on restriction, every citizen was isolated from the multitudes in society and shrank to the small circle of his family and friends. As a result, very few people showed concern for the social development and problems. The ideology of individualism only corrodes social ethics and morality in the beginning and will eventually and surely develop to the extent that people become selfish. Judging outwardly, individualists do not treat other people unfairly or expect anything from anybody and they rely on themselves alone. This is a good thing. However, they form a customary idea and hold that their destiny is totally related to individual struggle and that individuals are isolated. Finally, they will be divorced from their parents and will disregard their children and other people. Individualism is not different from egotism. Such individuals will forever feel lonely in their hearts.[4] A social system which makes citizens become isolated individuals is especially suitable to the rule of dictatorship. Tocqueville pointed out that competition in a capitalist society made individuals isolated and made them feel powerless before society and their own fate. This just runs counter to the democratic ideals. In the 1830s, the United States still regarded agricultural production as the main work, there was little movement of population, and the activities of the Christian religion and the idea of "loving one's neighbor" still greatly affected society. However, the textile industry which began to spring up in the northeastern part of the United States employed a large number of immigrants and women workers. This caused de Tocqueville to worry that the proprietors and managers of factories would dominate the fate of the workers and that the masses at the lower level would be unable to enjoy democratic rights.

After one and a half centuries had elapsed, the result of America's industrial social development gradually made de Tocqueville's worries come true. Not long ago, Robert Nisbet, professor emeritus of humanities at Columbia University, heavy-heartedly said: "Judging from Western ideology as a whole, it is now in a transition period and is somewhat similar to the change in French ideological circles after the French Revolution.

"In the United States, there was no outbreak of a social revolution which destroyed the original social order in a planned way, but it was apparent that the American social order disintegrated over a period of time. Whatever the reasons— families, neighborhoods, communities, religions, and all classes in society, particularly the middle class, have been shaken with corrosion. This is the reality of the American people's mental world. [. . .] In the 19th century, the mention of the belief in individualism would remind people of the spirit of blazing a new trail, with which people exploited the western frontier, ventured into the wilderness, or painstakingly built up small farms or small shops. Today, the reiteration of the creed of individualism can only remind people of the scenes of alien[ated] people, ranging from old lonely and worried people to thieves and terrorists. Like Comte de Tocqueville and Durkheim, American ideological circles [held] that individualism and individualized social organizations disintegrated and that society was no longer a mass organization where people's common aspirations and interests assembled and it evolved to the extent that it was a heap of sand at most. Considering its bad side, it was a tropical jungle where people were lonely, fierce, and malicious and lived by plunder."[5]

Some people hold that since the beginning of this century, individualism has been on the decline in the United States. Professor Nisbet pointed out [that] this is not true. It is even more colorful and even more remarkably expressed in people's life than in any previous period in the United States.[6]

A study of ideology and the American people's way of life to which American academic circles have attached importance in recent years is the book *Spiritual Customs: Individualism and Pursuit of Ideals in American Life*. The book was written by Robert Bellah, professor of sociology of the University of California, Berkeley, in the United States, three professors of sociology, and a professor of philosophy, from 1979 to 1984 on the basis of holding in-depth talks and conducting observation of some 200 selected members of the middle class in large cities and small towns in the northeastern, southern, and western parts of the United States.[7] *Spiritual Customs* was derived from the book *American Democracy* by de Tocqueville and the original text should be literally translated into "inner customs." The word "inner" here follows its usage in the Bible of the Christian religion and includes knowledge, will, desires, and emotions. Its contents are very extensive and it was therefore translated into *Spiritual Customs*. The aim of this book is to study in the aspect of culture the expression and social influence of individualism in the way of life of the middle class of United States. It has generally been held that the middle class is representative of American society and the way of life of the middle class has held sway on the American way of life; and what the lower class pursues, attains, and does its best to imitate is also the way of life of the middle class. Although the history, traditions, and economic levels of all developed capitalist countries are different and they have their own characteristics, we can, on the whole, study the ideology and way of life of the American middle class, which has held sway on the ideology and way of life of the capitalist society. What follows this paragraph are data collected on the basis of the practical investigation and analysis conducted by Bellah and others.[8]

Professor Bellah and others pointed out that over the past half century, the image of the United States has been represented by many members of the stratum of company managers who have had the spirit of forging ahead, carried out indomitable competition, put their heart and soul into accumulating wealth, and held that so long as they have money, they will have social status and everything. Large companies and the government have become the biggest employers. So far as the majority of the members of the middle class are concerned, life is divided into two parts: One part is employment, and people are intent on personal advancement in order to earn more and more money; another part is personal life, the great majority of whose contents are purchased with money. Only a very small number of people can regard their work as an ideal to which they devote themselves. From childhood, people have been taught to rise head and shoulders above the others. When a young person enters society, he clearly knows that in the eyes of others, he is valued by his profession and status. Because of this, he puts friendship and his family in the secondary position and works desperately at all costs. Having reached middle age and after acquiring a middle-class status, he hopes to be further promoted. Senior positions dwindle and the opportunities he can attain in the course of competition also dwindle. His youthful dreams begin to vanish and the prospects for getting more money and a higher position by relying on promotion gradually become gloomy. These gloomy practical prospects are always linked with desire for promotion and with dreams, and weigh heavily on people, causing nervousness and crisis. A person who is unable to bear such stress is weak and will be eliminated by society through competition. He therefore needs a psychiatrist for medical treatment. When age and health fail him, he leaves his work and his personal life is doomed to decline. This is the way of life designated for people by society.

Under these circumstances, people cannot find satisfaction and even feel oppressed in the course of their work. They will naturally try to find it in personal life other than their work. Personal life includes the way to spend leisure time, consumer lifestyles, what club to join, where to spend vacations, at what shop to buy goods, the selection of modern clothing and furniture, what school children go to, and so on. All this is determined by the amount of money a person has and is the reflection of his social status and social class. The individual way of life is therefore connected to his work. On the other hand, personal life has also become a harbor for people who feel tense and oppressed in their work. People hope that the farther the harbor is from their work, the better. The harbor has become an opposite to work. It seems that in personal life, after struggling hard in the wind and waves on the sea of society, people are exhausted, go to a small island, take breath for a while, and then go down to the sea to struggle again. To escape solitude, people must always look for friends. Even among people whose personal consciousness is very strong, everyone still wants to be the center of everything even among a small number of persons. If he cannot find satisfaction, he will fall into the sense of solitude again. Consequently, the solitary individual is regarded as "rational" and further described as a value of life.

Judging from the movies—the most popular amusement in the United States, those on Western cowboys, private detectives, and "superman" which attract a large audience also reflect the same mental state. The horsemanship of a cowboy is exceptionally good and he is a crack shot and has a sense of justice. He is a great person adept in martial arts and given to chivalrous conduct who takes up the cudgels for the injured party and is always incompatible with society. After rescuing the residents of a small town, he often rides off alone, galloping to a distant place in the setting sun. Detectives or reporters act as the heroes of detective stories and often disclose that police officers, influential families, and high-society people participate in criminal activities. For the sake of justice, a hero can only fight alone and cannot enjoy both a social and family life. He must also resist the temptation of money or women and becomes a lonely warrior who upholds justice. Films on "supermen" and [extra]-terrestrials often use as the main plot stories about a lonely giant fighting against the whole society. All these films therefore reflect an idea that only by standing outside society can a lonely individual uphold an ideal image or value. However, individuals are unable to transform society and the pursuit of morals and ideals is, therefore, frequently interwoven with disappointment in practical life, finally leading to moral cynicism. Sometimes they shrink into their small spiritual circle and pay attention to their own moral uplift without thought of others. In this way, individuals who are originally antagonistic to society finally adapt themselves to this society under the pressure of capitalist society. As de Tocqueville pointed out earlier, individualism and adapting oneself to the social environment are originally two contradictory sides, and the two contradictory sides are strangely united.

Judging from appearances, people work under stress, lay stress on efficiency, and are like a machine in motion; individual life is established according to modes 1, 2, 3, and 4 (one family, two cars, a house of three bedrooms, and four television sets and various domestic electric appliances). However, these modes [of] work and life with individualist ideology as the foundation are always accompanied by the sense of individual loneliness. Unless people try to escape spiritual depression by tense and busy work and life enjoyment, they will not stop to ask: What is all this for? What is the significance of life as a whole? The significance of everything exists in the relationship between it and other things. If a man lives not for an ideal collective cause but for himself, he himself is the significance. This "significance" is actually insignificant and as a result, "insignificance" becomes the significance of life. The life devoid of meaning and the sense of being fed up with life cannot be filled with any material things. Moreover, this individualism also greatly restricts people's ideology, field of vision, emotions, and contents of life and makes people lose their concern for the world and people at large, unwilling to conscientiously pursue knowledge, and to lose interest in culture. As a result, people degenerate spiritually and not only make other people feel flat and insipid but also feel flat and insipid themselves. They can only dress up and cover themselves up with colorful materials. This state is now generally called "poverty in material richness" or "poverty in material progress" by Western scholars.

Of course, not everyone in a society lives according to one mode. In the United States or any other developed capitalist countries, there are many organizations which show concern for world peace, oppose racial discrimination, uphold democratic rights, and are public-spirited, and there are many people who have ideals and a sense of justice and who participate in these activities, pay any price for them, and even make sacrifices. There are also many people who join cultural, art, and sports organizations and organizations which suit their interests, go to evening university, and develop their own knowledge, ability, and interests. In the United States, these mass organizations voluntarily set up are countless. De Tocqueville pointed out that this was a very important part of the American democratic society. Professor Robert Bellah and others surely knew that not all American people nor the people of developed capitalist countries live as mentioned above, and their works or the works of other sociologists in this aspect did not deliberately vilify the American way of life. From the angle of study of sociology, they analyzed the process of the development of individualism under the American capitalist system and the social life thus formed which occupies a dominant position. This solemn scientific study is necessary for us to understand a capitalist society.

We [China] must strengthen financial supervision, enforce rigorous financial discipline and check all unhealthy tendencies. Judging from the problems brought to light in the general review of taxation, finance and prices over the last few years, violations of financial and economic discipline have been widespread. Some people have evaded taxes, retained a larger share of profits than they were entitled to for their own enterprises, falsified accounts about losses to secure subsidies or diverted state funds to other uses than prescribed. Others have made unauthorized decisions on tax reductions and exemptions, raised the ceilings for funds allocated for special purposes, indiscriminately issued bonuses and subsidies in cash or in kind, diverted state property to collective use, appropriated public property for use by individual units or turned it into private property. Still others have been guilty of embezzlement, theft and accepting or offering bribes. Such practices have reached very serious proportions in some areas, departments and units. In the campaign to increase production, practice economy, raise revenues and reduce expenditures this year, we must focus on combatting extravagance and waste, unhealthy tendencies and violations of financial and economic discipline. The relevant departments—particularly banks and departments of finance, taxation, auditing, pricing and industrial and commercial administration—should mobilize the masses and organize special teams to go down to the grass-roots units and carry out a general inspection. When serious violations of financial and economic discipline are discovered, governments at all levels and departments concerned must deal with them severely, after investigating and verifying the facts and identifying the leaders and other personnel responsible. The laws and statutes on finance and taxation promulgated by the state must be strictly enforced. Tax reduction and exemptions may only be decided on by competent authorities and in accordance with the provisions of the tax law. No department or individual may violate the tax law or exceed authority by making tax decisions at will. The State Council will make special arrangements for this year's general review of taxation, finance and prices.

Fellow deputies,

Since the beginning of this the trend of development of the national economy has been encouraging, and the execution of the state budget has been correctly implemented. However, it will be a difficult task to fulfill the budgeted revenues and expenditures for the current year. From beginning to end we shall have to pay close attention to the campaign to increase production, practice economy, raise revenues and reduce expenditures. We must firmly rely on the people of all our nationalities, uphold the four cardinal principles, strengthen leadership of economic work, particularly leadership of the campaign, and do a good job in all fields of endeavor. Let us unite as one and make concerted efforts to execute the state budget for 1987 successfully.

RENMIN RIBAO ON MODERN WESTERN CULTURE—PART II

The Concept of the Value of Individualism

Fundamentally speaking, only by relying on society can individuals create and develop their own values. The fact that, since the Renaissance, Europe has stressed human value has its historical background in those times and a progressive significance in history as well.

However, in the course of the development of capitalism, the lopsided tendency of seeking individual interests and ignoring the social public welfare has gradually developed. By the 19th century, individualism occupied the central position in Western culture. In the United States, because the immigrants from Europe freed themselves from the restrictions of the traditional social behavior much earlier and people could establish themselves in the new land and stand out among their fellows only through individual struggle, the ideology of individualism is more prevailing. However, it is not an easy job to explain the exact meaning of individualism. This is because individualism has different meanings at different times and there are also different types of individualism which permeate one another in the same era. Therefore, people have different sorts of understandings about individualism.

The rise of the modern ideological concept of individualism can be said to be represented by John Locke (1632–1704), the British bourgeois democratic philosopher and political thinker in the second half of the 17th century. Locke thought that individuals existed before the society existed. The natural state of mankind is the state of individual freedom. Individuals began to have contact with others only when they wanted to gain greater interests. On this basis, individuals began to form a society. The natural rights of mankind are to protect their lives, freedoms, and property from attack. The basic task of the government is to protect the natural rights of the citizens. It was for this reason that the state emerged. John Locke's theory was developed in the 17th-century British bourgeois movement against the autocratic monarchy and exerted a great influence on the European immigrants in North America and on the ideological field in the United States later on. Therefore, John Locke's theory has become the philosophical basis for the modern ideology of individualism in Europe and America.

However, John Locke's theory only reflected the ideology of the rising bourgeoisie in the period of free capitalism. From the 17th century to the end of the 19th century, capitalism experienced the period of free capitalism and entered the period of monopoly capitalism. Individualism, which was described by Max Weber (1864–1920) as the sense of mission of the bourgeois Protestants and the spirit of Protestantism characterized by hard labor, a simple life, and the accumulation of capital for the purpose of production development, also experienced enormous changes. By the 1830s de Tocqueville had already discovered that individualism and the ideology of trying in every way to seek private gains occupied a dominant position in the society and thought that it constituted a hidden danger. By the middle of the 19th century, the social maladies caused by individualism had become very obvious. So some American thinkers and commentators, such as Ralph Waldo Emerson (1803–1882) and Henry David Thoreau (1817–1862), pointed out that individuals should not only pursue wealth, but should seek their own spiritual development. However, this view was also based on individualism. Over a century has now passed. However, the ideology of individual struggle and the strong desire to seek individual interests that prevailed at the beginning of capitalism are still the main contents of the concept of the value of individualism. Moreover, the ideology of seeking "self-expression" and "self-accomplishment" has also become the main content of the concept of the value of individualism.

In the following, I will mainly analyze the concept of the value of individualism in modern capitalist society. Here, we can divide the concept of the value of individualism into two levels, just as Western scholars divide Western culture into "high-grade culture" which has a relatively delicate form and "common culture" which has a relatively common form.

In Western "common culture," the most important attributes of the concept of value are the individual achievements which include fame, wealth, and position. The value lies in seeking individual interests. Another concept of value based on seeking self-expression is to first look at the appearance of a person, which means that men should be manly and should be bold, unconstrained, handsome, and natural, while women should have beauty, tenderness, and so on; in addition a person should have outstanding ability and a strong character. This has become the determination of the value of a person. Let us analyze it more carefully: The concept of value is a social consciousness and the value of an object is only evident through its relations with other objects. The value of a person is the same. It can only be shown through an individual's relations with the society. The contribution made by individuals to the welfare of the public is the criterion for assessing the value of individuals. If individuals lose their social consciousness and the sense of social responsibility and only pursue the satisfaction of individual desires or self-expression, then they will fundamentally lose their value in the society. What is more, if individuals take the satisfaction of individual desires as their goal, they will never satisfy their desires. As for seeking spiritual self-development, if individuals do not establish themselves among the people who create the spiritual culture and do not serve the social goal which surpasses that of the individuals, then individuals are bound to be spiritually poor. In Western "common culture," such spiritual self-development has two characteristics: an individual's life has to develop in the direction of subjective ideology and irrationalism by ideologically "surpassing" the social traditions and ethics, negating all the objective criteria governing literature, art, sexual relations, lifestyle, and moral concepts, believing that "what feels good is good," and replacing an objective standard of value with the individual's subjective feelings. All things, from surrealist paintings, music that only has strong rhythms but no melodies, and exotic costumes to sexual indulgence, homosexuality, and so on, have reflected the concept of value of individualism of self-expression. Because of such a concept of values, some young people have indulged in the stimulation of sensory organs, which can be seen in the "hippie–drug addiction–fanatical rock and roll" culture.

At the level of "high-grade" culture, the concept of the value of Western individualism is believed to be composed of two aspects: individual ethics and social public life. As far as individual ethics is concerned, a person is required to be just, reliable in social contacts, sympathetic, loyal to his or her own family, and so on. This is a self-perfection and a process of "moral self-accomplishment," which is still the publicly recognized standard individual behavior in modern Western society. Although such a person is worthy of respect, as far as the society is concerned, such a person is only a "good person" in the negative sense because his concern for the society is limited and his real concern is still himself.

In public social life, the Western bourgeois society regards freedom and justice as two main values, of which freedom occupies a very important position. In one sense, freedom is the criterion for assessing the individual's life and the political life. However, so-called individual freedom means to be free from the restrictions of any political and social authorities, free from the restrictions of any authorities in the individual's work and famil[y], and free from the restrictions of any historical and cultural traditions. It also means that individuals need not be responsible for society, the collectives, and other people. Therefore, the relationship between an individual and other people is only a relationship of interests. As a result, moral responsibility and emotional responsibility do not exist or almost do not exist, and the pursuit of individual freedom has brought about the individual's spiritual loneliness. When talking with people in the Western philosophical and sociological circles, I have found that Western scholars generally agree that what the West has paid most attention to is individual freedom and what the West fears most is individual loneliness. When I was invited to make a short speech at Harvard University, I said that just like the palm of the hand and the back of the hand, individual freedom and individual loneliness are the two inseparable aspects of individualism. What the people of the United States like most and what they fear most are actually the same thing. This is the cultural and ideological predicament of the United States and also the predicament of the concept of the value of individualism. Moreover, after a person gets freedom, what will he do with freedom? Will the satisfaction of the desires of individuals become a value? Can self-expression through freedom be different in nature from the satisfaction of the desires of individuals? Will a spiritually lonely person, who is outside society but tries to transform society by proceeding from individualism, be able to change society? These questions have made me recall the talk between me and Jürgen Habermas, a representative figure of the New School of Frankfurt in Munich a few years ago. I asked him: "What do you feel happy about and what do you feel worried about when you recall your own academic career?" In the usual manner of a philosopher, he spoke from the negative side of a question: "Here, I have absolute freedom to express my views, but I also know that what I have said is absolutely useless." In the realistic world, there can be no absolute objects. However, when thinking that a philosophical social scientist finally felt that his life-long academic career was "absolutely useless" and seeing him uttering the above remarks with an ironic look on his face, I was at a loss what to say.

What is more, besides being restricted by the economic conditions, individual freedom will also bring about loneliness and will not find the real meaning in the individual's small circle. If everyone demands individual freedom and shows no concern for others, then human society will even be inferior to a swarm of bees or a swarm of ants. Can this be the value pursued by mankind? The so called "free society" is almost a pet phrase of people in the West. However, people usually fail to see the contradiction in this pet phrase. Society is people's common living entity formed on the basis of the mode of material production, which will naturally include a restrictive relationship among the people. Without such a restrictive relationship or "limits of freedom," there cannot be a civilized society. If a society takes abstract individual freedom as its banner and calls on the people to pursue it, then the society is actually calling on the members of the society to destroy their own living environment and destroy the society. If such abstract individual freedom can actually get nowhere because it has to obey various conditions, but it is still flaunted as a banner by the society, then it is an untrue freedom, or to use an impolite term, a false freedom. Therefore, it is not strange that when Professor Barzun advertised "individual freedom" as the goal of the Western democratic society, as I have mentioned before, he also called it "something elusive."

However, since there is a big gap between the rich and the poor in capitalist countries, everything costs money, and money can buy everything, how can the rich and the poor have equal opportunities? Employment is a question with which the broad masses of the people are most concerned. In the United States, the increasingly low standard of the public secondary schools has caused a crisis. The children of the rich in the United States can go to expensive private secondary schools which have good equipment and better-qualified teachers, while the children of the poor can only go to cheap public schools whose standard is relatively low. In the keen competition, although the children of both rich and poor families can compete with one another on equal terms, the poor can only be "equally" defeated in the keen competition. Moreover, this situation is also guaranteed by the law and the government. When disputes appear in the social relations of the people and justice needs to be upheld, the poor cannot afford the protracted legal procedures and expensive attorney fees. Justice is just like a cake hanging in midair so that those who have the support of money can eat the cake while those who do not have money can only look at the cake but not eat it. In a society where there is a wide gap between the rich and the poor and everything costs money, how can there be equal opportunities for everyone, how can things be fair, and where can justice be found? Therefore, officially, everyone has freedom, but actually only those who have money can really enjoy freedom; officially, everyone has equal opportunities in the society, but actually only those who have money can enjoy justice. This is the vivid manifestation of the contradiction between the capitalist economic system and the capitalist culture and ideals in the concept of value in the West.

Nowadays, some hold [that] the advanced capitalist countries are entering an information society based on computers and electronics. In an information society, where information plays a decisive role in the economic life, great changes will take place in work style, lifestyle, ideological concepts, and so on, which can even be called a "revolution," as if a "new world would emerge." This view has made people think. Information provides only the change to obtain knowledge, but information itself is not knowledge, and cannot be lumped together with science and technology. We must carefully study the view that the development of computers and electronics will certainly have a great impact on the development of the productive forces and cause changes in work style, lifestyle, and ideological concepts. The development of computers and electronics cannot change the basic production relations, social structure, and the ideology of individualism which forms the basis of the concept of value. The so-called "concept renewal" in name cannot change the nature of the capitalist system. All the serious social scientists in the West have already clearly seen this fact.

"The Internal Cultural Contradictions of the Capitalist System"

Marxist scholars and non-Marxist scholars in the West have made a lot of analyses of the abnormal state of the capitalist culture. The present question is: To what extent has such an abnormal state of the capitalist culture already developed. The scholars' research group presided over by Robert Bellah believed: "What we are concerned about is that such individualism has probably developed into a cancer. Tocqueville once believed that it was necessary to rely on the social organizations to prevent the destructive role of individualism. The present situation is that the cancer of individualism is now probably damaging the skin of the society and is even threatening the freedom itself."[9]

As for why the destructive role of individualism has not been prevented, but, on the contrary, has developed into a cancer, Professor Bellah and his colleagues did not give an answer. In order to explore this question, we can look at the analysis made by Daniel Bell, professor of sociology at Harvard University. Professor Bell has never ideologically agreed to Marxism and has always advocated the theory of a post-industrial society, believing that in the modern world, politics plays the decisive role in the economic and cultural fields. After 13 years of research from 1963 to 1975, he published the book *The Cultural Contradictions of Capitalism*. In the preface to the second edition (1978), Professor Bell said: "In a broad sense, the theme of this book is not only the cultural contradiction of capitalism but also the cultural contradiction of bourgeois society."[10] This means that the author of this book tried to observe the internal cultural contradictions by combining the bourgeois society with its economic system. Bell believed that the demand of the capitalist economic system fundamentally contradicts the ideological principles flaunted by the capitalist culture. The production activities of the capitalist social and economic systems are aimed at continuously accumulating funds and expanding investment. In the huge organization of modern mass production, in which there is a high degree of division of labor, the various types of work have become increasingly specialized. A huge "institution" (which can also be directly translated as "bureaucratic institution") has been formed in the organization. In the institution, the style of the individual behavior is determined by the specific role played by the individuals, employees are regarded as instruments which can help the company to earn the biggest profit, and the personality of individuals is therefore lost when their specific roles are decided in the process of the division of labor. However, the capitalist culture advocates the self-development and self-expression of individuals, regards the self-satisfaction of individuals as the criterion in assessing everything, and negates any objective concepts of value. As a result, the self-demand of individuals and the demand of modern monopoly capitalism will naturally contradict each other. This is the fundamental contradiction between the modern capitalist economic system and modern bourgeois culture.

In the political field, since capitalism stresses individual freedom, it must put forward the principle of equality and stress that every citizen has equal rights in order to coordinate the relations among the people in the free competition. However, no matter whether it is in the government or in the big companies, the capitalist political and social structures are huge institutions in which the inferior must obey the superior and the employees must obey the boss regardless of the individual's personal quality and ability and the right and wrong. This contradiction between the bureaucratic organizations and the principle that everyone is equal has brought about enormous conflicts in society.

In social life, as far as work is concerned, all big companies demand that their employees work hard and be cold and indifferent. They try to train their employees to become "economic people" and "members of big organizations." On the other hand, in order to encourage individual consumption, capitalism must stimulate the desires of individuals and encourage individuals to enjoy themselves. As a result, some people have adopted a sick lifestyle. They strictly observe discipline and work very hard during office hours, but become completely different people who seek stimulation, get drunk, and give vent to their personal feelings in order to "realize themselves" in their spare time. The various types of recreation and colorful commercial advertisements in society all propagandize a lifestyle characterized by consumption and enjoyment. This consumption is not based on actual needs, but is based on people's desires. People's needs are limited, but people's desires are unlimited. In the bourgeois society, the amount of consumption represents the social status of an individual, and is not necessarily always aimed at economic results. Seemingly, the various types of commodity advertisements only publicize certain clothes, ornaments, food, furniture, and so on. However, they actually publicize an ideology of hedonism, which they regard as the goal of human life. In order to immediately enjoy such a lifestyle, people can buy the things they want on installment, which means that people can go into debt. Thus, work is for money and life is for enjoyment. Such an outlook on life and concept of value have corrupted people's social ideals and the whole society as well. This is another internal contradiction of the capitalist system.

Philosophically speaking, when capitalism was on the rise, the bourgeoisie was fully confident in its own strength. Because the bourgeoisie wanted capital to control everything, it had to study, understand, and have a good grasp of the objective world. Therefore, the bourgeoisie stressed rationalism. However, the internal contradictions of capitalism became increasingly obvious in the middle of the 19th century. By then, individualism had developed according to its own logic to the emergence of the philosophy of Friedrich Nietzsche, which advocated the unity of the individuals' will, desire, and action, and [which] expect[ed] the emergence of a superman who is capable of ruling the whole world. Since such a world is composed of power and will, all the capitalist traditional political theories, social ideologies, ethics, religions, and philosophies that hinder the superman from realizing his power and will and that have numerous internal contradictions should be negated. The philosophy of Friedrich Nietzsche not only exposed the morbid state of capitalism but was itself also a product of the morbid state of capitalism. The development of Western ideologies over the past one and a half centuries has always been characterized by interdependence and intercontradiction between capitalism and individualism.

The arguments of Professor Robert Bellah's group, Professor Daniel Bell, and Professor Jacques Barzun confirm one another, and the contents of their arguments supplement one another. The ideological theories and ideologies of Western capitalism are the historical products of Western capitalism and therefore cannot be exported and transplanted. Moreover, the ideologies of Western capitalism are in a morbid state and have developed into a cancerous state. All these are not the result of people's mismanagement but are determined by the internal factors of the capitalist system.[11]

In order to survive, a modern social system needs two conditions: one is guiding theories, and the other is goals for economic and social development so as to unite the broad masses of the people to make joint efforts to maintain that social system. However, the modern capitalist system simply lacks these two conditions. As far as political and economic theories are concerned, capitalism believes that social needs can be met through the automatic regulation of the market mechanism. Therefore, in terms of production, circulation, and distribution of wealth, capitalism only has a theory concerning the short-term regulations adaptable to the changing conditions, but no guiding theory which is capable of answering the structural questions; as far as social ethics are concerned, the capitalist system has not been able to put forward a social ideal which advocates long-term devotion to the public welfare. Without a social ideal and a goal of struggle that can mobilize hundreds of millions of people, it will be difficult for a society to really form a united force. On the other hand, the United States and all the West[ern] European capitalist countries initially had a spirit of hard struggle. However, by the second half of the 20th century, another trend had developed, which cast away the tradition of plain and economical living and advocated luxury and enjoyment.[12] That was the beginning of the spiritual decadence. The history of the world has enabled us to see this phenomenon. Although some powerful countries can develop without a relatively long period of time, the decline of the spiritual culture is always the omen of the decline of these countries, just like the blowing of the wind anticipating the death of the green leaves. The ancient Roman Empire, the Byzantine Empire, and some modern big colonial powers have all provided precedents in this aspect. This is why some Western scholars are worried about the developed capitalist countries at present. Some Western scholars have expressed such feelings in their works. These facts can help us acquire a relatively complete understanding of the modern world and think about the questions of China.

Over the past 3 centuries or so, the relationship between Western society and individuals formed in the process of the development of capitalism has caused increasing worries among Western scholars and growing concern among scholars in Third World countries. Modernization is not equal to Westernization. This has become the common understanding of the majority of the scholars of the Third World countries. Every developing country must develop its own economy, politics, and culture in light of its own realistic situation. Mechanically copying foreign things will only result in failure. It is wrong to carry out cultural construction divorced from its historical context. In China's cultural traditions, individuals have always been linked with society. Individuals are allowed to have their individuality, and the beliefs of individuals are always respected. However, individuals have never been placed above society, and the values of individuals have always been unified with the responsibilities of society. This is one of the important factors that have contributed to the continued powerful cohesion of the Chinese nation.

Is it true that we will naturally develop Western-style individualism and weaken the fine contents of the traditional culture of our nation in our development of the commodity economy and support for competition? The experiences over the past 100 years in Third World developing countries which have long-standing cultures have given a negative answer to this question. The important thing is what kinds of ideologies and cultures people will advocate according to their subjective initiative. This has been one of the pressing questions in our country's ideological field in recent years. This concern is also one of the reflections of the influx of various Western ideological trends during the process of our country's reform and opening up to the outside world over the past 8 years. The influx of Western ideological trends is unavoidable. Some of them are positive ones and helpful to us, while others can still provide us with reference from the opposite side and are therefore also useful. What is important is that we should make comparisons and appraisals so as to decide what to take in and what to reject. As a matter of fact, the Chinese people have had contacts with Western culture for nearly 4 centuries. Over the past 4 centuries, Western culture has had its own development while the Chinese people have also deepened their understanding of Western culture. They have also gained rich practical experiences and learned lessons in their appraisals of the Western culture. That the Chinese people have decided to take the socialist road is the most important conclusion made by the Chinese people. In order to acquire a better understanding of the four cardinal principles and the historical significance of the reform and opening up to the outside world, it is necessary for us to deepen our scientific understanding of modern Western culture and conscientiously sum up the modern history of China's contacts with Western culture. We must try hard to accomplish these two tasks.

NOTES

1. Jacques Barzun, "Can a Democratic Theory Be Exported?" 1986 edition of Carnegie Association of Ethics and International Affairs, pp. 5–7, 25, 26.

2. Arthur Schlesinger, "The United States 1968: Violent Politics" in *Philosophy and Contemporary Problems: A Reader,* compiled by Richard Popkin and Avrum Stroll (New York, 1984), pp. 435.

3. Ian Mills and John Irwin, *Material Progress and Poverty* (New York, 1982), pp. 137–206.

4. Alexis de Tocqueville, *American Democracy* (New York, 1969), pp. 506, 508.

5. Robert Nisbet, *Prejudice: A Dictionary of Philosophy* (Cambridge, MA: Harvard University Press, 1982), pp. 184–186.

6. Ibid., p. 187.

7. Robert Bellah and others, *Spiritual Customs: Individualism and Pursuit of Ideals in American Life* (Berkeley: University of California Press, 1985).

8. Ibid., chapters 2, 3, 5.

9. Bellah and others, *Spiritual Customs,* p. 8.

10. Daniel Bell, *The Cultural Contradictions of Capitalism,* 2nd ed. (New York, 1978), p. 16.

11. Professor Takahashi of the Tsukuba University of Japan reached the following conclusion from his research: "As far as the whole world is concerned, the life outlook and social outlook of the individualism born and developed in Europe and America now has no way out." See Gao Qiaojin, "The Modern Significance of Chinese Ideologies in World History" in *Study on Confucius* (1986), Vol. 3.

12. In 1980, the Broadcast Association of Japan carried out a social investigation in Japan and the United States. The result of the investigation showed that some 27 percent of the American people who answered the questionnaire thought that leisure activities were the most important. One of the questions in the questionnaire of the 1984 international investigation on youth was: "Which do you think is more important, work or other activities?" Some 67 percent of the American people who answered the

question believed that other activities were more important. See S. M. Lipset (professor of sociology, Stanford University), "The Traditions and Modernization of Japan and the United States," *Japan International Centre Quarterly,* Vol. 1 (1987).

REFERENCES

Barzun, Jacques. 1986. "Is Democratic Theory for Export?" In *Sixth Morgenthau Memorial Lecture on Ethics and Foreign Policy.* New York, NY: Carnegie Council on Ethics and International Affairs.

Cong, Yao. 2012. "Exclusive: A Chinese Intellectual's Honesty Forces Exile." *Epoch Times,* July 12, 2012. http://www.theepochtimes.com/n2/china-news/exclusive-a-chinese-intellectuals-honesty-forces-exile-264489.html. Accessed January 31, 2015.

De Tocqueville, Alexis. 2003 [1836]. *Democracy in America.* New York: Penguin Classics.

Zhen, Yang. 1979. *Jidujiao shigang* (The History of Christianity in China). Beijing: Sanlian Press.

18

Be Nice to the Countries
That Lend You Money

Interview of Gao Xiqing by James Fallows, 2008

In the December 2008 issue of the *Atlantic Monthly,* James Fallows, undoubtedly with the world financial crisis in mind, interviewed the man who oversees $200 billion of China's $2 trillion in foreign holdings. Gao Xiqing is president of the China Investment Corporation, a man who speaks fluent English and holds a law degree from Duke University (and has experience practicing in a Wall Street law firm). Fallows reports that Gao's father was a Red Army officer, and that Gao himself worked in railroad construction and also in an ammunition factory during the Cultural Revolution. In other words, Gao, at fifty-five when Fallows interviewed him, had gained a wide range of political and labor experiences as he moved up the ladder into the international scene.

Gao Xiqing is knowledgeable and frank, and, unlike authors in earlier selections, uses China for comparison sparingly. He does not strive to be polite. Instead he lumps together China, Japan, and Middle Eastern countries, all places of old civilizations, countries not only that lend money to the United States but whose people might teach Americans something about how to behave diplomatically and even how to make use of American pragmatism. Gao describes his challenge in trying to explain derivatives to the State Council of China by comparing derivatives to a bunch of mirrors that, when accumulated, convince investors that derivatives are real. The Chinese ministers laughed, and so, I might add, did the head of Lebanese banks who forbade his bankers to invest in derivatives. Dubai, however, "fell for derivatives" and along with the Americans ended up paying for it during the 2008 financial downturn. "But," Gao says, "you have to have someone tell the truth."

Gao Xiqing also gives more straightforward advice, for example, about the extravagant financial system, something American critics have also commented on. "Way too much money," he says. "And this is not right." American CEOs receive greater financial returns than CEOs in any other industrial country. On the other hand, on the financial bailout he again credits American pragmatism, while also cautioning Americans as to their feelings about supremacy and their refusal to demonstrate humility when it is needed. Humility is something Gao himself has learned by experience.

In the end Gao has a practical suggestion: why don't we get together and call a second Bretton Woods conference? But in the meantime he cautions, "Be nice to the countries that lend you money."

In contrast to other selections, in this case the interviewer selected from the responses he recorded and organized them according to Gao Xiqing's recurrent themes.

· · ·

In his first interview since the world financial crisis, Gao Xiqing, the man who oversees $200 billion of China's $2 trillion in dollar holdings, explains why he's betting against the dollar, praises American pragmatism, and wonders about enormous Wall Street paychecks. And he has a friendly piece of advice:

"BE NICE TO THE COUNTRIES THAT LEND YOU MONEY"

Americans know that China has financed much of their nation's public and private debt. During the presidential campaign, Barack Obama and John McCain generally agreed on the peril of borrowing so heavily from this one foreign source. For instance, in their final debate, McCain warned about the "$10 trillion debt we're giving to our kids, a half a trillion dollars we owe China," and Obama said, "Nothing is more important than us no longer borrowing $700 billion or more from China and sending it to Saudi Arabia." Their numbers on the debt differed, and both were way low. One year ago, when I wrote about China's U.S. dollar holdings, the article was called "The $1.4 Trillion Question." When Barack Obama takes office, the figure will be well over $2 trillion.

During the late stages of this year's campaign, I had several chances to talk with the man who oversees many of China's American holdings. He is Gao Xiqing, president of the China Investment Corporation, which manages "only" about $200 billion of the country's foreign assets but makes most of the high-visibility investments, like buying stakes in Blackstone and Morgan Stanley, as opposed to just holding Treasury notes.

Gao, whom I mentioned in my article, would fit no American's preexisting idea of a Communist Chinese official. He speaks accented but fully colloquial and very high-speed English. He has a law degree from Duke, which he earned in the 1980s after working as a lawyer and professor in China, and he was an associate in Richard Nixon's former Wall Street law firm. His office, in one of the more tasteful new glass-walled high-rises in Beijing, itself seems less Chinese than internationally "fusion"-minded in its aesthetic and furnishings. Bonsai trees in large pots, elegant Japanese-looking arrangements of individual smooth stones on display shelves, Chinese and Western financial textbooks behind the desk, with a photo of Martin Luther King Jr. perched among the books. Two very large, very thin desktop monitors read out financial data from around the world. As we spoke, Western classical music played softly from a good sound system.

Gao dressed and acted like a Silicon Valley moneyman rather than one from Wall Street—open-necked tattersall shirt, muted plaid jacket, dark slacks, scuffed walking shoes. Rimless glasses. His father was a Red Army officer who was on the Long March with Mao. As a teenager during the Cultural Revolution, Gao worked on a railroad-building gang and in an ammunition factory. He is 55, fit-looking, with crew-cut hair and a jokey demeanor rather than an air of sternness.

His comments below are from our one on-the-record discussion, two weeks before the U.S. elections. As I transcribed his words, I realized that many will look more astringent on the page than they sounded when coming from him. In person, he seemed to be relying on shared experience in the United States—that is, his and mine—to entitle him to criticize the country the way its own people might. The conversation was entirely in English. Because Gao's answers tended to be long, I am not presenting them in straight Q&A form but instead grouping his comments about his main recurring themes.

Does America wonder who its new Chinese banking overlords might be? This is what one of the very most influential of them had to say about the world financial crisis, what is wrong with Wall Street, whether one still-poor country with tremendous internal needs could continue subsidizing a still-rich one, and how he thought America could adjust to its "realistic" place in the world. My point for the moment is to convey what it is like to hear from such a man, rather than to expand upon, challenge, or agree with his stated views.

About the financial crisis of 2008, which eliminated hundreds of billions of dollars' worth of savings that the Chinese government had extracted from its people, through deliberately suppressed consumption levels:
We are not quite at the bottom yet. Because we don't really know what's going to happen next. Everyone is saying, "Oh, look, the dollar is getting stronger!" [As it was when we spoke.] I say, that's really temporary. It's simply because a lot of people need to cash in, they need U.S. dollars in order to pay back their creditors. But after a short while, the dollar may be going down again. I'd like to bet on that!

The overall financial situation in the U.S. is changing, and that's what we don't know about. It's going to be changed fundamentally in many ways.

Think about the way we've been living the past 30 years. Thirty years ago, the leverage of the investment banks was like 4-to-1, 5-to-1. Today, it's 30-to-1. This is not just a change of numbers. This is a change of fundamental thinking.

People, especially Americans, started believing that they can live on other people's money. And more and more so. First other people's money in your own country. And then the savings rate comes down, and you start living on other people's money from outside. At first it was the Japanese. Now the Chinese and the Middle Easterners.

We—the Chinese, the Middle Easterners, the Japanese—we can see this too. Okay, we'd love to support you guys—if it's sustainable. But if it's not, why should we be doing this? After we are gone, you cannot just go to the moon to get more money. So, forget it. Let's change the way of living. [By which he meant: less debt, lower rewards for financial wizardry, more attention to the "real economy," etc.]

About stock market derivatives and their role as source of evil:
If you look at every one of these [derivative] products, they make sense. But in aggregate, they are bullshit. They are crap. They serve to cheat people.

I was predicting this many years ago. In 1999 or 2000, I gave a talk to the State Council [China's main ruling body], with Premier Zhu Rongji. They wanted me to explain about capital markets and how they worked. These were all ministers and mostly not from a financial background. So I wondered, *How do I explain derivatives?,* and I used the model of mirrors.

First of all, you have this book to sell. [He picks up a leather-bound book.] This is worth something, because of all the labor and so on you put in it. But then someone says, "I don't have to sell the book itself! I have a mirror, and I can sell the mirror image of the book!" Okay. That's a stock certificate. And then someone else says, "I have another mirror—I can sell a mirror image of that mirror." Derivatives. That's fine too, for a while. Then you have 10,000 mirrors, and the image is almost perfect. People start to believe that these mirrors are almost the real thing. But at some point, the image is interrupted. And all the rest will go.

When I told the State Council about the mirrors, they all started laughing. "How can you sell a mirror image! Won't there be distortion?" But this is what happened with the American economy, and it will be a long and painful process to come down.

I think we should do an overhaul and say, "Let's get rid of 90 percent of the derivatives." Of course, that's going to be very unpopular, because many people will lose jobs.

About Wall Street jobs, wealth, and the cultural distortion of America:
I have to say it: you have to do something about pay in the financial system. People in this field have way too much money. And this is not right.

When I graduated from Duke [in 1986], as a first-year lawyer, I got $60,000. I thought it was astronomical! I was making somewhere a bit more than $80,000 when I came back to China in 1988. And that first month's salary I got in China, on a little slip of paper, was 59 yuan. A few dollars! With a few yuan deducted for my rent and my water bill. I laughed when I saw it: 59 yuan!

The thing is, we are working as hard as, if not harder than, those people. And we're not stupid. Today those people fresh out of law school would get $130,000, or $150,000. It doesn't sound right.

Individually, everyone needs to be compensated. But collectively, this directs the resources of the country. It distorts the talents of the country. The best and brightest minds go to lawyering, go to MBAs. And that affects our country, too! Many of the brightest youngsters come to me and say, "Okay, I want to go to the U.S. and get into business school, or law school." I say, "Why? Why not science and engineering?" They say, "Look at some of my primary-school classmates. Their IQ is half of mine, but they're in finance and now they're making all this money." So you have all these clever people going into financial engineering, where they come up with all these complicated products to sell to people.

About the $700 billion U.S. financial-rescue plan enacted in October:
Finally, after months and months of struggling with your own ideology, with your own pride, your self-righteousness . . . finally [the U.S. applied] one of the great gifts of Americans, which is that you're pragmatic. Now our people are joking that we look at the U.S. and see "socialism with American characteristics." [The Chinese term for its mainly capitalist market-opening of the last 30 years is "socialism with Chinese characteristics."]

It *is* joking, and many people are saying: "No, Americans still believe in free capitalism and they think this is just a hiccup." This is like our great leader Deng Xiaoping, who said that it doesn't matter if the cat is white or black, as long as it catches the mouse. It doesn't matter what we call this. It's pragmatic.

With so much of China's money at stake, did U.S. officials consult the Chinese about the rescue plan?
Not directly. We were talking to people there, and they were hoping that we would be supportive by not pulling out our money. We know that by pulling out money, we're not serving anyone's good. Including ourselves. [This is the famous modern "balance of financial terror." If Chinese officials started pulling assets out of the U.S. and touched off a run on the dollar, their vast remaining dollar holdings would plummet in value.] So we're trying to help, at least by not aggravating the problem.

But I think at the end of the day, the American government needs to talk with people and say: "Why don't we get together and think about this? If China has $2 trillion, Japan has almost $2 trillion, and Russia has some, and all the others, then—let's throw away the ideological differences and think about what's good for everyone." We can get all the relevant people together and think up what people are calling a second Bretton Woods system, like the first Bretton Woods convention did.

On what might make the Chinese government start taking its dollars out of America (I began the question by saying that China would hurt itself by pulling out dollar assets—at which he interjected, "in the short term"—and then asked about the long-term view):
Today when we look at all the markets, the U.S. still is probably the most viable, the most predictable. I was trained as a lawyer, and predictability is always very important for me.

We have a PR department, which collects all the comments about us, from Chinese newspapers and the Web. Every night, I try to pick a time when I'm in a relatively good mood to read it, because most of the comments are very critical of us. Recently we increased our holdings in Blackstone a little bit. Now we're increasing a little bit our holdings in Morgan Stanley, so as not to be diluted by the Japanese. People here *hate* it. They come out and say, "Why the hell are you trying to save those people? You are the representative of the poor people eating porridge, and you're saving people eating shark fins!" It's always that sort of thing.

And how should Americans feel about the growing Chinese presence in their economy? Isn't it natural for them to worry that China will keep increasing its stake in American debt and assets—or that China won't, essentially cutting America off?

I can understand why Americans might feel that way. But, talking with my lawyer head once again, it's not relevant to discuss how Americans "should" think. We should discuss how Americans *might* think.

This concern is not really about China itself. It could be any country. It could be Japan, or Germany. This generation of Americans is so used to your supremacy. Your being treated nicely by everyone. It hurts to think, *Okay, now we have to be on equal footing to other people.* "On equal footing" would necessarily mean that sometimes you have to stoop to appear to be humble to other people.

And you can't think as a soldier. You put yourself at the enemy end of everyone. I grew up during the Cultural Revolution, when people really treated other people like enemies. I grew up in an environment where our friends, our relatives, people I called Uncle or Auntie, could turn around and put a nasty face to me as a small child. One time, Vladimir Lenin told Gorky, after reading Gorky's autobiography, "Oh my god! You could have become a very nasty person!" Those are exactly the words one of my dear professors told me after hearing what I went through.

But over the years, I believe I learned to be humble. To treat other people nicely. I learned that, from a social point of view, no matter how lowly statured a person you are talking to, as a person, they are the same human being as you are. You have to respect them. You have to apologize if you inadvertently hurt them. And often you have to go out of your way to be nice to them, because they will not like you simply because of the difference in social structure.

Americans are not sensitive in that regard. I mean, as a whole. The simple truth today is that your economy is built on the global economy. And it's built on the support, the gratuitous support, of a lot of countries. So why don't you come over and . . . I won't say *kowtow* [with a laugh], but at least, *be nice* to the countries that lend you money.

Talk to the Chinese! Talk to the Middle Easterners! And pull your troops back! Take the troops back, demobilize many of the troops, so that you can save some money rather than spending $2 billion every day on them. And then tell your people that you need to save, and come out with a long-term, sustainable financial policy.

Although Gao has frequently mentioned Chairman Mao's maxim—"Go with the Republicans. They're predictable!"—he obviously was hoping for a "change" agenda under the Democrats:
The current conditions can't go on. It is time for the new government, under Obama or even McCain, to really tell people: "Look, this is wartime, this is about the survival of our nation. It's not about our supremacy in the world. Let's not even talk about that any more. Let's get down to the very basics of our livelihood."

I have great admiration of American people. Creative, hard-working, trusting, and freedom-loving. But you have to have someone to tell you the truth. And then, start realizing it. And if you do it, just like what you did in the Second World War, then you'll be great again!

If that happens, then of course—American power would still be there for at least as long as I am living. But many people are betting on the other side.

REFERENCES

Klimasinska, Kasia. 2013. "CIC Chief Gao Says China's Fund Treated Differently by U.S." *Bloomberg Businessweek Online,* April 25, 2013. http://www.businessweek.com/news/2013-04-25/cic-chief-gao-says-china-s-fund-treated-differently-by-u-dot-s-dot.

Sender, Henny. 2014. "Founding President to Step Down at China Wealth Fund." *Financial Times Online,* January 22, 2014. http://www.ft.com/cms/s/0/9c7a7934-8332-11e3-86c9-00144feab7de.html#axzz388C6vMTC.

19

Full Text of Human Rights Record of United States in 2008

Xinhuanet, 2008

Human rights as a concept gained stature with the 1948 United Nations Declaration of Human Rights following World War II. Eleanor Roosevelt, who chaired the UN Human Rights Commission, reminded her collaborators that they were charged with writing a declaration acceptable to all religions, ideologies, and cultures. Yet there were disagreements as well as nations absent from the table, if only because the Commission on Human Rights and the UN were predominately Western-led, largely by Americans, although Western Europeans, the Soviets, and the Chinese were involved. All but two of the drafts were written in English. The focus on individual rights versus collective rights was a problem for indigenous peoples, whose interests were not represented. In addition, the focus on international human rights versus universal (meaning Western) human rights encroached on issues of sovereignty and culture. The related issue of Western exceptionalism lurked in the background.

The idea that human rights are an American export has been increasingly irritating to other countries, especially with the growth of American empire. Since 1948, human rights advocates from countries outside Europe and North America have spoken up and have deparochialized human rights. From the Southern Hemisphere's point of view, claims to the universality of human rights as defined by Americans are unacceptable.

The Russian Parliament's cataloging of American human rights abuses was covered in a 2012 *New York Times* article with the headline "Stung by Criticism, Russian Lawmakers Point to Human Rights Abuses in U.S." The report included rights violations spanning the long

Xinhua News Agency. 2009. "Full Text of Human Rights Record of United States in 2008." Yan Liang, ed. *China View Online*. February 26. http://news.xinhuanet.com/english/2009–02/26/content_10904741 .htm. Accessed February 1, 2015.

period from Ku Klux Klan lynchings in the late nineteenth century to the death penalty, waterboarding, and detentions at the U.S. military prison at Guantanamo Bay. Such abuses were discussed during parliamentary hearings in Russia titled "On Problems on the Observation of Human Rights in the United States."

Another 2012 *New York Times* article quotes Khalid Shaikh Mohammed, accused of masterminding the September 11 attacks, as saying that the U.S. government was guilty of killing many more people than he was, all under the guise of national security: "Thousands of people, millions." The justification of murder and rights violations abroad as guaranteeing "national security" indicates that since 1948 the work of American human rights advocates has far been outweighed by the actions of their own government.

The article that follows, from the China News Agency in 2009, is all-encompassing and includes criminality via gun killings; violations of civil, political, economic, social, and cultural rights; racial discrimination; violations of the rights of women and children; and trampling on other nations' sovereignty and violating human rights in those countries. Pointing to U.S. human rights obligations under the international treaties, the article concludes that the United States has turned "a blind eye to its own violations of human rights" and is "applying double standards on human rights issues."

· · ·

BEIJING, Feb. 26 (Xinhua)—The Information Office of the State Council published a report titled "The Human Rights Record of United States in 2008" here on Thursday. Following is the full text:

The State Department of the United States released its Country Reports on Human Rights Practices for 2008 on February 25, 2009. As in previous years, the reports are full of accusations of the human rights situation in more than 190 countries and regions including China, but mentioned nothing of the widespread human rights abuses on its own territory. The Human Rights Record of the United States in 2008 is prepared to help people around the world understand the real situation of human rights in the United States, and as a reminder for the United States to reflect upon its own issues.

ON LIFE AND PERSONAL SECURITY

Widespread violent crimes in the United States pose serious threats to its people's lives, property and personal security.

According to a report published in September 2008 by the Federal Bureau of Investigation (FBI), the country reported 1.4 million violent crimes, including 17,000 murders (*The Washington Post*, June 10, 2008), and 9.8 million property crimes (*The World Journal*, September 16, 2008) in 2007. Throughout 2007, the estimated number of robberies counted 445,125, a 7.5 percent rise over the last five years (*The Washington Post*, September 16, 2008). In cities with 50,000 to 100, 000 inhabitants, the number of murders increased by 3. 7 percent [over] 2006 (*The*

Washington Post, June 10, 2008). In those with populations of 10,000 to 30,000, the number of violent crimes rose 2.4 percent [over] 2006 (*The Washington Post,* September 16, 2008). U.S. residents age 12 and older experienced an estimated 23 million crimes of violence or theft. The violent crime rate in 2007 was 20. 7 victimizations per 1,000 persons age 12 or older; for property crimes it was 146.5 per 1, 000 households. (Criminal Victimization, 2007, U.S. Department of Justice, http://www.ojp.usdoj.gov/bjs/abstract/cv07.htm). Among cities with relatively high violence and murders rates, New Orleans reported 95 murders per 100,000 population, Baltimore 45, Detroit 44, St. Louis 40, Philadelphia 27.8, Houston 16.2, and Dallas 16.1 (*The Philadelphia Inquirer,* June 10, 2008). In the United States, one murder is committed every 31 minutes, one rape every 5.8 minutes, and one burglary every 14. 5 seconds (*The Washington Post,* September 16, 2008).

Guns are widespread in the United States. The U.S. Supreme Court asserted that Americans had an individual right to possess and use firearms, even when the guns are not related to service in a government militia, *The Christian Science Monitor* reported on June 27, 2008. Statistics show that the U.S. citizens own about 200 million private guns, including 60 to 65 million pistols. A total of 48 states in the United States allow its residents to bear guns (*The China Press,* October 16, 2008), while it is believed that one can buy a gun at gun shows in 35 states without a background check (United Press International, October 3, 2008). A gun store outside Nashville, Tennessee, sold 70 guns on November 5, 2008 alone (http://www .usqiaobao.com). More than 20 airports in Philadelphia, Los Angeles, San Francisco and other cities allow people with gun permits to carry firearms in the general public areas of the terminal (*The China Press,* October 15, 2008). A local high school in north Texas even let some teachers carry concealed weapons (*The New York Times,* August 29, 2008). *The Washington Post* reported on December 5, 2007, that 10 states, including Virginia, South Carolina, West Virginia, and Mississippi, supplied 57 percent of the guns that were recovered in crimes in other states in 2007. The 10 states with the highest crime-gun export rates had nearly 60 percent more gun homicides than the 10 states with the lowest rates.

The frequent occurrences of gun killings were a serious threat to the lives of U.S. citizens. According to the U.S. Center for Disease Control and Prevention, 1.35 million high school students in 2007 were either threatened or injured with a weapon at least once on school property (United Press International, October 3, 2008). Young people represent an expanding proportion of all shooting victims, from 13 percent in 2002 to more than 21 percent in 2007. According to a Harvard University survey of high school students in 2006, a fifth of the 1,200 questioned in schools across Boston had witnessed a shooting. More than 40 percent believed it was easy to get a gun, and 28 percent said they did not feel safe on the bus or train (*The Boston Globe,* September 18, 2008). In the 2007–8 school year, a record 34 Chicago Public School students were killed (*The Chicago Tribune,* April 2,

2008). Within a week from February 7, 2008, the United States had seven shooting incidents, leading to 23 deaths and dozens of injuries. On March 27, 2008, five people in Georgia and Kentucky were shot dead (The Associated Press, March 27, March 28, 2008). On the night of April 18, nine shootings were reported in a period of less than two hours in Chicago (*The Chicago Tribune*, April 21, 2008). In November, Baltimore had 31 shootings (*The Baltimore Sun*, December 2, 2008). On December 24, 2008, a man dressed in a Santa costume shot at a Christmas Eve party at his ex-parents-in-law's house, causing eight deaths, three injuries and three missing persons (*The China Press*, December 26, 2008).

ON CIVIL AND POLITICAL RIGHTS

In the United States, an increasing number of restrictions have been imposed on civil rights.

According to a report on *The Washington Post* website on April 4, 2008, the deep-packet inspection, a brand new surveillance technology, which has been applied, is able to record every visited web page, every sent email and every online search. Statistics indicated that at least 100,000 U.S. Internet users had been tracked and the service providers had conducted tests on as many as 10 percent of the U.S. netizens (*The Washington Post*, April 4, 2008). The FBI has been engaged in illegal surveillance launched by the U.S. government nationwide, obtaining thousands of people's phone records, bank accounts and other personal information by unwarranted means.

The Seattle Times reported on July 15, 2008, that President Bush signed a bill on July 10 that overhauls government eavesdropping and called it "landmark legislation that is vital to the security of our people." The new law grants legal immunity to telecommunication companies that take part in wiretapping programs and authorizes the government to wiretap international communications between parties outside the U.S. for anti-terrorism purposes without court approval. The U.S. Department of Homeland Security disclosed in July 2008 that as part of border search policies, federal agents may take a traveler's laptop computer or other electronic device to an off-site location for an unspecified period of time without any suspicion of wrongdoing (*The Washington Post*, August 1, 2008). *The New York Times* reported on December 8, 2008, that the National Security Agency illegally wiretapped a Muslim scholar named Ali al-Timimi in northern Virginia and intentionally withheld materials gained through eavesdropping during a 2005 trial in which the scholar was convicted on terrorism charges. These materials may provide evidences that the U.S. government's eavesdropping program has violated its citizens' civil rights.

Police abuse of force infringed on the civil rights of Americans. According to a report by *The Chicago Tribune* on June 25, 2008, Chicago witnessed eight shootings by police officers in two weeks in June, causing five fatalities. Shapell Ter-rell, a 39-year-old sanitation worker, was fatally shot by police officers on June 22 at the entrance of a two-story building where all four apartments were filled with family members (*The Chicago Tribune,* June 23, 2008). Luis Colon, an 18-year-old man in Chicago, was shot and killed by a plainclothes police officer on June 24, when he was walking with his girlfriend to meet friends and eat at a restaurant (*The Chicago Tribune,* June 25, 2008). Daryl Battle, 20, was shot dead in his Brooklyn apartment in New York City on the morning of August 2, 2008. Michael Mineo was sodomized by a police officer's baton on October 15, on a busy Brooklyn subway platform (*The New York Times,* December 10, 2008). Gilberto Blanco was shot and killed when he was swinging a folding chair in front of a policewoman named Dawn Ortiz in a parking lot near the Coney Island church (*The New York Times,* December 1, 2008).

The proportion of U.S. prisoners to its population has hit a new high. *The Wash-ington Post* reported on July 11, 2008, that the United States has 2.3 million crimi-nals behind bars, more than any other nation in the world. A report issued by the U.S. Department of Justice on December 11, 2008, said that over 7.3 million people were on probation, in jail or on parole at the end of 2007, equivalent to 3.2 percent of all U.S. adult residents or one in every 31 adults. (United Press International, December 11, 2008). For black men age 20–34, one in nine was in jail. (*The Guard-ian,* March 1, 2008). The rate of prisoners, higher than any period in the U.S. his-tory, was almost six times the world average (125 of every 100,000 people). Accord-ing to statistics, the recidivism rate stayed high in the United States. Half the people of previous convictions were sentenced to prison again within three years.

There is no proper protection of prisoners' basic rights. Information released in August 2008 by the U.S. Department of Justice showed that the rate of conviction by U.S. courts has been on a rise since 1993. Convicts who committed violent crimes accounted for more than 50 percent of the total. California had 172,000 inmates in its 33 prisons, which were designed for just over half that number, leav-ing each inmate a space of only 6 square feet ("Prison Overcrowding Blamed for Health Woes," http://www.sfgate.com, November 19, 2008). In Prince George['s County] in Maryland, the Upper Marlboro jail held an estimated 1,500 prisoners while it was designed for about 1,330 (*The Washington Post,* July 25, 2008). There were frequent reports of inmates dying from prison officers' violence. An Amnesty International report in 2008 said the Taser was widely used to control inmates in the U.S. prisons and detention centers. It had tracked more than 300 cases since 2001 in which people died after being shocked by a Taser. Among them, 69 died in 2008. According to a report by *The Washington Post* on July 25, more than 10 jail officers in Prince George['s County], Maryland, have arrest records. At least six officers were suspended in the past seven months and nine others still worked in the prison though they were accused of crimes or violence. Baron Pikes, arrested on a cocaine charge, died in January 2008 after a police officer had shocked him nine times with a Taser (CNN website, July 22, 2008). Ronnie L. White, 19, died of strangulation on June 29, 2008, when he was held in solitary confinement at a correction center in Prince George's County, Maryland (*The Washington Post,* September 23, 2008). According to the latest statistics released by the U.S. Department of Justice in June 2008, 1,154 inmates in the federal and state prisons died of AIDS between 2001 and 2006 (*Ming Pao Daily,* July 3, 2008). Some U.S. jails have become the "new asylums" for drug addicts and mental patients, with six out of 10 people in jail living with a mental illness (Jails bulging with people with mental illnesses, the homeless and people detained for immigration offenses; costing counties billions ["New Report: Jail Populations Exploding; Massive Growth Devastating Local Communities"], http://justicepolicy.org). *The Economist* reported on May 10, 2008, that the U.S. was one of the few countries where the felons were deprived of rights. Some U.S. states even forbid felons to vote.

ON ECONOMIC, SOCIAL AND CULTURAL RIGHTS

American people's economic, social and cultural rights are not properly protected.

There is a wide wealth gap in the American society. According to a *New York Times* report on October 5, 2008, the United States developed the most unequal distribution of income and wages of any high-income country over the past 30 years. The richest fifth of the Americans earn an average of 168,170 U.S. dollars a year, about fifteen times the figure for the bottom fifth—11,352 U.S. dollars. The top one percent of New York City tax filers received 37 percent of the city's adjusted gross income—which includes wages, business income and capital gains, among other earnings (*The New York Times,* April 9, 2008). There are 64 billionaires in New York City with a combined net worth of 344 billion U.S. dollars, 469 percent more than the collective worth of the city's billionaires two years ago (*The Washington Post,* September 29, 2008). A UN report released on October, 22, 2008, showed that the wealth gap in big American cities, including New York, Washington, Atlanta and New Orleans, was almost as wide as some African cities, and the ratio of income inequality in American cities was very high.

The number of people who are homeless, in poverty and hunger increased in the United States in 2007. Figures released in August 2008 by the U.S. Census Bureau showed that 12.5 percent of Americans, or 37. 3 million people, were living in poverty in 2007, up from 36.5 million in 2006. Eighteen percent of children (13.3 million) were impoverished in 2007, up from 17.4 percent (12.8 million) in 2006 (Reuters, August 27, 2008). Some 7.6 million American families, or 9.8 percent of the total, were living in poverty.

In 2007, the annual income of 1.56 million American people, 41.8 percent of the country's population in poverty, reached only half of the poverty threshold. In

New York City, [the] latest study shows 23 percent of the people are living in poverty (*The Washington Post,* July 14, 2008).

"According to a nationwide survey jointly conducted by the Washington Post, Harvard University and others in 2008, about 80 percent of low-income workers could not afford to buy fuel or save for pension insurance under the influence of the financial crisis." More than 60 percent of them could not afford medical insurance and 50 percent could not pay for food or housing. Reuters reported that food stamps, the main U.S. anti-hunger program which helps the needy buy food, set a record in September 2008, as more than 31.5 million Americans used the program, a year-on-year increase of 17 percent (Reuters, December 3, 2008). About 48 percent of New York City residents had difficulty affording food for themselves and their families in 2008, doubling [the percentage for] 2003. Already, 1.3 million New York City residents rely on emergency food organizations, up 24 percent from 1 million in 2004 (*The NYC Hunger Experience 2008 Update: Food Poverty Soars as Recession Hits Home*). Some 68.8 percent of emergency food agencies reported that they did not have enough food to fulfill demand ("Survey Shows Impact of Hunger Crisis," http://www.nyccah.org). More than 2 million American families were unable to pay back house loans. Statistics released on November 13, 2008, showed that foreclosure filings grew 25 percent nationally in October 2008 over the same month in 2007. More than 84,000 properties were repossessed by banks in October (*The China Press,* November 14, 2008).

Statistics collected by the U.S. Department of Housing and Urban Development showed that the number of chronically homeless people living in the nation's streets and shelters reached 123,833 in 2007. About 1.6 million people experienced homelessness and found shelter between October 1, 2006, and September 30, 2007 (*The New York Times,* July 30, 2008). The number of requests for emergency shelter doubled from fiscal year 2007 to fiscal 2008 (*World Journal,* October 22, 2008). In Louisiana and Kentucky, the number of homeless families increased to 931. In December 2008, 19 of the 25 American cities surveyed reported some kind of increase in homelessness between October 1, 2007, and October 30, 2008. And 16 cities reported an increase in family homelessness ("Advocacy Groups Fear New Wave of Homeless," http://ipsnews.net). The Washington Legal Clinic for the Homeless estimated that more than 6,000 people were homeless in the District [of Columbia] on an average day. Among them, 47 percent were "chronically homeless" ("District Agrees on Homeless Shelter Access; Faces $5 Million Cost," *The Washington Times,* December 13, 2008).

The rights of laborers are not properly protected. The unemployment rate in America keeps high. Statistics released by the U.S. Department of Labor on January 9, 2009, showed that the unemployment rate increased from 4.6 percent in 2007 to 5.8 percent in 2008, the highest since 2003. A total of 2.6 million jobs were lost in 2008, the biggest loss since 1945. In December 2008 alone, 524,000 jobs were lost, driving the unemployment rate to a 16-year-high of 7. 2 percent (*The New York Times*, January 10, 2009). The number of long-term unemployed (those jobless for 27 weeks or more) reached 2.2 million in November, up by 822,000 over the past 12 months (Employment Summary, http://data.bls.gov). According to a poll conducted by Harris Interactive, the median time Americans spent working in 2008, which included housekeeping and studying, was 46 hours, which was one hour more than that of 2007. One in every four Americans said their working hours increased in 2008. The median time Americans spent playing in 2008 was 16 hours, a decline of four hours from a year ago and the lowest since 1973 (Agence France Presse, December 10, 2008). A survey of day-laborer sites in 25 states found that half of all workers had been underpaid or not paid at least once (*The Washington Post*, July 8, 2008). In July 2008, a Minnesota court ruled Wal-Mart Stores Inc. violated state wage and hour laws, failing to give workers their full rest breaks and requiring hourly employees to work off-the-clock during training (*The China Press*, December 10, 2008). On July 23, 2008, New York's State Labor Department said a clothes factory called "Jin Shun" in Queens was found to have cheated its workers of 5.3 million U.S. dollars in the past six years by paying them salaries far below the minimum wage and not paying for overtime work (*World Journal*, July 24, 2008). On September 6, about 27,000 machinists at Boeing went on strike, requiring the company to raise their salaries and welfares (http://news. bbc.co.uk/chinese/simp /hi/newsid-7600000). On October 20, the U.S. District Court in Manhattan, New York, ordered Saigon Grill Restaurant to compensate 4.6 million U.S. dollars to 36 delivery workers for violations of minimum wage and overtime laws (*The China Press*, December 23, 2008).

Employees' pension plans shrank considerably. A senior budget analyst with the U.S. Congress estimated in October 2008 that Americans' pension accounts lost 2 trillion U.S. dollars in the past 15 months. More than half the people surveyed in an Associated Press–GfK poll said they would have to delay their retirement. A survey conducted by the American Association of Retired Persons (AARP) released in October 2008 said one out of five Americans above the age of 45 stopped putting money into a 401(k), IRA (Individual Retirement Account) or other retirement account (*The China Press*, October 8, 2008). A study by Hewitt Associates found the average U.S. 401(k) plan balance was down 14 percent in 2008 to 68,000 U.S. dollars from 79,000 U.S. dollars in 2007. 401(k) refers to a section of the U.S. Tax Code that allows retirement plan investors to defer paying taxes (*The China Press*, November 25, 2008).

The realization of Americans' education rights is not guaranteed. The American Human Development Report for 2008–2009 showed that 14 percent of Americans (about 40 million), with inadequate ability to read or write, were not able to understand the articles in newspapers or user manuals (*The China Press*, July 17, 2008). A report published on December 3, 2008, by the U.S. National Center for

Public Policy and Higher Education said college tuition and fees increased 439 percent from 1982 to 2007 while median family income rose 147 percent. Tuition for the 2008 fall semester increased by 6.4 percent on average for state universities. Many states planned to sharply increase tuition for public universities in 2009. Florida and Washington State were considering an increase of 15 percent and 20 percent, respectively. Among the poorest families—those with incomes in the lowest 20 percent—the net cost of a year at a public university was 55 percent of median income, up from 39 percent in 1999–2000. At community colleges, that cost was 49 percent of the poorest families' median income in 2008, up from 40 percent in 1999–2000 (*The New York Times,* December 3, 2008). Only 11 percent of the children from the most impoverished families were college graduates. The figure for children from the top-earning 20 percent of families was 53 percent (*The New York Times,* February 22, 2008).

[The number of] Americans without health insurance has been increasing. According to the *American Human Development Report* published in July 2008, despite spending 230 million U.S. dollars an hour on healthcare, Americans live shorter lives than citizens of almost every other developed country, ranking 42nd in terms of life expectancy. One out of six Americans does not have health insurance. The Census Bureau said in a report published on August 26, 2008, that there are 45.7 million Americans without health insurance. Nineteen states had already made cuts or were planning to make cuts in Medicaid and/or the State Children's Health Insurance Program (SCHIP) (*The China Press,* December 12, 2008). As medical expenses were rising, many companies quit buying health insurance for their employees. Research conducted by the National Federation of Independent Business in March 2008 found that only 47 percent of small-size companies provide health aids [*sic*] for their employees. Among companies of 50 employees or less, only 24 percent offer health aids. Many gave up seeing a doctor or receiving treatments as they couldn't afford it.

Drugs, suicide and other social problems prevail in the United States. America has the largest population of cocaine and marijuana users in the world. A survey of 54,000 people from 17 countries found that 16 percent of U.S. survey respondents had at least tried cocaine in their lifetime, and more than 42 percent had tried marijuana ("WHO Global Drug Survey Finds High Rates of Cocaine, Marijuana Use in U.S.," http://www.thebostonchannel.com). The suicide rate among middle-aged white Americans has been on the rise. A research report issued on October 21, 2008, by the Johns Hopkins Bloomberg School of Public Health said between 1999 and 2005, the overall suicide rate in the United States rose by 0.7 percent every year. The figure for white men aged 40 to 64 rose 2.7 percent and for middle-aged white women 3.9 percent. In 2007, a total of 138 people in the city of St. Louis committed suicide. As of June 2, 2008, 61 in the city committed suicide, up by 15 year-on-year (*The Washington Post,* June 2, 2008). The suicide rates in

Baltimore, Detroit and New Orleans were all on the rise (*The Christian Science Monitor,* January 4, 2008). Many young Americans have personality disorders. Researchers found that almost one in five young American adults has a personality disorder that interferes with everyday life, and nearly half of young people surveyed have some sort of psychiatric condition. Less than 25 percent of college-aged Americans with mental problems get treatment ("1 in 5 Adults Has Personality Disorder," http://www.archgenpsychiatyr.com).

ON RACIAL DISCRIMINATION

In the United States, racial discrimination prevails in every aspect of social life. Black people and other minorities are still suffering from unequal treatment and discrimination.

Black people and other minorities live at the bottom of the American society. A report issued by the U.S. Census Bureau on August 26, 2008, said the real median income for American households was 50,233 U.S. dollars in 2007. That of the non-Hispanic White households was 54,920 U.S. dollars, Hispanic households 38,679 U.S. dollars, Black households 33, 916 U.S. dollars. The median income of Hispanic and Black households was roughly 62 percent of that of the non-Hispanic White households. The poverty rate of Hispanics stood at 21.5 percent, higher than the 20.6 percent in 2006 (Income, Poverty, and Health Insurance Coverage in the United States: 2007, issued by the U.S. Census Bureau in August 2008, http://www.census.gov). According to *The State of Black America,* issued by the National Urban League in March 2008, nearly one quarter of Black American households live below the poverty line, three times that of White households. A report released by the Working Poor Families Project on October 14, 2008, said that in 2006, among all non-Hispanic White Households, those with low income accounted for 20 percent, while among minorities, the proportion was 41 percent. In New York City, the poverty proportion of Hispanic, Asian, African Americans and non-Hispanic White people were 29.7 percent, 25.9 percent, 23.9 percent and 16.3 percent, respectively (*World Journal,* July 14, 2008). Immigrants find it hard to own a house in the United States. The New York Immigrant Housing Collaborative and Pratt Center for Community Development said in a report issued on December 3, 2008, that around 25 percent of the native Americans spent half of their income on housing rent, while the ratio was about 31. 5 percent among immigrants. Immigrants from South America and Mexico spent 71.1 percent and 79.8 percent of their incomes on rent, respectively (*The China Press,* December 4, 2008). AIDS threatens the life of African Americans. A study released by the New York City Department of Health and Mental Hygiene in August 2008 said that among the newly infected HIV-positive [people] in the city in 2006, 46 percent were Blacks while 32 percent were Hispanics (*New York Times,* August 28, 2008). Black women are 15 times as likely to be infected with HIV as White women ("Hot Docs: AIDS in America, Criminal-izing HIV, Obama's National Security Team," http://www.usnews.com). Currently, there are at least 500,000 Black Americans infected with HIV/AIDS.

Discrimination in employment is commonplace. According to statistics from the U.S. Labor Department, the jobless rate in the United States was 6 percent in the third quarter of 2008. The jobless rate for Blacks was 10.6 percent, twice that of the Whites (5.3 percent) (The Employment Situation: November 2008, issued by the U.S. Department of Labor, http://www.bls.gov). The Equal Employment Opportunity Commission said it received 30,510 charges concerning employment discrimination in 2007 (Charge Statistics FY1997 through FY 2007, http://www.eeoc.gov/stats/charges.html). An accusation was filed by Oswald Wilson, an Afri-can American, on February 11, 2008, against the American Broadcast Company (ABC) and its parent company, Disney. He said a pattern of racial discrimination had caused him physical pain and emotional suffering ("Black Worker Hits ABC in Racism Suit," http://www.nydailynews.com/news). On December 5, 2008, former New York state governor Eliot Spitzer's father, Bernard Spitzer, was found guilty of racial discrimination by a jury. Four African Americans who had worked as door-men or porters at a 34-story building owned by Bernard Spitzer claimed that they lost their jobs because of the color of their skins. They were fired a decade ago, replaced by someone with lighter skin color (The China Press, December 8, 2008).

The ugly head of racial discrimination emerges from time to time in the educa-tion sector. The State of Black America issued by the National Urban League in 2008 said African Americans' high school graduation rate and college entry rate still lingered at the level of the Whites two or three decades ago. Fewer African American students get college degrees than the Whites. A news report said that African American students in public schools were more likely to get physical pun-ishment than White children, while African American girls were twice as likely to get paddled than White girls ("US: End Beating of Children in Public Schools," http://www.hrw.org/en/news/2008/08/19). Racial segregation in schools is getting worse. A report by the Civil Rights Project at the University of California found that Blacks and Hispanics are more separate from white students than at any time since the civil rights movement. Some 39 percent of Black students and 40 percent of Hispanic students are isolated in schools in which there is little racial mixing. The report also found that the average Black and Latino students is now in a school that has nearly 60 percent of students from families who are near or below the poverty line (Reuters, January 14, 2009).

Racial discrimination in the judicial system is appalling. The U.S. Department of Justice said on June 5, 2008, that jailed Black men were six times as many as the Whites by July 30, 2007. Nearly 11 percent of the Black men between 30 and 34 were in prison. The New York-based Human Rights Watch said in a report released in February 2008 that African American youth arrested for murder are at least three times more likely than their White peers to receive life imprisonment without the possibility of parole [LWOP] ("US: Uphold Treaty against Racial Discrimination," http://www.hrw.org/en/news/2008/02/06). In California, they are almost six times more likely to receive a sentence of LWOP ("The United States Was Not Forthcoming and Accurate in its Presentation to CERD," http://www.hrw.org/en/news/2008/02/06). *The New York Times* carried a report on May 6, 2008, saying that although most drug offenders are White, 54 percent of the drug offenders sent to prison are Black. In 16 states, African Americans are sent to prison for drug offenses at rates between 10 and 42 times greater than the rate for Whites. A study of 34 states shows that a Black man is 11.8 times more likely than a White man to be sent to prison on drug charges, and a Black woman is 4.8 times more likely than a white Woman ("US: 'Drug War' Unjust to African Americans," http://www.hrw.org/en/news/2008/05/04). According to media reports, Sean Bell, a black youngster, died after being shot at 50 times the day he was to be married. But the three police officers were acquitted of all charges in his death ("National Urban League Urges U.S. Justice Department to Prosecute Acquitted Officers in Sean Bell Shooting Case," http://www/nul.org/PressReleases/2008/2008pr430.htm). Statistics from the Los Angeles police showed that for every 100 Hispanics stopped by the police for questioning, there is only one White person being stopped. African Americans are even more likely to be intercepted by police. Blacks and Hispanics are also frequently ordered to get out of their vehicles, frisked, shoved and detained. In the past five years, the L.A. police received nearly 1,200 complaints against police officers over racial discrimination, but none was handled (*The China Press*, October 21, 2008). Muslims, Arabic Americans and other minority groups are also targets for anti-terrorism investigation of FBI (*Ming Pao Daily*, July 3, 2008). On New Year's Day of 2009, an unarmed black man, 22-year-old Oscar Grant, was pressed face-down on an Oakland train platform by police officers and shot in the back. Such atrocity aroused protest from local people, who took to streets on January 7 (Associated Press, February 13, 2009).

The basic rights of Indigenous Americans were infringed on. The United States erected a 18-feet-high wall along the U.S.-Mexico border, which severely impaired life of local Apache people. Indigenous women fell victim to violence of American soldiers. In border cities and townships like Juarez, more than 4,000 Indigenous women were killed or reported missing. The population of Indigenous youth accounts for less than 2 percent of the total youth population in the United States. But among those in jail, the Indigenous accounted for 15 to 20 percent, and 30 percent of them received the toughest penalty. On April 15, 2008, people of the Yankton Sioux ethnic group in South Dakota staged a peaceful demonstration against building a hoggery, which they considered as highly pollutant. More than 70 officers from the county, state and federal law enforcement agencies, with the help of a special police squad, police dogs, snipers as well as helicopters, cracked down [on] the peaceful protest. Thirty-eight people, including children and the elderly, were arrested. The United States deployed troops and built navy and air force bases in Guam, taking up one third of the land there. Local Chamoru people were victimized by the weapons left by the U.S. Army during the World War II and nuclear tests. The incidence of rhino pharyngeal cancer among them is 1,999 percent higher than the average for Americans.

Immigrants received inhumane treatment. Harriett Olson, deputy general secretary of the Women's Division of the General Board of Global Ministries of the United Methodist Church, said that once arrested, the illicit immigrants were always mistreated. They were often jailed with criminals and denied fundamental human rights and basic medical service. Each year, dozens of them die in jail (*The China Press*, December 14, 2008). Human Rights Watch said in June 2008 that the Department of Homeland Security had more than 30,000 individuals in detention, and that more than 80 immigrants have died in the last five years while in the care of the department or immediately after their release from custody, due to inconsistent standards of care and inadequate oversight ("US: Protect Health of Immigration," http://www .hrw.org/en/news). According to a report by *The New York Times*, computer engineer Hiu Lui Ng, who moved to New York from Hong Kong in 1992, was sent to a detention center in 2007 after his visa expired, and was then jailed in three states in New England. He died in custody in August 2008 with his spine fractured and his body riddled with cancer that had gone undiagnosed and untreated for months (*The New York Times*, August 12, 2008). More than 2,900 illegal laborers were detained since October 2007, but only 75 employers or managers faced accusation. This number was just 2 percent of the laborers (*The New York Times*, July 1, 2008).

There is serious racial hostility in the United States. According to [the] Voice of America, a research report released by the U.S. Department of Justice at the end of 2005 shows that the United States reports about 191,000 hate crime each year (Voice of America's Chinese website, November 7, 2008). An FBI report released on October 27, 2008, indicated that 7,624 hate crime incidents were reported in the United States in 2007. Among them, 50.8 percent were motivated by a racial bias, and 62.9 percent of the known offenders were white ("FBI Releases 2007 Hate Crime Statistics," http://www.fbi.gov/hc2007/summary.htm). *The Chicago Tribune* reported on November 23, 2008, that there were 602 organizations based on racial bias [*sic*] in the United States in 2000. The number surged to 888 by 2008. On the same day, *The Boston Globe* reported a survey by a professor from Northwestern University, saying that the ratio of black men being murdered soared by 33 percent from 2002 to 2007.

ON THE RIGHTS OF WOMEN AND CHILDREN

The conditions of women and children in the United States are worrisome.

Women account for 51 percent of the U.S. population, but only 88 women serve in the 110th U.S. Congress. Sixteen women serve in the Senate, or 16 percent of the seats, and 72 women serve in the House, or 16.6 percent of the seats. As of December 2007, 73 women held statewide elective executive offices across the country, or 23.2 percent of the available positions. The proportion of women in state legislatures is at 23.7 percent. As of July 2008, among the 100 largest cities in the U.S., only 11 had women mayors ("Women Serving in the 110th Congress, 2007–09," Center for American Women and Politics, http://www.cawp.rutgers.edu).

Gender-based discrimination in employment is quite serious. The U.S. Equal Employment Opportunity Commission said it received 24,826 charges of discrimination on the basis of sex in 2007, accounting for 30.1 percent of the total discrimination charges (Charge Statistics FY 1997 through FY 2007, http://eeoc.gov /stats/charges.html). A growing number of women are being treated unfairly by employers because they are pregnant or hope to be ("Mom-to-Be Claim Work Bias," http://www.nydailynews.com, May 19, 2008). According to statistics released by the U.S. Census Bureau in August 2008, the real median earnings of women who worked full time in 2007 were 35,102 U.S. dollars, 78 percent of those of corresponding men, whose median earnings were 45,113 U.S. dollars (Current Population Survey, http://www.census.gov/press-release/www/releases/archives /income_wealth/012528.html). The unemployment rate for adult women continued to trend up. It reached 5.5 percent as of November 2008 (*The Employment Situation: November 2008*, issued by the U.S. Department of Labor, December 5, 2008, http://www.bls.gov).

American women are victims of domestic violence and sexual violence. Statistics showed that among women receiving emergency treatment, one third of them are victims of domestic violence. Sexual violence poses a serious threat to American women. It is reported that the United States has the highest rape rate among countries which report such statistics. It is 13 times higher than that of England and 20 times higher than that of Japan (Occurrence of Rape, http://www.sa .rochester.edu/masa/stats.php). Sexual assault against Indigenous women in the United States is widespread. Some women interviewed by Amnesty International said they didn't know anyone in their community who had not experienced sexual violence ("Maze of Injustice: The Failure to Protect Indigenous Women from Sexual Violence in the USA," http://www.amnestyusa.org). Statistics showed that the Equal Employment Opportunity Commission received 12,510 charges of sexual harassment in 2007, 84 percent of which were filed by females ("Sexual Harassment Charges EEOC & FEPAs Combined: FY 1997–FY 2007," http//www.eeoc .gov). A *USA Today* report on October 28, 2008, citing a study, said about one out of seven female veterans of Afghanistan or Iraq who visit a Veterans Affairs center for medical care reported being a victim of sexual assault or harassment during military duty. More than half these women have post-traumatic stress disorder ("15% of Female Veterans Tell of Sexual Trauma, More Than Half of Them Experience Stress Disorder," http://global.factiva.com).

An increasing number of children are living in poverty. Children under 18 account for one third of the people in poverty in the United States. Statistics show that as of the end of 2007, the poverty rate of children younger than 18 was 18 percent, up from 17.4 percent in 2006. The poverty rate of children in single female-headed families reached as high as 43 percent (*Income, Poverty, and Health Insurance Coverage in the United States: 2007*, issued by the U.S. Census Bureau, August 2008, www.census.gov.). According to a report released on October 14, 2008, by the Working Poor Families Project, one third of children lived in low-income working families in 2006. In New York City, 41.6 percent of children in single-parent families live under the poverty line. At the end of 2007, 8.1 million children under 18, or 11 percent of the total, were uninsured (*Income, Poverty, and Health Insurance Coverage in the United States: 2007*, issued by the U.S. Census Bureau, August 2008, www.census.gov).

The conditions of American students are worrisome. According to the U.S. Department of Education, more than 223,000 students were corporally punished in 2007. More than 200,000 public school students were punished by beatings during the 2006–2007 school year. In 13 states, more than 1,000 students were corporally punished per year ("US: End Beating of Children in Public Schools," http://www.hrw.org/en/new/2008/08/19). Corporal punishment is legal in 21 states, according to a report released by the American Civil Liberties Union and Human Rights Watch on August 19, 2008. Alcohol abuse, gambling and drug use are pervasive on campus. Between 1999 and 2005, 157 college students died of alcoholism and 750,000 youths were addicted to drugs. A report on teen drug use issued by University of Michigan researchers on December 11, 2008, shows that 11 percent of eighth graders, 24 percent of tenth graders and 32 percent of 12th graders reported using marijuana in the prior year. Use of any illicit drug in the prior year was reported by 37 percent of 12th graders, 27 percent of 10th graders and 14 percent of eighth graders (*The China Press*, December 12, 2008).

There is no guarantee of children's security. The Children's Defense Fund said in its 2008 annual report that 3,006 children and teens died in 2005 from firearms. According to a survey by the Center for Children, Law and Policy, University of Houston, guns kill eight children and teens every day in America, which means the Virginia Tech shooting occurring every four days, or a child or teen being killed by guns every three hours ("Children and Teens Firearm Deaths Increase for First Time since 1994," http://www.childrenandthelawblog.come/2008/06/19). Each year about 1.8 million children are reported lost. More than 3 million children are reported as victims of physical, sexual, verbal and emotional abuse, neglect, abandonment, and death ("Facts You Should Know about Violence against Children," http://www.loveourchildrenusa.org). There are about 1,500 child-abuse fatalities every year ("Abuse More a Risk in Non-traditional Families," http://usa-today.com). Sexual abuse against children is serious. One in five children were reportedly sexually abused by the age of 18 ("Facts You Should Know about Violence against Children," http://www.loveourchildrenusa.org). In a Texas polygamist sect, some girls as young as 12 were forced into marriage with middle-aged men (*The China Press*, September 23, 2008). Research by the U.S. Centers for Disease Control and Prevention found that one fourth of teenage American girls, or 3 million, had a sexually transmitted disease (STD). African American teenage girls were most severely affected. Nearly half of the young African American women were infected with an STD, compared with 20 percent of young White women (*Sing Tao Daily*, March 12, 2008).

The United States is one of the few countries in the world where minors receive the same criminal punishments as adults do. It is the only country in the world that sentences children to life in prison without possibility of parole or release. There are 2,381 such inmates in U.S. prisons currently ("The United States Was Not Forthcoming and Accurate in Its Presentation to CERD," http://www.hrw.org). Seventy-three of them are serving a death-in-prison sentence for offenses at the age of 13 or 14. Among them, 49 percent are African Americans, and most of them come from needy families, without enough legal aids. These children will die in prison without parole no matter how they are corrected (Equal Justice Initiative, http://eji.org). According to the general comments made by the United Nations Committee on the Rights of the Child in April 2007, sentencing minors to death or life in prison without possibility of release violates Article 37 of the [UN] Convention on the Rights of the Child. When reviewing the human rights record of the United States in 2006, the United Nations Human Rights Council said sentencing minors to life in prison without possibility of release violates Article 7 and Article 24 of the International Covenant on Civil and Political Rights.

Thousands of innocent children have been put into prison by corrupt judges. According to a report of the Spanish newspaper *Rebelion* on February 20, 2009, among the 5,000 juvenile prisoners in Pennsylvania, an estimated 2,000 were wrongly put into prison by two bribe-taking judges. According to the report, Judge Mark A. Ciavarella Jr. and Michael T. Conahan in Luzerne County took more than 2.6 million U.S. dollars in kickbacks to send teenagers to two private youth detention centers run by PA Child Care and a sister company, Western PA Child Care. Most of the teenagers did not have a lawyer to turn to. Jamie Quinn, 18, stayed in prison for one year when she was 14 after she and a friend quarreled and slapped each other's face. Jamie was taken to a juvenile detention center and later transferred to several other jails. In her captivity, Jamie was forced to take some medicines so she could be "obedient." The girl is just one of the thousands of innocent children.

The use of child labor is serious in the United States. The Associated Press reported that the owner and managers of a meatpacking plant in Iowa was in September 2008 charged with more than 9,000 misdemeanors alleging they hired minors and in some cases had children younger than 16 handle dangerous equip-ment. The Iowa attorney general's office said the violations involved 32 illegal immigrant children under age 18, including seven who were younger than 16 ("Iowa Files Child Labor Charges against Meat Plant," Associated Press, Septem-ber 10).

ON THE VIOLATION OF HUMAN RIGHTS
IN OTHER NATIONS

The United States has a string of records of trampling on the sovereignty of, and violating human rights in, other countries.

The war in Iraq has led to the death of more than a million civilians, made the same number of people homeless, and incurred huge economic losses. Xe, for-merly known as Blackwater Worldwide and connected to the U.S. Department of State, and DynCorp hired 6,000 private security guards in Iraq. Victims of activi-ties of the two companies are frequently Iraqi civilians. A report issued by a super-vision team under the U.S. House of Representatives in October 2007 said Xe employees had been involved in at least 196 shooting incidents in Iraq since 2005, which translates into 1.4 incidents a week. Xe employees fired first in 84 percent of these incidents. The United States established prisons across Iraq, where prisoners were routinely abused. Human Rights Watch said on April 27, 2008, that the U.S.-led Multi-national Force–Iraq (MNF) was holding 24,514 detainees at the end of 2007 ("UN: Tell US to End Illegal Detention Practices in Iraq," http://www.hrw .org/en/news/2008/04/27). On average, detainees remain in custody for more than 300 days, and all Iraqi detainees are denied their basic rights ("America's Iraqi Prisoners," http://www.hrw.org/en/news/2008/08/07). According to a Human Rights Watch report on May 19, 2008, the United States has detained some 2,400 children in Iraq, including those as young as 10, since 2003. U.S. forces were also holding 513 Iraqi children as "imperative threats to security." Children in Iraqi custody are at risk of physical abuse ("US: Respect Rights of Child Detainees in Iraq," http//www.hrw.org/en/news/2008/05/19).

The United States has maintained its economic, commercial and financial embargo against Cuba for nearly 50 years. Cuban foreign minister Felipe Perez Roque said the U.S. blockade has caused an accumulated direct economic loss of more than 93 billion U.S. dollars for Cuba. Seven out of 10 Cubans have spent their entire lives under the U.S. embargo ("Overwhelming International Rejection of US Blockade of Cuba at UN," www.cubanews.ain.cu/2008/1029votacion_onu .htm). On October 29, 2008, the 63rd session of the United Nations General Assembly adopted a resolution entitled "Necessity of Ending the Economic, Com-mercial and Financial Embargo Imposed by the United States of America against Cuba" with a vote of 185 for, three against, urging the United States to immediately end its unilateral embargo against Cuba. It is the 17th consecutive year that an overwhelming majority in the assembly have supported the measure. It is a demonstration of the international community expressing their strong dissatisfaction over the United States acting against the international law and UN Charter by viciously violating Cuban peoples' rights to live and develop.

The United States is the world's biggest seller of arms. Its arms sales greatly intensified instability across the world and severely violated human rights of foreign nationals. [According to] a report by the New America Foundation, U.S. arms sales reached 32 billion U.S. dollars in 2007, more than three times the level in 2001. The weapons were sold to more than 174 nations and regions ("Study: US Arms Sales Undermine Global Human Rights," http://sfgate.com).

The United States is haunted by scandals of prisoner abuses. *The Washington Post* reported on September 25, 2008, that U.S. interrogators poking, slapping or shoving detainees would not give rise to criminal liability, according to an internal memo declassified by the Department of Defense. The same newspaper reported on April 22, 2008, that U.S. interrogators used practices such as keeping detainees from sleeping, forced drugging, and coercing confession through torture during questioning detainees at the military prison in Guantanamo. Human Rights Watch said in a February 6, 2008, report that about 185 of the 270 detainees are housed in facilities akin to "supermax" prisons in various "camps" at the detention center in Guantanamo even though they have not yet been convicted of a crime. These detainees have extremely limited contact with other human beings, spend[ing] 22 hours a day alone in small cells with little or no natural light or fresh air ("News Report Finds Treatment of Detainees Unnecessarily Harsh," http//www.hrw.org /en/news/2008/06/10). The Associated Press reported that more than 20 detainees under the age of 18 have been brought to the prison camp in Guantanamo since 2002 to fall victim to mistreatment from U.S. Army service people. In June 2008, Mohammed Jawad described his experience in May 2004 when he, [under age] 18 then, was brought to the detention center in Guantanamo and was denied his time for sleep. Jawad was moved from cell to cell 112 times in 14 days, usually left in one cell for less than three hours before being shackled and moved to another. He was moved more frequently between midnight and 2 A.M. to ensure maximum disruption of sleep ("The War on Teen Terror," http://www.hrw.org/en/news/2008/06/23).

The United States is inactive towards its international human rights obligations under the international treaties. The U.S. signed the International Covenant on Economic, Social and Cultural Rights 31 years ago, the Covenant on the Elimination of All Forms of Discrimination against Women 28 years ago, and the Convention on the Rights of the Child 14 years ago, but none of the above treaties has been approved yet. The Convention on Rights of Disabled Persons is the most important progress the United Nations has achieved in protecting the rights of disabled persons in the new century, and the convention is highly valued by different nations. So far, 136 countries have signed the convention, and 41 already approved it. But the United States has yet to endorse and sign the convention. The U.S. has refused a pledge to promote and protect the rights of Indigenous people, and also failed to acknowledge their rights of self-govern[ment], of land and of natural resources in the United Nations and in the international community. On September 13, 2007, the 61st session of the United Nations General Assembly adopted the Declaration of Aboriginal Rights by a vote of 143 in favor, while the United States was one of the only four countries that voted against it.

The United States has always obstinately followed double standards in dealing with international human rights affairs, and failed to fulfill its international human rights obligations. The Special Rapporteur on the Human Rights of Migrants of the United Nations visited the United States in 2007. However, the original plans to visit the detention centers in Hutto, Texas, and Monmouth, New Jersey, were canceled with no satisfactory explanations from the U.S. government, although the plans had been sanctioned by the U.S. government in advance. In 2008, the UN Special Rapporteur on the Human Rights of Migrants said in the U.S.-visit report that the United States detained 230,000 migrants every year, more than three times the number nine years ago. The U.S. deportation procedures lack proper procedures about "non-citizens," and non-citizens are rendered incapable of questioning whether they are detained lawfully, or whether for too long. The Special Rapporteur said the United States had failed to fulfill its international obligations, and also failed in adopting comprehensively coordinated national policies in light of explicit international obligations to prioritize the human rights of more than 37.5 million migrants living in the country.

The outbound humanitarian aid offered by the United States are dwarfed by its status as the richest country in the world. According to a report from the Development Assistance Research Associates, a non-profit organization based in Spain, the United States is listed as one of the countries with the worst records in providing independent, righteous [sic], and unbiased humanitarian aid to other countries. The report said the U.S. aid to other countries came frequently linked to its military or political ambitions.

Respect to and protection of human rights is an important indication of civilization and progress of human society. Every government shoulders a common responsibility in committing itself to improvement of human rights conditions in the country. For years, the United States has positioned itself over other countries and released the *Country Reports on Human Rights Practices* annually to criticize human rights conditions in other countries, using it as a tool to interfere with and demonize other nations. In the meantime, the U.S. has turned a blind eye to its own violations of human rights. The U.S. practice of throwing stones at others while living in a glass house is a testimony to the double standards and hypocrisy of the United States in dealing with human rights issues, and has undermined its international image. We hereby advise the U.S. government to begin anew, face its own human rights problems with courage, and stop the wrong practice of applying double standards on human rights issues.

REFERENCES

Barry, Ellen. 2012. "Stung by Criticism, Russian Lawmakers Point to Human Rights Abuses in U.S." *New York Times,* October 23, p. A9.

Branigan, Tania. 2011. "China Accuses US of Human Rights Double Standards." *The Guardian,* April 11. http://www.theguardian.com/world/2011/apr/11/china-us-human-rights-double-standards. Accessed February 1, 2015.

Zakaria, Fareed. 2011. "What in the World? China Calls Out the U.S. on Human Rights." *CNN World Online,* April 18. http://globalpublicsquare.blogs.cnn.com/2011/04/18/what-in-the-world-china-calls-out-the-u-s-on-human-rights/. Accessed February 1, 2015.

PART THREE

Indian Travelers and Their Observations

20

From Travels of Mirza Abu Taleb Khan

Mirza Abu Taleb Khan, 1810

Mirza Abu Taleb Khan, of Persian and Turkish descent, was born in 1752 in Lucknow, India, where his father, Mohammed of Ispahan, served in the royal courts. With his courtier lineage, Abu Taleb understood the appropriate behavior for those admitted to these courts. Persian was the language of the Mughal courts and the language of empire in South Asia. British officials had to learn Persian as they assumed power over Indian regional kingdoms from the mid-eighteenth century onward. It was not until 1837 that English officially replaced Persian as the official language of British rule.

With the intention of opening a public-financed academy for the instruction of the "Hindoostany, Persian, and Arabic languages," in 1799 Abu Taleb embarked on a journey to England in the company of a Scottish friend. While working in Bengal for officers of the East India Company, he encountered "many individuals [who] were so desirous of learning the Oriental languages, that they attended self-taught masters ignorant of every principle of the science, and paid them half-a-guinea a lesson" (Abu Taleb Kahn 1810 [1]:164). His European journey, which started in Dublin, Ireland, lasted four and a half years.

Abu Taleb was from a well-to-do and cultured family from Lucknow, where the nobility and courts were famous for their refinement and their patronage of and familiarity with the arts, literature, and poetry. By 1799 he was thus ready for an adventure. He enjoyed his three years traveling in Europe. Upon arrival in London, he was presented to the king and queen, dubbed "the Persian prince," and immediately accepted by the English aristocracy. He understood a great deal about the British before he ever saw England, and evaluated them with many of their own criteria.

Abu Taleb Khan, Mirza. 1810. *Travels of Mirza Abu Taleb Khan in Asia, Africa, and Europe during the Years 1799, 1800, 1801, 1802, and 1803.* Charles Stewart, transl. London: R. Watts, Broxbourne, Herts. Vol. 1, pp. 3–17; Vol. 2, pp. 401–418.

Abu Taleb reserves his highest praise for the scientific advances of the English, which he sees as the positive effects of a liberal education, and is struck by everything from the regularity of English streets, to the great "economy" of their farmyard and dairy systems, to the science of anatomy. While he opines on the many drawbacks to the constant focus among the English on fashion and their apparent ongoing need to acquire new belongings, Abu Taleb is also impressed by the ingenuity and perseverance of invention that this inspires.

Although Abu Taleb is irritated by some of the most personal and intimate practices of the British, such as sleeping on a bed of feathers (on which he has never been able to get a good night's rest), his strongest critiques concern systems that do not work in accord with the rationale that justifies them. He notes with disgust that English law often overrules equity, rather than promoting it, and argues that the jury system is not the bastion of English liberty that it claims to be. In his opinion, Islamic law is the model for removing the profit motive from the legal profession ([1]:16–17). Upon returning home, he identifies some of the problems that arise when the English way of life is translated into an Indian context. Abu Taleb takes a supposedly universal principle, "law," and shows how it can be utilized in a way not universally beneficial. By critically reflecting on the practices of the British in his own country, he shows how untenable it is to impose a way of life onto another society without causing major disruptions.

One of the most interesting selections from Abu Taleb's narrative is his response to accusations by English women that Eastern women are oppressed. What is seen as oppression in Asia, he frames as privilege—"rights," "freedom," and natural law. According to him, Eastern families have the wealth to provide separate parts of the house for the husband and wife, and women are free from participating in business and the affairs of the world while having rights over property, children, and servants. Abu Taleb wryly comments on the custom whereby English women sleep in the same quarters as their husbands, attributing it to the cold climate, and notes that English women do not have real power in marriage when it comes to finances and children.

On his journey back to India in 1803 he visited the Rhone Valley, Marseilles, Geneva, Malta, and Constantinople, then Iraq and Iran. On his return to India Abu Taleb wrote *Travels of Mirza Abu Taleb Khan* in Persian, based on the reflections that occurred to him while traveling and written in a journal. Once home, he revised, abridged, and arranged his journal notes. His catalogue of the vices of English elites—their irreligious behavior, love of luxury, incurable materialism—all made them unfit to rule a religious country like India, he believed. Of more fundamental interest are his comments on the Western belief in progress and perfectibility of human knowledge (165–66). "This boasted knowledge is but vanity," he writes, in a preview of Gandhi's nationalist writings a century later. A "professor" of the East India Company translated the account into English and this first translation was published in London in 1810. Since then many English versions have appeared.

In the end Abu Taleb finds much to admire as well as much that displeases him. Most important, he does not attribute these differences to a "natural" superiority or deficiency, but sees them as simple differences that arise between people with diverse histories, customs, and beliefs. Abu Taleb's writing between 1799 and 1803 makes his account contemporaneous with Al-Jabarti's. But unlike Al-Jabarti, he was not witness to an abrupt invasion.

. . .

CHAP. XVII

Description of the Courts of Law in London—of English Juries—of the Judges and Lawyers. The Author prosecuted by a tailor—his reflections and determination thereon—Censures the establishment of English Courts of Judicature in India—Anecdote of a Witness. Ambiguity of the English Law—Remedy proposed by the Author.

In London, there are several public courts of justice, each of which has its particular department, and separate judges. The court in which criminals are tried is called the *Old Bailey.*

As I had the happiness to be acquainted with several of the judges of this court, and was anxious to obtain some insight of English jurisprudence, I frequently attended their sittings.

The first circumstance that attracted my attention, and consequent applause of the English law, was the right which every British subject possesses, of being tried by a jury. These juries are composed of twelve respectable inhabitants of the city, and, being summoned to attend without having any previous information of the subject to be tried, or any opportunity of conversing with the parties, come into court perfectly disinterested and unbiased, they then take an oath to act impartially, and to decide according to the evidence. It is the duty of the jury to attend scrupulously to the whole of the proceedings, and particularly to the examination of the witnesses, both by the counselors and the judge; they are then to determine, whether the person accused is guilty, or not, of the crime laid to his charge. If they are unanimous in their opinions, the affair is immediately determined, and the judge pronounces the sentence of the law; but if they are of contrary opinions, they are locked up in an adjoining apartment, until they come to a decision on the case. Notwithstanding this is the boasted palladium of English liberty, it does not appear to me free from imperfections. The judge, being a person of great consequence and superior abilities, often impresses the jury with such awe, that, if he is inclined to pass an unjust sentence, he can, in his interpretation of the law, and his address to them, dictate what they are to do. I have frequently seen the judge reprehend the jury for their decisions, and send them back, once or twice, to reconsider their verdict. If, by the above means, the judge can bring a few of the jury over to his opinion, he can frighten the rest, by threatening to lock them up without food; while he and the lawyers retire from the court, and refresh themselves, for three or four hours. From the above circumstance, it appears to me, that the decision in all cases depends more on the judge than on the jury.

The English judges are doubtless men of the strictest honor and probity, and, being independent both in their fortunes and situation, are above all temptation to act unjustly; but the laws being excessively voluminous, and in many instances either contradictory or obscure, the lawyers, whose only income arises from their practice (that is, the fees they receive from the plaintiff and defendant), endeavor to delay the decision of the business as much as possible, and frequently prevail on the judge to postpone the trial to another year: in this manner, civil causes are often carried on for twenty years, to the ruin of both parties. In other instances, the judges allow the lawyers to puzzle and intimidate the witnesses, in such a manner, that it is impossible for a person, unaccustomed to their proceedings, to give his evidence correctly; and it sometimes happens, that the judge yields his own better judgment to the interested arguments of a bribed counselor, who, to serve his client, will undertake to prove that black is white.

I was disgusted to observe, that, in these courts, law very often overruled equity, and that a well-meaning honest man was frequently made the dupe of an artful knave; nor could the most righteous judge alter the decision, without transgressing the law.

I myself had the misfortune to acquire a little experience in this way. Having purchased some cloth, I agreed with a tailor to make me a coat for ten shillings. Although there were two witnesses present, and I even had the agreement in his own hand-writing, he denied it, and sent me a bill for twenty shillings. I gave him the ten, but refused to pay him any more: he said it was well, he should complain to the court of justice, and make me pay the remainder. He went immediately, and procured a summons for me to appear, but this he never delivered; and, after a certain time, produced a decree from one of the courts, ordering me immediately to pay the ten shillings, and a further fine of six shillings, for not having obeyed the summons. This I thought extreme injustice, and consulted one of my friends, who was an attorney, what I should do. He replied, "Although the case is very hard, you must *immediately* pay the money: you may then sue him for having withheld the summons, and for having, by that means, obtained an unjust decision against you." I was however perfectly satisfied with the experience I had already gained, and quietly paid the money. After that transaction, whenever any *unjust claim* was made on me, I endeavored to compromise the matter, by offering to pay a third, or a half, of the amount; and, as my adversaries found it troublesome to go backward and forward, in attendance on the court, they were, in general, reasonable enough to comply with my wishes. This is the plan adopted by many, sensible Englishmen, who find it easier to settle with their opponents in this manner, than to contend the point in a court of law.

I cannot pass over this opportunity of freely expressing my sentiments with respect to the establishment of British courts of law in India; which, I contend, are converted to the very worst of purposes, and, unless an alteration takes place in the system, will some time or other produce the most sinister consequences.

In Calcutta, few months elapse that some respectable and wealthy man is not attacked by the harpies who swarm round the courts of judicature. Various are their modes of extorting money: and many of them have acquired such fortunes by these nefarious means, as to live in great splendor, and quite eclipse the ancient families.

Their general mode of proceeding is this: having, by some means, connected themselves with one of the attorneys of the court, they then, under a fictitious name, purchase a large quantity of goods, on credit, from some country trader; and when the time of payment arrives, they bring forward false witnesses, to prove that the merchandise was bought for half the price actually agreed on.

Another mode of acquiring money, is by frightening people with the terrors of the English law. They first make a demand on a person for a large sum of money, which they say is owing to them, either by himself or his father; to prove which, they frequently forge bonds. If he is alarmed, and compromises the matter with them, it is well; but if he disputes their claim, they proceed to the court, and, in the most hardened and villainous manner, make oath, or twenty oaths if requisite, that such a person owes them 50,000 rupees (£.6250), and is about to abscond to one of the foreign settlements within twenty miles of Calcutta. A summons is *instantly* issued; and the person accused, being seized and brought to the court, is told, he must either give immediate security for a lac of rupees (£.12,500), or go to jail: if he is fortunate enough to have opulent friends, who will immediately come to his assist-ance, and give their security, he may escape the disgrace of being carried to prison, on condition of agreeing to attend on the day of trial: if, on that day, he should arrive in the court an hour too late, he is fined, perhaps a hundred or two hundred pounds; but if he should, by any accident, neglect to attend, his securities are obliged to pay the whole of the lac of rupees. These circumstances are all very distressing to a native of India, unacquainted with the English laws and customs; and many of them, rather than have the trouble and run the risk, willingly pay a sum of money: but if the person accused is a resolute man, who determines to go through the whole process, he is obliged to employ an attorney, who understands not a word of his language, and to entrust an important concern in the hands of a counselor, whom he cannot understand, but through the medium of an interpreter; and the attorney, not being paid by the year, month, or day, as is the custom of India, makes what charges he pleases, and postpones the trial till it suits his convenience. After a lapse of many months, or perhaps years, the cause comes on; and if the defendant is fortunate enough to prove that the plaintiff and his witnesses have perjured them-selves, he obtains a verdict in his favor, and the plaintiff is ordered to pay the *costs of suit*. It frequently happens, that the plaintiff, aware of the event, absconds on the day of trial: if he does not, he may be arrested for the amount of the costs, and carried to jail; he there pleads poverty, and the defendant, after such injuries, is obliged to pay him a weekly allowance; in failure of which, the scoundrel is liberated, and again let loose on the world, to recommence his villainies.

Hitherto we have taken the favorable side of the question. But suppose the defendant unable to give security for so large a sum of money: He is detained, the first day, in the court-house, under charge of the constables; where, if he is a Hindoo, he cannot eat; and if a Mohammedan, he is precluded from performing the duties of his religion. The following day, he is carried to the same prison in which the felons are confined, to the great disgrace of himself and family: there he is every night shut up in a dark and hot cell, where he lingers for months. Many are the respectable persons who die under such misfortunes, before the trial comes on. If the supposed debtor survive till the day of trial arrives, he is then conveyed, under a guard, to the court, where, probably, the plaintiff plays the same tricks as before described; and the only consolation the poor man receives, is, that the court are very sorry he should have suffered so much trouble.

The hardships and inconvenience which witnesses also suffer, when summoned to Calcutta, are so great, that no man in India will now give voluntary evidence in any cause. The witnesses are sometimes brought down the country a month's journey; they are then detained five or six months in Calcutta: when brought into court, they are kept standing for two or three hours; and if pulled by the various questions and cross-questioning of the lawyers and judges, they are then accused of being liars; and obliged to return home, at their own expense, without any remuneration for their loss of time and trouble.

An anecdote is related of a clever woman, who, having been summoned to give evidence before the court of judicature in Calcutta, deposed that such a circumstance occurred in her presence. The judge asked where it happened: she replied, In the verandah of such a house. "Pray, my good woman," said the judge, "how many pillars are there in that verandah?" The woman, not perceiving the trap that was laid for her, said, without much consideration, that the verandah was supported by four pillars. The counsel for the opposite party immediately offered to prove that the verandah contained five pillars, and that, consequently, no credit could be given to her evidence. The woman, perceiving her error, addressed the judge, and said, "My lord, your lordship has for many years presided in this court, and every day, that you come here, ascend a flight of stairs: may I beg to know how many steps these stairs consist of?" The judge confessed he did not know: "Then," replied she, "if your lordship cannot tell the number of steps you ascend, daily to the *seat of Justice,* it cannot be astonishing that I should forget the number of pillars in a balcony, which I never entered half a dozen times in my life." The judge was much pleased with the woman's wit, and decided in favor of her party.

In short, the ambiguity of the English law is such, and the stratagems of the lawyers so numerous, as to prove a source of misery to those who are unfortunate enough to have any concern with it or them.

As it may not appear fair or candid to censure any system so freely, without an endeavor to point out some remedy to correct its defects, I shall here take the liberty of suggesting a few hints, which, I think, might be usefully applied.

For many years after the establishment of the Mohammedan religion, every person pleaded his own cause; and the cazies, being then men of great learning and sanctity, gave their decisions gratuitously.

As the English judges are at present paid from the public funds, and therefore cannot benefit themselves by prolonging suits, I recommend, that the counselors, attorneys, &c. shall be placed on a similar footing, and that they shall not receive any fee or bribe, from the litigating parties, under a severe penalty. In order to defray the expense of this establishment, either let a small additional tax be laid on the nation at large, or a duty of so much per cent, be levied on all litigated property. By this plan, I am convinced that the number and length of suits would be much curtailed, the time of the witnesses would be saved, the law would be purified from those imperfections which are now a reproach to it, and the courts purged of those pettifogging lawyers, who are a disgrace to their profession.

APPENDIX B

The following Tract, on the Liberties of the Asiatic Women, was written by Mirza Abu Taleb Khan, during his residence in England, and was translated by his friend and shipmate, Captain David Richardson, who, it is to be feared, has perished in one of the missing ships from India. It was published by the intelligent author and compiler, Mr. Dundas Campbell, in the Asiatic Annual Register of the year 1801.

Vindication of the Liberties of the Asiatic Women

By Mirza Abu Taleb Khan

One day, in a certain company, the conversation turned upon LIBERTY, in respect of which the ENGLISH consider their own customs the most perfect in the world. An English lady, addressing herself to me, observed, that the women of Asia have no liberty at all, but live like slaves, without honor and authority, in the houses of their husbands; and she censured the men for their unkindness, and the women, also, for submitting to be so undervalued. However much I attempted, by various ways, to undeceive her (and in truth, said I, the case is exactly the reverse, it is the European women who do not possess so much power), yet it did not bring conviction to her mind. She however began to waver in her own opinion; and falling into doubt, requested of me to write something on the subject, the purport of which she might comprehend at one view, and be enabled to distinguish the truth from falsehood. Since the same wrong opinion is deeply rooted in the minds of all other Europeans, and has been frequently before this held forth, I considered it necessary to write a few lines concerning the privileges of the female sex, as established, both by law and custom, in Asia and in Europe; omitting whatever was common to both, and noticing what is principally peculiar to each, in the manner of comparison, that the distinction may be the more easily made, and the real state of the case become evident to those capable of discernment.

It must be first laid down as a general maxim, that, in social order, respect to the rules of equity and politeness, and forbearance from injury, is a necessary condition; for, otherwise, the liberty of one would be destructive of the liberty of another: thus, if a person be at liberty to do with his own house what may endanger the safety of his neighbor's, this must be in direct opposition to the liberty of that neighbor; or if, in order to free himself from the inconveniences of the hot weather, he should visit his friends in his dressing-gown or night-shirt, although it would be ease and liberty to him, yet it would be sowing the seeds of ill-breeding: therefore the observance of these rules is essential.

Those things which make the liberty of the Asiatic women appear less than that of the Europeans, are, in my opinion, *six*.

The *first* is, "The little intercourse with men, and concealment from view," agreeably to law and their own habits; and this is the chief of these six; for it has been the cause of those false notions entertained by the European women, that the inclination of the Asiatic women leads them to walk out in the streets and market-places, but that their husbands keep them shut up, and set guards over the door. It may be here observed, that the advantages of this *little intercourse*, which prevents all the evils arising from the admittance of strangers, and affords so much time for work and useful employments, are so very manifest, that they need not be enlarged upon; and besides, the practice, in London, of keeping the doors of the houses shut, and the contemptible condition of the Dutch at the Cape, are sufficient proofs. Notwithstanding this, the custom of the intercourse of the sexes is allowed in England, and it is owing both to the force of virtue and good manners generally to be found in the English, and to the apprehension of other greater inconveniences, the chief of which are four, as here mentioned, and whose effects are not felt in Asia. *One of these* is, the high price of things, and the small number of servants and rooms; for were there a separate house and table and equipage for the wife, the expense would be too great to be borne; and therefore, of necessity, both husband and wife eat their food, with their guests, in one place, sleep together in the same chamber, and cannot avoid being always in each other's company; contrary to the custom in Asia, where, by reason of the cheapness of work, the women have separate apartments for themselves, and have not to make their time and convenience suit that of their husbands; and when their particular friends are with them, they do not desire their husband's company for several days, but send his victuals to him in the murdannah (or male apartments); and, in like manner, when the husband wishes to be undisturbed, he eats and sleeps in the murdannah.

A second cause is "The coldness of this climate, which requires exercise and walking, and the husband to sleep in the same bed with his wife: but concealment from view is incompatible with walking; and as for the second case, another cause is the want of room; for, otherwise, it is the natural disposition of mankind, when under distress and affliction of mind, to wish frequently for privacy and unrestraint, and sleep in a room alone."

A third cause is "The people here being all of one kind"; for, in this kingdom, placed in a corner of the globe where there is no coming and going of foreigners, the intercourse of the sexes is not attended with the consequences of a corruption of manners, as in Asia, where people of various nations dwell in the same city; and to allow the women such a liberty there, where there is such danger of corruption, would be an encroachment upon the liberty of the men, which (as shown in the beginning) is contrary to justice; and that a corruption of manners must ensue, where various kinds of people mix together, is too evident to require demonstration. Before the Mussulmans entered Hindustan, the women did not conceal themselves from view; and even yet, in all the Hindu villages, it is not customary: and it is well known how inviolable the Hindus preserve their own custom, and how obstinately they are attached to them; but now so rigidly do the women in the great towns observe this practice of concealment from view, that the bride does not even show herself to her father-in-law, and the sister comes but seldom into the presence of her brother.

A fourth cause is "The necessity which the European women have to acquire experience in the affairs of the world, and in learning various arts, on account of the duty that belongs to them, to take part in their husband's business," which experience could not be obtained by keeping in concealment: whereas the duties of the Asiatic women, consisting only in having the custody of the husband's property, and bringing up the children, they have no occasion for such experience, or for laying aside their own custom of concealment. What has been just said, was to show that the Asiatic women have no necessity to expose their persons; but it must also be observed, that they have many reasons for preferring privacy. One is, the love of leisure, and repose from the fatigue of motion: a second is, the desire of preserving their honor, by not mixing with the vulgar, nor suffering the insults of the low and rude, who are always passing along the streets; a feeling in common with the wives of European noblemen, who, to preserve their dignity, are never seen walking in the streets; and also with ladies in private life, who when walking out at night, and even in the day, are always attended by a male friend or servant to protect them. The notions which the European women have, that the women of Asia never see a man's face but their husband's, and are debarred from all amusement and society, proceed entirely from misinformation: They can keep company with their husband and father's male relations, and with old neighbors and domestics; and at meals there are always many men and women of this description present; and they can go in their palankeens to the houses of their relations, and of ladies of their own rank, even although the husbands are unacquainted; and also to walk in gardens after strangers are excluded; and they can send for musicians and dancers, to entertain them at their own houses; and they have many other modes of amusement besides these mentioned.

The *second* is, "The privilege of the husband, by law, to marry several wives." This, to the European women, seems a grievous oppression; and they hold those very cheap who submit to it. But, in truth, the cause of this law and custom is the nature of the female sex themselves, which separates them from the husband, the several last months of pregnancy, and time of suckling; and besides these the Asiatic women have many other times for being separate from their husbands. This privilege not being allowed by the English law, is indeed a great hardship upon the English husbands; whereas the Asiatic law permitting polygamy, does the husband justice, and wrongs not the wife; for the honor of the first and *equal* wife is not affected by it; those women who submit to marry with a married man, not being admitted into the society of ladies, as they are never of high or wealthy families, no man of honor ever allowing his daughter to make such a marriage. The mode in which these other wives live is this: they who are of a genteel extraction, have a separate house for themselves, like kept mistresses in England; and they who are not, live in the house of the equal wife, like servants, and the husband at times conveys himself to them in a clandestine manner. Besides, these wives cannot invade any of the rights of the equal wife; for although they and their children are by law equally entitled to inheritance, yet, since the equal wife never marries without a very large dowry settled upon her, all that the husband leaves goes to the payment of this dowry, and nothing remains for his heirs. The opinion that the men of Asia have generally three or four wives, is very ill founded, for in common they have only one; out of a thousand, there will be fifty persons, perhaps, who have from one to two, and ten out of these who have more than two. The fear of the bad consequences of polygamy makes men submit with patience to the times of separation from the equal wife, as much the better way; for, from what I know, it is easier to live with two tigresses than two wives.

The *third* is, "The power of divorce being in the hands of the husband." This is ordained by law, but not practiced; for if a great offense be the motive to divorce a wife, and if it be proved against her, she receives punishment by the order of the magistrate, or from the husband, with the concurrence of all her relations; and if the offense be of a trivial nature, such as a difference of temper and unsociability, the husband punishes her, by leaving the female apartments, and living in his own. But the reason for divorce being at the will of the husband, lies in the very justice of the law, and the distinction of the male sex over the female, on account of the greater share they take in the management of the world; for all the laborious work falls to their lot, such as carrying heavy burthens, going to war, repulsing enemies,

&c. and the women generally spend their lives in repose and quiet. Nevertheless, if the wife establishes a criminal offence against the husband, such as an unfair distribution of his time among his wives, or a diminution of the necessaries of life, she can obtain a divorce in spite of him.

The *fourth* is, "The little credit the law attaches to the evidence of women in Asia"; for, in a court of justice, every fact is proved by the testimony of two men; but if women be the witnesses, four are required. This does not arise from the superiority of the one over the other, but it is founded upon the little experience and knowledge women possess, and the fickleness of their dispositions.

The *fifth* is, "The Asiatic women having to leave off going to balls and entertainments, and wearing showy dresses and ornaments, after their husband's death." This is owing to their great affection for their husband's memory, and their own modes and habits; for there is nothing to prevent a woman's doing otherwise, or marrying a second husband, but the dread of exposing herself to the ridicule and censure of women of her own rank.

The *sixth* is, "The Asiatic daughters not having the liberty of choosing their husbands." On this head nothing need be said; for in Europe this liberty is merely nominal, as, without the will of the father and mother, the daughter's choice is of no avail; and whatever choice they make for her, she must submit to; and in its effects, it serves only to encourage running away (as the male and female slaves in India do), and to breed coldness and trouble amongst the members of a family. But granting that such a liberty does exist in England, the disgrace and misery it must always entail is very evident. The choice of a girl just come from the nursery, and desirous by nature to get a husband, in an affair on which the happiness of her whole life depends, can neither deserve that respect nor consideration which is due to the choice of her parents, who have profited by experience, and are not blinded by passion.

But what the Asiatic women have more than the European, both by law and custom, may be ranked under *eight* heads.

First, "Their power over the property and children of the husband, by custom"; for the men of Asia consider the principal objects of marriage, after the procreation of their species for the worship of God, two things—the one to have their money and effects taken care of, and the other to have their children brought up; so that they themselves, being left entirely disengaged of these concerns, may turn their whole endeavors to the attainment of their various pursuits. The chief part, therefore, of whatever wealth they acquire, they give in charge to their wives; and thus the women have it in their power to annihilate in one day the products of a whole life. Although this seldom happens, yet it is often the case, where the husband having amassed a large fortune in youth and power, has delivered it in charge to his wife, and requires it back in his old age and necessity, she does not allow him more than sufficient for his daily support, and lays the rest up, in a place of security, for the sake of her children. And so great is the power they possess, as to the disposal of their children, that frequently they are brought up without any education, or die in childhood; for the women, on account of their little sense, are never pleased to part with their children, by sending them to school, and to acquire experience by traveling; and when they fall sick, they give them improper medicines, by the advice of their own confidants, or, from their softness of heart, indulge them in whatever it is the nature of the sick to take a longing for, and thus they cause their death.

Second, "Their power, by custom, as to the marriage of their children, and choice of their religious faith"; for if the husband wishes to give one of them in marriage to a person the wife disapproves of, the match does not take place, but the other way it generally does. All the children, both male and female, from being mostly in the company of their mother, and looking upon her as their protector against their father, whom, on account of his wishing to have them educated, they consider their tormentor, follow the religious tenets of their mother, and remain perfect strangers to those of their father. It often happens, where the wife is a Shya, and the husband a Soony, the children, having been Shyas, from their own natural disposition and the instructions of the mother, speak disrespectfully of the chiefs of the Soony sect in their father's presence; and he, who all his life never bore such language from any person, but was even ready to put the speaker of it to death, has no redress, but patiently submitting to hear it from them, as, on account of their want of understanding, they are excusable; and thus, by frequent repetition, his attachment to his faith is shaken, and, in the course of time, he either entirely forsakes it, or remains but lukewarm in it.

Third, "Their authority over their servants"; for the servants of the male apartments, the keeping and changing of whom are in the hands of the husband, through fear of exposing themselves to the displeasure or complaints of the wife, when she finds a proper opportunity, by their committing some fault, which servants are continually doing, are more obedient to her than to their own master; and the servants of the zenana, whom the wife has the care of retaining or turning off, stand so much in awe of their mistress, that many of them pass their whole lives in the zenana, without ever once coming into the presence of the husband: some of them never perform any service for him at all; and others, who do, enter not into discourse with him: and the women are so obstinate in this respect, their husbands never can turn off one of these servants, but his very complaint against them is a recommendation in their favor; and his recommendation has the effect of complaint, by subjecting them to their mistress's resentment. Contrary to this is the manner of the European ladies, who have not their own will with their children and servants, but live more like free and familiar guests in their husband's houses: and the household establishment and equipage being in common to both, if any part, as the carriage for example, is previously employed by the one, the other has to wait till it is disengaged. Of this there is no doubt, that if a quarrel ensues between an English husband and wife, the wife has to leave the house, and seek her dinner either at her father's or a friend's; whereas in Asia, it is the husband that has to go out; for frequently the utensils of cookery are not kept in the male apartments.

Fourth, "The freedom, by custom, of the Asiatic women from assisting in the business of the husband, or service of his guests"; whereas this is generally the duty of European wives, whether their husbands be of a genteel business, such as jewelry, mercery, or perfumery, or the more servile ones: I have seen many rise from their dinner, to answer the demands of a purchaser: and although all these duties are not required of the ladies, yet some, especially the entertaining the guests, carving and helping the dishes at table, and making the tea and coffee, are generally performed by them. Now the Asiatic ladies have no such duties at all, but live in the manner before described.

Fifth, "The greater deference the Asiatic ladies find paid to their humors, and a prescriptive right of teasing their husbands by every pretext," which is considered as constituting an essential quality of beauty; for if a wife does not put these in practice, but is submissive to her husband's will in every thing, her charms very soon lose their brilliancy in his eyes. Thus, when a wife goes to visit her father, she will not return to her husband, till he has come himself several times to fetch her, and been as often vexed by her breaking her promise; and every day when dinner is served, by pretending to be engaged at the time, she keeps her husband waiting, and does not come till the meat has grown cold; and in the same manner at bedtime—for returning quickly from their father's house is considered as a sign of fondness for the husband, which, in their opinion, looks very ill; and coming soon to dinner they think betrays the disposition of a hungry beggar. In these, and such like, the husband has nothing for it but patience; nay, it ever pleases him. I have known of many beautiful women, constant in their affection, and obedient to their husbands night and day, whom, for not having these qualities, the husbands have quickly tired of, and unjustly deserted, for the sake of plain women who possessed them.

Sixth, "The greater reliance placed by the Asiatic husbands on their wives' virtue, both from law and custom." For as to the European ladies, although they can go out of doors, and discourse with strangers, yet this is not allowed, unless they have a trusty person along with them, either of the husband's or the father's; and sleeping out all night is absolutely denied them—contrary to the way of the Asiatic ladies, who, when they go to the house of a lady of their acquaintance, though their husbands be entire strangers, are not attended by any person of the husband's or father's, and they spend not only one or two nights in that house, but even a whole week; and in such a house, although the master is prohibited entering the apartments where they are, yet the young men of fifteen, belonging to the family or relations, under the name of children, have free access, and eat with and enter into the amusements of their guests.

Seventh, "Their share in the children, by law." For if a divorce happens, the sons go to the father, and the daughters to the mother; contrary to the custom here, where, if a divorce takes place, the mother, who for twenty years may have toiled and consumed herself in bringing up her children, has to abandon all to the father, and, full of grief and affliction, leave his house.

Eighth, "The ease, both by law and custom, with which the wife may separate herself from her husband, when there may be a quarrel between them, without producing a divorce." Thus the wife, in an hour's time after the dispute, sets off with the children and her property to the house of her father or relations, and until the husband makes her satisfaction she does not return: and this she can always do, without a moment's delay.

Besides these eight, as above noticed, of the superior advantages the Asiatic women enjoy over the European, there are many others, here omitted for brevity's sake. What has been said, is enough for people of discernment. Farewell.

> "I'll fondly *place on either eye,*
> "The man that can to this reply."

REFERENCE

Sen, Amrit. 2008. "'The Persian Prince in London': Autoethnography and Positionality in *Travels of Mirza Abu Taleb Khan.*" *Asiatic: IIUM Journal of English Language and Literature,* Vol. 2, No. 1, pp. 58–68.

21

Remarks on Settlement in India by Europeans

Raja Rammohun Roy, 1832

Raja Rammohun Roy is referred to as both a father and a maker of modern India, as both a scholar and a builder of infrastructure. He was born in Bengal in 1772, into a Brahmin caste to parents of different religious backgrounds—one of whom encouraged him to be a scholar, the other to work in public administration. By the age of fifteen Roy had learned Bangala, Persian, Arabic, and Sanskrit, adding English later. Differences with his father led him to leave home and travel in the Himalayas and then in Tibet. When his father died, Roy took a position in Calcutta involving work in the Revenue Department of the East India Company. He therefore knew how much revenue Western traders and others were taking out of India—at least half, with the remainder left in India—and he saw firsthand how Westerners discriminated against Indians and disrespected Hindu traditions. This experience motivated him to both legitimize and reform Hindu traditions.

Even though his father was an orthodox Brahmin, Roy was critical of orthodox Hindu rites. Seeking to initiate education reform, he advocated for the right of women to hold property and to remarry in the case of their husband's death, rather than having to perform *sati* (in which the widow immolates herself on her husband's funeral pyre). In part, Roy's efforts were an attempt to deal with the growing influence of Christianity on Hindu society. He started a number of colleges in which he insisted on a synthesis of Western and Indian learning and encouraged the study of science, technology, Western medicine, and the English language.

Roy's reformist educational pursuits were instigated as a reaction to the moral superiority that the English projected, which he thought could be dealt with by creating a fair and just society with humanitarian practices consonant with Christian ideals. Roy was no wide-eyed

Roy, Raja Rammohun. 1947. "Remarks on Settlement in India by Europeans." In *The English Works of Raja Rammohun Roy: Part III*. Kalidas Nag and Debajyoti Burman, eds. Calcutta: Sadharan Brahmo Samaj. Pp. 81–85.

innocent. He knew what he was up against, and as a journalist he published his views in magazines in English, Hindi, Persian, and Bengali, covering topics such as freedom of the press while steadily opposing social practices like *sati* and child marriage. His influence was wide—not only in the fields of education but also in politics, public administration, and religion.

In 1830 Rammohun Roy was among the first educated Indians to visit England. By this time the British had conferred on him the title of Raja as ambassador of the Mughal Emperor Akbar II. The remarks he made during his visit on European settlement in India appeared in the appendix of the 1832 "Report of the Select Committee of the House of Commons on the Affairs of the East India Company." Tragically, he died in Britain in 1833 of meningitis and was buried in Bristol.

In those of his writings excerpted below, Roy first notes some of the advantages to India of European settlement and then follows with a discussion of disadvantages. The advantages include the spread of European knowledge to India, the possibility of equality in governance, communication across the globe, better schools and more widespread education, and protection from external attack. He weighs all of these against the problems of discrimination that might result, which would necessitate the enactment of equality laws. Roy observes that the foreigners would be in a privileged position relative to the subject population with regard to law, and also that there would be discriminatory consequences for the subject population. Only knowing a privileged sample of English people might provoke the subject masses to insult and then revolt, much as the Americans were driven to rebellion by English misgovernment. To each of these problems listed as disadvantages he adds remedies. His suggestions are intended to encourage the British to rule better by resolving some of the fundamental problems of rule. In that sense his is a limited prescription: "Be nice to the natives and treat them as you would treat your English."

Bengalis were never totally opposed to British rule and, though they were not treated equally by the British, saw themselves as elites equal to any other elite from foreign lands. Roy also saw British expansion into India as an "experiment," one that might lead to an improvement in his fellow Indians' social, cultural, and religious life.

. . .

Much has been said and written by persons in the employ of the Hon. East India Company and others on the subject of the settlement of Europeans in India, and many various opinions have been expressed as to the advantages and disadvantages which might attend such a political measure. I shall here briefly and candidly state the principal effects which, in my humble opinion, may be expected to result from this measure.

2. I notice, first, some of the advantages that might be derived from such a change.

ADVANTAGES

First.—European settlers in India will introduce the knowledge they possess of superior modes of cultivating the soil and improving its products (in the article of sugar, for example), as has already happened with respect to indigo, and improvements in the mechanical arts, and in the agricultural and commercial systems generally, by which the natives would of course benefit.

Secondly.—By a free and extensive communication with the various classes of the native inhabitants the European settlers would gradually deliver their minds from the superstitions and prejudices, which have subjected the great body of the Indian people to social and domestic inconvenience, and disqualified them from useful exertions.

Thirdly.—The European settlers being more on a par with the rulers of the country, and aware of the rights belonging to the subjects of a liberal Government, and the proper mode of administering justice, would obtain from the local Governments, or from the Legislature in England, the introduction of many necessary improvements in the laws and judicial system; the benefit of which would of course extend to the inhabitants generally, whose condition would thus be raised.

Fourthly.—The presence, countenance and support of the European settlers would not only afford to the natives protection against the impositions and oppression of their landlords and other superiors, but also against any abuse of power on the part of those in authority.

Fifthly.—The European settlers, from motives of benevolence, public spirit and fellow-feeling towards their native neighbors, would establish schools and other seminaries of education for the cultivation of the English language throughout the country, and for the diffusion of a knowledge of European arts and sciences; whereas at present the bulk of the natives (those residing at the Presidencies and some large towns excepted) have no more opportunities of acquiring this means of national improvement than if the country had never had any intercourse or connection whatever with Europe.

Sixthly.—As the intercourse between the settlers and their friends and connections in Europe would greatly multiply the channels of communication with this country, the public and the Government here would become much more correctly informed, and consequently much better qualified to legislate on Indian matters than at present, when, for any authentic information, the country is at the mercy of the representations of comparatively a few individuals, and those chiefly the parties who have the management of public affairs in their hands, and who can hardly fail therefore to regard the result of their own labors with a favorable eye.

Seventhly.—In the event of an invasion from any quarter, east or west, Government would be better able to resist it, if, in addition to the native population, it were supported by a large body of European inhabitants, closely connected by national sympathies with the ruling power, and dependent on its stability for the continued enjoyment of their civil and political rights.

Eighthly.—The same cause would operate to continue the connection between Great Britain and India on a solid and permanent footing; provided only the latter country be governed in a liberal manner, by means of Parliamentary superintend-ence, and such other legislative checks in this country as may be devised and established. India may thus, for an unlimited period, enjoy union with England, and the advantage of her enlightened Government; and in return contribute to support the greatness of this country.

Ninthly.—If, however, events should occur to effect a separation between the two countries, then still the existence of a large body of respectable settlers (consisting of Europeans and their descendants, professing Christianity, and speaking the Eng-lish language in common with the bulk of the people, as well as possessed of supe-rior knowledge, scientific, mechanical, and political) would bring that vast Empire in the east to a level with other large Christian countries in Europe, and by means of its immense riches and extensive population, and by the help which may be rea-sonably expected from Europe, they (the settlers and their descendants) may suc-ceed sooner or later in enlightening and civilizing the surrounding nations of Asia.

3. I now proceed to state some of the principal disadvantages which may be apprehended, with the remedies which I think calculated to prevent them, or at any rate their frequent occurrence.

DISADVANTAGE

First.—The European settlers being a distinct race, belonging to the class of the rulers of the country, may be apt to assume an ascendancy over the aboriginal inhabitants, and aim at enjoying exclusive rights and privileges, to the depression of the larger, but less favored class; and the former being also of another religion, may be disposed to wound the feelings of the natives, and subject them to humili-ations on account of their being of a different creed, color and habits.

As a remedy or preventive of such a result, I would suggest, 1st, That as the higher and better educated classes of Europeans are known from experience to be less disposed to annoy and insult the natives than persons of lower class, European settlers, for the first twenty years at least, should be from among educated persons of character and capital, since such persons are very seldom, if ever, found guilty of intruding upon the religious or national prejudices of persons of uncultivated minds; 2nd. The enactment of equal laws, placing all classes on the same footing as to civil rights, and the establishment of trial by jury (the jury being composed impartially of both classes), would be felt as a strong check on any turbulent or overbearing characters amongst Europeans.

The second probable disadvantage is as follows: the Europeans possess an undue advantage over the natives, from having readier access to persons in author-ity, these being their own countrymen, as proved by long experience in numerous instances; therefore, a large increase of such a privileged population must subject the natives to many sacrifices from this very circumstance.

I would therefore propose as a remedy, that in addition to the native vakeels, European pleaders should be appointed in the country courts in the same manner as they are in the King's courts at the Presidencies, where the evil referred to is consequently not felt, because the counsel and attorneys for both parties, whether for a native or a European, have the same access to the judge, and are in all respects on an equal footing in pleading or defending the cause of their clients.

The third disadvantage in contemplation is, that at present the natives of the interior of India have little or no opportunity of seeing any Europeans except persons of rank holding public offices in the country, and officers and troops stationed in or passing through it under the restraint of military discipline, and consequently those natives entertain a notion of European superiority, and feel less reluctance in submission, but should Europeans of all ranks and classes be allowed to settle in the country, the natives who came in contact with them will materially alter the estimate now formed of the European character, and frequent collisions of interests and conflicting prejudices may gradually lead to a struggle between the foreign and native race till either one or the other obtain a complete ascendancy, and render the situation of their opponents so uncomfortable that no government could mediate between them with effect or ensure the public peace and tranquility of the country. Though this may not happen in the interior of Bengal, yet it must be kept in mind, that no inference drawn from the conduct of the Bengalese (whose submissive disposition and want of energy are notorious) can be applied with justice to the natives of the Upper Provinces, whose temper of mind is directly the reverse. Among this spirited race the jarrings above alluded to must be expected, if they be subjected to insult and intrusion—a state of things which would ultimately weaken, if not entirely undermine, the British power in India, or at least occasion much bloodshed from time to time to keep the natives in subordination.

The remedy already pointed out (para. 3rd, art. 1st, remedy 1st), will, however also apply to this case, that is, the restriction of the European settlers to the respectable intelligent class already described, who in general may be expected not only to raise the European character still higher, but also to emancipate their native neighbors from the long standing bondage of ignorance and superstition, and thereby secure their affection, and attach them to the government under which they may enjoy the liberty and privileges so dear to persons of enlightened minds.

Some apprehend, as *the fourth probable danger,* that if the population of India were raised to wealth, intelligence, and public spirit, by accession and by the example of numerous respectable European settlers, the mixed community so formed would revolt (as the United States of America formerly did) against the power of Great Britain, and would ultimately establish independence. In reference to this, however, it must be observed that the Americans were driven to rebellion by misgovernment, otherwise they would not have revolted and separated themselves from England. Canada is a standing proof that an anxiety to effect a separation from the mother country is not the natural wish of a people, even tolerably well-ruled. The mixed community of India, in like manner, so long as they are treated liberally, and governed in an enlightened manner, will feel no disposition to cut off its connection with England, which may be preserved with so much mutual benefit to both countries. Yet, as before observed, if events should occur to effect a separation (which may arise from many accidental causes, about which it is vain to speculate or make predictions), still a friendly and highly advantageous commercial intercourse may be kept up between two free and Christian countries, united as they will then be by resemblance of language, religion, and manners.

The fifth obstacle in the way of settlement in India by Europeans is, that the climate in many parts of India may be found destructive, or at least very pernicious to European constitutions, which might oblige European families who may be in possession of the means to retire to Europe to dispose of their property to disadvantage, or leave it to ruin, and that they would impoverish themselves instead of enriching India. As a remedy I would suggest that many cool and healthy spots could be selected and fixed upon as the head-quarters of the settlers (where they and their respective families might reside and superintend the affairs of their estates in the favorable season, and occasionally visit them during the hot months, if their presence be absolutely required on their estates), such as the Suppatoo, the Nielgherry Hills, and other similar places, which are by no means pernicious to European constitutions. At all events, it will be borne in mind that the emigration of the settlers to India is not compulsory, but entirely optional with themselves.

To these might be added some minor disadvantages though not so important. These (as well as the above circumstances) deserve fair consideration and impartial reflection. At all events, no one will, I trust, oppose me when I say, that the settlement in India by Europeans should at least be undertaken experimentally, so that its effects may be ascertained by actual observation on a moderate scale. If the result be such as to satisfy all parties, whether friendly or opposed to it, the measure may then be carried on to a greater extent, till at last it may seem safe and expedient to throw the country open to persons of all classes.

On mature consideration, therefore, I think I may safely recommend that educated persons of character and capital should now be permitted and encouraged to settle in India, without any restriction of locality or any liability to banishment, at the discretion of the government; and the result of this experiment may serve as a guide in any future legislation on this subject.

REFERENCE

Collett, Sophia D. 1914 [1900]. *The Life and Letters of Raja Rammohun Roy.* Calcutta: A. C. Sarkar.

22

My Impressions of England

Keshub Chunder Sen, 1870

Keshub Chunder Sen was born in 1838 into an affluent Brahmin family of Calcutta. As a young activist in 1855, he founded a school for children. For a brief time he worked as a bank clerk in Bengal, before resigning to study literature and philosophy. He wrote articles for the *Indian Mirror,* a weekly Calcutta journal in which social issues were debated.

In 1870 Sen traveled from India to England as a student, missionary, and advocate of social reform. His purpose, as Prem Sundar Basu (1938) quotes Sen, was "to survey Christian life in all its aspects and bearings" (iii). "The eminent scholar and divine J. Estlin Carpenter," Basu also notes, described Sen as "a voice of rare power, eloquence, and charm" (iii). Basu finds that Sen was nonetheless "not slow to admonish when he found it necessary to do so" (iv), and gives examples of Sen's critiques: "English Christianity is too sectarian; it is not large enough, not broad enough. . . . I do honestly believe in India there is such a thing as spirituality. In England there is too much materialism. . . . England is not yet a Christian nation . . . look at that awful amount of pauperism which surrounds you still; look at the . . . immorality and impurity that still rides rampant." (iv). Sen had thought of Christianity as a tradition from which Indians could learn and, in his meeting with Queen Victoria, even expressed acceptance of British rule, making him a target of criticism at home.

Sen knew his origins: "While other nations that are now in a state of refinement and civilization were sunk in ignorance and barbarism, India possessed a very high order of civilization" (Sen 1938:v). Sen was an Eastern missionary in the West. In sermon after sermon his message was to "unite and co-operate harmoniously in order to bring . . . the blessings of true salvation" to his English listeners (v). Basu notes that Sen was able to bring together people of different persuasions by his straightforward manner, and able to put

Sen, Keshub Chunder. 1938. "My Impressions of England." In *Keshub Chunder Sen in England: Diary, Sermons, Addresses, and Epistles.* Prem Sundar Basu, ed. Calcutta: Navavidhan Publication Committee. Pp. 481–496.

aside his own doctrinal differences in striving to create a new Hinduism, combining Yoga, Bhakti, and Christianity, a blend suited to modern civilization and science.

As a reform advocate, he was clear in his positions. "There are many serious defects in the [colonial] administrative machinery which have to be rectified, many just grievances of the people to be redressed, many instances of injustice and oppression. . . . For these you [British colonial administrators] are responsible." He balanced his comments by noting what he saw as serious defects in Indian society, such as the lack of education and the practice of plural marriage. But when invited to give his impressions of England before he left his "Father's Western house" to return to India, he agreed that the English had a right to know what he thought of them. "In England," he said, "there is hardly anything like meditation or solitary contemplation" (Sen 1938:v). On the other hand, he continued, "from England I go away, but my heart will always be with you, and England will always be in my heart. Farewell, dear England; 'with all thy faults I love thee still.' Farewell, country of Shakespeare and of Newton, land of liberty and charity! Farewell, temporary home where I realized, and tasted, and enjoyed the sweetness of brotherly and sisterly love. Farewell, my Father's Western house. Farewell, my beloved brothers and sisters" (496).

Upon returning home to India, Sen established the India Reform Association to help change attitudes about education, charity, and women's lives (a most contested topic) and, according to some, continued to eloquently protest the Europeanization of Asia and Western sectarianism, which pitted one ethnic or religious group against another.

. . .

Nearly six months have elapsed since I arrived in this country, and during that time I have studied men and things according to my means and opportunities, and I have attended several meetings, both public and private, with a view to excite the interest of the British people in Indian affairs, and to unite as far as possible these two great countries in the closest ties of social and religious fellowship. Before I proceed to the graver topics I have to dilate upon, allow me to give out my first impressions of this country. The first thing that struck me and dazzled my eyes in London was the brilliancy and splendor of your shops. The neat arrangement of the various shops I saw on both sides of the streets pleased me very much; but their number bewildered me. I thought, "Surely the English must be a nation of shopkeepers; but if everybody sells, where are the buyers?" (Laughter) The next thing to which my attention was forcibly drawn was the art of puffing. East, west, north, south, everywhere I saw handbills and advertisements. No place was free from them. If I wished to move from one place to another, I must get into the *Daily Telegraph* omnibus or the *Echo* omnibus; if I wanted to go by railway from one city to another, I was driven from station to station, and I could not possibly make out what those stations were, for I passed through a forest of advertisements. I should not wonder if in future you send out every man and woman through the streets with a placard posted on the forehead. (Laughter) Thirdly, the Englishman's activity troubled me very much. John Bull's whole life seems to be concentrated in the right hand. He works and works, and cannot live for anything like contemplation or thought. He is a machine made for work, eternal and everlasting work, and he does not like rest. He is like Hamlet's ghost, *hic et ubique,* here, there, everywhere—always moving about.

I may say also a few words about eating. An English dinner party, I always think, is a hunting party (laughter); and what confirms this view of the case is the fact that ladies always seek the protection of gentlemen before entering the dining-room, lest there should be, perhaps, some accident. (Laughter) They always go armed with spoons and forks and knives, in order to attack the fowls of the air, the beasts of the wilderness, and the fishes of the sea that are gathered on the table. (Continued laughter) It troubled me very much, may I say it frightened me, when I saw birds and beasts on the table almost ready to start into existence again. Why, if you go on at this rate, you may hereafter feel afraid of sitting in each other's company. My flesh creeps on my bones when I see a huge piece of roast English beef on the table. (Renewed laughter)

Lastly, I must say one or two words about ladies' dress. Perhaps John Bull will not tolerate such a thing, but I am one of those who, fortunately or unfortunately, do not believe in man's infallibility or in woman's infallibility. The Girl of the Period is really a peculiar creature. I hope she will never make her appearance in India. There are two things in particular which I object to—the head and the tail. (Much laughter) In these days of "woman's rights," may I not seriously suggest that women ought not to occupy more ground than men. (Laughter) It is a fact that a civilized and refined lady of the West occupies five times as much space as a gentleman. The fair sex ought to be fair. (Renewed laughter) And as regards the head. At first sight the hair on women's heads in England and in European countries generally seemed to me to be much longer than that on women's heads in India. But I am told there is a secret inside that huge protuberance at the back of the head, which would not bear criticism. (Continued laughter) I hope educated and sensible ladies of the present day will give better proof in future of the fertility of their brains. (Laughter and applause)

Let me turn to the deeper social life of the people. It is with feelings of grief and distress that I have witnessed the vast amount of poverty and pauperism which prevails in this city. God help and bless the poor of London! The sight of London beggars is very painful. My surprise was great when I found in this civilized Christian country so much moral and spiritual destitution and physical suffering, caused by the curse of intemperance. I was also pained to notice an institution which I certainly did not expect to find in this country—I mean *caste.* Your rich people are really Brahmins, and your poor people are Sudras. (Hear hear) I thought caste was peculiar to India; certainly in a religious sense it is, but as a social institution it perpetrates prodigious havoc in this country. Cases of baby-farming, and breaches of promise of marriage constantly figure in the columns of your daily paper and my attention has been several times drawn to these frightful disclosures. But nothing has distressed me so much as the obstinacy with which the government of this country has afforded, indirectly if not directly, vast and potent encouragement to intemperance and prostitution by unwise legislative enactments. It is the duty of every humane and civilized government to discourage and put down with a high hand the two great social evils of the day—drunkenness and prostitution. (Applause) I have noticed these defects in the social life of the nation with feelings of concern and regret, and, as one of your best friends, I sincerely wish to see them rectified. (Applause) Turning to the other side of the picture, I must express my admiration of the charities in London—of the noble work which is being carried on in hospitals, in reformatories, and in schools. I am amazed at the fact that the aggregate annual income of London charities is upwards of £8,000,000. Certainly it is the spirit of Christianity which has produced this great result. If there are evils in England whose parallel it would be difficult to find in any other country of the world, there are, on the other hand, means and agencies at work for crushing and extinguishing those evils. One institution in England I have looked upon with peculiar feelings of delight—the happy English home, in which the utmost warmth and cordiality of affection and sympathy are mingled with highest moral and religious restraint and discipline. The spirit of prayer and worship seems mixed up with daily household duties, and the influence of the spirit of Christ is manifest in domestic concerns. The bright and loving faces of English children have deeply impressed me, and I have frequently said, "Happy is that family where such children dwell." The power of English public opinion, too, is a great blessing, for it has obliterated many of the evils from which this country for a long time suffered. I trust that India may soon have such a thing as public opinion, for its want is daily felt. As I am now about to return home, I can ask for nothing better than the co-operation of Englishmen in obtaining for my native land English charity, English homes, and English public opinion. True, thousands of Englishmen have gone out to India, and many have settled there; but where in that country is Christian charity exhibited in its extended dimensions, in its untiring industry and disinterested earnestness as it is here? I hope that attempts will soon be made there to extend the light of education amongst the masses, to establish reformatories and sanitary societies, and to found work-houses, schools for the blind and deaf, and other charitable institutions. At all the meetings I have attended, every demand I have made for India in the name of justice and humanity has received a favorable response, and tens of thousands have indicated their love and sympathy towards that country, and their anxious desire to do justice to the hundred and eighty millions of its population. (Applause) Whatever may have been the shortcomings of the rulers of India hitherto, I thankfully acknowledge that if evils are pointed out, no other nation is so anxious as England to remedy those evils. (Hear) Unfortunately, English people are profoundly ignorant of the actual state of things in India, and the requirements of the people confided to their care. What I ask for may be briefly said—the education of the masses, the improvement of women, the suppression of the liquor and opium traffic, the introduction of those charities which constitute the glory of England, and, lastly, an Act for reforming marriage customs. The Reform party in India are protesting against, and trying practically to put down, if possible, such evils as bigamy and polygamy, the cruel custom which prohibits the re-marriage of widows, premature and untimely marriage; while at the same time we primarily declare a violent crusade against idolatry and caste. (Loud applause) For God's sake, for truth's sake, let the English nation and the Indian legislature assist them in this great work. (Applause)

The last and the most important subject I have to deal with is the religious life of England. What do I think of English Christianity? I shall notice three characteristics of Christian life as it exists in this part of the world, and these three are, no doubt, great drawbacks. English Christianity is too sectarian; it is not large enough, not broad enough. It appears to me that the waters of immortal life, bounded by the barriers of sects, are small in quantity, and therefore, in order that they may be deep, the channels through which they run have been made narrow. Thus Christian sects have become narrow—too narrow indeed, for large human hearts and souls. I have often been amused at the patronizing way in which your countrymen have talked to me about my country. The Thames is a little stream compared with the mighty Ganges, and your mountains are mole-hills in comparison with the Himalayas. The houses here, too, are small, and I am afraid that the houses for the soul are smaller still. (Applause) God's Church has been split up into a thousand little sectarian huts. Differences of opinion are inevitable: where honest differences do not exist, there must be stagnation and lifelessness; where there is life there must be disunion, and against this I have naught to say; but what I protest against is the spirit of sectarian antipathy and antagonism which ill becomes a Christian. Christians of all denominations, Catholics and Protestants, Trinitarians and Unitarians, are bound to stand together on the same platform. This is what Christ has told them, "By this shall all men know that ye are my disciples, if ye have love one to another." (Applause) I am distressed to find that such a spirit does not exist now, but I have hopes for the future. Secondly, English Christianity appears to be too muscular and hard. It is not soft enough for the purposes of the human heart. On the battlefield, amid the crash of war, Western Christianity offers prayers to God that thousands of men may be slaughtered and butchered. (Applause) That is not the right sort of Christianity. (Hear) Where there is true Christianity there must be soft, gentle hearts; not hard muscles stretched out for the extermination of the foe, but hearts expanded with love and charity, offering prayers that the foe may be forgiven. Unfortunately, soft Christianity is not found here, at least not to that extent to which it ought to exist in a Christian nation. Thirdly, Christian life in England is more materialistic and outward than spiritual and inward. English

Christianity looks forward to something visible, tangible, outward; men do not close their eyes in order to see within the recesses of their hearts and souls the reality, and grandeur of the spiritual universe, vaster, nobler, grander far than the outward universe. There is a spiritual life as there is a material life, and the spirit, if I may so say, has its eyes, and its ears, and its hands, as the body has. The spirit can see things of the spiritual world just as external eyes can see external objects, and the spiritual ears can hear the direct utterances of God's lips in the same way that our outward ears can hear man's voice and the sounds of the material world. If God is to be worshipped, He must be worshipped in spirit and in truth. In England there is hardly anything like meditation or solitary contemplation. Englishmen seek their God in society; why do they not, now and then, go up to the heights of the mountains in order to realize the sweetness of solitary communion with God? There is a tendency to see God outside, in forms, in rites, in dogmas, and in propositions, and there is very little spiritual insight.

As regards the distinguishing tenets of Christianity, I may say, without entering the arena of theological controversy, that there are three great ideas in true Christianity—first, the Father; second, the Son; third, the Holy Ghost. Though these three words, Father, Son, and Holy Ghost, are often repeated from pulpits and in the theological literature of the present day, the world has yet to realize their deep significance. The Trinity is recognized, but the Unity is not yet understood, though all Christendom is struggling to attain and realize it. Where is this Unity? This is a problem which has been put aside as incapable of solution, but humanity demands that it should be solved. Can this Unity be realized? Is it a mystery? No; it is not inexplicable—it is no mystery. The doctrine of divine unity was grasped by the Jews. The mighty Jehovah was worshipped by them—Jehovah seated on His glorious throne, clad in the robes of celestial righteousness and purity, with wide-extended hand ruling the destinies of nations and exhibiting in a variety of ways His infinite mercy and power. To whom were the Psalms of David addressed but to the One Supreme Being? Not to things of clay and stone, not to beasts or creeping things, not even to man, but to the One God of spirit and of truth. But mankind wanted to know the way to the God of Spirit, to the invisible and everlasting Jehovah. They must not only adore and worship Him as the God of Spirit, but they must also see righteousness in human life in order to attain a godly and righteous life. They wanted to see righteousness in life, divinity in the life of man, the manifestation of God's truth and love in human character—"God manifest in the flesh." To that the world looked forward hopefully and anxiously, and according to the promise in the Jewish theocracy, in the fullness of time, the Son of God came, and was received and accepted by many as the promise fulfilled but he was not perfectly honored, and up to the present time even in the heart of Christendom he has not been properly honored. It grieves me to find that the once crucified Jesus is crucified hundreds of times every day in the midst of Christendom. The Christian world has not imbibed Christ's spirit. Many, it is true, have deified him, many have accepted him as God Himself in human form, but even these have not truly honored him. Christ has received honors which he himself would protest against with all his heart and soul; but he has not received the honor which he wants and claims. And what is that honor? That he may be made the flesh and the blood of his disciples and followers. We find him in the dogma of Atonement, in the pages of the Bible, in the utterances of ministers, in the creed of believers, perhaps also in the heart of the devout and in the right hand of the philanthropist and the reformer, but he is not seen in the flesh and blood of Christendom. Every man must be Christlike in order to be worthy of Christ. (Applause) The true Christ of all nations is not the Christ of flesh and blood that lived some time ago, not the Christ of pictures and representations, not the visible—but the spiritual Christ. When Christ was about to leave this world, he said—"I have yet many things to say unto you, but ye cannot bear them now: howbeit when he, the Spirit of truth, is come, he will guide you into all truth. If I go not away, the Comforter will not come." But, alas! The Spirit of truth has not yet come. The promise of the Son of God was fulfilled; the promise of the Spirit of God has not yet been fulfilled. Christ knew that his followers would give him external homage and doctrinal worship, but he was not to be satisfied with that, and hence, just before leaving the world he entered his protest against it, both by direct counsel and by the ceremony known as the Last Supper. He told his disciples there were many things they could not understand, and so he did not give them the whole truth. They had yet to learn better truth, higher truth, and fuller truth; and who would reveal that? The Spirit of God. The Jew beheld God in Nature, and the Christian sees God manifest in Christ, but God manifest in the spirit of the individual believer few have seen, and unless that is seen, the Father is lost in the Son, and the Son lost in the Father, as is painfully the case in Christendom. Do Christians see God as Spirit? Do they worship Him as Spirit? Do they not rather start from the proposition that man cannot conceive of Divinity except in human form? Therefore they bow down to Christ, and, in so doing, dishonor both God and Christ. Must a visible incarnation be worshipped because men cannot realize the invisible God? God forbid. He needs not flesh to reveal Himself; He is present, filling the whole universe, one vast spiritual Entity, before whose reality the world is but a delusion. What is the world's reality, what is man's reality, what is even Christ's reality, before the reality, the grandeur, the majesty of the Supreme Jehovah? I protest against the doctrine of the heart's inability to conceive of God as a reality. It is consistent both with philosophy and true theology to maintain that man can by prayer and by faith, not by the all-sufficiency of human reason, not by the dim light of human judgment, realize God, though he cannot comprehend Him. To honor Christ, therefore, the first thing needed is to honor God, and, like the Jew, to be able to worship Him without Christ, without mediation, without dogmas of Atonement, proceeding to the Father directly and immediately; then God will come out to receive the penitent sinner with His own hands, and will kiss him as the father kisses his dear son who was lost but is found. He who does not understand God cannot understand Christ. How then can Christ be known? Not through a book, not through doctrines, not by having recourse to ministers or priests, but by having recourse to the Spirit of God. The world has tried the experiment of the worship of incarnation, and that experiment has sadly failed; for man, by logic and dogmas, has broken up the Divine Unity into three persons. That was not the promise made to the Jew, that was not what Christ meant. Goodness as goodness is God's goodness, and cannot belong to any other being; truth as truth is Divine, and is God's property wherever met with, in Socrates, in Confucius, in the Bible, in Christ, in the Hindu Scriptures, or in the Mahometan Scriptures. Here behold the unity of Truth and Goodness. Christ identified the spirit of truth in himself with God, and he never for a moment allowed his disciples to believe that he came into the world to do his own will and not his Father's. He was the willing and humble servant of the great Father. God's will was his will, God's delight his delight. The object, then, of all men should be to attain and realize that unity of spirit which is to be perceived in all forms of truth and practical goodness in this world. The Hindu, so far as he believes in God, is true to Christ. If purity, truth, charity, resignation, self-sacrifice constitute Christianity, then, in whomsoever they are found, there is Christianity, whether the man be called a Christian, or a Hindu, or a Mahometan. None would rejoice so heartily as the living spirit of Jesus Christ to see his followers give all the glory to God and reserve nothing for him or for themselves. If all the glory be given to God, there will be unity; if not, all must be confusion. Why is it that many Hindus are far better Christians than some who take the name of Christian? Because the same God inspires them, because from the same fountain comes truth to all. God is no respecter of persons, and all men who are true to Him will be accepted by Him, rich or poor, ministers or laymen, Hindus or Christians. The great secret of revelation, inspiration, and salvation lies in this third ideal—Holy Ghost. So long as the Holy Ghost comes not to an individual or to a nation, so long God cannot be worshipped as He ought to be, and Christ cannot be honored as he ought to be. Christ has been in the world for the last eighteen hundred years, yet how far is Christendom still from the kingdom of heaven! And why? Because people do not look within—they do not sufficiently acknowledge the Spirit. John the Baptist paved the way for Christ; another John the Baptist is needed now, to prepare the way for the Spirit of God. I must say that I hopefully look forward to this, for I believe that the spirit of Christ is the spirit of truth in humanity, not Christ as God, but Christ as manifesting God—not another God, but God's spirit, working practically in the human heart. In England two great forces are at work—one inside and the other outside the Church—bringing the whole Church of Christ nearer to Christ and nearer to God; the Broad Church movement, breaking down the barriers of sect and extending the sympathies of the Christian heart; and Dissenters and Liberal thinkers, helping, by a pressure from without, to bring about a more rational and liberal interpretation of the doctrines of Christianity.

The result of my visit to England is that as I came here an Indian, I go back a confirmed Indian; I came here a Theist, I return a confirmed Theist. I have learnt to love my own country more and more. English patriotism has by a sort of electric process quickened my own patriotism. I came here a believer in the Fatherhood of God and the Brotherhood of Man, and I shall return confirmed in this belief. I have not accepted one single new doctrine that God had not put into my mind before; I have not accepted new dogmas or doctrines, but I have tried as far as possible to imbibe the blessed influence of Christian lives. I have placed myself at the feet of Christians of all shades of opinion, and tried to gather from their lives and examples all that was calculated to enlighten me and to purify me, and to sanctify my native land; and I have been amply repaid for all my exertions. I have learnt a great deal, but all in confirmation of my views of God. On the banks of the Thames, as on the banks of the Ganges, I have opened the secrets of my aspirations and prayers to the one loving and holy God, and He has heard me here as He did there. As on the heights of the Himalayas I have entered into sweet, undisturbed and solitary communion with my Divine Master, so, while gliding on the placid waters of Loch Lomond and Loch Katrine I have looked devoutly at the hills which surrounded me and seen the majesty of the Supreme God in the solemn stillness of those solitary heights. Whatever city I have visited, I have seen everywhere the same God, the same dear Father. Were it not for this, existence would be a burden, and my visit to England ineffectual. I am now, thank God, a man of the world, and can say that England is as much my Father's house as India. Often in the midst of my friends and companions in India I have glorified God with the most enthusiastic rejoicing, and I have done the same amid large congregations of fellow-worshippers in England. Wherever I have been I have met with a cordial welcome. From Her Majesty down to the poorest peasant in the kingdom, I have received sympathy and kindness. People of all denominations, putting aside their doctrinal differences, have loved me as a brother. I have been in official circles, and from the authorities I have received emphatic assurances that earnest efforts will be made in order to do justice to India. (Applause) I was always a faithful and loyal subject of Her Majesty Queen Victoria, but since my interview with her, my attachment to her has been deeper than ever. What can I give you as an adequate return for all the kindness and sympathy which you have shown me? I have not told you the whole truth with regard to your kindness; for I came here almost penniless, and you have not only given me a public welcome, but you have fed me and clothed me during my residence in this country; and for that with my whole heart I give thanks unto my Father and your Father. All this weight of obligation presses heavily on my heart now that the day is coming when I shall depart from the shores of beloved

England. How can I show in an outward manner my grateful appreciation of your unusually generous interest and your unbounded kindness? Gold and silver have I none; in wisdom as in wealth am I poor. When I came here I knew not that I should be honored in the way I have been; such honors came spontaneously from your sympathizing and generous hearts, but I assure you most strongly I deserved not honors such as these. I have humbly served you, and that is my only consolation. That will gladden my heart, and all the sympathy you have shown me during my short sojourn in your country will always encourage me to be good and to do good. I deeply regret that I have absolutely failed to show my inmost and heartfelt gratitude, which lies stifled in the recesses of my heart. God alone who searches the depths of human hearts knows it. To Him I offer my prayers that He may bless you. Prayers and good wishes alone can I give. My God is the God of Love. That truth I learnt when it pleased my Father to reveal Himself to me, and that truth He has revealed more and more unto me, and up to the present moment, that has been my doctrine, my theology, my ethics, my riches, my treasure, my joy, my hope, my consolation in the midst of trials and tribulation, my strength and my fortress in the season of difficulty and doubt. That I leave with you. God is love. Know that, realize the deep truth that lies therein, and you will find comfort in it. May that be your religion, your life, your light, your strength, your salvation! My God is a sweet God, and if you love Him as your Father, He will show His sweetness unto you. Forget and forgive all the offense that I may have given you during my stay in this country. If I have not treated you well, if I have not honored you as I ought, pardon me, for I knew not the customs of your country. If I have shown any indifference, it proceeded from ignorance, not from any deficiency in the heart. My brethren, the time has come for me to say the last word of farewell. From England I go away, but my heart will always be with you, and England will always be in my heart. Farewell, dear England; "with all thy faults I love thee still." Farewell, country of Shakespeare and of Newton, land of liberty and of charity. Farewell, temporary home where I realized, and tasted, and enjoyed the sweetness of brotherly and sisterly love. Farewell, my Father's Western house. Farewell, my beloved brothers and sisters. (Long-continued applause)

REFERENCE

Mozoomdar, Protap C. 1887. *The Life and Teachings of Keshub Chunder Sen.* Calcutta: J. W. Thomas Baptist Mission Press.

23

From Poverty and Un-British Rule in India

Dadabhai Naoroji, 1901

Dadabhai Naoroji wrote in the late nineteenth and early twentieth centuries. Differing from Roy in style and content, he argues in the following text not to "be nice to the natives," but rather to oppose British hypocrisy. In his introduction he describes British rule as despotic, destructive of Indian society, and not even good for Britain. Like Roy, he first sketches the benefits derived from the British presence and also the importance of India to Britain's empire, using quotes from British notables themselves. He then discusses poverty in India, which he believes is a consequence of British rule.

His topic is extreme poverty in India, a country that in the mid-eighteenth century accounted for nearly 25 percent of global trade. As a member of the Bombay town council, he was in a position to review the finances of India at the local level. He later drew on this fiscal experience to develop his broad-gauged analysis in *Poverty and Un-British Rule in India* (1901). Indicating a deep understanding of the economic dynamism of colonialism, Naoroji convincingly argued that England drained India of resources worth millions annually, thereby creating poverty and famine in the subcontinent.

Born in 1825 in Bombay, Naoroji was a Zoroastrian, and lived a full ninety-three years. During his long life he became known as the Father of Indian Politics and Economics and early on as a promoter of self-government in India within the British Empire. His influence as a mentor was later to be acknowledged by Gandhi and others. Naoroji's political career started with the Bombay Association, a pressure group seeking reforms in British rule—albeit limited ones such as the admittance of Indians to the civil service. He himself sought to educate both Indians and British about the Indian situation, and his first relocation to Britain, in 1855, had as its purpose to reform both countries. He established a number of organizations, including the London Indian Society (1865), and several active local associations.

Naoroji, Dadabhai. 1901. "Introduction" and "The Poverty of India." In *Poverty and Un-British Rule in India*. London: Swan Sonnenschein and Co., Ltd. Pp. v–xiv, 203–219.

Until 1881 he ran a business in Britain and moved between England and India, remaining politically active in both countries. His position on Indian self-rule grew more radical with the years, and he even ran and was elected in Britain as a Liberal member of Parliament in 1892, losing his seat three years later. Nevertheless, along with some Pan-Africanists he continued to be involved with the Liberal Party. His speech to the Socialist International in 1904 was a major event indicating both his growing influence and his ever-increasing activism.

He is remembered as the first "black" man to be elected to the British Parliament and his maiden speech has been repeatedly reproduced—a unique event in the history of India and of the British Empire. Remembered also for intense passion in his political and economic pursuits for a regenerated India, the Father of Indian Politics left this world respected and beloved by his countrymen—the ideal patriot who worked tirelessly on a variety of fronts: economics, politics, organizing. His analysis of poverty embedded in the concept of "drain"—excess of exports over imports—is as sound now as it was then. He called the taxation of India crushing, noting external and internal drain. But he also noted a moral drain in India: "Europeans occupy almost all the higher places in every department of Government ... (they) eat the substance of India, material and moral, while living there, and when they go, they carry away all they have acquired, and their pensions and future usefulness besides" (Naoroji 1901:205–206). Meanwhile, "the thousands [of Indian students] that are being sent out by the universities every year find themselves in a most anomalous position. ... There is no place for them in their mother-land" (205). Naoroji speaks vehemently about those who retire "with their plunder and booty" (211). A man with a vision of what was ahead for India.

. . .

INTRODUCTION
"Britain's Solemn Pledges"

ACT OF PARLIAMENT, 1833 (INDIA)

That no Native of the said territories, nor any natural-born subject of His Majesty resident therein, shall by reason only of his religion, place of birth, descent, or any of them, be disabled from holding any place, office, or employment under the said Company.

[The East India Company's duties on imports and exports were transferred to the Crown.]

THE QUEEN'S PROCLAMATION OF 1858

We hold ourselves bound to the Natives of our Indian territories by the same obligations of duty which bind us to all our other subjects, and these obligations, by the blessing of Almighty God, we shall faithfully and conscientiously fulfil.

And it is our further will that, so far as may be, our subjects, of whatever race or creed, be freely and impartially admitted to offices in our service, the duties of

which they may be qualified, by their education, ability, and Integrity, duly to discharge.

When, by the blessing of Providence, internal tranquility shall be restored, it is
our earnest desire to stimulate . . . and to administer its government for the benefit of
all our subjects resident therein. In their prosperity will be our strength, in their
contentment our security, and in their gratitude our best reward. And may the God
of all power grant to us and to those in authority under us strength to carry out these
our wishes for the good of our people.

LORD LYTTON (THE VICEROY), ON THE ASSUMPTION OF THE TITLE OF
EMPRESS, 1ST JANUARY, 1877, AT THE DELHI ASSEMBLAGE

But you, the Natives of India, whatever your race and whatever your creed, have a recognized claim to share largely with your English fellow-subjects, according to your
capacity for the task, in the administration of the country you Inhabit. This claim is
founded in the highest justice. It has been repeatedly affirmed by British and Indian
statesmen and by the legislation of the Imperial Parliament. It is recognized by the Government of India as binding on its honor, and consistent with all the aims of its policy.

LORD LYTTON (THE VICEROY), AS CHANCELLOR OF THE CALCUTTA
UNIVERSITY, MARCH, 1877

The Proclamation of the Queen contains solemn pledges, spontaneously given, and
founded upon the highest justice.

JUBILEE OF 1887. THE QUEEN-EMPRESS, IN REPLY TO THE JUBILEE ADDRESS OF
CONGRATULATION OF THE BOMBAY MUNICIPAL CORPORATION

Allusion is made to the Proclamation issued on the occasion of my assumption of the
direct government of India as the charter of the liberties of the Princes and Peoples
of India. It has always been and will be continued to be my earnest desire that the
principles of that Proclamation should be unswervingly maintained.

In order to give briefly some indication of the scope and object of this book, I
make some introductory remarks.

The title of the book is "POVERTY AND UN-BRITISH RULE IN INDIA," *i.e.,* the
present system of government is destructive and despotic to the Indians and un-
British and suicidal to Britain. On the other hand, a truly British course can and
will certainly be vastly beneficent both to Britain and India.

Before dealing with the above evil qualities of the present system of government I would first give a very brief sketch of the benefits which India has derived
from British connection, and of the immense importance of India to Britain for
Britain's own greatness and prosperity.

The Benefits to India

The present advanced humanitarian civilization of Britain could not but exercise
its humane influence to abolish the customs of *sati* and infanticide, earning

the everlasting blessings of the thousands who have been and will be saved thereby.

The introduction of English education, with its great, noble, elevating, and civilizing literature and advanced science, will for ever remain a monument of good work done in India and a claim to gratitude upon the Indian people. This education has taught the highest political ideal of British citizenship and raised in the hearts of the educated Indians the hope and aspiration to be able to raise their countrymen to the same ideal citizenship. This hope and aspiration as their greatest good are at the bottom of all their present sincere and earnest loyalty, in spite of the disappointments, discouragements, and despotism of a century and half. I need not dwell upon several consequential social and civilizing benefits. But the greatest and the most valued of all the benefits are the most solemn pledges of the Act of 1833, and the Queen's Proclamations of 1858, 1877, and 1887, which if "faithfully and conscientiously fulfilled" will be Britain's highest gain and glory and India's greatest blessing and benefit.

Britain may well claim credit for law and order, which, however, is as much necessary for the existence of British rule in India as for the good of the Indian people; for freedom of speech and press, and for other benefits flowing therefrom.

The Immense Importance of India to Britain's Empire, to Its Greatness and Its Prosperity

Lord Curzon, before he went out to India as Viceroy, laid great and repeated emphasis, two or three times, upon the fact of this importance of India to Britain. "India," he said, "was the pivot of our Empire. (Hear, hear.) If this Empire lost any other part of its dominion we could survive, but if we lost India, the sun of our Empire would be set" (*Times,* [December 3] 1898).

Lord Roberts, after retiring for good from India, said to the London Chamber of Commerce:—

"I rejoice to learn that you recognize how indissolubly the prosperity of the United Kingdom is bound up with the retention of that vast Eastern Empire" (*Times,* [May 25] 1893). He repeated "that the retention of our Eastern Empire is essential to the greatness and prosperity of the United Kingdom" (*Times,* [July 29] 1893). And with still more emphasis he pointed out upon what essential condition such retention of the Indian Empire depended—not upon brute force; but "however," he said, "efficient and well-equipped the army of India may be, were it indeed absolute perfection, and were its numbers considerably more than they are at present, our greatest strength must ever rest on the firm base of a united and contented India."

I now come to the faults of the present un-British system of Government, which unfortunately "more than counterbalances the benefits."

Destructive and Despotic to the Indians

The Court of Directors, among various expressions of the same character, said, in their letters of [May 17] 1766 and others about the same time: "Every Englishman throughout the country . . . exercising his power to the oppression of the helpless Natives. . . . We have the strongest sense of the deplorable state . . . from the corruption and rapacity of our servants . . . by a scene of the most tyrannic and oppressive conduct that ever was known in any age or country!" Such unfortunately was the beginning of the connection between Britain and India—based on greed and oppression. And to our great misfortune and destruction, the same has remained in subtle and ingenious forms and subterfuges up to the present day with ever increasing impoverishment.

Later, as far back as 1787, Sir John Shore (subsequently Governor-General) prophesied the evils of the present system of the British Indian Government which is true to the present day.

He said in a deliberate Minute:—

Whatever allowance we may make for the increased industry of the subjects of the State, owing to the enhanced demand for the produce of it (supposing the demand to be enhanced), there is reason to conclude that *the benefits are more than counterbalanced by evils inseparable from the system of a remote foreign dominion.* . . .[1]

Commonsense will suggest this to any thoughtful mind. These evils have ever since gone on increasing, and more and more counterbalancing the increased produce of the country, making now the evil of the "bleeding" and impoverishing drain by the foreign dominion nearly or above £30,000,000 a year in a variety of subtle ways and shapes; while about the beginning of the last century the drain was declared to be £3,000,000 a year—and with private remittances, was supposed to be near £5,000,000—or one-sixth of what it is at present. If the profits of exports and freight and insurance, which are not accounted for in the official statistics, be considered, the present drain will be nearer forty than thirty millions; speaking roughly on the old basis of the value of gold at two shillings per rupee.

Mr. Montgomery Martin, after examining the records in the India House of a minute survey made in 1807–1814 of the condition of some provinces of Bengal and Behar, said in 1835 in his "Eastern India":—"It is impossible to avoid remarking two facts as peculiarly striking—first the richness of the country surveyed, and second, the poverty of its inhabitants. . . . The annual drain of £3,000,000 on British India has amounted in thirty years, at 12 per cent (the usual Indian rate) compound interest to the enormous sum of £723,900,000 sterling. . . . So constant and accumulating a drain, even in England, would soon impoverish her. How severe then must be its effects on India when the wage of a laborer is from twopence to threepence a day." He also calculates the result of the drain of £5,000,000 a year. What then must be or can be the effect of the unceasing drain which has now grown to the enormous amount of some £30,000,000 a year, if not famines and plagues, destruction and impoverishment?

Mill's "History of India" (Vol. VI, p. 671; "India Reform Tract" II, p. 3) says: "It is an exhausting drain upon the resources of the country, the issue of which is replaced by no reflex; it is an extraction of the life blood from the veins of national industry which no subsequent introduction of nourishment is furnished to restore."

Sir George Wingate has said (1859): "Taxes spent in the country from which they are raised are totally different in their effect from taxes raised in one country and spent in another. In the former case the taxes collected from the population . . . are again returned to the industrious classes. . . . But the case is wholly different when the taxes are not spent in the country from which they are raised. . . . They constitute . . . an absolute loss and extinction of the whole amount withdrawn from the taxed country . . . might as well be thrown into the sea. . . . Such is the nature of the tribute we have so long exacted from India. . . . From this explanation some faint conception may be formed of the cruel, crushing effect of the tribute upon India. . . .

The Indian tribute, whether weighed in the scales of justice or viewed in the light of our own interest, will be found to be at variance with humanity, with common sense, and with the received maxims of economic science" ("A Few Words on Our Financial Relation with India," London: Richardson Bros., 1859).

Lord Salisbury, as Secretary of State for India, in a Minute ([April 26] 1875) said [. . .]:

> The injury is exaggerated in the case of India, where so much of the revenue is exported without a direct equivalent. As *India must be bled* the lancet should be directed to the parts where the blood is congested or at least sufficient, not to those (the agricultural people) which are *already feeble from the want of it.*

This was said twenty-six years ago, and those who were considered as having sufficient blood are also being brought lower and lower. The "want of blood" among the agricultural population is getting so complete that famines and plagues like the present are fast bleeding the masses to death.

Lord Lawrence, Lord Cromer, Sir Auckland Colvin, Sir David Barbour, and others have declared the *extreme poverty* of India.

But the drain is not all. All the wars by which the British Indian Empire is built up have not only been fought mainly with Indian blood, but every farthing of expenditure (with insignificant exceptions) incurred in all wars and proceedings within and beyond the frontiers of India by which the Empire has been built up and maintained up to the present day has been exacted from the Indian people. Britain has spent nothing.

There is the great injustice that every expenditure incurred even for British interest is charged to India. Under the recommendation of the late "Royal Commission on Indian Expenditure and Apportionment" the British Government has done a very small justice in refunding about £250,000 a year. Even for such trifle of justice we are thankful, and hope that this may lead to further justice. But it is necessary for us to have the help of the recognition and voice of the British public to ensure this.

The utter exhaustion and destruction from all these causes is terrific, and cannot but produce the present famines, plagues, etc. What would Britain's condition be under a similar fate? Let her ask herself that question. The Anglo-Indians always shirk that question, never face it. Their selfishness makes them blind and deaf to it.

Despotism

I need only say that the people of India have not the slightest voice in the expenditure of the revenue, and therefore in the good government of the country. The powers of the Government being absolutely arbitrary and despotic, and the Government being alien and bleeding, the effect is very exhausting and destructive indeed.

Sir William Hunter has truly said:

> I cannot believe that a people numbering one-sixth of the whole inhabitants of the globe, and whose aspirations have been nourished from their earliest youth on the strong food of English liberty, can be permanently denied a voice in the government of their country. I do not believe that races . . . into whom we have instilled the maxim of "no taxation without representation" as a fundamental right of a people, can be permanently excluded from a share in the management of their finances.

Un-British and Suicidal to Britain

A committee of five members of the Council of the Secretary of State for India have declared the British Government to be "exposed to the charge of keeping promise to the ear and breaking it to the hope" (Report, 20th January, 1860).

Lord Lytton, as Viceroy of India, in a Minute referred to in the dispatch of the Government of India of 2nd May, 1878, said: "No sooner was the Act (1833) passed than the Government began to devise means for practically evading the fulfilment of it. . . . We have had to choose between prohibiting them and cheating them, and we have chosen the least straightforward course . . . are all so many deliberate and transparent subterfuges for stultifying the Act and reducing it to a dead letter. . . . I do not hesitate to say that both the Government of England and of India appear to me up to the present moment unable to answer satisfactorily the charge of having taken every means in their power of breaking to the heart the words of promise they had uttered to the ear." (First Report of the Indian National Congress)

The Duke of Argyll has said: "We have not fulfilled our duty or the promises and engagements which we have made." (*Hansard*, [March 11] 1869.)

Lord Salisbury, in reply to Lord Northbrook's pleading for the fulfilment of British solemn pledges, said it was all "political hypocrisy." (*Hansard,* [April 9] 1883.)

Suicidal to Britain

Sir John Malcolm says: "We are not warranted by the history of India, nor indeed by that of any other nation in the world, in reckoning upon the possibility of pre-serving an Empire of such a magnitude by a system which excludes, as ours does, the Natives from every station of high rank and honorable ambition. . . . If we do not use the knowledge which we impart it will be employed against us. . . . If these plans are not associated with the creation of duties that will employ the minds which we enlighten, we shall only prepare elements that will hasten the destruc-tion of our Empire. The moral evil to us does not thus stand alone. It carries with it its Nemesis, the seeds of the destruction of the Empire itself."

Mr. John Bright: "I say a Government like that has some fatal defect which at some not distant time must bring disaster and humiliation to the Government and to the people on whose behalf it rules." (Speech in the Manchester Town Hall, [December 12] 1877)

The Duke of Devonshire pointed out that "it is not wise to educate the people of India, to introduce among them your civilization and your progress and your lit-erature and at the same time to tell them they shall never have any chance of taking any part or share in the administration of the affairs of their country *except by their getting rid in the first instance of their European rulers.*" (*Hansard,* [August 23] 1883.)

Lord Randolph Churchill, as Secretary of State for India, has said in a letter to the Treasury:

> The position of India in relation to taxation and the sources of public revenue is very peculiar, not merely from the habits of the people and their strong aversion to change, which is more specially exhibited to new forms of taxation, but likewise from *the character of the Government* which is *in the hands of foreigners who hold all the principal administrative offices, and form so large a part of the army.* The impatience of the new taxation, which will have to be borne *wholly as a consequence of the foreign rule imposed on the country,* and virtually to meet additions to charges arising outside of the country, would constitute a *political danger,* the real magnitude of which it is to be feared is not at all appreciated by persons who have no knowledge of or concern in the Government of India, but which those responsible for that Government have long regarded as of *the most serious order.*[2]

Lord George Hamilton candidly admits:—"Our Government never will be popular in India." Again, "our Government never can be popular in India." (*Times,* [June 16] 1899.)

How can it be otherwise ? If the present un-British and suicidal system of gov-ernment continues, commonsense tells us that such a system "can never" and "will never" be popular. And if so, such a deplorable system cannot but perish; as Lord Salisbury truly says, "Injustice will bring the highest on earth to ruin." Macaulay has said, "The heaviest of all yokes is the yoke of the stranger." And if the British rule remains, as it is at present, a heavy yoke of the stranger and the despot, instead of being a true British rule and a friendly partner, it is doomed to perish. Evil is not, and never will be, eternal.

True British Rule

True British rule will vastly benefit both Britain and India. My whole object in all my writings is to impress upon the British People, that instead of a disastrous explosion of the British Indian Empire, as must be the result of the present dishonorable un-British system of government, there is a great and glorious future for Britain and India to an extent unconceivable at present, if the British people will awaken to their duty, will be true to their British instincts of fair play and justice, and will insist upon the "faithful and conscientious fulfilment" of all their great and solemn promises and pledges.

Mr. John Bright has truly said: "The good of England must come through the channels of the good of India. There are but two modes of gaining anything by our connection with India. The one is by plundering the people of India and the other by trading with them. I prefer to do it by trading with them. But in order that England may become rich by trading with India, India itself must become rich." Cannot British authorities see their way to such intelligent selfishness? Hitherto England has to some extent made herself rich by plundering India in diverse subtle and ingenious ways. But what I desire and maintain is that England can become far richer by dealing justly and honorably with India, and thereby England will not only be a blessing to India and itself, but will be a lesson and a blessing to mankind.

Macaulay, in his great speech of 1833, said: "I have no fears. The path of duty is plain before us; and it is also the path of wisdom, of national prosperity, of national honor. . . . To have found a great people sunk in the lowest depths of slavery and superstition, to have so ruled them as to have made them desirous and capable of all the privileges of citizens would indeed be a title to glory all our own. The scepter may pass away from us. Unforeseen accidents may derange our most profound schemes of policy. Victory may be inconstant to our arms. But there are triumphs which are followed by no reverses. There is an empire exempt from all natural causes of decay. Those triumphs are the pacific triumphs of reason over barbarism; that empire is the imperishable empire of our arts and our morals, our literature and our laws."

Sir William Hunter, after referring to the good work done by the Company, said: "But the good work thus commenced has assumed such dimensions under the Queen's government of India that it can no longer be carried on, *or even supervised,* by imported labor from England except at a cost which India cannot sustain. . . . Forty years hereafter we should have had an Indian Ireland multiplied fifty fold on our hands. . . . You cannot work with imported labor as cheaply as you can with Native labor, and I regard the more extended employment of the Natives not only as an act of justice but as a financial necessity." "The appointment of a few Natives annually to the Covenanted Civil Service will not solve the problem. . . . If we are to govern the Indian people efficiently and cheaply we must govern them by means of themselves and pay for the administration at the market rates of Native labor." ("England's Work in India," pp. 118–119.)

The Duke of Devonshire has said: "If the country is to be better governed that can only be done by the employment of the best and most intelligent of the Natives in the Service."

Events are moving now at lightning pace, and it is difficult to say what tomorrow may bring, as forces evil or beneficent when once set in motion will move with accelerated speed to their natural results—evil out of evil, good out of good.

In the "faithful and conscientious fulfilment" of solemn pledges, India expects and demands that the British Sovereign, People, Parliament, and Government, should make honest efforts towards what the Bishop of Bombay described as the aspirations and necessities of India—"Self-government under British paramountcy" or true British citizenship.

This book contains a selection from my papers written from time to time as occasion arose, and I think giving them in the same order here will be the most intelligible form for a subject which is so complicated and whose important points are so much intermixed with each other.

THE POVERTY OF INDIA

Papers Read before the Bombay Branch of
the East India Association of London in 1876

[. . .]

16th November, 1880.

MEMORANDUM NO. 2: *The Moral Poverty of India and Native Thoughts on the Present British Indian Policy.*

In my last paper I confined myself to meeting Mr. Danvers' line of argument on the question of the material destruction and impoverishment of India by the present British Indian policy. I endeavored to show that this impoverishment and destruction of India was mainly caused by the unnatural treatment it received at the hands of its British rulers, in the way of subjecting it to a large variety of expenditure upon a crushing foreign agency both in India and England, whereby the children of the country were displaced and deprived of their natural rights and means of subsistence in their own country; that, by what was being taken and consumed in India itself, and by what was being continuously taken away by such agency clean out of the country, an exhaustion of the very life-blood of the country was unceasingly going on; that not till this disastrous drain was duly checked, and not till the people of India were restored to their natural rights in their own country, was there any hope for the material amelioration of India.

In this memorandum I desire to submit for the kind and generous consideration of his Lordship the Secretary of State for India that, from the same cause of the deplorable drain, besides the material exhaustion of India, the moral loss to her is no less sad and lamentable.

With the material wealth go also the wisdom and experience of the country. Europeans occupy almost all the higher places in every department of Government directly or indirectly under its control. While *in* India they acquire India's money, experience, and wisdom; and when they go, they carry both away with them, leaving India so much poorer in material and moral wealth. Thus India is left without, and cannot have those elders in wisdom and experience who in every country are the natural guides of the rising generations in their national and social conduct, and of the destinies of their country; and a sad, sad loss this is!

Every European is isolated from the people around him. He is not their mental, moral, or social leader or companion. For any mental or moral influence or guidance or sympathy with the people he might just as well be living in the moon. The people know not him, and he knows not, nor cares for, the people. Some honorable exceptions do, now and then, make an effort to do some good if they can, but in the very nature of things these efforts are always feeble, exotic, and of little permanent effect. These men are not always in the place, and their works die away when they go.

The Europeans are not the natural leaders of the people. They do not belong to the people; they cannot enter their thoughts and feelings; they cannot join or sympathize with their joys or griefs. On the contrary, every day the estrangement is increasing. Europeans deliberately and openly widen it more and more. There may be very few social institutions started by Europeans in which Natives, however fit and desirous to join, are not deliberately and insultingly excluded. The Europeans are, and make themselves, strangers in every way. All they effectually do is to eat the substance of India, material and moral, while living there, and when they go, they carry away all they have acquired, and their pensions and future usefulness besides.

This most deplorable moral loss to India needs most serious consideration, as much in its political as in its national aspect. Nationally disastrous as it is, it carries politically with it its own Nemesis. Without the guidance of elderly wisdom and experience of their own natural leaders, the education which the rising generations are now receiving is naturally leading them (or call it misleading them if you will) into directions which bode no good to the rulers, and which, instead of being the strength of the rulers, as it ought to be and can be, will turn out to be their great weakness. The fault will be of the rulers themselves for such a result. The power that is now being raised by the spread of education, though yet slow and small, is one that in time must, for weal or woe, exercise great influence; in fact, it has already begun to do so. However strangely the English rulers, forgetting their English manliness and moral courage, may, like the ostrich, shut their eyes, by gagging acts or otherwise, to the good or bad influences they are raising around them, this good or evil is rising nevertheless. The thousands that are being sent out by the universities every year find themselves in a most anomalous position. There is no place for them in their mother-land. They may beg in the streets or break stones on the roads for ought the rulers seem to care for their natural rights, position and duties in their own country. They may perish or do what they like or can, but scores of Europeans must go from this country to take up what belongs to them, and that in spite of every profession, for years and years past and up to the present day, of English statesmen, that they must govern India for India's good, by solemn Acts and declarations of Parliament, and, above all, by the words of the august Sovereign herself. For all practical purposes all these high promises have been hitherto almost wholly the purest romance, the reality being quite different.

The educated find themselves simply so many dummies, ornamented with the tinsel of school education, and then their whole end and aim of life is ended. What must be the inevitable consequence? A wild spirited horse, without curb or reins, will run away wild, and kill and trample upon every one that comes in his way. A misdirected force will hit anywhere, and destroy anything. The power that the rulers are, so far to their credit, raising will, as a Nemesis, recoil against themselves, if, with this blessing of education, they do not do their whole duty to the country which trusts to their righteousness, and thus turn this good power to their own side. The Nemesis is as clear from the present violence to nature, as disease and death arise from uncleanliness and rottenness. The voice of the power of the rising education is, no doubt, feeble at present. Like the infant, the present dissatisfaction is only crying at the pains it is suffering. Its notions have not taken any form or shape or course yet, but it is growing. Heaven only knows what it will grow to! He who runs may see that if the present material and moral destruction of India continues, a great convulsion must inevitably arise, by which either India will be more and more crushed under the iron heel of despotism and destruction, or may succeed in shattering the destroying hand and power. Far, far is it from my earnest prayer and hope that such should be the result of the British rule. In this rule there is every element to produce immeasurable good, both to India and England, and no thinking Native of India would wish harm to it, with all the hopes that are yet built upon the righteousness and conscience of the British statesman and nation.

The whole duty and responsibility of bringing about this desired consummation lies upon the head and in the hands of the Indian authorities *in England*. It is no use screening themselves behind the fiction and excuse that the Viceroys and authorities in India are difficult to be got to do what they ought, or that they would do all that may be necessary. They neither can nor will do this. They cannot go against Acts of Parliament on the one hand, and, on the other, the pressure of European interests, and of European selfishness and guidance, is so heavy in India, that the Viceroys in their first years are quite helpless, and get committed to certain courses; and if, in time, any of them, happening to have sufficient strength of character and confidence in their own judgment, are likely to take matters in their own hands, and, with any moral courage, to resist interests hostile or antagonistic to the good of the people, the end of their time begins to come near, their zeal and interest begin to flag, and soon they go away, leaving India to roll up Sisyphus's stone again with a new Viceroy. It is the highest Indian authority here, the Secretary of State for India, upon whom the responsibility wholly rests. He alone has the power, as a member of and with the weight of the British Cabinet, to guide the Parliament to acts worthy of the English character, conscience, and nation. The glory or disgrace of the British in India is in his hands. He has to make Parliament lay down, by clear legislation, how India *shall* be governed for "*India's good*," or it is hopeless for us to look forward for any relief from our present material and moral destruction, and for future elevation.

Englishmen sometimes indulge the notion that England is secure in the division and disunion among the various races and nationalities of India. But even in this, new forces are working their way. Those Englishmen who sleep such foolish sleep of security know very little of what is going on. The kind of education that is being received by thousands of all classes and creeds is throwing them all in a similar mold; a sympathy of sentiment, ideas, and aspirations is growing amongst them; and, more particularly, a political union and sympathy is the first fruit of the new awakening, as all feel alike their deprivation and the degradation and destruction of their country. All differences of race and religion, and rivalry, are gradually sinking before this common cause. This beginning, no doubt, is at present insignificant; but it is surely and steadily progressing. Hindus, Mahomedans, and Parsees are alike asking whether the English rule is to be a blessing or a curse. Politics now engross their attention more and more. This is no longer a secret, or a state of things not quite open to those of our rulers who would see. It may be seen that there is scarcely any union among the different nationalities and races in any shape or ways of life, except only in political associations. In these associations they go hand in hand, with all the fervor and sympathy of a common cause. I would here touch upon a few incidents, little though they are, showing how nature is working in its own quiet way.

Dr. Birdwood has brought to the notice of the English public certain songs now being spread among the people of Western India against the destruction of Indian industry and arts. We may laugh at this as a futile attempt to shut out English machine-made cheaper goods against hand-made dearer ones. But little do we think what this movement is likely to grow into, and what new phases it may take in time. The songs are at present directed against English wares, but they are also a natural and effective preparation against other English things when the time comes, if the English in their blindness allow such times to come. The songs are full of loyalty, and I have not the remotest doubt in the sincerity of that loyalty. But if the present downward course of India continue, if the mass of the people at last begin to despair of any amelioration, and if educated youths, without the wisdom and experience of the world, become their leaders, it will be but a *very, very* short step from loyalty to disloyalty, to turn the course of indignation from English wares to English rule. The songs will remain the same; one word of curse for the rule will supply the spark.

Here is another little incident with its own significance. The London Indian Society, a political body of many of the Native residents of London, had a dinner the other day, and they invited guests. The three guests were, one Hindu, one Mahomedan, and one Parsee. The society itself is a body representing nearly all the principal classes of India. It is small, and may be laughed at as uninfluential, and can do nothing. But it shows how a sympathy of political common cause is bringing the different classes together, and how, in time, such small seeds may grow into large trees. Every member of this little body is carrying back with him ideas which, as seeds, may produce crops, sweet or bitter, according to the cultivation they may receive at our rulers' hands.

I turn to one bright incident on the other side. True to their English nature and character, there are some Englishmen who try to turn the current of Native thought towards an appreciation of English intentions, and to direct English thought towards a better understanding of England's duty to India. The East India Association is doing this beneficent work, more especially by the fair and English character of its course of bringing about free and full discussion upon every topic and from every point of view, so that, by a sifting of the full expression of different views, truth may be elicited. Though yet little appreciated by the English public, the English members of this Association are fulfilling the duty of patriotism to their own country and of benefaction towards India. How far their good efforts will succeed is yet to be seen. But they at least do one thing. These Englishmen, as well as public writers like Fawcett, Hyndman, Perry, Caird, Knight, Bell, Wilson, Wood, and others, vindicate to India the English character, and show that when Englishmen as a body will *understand* their duty and responsibility, the Natives of India may fairly expect a conduct of which theirs is a sample—a desire, indeed, to act rightly by India. The example and earnestness of these Englishmen, though yet small their number, keep India's hope alive—that England will produce a statesman who will have the moral courage and firmness to face the Indian problem, and do what the world should expect from England's conscience, and from England's mission to humanity.

I have thus touched upon a few incidents only to illustrate the various influences that are at work. Whether the result of all these forces and influences will be good or bad remains, as I have said, in the hands of the Secretary of State for India.

In my last paper I said the thinking Natives were as yet staunch in their loyalty to the British rule, as they were yet fully hopeful of the future from the general character and history of the English people. They believe that when the conscience of the English nation is awakened, it will not be long before India receives full and thorough redress for all she has been suffering. While thus hopeful of the future, it is desirable that our rulers should know and consider what, as to the past, is passing in many a thinking Native mind.

They are as grateful as any people can be for whatever real good of peace and order and education has been done for them, but they also ask what good, upon the whole, England has done to India. It is sadly poor, and increasing in poverty, both material and moral. They consider and bewail the unnatural treatment India has been receiving.

They dwell upon the strange contrast between the words and deeds of the English rulers; how often deliberate and solemn promises are made and broken. I need not here instance again what I have at some length shown in my papers on the Poverty of India under the heading of "Non-Fulfilment of Solemn Promises."[3]

I would refer here to one or two characteristic instances only. The conception for an Engineering College in London was no sooner formed than it became an accomplished fact; and Mr. Grant Duff, then Under-Secretary of State, in his place in Parliament, proclaimed what great boons "we" were conferring on the English people, but quite oblivious at whose sacrifices. It was an English interest, and the thing was done as quick as it was thought of. On the other hand, a clause for Native interests, proposed in 1867, took three years to pass, and in such a form as to be simply ineffectual. I asked Sir Stafford Northcote, at the time of the proposal, to make it some way imperative, but without effect. Again, after being passed after three years, it remained a dead letter for seven years more, and might have remained so till Doomsday for aught any of the Indian authorities cared. But, thanks to the persevering exertions of one of England's true sons, Sir Erskine Perry, some steps were at last taken to frame the rules that were required, and it is now, in the midst of a great deal of fine writing, making some, though very slow, progress. For such, even as it is, we are thankful; but greater efforts are necessary to stem the torrent of the drain. Turning to the Uncovenanted Service, Sir Stafford Northcote's dispatch of 8th February, 1868, declared that Europeans should not be allowed in this service to override "the inherent rights of the Natives of the country." Now, in what spirit was this dispatch treated till very lately? Was it not simply, or is it not even now, almost a dead letter?

In the matter of the load of the public debt of India, it is mainly due to the wars of the English conquests in India, and English wars abroad in the name of India.

Not a farthing has been spent by England for its British Indian Empire. The burden of all England's wars in Asia has been thrown on India's shoulders. In the Abyssinian War, India narrowly and lightly escaped; and in the present Afghan War, her escape from whatever portion she may be saved is not less narrow. Though such is the character of nearly the whole of the public debt (excluding for public works), being caused by the actions by which England has become the mistress of a great Empire, and thereby the first nation in the world, she would not move her little finger to give India any such help as is within her power, without even any material sacrifice to herself—viz., that of guaranteeing this public debt, so that India may derive some little relief from reduced interest.

When English interests are concerned, their accomplishment is often a foregone conclusion. But India's interests always require long and anxious thought—thought that seldom begins, and when it does begin, seldom ends in any thorough good result. It is useless to conceal that the old pure and simple faith in the honor and word of the English rulers is much shaken, and were it not for the faith in the conscience of the statesmen and people in *this* country, any hope of good by an alteration of the present British Indian policy would be given up.

The English rulers boast, and justly so, that they have introduced education and Western civilization into India; but, on the other hand, they act as if no such thing had taken place, and as if all this boast was pure moonshine. Either they have educated, or have not. If they deserve the boast, it is a strange self-condemnation that after half a century or more of such efforts, they have not yet prepared a sufficient number of men fit for the service of their own country. Take even the Educational Department itself. We are made B.A.'s and M.A.'s and M.D.'s, etc., with the strange result that we are not yet considered fit to teach our countrymen. We must yet have forced upon us even in this department, as in every other, every European that can be squeezed in. To keep up the sympathy and connection with the current of European thought, an English head may be appropriately and beneficially retained in a few of the most important institutions; but as matters are at present, all boast of education is exhibited as so much sham and delusion.

In the case of former foreign conquests, the invaders either retired with their plunder and booty, or became the rulers of the country. When they only plundered and went back, they made, no doubt, great wounds: but India, with her industry, revived and healed the wounds. When the invaders became the rulers of the country, they settled down *in* it, and whatever was the condition of their rule, according to the character of the sovereign of the day, there was at least no material or moral drain in the country.[4] Whatever the country produced remained in the country; whatever wisdom and experience was acquired in her services remained among her own people. With the English the case is peculiar. There are the great wounds of the first wars in the burden of the public debt, and those wounds are kept perpetually open and widening, by draining away the life-blood in a continuous stream. The former rulers were like butchers hacking here and there, but the English with their scientific scalpel cut to the very heart, and yet, lo! there is no wound to be seen, and soon the plaster of the high talk of civilization, progress, and what not, covers up the wound! The English rulers stand sentinel at the front door of India, challenging the whole world, that they do and shall protect India against all comers, and themselves carry away by a back-door the very treasure they stand sentinel to protect.

In short, had England deliberately intended to devise the best means of taking away India's wealth in a quiet continuous drain, without scandalizing the world, she could not have hit upon a more effectual plan than the present lines of policy. A Viceroy tells us the people of India enjoy but scanty subsistence; and this is the outcome of the British rule.

No doubt the exertions of individual Europeans at the time of famines may be worthy of admiration; the efforts of Government and the aid of the contributions of the British people to save life, deserve every gratitude. But how strange it is that the British rulers do not see that after all they themselves are the main cause of the destruction that ensues from droughts; that is the drain of India's wealth by *them* that lays at their own door the dreadful results of misery, starvation, and deaths of millions; England does not know famines, be the harvest however bad or scanty. She has the means of buying her food from the whole world. India is being unceasingly deprived of these means, and when famine comes the starving have to be taxed so much more to save the dying.

England's conduct in India is in strange contrast with her conduct with almost any other country. Owing to the false groove in which she is moving, she does violence to her own best instincts. She sympathizes with and helps every nationality that struggles for a constitutional representative government. On the one hand, she is the parent of, and maintains, the highest constitutionalism; and, on the other, she exercises a clear and, though thoughtlessly, a despoiling despotism in India, under a pseudo-constitutionalism, in the shape of the farce of the present Legislative Councils.

Of all countries in the world, if any one has the greatest claim on England's consideration, to receive the boons of a constitutional representative government at her hands, and to have her people governed as England governs her own, that country is India, her most sacred trust and charge. But England, though she does everything she can for other countries, fights shy of, and makes some excuse or other to avoid, giving to the people of India their fair share in the legislation of their country. Now I do not mean to say that India can suddenly have a full-blown Parliament, and of such widespread representation as England enjoys. But has England made any honest efforts to gradually introduce a true representation of the people, excepting some solitary exceptions of partial municipal representation? I need not dwell upon the present farce of the nomination system for the

Legislative Councils, and of the dummies that are sometimes nominated. I submit that a small beginning can be well made now. I would take the Bombay Presidency as an instance. Suppose the present Legislative Council is extended to twenty-one members, thirteen of these to be nominated from officials and non-officials by the Government, and eight to be elected by the principal towns of the Presidency. This will give Government a clear majority of five, and the representative element, the minority, cannot do any harm, or hamper Government; in England the majority determines the Government. In India this cannot be the case at present, and so the majority must follow the Government. It would be, when something is extremely outrageous, that the minority would, by force of argument and truth, draw towards it the Government majority; and even in any such rare instance, all that will happen will be that Government will be prevented from doing any such outrageous things. In short, in such an arrangement, Government will remain all-powerful, as it must for a long time to come; while there will be also independent persons, actually representing the people, to speak the sentiments of the people; thereby giving Government the most important help, and relieving them from much responsibility, anxiety, and mistakes. The representative element in the minority will be gradually trained in constitutional government. They will have no inducement to run wild with prospects of power; they will have to maintain the reasons of their existence, and will, therefore, be actuated by caution and good sense. They can do no harm, but a vast amount of good, both to the Government and the governed. The people will have the satisfaction that their rulers were doing their duty, and endeavoring to raise them to their own civilization.

There are in the Bombay Presidency the following towns of more than 50,000 population. Bombay having by far the largest, and with its importance as the capital of the Presidency, may be properly allowed three representatives.

The towns are—

Bombay: 644,405[5]
Poona: 118,886
Ahmedabad: 116,873
Surat: 107,149
Kurrachi: 53,536
Sholapore: 53,403

Thus, Bombay having three, the Gujerati division of the Presidency will be represented by Ahmedabad and Surat, the Maratha portion by Poona and Sholapore, and Sind by Kurrachi, making altogether eight members, which will be a fair, though a small, representation to begin with. Government may with advantage adopt a larger number; all I desire and insist is, that there must be a fair *representative* element in the Councils. As to the qualifications of electors and candidates for election, Government is quite competent to fix upon some, as they did in the case of the Bombay Corporation, and such qualifications may from time to time be modified as experience may suggest. With this modification in the present Legislative Council, a great step will have been taken towards one of the greatest boons which India asks and expects at England's hands. Without some such element of the people's voice in all the Legislative Councils, it is impossible for Englishmen, more and more estranged and isolated as they are becoming, to be able to legislate for India in the true spirit and feeling of her wants.

After having a glorious history of heroic struggles for constitutional government, England is now rearing up a body of Englishmen in India, trained up and accustomed to despotism, with all the feelings of impatience, pride, and highhandedness of the despot becoming gradually ingrained in them, and with the additional training of the dissimulation of constitutionalism. Is it possible that such habits and training of despotism, with which Indian officials return from India, should not, in the course of time, influence the English character and institutions? The English in India, instead of raising India, are hitherto themselves descending and degenerating to the lower level of Asiatic despotism. Is this a Nemesis that will in fullness of time show to them what fruit their conduct in India produced? It is extraordinary how nature may revenge itself for the present unnatural course of England in India, if England, not yet much tainted by this demoralization, does not, in good time, check this new leaven that is gradually fermenting among her people.

There is the opium trade. What a spectacle it is to the world! In England no statesman dares to propose that opium may be allowed to be sold in public houses at the corners of every street, in the same way as beer or spirits. On the contrary, Parliament, as representing the whole nation, distinctly enacts that "opium and all preparations of opium or of 'poppies,' as 'poison,' be sold by certified chemists only, and every box, bottle, vessel, wrapper, or cover in which such poison is contained, be distinctly labeled with the name of the article and the word 'poison,' and with the name and address of the seller of the poison." And yet, at the other end of the world, this Christian, highly civilized, and humane England forces a "heathen" and "barbarous" Power to take this "poison," and tempts a vast human race to use it, and to degenerate and demoralize themselves with this "poison"! And why? Because India cannot fill up the remorseless drain; so China must be dragged in to make it up, even though it be by being "poisoned." It is wonderful how England reconciles this to her conscience. This opium trade is a sin on England's head, and a curse on India for her share in being the instrument. This may sound strange as coming from any Natives of India, as it is generally represented as if India it was that benefited by the opium trade. The fact simply is that, as Mr. Duff said, India is nearly ground down to dust, and the opium trade of China fills up England's drain. India derives not a particle of benefit. All India's profits of trade, and several millions from her very produce (scanty as it is, and becoming more and more so), and with these all the profit of opium, go the same way of the drain—to England. Only India shares the curse of the Chinese race. Had this cursed opium trade not existed, India's miseries would have much sooner come to the surface, and relief and redress would have come to her long ago; but this trade has prolonged the agonies of India.

In association with this trade is the stigma of the Salt-tax upon the British name. What a humiliating confession to say that, after the length of the British rule, the people are in such a wretched plight that they have nothing that Government can tax, and that Government must, therefore, tax an absolute necessary of life to an inordinate extent! The slight flash of prosperity during the American War showed how the people of India would enjoy and spend when they have anything to enjoy and spend; and now, can anything be a greater condemnation of the results of British lines of policy than that the people have nothing to spend and enjoy, and pay tax on, but that they must be pinched and starved in a necessary of life?

The English are, and justly and gloriously, the greatest champions of liberty of speech. What a falling off must have taken place in their character when, after granting this boon to India, they should have even thought of withdrawing it! This act, together with that of disarming the people, is a clear confession by the rulers to the world that they have no hold as yet upon the affection and loyalty of the people, though in the same breath they make every profession of their belief in the loyalty of the people. Now, which is the truth? And are gagging and disarming the outcome of a long benign rule?

Why do the English allow themselves to be so perpetually scared by the fears of Russian or any other foreign invasion? If the people of India be satisfied, if their hearts and hands be with England, she may defy a dozen Russias. On the other hand, do British statesmen think that, however sharp and pointed their bayonets, and however long-flying their bullets, they may not find the two hundred millions of the people of India her political Himalaya to be pierced through, when the present political union among the different peoples is more strengthened and consolidated?

There is the stock argument of over-population. They talk, and so far truly, of the increase by British peace, but they quite forget the destruction by the British drain. They talk of the pitiless operations of economic laws, but somehow they forgot that there is no such thing in India as the natural operation of economic laws. It is not the pitiless operations of economic laws, but it is the thoughtless and pitiless action of the British policy; it is the pitiless eating of India's substance in India, and the further pitiless drain to England; in short, it is the pitiless *perversion* of economic laws by the sad bleeding to which India is subjected, that is destroying India. Why blame poor Nature when the fault lies at your own door? Let natural and economic laws have their full and fair play, and India will become another England, with manifold greater benefit to England herself than at present.

As long as the English do not allow the country to produce what it can produce, as long as the people are not allowed to enjoy what they can produce, as long as the English are the very party on their trial, they have no right, and are not competent, to give an opinion whether the country is over-populated or not. In fact, it is absurd to talk of over-population—*i.e.,* the country's incapability, by its food or other produce, to supply the means of support to its people—if the country is unceasingly and forcibly deprived of its means or capital. Let the country keep what it produces, for only then can any right judgment be formed whether it is over-populated or not. Let England first hold hands off India's wealth, and then there will be disinterestedness in, and respect for, her judgment. The present cant of the excuse of over-population is adding a distressful insult to agonizing injury. To talk of over-population at present is just as reasonable as to cut off a man's hands, and then to taunt him that he was not able to maintain himself or move his hands.

When persons talk of the operation of economic laws they forget the very first and fundamental principles. Says Mr. Mill: "Industry is limited by capital." "To employ industry on the land is to apply capital to the land." "Industry cannot be employed to any greater extent than there is capital to invest." "There can be no more industry than is supplied by materials to work up, and food to eat; yet in regard to a fact so evident, it was long continued to be believed that laws and Governments, without creating capital, could create industry." And while Englishmen are sweeping away this very capital, they raise up their hands and wonder why India cannot have industry.

The English are themselves the head and front of the offending, and yet they talk of over-population, and every mortal irrelevant thing but the right cause—viz., their own drain of the material and moral wealth of the country.

The present form of relations between the paramount Power and the Princes of India is un-English and iniquitous. Fancy a people, the greatest champions of fair-play and justice, having a system of political agency by which, as the Princes say, they are stabbed in the dark; the Political Agents making secret reports, and the Government often acting thereon, without a fair enquiry or explanation from the Princes. The Princes, therefore, are always in a state of alarm as to what may befall them unawares. If the British authorities deliberately wished to adopt a method by which the Princes should always remain alarmed and irritated, they could not have hit upon a more effective one than what exists. If these Princes can feel assured that their treaty rights will be always honorably and faithfully observed, that there will be no constant nibbling at their powers, that it is not the ulterior policy of the British to pull them down gradually to the position of mere nobles of the country, as the Princes at present suspect and fear, and if a more just and fair mode of political agency be adopted, I have not the least hesitation in saying that, as much from self-interest alone as from any other motive, these Princes will prove the greatest bulwark and help to perpetuate British supremacy in India. It stands to reason and common-sense that the Native Princes clearly understand their interest, that by a power like the British only, with all the confidence it may command by its fairness as well as strength, can they be saved from each other and even from themselves. Relieved of any fear from the paramount Power, they will the more readily listen to counsels of reform which they much need. The English can then exercise their salutary influence in advising and helping them to root out the old corrupt *régimes,* and in making them and their courtiers to understand that power was not self-aggrandizement, but responsibility for the good of the people. I say, from personal conversation with some of the Princes, that they thoroughly understand their interest under the protection of the present paramount Power.

It is useless for the British to compare themselves with the past Native rulers. If the British do not show themselves to be vastly superior in proportion to their superior enlightenment and civilization, if India does not prosper and progress under them far more largely, there will be no justification for their existence in India. The thoughtless past drain we may consider as our misfortune, but a similar future will, in plain English, be deliberate plunder and destruction.

I do not repeat here several other views which I have already expressed in my last memorandum.

I have thus given a general sketch of what is passing in many Natives' minds on several subjects. It is useless and absurd to remind us constantly that once the British fiat brought order out of chaos, and to make that an everlasting excuse for subsequent shortcomings and the material and moral impoverishment of the country. The Natives of the present day have not seen that chaos, and do not feel it; and though they understand it, and very thankful they are for the order brought, they see the present drain, distress and destruction, and they feel it and bewail it.

By all means let Englishmen be proud of the past. We accord them every credit for the order and law they brought about, and are deeply thankful to them; but let them now face the present, let them clearly realize, and manfully acknowledge, the many shortcomings of omission and commission by which, with the best of intentions, they have reduced India to material and moral wretchedness; and let them, in a way worthy of their name and history, repair the injury they have inflicted. It is fully in their power to make their rule a blessing to India, and a benefit and a glory to England, by allowing India her own administration, under their superior controlling and guiding hand; or, in their own oft-repeated professions and words, "by governing India for India's good."

May the God of all nations lead the English to a right sense of their duty to India, is my humble and earnest prayer.

NOTES

1. The italics are all mine [Naoroji's], except when stated otherwise.

2. "Parliamentary Return" [. . .], 1886.

3. The Duke of Argyll, as Secretary of State for India, said in his speech of 11th March, 1869, with regard to the employment of Natives in the Covenanted Service: "I must say that we have not fulfilled our duty, or the promises and engagements which we have made."

4. Sir Stafford Northcote, in his speech in Parliament on 24th May, 1867, said: "Nothing could be more wonderful than our Empire in India, but we ought to consider on what conditions we held it, and how our predecessors held it. The greatness of the Mogul Empire depended upon the liberal policy that was pursued by men like Akbar availing themselves of Hindu talent and assistance, and identifying themselves as far as possible with the people of the country. He thought that they ought to take a lesson from such a circumstance, and if they were to do their duty towards India, they could only discharge that duty by obtaining the assistance and counsel of all who were great and good in that country. It would be absurd in them to say that there was not a large fund of statesmanship and ability in the Indian character."—*Times*, of 25th May, 1867.

5. "Statistical Abstract of British India, 1879," page 21.

REFERENCES

Bakshi, S. R. 1991. *Dadabhai Naoroji: The Grand Old Man.* New Delhi: Anmol.

Ganguli, B. N. 1965. *Dadabhai Naoroji and the Drain Theory.* New York: Asia Publishing House.

Grover, Verinder. 1998. *Dadabhai Naoroji: A Biography of His Vision and Ideas.* New Delhi: Deep and Deep.

Masani, Rustom P. 1968 [1939]. *Dadabhai Naoroji: The Grand Old Man of India.* Mysore, India: Kavyalaya.

Rawal, Munni. 1989. *Dadabhai Naoroji: A Prophet of Indian Nationalism, 1855–1900.* New Delhi: Anmol.

24

The Condition of England
and Civilization

Mohandas K. Gandhi, 1909

Gandhi's *Hind Swaraj*, or *Indian Home Rule*, is widely regarded as the text that sparked the Indian Nationalist Movement in 1909. Having first appeared in installments in the newspaper founded by Gandhi, *Indian Opinion*, it was immediately prohibited by the government of Bombay. In defiance of government restrictions, Gandhi chose to publish the short tract, which was widely circulated and earned its fame as a condemnation of modern civilization and a call for nonviolent resistance. The edition reproduced here is a reprint from *Indian Opinion* in 1922, when Gandhi was imprisoned by the British for leading the Indian campaign of civil disobedience.

Indian Home Rule has been read in various ways. The somewhat asymmetric conversation between the editor and reader that structures the text permits Gandhi to speak through the voice of "the editor" via an imaginary interlocutor. He uses the opportunity to deploy harsh critiques of colonialist modernization: the British government, political (in)effectiveness in India, irreligious (im)morality, and the materialism spawned by self-interested trade. His conclusion is clear: "If India copies England, it is my firm conviction that she will be ruined" (Gandhi 2010 [1909]:47).

Writing *Indian Home Rule* after having lived in South Africa and traveled to London, Gandhi was accomplishing a double objective: first, he was responding to the Indian "extremists" whom he had met in London and who resorted to violence to achieve Indian independence; second, he was drawing upon his experiences with nonviolent resistance in South Africa, which ultimately led to the South African government's commitment to counteract anti-Indian discrimination.

The "editor" in these short excerpts from *Indian Home Rule* proposes a startling and curious hypothesis: "The English have not taken India; we have given it to them. They are

Gandhi, Mohandas K. 2010 [1909]. "The Condition of England" and "Civilisation." In *Indian Home Rule* [*Hind Swaraj*]. New Delhi: Promilla and Co. Pp. 129–138.

not in India because of their strength, but because we kept them" (36). The "editor" rejects the ruler-victim model of colonialism and instead suggests that Indians are largely respon- sible for the political conditions of the time. Such a move transforms colonialism from a top-down paradigm (the stronger overcoming the weaker) to a more equal, side-to-side relationship (they are here because we let them). There is nothing inherently superior about the English that allowed them to conquer the Indians, Gandhi maintains. In fact, English society, especially its government, is so corrupt that the "editor" would prefer Indians not copy it. He likens the government structure to "a sterile woman and a prostitute" (26). What is surprising about the editor's critique is that he claims this state of affairs is not "due to any peculiar fault of the English people, but . . . to modern civilization" (30). Just as there is nothing about the English that naturally makes them stronger, there is nothing about the English that naturally makes them corrupt. In Gandhi's view, they are afflicted by a disease called modern civilization, which unfortunately the Indians have caught.

In *Indian Home Rule,* Gandhi examines India as much as England and exposes the weaknesses of both societies without reducing either side to essential qualities and oppos- ing them directly to each other. In fact, in his analysis, both are victims together and impris- oned by the vicissitudes of modern civilization. Both have lost their morality, and only by regaining this morality can the Indians begin to fight against the British. Gandhi would have Indians remember that "strength lies in absence of fear, not in the quantity of flesh and muscle we may have on our bodies" (42).

In considering the Gandhian point of view, it is worth asking whether it really is a rejec- tion of Western civilization and its ideas, or are Gandhi's views in fact strongly compatible with those of some Western thinkers? In a letter to Henry Salt in 1929, Gandhi noted that his first introduction to Henry David Thoreau's writing was around 1907, when he was in the thick of the passive resistance struggle. Shiv Visvanathan (1998), an anthropologist of sci- ence, recently proposed a rethinking of Gandhi: "To portray Gandhi as anti-science or Lud- dite . . . is superficial. His ashrams . . . were locations for scientific experiments, especially on waste management. His theory of Khadi (homespun cloth) was a theory of technological innovation" (42). Visvanathan concludes that "Gandhi's *Hind Swaraj* . . . was one of the great critiques of science and technology," and relates this to the claim that "'the scientific method' as an ideology became a Victorian corset constricting creativity" (43), a claim later pursued and developed by anthropologists within and outside India (Malinowski 1948; Nader 1996).

. . .

THE CONDITION OF ENGLAND

READER: *Then from your statement I deduce that the Government of England is not desirable and not worth copying by us.*

EDITOR: Your deduction is justified. The condition of England at present is pitiable. I pray to God that India may never be in that plight. That which you consider to be the Mother of Parliaments is like a sterile woman and a prostitute. Both these are harsh terms, but exactly fit the case. That Parliament has not yet of its own accord done a single good thing, hence I have compared it to a sterile woman. The natural condition of that Parliament is such that, without outside pressure, it can do nothing. It is like a prostitute because it is under the control of ministers who change from time to time. Today it is under Mr. Asquith, tomorrow it may be under Mr. Balfour.

READER: *You have said this sarcastically. The term "sterile woman" is not applicable. The Parliament, being elected by the people, must work under public pressure. This is its quality.*

EDITOR: You are mistaken. Let us examine it a little more closely. The best men are supposed to be elected by the people. The members serve without pay and, therefore, it must be assumed, only for the public weal. The electors are considered to be educated and, therefore, we should assume that they would not generally make mistakes in their choice. Such a Parliament should not need the spur of petitions or any other pressure. Its work should be so smooth that its effect would be more apparent day by day. But, as a matter of fact, it is generally acknowledged that the members are hypocritical and selfish. Each thinks of his own little interest. It is fear that is the guiding motive. What is done today may be undone tomorrow. It is not possible to recall a single instance in which finality can be predicted for its work. When the greatest questions are debated, its members have been seen to stretch themselves and to doze. Sometimes the members talk away until the listeners are disgusted. Carlyle has called it the "talking shop of the world." Members vote for their party without a thought. Their so-called discipline binds them to it. If any member, by way of exception, gives an independent vote, he is considered a renegade. If the money and the time wasted by the Parliament were entrusted to a few good men, the English nation would be occupying today a much higher platform. The Parliament is simply a costly toy of the nation. These views are by no means peculiar to me. Some great English thinkers have expressed them. One of the members of that Parliament recently said that a true Christian could not become a member of it. Another said that it was a baby. And, if it has remained a baby after an existence of seven hundred years, when will it outgrow its babyhood?

READER: *You have set me thinking; you do not expect me to accept at once all you say. You give me entirely novel views. I shall have to digest them. Will you now explain the epithet "prostitute"?*

EDITOR: That you cannot accept my views at once is only right. If you will read the literature on this subject, you will have some idea of it. The Parliament is without a real master. Under the Prime Minister, its movement is not steady, but, it is buffeted about like a prostitute. The Prime Minister is more concerned about his power than about the welfare of the Parliament. His energy is concentrated upon securing the success of his party. His care is not always that the Parliament shall do right. Prime Ministers are known to have made the Parliament do things merely for party advantage. All this is worth thinking over.

READER: *Then you are really attacking the very men whom we have hitherto considered to be patriotic and honest?*

EDITOR: Yes, that is true; I can have nothing against Prime Ministers, but what I have seen leads me to think that they cannot be considered really patriotic. If they are to be considered honest because they do not take what is generally known as bribes, let them be so considered, but they are open to subtler influences. In order to gain their ends, they certainly bribe people with honors. I do not hesitate to say that they have neither real honesty nor a living conscience.

READER: *As you express these views about the Parliament, I would like to hear you on the English people, so that I may have your view of their Government.*

EDITOR: To the English voters their newspaper is their Bible. They take their cue from their newspapers, which latter are often dishonest. The same fact is differently interpreted by different newspapers, according to the party in whose interests they are edited. One newspaper would consider a great Englishman to be a paragon of honesty, another would consider him dishonest. What must be the condition of the people whose newspapers are of this type?

READER: *You shall describe it.*

EDITOR: These people change their views frequently. It is said that they change them every seven years. These views swing like the pendulum of a clock and are never steadfast. The people would follow a powerful orator or a man who gives them parties, receptions, etc. As are the people, so is their Parliament. They have certainly one quality very strongly developed. They will never allow their country to be lost. If any person were to cast an evil eye on it, they would pluck out his eyes. But that does not mean that the nation possesses every other virtue or that it should be imitated. If India copies England, it is my firm conviction that she will be ruined.

READER: *To what do you ascribe this state of England?*

EDITOR: It is not due to any peculiar fault of the English people, but the condition is due to modern civilization. It is a civilization only in name. Under it the nations of Europe are becoming degraded and ruined day by day.

CIVILIZATION

READER: *Now you will have to explain what you mean by civilization.*

EDITOR: It is not a question of what I mean. Several English writers refuse to call that civilization which passes under that name. Many books have been written upon that subject. Societies have been formed to cure the nation of the evils of civilization. A great English writer has written a work called "Civilization: Its Cause and Cure." Therein he has called it a disease.

READER: *Why do we not know this generally?*

EDITOR: The answer is very simple. We rarely find people arguing against themselves. Those who are intoxicated by modern civilization are not likely to write against it. Their care will be to find out facts and arguments in support of it, and this, they do unconsciously, believing it to be true. A man, whilst he is dreaming, believes in his dream; he is undeceived only when he is awakened from his sleep. A man laboring under the bane of civilization is like a dreaming man. What we usually read are the works of defenders of modern civilization, which undoubtedly claims among its votaries very brilliant and even some very good men. Their writings hypnotize us. And so, one by one, we are drawn into the vortex.

READER: *This seems to be very plausible. Now will you tell me something of what you have read and thought of this civilization?*

EDITOR: Let us first consider what state of things is described by the word "civilization." Its true test lies in the fact that people living in it make bodily welfare the object of life. We will take some examples. The people of Europe today live in better-built houses than they did a hundred years ago. This is considered an emblem of civilization, and this is also a matter to promote bodily happiness. Formerly, they wore skins, and used spears as their weapons. Now, they wear long trousers, and, for embellishing their bodies, they wear a variety of clothing, and, instead of spears, they carry with them revolvers containing five or more chambers. If people of a certain country, who have hitherto not been in the habit of wearing much clothing, boots, etc., adopt European clothing, they are supposed to have become civilized out of savagery. Formerly, in Europe, people ploughed their lands mainly by manual labor. Now, one man can plough a vast tract by means of steam engines, and can thus amass great wealth. This is called a sign of civilization. Formerly, the fewest men wrote books, that were most valuable. Now, anybody writes and prints anything he likes and poisons people's minds. Formerly, men traveled in wagons; now they fly through the air in trains at the rate of four hundred and more miles per day. This is considered the height of civilization. It has been stated that, as men progress, they shall be able to travel in airships and reach any part of the world in a few hours. Men will not need the use of their hands and feet. They will press a button, and they will have their clothing by their side. They will press another button, and they will have their newspaper. A third, and a motorcar will be in waiting for them. They will have a variety of delicately dished-up food. Everything will be done by machinery. Formerly, when people wanted to fight with one another, they measured between them their bodily strength; now it is possible to take away thousands of lives by one man working behind a gun from a hill. This is civilization. Formerly, men worked in the open air only so much as they liked. Now, thousands of workmen meet together and for the sake of maintenance work in factories or mines. Their condition is worse than that of beasts. They are obliged to work, at the risk of their lives, at most dangerous occupations, for the sake of millionaires. Formerly, men were made slaves under physical compulsion, now they are enslaved by temptation of money and of the luxuries that money can buy. There are now diseases of which people never dreamt before, and an army of doctors is engaged in finding out their cures, and so hospitals have increased. This is a test of civilization. Formerly, special messengers were required and much expense was incurred in order to send letters; today, anyone can abuse his fellow by means of a letter for one penny. True, at the same cost, one can send one's thanks also. Formerly, people had two or three meals consisting of home-made bread and vegetables; now, they require something to eat every two hours, so that they have hardly leisure for anything else. What more need I say? All this you can ascertain from several authoritative books. These are all true tests of civilization. And, if anyone speaks to the contrary, know that he is ignorant. This civilization takes note neither of morality nor of religion. Its votaries calmly state that their business is not to teach religion. Some even consider it to be a superstitious growth. Others put on the cloak of religion, and prate about morality. But, after twenty years' experience, I have come to the conclusion that immorality is often taught in the name of morality. Even a child can understand that in all I have described above there can be no inducement to morality. Civilization seeks to increase bodily comforts, and it fails miserably even in doing so.

This civilization is irreligion, and it has taken such a hold on the people in Europe that those who are in it appear to be half-mad. They lack real physical strength or courage. They keep up their energy by intoxication. They can hardly be happy in solitude. Women, who should be the queens of households, wander in the streets, or they slave away in factories. For the sake of a pittance, half a million women in England alone are laboring under trying circumstances in factories or similar institutions. This awful fact is one of the causes of the daily growing suffragette movement.

This civilization is such that one has only to be patient and it will be self-destroyed. According to the teaching of Mahomed this would be considered a Satanic civilization. Hinduism calls it the Black Age. I cannot give you an adequate conception of it. It is eating into the vitals of the English nation. It must be shunned. Parliaments are really emblems of slavery. If you will sufficiently think over this, you will entertain the same opinion, and cease to blame the English. They rather deserve our sympathy. They are a shrewd nation and I, therefore, believe that they will cast off the evil. They are enterprising and industrious, and their mode of thought is not inherently immoral. Neither are they bad at heart. I, therefore, respect them. Civilization is not an incurable disease, but it should never be forgotten that the English people are at present afflicted by it.

REFERENCES

Chakrabarty, Bidyut. 2007. *Mahatma Gandhi: A Historical Biography.* New Delhi: Lotus Collection.
Jack, Homer A., ed. 1994. *The Gandhi Reader: A Source Book of His Life and Writings.* New York: Grove Press.
Malinowski, Branislaw. 1948. *Magic, Science, and Religion, and Other Essays.* Glencoe, IL: The Free Press.
Nader, Laura. 1996. *Naked Science: Anthropological Inquiry into Boundaries, Power, and Knowledge.* New York: Routledge.
Visvanathan, Shiv. 1998. "A Celebration of Difference: Science and Democracy in India." *Science,* Vol. 280, no. 5360 (April 3): 42–43.

25

Passage to and from India

Nirad C. Chaudhuri, 1954

Nirad Chaudhuri was born in Bengal (today part of Bangladesh) in 1897 and died in England in 1999. Educated in Calcutta, he attended the Scottish Church College, where he partially completed his MA in history. Although he began his work life in the accounting department of the Indian Army, his life's preoccupation was writing articles in popular magazines, and he made his career as a writer and editor. Chaudhuri was a prolific author over his 101 years.

In 1938 Chaudhuri worked for the Indian Nationalist Movement in India and interacted with political leaders such as Gandhi and Nehru. His most renowned work was *The Autobiography of an Unknown Indian,* published in 1951, after independence. The book's dedication sarcastically praised British rule, was taken at face value by Indian officials, and resulted in Chaudhuri's blacklisting by the Indian government. He became jobless even though his work was really a condemnation of the British rulers for not treating the Bengalis as equals. As part of the Bengali intelligentsia, Chaudhuri was obsessed with the West, torn between the British and their Westernizing policies on the one hand and the Muslims, for whom he had an obsessive dislike, on the other. This put Chaudhuri's sympathies with the right-wing nationalists in India and with defending the vanishing civilization unique to the Bengali aristocracy because of British racism and an independent India. No doubt he was a contrarian—as much as he admired the British, he made fun of them. His approach was often described as offbeat by others and by himself—self-confident, sometimes arrogant, but always of great erudition. The pictures he paints of Indian society and the British satirize both.

In 1955 the British Broadcasting Company invited Chaudhuri to England to lecture. He was fifty-seven years old and was visiting for the first time an England he had only read

Chaudhuri, Nirad C. 1954. "Passage to and from India." *Encounter,* Vol. 2, No. 6, pp. 19–24. Reprinted with the permission of the author's estate.

about. His book *Why I Mourn for England* (1955) describes a nation that has given itself over to money-making in politics and economics—the new religion. Yet without achieving contentment, the wealthy of his day were worse than those of the East India Company. In a series of short essays he wrote about the real East-West conflict. He thought that the conflict between Muslims and Hindus was provoked by Europeans, because of an irreconcilable antagonism that has continued to the present.

The selection that follows is a thoughtful and nuanced commentary on the real impact of E. M. Forster's novel *A Passage to India* (1924), "a powerful weapon in the hands of the anti-imperialists" (Chaudhuri 1954:19). He thought the novel had the effect of alienating the British people, who he believed were only marginally aware of their empire, by satirizing a small sector of India and Anglo-Indian life, a satire that prompted many British to want to leave India since it is critical of both Anglos and crude Indians. While Forster may not have intended his work to have the impact Chaudhuri speaks of, the novel nevertheless helped create a "mood which enabled the British people to leave India." Chaudhuri thought Forster too charitable in his description of the Indians (mainly Muslim Indians) and that the shortcoming of the British was "not in courage, but in intelligence." He attributes the British tendency to favor Muslims over Hindus to the Hindus' more bizarre and rococo appearance. Once again he speaks to the class of Indians who enthusiastically embraced the Westernization of their country, only to be shunned by the British. He concludes with a critique of the contemporary West's proselytizing impact on the non-West, betraying the continued Bengali preoccupation with the West, both as attraction and as repulsion.

. . .

Reading *A Passage to India* some time ago, I was led to think not only of the final collective passage of the British from India but also of Mr. Forster's contribution to that finale. Such an association of ideas between a novel and an event of political history may be objected to, but in this case I think the association is legitimate. For *A Passage to India* has possibly been an even greater influence in British imperial politics than in English literature.

From the first, the more active reaction to it followed the existing lines of political cleavage, its admirers being liberal, radical, or leftist sheep and its detractors conservative, imperialist, and diehard goats. The feud between English liberalism and the British empire in India was as old as the empire itself. Except for a short period of quiescence when Liberal-Imperialism was in vogue, it raged till 1947. Mr. Forster's novel became a powerful weapon in the hands of the anti-imperialists, and was made to contribute its share to the disappearance of British rule in India.

On those, also, who did not follow clear party cues in respect of India, its influence was destructive. It alienated their sympathy from the Indian empire. As it was, the British people taken in the mass were never deeply involved in this empire, emotionally or intellectually. To them it was rather a marginal fact of British history than what it really was—a major phenomenon in the history of world civilization. Mr. Forster's book not only strengthened the indifference; it also created a positive aversion to the empire by its unattractive picture of India and Anglo-Indian life and its depiction of Indo-British relations as being of a kind that were bound to outrage the English sense of decency and fair play. Thus, the novel helped the growth of that mood which enabled the British people to leave India with an almost Pilate-like gesture of washing their hands of a disagreeable affair.

Even intrinsically, the novel had a political drift. There is of course no necessary connection between a writer's own intentions and the manner in which he is accepted or exploited by his public. It has even been said that it is only when they are debased or deformed that philosophical ideas play a part in history. But in regard to *A Passage to India,* it can be said that the author's purpose and the public response more or less coincided. The novel was quite openly a satire on the British official in India. Perhaps in a veiled form it was also a satire on the Indians who were, or aspired to be, the *clientes* of the foreign patriciate. As such it was, at one remove, a verdict on British rule in India. At the risk of depriving it of its nuances, but perhaps not misrepresenting its general purport, I might sum it up as follows. This rule is the cause of such painful maladjustment in simple human relations that even without going deeply into the rights and wrongs of the case it is desirable to put an end to it. The intention seems to have been to bring even English readers to agree with the last outburst of the hero of the novel, Aziz: "We shall drive every blasted Englishman into the sea, and then you and I shall be friends."

Accordingly, one is almost forced to appraise the novel as a political essay on Indo-British relations, and as soon as it is considered as such, a striking gap in Mr. Forster's presentation of these relations fixes attention. It is seen that the novel wholly ignores the largest area of Indo-British relations and is taken up with a relatively small sector. The ignored area is the one I watched at first hand from the age of seven to the age of fifty. The other sector, in contrast, was known to me only by hearsay, because I feared its contact almost as much as a Pharisee feared the contact of publicans and sinners.

The Indo-British relations I was familiar with were contained, for the most part, within the conflict between Indian nationalists and the British administration. Here I saw great suffering and distress, but also exultation, a brave acceptance of ill-treatment and conquest of weak tears. The longer the men had been in jail, the more they had been persecuted, the more "sporting" they seemed to be. In the other sector, the conflict was between associates, the British officials and their Indian subordinates or hangers-on, and had all the meanness of a family quarrel. It sizzled without providing any ennobling or even chastening release for passion, only distilling rancor. It contributed much to the pathology of Indo-British relations but virtually nothing to the final parting of ways. If we can at all speak of having driven the "blasted Englishman into the sea," as Aziz puts it, it was not men of his type who accomplished the feat. Those who fought British rule in India did not do so with the object of eventually gaining the Englishman's personal friendship. Just as personal humiliation did not bring them into the conflict, personal friendship did not also lure them as a goal.

But of course there was good reason for Mr. Forster's choice. The reason is not however that the political conflict was impersonal and could not be treated in a novel. It could be, though the result would have been a tragedy of mutual repulsion and not a tragi-comedy of mutual attraction. Mr. Forster chose the sector of which he had personal knowledge. As an Englishman paying a short visit to India, he naturally saw far less of Indians in general than of his own countrymen and of the Indians with whom the latter had official business or perfunctory social relations. Being an Englishman, of humane sensibilities, he was also shocked by the state of these relations, as among others Wilfrid Blunt was before him. On the other hand, he could not observe the larger and the more important area without going considerably out of his way and making a special effort.

There is also another and not less fundamental reason for Mr. Forster's choice. That is the character of his political consciousness. I should really call it humanitarian consciousness. For his is an appeal in a political case to the court of humane feelings to what he himself calls "common humanity" in a later essay. Now, the relationship between common humanity and politics is even more complex than that which exists between morality and politics. I firmly believe that ultimately, politics and morals are inseparable; even so, the most obvious moral judgment on a political situation is not necessarily a right judgment, and for humane feelings to go for a straight tilt at politics is even more quixotic than tilting at windmills.

The consequences of pitting humane feelings against a political phenomenon are well illustrated in A Passage to India. One consequence is that it leads to pure negation. In the sphere of Indo-British relations the novel has no solution to offer except a dissolution of the relationship, which is not a solution of the problem but only its elimination. The good feeling that such a dissolution can generate, and has in actual fact generated between Indians and the British after 1947, is the sort of kindly feeling one has for strangers or casual acquaintances. It is of no use whatever for a sane ordering of political relations which one is struggling to raise from an amoral or even immoral level to a moral one.

Another consequence is that the humanitarian prepossession leads Mr. Forster to waste his politico-ethical emotion on persons who do not deserve it. Both the groups of characters in A Passage to India are insignificant and despicable. I have, however, my doubts about Mr. Forster's delineation of his countrymen. I am no authority on the life of White officials in India, for I never cultivated them. Still, observing them in their public capacity, and at times laying incredible stupidities at their door, I did not consider them quite so absurd a class as Mr. Forster shows them to be.

Of one implied charge I will definitely acquit them. Mr. Forster makes the British officials of Chandrapore nervous about the excitement of the Muharram to the extent of making the women and children take shelter in the club, and after the trial of Aziz he makes them reach home along by-ways for fear of being man-handled by a town rabble. Of this kind of cowardice no British official in India was to my mind ever guilty, even in their worst time since the Mutiny, in the years 1930 to 1932, when the Auxiliary Force armory at Chittagong in Bengal was raided by a band of young revolutionaries, British officials were shot dead in Calcutta and the districts, and attempts were made on the life of the Governor of Bengal and the Police Commissioner of Calcutta. As a class, the British officials kept their head. The courage shown by the District Magistrate of Chittagong on the night of the raid, when an insurrection of unknown magnitude and danger faced him, was admirable. The shortcoming of the British official was not in courage, but in intelligence.

On the other hand, Mr. Forster is too charitable with the Indians. Aziz would not have been allowed to cross my threshold, not to speak of being taken as an equal. Men of his type are a pest even in free India. Some have acquired a crude idea of gracious living or have merely been caught by the lure of snobbism, and are always trying to gain importance by sneaking into the company of those to whom this way of living is natural. Another group of men are more hardboiled. They are always out to put personal friendship to worldly profit, perhaps the most widespread canker in Indian social life even now. Indian ministers and high officials feel this even more strongly than Ronny in Mr. Forster's novel. These attempts at exploitation are making them more outrageously rude than any British official, and all the more so because in India there is no tradition of kindliness among people in power. In British days this bickering gave rise to a corrosive race conflict; now it is fomenting an equally corrosive class conflict. But it is futile to grow censorious over this, no sane or satisfactory human relations can be built up with such material.

Mr. Forster appears to have felt this himself. He is too intelligent to be able to overlook the weak points in the Indian character, and too honest to suppress them in his book. Indeed, he shows himself so acute in seizing them that it is impossible to imagine that he was representing Aziz and his associates as fine fellows who deserved to be treated as equals by the British, and was not conscious of their utter worthlessness. I detect a personal admission in the comment he puts in the mouth of Ronny about the Nawab Bahadur, the "show Indian": "Incredible, aren't they, even the best of them?" So I am not surprised to find a streak of satire even in his presentation of Indians. But such satire not being his aim, he is driven into a corner, from where he can plead for satisfactory Indo-British relations on the only basis which could be proof against disillusionment, the basis of the least respect and the largest charity. Inevitably he has also to make a moralist's impossible demand on human nature.

But even if Mr. Forster's Indians had been good as individuals as they are malodorous, he would not have had a very much stronger case. For he had not chosen his Indian types happily. In regard to the Hindu characters, he relied mostly on the types found in the Princely States. Certainly they were more traditional than those in British India, but they were so traditional that they did not represent modern India at all. For instance, to those of us who are familiar with the teachings of the Hindu reformers of the 19th century, Godbole is not an exponent of Hinduism, he is a clown. Even for us, friendly personal relations with these men became possible only if we assumed we were in an anthropological reserve. Although the States have now been incorporated in India, the unevenness persists, and it presents a serious problem of *Gleichschaltung* for the future.

But Mr. Forster's more serious mistake was in taking Muslims as the principal characters in a novel dealing with Indo-British relations. They should never have been the second party to the relationship in the novel, because ever since the nationalist movement got into its stride the Muslims were playing a curiously equivocal role, realistic and effective politically, but unsatisfying in every other respect. The Muslims hated the British with a hatred even more vitriolic than the Hindu's, because it was they who had been deprived of an empire by the British. Yet they found themselves wooed by the latter as a counterpoise to the Hindu nationalists, and they did not reject these overtures.

They were shrewd in their calculations. They knew that their own battle was being fought by the Hindus and that in an eventual victory their share of the spoils was guaranteed. In the meanwhile, it was profitable to exploit the British, make the best of both worlds. This game, played with boldness and hardheaded realism, succeeded beyond expectation and created an independent state for the Muslims of India.

But a colossal Machiavellian game of politics like this could be played without moral risks only by men of very great strength of character, as indeed all the Muslim leaders, from Sir Sayyid Ahmad Khan to M. A. Jinnah, were. On the rank and file of the Muslims, so far as this policy influenced them, it had a deplorable effect. It left one section unweaned from its barren and rancorous hatred and made another pine for British patronage. Aziz and his friends belong to the servile section and are all inverted toadies. With such material, a searching history of the Muslim destiny in India could have been written, but not a novel on Indo-British relations, for which it was essential to have a Hindu protagonist.

But I think I know why Mr. Forster would not have a Hindu. He shares the liking the British in India had for the Muslim, and the corresponding dislike for the Hindu. This was a curious psychological paradox and in every way unnatural, if not perverse. On the one hand, the Islamic order was the natural enemy of the Christian-European, and the British empire in India was in one sense the product of the secular conflict between the Christian West and the Islamic Middle East, which is still running its course. More than one British Foreign Secretary found the pitch of British policy queered by the incurable phil-Islamic attitude of the

British Indian Government, and once Sir Edward Grey expressed frank annoyance at it.

On the other hand, there was between European civilization and the Hindu in its stricter form a common Indo-European element, which was discovered and described by British Orientalists in the first century or so of British rule, but which came to be forgotten and ignored by Englishmen in later times. Modern Hindu thinkers did not, however, lose sight of the affinity. Swami Vivekananda, speaking at the end of the last century, said that two branches of the same people placed in different surroundings in Greece and India had worked out the problems of life, each in its own particular way, but that through the agency of the British people the ancient Greek was meeting the ancient Hindu on Indian soil, and thus "slowly and silently the leaven has come, the broadening out, the life-giving revivalist movement that we see all around us." The British in India never gave this fruitful idea any encouragement. They were taken in by the deceptive simplicity of the Muslim and repelled by the apparent bizarrerie of Hinduism and its rococo excrescences. I wonder if it was the Hebraic element in the British ethos which was responsible for this.

This leads me straight to my objections to the politics of *A Passage to India* and my one positive comment on its central theme. My most serious criticisms are the following. It shows a great imperial system at its worst, not as diabolically evil but as drab and asinine; the rulers and the ruled alike are depicted at their smallest, the snobbery and pettiness of the one matching the imbecility and rancor of the other. Our suffering under British rule, on which a book as noble as Alfred de Vigny's *Servitude et Grandeur militaires* could have been written, is deprived of all dignity. Our mental life as depicted in the book is painfully childish and querulous. Lastly, attention is diverted away from those Indians who stood aloof from the world the book describes and were aristocratic in their way, although possessing no outward attribute of aristocracy. When I consider all this I feel Mr. Forster's literary ability, which has given the book its political importance, as a grievance.

At the root of all this lies the book's tacit but confident assumption that Indo-British relations presented a problem of personal behavior and could be tackled on the personal plane. They did not and could not. The great Indians who brought about the Westernization of their country and created its modern culture had none of the characteristic Indian foibles for which Mr. Forster invokes British compassion. They were men of the stature of an Erasmus, Comenius, or Holberg, who could hold their own with the best in Europe. Yet some of them were assaulted, some insulted, and others slighted by the local British. None of them had any intimate personal relations with any member of the British ruling community. There were also thousands of Indians who had adopted Western ideals and were following them to the best of their ability, who were not only not cultivated but shunned with blatant ostentation by the British in India. "What you have got to stamp on is these educated classes," they all said, like the subaltern in the novel. This was due, not to any personal snobbery, but to that massive national snobbery which refused to share British and Western civilization with Indians.

Those who remember the powerful championship of Westernization by Macaulay usually forget that his best supporters were Indians and his most determined opponents his own countrymen. In spite of the formal adoption of this policy, the British ruling class in India never felt happy about it and carried it out half-heartedly. Towards the result, the attitude of the thoughtful Englishman was one of regret, while the average Englishman grew maliciously quizzical.

To give only one example, there was hardly one Englishman who had a good word to say about our employment of the English language. I still remember the pleasure I felt when for the first time in my experience, I read praise of our English in Sir Michael Sadler's report on Calcutta University. Normally the better our English the more angry did the Englishman become, and the worse it was the greater was the entertainment of the Memsahib and *ergo* the larger the favors of the Sahib. Even so great a personage as Lady Minto was not above the weakness, and in his kindly manner even Mr. Forster has felt amused by our English.

Of course, I cannot deny that much of our English as indeed much of our Westernization was quaint. But ours were the shortcomings of self-taught and unguided men everywhere. If, in their days of power, the British had not looked askance at our employment of English, today the battle for English in India would not have been already lost, and we should not have needed the forlorn crusade of the British Council, too late for love, too late for joy, too late, too late!

Once the premise of cultural apartheid was admitted, there could be no advance on the personal plane, for men do not treat as equals those who are not of their psychological species. The British in India clinging to the obsolete idea of zoological speciation for mankind, could only cry as the District Collector does in *A Passage to India:* "I have never known anything but disaster result when English people and Indians attempt to be intimate socially. Intercourse, yes. Courtesy by all means. Intimacy—never, never."

A real Englishman, greater than Mr. Forster's Turton, had come to the same conclusion. Sir Edwin Lutyens, the builder of New Delhi, tried friendship with Indians and wrote in disenchantment: "The natives do not improve on acquaintance. Their very low intellects spoil much and I do not think it is possible for the Indians and Whites to mix freely and naturally. They are very different, and even my ultrawide sympathy with them cannot admit them on the same plane as myself. They may be on a higher plane or a lower one than a White, but the ethics of their planes are different to ours, and for one or the other to leave his plane is unclean and unforgivable."

On the other hand, putting the cultural impact in the foreground, Indians propounded a strikingly contrasted thesis. At that level our personal humiliations ceased to matter and even our great *injuria temporum*, political subjection, presented a second face. Rammohun Roy was grossly insulted by a British baronet and official. He protested against it to the Governor-General but did not allow it to influence his views on Westernization or even those about British rule in India. He surprised a young French scientist, Victor Jacquemont, who saw him in Calcutta, by an expression of opinion which the Frenchman set down verbatim in his journal: "*La conquête est bien rarement un mal, quand le peuple conquérant est plus civilisé que le peuple conquis, parce qu'elle apporte à celui-ci les biens de la civilisation. Il faut d l'Inde bien des années de domination anglaise pour qu'elle puisse ne pas perdre beaucoup en ressaisissant son indépendance politique.*"

Bankim Chandra Chatterji, the creator of Hindu nationalism, was actually assaulted by a British official though a magistrate himself, but he too, when it came to assessing the larger consequences of British rule in India, argued persuasively that it was in many ways providential. Personal grievance, even when well-founded, did not influence men of this type.

The contrast between the generosity of such Indians and the British narrowness furnishes the key to the real failure of the British in India. It was the failure to see that a nation which was not willing to propagate its civilization and extend its spiritual citizenship was also incapable of perpetuating, not only an empire, but even friendly political relations with other nations not belonging to its own culture complex. The challenge before the British was to create an open society in the order of the mind. Their opportunity was to make India an extension of the Western world. But they failed as completely in using their opportunity as they did in meeting the challenge. Compared with this failure, which was a betrayal of the West in India, their bad manners were mere peccadillos.

This political evaluation of *A Passage to India* has not been attempted for its historical interest, great as that interest is. I believe that the questions which British rule raised in India have only been put aside and not answered by what happened in 1947. I also believe that the British failure to understand the true nature of the Indo-British relationship has a moral, whose application is likely to widen as time passes, for a new set of international relations taking shape today over an area very much larger than India. It is this moral that I have to draw now.

But as a preliminary I should define my position. I represent no school of thought in India, past or present, and there is nothing characteristically Indian in my views except the fact that they are those of an Indian by birth and are based on Indian experience. I differ fundamentally from the nationalistic majority of my countrymen who speak of 19th century imperialism but forget that the century also had its nationalism. I differ no less fundamentally from the influential minority in India who believe in world government, who pin their faith to a world government of the contractual type, carried on by means of a world assembly in which the national representatives will be wise, reasonable, and just. I cannot say, like a

Christian, that this conception is bound to be wrecked on the innate sinfulness of man, but I would say that it would hurtle against man's inherent urge to power.

It seems to me that the West is now showing the same incomprehension which destroyed British power in India. The economic and the political impact of the West is being felt. What is absent is that proselytizing cultural impact which alone can counteract the mental resistance to the extension of Western culture into the non-Western parts of the world. Instead, there is the same uncritical faith in the promotion of economic prosperity and the converting power of *Pecunia Americana* as there was in the maintenance of law and order and the indispensability of *Pax Britannica*. The West ought to, and in my opinion can, think in terms of something higher than effective diplomacy, higher even than world government, for converting the single zoological species called man into one psychological species. Of course, that might not be possible. But one can never speak of impossibility before an effort has been made.

REFERENCES

Chaudhuri, Dhruva N. 2011. *Nirad C. Chaudhuri: Many Shades, Many Frames.* New Delhi: Niyogi Books.

Chaudhuri, Nirad C. 1951. *The Autobiography of an Unknown Indian.* London: Macmillan.

———. 1999 [1955]. *Why I Mourn for England.* Mitra and Ghosh.

Dasgupta, Swapan, ed. 1997. *Nirad C. Chaudhuri, the First Hundred Years: A Celebration.* New Delhi: Harper Collins.

Dhawan, R. K., ed. 2000. *Nirad C. Chaudhuri: The Scholar Extraordinary.* New Delhi: Prestige Books.

Forster, E. M. 1965 [1924]. *A Passage to India.* New York: Mariner Books.

26

Indian Economic Policy

Birendra Narayan Chakravarty, 1966

Birendra Narayan Chakravarty was educated in Calcutta and London. After receiving his bachelor's in chemistry, he returned to India, where he held posts under the British colonizers. Following independence he served in a number of governmental posts. He was ambassador to the Netherlands and high commissioner for India to London and Canada, and mainly worked for the Indian Ministry of External Affairs. Much of what he writes about has been iterated by other well-known Indian scholars, which does not make it less important, though similar views of the West and of the United States in particular are repeated.

Chakravarty spent thirty-six years in the Indian Civil Service and Diplomatic Service, including three years as the Permanent Representative of India to the United Nations. In *India Speaks to America* he writes about the relations between the world's "two largest democracies." Writing for the general public, the author includes chapters on nonalignment, colonialism, Indian economic policy, the partition of India, American military aid to Pakistan, Goa, and democracy in India—all of which are written on the basis of experience and passion, inviting criticism from both Americans and Indians. Although he recognizes the Gandhian philosophy of nonviolence as a first-choice strategy, he does not rule out violence as a follow-up strategy for achieving justice.

The following selection, "Indian Economic Policy," might be read as an attempt to explain just that, along with India's foreign policy, while explaining the observation that "socialism is something which is anathema to the average American," an idea conjuring images of "loss of freedom and individuality, and killing of free enterprise." Chakravarty adds at the start, "For a proper appreciation of our economic policy it is necessary to have

Chakravarty, B. N. 1966. "Indian Economic Policy." In *India Speaks to America*. Bombay, India: Orient Longmans. Pp. 56–72.

some knowledge of the shattered economy we inherited on our independence," economic conditions that have been written about since the earliest days of British colonialism in India, but which he believed needed repetition due to the American general public's ignorance of colonial history.

To understand what is not obvious about contemporary Indian economic policy, one must know of the plunder of India's natural resources during colonialism. Rather than elaborate further on that which he says is anathema to the average American, Chakravarty focuses on how American enlightenment might help India. Although this is not an uncommon priority among government personnel who have traveled West, in the examples from India and Japan we see the need to privilege the home country over mere curiosity about the Other.

· · ·

INDIAN ECONOMIC POLICY

The foreign policy of a country is naturally closely linked with its economic policy. There is still some misconception in the U.S.A. about the Indian economic policy. Our declared objective of achieving the goal of a socialistic pattern of society has been very much misunderstood. This objective is in conformity with the provisions in our Constitution which require the State to secure a social order in which justice, social, economic and political, shall prevail. Broadly speaking, what we mean to develop is a society in which there is social cohesion, a society which is classless and casteless and in which there is equality of opportunity for all and the possibility for every one to live a full life. Obviously this goal cannot be attained, unless we can produce more wealth for distribution. When we lay stress on the need for the removal of disparities, we do not intend to reach that goal by expropriating the few rich and spread out poverty. We desire to develop an economic system which "does not result in the concentration of wealth and means of production to the common detriment." Whether one calls these principles socialistic or not, they have undoubtedly been the objectives in all Western democracies over a long period. Equality of opportunity and social justice, which are our objectives, have reached a much higher level in the U.S.A. today than what we can hope to achieve in many years to come.

Socialism is something which is anathema to the average American. It conjures up all kinds of images, loss of freedom and individuality, and killing of free enterprise. To the American, socialism and communism are apparently synonymous. Many communists call themselves socialists as indeed many communist countries call themselves "peoples' democracies." We are trying to bring about a socialistic pattern of society but there is no country which has greater freedom and individuality than one finds in India. In fact, in India individualism not only prevents regimentation but sometimes goes to the other extreme and stands in the way of organized, collective or co-operative action. True, there is governmental control in certain sectors of Indian industry but even so the public sector in Indian economy today is proportionately much smaller than that in the U.S.A. While we are still talking of a socialistic pattern of society, this has already been achieved to a far greater extent in the U.S.A. Free enterprise is still responsible for almost 90 per cent of India's national output while the comparable figure for the U.S.A. is about 80 per cent. American suspicion of our economic policy is thus largely misplaced. The Indian policy does not venture to go as far as the policies followed by the Labour government in the United Kingdom. All that we want is that the State should step in only in those fields of production in which private capital is shy either because of the risk involved or because of the lack of adequate or immediate return.

For a proper appreciation of our economic policy it is necessary to have some knowledge of the shattered economy we inherited on our independence. During the long period of colonial rule our economy had been practically stagnant and had failed to meet the demands of a rapidly growing population or to relieve the pressure on agriculture—about 70 per cent of the working population is engaged on agriculture. Agricultural yields were, however, low in comparison with those in most other countries. Large-scale industries provided employment for about only 10 per cent of the working population; medium-and-small-scale industries engaged another 10 per cent and the remaining 10 per cent found employment in services and in the distributive trade. Scarcity of the barest essentials of life, relatively high prices and a low level of consumption underlined the inadequacy of the country's economy.

On top of these long-term trends which explain the persistence of mass poverty, an extraordinarily severe strain was put on the Indian economy by the Second World War and by the partition of the country. Under the stimulus of war demands, some increase in agricultural and industrial production did take place. But as India became the supply base for the allied armies East of Suez, this increase in production was more than offset by the diversion to war purposes, of a large proportion of the total supplies available. The value of goods and services provided by the economy of undivided India for war purposes, was roughly equivalent to four and a half billion dollars. The diversion of the limited resources of such a poor people inevitably led to under-nourishment, poor health and a consequent reduction in productive capacity culminating in the death by starvation, of a couple of million people during the Bengal famine in 1943. A further severe shock was received when the country was partitioned, on our independence. Partition resulted in certain fundamental changes in the economic structure of the country. A part of what had previously been internal trade in cotton, jute and foodgrains now became a feature of external trade resulting in an aggravation of the balance of payments problem. While 82 per cent of the population of the Indo-Pakistan sub-continent remained in India after partition, only 69 per cent of the irrigated area; 65 per cent of the wheat and 68 per cent of the rice-growing area fell to India's share. In consequence, food shortage was more aggravated. The jute mills remained in India, but the area growing jute went mostly to Pakistan. Similarly, the cotton textile mills remained mostly in India while the area growing the best quality cotton went to Pakistan. Production in two of our most important foreign exchange-earning industries, viz. jute and cotton textiles, was thus adversely affected by the partition. The evacuation, relief and rehabilitation of millions of people who migrated into India following partition resulted in refugee problems unparalleled in history, and the abnormal expenditure year after year on this account intensified budgetary problems.

This formidable array of problems needed immediate attention from Government and a planned utilization of the available meager resources became essential.

There is now a general consensus that unless there is rapid industrialization, India cannot survive—any rate, as a democracy. When, however, our First Five Year Plan was put forward, it aroused a lot of suspicion in the United States. Many people had then looked upon planning for development as a totalitarian concept. No such planning had been necessary in democratic countries of the West. Why should a plan of development be necessary in a democratic set-up like the one in India? It was not appreciated that circumstances were indeed very different. In the case of countries like England and West Europe, the industrial revolution preceded the full development of democracy with universal adult franchise. The industrial revolution was accompanied, at least in the initial stages, by enormous social upheaval, uprooting of large sections of population and subjecting them to untold misery, but the governments which did not have to depend so much on popular votes, could survive. The hardships and sacrifices were no doubt to some extent mitigated by the exploitation of the resources of the colonies but it was only after political democracy had been fully established, enabling the masses effectively to demand improvement, that a semblance of economic justice could be secured. The newer countries like the U.S.A., Canada and Australia, on the other hand, because of their vast areas, richly endowed with natural resources, could develop through a system of free enterprise, without suffering too much from the evils of the industrial revolution. Even so, they needed a century or more to develop despite the very substantial foreign capital that flowed from Britain and other European countries. While the methods followed in these countries and their experiences provide us with valuable lessons, we cannot follow them in their entirety to solve our problems, because they are of a different nature. Our political freedom, bringing with it adult franchise, came before the beginning of an industrial revolution. The people naturally demand some improvement in their economic condition; otherwise political independence has no meaning for them. We have, therefore, to develop our economy in a much shorter time, and at the same time avoid the hardship caused by the industrial revolution in Europe. The methods of rapid growth adopted in the U.S.S.R., Eastern Europe and in China—although some of their problems are similar to those in India—are also of limited interest to us. These methods, too, have some lessons for us but despite their promise of quick results, they cannot be adopted in a democratic set-up. While wishing to benefit from the experience of others, we also like to avoid regimentation, class conflicts, social waste, as well as oppressive concentration of power and wealth. We welcome and wherever possible, draw upon the ideas, the experience, the advice and assistance of other people but the final decision as to the methods most suitable for us, must be our own.

It is true that affluent and highly developed societies in the Western world have not found it necessary in the past to plan for development except perhaps in a period of crisis, such as war. They had enough time—many decades—to arrange for high-grade technical training to build up trained manpower on an adequate scale, and to provide for banking and credit facilities for financing both agriculture and industry. We in India have to arrange for training and to develop these facilities for financing both agriculture and industry. We have to arrange for training and to develop these facilities—practically from scratch—in a comparatively much shorter period. We have even to provide our people with basic education which was sadly neglected during the colonial era. We have to revive our agriculture and industries which had remained moribund for a long time, to set up new institutions and to introduce new improved methods. All this needs urgent and positive action in a coordinated manner and cannot be left entirely to private enterprise. Our resources are limited while the demands are so varied and numerous. It is necessary to decide on priorities and make necessary allotment of funds. All these requirements can be met only through careful and proper planning so that the scarce capital is not frittered away on less important projects. The plan must provide for first things first, lay the foundation for economic advance and ensure that the limited resources are utilized to the best advantage of the nation. It is unnecessary to elaborate this point further since the need for planning in underdeveloped countries has now been generally recognized. In fact, the pendulum has now swung to the other extreme and today a developing country which has no proper plan finds it difficult to convince donor countries that foreign aid is at all needed, or that if granted, would be used efficiently and to its best advantage. If there is no adequate planning, it is difficult to find out how much local resources would be available and how much of it could in fact be diverted to social and economic development. For developing countries, planning has thus become an absolute necessity. At the same time, the plan must avoid too much centralization so that enough initiative and opportunities are left to individual or local authorities.

While planning for development is no longer exclusively associated with a totalitarian regime, most Americans still find it difficult to understand why economic development cannot be left to private enterprise or why there should be any need for a public sector in India. These aspects of Indian economic development are still looked upon with suspicion as if these are necessarily totalitarian concepts. It is important to remove these misconceptions. We obtained our political freedom through non-violent means. We want to achieve our economic freedom equally without violence, injustice or too much social upheaval. At the same time, we cannot afford to wait too long. Indians are a proverbially patient people, but if no tangible improvement can be brought about in a few years' time, their patience might be exhausted. If our efforts to bring about economic and social betterment through democratic means fail, there may be a popular demand to try the alternative—the totalitarian method of development—which already has attraction for some people. It is therefore essential to ensure that our experiment of democratic planning proves to be a success. Having regard to the enormity and the complexity of our problem, we decided to choose a mixed economy incorporating all three methods of economic development which have proved effective in other democratic countries. In our planned development there is therefore room for private enterprise, public enterprise and also for co-operative enterprise in fields which are specially suited to it such as agriculture and rural industries. New heavy industries and machine tool plants would normally be set up in the public sector. Government would also be responsible for development and expansion of the public utilities, power and transport facilities which are essentially needed to serve other basic industries. With limited resources, private enterprise would either have been unable to finance such gigantic projects or would have been unwilling to take up irrigation or power projects which would yield no profit for several years. Indian industry is also not sufficiently developed to have surplus technical and managerial staff to organize and administer a rapidly expanding program in the public sector in addition to what it has to do to expand its own program. It is well to remember that for similar reasons, even the highly developed private sector in America, with no shortage of capital, could not be left alone to deal with the development of atomic energy or of the space program. The U.S. Government had to take a hand in both.

The field in which the private sector can function, is, however, still a very large one. Private enterprise still produces 90 per cent of India's national output. All agriculture is in the private sector. Small and medium industries, as also cottage industries, are entirely in the private sector. Even in heavy industries meant normally for public enterprise, private enterprise continues and expands side by side. Private industries like the Tata Iron and Steel Company, as also the Indian Iron and Steel Company, have nearly doubled their production not only with encouragement but also with substantial assistance from Government. Heavy engineering and construction plants are all in the private sector. Jute and cotton textile industries and the tea industry are entirely in the private sector. The controversy about the public sector is very much exaggerated; in reality one is complementary to the other. The rate of growth in the private sector during the plan period, has been very much higher than that in the public sector. Any suspicion that a growth of the public sector stands in the way of the development of the private sector is thus completely unfounded. On the contrary, by taking over the main responsibility of developing power, transport facilities etc., Government has made it possible for private enterprise to develop many new industries, and promote faster growth in other sectors of our economy.

While one set of people complain that we are too closely following totalitarian methods and drawing up much too ambitious plans, others criticize us for the slower rate of progress in India as compared to that in China. Our plans, no doubt, appear large in terms of our resources but they are by no means ambitious in relation to our needs. Merely to keep pace with the annual increase in population, even to maintain its existing poor standard of living, India has to make real efforts to go forward. Our struggle to move forward can be compared with the efforts of a man trying to run up a descending escalator. We must struggle hard even if we are to stand still. Without such a struggle we would go backwards. For India, time is short and we cannot afford a slower rate of progress. The speed with which improvement is brought about is no less important than the changes themselves.

The criticism about the slower rate of progress in India as compared to that in China is not without substance. One must, however, try to understand the reasons for this difference. Social and economic conditions in India and in China were in many ways comparable. Both had a glorious past, both had become static, had fallen behind Europe in the race for industrialization and both are now trying to rebuild their respective economies. The difference, however, lies in the method of approach. India wants economic progress and social justice without detriment to the principle of individual freedom and tolerance of different views. Our Five Year Plans are evolved democratically, at the village level, at the district level, at the state level and finally endorsed by the Indian Parliament. The plan is discussed by different sections of our people and modified in accordance with their wishes, as far as possible. China, on the other hand, has preferred to choose the totalitarian methods of development subordinating the individual to the party and the State.

India is committed to raising its resources by democratic means. In advanced and industrially developed countries, savings available for investment are at least 10 to 15 per cent of the national income—sometimes even more. Such substantial savings are possible without depressing the relatively high standards of living. Underdeveloped countries like India which produce little, and have little surplus wealth, consume most of what they are able to produce. The rate of investment is naturally low, seldom exceeding 5 per cent of the national income. One way of securing a larger investment would be by deliberately lowering the standard of living and consumption of goods. In a democracy one cannot raise resources by forced contributions or by compulsory delivery of agricultural surpluses to the State. It is possible for a totalitarian government to compel its people to accept a low or static standard of living and thus collect funds for development, by heavy taxes, forced savings and compulsory sale of a large share of crops. Some nations have indeed gone too far in order to achieve spectacular growth even at great human and social cost. The standard of living in India is pitifully low and we have no desire to force it down still lower nor as a democratic country could we do so. We cannot subject our people to any greater suffering and misery. We must keep the standard of living rising and at the same time draw off as much funds for development as possible.

In a democracy we cannot also force the adoption of new and improved methods without regard to the cost in terms of human life and dignity. We have to follow the more difficult method of persuasion. Each farmer has to be taught, not forced, to use improved methods, better implements, fertilizers and so on. Each craftsman has to be trained so that he can be made to understand how to use new tools and follow modern methods. Even in heavy industries, the introduction of more up-to-date machinery must be so paced that workers are not thrown out without hope of securing new jobs. This is a most important consideration in a country where there is surplus labor and unemployment is already at a very high level. The need for technological advance has thus to be balanced against the need for finding employment. No such problem faces the industrially more advanced countries with a high level of employment or countries which are not committed to democratic methods of development. Because of the existence of this problem in India, we have often to make compromises. To find fresh avenues of employment is an important objective in itself and is indeed a social and a political necessity. Labor-saving devices cannot, therefore, be promptly introduced before finding alternative employment for workers rendered surplus to requirement. Small enterprises and cottage industries employing many must therefore continue, competing with highly mechanized industries employing a few. That is why we have to allot a substantial quantity of cotton yarns for the employment of our handloom workers. This process of democratic persuasion, co-operation and compromise is naturally slower in yielding results than the totalitarian method of force and coercion.

We have chosen to follow the democratic method of development since that is more in keeping with our history and culture. This method involves consultation and co-operation at all levels from the village right up to the Central Government and takes note of differing points of view. The reason for adopting this method can be best explained in the words of the late Prime Minister Nehru:

> We have definitely accepted the democratic process. . . . Because we think that in the final analysis it promotes the growth of human beings and of society; because. . . . we

attach great value to individual freedom and dignity. . . . We do want high standards of living, but not at the expense of the spirit of man, not at the expense of his creative energy, not at the expense of all those fine things of life which have ennobled man all through the ages.[1]

By contrast, China has given up such ideals for the sake of achieving a faster development. There is a complete regimentation of men, women and children and the entire people have been forced into service for the government. China has taken full advantage of its huge manpower but in the process has given up any pretense of maintaining even a modicum of human dignity and freedom. The Chinese argument seems to be that in any case, there never was much civil liberty in China and the denial of what little there may have been, makes no difference. It is no use bothering about human dignity when one would otherwise have to go without enough food and clothing. Human freedom and dignity are luxuries which can wait for the moment. The present generation must be condemned to work like slaves. Then only can the Chinese people hope to make adequate progress—at least in the next generation. It is perhaps on some such considerations that the rural and urban industrial communes in China were left with very little personal freedom or relaxation. Few women can stay at home. Most of them have to work in factories and have little family life. These stringent authoritarian methods are naturally more effective and they do yield quicker results but are not methods which can be adopted under any system of parliamentary democracy. The reasons for the comparatively more rapid development in China are thus clear. Admittedly totalitarian methods are likely to bring about rapid results and imposed methods are more effective than persuasion, at least in the short run. The failure of the great leap forward program in China has, however, now given rise to some doubts in this respect. In any case, we believe that democratic changes are more successful in gaining acceptance of the people and are thus more enduring from the point of view of final results. We are not, therefore, prepared to give up the democratic method of development which we have chosen to adopt.

There is a school of thought which believes that India is overpopulated and no matter what is done, there is no hope for the country unless the problem of population is tackled and solved first. It is true that India has a population of 460 million—larger than the combined populations of Africa and South America. The density of population of 383 per square mile still compares favorably with the world's highly populated countries—800 in England and Wales, 782 in Belgium, 909 in Holland, 432 in Italy and 665 in Japan.[2] India's rate of increase in population again is no higher than that in many countries and is lower than that in the South American countries. The problem, however, has been acute because India's already vast population is increasing by about 10 million a year. Even so, basically India's problem is not one of overpopulation but one of under-production. It is not a question of too many people but of too little productivity—both agricultural and industrial. India's greatest potential asset is its large population; its greatest challenge is to put their energies and skills to exploit the vast natural resources of the country. At present India is faced with a seeming paradox. On the one hand, there is acute and chronic unemployment and enforced idleness of a large number of people for about five months in the year; on the other hand, there is a severe shortage of trained men and women—doctors, nurses, scientists, engineers, technicians, and skilled workers. We are now trying to remove the anomaly by adapting the Indian education system to the needs of national development and diverting people from white collar jobs. Attempts are being made to harness our underemployed manpower through community development programs. The results have been most encouraging in every place where there was good leadership.

We realize, of course, that so long as under-production continues, there can be no substantial increase in the per-capita income or an improvement in the standard of living, unless there is an effective curb on the growth of population. The first results of our health programs have been to lower the death rate and to increase life expectancy. We have now to counteract this development by well-organized and widespread efforts at birth control. With a view to control the terrible growth in population, energetic action is being taken to popularize family planning. Birth control clinics have been set up in different parts of the country. India is one of the few countries which is officially supporting a program of birth control. Fortunately, there has been no opposition to this program on religious grounds. Thousands of people have in fact voluntarily gone in for sterilization. It is the abject poverty of the people that stands in the way of their buying contraceptives. Government has now set aside comparatively large funds for their free supply.

There is also considerable ignorance about the treatment of foreign capital in India. We welcome foreign capital, but we wish foreign investors to associate Indian enterprises and capital with themselves. No rigid formula has been laid down prescribing the extent or proportion of foreign participation. Naturally, we prefer that the major proportion of the capital and effective control of the enterprise should remain in Indian hands. In cases where rapid development of an industry is in the national interest and foreign participation is considered essential, exceptions are made and foreign investors are allowed to retain major interests in ownership and effective control. Foreign investment is, however, welcome mainly in manufacturing industries, in which Indian enterprise is not yet fully developed. It is also welcome if the produce of these industries helps to augment India's foreign exchange resources either by increasing exports or by reducing imports from foreign countries. Foreign investment is not normally desired in purely trading or financial ventures not involving manufacture. It has been the policy of the Government of India all along to give every facility to foreign investors for remittance of profits and for repatriation of capital. A variety of tax incentives and rebates, tax holiday and a virtual monopoly of the Indian market have been given to attract foreign capital. The fear about the safety and security of the investment is completely unfounded. In fact, President Eisenhower had said, "India is becoming one of the great investment opportunities of our time." It is the policy of Government to encourage the flow of foreign capital in every possible way. If we have not succeeded in attracting substantial private capital the reasons are not due to any unwillingness on our part to have such capital. Foreign investment in India is so small that for a long time, we will have no reason to fear such economic domination as is evident in some countries of Europe. President de Gaulle, for example, called for new vigilance against economic domination by the U.S.A. Canada has also at some stage showed some concern on this account. The distrust with which new countries are viewed and ignorance of the opportunities of investment are mainly responsible for the reluctance of private capitalists to invest in distant lands. We welcome private investment so long as it does not go against our economic policy and promotes industrial development in India.

Our per-capita income is one of the lowest in the world. Even so, more than 80 per cent of our investment in the Indian economy during the plan periods has come from the Indian people themselves. The next few years would be the most crucial period in India's economic history. If the Indian economy is to be given a big enough push so that it can go ahead, expanding and producing more under its own power, it would be necessary to step up the investment on a relatively larger scale. At a time when living standards and the saving potential are already low, we need urgently some measure of foreign capital and assistance in order to cross the take-off point of economic development. We have set our economy in motion as never before. Acute shortage of foreign exchange, however, stands in the way of importing essential components and raw materials with the result that even the manufacturing capacity already installed often remains unutilized. India's social stability and its future as a democracy depend on the speed with which it pushes ahead the pace of its economic and social growth. What is on trial is whether democracy can solve the problems of mass poverty and unemployment and can bring about a rate of economic progress comparable to what can be achieved by totalitarian methods. Many doubt that problems of such magnitude can be solved through democratic processes, and assert that they cannot in any case be solved fast enough. We, in India, have faith that the democratic method of development can deliver the goods fast enough. If India can make adequate progress under democracy, it may indeed serve the cause of democracy. In meeting this great challenge to democracy, India hopes to receive the friendly assistance of other nations who share its belief in the democratic principles of human dignity and individual freedom.

The misconceptions in the United States about Indian economic policy have been partially responsible for much of the criticism that has been made about U.S.

aid to India. Some Americans believe that India's policy of non-alignment has in fact worked more often in favor of communist countries. They, therefore, do not think that India deserves any aid from the U.S. when there are so many differences between India and the U.S.A. on important political issues. Another criticism has been that Americans, believing as they do in free enterprise, ought not to assist a country set on having some sort of a controlled economy in which the public sector is destined to play an important role. These critics see no difference between the mixed economy chosen by India and some form of State capitalism. On the other hand, the great majority of Americans do not think that an agreement on political issues should be a condition precedent to the granting of aid. They recognize that it is in the American national interest to help in the development of a democratic India. In their view "slavish compliance is a characteristic for which a free society has no use." In his presidential campaign speech on June 14, 1960, President Kennedy had underlined the importance of assisting India's development programs and had then said that: "It is vital that we aid India to make a success of her new Five Year program—a success that will enable her to compete with Red China for economic leadership of all Asia, and we must undertake this effort in a spirit of generosity motivated by a desire to help our fellow citizens of the world, not as narrow bankers or self-seeking politicians." It has also been pointed out by many Americans that India qualifies for aid, on each one of the grounds on which foreign aid can be justified. If the grounds are humanitarian, if the reason for granting aid is to reduce the grinding poverty, there is hardly any country which is poorer and which is in greater need of help. If the object is to help countries which show the greatest promise of sustained growth and also offer the prospect of developing soon to the take-off point, India's claims are equally strong. If the object is to open up new markets, India with a population of 160 million—a population larger than that of Africa and South America combined—is potentially one of the most promising markets.

Aid to India has often been sanctioned after heated and sometimes acrimonious discussions in the United States. It is unfortunate that statements of the few who oppose aid hit the headlines in newspapers while those of the many that support it do not get as much publicity and often go unnoticed. Too much importance is given to the criticisms without appreciating that the aid would not have been granted if the majority had not been in its favor. In their annoyance, Indians argue that, after all, the aid is mostly in the form of loans, all of which would have to be repaid with interest, that much of this loan has to be spent in the donor country with resulting increase in its export and that left to ourselves we would have preferred trade to aid. This line of argument ignores how important it is for the receiving country to acquire foreign exchange which cannot otherwise be earned by normal trade and without which further economic development comes to a grinding halt. Americans then complain that there is not enough recognition of the generous economic aid given by the U.S.A. to India. This complaint is not quite justified since American aid receives wide publicity and the extent of the assistance is well known in India. There is thus a vicious circle creating some irritation for no good reason. We should not be over-sensitive. We should remember that in a democracy a debate is essential and it is not unusual to have heated discussions when the opposition attempts to marshal all possible arguments in support of its views. The democratic processes are also slower. The delay in getting aids approved ought not to be misunderstood particularly in India where we go through the same process. At the same time, when an aid is given after an unpleasant debate the grace is often taken away, even though people may, nevertheless, express their gratitude for the help they receive.

Many Americans visiting India are struck with the fact that Britain, West Germany and the Soviet Union have received a lot of credit by setting up steel plants which serve as standing monuments to their contributions to Indian economic development. They naturally feel unhappy that although American economic aid has been of a much larger order, there are no similar projects which could be shown as visible symbols of Indo-American collaboration. With a view to removing this anomaly, a proposal was made to secure American collaboration for a large new steel plant at Bokharo. There were protracted and long-drawn-out negotiations, but despite strong support from the American administration, despite the recommendations of the late President Kennedy himself, the proposal could not get through. India ultimately had to withdraw the request with a view to saving the embarrassment that was being caused to the administration. It was an open secret that although many criticisms were made, the project fell through not on technical grounds but on the ground that no assistance should be given to this project in the public sector, which, it was wrongly assumed, would compete with private sector steel plants. The Bokharo project is now going to be executed with Soviet technical and financial assistance.

NOTES

1. Speech to All India Congress Committee, Indone, on January 4, 1957, reproduced in Jawaharlal Nehru's *Speeches*, Vol. III, p. 53.
2. *U.N. Demographic Year Book*, 1963.

REFERENCE

Levit, William H., Jr. 1966. "*India Speaks to America* (review)." *World Affairs*, Vol. 129, No. 3, pp. 202–204.

27

The Eurocentric History of Science *and* Multicultural Histories of Science

Arun Bala, 2006

In the following selection, Arun Bala grapples with the politics of knowledge and the coexistence of different forms of knowledge without privileging state-sponsored sciences. Bala, a Singaporean of Indian ancestry, completed his BA and MA degrees in physics at the University of Singapore in the late 1960s and early 1970s, before traveling west to the United Kingdom and Canada, where he completed a PhD in philosophy. He authored *The Dialogue of Civilizations in the Birth of Modern Science* in 2006 and, in 2012, *Asia, Europe, and the Emergence of Modern Science: Knowledge Crossing Boundaries*.

The excerpt that follows reflects Bala's research for a history that acknowledges the birth of modern science as the result of the integration of several civilizations—Chinese, Indian, and Arabian. Bala acknowledges that European overseas exploration opened corridors of communication between India, China, Arabia, and Europe. He argues that the ensuing exchange of ideas and texts sparked the development of modern science and philosophy in Europe. In his endeavor, he recognizes that he is in the good company of Joseph Needham, George Saliba, Paul Feyerabend, and other historians of science who challenge the idea of an independent emergence of European science.

One reviewer of his 2006 book (Hunter 2008) begins with a quote from *Anne of Green Gables* that encapsulates Bala's multicultural conception of science: "If it hadn't been for you, if it hadn't been for me, if it hadn't been for all of us I don't know where she'd be." From this perspective, the nation-state and nationalism moved the historiography to attend to the ideological components of science that began with the European colonization of the other sciences throughout the world. The spread of Western hegemonic ideas of what science is

Bala, Arun. 2006. "The Eurocentric History of Science" and "Multicultural Histories of Science." In *The Dialogue of Civilizations in the Birth of Modern Science*. New York: Palgrave Macmillan. Pp. 21–24, 32–39. Reproduced with the permission of Palgrave Macmillan.

led up to Bala's concern with the developing world, in which he claims that traditional sci-entific cultures can sometimes address problems better than modern science when the lat-ter is in conflict with traditional knowledge. He wants to make room for *all* the building blocks of true science. Such a position often conflicts with "knowledge" generated from ideologies of European exceptionalism. He integrates his research on knowledge in Asian traditions with modern science, examining the hypothesis that the European Renaissance in science cannot be understood if one ignores the European conquest of non-European civilizations. This *exchange* of ideas prompted by colonialism, Bala holds, inspired the Copernican Revolution as well as the work that followed. From this viewpoint, ancient Greek influences were only the beginning of a dialogue that occurred over the centuries between the Chinese, Indian, Egyptian, and Arab precursors.

The further we move into the twenty-first century, the more we change from earlier times. A possible shift in power relations may mean incorporation of all the sciences, local and global.

• • •

THE EUROCENTRIC HISTORY OF SCIENCE

By a Eurocentric history of science I mean any account of the birth and growth of modern science that appeals solely to intellectual, social, and cultural influences, causes, and ideas within Europe, and that marginalizes the importance of contri-butions, if any, of cultures beyond Europe to the birth and growth of modern sci-ence. Indeed, until quite recently, the possibility that Europe could have been cru-cially influenced by other cultures in constructing modern science was hardly entertained.[1] A typical view of this kind is expressed by Rupert Hall: "Europe took nothing from the East without which modern science could not have been created; on the other hand, what it borrowed was valuable only because it was incorporated in the European intellectual tradition. And this, of course, was founded in Greece" (Hall 1962, p. 6).

The situation began to change with the publication of Needham's monumental series *Science and Civilization in China*. For the first time Needham and his col-laborators presented an impressive body of evidence of both technologies and ideas that had originated in China and, after transmission to the West, crucially conditioned the birth and growth of scientific ideas there in the modern era. Though Needham's view regarding the extent of the influence has been contested, he opened the door to the possibility that the development of science within Europe may not have been as insular a process as hitherto assumed. There have been since then widening attempts to document the influence of non-European cultures on the development of modern science. Nevertheless, these dialogical counterperspectives remain on the periphery, and dominant histories of modern science continue to remain Eurocentric.

Although the Eurocentric position is orthodox and well established, any attempt to identify it more precisely immediately leads us into a host of difficulties. What appears to be a clearly defined position begins to lose its sharp definition as we attempt to make a closer approach. Even among those who share the Eurocentric presumption that the history of modern science is the outcome of ideas, values, institutions, and practices autogenerated within Europe, there exists considerable divergence in views about what these actually are. One major divide is between internalists and externalists. Internalist historians explain the changes that led to modern science by invoking intellectual factors such as philosophical, methodological, and scientific ideas. Externalists seek for causes in the social, political, and economic conditions within Europe at the time of the birth of modern science.

Even inside these broad categories, there are further divisions. Among internalists, some stress the role of method in shaping the growth of scientific knowledge; others emphasize metaphysics; and some see the significant variable as a scientific theory. Historians like Whewell lay stress on the inductive method—what he terms the explication or conceptions, the colligation of facts, and the consilience of inductions. Kant emphasizes the importance of the change brought about by Bacon's active experimental method in contrast to the passive collection of facts that had been the guiding strategy of Aristotelian science.[2] In the early years of the twentieth century, historians such as Koyré (1957), Burtt (1959), and Dijksterhuis (1961) believed that the emergence of science can be attributed to a metaphysical orientation that promoted the mathematization of nature. They identified Galileo as the seminal figure who promoted this turn by arguing that mathematics constituted the language of nature. Others such as Duhem (1985) and Kuhn (1957) go beyond such metascientific explanations and see the rise of science in the development of a specific scientific theory. For Duhem the impetus theory in the fourteenth century, and for Kuhn the Copernican theory in the seventeenth century, played the key role in the Scientific Revolution. However, even if they do not see metaphysics and method as major factors, they do not ignore them altogether.

In contrast to the internalists, who hold positions that at least can be categorized into clear-cut alternatives even if these sharp distinctions become fuzzy as we examine their positions more closely, the externalist views are so diverse and multifaceted that they elude categorization altogether. Religion, technology, history, geography, politics, economics, society—and in the not-too-distant past, even race—have been invoked as factors contributing to the emergence of science from conditions within Europe. Hooykaas appeals to the biblical worldview, Merton to Puritan values, Marxists to the needs of an emerging capitalism, Landes to the revolution in the conception of time brought about by the clock, and so on. Going through these diverse explanations one gets the sense that nearly every factor conceivable has been identified as crucial for the emergence of modern science in Europe.[3]

More recently some historians of science have even contested the notion that there was a scientific revolution within Europe that led to the modern era. They argue that there is so much continuity in the science that followed Copernicus with the science that preceded him that it is difficult to conceive of any revolutionary break with tradition separating them. One of the pioneers of this approach is Herbert Butterfield, who, in his seminal study *The Origins of Modern Science*, traces the beginning of contemporary science to the thirteenth century. The social constructivist Steven Shapin also claims that his book *The Scientific Revolution* was really about showing that there was no such thing.[4] Peter Dear, in *Discipline and Experience: The Mathematical Way in the Scientific Revolution*, takes a similar stand. Dear acknowledges that many mathematicians and natural philosophers, such as Mersenne, Descartes, Pascal, Barrow, Newton, and Boyle, did break with the heritage of the medieval period, but it had less to do with the contents of their claims and more to do with their appeal to personal experience than to traditional authority. However, the changes in ideas they wrought did not occur suddenly, or break radically with the past. Rather, the shift of ideas involved a much more gradual and halting process that extended over more than a century. Hence Dear rejects the notion of a revolutionary intellectual mutation leading to modern science. These new histories lead Margaret Osler (2000), in the introduction of her edited work *Rethinking the Scientific Revolution*, to wonder whether the notion of a scientific revolution may not itself be a construct of historiography with its narrative of canonical heroes, such as Copernicus, Kepler, Galileo, [and] Newton, and canonical subjects, such as astronomy, physics, and mathematics.[5]

These no-revolution views have been attacked by the social historian Howard Margolis in his study *It Started with Copernicus: How Turning the World Inside Out Led to the Scientific Revolution*. He maintains that the notion that there was no such thing as a scientific revolution does not make sense, especially if we note the fact that within Europe there was barely any noticeable change for fourteen centuries before most of the major discoveries associated with the rise of modern science came to be made within a few years around 1600 CE. This change was nothing short of revolutionary and requires explanation—it cannot simply be explained away. He attributes the shift to a novel transformation in the psychological orientation of the canonical heroes of the revolution—every one of whom came to be inspired by Copernicus' idea of a sun-centered universe. The counterintuitive claims of the theory led them to look, as Aristotle and the ancient Greeks did not, for hidden evidence and explanations for phenomena—even though such evidence and explanations had always been available at hand but had gone unnoticed. In this respect, the revolution could have happened earlier but did not—until Copernicus turned the world inside out and triggered a new orientation to nature.

Yet what is striking about the diverse internalist, externalist, and no-revolution approaches is their silence concerning the impact of non-European cultures on the

Scientific Revolution in Europe. This even includes recent theorists such as Shapin, Dear, and Osler, who question the notion of a scientific revolution, as well as their critics such as Margolis—all of them ignore much of the recent literature documenting multicultural impacts. Even where they are prepared to acknowledge that some ideas did enter Europe from China, the Arabic world, or India, these are not seen as being crucial. Their accounts easily lead us to suppose that the transition to modern science from medieval science could have occurred without such multicultural contributions, even though European thinkers exploited them opportunistically when they were available. Thus the new historians also assume, like their predecessors of earlier decades, that modern science is not the outcome of vital contributions of ideas and influences from cultures outside Europe.

Indeed there is often great resistance to probing more carefully the role of such influences even when their possibility is acknowledged. In his study *The Scientific Revolution: A Historiographical Inquiry,* historian Floris Cohen acknowledges the possibility of dialogical influences but quickly dismisses it by questioning the motives of those who raise the issue. [. . .]

MULTICULTURAL HISTORIES OF SCIENCE

In recent years there have been numerous calls to reconsider the historical narrative of modern science as solely (or mainly) rooted in the Western or European tradition. This narrative has come to be suspect as historians examining traditions of natural knowledge outside Europe before modern times have increasingly come to recognize the contributions of non-European cultures to modern science. A major pioneer in this direction was Joseph Needham, with his series *Science and Civilization in China,* the first volume of which was published in 1954. Needham argued that many scientific ideas and technological discoveries earlier attributed to Europe had actually originated in China. Needham's groundbreaking studies— the most comprehensive modern survey of the scientific and technological accomplishments of any civilization outside Europe—were followed in 1968 by Nasr's *Science and Civilization in Islam,* which, although concerned only with documenting Arabic science on its own terms, nevertheless examined the profound influence of Arabic scientists on their modern counterparts. Shortly thereafter, Bose, Sen, and Subbarayappa attempted to do for Indian civilization what Needham and Nasr had done for Chinese and Arabic cultures. Their study in 1971, *A Concise History of Science in India,* constitutes a comprehensive survey of the main achievements of classical Indian science and the contributions it made to modern science. More recently, Martin Bernal, in his *Black Athena: The Afro-Asiatic Roots of Classical Civilization,* whose first volume appeared in 1987, argued that Greek civilization—generally considered by Eurocentric historians to be the sole ancient foundation for modern science—was profoundly influenced by the traditions of ancient Egypt and the Levant.[6]

These multicultural influences on the construction of modern science traced by Needham, Nasr, Bose et al., and Bernal have been made mainly from the point of view of the impact of one specific culture—Chinese, Arabic, Indian, or Egyptian—on European science, but taken together, they open the door to the possibility that modern science itself is a phenomenon with much wider multicultural roots than hitherto suspected. However, this multicultural turn itself may have been inspired by attempts made much earlier to trace the roots of modern science to medieval European culture. At the beginning of the twentieth century the French philosopher Duhem argued that modern science was crucially influenced by the scholastic tradition of the fourteenth century. Prior to Duhem it was customary to assume that the birth of modern science occurred with Copernicus, Galileo, Kepler, and others, who liberated thought from the servile subservience of scholasticism to Aristotelian doctrines. Going against this dominant view Duhem wrote:

> When we see the science of Galileo triumph over the hard-headed Peripateticism of a Cremonini [one of Galileo's adversaries in Padua], we believe, badly informed as we are about the history of human thought, that we are witnessing the victory of young modern Science over medieval Philosophy and its obstinate parrotry. But in reality, we are watching the triumph, prepared long in advance, of the science which was born in Paris in the 14th century over the doctrines of Aristotle and Averroes, which in the meantime had been restored to honor by the Italian Renaissance.[7]

By tracing the beginnings of science to the fourteenth century, Duhem put into question the key assumption behind the so-called "War of the Ancients and the Moderns" that had characterized previous historical writing—namely that while the moderns broke away from the ancients, the medieval scholastics slavishly imitated them. The end of this intellectual war was seen as the triumph of the modern science over the Hellenistic tradition. By tracing the roots of modern science to the scholastic heritage, Duhem not only proposed that modern science shared continuity with the scholastic tradition but, since the scholastic tradition saw itself as an attempt to come to terms with Greek thought, he made it possible for others to link modern science with the Greek corpus of knowledge. Many historians of science who followed him were to take up this theme and develop it much further. With the writings of Koyré, Dijksterhuis, and Burtt, we reach the current dominant view that Greek science was a precursor, rather than an obstacle, to modern science.

There was also another unintended consequence of Duhem's account—one he never addressed or even considered as a possibility. By locating the birth of modern science in the medieval era, Duhem led historians into a period in the history of Europe when it became connected to the more intellectually and technologically advanced Arabic and Chinese civilizations. At this time the Arabic-Muslim world stretched along the whole of the southern borders of Europe and also ruled European territories in the Iberian Peninsula in the west. The Chinese civilization also became linked to Europe through the territories of the Mongol Empire—an empire that included Russia in Eastern Europe. Sandwiched between the Arabic and Mongolian worlds, with territories in Western Europe ruled by Arab-Muslims and in Eastern Europe by Mongols, Europe was more open to external cultural influences than at any time since the Persian Empire ruled the Ionian Greeks during the lifetimes of Socrates, Plato, and Aristotle.[8]

By drawing attention to the role of medieval Europe in the genesis of modern science, Duhem prepared the way for Needham's and Nasr's histories, in which the impact of Chinese and Arabic sciences on Europe are first traced back to this seminal era. Moreover, Duhem made it possible to entertain the notion that if medieval science—with its religiously motivated philosophy, its organic metaphysics, its theory of five elements, its belief in qualities like hot, cold, wet, and dry—could serve as the precursor of modern science, then Chinese and Arabic cultures with a similar science of elements and qualities could also have played a role in the birth of modern science. He opened the door to the possibility that modern science might have a history that went further into the past than hitherto suspected—it did not simply emerge de novo in the sixteenth and seventeenth centuries. Thus the new historiography that traces the contributions of the Chinese, Arabic, Indian, and Egyptian traditions of knowledge to modern science can be considered as only taking further, into a wider geographical arena, Duhem's attempt to trace the roots of modern science to medieval Europe.

The most recent multicultural approaches to the history of modern science combine the earlier studies on the separate contributions of the Chinese, Arabic, Indian, and Egyptian traditions into more comprehensive accounts that trace the roots of modern science to the interaction of a plurality of non-European cultural influences. Although Needham did not himself undertake this task (focusing mainly on Chinese contributions), he pointed the way to such an approach when he wrote: "It is necessary to see Europe from the outside—to see European history and European failure no less than European achievement, through the eyes of that large part of humanity, the peoples of Asia and indeed also of Africa" (Needham 1979, p. 11).

Needham is calling into question Eurocentric constructions of the history of science. There are those who would interpret this as tarnishing the repute of science by linking it to mythical, pseudoscientific traditions of knowledge from non-European cultures. Since science, as the Indian psychologist and culture critic Ashis Nandy has argued, is the dominant ideology today, this can also be easily interpreted as calling into question the unique status of modern science. Hence calls to transcend Eurocentrism tend to be perceived as extremist positions—and often evoke equally extreme counter-reactions. In his study *Eurocentricism,* Samir Amin writes: "Resistance to the critique of Eurocentricism is always extreme, for we are here entering the realm of the taboo. The calling into question of the Euro-centric dimension of the dominant ideology is more difficult to accept even than a critical challenge to its economic dimension" (Amin 1989, p. 116).

In his study *Science and Technology in a Multicultural World,* the social anthro-pologist David Hess attempts to break this taboo by articulating a multicultural perspective on the history of science that traces the roots of modern science to non-Western cultures as well. Hess begins by questioning the conventional narra-tive of the Scientific Revolution of the seventeenth century told, as he describes it, "in the form of a dialogue between the Old Europe (ancient thinkers) and the New Europe (modern thinkers)" (Hess 1995, p. 63).[9]

He argues that this narrative ignores not only events prior to Old Europe but also those in the period intervening between Old and New Europe. According to him, during these eras, important exchanges took place between Europe and other cultures that are either completely ignored or only given a secondary plot status in Eurocentric narratives. Even though individual elements of the Eurocentric narra-tive, taken in isolation, do occasionally get questioned, such critiques are never brought together to subvert the overall Eurocentric structure of the story offered. They only appear as qualifying subplots designed to strengthen the Eurocentric main plot by acknowledging contributions that cannot avoid being recognized.

Hess refers to Needham's studies that show China to have been more advanced technologically than the West until the sixteenth century, and documents the numerous transfers of Chinese science and technology to the West in the medieval and later periods. Referring to one of Needham's lists—which includes magnetic science, equatorial celestial coordinates, quantitative cartography, the technology of cast iron, essential components of the reciprocating steam-engine, the mechan-ical clock, the boot-stirrup, the efficient equine harness, gunpowder—he argues that much of the technological infrastructure of modern science rests on borrow-ings from China (Hess 1995, p. 64). Mention could also be made of many other Chinese inventions such as weight-driven and water clocks, glass-making tech-niques, orgival (Gothic) architecture, water-raising machines, and paper making.[10]

Hess also draws our attention to the Arabic contribution. According to him, this influence was not only technological but also methodological and theoretical. He refers to the discovery of the lesser circulation of blood by al-Nafis as a possible influence on Harvey's discovery of the larger circulation. Moreover, following But-terfield, he argues that Harvey's experimental approach to biology was inspired by Averroes (Ibn Rushd, 1126–1198 CE),[11] who taught a secular and critical orientation toward the study of nature and medicine. Averroism (or at least Aristotelianism as seen through Averroes) was an important influence at the University of Padua when Harvey studied there (Hess 1995, p. 65).

Galileo was also a student at Padua and, moreover, did much of his work there. He too adopted the Averroist secular and critical approach to science. Moreover, Galileo was also influenced by the Arabic scientist Alhazen (Ibn al-Haytham),[12] known for his experimental approach to science, since he used the Alhazen theory of optics to show that the moon was not a polished mirror. Like Galileo, the mathematical astronomer Kepler also studied Alhazen's optics. Hence it is reasonable to suppose that both Galileo and Kepler could have been inspired by Alhazen's general approach to the practice of theoretical and experimental science (Hess 1995, p. 66).

Apart from optics, Hess also refers to Saliba's studies on the Maragha School of astronomy that flourished in the thirteenth and fourteenth centuries. Saliba argues that there are many parallels between the models of planetary motion and mathematical techniques deployed by Copernicus and the Damascene astronomer al-Shatir, which strongly suggests that Copernicus was aware of the latter's studies.[13]

Hess also considers the numerous and complex multicultural exchanges that took place in mathematics among different cultures over long historical periods. These led to significant mathematical achievements that were inherited by Europe and played a crucial role in the modern Scientific Revolution. There were the mathematical contributions of Egypt and Mesopotamia to Greek science, and the Arabic synthesis of the geometrical tradition of the Greeks with the algebraic and arithmetical traditions of Babylonia, India, and China. Hess also considers the influence of the Kerala School of mathematics in India during the medieval period that approached discoveries close to the calculus, although he acknowledges that the question of whether they influenced Europe continues to generate controversy. He concludes that cultures from Egypt and Mesopotamia to the Arabic world, India, and China made important contributions to the mathematical tools that made modern science possible.

After tracing the many multicultural influences on Europe, Hess proceeds to draw a number of highly dubious conclusions. First, he questions the notion that there was a Scientific Revolution in Europe at the dawn of the modern era. He thinks that the continuities between modern science and other traditions that preceded it make the notion of revolutionary break implausible. In this regard his views parallel those of historians Butterfield, Shapin, and Dear, although his conclusion is based on continuities within modern science and multicultural, not just medieval European, traditions.

Hess adopts the continuity thesis precisely because he thinks postulating a radical break separating modern science from earlier traditions would be ethnocentric, since it would marginalize the contributions of other cultures—especially the Arabic. However, a multicultural history of modern science acknowledging non-Western contributions can be written without denying that there was a revolutionary break involved in the emergence of modern science. Even if modern science was forged out of ideas, methods, and technologies developed in multicultural contexts, it is a sufficiently radical and unique achievement to be rightly described as revolutionary. Consequently, it is hardly ethnocentric to claim that a scientific revolution occurred in Europe—unless one denies the plausible claim that modern science first emerged in Europe. What would be ethnocentric is to deny the dialogical contributions that made the revolutionary break possible.

Equally questionable is the second conclusion Hess draws from his multicultural approach. He argues that we should replace the term "Western science" by the term "modern science" or "cosmopolitan science" since it absorbed contributions from many cultures. Yet somewhat inconsistently, he also wants to treat modern science as Western "ethnoscience" so that it cannot be used to ignore the valuable knowledge still carried by non-Western cultures, especially their environmental and medical knowledge (Hess 1995, pp. 67–68). His ambivalence appears to be related to the dual perspective he wants to adopt with respect to modern science: by virtue of its multicultural roots it is cosmopolitan; by virtue of its limitations relative to non-Western traditions, it is Western. Referring to modern science as "Western science" would be to ignore the contributions of other cultures that made it possible; referring to modern science as "cosmopolitan science" would marginalize other traditions of knowledge by implying that they have been completely displaced by this science synthesized in the West.

The aforementioned difficulties that Hess confronts can be easily resolved if we make a distinction between premodern and modern traditions of science. Then we can treat modern science as Western science—should we want to—provided we recognize its multicultural roots. Since we are prepared to refer to the science that developed in the Arabic-speaking world as "Arabic science" in spite of its roots in Greek, Persian, Indian, and (to an extent) Chinese traditions, there is no reason to deny the term "Western science" to the tradition that developed in the West in spite of its roots in other traditions. The universal or cosmopolitan status of modern (or Western) science can also be left as an open question. It is quite possible that, in effecting the synthesis of modern science from premodern traditions, Europeans created a science that has obscured our understanding of some areas of reality now understood better by other traditions of science. It may well be correct for many environmentalists, feminists, and multiculturalists to turn to what they think are the more holistic or organic perspectives of premodern traditions to remedy the blind spots they perceive in modern science. If they are right, then modern science cannot legitimately claim to be universal science.

Indeed the historical question of the roots of modern science and the epistemological question regarding its universal scope or cosmopolitan status are intimately connected. If modern science has roots in Europe alone, and grew independently of other traditions, it lends credibility to its universalist and cosmopolitan claims— it is quite possible that a universal science emerged once in Europe through the discovery of how to discover, that is, through the finding of the one and only scientific method, and then spread elsewhere. However, if modern science drew on earlier traditions of science, then it is conceivable that a new order of science may yet emerge in the future by drawing on modern science and other premodern traditions. This would lead us to be wary of claims that modern science is both universal and cosmopolitan and that we can discount the claims of other traditions to reveal aspects of nature ignored by modern science. Thus, whether we take a Eurocentric or a dialogical approach to the birth of modern science would have significant implications for our evaluation of the future relationship between traditional cultural reservoirs of knowledge and modern science.

NOTES

1. Of course there have always been early isolated dissenting voices. For example, Muhammad Iqbal (1934) had argued that Islam gave birth to the "inductive intellect" which led to modern science. He maintained that the reactions of Muslim theologians—like Ibn Hazm and Ibn Taymiyah—against the logic of Aristotle provided the stage for Mill's inductive logic. He also notes that Roger Bacon, often credited with the discovery of the scientific spirit of inquiry, was himself educated in universities in Spain set up by Muslims (p. 23). See Fakhry (2004, pp. 363–368) for a more detailed discussion of Iqbal's views. Nevertheless, none of these dissenting perspectives have been articulated in detail so as to provide a systematic alternative to the Eurocentric interpretations of the rise of modern science. Iqbal's views can also be seen as one-sided because they fail to see the unique achievements of the moderns as the result of the dialogical integration of not just Arabic but also other traditions.

2. For Kant's view, see the preface to the second edition of his *Critique of Pure Reason* (trans. Kemp, 1950). Much of the discussion here depends on Cohen's excellent exposition of various approaches to the history of science, especially the Scientific Revolution, associated with the birth of modern science. However, I have not followed Cohen (1994) in the way he categorizes the approaches of Kant, Whewell, Koyré, Burtt, Dijksterhuis (1961), and others.

3. See Blaut (2000) and Hobson (2004) for a critical discussion of many of these invoked factors. For a typical Marxist position see Bernal (1971).

4. Butterfield (1957) was preceded in this regard by Duhem (1985), and followed by Shapin (1996). Indeed once we stress the importance of medieval contributions as crucial to the emergence of modern science in the seventeenth century, it is easy to reject the discontinuity thesis. Such a discontinuity between modern science and its medieval antecedents might appear to militate against the idea that the medieval contributions were crucial.

5. Of course, it is possible to make a more nuanced argument that sees the medieval contributions as necessary, but not sufficient for the rise of modern science. This would preserve the discontinuity thesis but acknowledge the indispensability of these contributions. This third position is adopted by Needham, who goes further by suggesting that not just medieval European science but also Chinese science made crucial contributions to modern science, but acknowledges discontinuities between the two.

6. Diop pioneered the study of the impact of Egyptian philosophy and science on the Hellenic world more than three decades before Bernal, although he did not examine the Levantine influence on Hellenism. See Diop (1991). There is also now an emerging awareness of the impact of Indian influences on Greek and Hellenistic science. See Goonatilake (1984). It is also likely that such dialogical impacts

involved a two-way process in which Indian and Greek ideas influenced each other. See McEvilley (2002).

7. Duhem quoted in Cohen (1994, p. 45).

8. There is no better record of the Persian influence on the Greek world than Herodotus' *Histories* (1998). Surprising as it might appear, most of his history is concerned with the politics and military actions of Persian kings. By contrast Thucydides' history is more concerned with the actions and motives of Greek personalities.

9. Hess also sees wider implications for his dialogical approach to history. It could promote greater awareness of traditional knowledge as a reservoir of resources for advancing knowledge in the future and exposing the limits of current scientific thinking. He writes:

> By showing that non-Western knowledges, technologies and medicines are often coherent and elaborate, an intellectual resource emerges that can be used to resist the ideology of development interests who wish to impose unwanted Western knowledges and technologies in the name of civilization. Furthermore, by showing that non-Western ways of knowing and doing are often efficacious and in some cases superior to Western or cosmopolitan alternatives, it is possible to build a resource base for critiquing and contributing to changing development projects.... At another level, the study of ethno-knowledges makes it possible to put into question the universalistic assumptions of cosmopolitan science and technology. (Hess 1995, p. 210)

10. For a more detailed historical discussion of the origin and spread of these technologies, see Pacy (1990) and Hobson (2004).

11. We will be using the Latinized name Averroes, instead of the Arabic name Ibn Rushd, since this was the name by which he was better known in the Western world, and all discussion of his views in this study will be focused on his influence on European thought.

12. We will be using the name Alhazen in this study because we are concerned with Ibn al-Haytham's impact on European thought in the medieval and early modern era, when he was better known by his Latinized name.

13. The discoveries of these historical parallels were made by a chain of historians beginning with Victor Roberts in 1957, followed by Kennedy, Neugebauer, Swerdlow, and Saliba. See Saliba (1994, p. 254). See also King (2000).

REFERENCES

Amin, Samir. 1989. *Eurocentrism*. Russell Moore, trans. New York: Monthly Review Press.

Bala, Arun. 2012. *Asia, Europe, and the Emergence of Modern Science: Knowledge Crossing Boundaries*. Palgrave Macmillan.

Bernal, Martin. 1971. *Science in History*. Cambridge, MA: MIT Press.

Blaut, James M. 2000. *Eight Eurocentric Historians*. New York: Guildford Press.

Burtt, E. A. 1959. *The Metaphysical Foundations of Modern Physical Science: A Historical and Critical Essay*. London: Routledge and Kegan Paul.

Butterfield, Herbert. 1957. *The Origins of Modern Science, 1300–1800*. New York: Free Press.

Cohen, H. Floris. 1994. *The Scientific Revolution: A Historiographical Inquiry*. Chicago: University of Chicago Press.

Deuraseh, Nurdeng. 2008. "The Dialogue of Civilizations in the Birth of Modern Science (review)." *Journal of World History*, Vol. 19, No. 4 (December): 552–556.

Dijksterhuis, E. J. 1961. *The Mechanization of the World Picture*. Oxford: Oxford University Press.

Diop, Cheikh Anta. 1991. *Civilization or Barbarism: An Authentic Anthropology*. New York: Lawrence Hill Books.

Duhem, Pierre. 1985. *Medieval Cosmology: Theories of Infinity, Place, Time, Void, and the Plurality of Worlds*. R. Ariew, trans. Chicago: University of Chicago Press.

Fakhry, Majid. 2004. *A History of Islamic Philosophy*. New York: Columbia University Press.

Goonatilake, Susan. 1984. *Aborted Discovery: Science and Creativity in the Third World*. London: Zed Books.

Hall, Rupert. 1962. "General Introduction" to Marie Boas Hall. *The Scientific Renaissance: 1450–1630*. London: Collins.

Herodotus. 1998. *The Histories*. Robin Waterfield and Carolyn Dwald, trans. and intro. Oxford: Oxford University Press.

Hess, David. 1995. *Science and Technology in a Multicultural World: The Cultural Politics of Facts and Artifacts*. New York: Columbia University Press.

Hetherington, Norriss S. 1996. "Plato and Eudoxus: Instrumentalists, Realists, or Prisoners of Themata?" *Studies in History and Philosophy of Science*, Vol. 17, No. 2, pp. 271–289.

Hobson, John M. 2004. *The Eastern Origins of Western Civilisation*. Cambridge: Cambridge University Press.

Hunter, Graeme. 2008. "The Dialogue of Civilizations in the Birth of Modern Science (review)." *University of Toronto Quarterly*, Vol. 77, No. 1, pp. 142–143.

Iqbal, Muhammad. 1934. *The Reconstruction of Religious Thought in Islam*. London: Oxford University Press.

Kemp, Norman, trans. 1950. *Critique of Pure Reason*, by Immanuel Kant. 2nd ed. New York: Macmillan.

King. 2000. "Mathematical Astronomy in Islamic Civilisation." In *Astronomy Across Cultures: The History of Non-Western Astronomy*. Helaine Selin, ed. Pp. 585–613. New York: Springer.

Koyré, Alexandre. 1957. *From the Closed World to the Infinite Universe*. Baltimore: Johns Hopkins University Press.

Kuhn, Thomas. 1957. *The Copernican Revolution: Planetary Astronomy in the Development of Western Thought*. Cambridge, MA: Harvard University Press.

Needham, Joseph. 1979. *Within the Four Seas: The Dialogue of East and West*. Toronto: University of Toronto Press.

Osler, Margaret, ed. 2000. *Rethinking the Scientific Revolution*. Cambridge: Cambridge University Press.

Pacy, Arnold. 1990. *Technology in World Civilization: A Thousand-Year History*. Cambridge, MA: MIT Press.

Saliba, George. 1994. *A History of Arabic Astronomy: Planetary Theories during the Golden Age of Islam*. New York: New York University Press.

———. 2009. "Development and Dialogue: Review of *The Dialogue of Civilizations in the Birth of Modern Science*, by Arun Bala." *Metascience*, Vol. 18, No. 1 (March): 61–64.

Shapin, Steven. 1996. *The Scientific Revolution*. Chicago: University of Chicago Press.
Visvanathan, Shiv. 2003. "Cultural Encounters and the Orient: A Study in the Politics of Knowledge." *Diogenes,* Vol. 50, No. 4, pp. 69–81.
Wahba, Mourad, and Mona Abousenna, eds. 1996. *Averroes and the Enlightenment.* Amherst, NY: Prometheus Books.

28

From The Thistle and the Drone

Akbar Ahmed, 2013

Akbar Ahmed is an author, playwright, and poet who obtained his PhD in anthropology in 1978 from the School of Oriental and African Studies at the University of London. While he was working on his MA at Cambridge University, Ahmed completed a set of four projects entitled the Jinnah Quartet—an academic study, a graphic novel, a feature film, and a documentary film—named in commemoration of the fiftieth anniversary of the founding of Pakistan.

After the September 11, 2001, attacks on the United States, Ahmed began a series of studies published by the Brookings Institution Press that covered relations between the West and Islam post-9/11. He has received many honors for his books and films, including Pakistan's Star of Excellence. As of this writing, he holds the Ibn Khaldun Chair of Islamic Studies at American University in Washington, DC, having taught at Princeton University, Harvard University, and the U.S. Naval Academy in Annapolis, Maryland.

In 1966, Ahmed joined the Civil Service of Pakistan and eventually became Pakistan's ambassador to the UK and Ireland. His book *The Thistle and the Drone* is the culmination of his life's work among Islamic hill peoples from Pakistan, Yemen, North Africa, and as far away as the Philippines. The selection that follows, from the introduction to this book, addresses U.S. drone operations not only in Pakistan's Waziristan, where he was ambassador, but also elsewhere in the Islamic world. Ahmed argues that wise planning is being outpaced by technology, something that Albert Einstein wrote about decades ago. For victims and observers alike, the United States' reputation, according to Ahmed, is symbolized by the drone.

Ahmed, Akbar. 2013. *The Thistle and the Drone: How America's War on Terror Became a Global War on Tribal Islam*. Washington, DC: Brookings Institution Press. Pp. 1–3. Reprinted with the permission of the author.

. . .

"The Jonas Brothers are here. They're out there somewhere," a smiling and confident President Barack Obama told the expectant and glittering audience attending the White House Correspondents' Dinner in Washington on May 1, 2010. "Sasha and Malia are huge fans, but boys, don't get any ideas. I have two words for you: 'predator drones.' You will never see it coming. You think I'm joking?"

Obama's banter may have seemed tasteless, given that he had just been awarded the Nobel Peace Prize, but this was not a Freudian slip. The president was indicating he possessed Zeus-like power to hurl thunderbolts from the sky and obliterate anyone with impunity, even an American pop group. One report said he had a "love" of drones, noting that by 2011 their use had accelerated exponentially.[1] It was also revealed that Obama had a secret "kill list."[2] Having read Saint Augustine and Saint Thomas Aquinas, and their ideas of the "just war" and "natural law," which promote doing good and avoiding evil, did not deter Obama from a routine of going down the list to select names and "nominate" them, to use the official euphemism, for assassination.[3] I wondered whether the learned selectors of the Nobel Peace Prize had begun to have second thoughts.

As its use increased, the drone became a symbol of America's war on terror. Its main targets appeared to be Muslim tribal groups living in Afghanistan, Pakistan, Yemen, and Somalia. Incessant and concentrated strikes were directed at what was considered the "ground zero" of the war on terror, Waziristan, in the Tribal Areas of Pakistan. There were also reports, however, of U.S. drones being used against other Muslim tribal groups like the Kurds in Turkey and the Tausug in the Philippines, and also by the United Kingdom against the Pukhtun tribes of Afghanistan, by France in northern Mali against the Tuareg, and even by Israel in Gaza. These communities—some of the most impoverished and isolated in the world, with identities that are centuries-old—had become the targets of the twenty-first century's most advanced kill technology.

The drone embodied the weaponry of globalization: high-tech in performance, sleek in appearance, and global in reach. It was mysterious, distant, deadly, and notoriously devoid of human presence. Its message of destruction resounded in its names: Predator and Reaper. For its Muslim targets, the UAV, or unmanned aerial vehicle, its official title, had an alliterative quality—it meant death, destruction, disinformation, deceit, and despair. Flying at 50,000 feet above ground, and therefore out of sight of its intended victims, the drone could hover overhead unblinkingly for twenty-four hours, with little escaping its scrutiny before it struck. For a Muslim tribesman, this manner of combat not only was dishonorable but also smacked of sacrilege. By appropriating the powers of God through the drone, in its capacity to see and not be seen and deliver death without warning, trial, or judgment, Americans were by definition blasphemous.

In the United States, however, the drone was increasingly viewed as an absolutely vital weapon in fighting terrorism and keeping America safe. Support for it demonstrated patriotism, and opposition exposed one's anti-Americanism. Thus the debate surrounding the drone rested on its merits as a precisely effective killing machine rather than the human or emotional costs it inflicted. Drone strikes meant mass terror in entire societies across the world, yet little effort was made on the part of the perpetrators to calculate the political and psychological fallout, let alone assess the morality of public assassinations or the killing of innocent men, women, and children. Even those who rushed to rescue drone victims were considered legitimate targets of a follow-up strike. Nor did Americans seem concerned that they were creating dangerous precedents for other countries.

Instead, boasting with the pride of a football coach, CIA director, and later secretary of defense, Leon Panetta referred to the drones as "the only game in town."[4] Fifty-five members of Congress organized what was popularly known as the Drone Caucus and received extensive funds for their campaigns from drone manufacturers such as General Atomics and Lockheed Martin. The drones' enthusiastic public advocates even included "liberal" academics and self-avowed "hippies" such as philosophy professor Bradley Strawser of Monterey, California.[5] Americans exulted in the fact that the drone freed Americans of any risk. It could be operated safely and neatly from newly constructed high-tech, air-conditioned offices. Like any office worker in suit and tie, the "pilot" could complete work in his office and then go home to take his family bowling or join them for a barbecue in the backyard. The drone was fast becoming as American as apple pie.

Typical of its propensity for excess in matters of security, by 2012 America had commissioned just under 20,000 drones, about half of which were in use. They were proliferating at an alarming rate, with police departments, internal security agencies, and foreign governments placing orders. In September 2012 Iran unveiled its own reconnaissance and attack drone with a range of over 2,000 kilometers. The following month, France announced it was sending surveillance drones to Mali to assist the government in fighting the Tuareg rebels in the north. In October 2012 the United Kingdom doubled its number of armed drones in Afghanistan with the purchase of five Reaper drones from the United States, to be operated from a facility in the United Kingdom. It was estimated that by the end of the decade, some 30,000 U.S. drones would be patrolling American skies alone. There was talk in the press of new and deadly varieties, including the next generation of "nuclear-powered" drones. Despite public interest, drone operations were deliberately obscured.

Ignoring the moral debate, drone operators are equally infatuated with the weapon and the sense of power it gives them. It leaves them "electrified" and "adrenalized"—flying a drone is said to be "almost like playing the computer game *Civilization*," a "sci-fi" experience.[6] A U.S. drone operator in New Mexico revealed the extent to which individuals across the world can be observed in their most private moments. "We watch people for months," he said. "We see them playing with their dogs or doing their laundry. We know their patterns like we know our neighbors' patterns. We even go to their funerals." Another drone operator spoke of watching people having sex at night through infrared cameras.[7] The last statement, in particular, has to be read keeping in mind the importance Muslim tribal peoples give to notions of modesty and privacy.

The victims are treated like insects: the military slang for a successful strike, when the victim is blown apart on the screen in a display of blood and gore, is "bug splat." Muslim tribesmen were reduced to bugs or, in a *Washington Post* editorial by David Ignatius, cobras to be killed at will. Any compromise with the Taliban in the Tribal Areas of Pakistan, officially designated as the Federally Administered Tribal Areas (FATA), is "like playing with a cobra," he wrote.[8] And do we "compromise" with cobras? Ignatius asked. "No, you kill a cobra." Bugs, snakes, cockroaches, rats—such denigration of minorities has been heard before, and as recent history teaches, it never ends well for the abused people.

NOTES

1. Michael Hastings, "The Rise of the Killer Drones: How America Goes to War in Secret," *Rolling Stone,* April 16, 2012.

2. Jo Becker and Scott Shane, "Secret 'Kill List' Proves a Test of Obama's Principles and Will," *New York Times,* May 29, 2012.

3. David Luban, "What Would Augustine Do?: The President, Drones, and Just War Theory," *Boston Review,* June 6, 2012.

4. "U.S. Airstrikes in Pakistan Called 'Very Effective,'" CNN, May 18, 2009, http://articles.cnn.com/2009-05-18/politics/cia.pakistan.airstrikes_1_qaeda-pakistani-airstrikes?_s=PM:POLITICS.

5. Rory Carroll, "The Philosopher Making the Moral Case for U.S. Drones," *Guardian* (Manchester), August 2, 2012.

6. Hastings, "The Rise of the Killer Drones."

7. Nicola Abé, "Dreams in Infrared: The Woes of an American Drone Operator," *Der Spiegel,* December 14, 2012.

8. David Ignatius, "Pakistan Blew Its Chance for Security," *Washington Post,* May 16, 2012.

REFERENCE

Ahmed, Akbar. 2001. Interview by Jennifer Byrne. *Foreign Correspondent.* New York: ABC, September 19, 2001. Television broadcast.

PART FOUR

Japanese Travelers and Their Observations

29

From The Record of a Pilgrimage to China in Search of the Law

Ennin, 838–847

Ennin, or Jikaku Daishi, was a Japanese Buddhist monk who lived from 793 (or 794) to 854 AD. He traveled to China between the years 838 and 847. His diary, *The Record of the Pilgrimage to T'ang in Search of the Law,* was written on four scrolls or booklets and later handcopied by Buddhist monks, one scroll in 1291 and another in 1805. The title refers to the ruling Chinese Tang Dynasty, and "the Law" was a term used by Buddhists to designate their own religion. Ennin's diary was first printed commercially in 1907 in Tokyo, and it also appeared in three later editions. The present selection is based on the first manuscript (1291) and third printing (1918) of the diary, which was part of a varied collection of Buddhist works.

The four booklets of Ennin's diary as it now exists consist mostly of daily entries in Chinese, which was a foreign tongue for him. He wrote in a combination of classical and vernacular. The precious books, the first written documents about China by a foreigner, offer a rare glimpse of the practice of popular Buddhism in China, as well as everyday life in mid-ninth-century China. In addition, Ennin records details of Korea's active trade with northeastern China and the Korean role in trade between China and Japan.

Ennin was born in what is now Tochigi Prefecture, Japan, and entered the Buddhist priesthood on Mount Hiei near Kyoto at the age of fourteen. He accompanied a Japanese diplomatic mission to the Tang imperial court in China in 838. For Ennin, this was the beginning of a series of adventures. He studied under masters at the Buddhist temple on Mount Utai in Shanxi Province, and later went to Chang'an, then the capital of China.

Ennin was in China when the anti-Buddhist Tang emperor Wuzong took the throne in 840, and during the Great Anti-Buddhist Persecution of 842–846. As a result of the emperor's actions, Ennin was deported from China and returned to Japan in 847. In 854, he

Ennin. 1955. *Ennin's Diary: The Record of a Pilgrimage to China in Search of the Law.* Edwin O. Reischauer, ed. New York: Ronald Press. Pp. 66–76, 320–342 (some footnotes edited or omitted). Reprinted with the permission of the Reischauer estate.

became the chief priest of the Tendai sect, and in Emryakuji he founded a temple and safe storage for the sutras and instruments he had brought back from China. Of the many books he authored, Ennin's best known is his diary, translated into English by Edwin O. Reischauer, an East Asia specialist.

The longevity of Ennin's impact prompted Virginia Stibbs Anami to replicate his journey and write *Following the Tracks of Ennin's 9th Century Journey* (2007), in which the author emphasizes the role of Buddhism in knitting together people from three countries—Japan, China, and Korea—and stimulating trade in art and culture.

. . .

K'AI-CH'ENG • FOURTH YEAR (*CHI-WEI*)

WHICH IS THE SAME AS

JŌWA • SIXTH YEAR IN JAPAN (*TSUCHINOTO HITSUJI*)

FIRST MOON: 1st DAY: chia-yin[1].   This is New Year's Day. Officials and laymen have a three-day holiday, and this monastery will have three days of maigre feasts. Early in the morning the Minister of State came to the monastery and worshiped the Buddha and then went back.

3rd DAY.   We started the drawing of three pictures each of Nan-yo and T'ien-t'ai Ta-shih. Of old, during the Liang period, there lived [a man called] Han Kan,[2] who was the leading painter of the Liang dynasty. When, in painting pictures of birds or animals, he drew in their eyes, they were able to fly or run. He investigated the appearance of Nan-yo Ta-shih and drew a likeness of him in the Lung-hsing-ssu of Yang-chou, which the Emperor placed on the wall of the south gallery of the Lapis Lazuli Hall of the Lotus Place of Ritual.[3] Now I have had the Ambassador's attendant, Awada no Ietsugu, make copies of this, which [he has done] without a single error. Next I am having Ietsugu draw on silk in the K'ai-yüan-ssu the visage and clothing [of Nan-yo], entirely in the manner of Han Kan.[4]

On the walls of the same gallery in that cloister is drawn the "Reciting of the *Lotus Sutra*," which again and again I find quite moving. Since there are about twenty pictures of monks, it cannot be described in detail. To the east of the Lapis Lazuli Hall is the Hall of Fugen's[5] Counter-Wind. In olden times there was a fire which destroyed the whole monastery, but, when it reached the Fa-hua-yüan, the master of scripture-reciting, Ling-yu, recited the *Lotus Sutra* in the Hall of Fugen, whereupon a great wind suddenly arose, blowing from within this cloister, and drove back the fire so that the hall was not consumed. The people nowadays accordingly call it the "Hall of Fugen's Counter-Wind."

In the Tung-t'a-yüan ("Eastern Pagoda Cloister") there is placed a portrait of Chien-chen Ho-shang. The inscription on the pavilion says, "The portrait of the monk who crossed the sea." On the eastern side within the inner gate stands a stele with an inscription to "the monk who crossed the sea." The introduction of the inscription tells how Chien-chen Ho-shang crossed the sea in the cause of Buddhism. It says, "In crossing the sea, the monk encountered evil winds. First he came to a sea of serpents, which were several tens of feet long. After proceeding a whole day, he came to the end of it and then reached a black sea, where the color of the sea was like India ink," and so on.

I hear that an Imperial document has reached the prefecture, the text of which says, "In accordance with the petition of the tributary embassy, notice is being sent to Ch'u-chou to hire ships for the Japanese embassy which then is ordered to [return home] across the sea in the third moon." The meaning of this is not yet clear.

6th DAY.   The Minister of State's military aide, Shen Pien, came and reported as a message from the Minister of State that, starting the fifth day of this moon, everyone was going to collect money, on behalf of the country, in order to repair the Balcony of the Auspicious Sandalwood Images in the K'ai-yüan-ssu. They were going to hold lectures on scriptures and the raising of funds[6] at the Hsiao-kan-ssu,[7] and he asked us Japanese monks in particular to come to hear the lectures and at the same time urged the Japanese officials to establish karma affinities[8] and donate money.

7th DAY.   Shen Pien came and gave us a message from the Minister of State to the effect that the officials of the prefecture and regional commandery intended to assemble on the next day at the Hsiao-kan-ssu and were going to invite us Japanese monks to come and listen to the lecture. There also was a fund-raising statement[9] by the Scripture-Lecturing Priest, . . . -fan.[10] I examined the document, and it said:

[In order to] repair the Balcony of the Auspicious Images, we are lecturing on the *Diamond Sutra*.[11] What we ask for [from you] is fifty strings of cash.[12] We have petitioned the Minister of State and have had our raising of funds approved by him. Let those of like karma affinities and relationships come to the Hsiao-kan-ssu, where we shall lecture on the scriptures and await their pleasure.[13]

This document is as separately [recorded].

Shen Pien tells us that the Minister of State has donated 1,000 strings of cash, and that the lectures are to last for a period of two moons.[14] There are many persons who come daily to listen to the Law. They estimate that with 10,000 strings of cash they can repair the balcony. Persia[15] has given 1,000 strings of cash, and some men from Champa[16] have donated 200 strings. Since our national group is few in number, [only] 50 strings are being solicited from us. With their repeated urging, I feel [this sum] to be small.

8th DAY.   A Korean, Wang Chŏng, came, and we met. He was a man who had been on the same boat with the Chinese Chang Chüeh-chi and others who drifted to the Province of Dewa[17] in the tenth year of the Japanese [year period of] Kōnin (819). When we asked him the circumstances of his having drifted there, he said that in order to trade various goods, they left here and crossed the seas, but that suddenly they encountered evil winds and drifted southward for three moons, drifting ashore in the Province of Dewa. When they were about to leave, Chang Chüeh-chi and his brother together deserted and stayed in Dewa. [The others] set out from northern Dewa on the "north sea," and with favorable winds drifted to the province of Nagato[18] in fifteen days. [Wang Chŏng] understands the Japanese language very well.

9th DAY.   The copying of the pictures of Nan-yo and T'ien-t'ai [Ta-shih] was completed.

14th DAY.   It was the beginning of spring. The townsmen made orioles and sold them, and people bought them and played with them.[19]

15th DAY.   At night they burned lamps in the private homes along the streets to the east and west. It was not unlike New Year's Eve in Japan. In the monastery they burned lamps and offered them to the Buddha. They also paid reverence to the pictures of their teachers. Laymen did likewise.

In this monastery they erected a lamp tower in front of the Buddha Hall.[20] Below the steps, in the courtyard, and along the sides of the galleries they burned oil. The lamp cups were quite beyond count. In the streets men and women did not fear the late hour, but entered the monastery and looked around, and in accordance with their lot cast coppers before the lamps which had been offered. After looking around they went on to other monasteries and looked around and worshiped and cast their coppers.

The halls of the various monasteries and the various cloisters all vie with one another in the burning of lamps. Those who come always give coppers before departing. The Wu-liang-i-ssu sets up a "spoon-and-bamboo lamp."[21] I estimated that it has a thousand lamps. The spoon-and-bamboo lamp is constructed like a tree and looks like a pagoda. The way in which it is bound together is most ingenious. It is about seven or eight feet in height. [This festival] lasts for a period of three nights from this night to the night of the seventeenth.

17th DAY.   Shen Pien came and joined us in lamenting our late departure [for Mt. T'ien-t'ai]. Then we asked him whether or not we could go to T'ai-chou if we were especially to receive a document from the Minister of State. Shen Pien wrote in reply that he, Pien, had asked the Minister of State about this three or four times in all, explaining that we Japanese monks wondered whether or not we could get [something from him] like a permit in order to go to T'ai-chou, but that the Minister of State said that, even if a Yang-chou document were issued, it would do nothing for us in Che-hsi-tao and Che-tung-tao[22] and that we should make a petition to the throne. If there were an Imperial order, we could go, but otherwise we could not. With a permit from the Minister of State we could come and go in the eight prefectures which the Minister of State administers, but Junchou[23] and T'ai-chou have other Ministers of State,[24] who have their own areas of jurisdiction. The respective officials have no relations with one another, and it is feared that if we have no Imperial order, we shall not be able to go easily.

After the forenoon meal they spread out in front of the halls of the monastery the treasures [of the establishment], laying out forty-two portraits of sages and saints[25] and all sorts of rare colored silks beyond count. As for the countenances of the sages and saints, some were concentrating with closed eyes, others with faces uplifted were gazing into the distance, others looking to the side seemed to be speaking, and others with lowered visages regarded the ground. The forty-two pictures had forty-two different types of countenances. As for the differences in their sitting postures, some sat in the full cross-legged position and others in the half cross-legged position.[26] Their postures thus differed. Besides the forty-two sages and saints, there were pictures of Fugen and Monju[27] and of *Gumyō-chō* and *Karyōbinga-chō.*[28]

At sunset they lit lamps and offered them to the pictures of the saints. At night they chanted praises and worshiped Buddha and recited Sanskrit hymns of praise. The monks reciting Sanskrit came in together, some of them holding golden lotuses and jeweled banners, and sat in a row in front of [the pictures of] the saints and intoned together Sanskrit hymns of praise. They went through the night without resting, lighting a cup lamp in front of each saint.

18th DAY. At dawn they made offerings of medicines and gruel, and at the time of the forenoon meal they made offerings of food of all sorts and of all flavors. Men and women onlookers gathered in large numbers both day and night. In the [dining] hall they arranged a maigre feast for the monks. In the night they again lit lamps and made offerings and chanted Sanskrit hymns of praise. In all [this lasted] two days and two nights.

The great officials, the military, and the monks in the monasteries on this day all pick over the hulled rice. The number of days [for this work] is not limited. They bring the rice from the prefectural government and divide it among the monasteries according to the size of the congregation [of monks]. The number of bushels is not fixed, being either ten or twenty bushels [per monastery]. The monastery storehouse receives it and then apportions it out to the monks, either one *tou* or one *tou* and five *sheng* apiece. The monks on receiving the rice select the good from the bad [grains]. The broken ones are bad and the unbroken good. If one receives one *tou* of rice and divides it into the two types, the good will amount to only six *sheng*. The good and the bad are put into different bags and returned to the government. All the monasteries also follow this same practice, each selecting the good from the bad, and returning both to the government, which, on receiving the two types, presents the good to the Emperor as Imperial rice and retains the bad in the [local] government.

[The work of picking] is assigned to the civil and military [officials], including monks among the civil [officials], but not to the common people. When they pick over millet[29] in the prefecture, it is harder to do. The rice selected in Yang-chou is extremely black in color, but they reject unhulled and damaged grains, taking only the perfect ones. The other prefectures differ from this. I hear that the Minister of State picks over five bushels, the Military Inspector's Office the same, the Senior Secretaries two bushels, the Deputy Secretaries one bushel, and the military and monks one *tou* and five *sheng* or one *tou*.

The Minister of State recently invited Kuang-i, a Reverence of the *Vinaya* of the Hao-lin-ssu of Jun-chou,[30] to stay temporarily at the Hui-chao-ssu. Since the Minister of State intends to make this monk the Bishop[31] of this prefecture, he is now having him live at the K'ai-yüan-ssu. The Bishop will look after the affairs of the monasteries and also the monks of the Government General of Yang-chou. As a rule in China there are three categories [of Buddhist officers], Archbishops,[32] Bishops, and Monastery Supervisors. Archbishops control the monasteries of the whole land and regulate Buddhism. Bishops are only for the area of jurisdiction of a single Government General, and Monastery Supervisors are limited to a single monastery. Aside from these there are also the monastic officers and the Monastery Stewards.

At sundown the Bishop [came to] dwell in this monastery.

20th DAY.   At sunset the Bishop came, and he saw us and was sympathetic.

21st DAY.   After the forenoon meal they brought a letter of the sixth day of the twelfth moon of last year from the Ambassador and the others. I examined it, and it said that on the third day of the twelfth moon they safely reached the capital and were lodged in the Foreign Guest Court in the eastern half of the capital.[33] This document is as separately [recorded]. A letter of the same date from Murakiyo, an attendant of the Administrative Officer Naga[mine], said that at 8 A. M. on the third day of that moon they arrived at Ch'ang-lo Post Station[34] and were met by an Imperial representative who transmitted to them the Imperial inquiries. The envoys went to the Foreign Guest Court and have also had their audience with the Emperor. [From this] we have some idea of what has happened [at the capital].

25th DAY.   Through the monk Hui-wei of the Yen-kuang-ssu[35] I got hold of the *Hokke-enkyō*[36] in three scrolls.

[...]

TENTH MOON: 13th DAY.[37]   Ishō returned to the capital from Ch'u-chou, and I received two letters from the national government, one letter from the Ryōgon'in,[38] one letter from ... -kō Shōnin, and four knives. The twenty-four small ounces of gold which had been entrusted to T'ao Chung had already been used by Yu Sinŏn, the Interpreter of Ch'u-chou, and [Ishō] did not get any at all and returned empty handed. I received a note from the Interpreter saying that he had already used [the gold] in accordance with Master Ensai's instructions.[39] The letters, boxes, and envelopes had already been broken open.

On the 9th DAY *of the* TENTH MOON an Imperial edict was issued [to the effect that] all the monks and nuns of the empire who understand alchemy, the art of incantations, and the black arts,[40] who have fled from the army, who have on their bodies the scars of flagellations and tattoo marks [for former offenses, who have been condemned to] various forms of labor, who have formerly committed sexual offenses or maintain wives, or who do not observe the Buddhist rules, should all be forced to return to lay life. If monks and nuns have money, grains, fields, or estates, these should be surrendered to the government. If they regret [the loss of] their wealth and wish to return to lay life [in order to retain it], in accordance with their wishes, they are to be forced to return to lay life and are to pay the "double tax"[41] and perform the corvee. The text of the Imperial edict is separately [recorded].

The Commissioners of Good Works for the two halves of the capital notified the monasteries not to let the monks and nuns out, and they kept the monastery gates closed.

The monk Hsüan-hsüan made a memorial to the throne [to the effect] that he would make a "sword wheel"[42] and would himself lead the troops to defeat the land of the Uighurs. An Imperial edict ordered him to try to make the "sword wheel," but he did not succeed. It was because of the petition of the Minister of State Li Shen that this regulation [of the clergy] was started. The monk Hsüan-hsüan was guilty of falsehood, and he has been decapitated in accordance with Imperial command.[43]

The Commissioners of Good Works for the Streets of the Left and Right have notified the monasteries, investigated the monks and nuns and their wealth, and regulated them in accordance with the Imperial edict. It has been generally the same throughout the land. The various prefectures and commanderies have been notified by the Imperial Secretariat and Imperial Chancellery and are carrying out [the edict].

In the capital the Army Inspector Ch'iu opposed the Imperial edict and did not wish to regulate [the clergy]. Because of the Emperor's desires, this was not permitted, but he was allowed to request a stay of one hundred days, and he notified the monasteries not to let the monks and nuns leave the monasteries.

The Commissioner of Good Works for the Streets of the Left made a memorial to the throne [to the effect] that in the regulation of monks and nuns in accordance with the Imperial edict, aside from those who were decrepit with age and those who were strict in their observance of the rules, there were in all 1,232 [monks] and nuns who, because they valued their wealth, had voluntarily returned to lay life. The Commissioner of Good Works for the Streets of the Right memorialized the throne that, in the regulation of the monks and nuns in accordance with the Imperial edict, aside from those who were already decrepit with age and those who were strict in their observance of the rules, there were in all 2,219 monks and nuns who, because they valued their wealth, returned to lay life of their own volition.[44]

Receiving the Imperial edict, the Commissioners of Good Works for the Streets of the Left and Right memorialize the throne:

As for the monks and nuns who, in accordance with the Imperial edicts of the seventh and sixteenth days of the tenth moon of last year,[45] have been regulated and forced to return to lay life, those who, because they value their wealth, wish to return to lay life should be handed over to their respective places of origin and should be included among the payers of the "double tax."[46] Hereafter, cases such as this in the various provinces should all be handled in this manner.

As for the slaves they possess, monks may retain one male slave and nuns two female slaves. The others are to be returned and given over to the custody of their original families. Those who have no family should be sold by the government. Likewise, aside from their clothes and alms bowls, the wealth [of the monks and nuns] is to be stored up and its disposition is to await subsequent Imperial decree. If among the slaves retained by monks and nuns there are those who [are versed in] the military arts or understand medicine or the other arts, they may not be retained at all, nor may their heads be shaved in secret.[47] If there are violations [of these orders], the Monastery Administrators and Supervisors are to record them and notify the government. The other property and money should all be turned over to the Commissioners of Good Works to be regulated by them. So it is petitioned.

NOTES

1. January 19, 839. *Chi-wei* (*tsuchinoto hitsuji* in Japanese), referring to the year, is fifty-six in the hexagenary cycle, and *chia-yin*, referring to the day, is fifty-one. "Sixth year (*tsuchinoto hitsuji*)" is copied twice in *Tōji* and then is set off the second time with brackets.

2. Han Kan, who is famous for his paintings of horses, was active in the middle decades of the eighth century. Ennin has obviously confused one of his reputed places of origin, Ta-liang in Honan, with the name of the Liang dynasty (502–557).

3. *Fa-hua tao-ch'ang* (J. *hokke dōjō*), a place for the performance of *hokke-zammai*, one of the four types of religious concentration of the Tendai Sect. (Cf. Coates and Ishizuka 208.) This hall probably was

part of the Fa-hua-yüan ("Lotus Cloister") mentioned [. . .] below. The term *tao-ch'ang* (*dōjō*), "place of ritual," appears frequently in later parts of the text, and occasionally is used for the ritual itself [. . .].

4. Implying that Ietsugu made a sketch of the original painting and then made final copies on silk in the K'ai-yüan-ssu.

5. (Skr. Viśvabhadra or Samantabhadra), a Bodhisattva often pictured on a white elephant on the right-hand side of the Buddha Shakamuni.

6. *Bōen,* a Buddhist term meaning "to urge the establishment of karma affinities" by good acts such as the donation of money.

7. . . . in existence since at least the beginning of the eighth century. Cf. the *Ch'ung-hsiu Yang-chou-fu chih* 28.3b.

8. *Kechien.* See footnote 6.

9. See footnote 6.

10. The title is *Kōkyō Hosshi.* As frequently in this text, only the second character of the name (fan) is given.

11. *Kongō-kyō,* or more fully *Kongō-hannya-haramitsu-kyō* (Skr. *Vajracchedikā-prajñā-pāramitā-sūtra*).

12. As we learn below, this was the assessment for the whole Japanese party.

13. (see note 8) . . . presumably a Buddhist variation of a typical Chinese phrase of invitation.

14. It was concluded on Intercalary I 8 (see Intercalary I 5). In China anything lasting more than one full moon is said to have lasted two moons.

15. . . . presumably standing for Po-ssu-kuo and referring to an official emissary or, more probably, some merchants from Persia.

16. It is likely that this stands for Chan-p'o-kuo, or Champa, an ancient country on the southeastern coast of Indochina.

17. . . . may be Dewa, the northwestern province of the main island of Japan, but in that case the subsequent statement that they drifted south to reach this area cannot be correct. *DBZ* and *KIK* believe that this may have reference to the drifting of twenty Chinese to Dewa recorded in the *Nihon kiryaku* on 820 IV 27. The same source also records that some Chinese arrived in Japan on board a Korean ship on 819 VI 16.

18. . . . the western tip of the main island of Japan.

19. This custom may have some connection with the festivals held in Kyūshū and other parts of Japan on certain days in the first moon in which man-made figures of birds are exchanged. Cf. Nishimura Shinji, *Nihon kodai keizai (Kōkan-en)* 1.228 ff.

20. *Butsuden* (Ch. *Fo-tien*), a hall containing Buddhist images and often the main building of a monastery.

21. . . . Apparently this was a tree-like tower constructed of bamboo, with metal or pottery spoons for burning oil tied to the ends of the bamboo branches.

22. Che-hsi Province and Che-tung Province were late T'ang divisions corresponding roughly to the western and eastern halves of the modern Chekiang in the northeastern corner of the original Chiang-nan Province . . .

23. . . . the modern Chen-chiang across the Yangtse from Yang-chou.

24. The term is used incorrectly here, as if all Prefects or Regional Commanders were Ministers of State.

25. . . . *KIK* suggests a possible identification of these forty-two pictures. On 840 V 2 and 5 references are made to "seventy-two sages and saints."

26. The *kekkafuza* or *kafuza,* in which the sole of each foot faces upwards in the crook of the knee of the opposite leg, is the proper sitting posture for meditation (*enza*). In the *hankaza* or *hankafuza* the sole of only one foot faces upwards, and the other foot is under the knee of the opposite leg.

27. Monju or more fully Monjushiri (Skr. Mañjuśrī), the Bodhisattva of Wisdom, often pictured riding on a lion on the left side of Shakamuni and opposite Fugen. [...]

28. (Skr. *Jīvamjīvaka*) and (Skr. *Kalaviṅka*), both mythical Indian birds.

29. *Su-mi,* which occurs occasionally in this text, appears to be a term for millet.

30. There was a famous Hao-lin-ssu at Jun-chou (see note 23). . . .

31. *Sōjō* (Ch. *Seng-cheng*), whose functions in China are described below. In Japan this was the highest of the three categories of general officers of the church . . .

32. *Sōroku* (Ch. *Seng-lu*).

33. Ch'ang-an was divided for administrative purposes into eastern and western halves, called "the streets of the left" *(tso-chieh)* and "the streets of the right." Here we actually have "Eastern Capital," which was Lo-yang, [...] but Ennin no doubt means the eastern half of Ch'ang-an. The Foreign Guest Court (*Li-pin-yüan*) was established in 754 under the Bureau of Ceremonies for Foreigners (*Hung-lu-ssu*) for the reception of foreign emissaries (cf. Des Rotours 408–417).

34. Presumably at Ch'ang-lo Slope . . . about three km. due east of the eastern gates of the T'ang city of Ch'ang-an and near the present Shih-li-p'u.

35. . . . mentioned in the *Ch'ung-hsiu Yang-chou-fu chih* 28.20a, double column 7.

36. . . . listed in the *Bussho kaisetsu daijiten* 10.17 as no longer preserved.

37. The first day was November 6, 842.

38. Or more fully the Shuryōgon'in, one of the subdivisions of the Enryakuji (see note 7).

39. Waley 154 suggests that Ensai had appropriated it to pay his own debts.

40. This is the only known rendition of this important document, but it is so abbreviated and garbled in parts as to be scarcely intelligible. However, Okada (12.164–166) has interpreted it on the basis of the somewhat similar edict against Buddhism issued by Shih-tsung of the Chou dynasty almost three centuries earlier. (The latter document is the eleventh in *Ch'üan T'ang wen* 125.) Okada interprets [one of the terms] by equating it with two passages from Shih-tsung's edict [...] which refer to magical practices, including self-mutilation, which was particularly abhorrent to Chinese intellectuals.

41. *Liang-shui,* the chief land taxes during the second half of the T'ang period.

42. *Kenrin* or *kenrinhō* was a Buddhist magical practice intended to subdue evil forces.

43. Ennin apparently meant to indicate either that it was the unfortunate incident regarding Hsüan-hsüan which inspired Li Shen's petition (first mentioned on III 3) or that the two together were the immediate causes of the persecution. Beginning with the words "and he has been decapitated" and carrying through the words "notified the monasteries and investigated" in the next paragraph, the translation is based on seventeen small characters written on the margin of *Tōji* 137. . . .

44. This statement, of course, could not have been written until after the completion of the regulating, which Ennin records on 843 I 18, when he again gives the figure of 1,232 for the left streets but 2,259 for the right streets.

45. Since the first of these is presumably the edict Ennin described on 842 X 9, this document also clearly dates from 843. Okada (12.168–169) feels that, although this document is ostensibly a petition, the bulk of it sounds more like an edict, indicating that part of the text has been lost at this point and two different documents have thus been run together. It may, however, be that Ennin, in paraphrasing or abbreviating the document, inadvertently changed its tone from a petition to that of an edict.

46. See note 41.

47. That is, non-official ordination. . . .

REFERENCES

Coates, Harper Havelock, and Ryu-gaku Ishizuka, trans. 1925. *Honen the Buddhist Saint: His Life and Teaching.* Kyoto, Japan: Chionin.

Des Rotours, Robert. 1947. *Traité des fonctionnaires et traité de l'armée, traduits de la nouvelle histoire des T'ang* (Chap. XLVI-L). Leiden, The Netherlands: Brill.

Okada, Masayuki. "Jikaku Daishi no nitto kiko nit suite." Toyo gakuho.

Reischauer, Edwin O. 1955. *Ennin's Travels in T'ang China*. New York: Ronald Press.

Stibbs Anami, Virginia. 2007. *Following the Tracks of Ennin's 9th Century Journey: Diary of a Japanese Monk Revived in Today's China*. Beijing: China Intercontinental Press.

Waley, Arthur. 1952. *The Real Tripitaka and Other Pieces*. London: Allen and Unwin.

30
_____

From A Secret Plan of Government *and* Tales of the West

Honda Toshiaki, 1798

Honda Toshiaki's two chief works are *A Secret Plan of Government* (1798) and *Tales of the West* (1798). He embraced Western ideas and success not because he was necessarily pro-Western, but because he was pragmatic. He wanted to change Japan's economy and political power after two centuries of isolation. In *A Secret Plan of Government,* he focused on the need to create new shipping channels and to improve internal transportation. He envisioned overseas expansion even reaching the Aleutians, North America, and the frontier with Russia. He had big plans for Japan, but not all the admirers of European science and civilization were similar advocates of opening the country to foreign intercourse. Toshiaki was far ahead of his contemporaries in this regard, reacting strongly against the Tokugawa Shogunate's *sakoku,* or "closed country," policy.

Honda Toshiaki was born in 1744 in Echigo Province, Japan, and died in 1822 in what is today Tokyo. He was one of many scholars of "Dutch Studies" (*rangaku*), Dutch texts being the only Western books then accessible to the Japanese, thanks to the Dutch trading post at Nagasaki. He has been described as a mathematician and political economist who was also interested in astronomy and navigation—he even sailed to the northernmost Japanese island, known today as Hokkaido. His statistical studies of the Japanese economy stimulated his ideas about the relation of population growth and food supply, around the same time as both the English demographer Thomas Malthus and the Chinese scholar Hung Liang-chi were writing.

The second excerpt comes from Honda Toshiaki's two-volume *Tales of the West*, an investigation of Western techniques and ideas written to advocate the end of Japanese isolationism. Toshiaki goes to great—some would say fanciful—lengths in this work to praise European practice and usage at the expense of his own people and culture. Exaggerated though his claims are, Toshiaki and his few like-minded colleagues set the stage for Japan to rise to the challenge of the West, before Commodore Perry burst in on them in 1853. One of the reviewers of Donald Keene's edited volume *The Japanese Discovery of Europe, 1720–1830* describes Honda Toshiaki: "He was a wild man whose originality bordered on crankiness and whose patriotic ambitions spilled over into wishful thinking, but in his concern for doing something about the west, not just knowing about it—principally colonizing northwards—he was nevertheless an important predecessor of many much more influential men."

Translations such as this of Toshiaki's are rare in the literature of Japan. Unlike most of the selections in this anthology, Toshiaki's writings result not from actual contact through travel and face-to-face interaction, but rather from philosophical travel to the West—with pragmatic intentions. His work helped configure Japanese attitudes toward the West before Japanese travelers actually went west to Europe and the United States.

• • •

A SECRET PLAN OF GOVERNMENT

[...]

Of all the countries of Europe, Africa, Asia, and America, the one with the longest history is Egypt, which lies on the eastern shores of Africa. Over six thousand years ago Egypt was civilized. The Egyptians knew the art of writing, had a calendar at that remote date, and had a system of time notation that was in use throughout the country.

There later appeared a man named Christ in a country called Judea at the northwest end of Asia; he established the Catholic religion, which spread northward to Europe. In India, to the east, Sakyamuni appeared, and in China there were the sage-rulers Yao, Shun, Yu, T'ang, Wen, and Wu. All these men were teachers. Although what they taught differed, their doctrines amounted in each instance to an explanation of the way countries should be ruled and kept at peace. The particulars differed from country to country, but in all cases their meaning could be reduced to the principle of encouraging virtue and punishing vice.

Every country has a system of writing with which it transmits the teachings of its sages. Our country adopted Chinese writing and philosophy. Thus there are persons who enjoy a reputation for wide scholarship when all they know is the origin and history of one country, China. China became civilized three thousand years ago, and was thus over three thousand years slower than Egypt. Because of this difference in antiquity there are many faults in Chinese state policies that time has not as yet corrected.

The great number and inconvenience of Chinese characters make them useless in dealings with foreign countries. There are now barely three countries besides

China where they may be understood: Korea, the Ryukyus, and Japan. And even in these countries it is considered a difficult task to gain a thorough knowledge of them. The European alphabet has twenty-five letters, each of which may be written in eight different forms.[1] With these letters one can describe anything in the world. Nothing could be simpler. If one tried to memorize all the hundreds of thousands of Chinese characters and devoted one's life's energies to the task, how many could one actually learn? One would be sure to forget a great many. Even supposing that some man could learn them all, the best he could do would be to copy in Japan all the old Chinese stories. Rather than attempt to help the nation in this way, it would be simpler to turn to profit those resources with which Japan is naturally endowed.

There is a country called Italy at the southern end of Europe, lying between 35 [degrees] and 36 [degrees] N[orth] Lat[itude]. The good laws of Judea, which is separated from the southern tip of Italy by the Mediterranean Sea, appear to have been transmitted there. Thus it was that an enlightened ruler established a benevolent rule in Italy that was cheerfully obeyed by the people. He was considered so wise a man that he was given the title of Emperor of Europe, and for many generations afterward all Europe was under one sovereign. However, there came a foolish emperor whose regime was disordered. The subject countries then rebelled, and now all the countries formerly under one emperor are independent.

The capitals of France, Spain, England, and Holland have become thriving places. There are reasons for their prosperity that I shall attempt to explain by using the example of one of them. France long ago became the first country to manufacture cannon, and she also invented the method of making gunpowder for military use.[2] This gave her supremacy over the neighboring countries. She afterward used her inventions against those countries that were at war, thus compelling them to cease fighting. This was the great achievement of France. No matter how well equipped a nation was, even if it possessed mighty fortresses of steel, when French cannons were brought to bear or French privateers[3] attacked, not only would its fortresses fall, but very few of its people would be left to tell the tale. For fear of loss of human life France has not yet transmitted her inventions to other countries.

Europe was first with all other important inventions as well. Because astronomy, calendar making, and mathematics are considered the ruler's business, the European kings are well versed in celestial and terrestrial principles, and instruct the common people in them. Thus even among the lower classes one finds men who show great ability in their particular fields. The Europeans as a result have been able to establish industries with which the rest of the world is unfamiliar. It is for this reason that all the treasures of the world are said to be attracted to Europe. There is nowhere the Europeans' ships do not go in order to obtain the different products and treasures of the world. They trade their own rare products, superior implements, and unusual inventions for the precious metals and valuable goods of others, which they bring back to enrich their own countries. Their prosperity makes them strong, and it is because of their strength that they are never invaded or pillaged, whereas for their part they have invaded countless non-European countries. Spain has conquered many of the best parts of North and South America, and has moved her capital there.[4] Portugal, England, and France also have possessions in the Americas. The islands of the eastern oceans, such as Java, Sumatra, Borneo, and Luzon, are all European possessions. In those countries that have not as yet submitted to the Europeans, they have set up trading stations where they trade with the local rulers, seeking only to obtain the greatest possible profits. Even countries that have not yielded to European might are devoting all their energies to producing things for Europe. The real objectives of the European nations are thus achieved anyway.

There is no place in the world to compare with Europe. It may be wondered in what way this supremacy was achieved. In the first place, the European nations have behind them a history of five to six thousand years. In this period they have delved deep into the beauties of the arts, have divined the foundations of government, and have established a system based on a thorough examination of the factors that naturally make a nation prosperous. Because of their proficiency in mathematics, they have excelled also in astronomy, calendar making, and surveying. They have elaborated laws of navigation such that there is nothing simpler for them than to sail the oceans of the world.

There is no positive evidence on when European ships first reached the nations of the Far East, but it would appear from the descriptions in the "Foreign Events" section of the *Ming History* that they first came to China during the Wan-li era.[5] It cannot have been so very long, in any case, since they first came. As far as our country's history is concerned, it was not until the opening years of the seventeenth century that Dutch ships came regularly every year for trade. It is by such trade that the European nations have become so wealthy.

Nothing can compare in size with the great bell of Moscow or the copper lantern of France.[6] Nor is there elsewhere in the world anything to compare with their practice of building houses of stone. These are a product of their achievements in sailing over the world. To complete any great undertaking—for example, a major public works project or a powerful fortress—with the resources of one country alone is very difficult, and results in the exhaustion of the people; but when the resources of foreign countries are added, there is no undertaking, however great, that cannot be accomplished. This is true in particular of those nations of Europe celebrated for their strength and prosperity. Because they are cold northern countries, they could not afford any large-scale expenditures if they had only the resources of their own country to depend on. In spite of this example, however, the Japanese do not look elsewhere than to China for good or beautiful things, so tainted are the customs and temperament of Japan by Chinese teachings. Japanese are therefore unaware of such things as the four imperative needs, since they do not figure in the teachings of the Chinese sages.

[. . .]

The Dutch have been coming to Japan for over a hundred and fifty years. During this time their writings for the people of their country must have included many amusing descriptions of Japanese religious and popular observances. I shall relate a few of the things I have heard. When the Dutch go into temples and see peculiarly shaped images like those of Aizen, the Guardian King, or Kōjin, the Hearth God, or Shōten, with three eyes, six or seven arms sticking out of their backs, and their whole bodies colored vermilion and green, or like Fudō, with fire flaming from his back, they think that these must all be false gods, and that the Japanese people believe only in empty idols. Japan harbors an exceptionally great number of foolish customs, but among them the one of having the common people pray to such things must count as the most absurd. However, since this practice is of many years' standing, I suppose nothing can be done about it now.

Among the factory directors who have come to Japan was one named Kaempfer. He remained in Nagasaki for three years and studied Japanese history with the interpreters. After he had sailed home, he wrote a book about events in Japan from the Age of the Gods to the present. Later, when Natsume, Lord of Izumi, was governor of Nagasaki, a factory director named Arend Willem Feith visited Edo twice. He was especially familiar with Japanese institutions and wrote a book called *Amoenitatum*. When I examined this book, the first thing I saw was an account of the imperial palace giving a detailed description of various ceremonies observed, of the appearance of the lords assembled in the palace on the occasion of a performance of *nō* and *kyōgen*, and of various minor matters as well.[7]

In certain of their books of miscellaneous essays resembling our *Tsurezuregusa*,[8] the Dutch include illustrations of everything from people and beautiful scenery down to implements. These pictures, which are copperplate engravings of the type used in Holland, are even more beautiful than the real things. Since there have been a number of Japanese in times past who have left Japan for good and never returned, the Westerners have been able to learn everything about our country from them.

Someone asked me, "Are there formal, running-hand, and cursive forms to the European letters?" I answered, "In Europe they do not use characters such as we have in China or Japan. They have only twenty-five letters, and these have eight forms that differ from one another in much the same way as the formal, running-hand, and cursive scripts do. These twenty-five letters suffice for writing anything. In Japan there is a particular character used for every single thing, in imitation of Chinese usage, which means that there is an inconveniently large number of characters. For example, *ten* in Japanese is written with one character, while in Dutch it is *hemel*, four letters.[9] *Chi* in Japanese is another character, while *aard* has four letters. It might seem simpler to use one character than four letters, but if a man were to attempt to memorize the tens of thousands of Chinese characters, he might not succeed even if he devoted his life's energies to it. This would certainly be a great waste of time. Even supposing there were someone who could memorize them all, I doubt whether it would be of any service to the nation. It must have been because the Europeans realized this fact that they adopted a simpler method. Since the chief function of writing is considered to be the recording of facts and opinions, it would be far more expedient to do so with our Japanese kana instead of attempting to memorize all the thousands of Chinese characters.

A person may acquire the reputation of being a great Confucian scholar and yet not be really familiar with the affairs of even one country. However, I understand that in the West a man who has a reputation for wide learning will know the languages of over thirty foreign countries, and will be perfectly acquainted with their conditions and products as well. This must be because, having few letters to learn, Westerners can devote all their energies to the study of more important things.

In Europe a large goose quill is used for writing. The Europeans sharpen the end to a point and fill the opening with ink. They start writing from the top left, and write across to the top right. The sentences are written underneath one another in layers. Most of the world uses this kind of writing. Chinese characters are used only in Korea, the Ryukyus and Japan (to the east of China), in the various provinces of Manchuria (to the north), and in eastern India. European letters are used in the countries of Europe and America, along the southern and western coasts of Africa, from the islands south of eastern India to the islands south of China, in the islands south of Japan, in the eastern Ezo islands, in the area of Kamchatka, and as far as the continent of North America. All of these places use twenty-five letters in writing. Although each country has a different language, all of them may be recorded with the twenty-five letters. The alphabet resembles the Japanese kana, but the latter has twice as many symbols as there are letters. One might expect that any sound could be recorded exactly by means of the kana, but this is not so. The kana cannot represent even the forty-three tables of sound changes listed in the *Mirror of Sounds*,[10] and these are still not all the possible sounds.

If a careful study is made of their system of writing and ours, it will become apparent which is correct and which false. The failings in our way of life cause people to spend most of their time in idle and elegant pursuits, the number of which constantly increases. They are forgetful of themselves, and when they reach old age it is too late for them to repent. It was fortunate for the Westerners that they foresaw this eventuality and took steps to avoid a system of writing so profitless to the nation.

"Why is it that European painting differs from Japanese and Chinese painting?" someone asked. I replied, "European paintings are executed in great detail, with a view to making them resemble exactly the objects portrayed, so that they may be of some use. There are rules of painting to achieve this effect. They observe the division of sunlight into light and shade, and also what are called the rules of perspective. For example, if one wishes to depict a person's nose from the front, there is no way in Japanese painting to represent the central line of the nose. In the European style of painting, shading is used on the sides of the nose, and one may thereby perceive the height of the nose. Again, if one wishes to draw a sphere, there is no way to make the center appear to stand out in Japanese painting, but the Europeans shade the edges to permit one to see the height of the center. In Japan this is called *ukie*. Since it is the custom in Europe to consider above all whether something is of use to the nation, there is an academy that examines all books before they are printed so that no books of a frivolous or indecent nature will be published."

In Europe and Africa are the huge edifices known as the Seven Wonders, considered the most remarkable sights of the world. The pyramids of Egypt and the tower of Babylon were both built for worshiping God. The latter, constructed of stone and ornamented with sculptures, was round in shape, and of a splendor difficult to describe. A spiral staircase ascended to the summit, at which point the tower was very broad, with balconies on every side from which the mountains and oceans could be seen. There one was truly above the clouds. These two wonders were both located in countries at the eastern end of Africa.

There was also the Colossus of Rhodes, which stood astride the mouth of the harbor of that island. It is said that large ships with full sail could pass between its legs. It was built because ships traveling to and from the island at night were apt to run aground on the concealed rocks in the Mediterranean some six or seven miles around the harbor mouth. The Lord of Rhodes, deploring this situation, decided to erect an all-night beacon in the form of a human figure built with two bodies, holding aloft beacons on both sides. It was so constructed that ships had no trouble sailing through. Some years ago, when war broke out in that country, the Colossus was destroyed, and it is no longer standing. Its remains are nevertheless very considerable, and people from many countries come to view them. The destruction of the Colossus demonstrates that even in Europe the failure to obtain natural good government has resulted in disorder of the kind that prevailed in Japan up to the end of the sixteenth century.

The wonders that still exist at present are the Great Bell of Muscovy and the Stone Bridge of London. When Kōdayū returned to Japan a few years ago after seeing the Great Bell, he said that it looked like a small mountain. In the capital city of London there is a broad river called the Thames. A stone bridge spans its width of about three ri, and at both ends there are markets and temples. Large ships with sails raised can pass under the bridge. The construction of the stone embankment along the river and of the bridge itself is so magnificent that one doubts it was accomplished by human labor. When it comes to grand edifices, no country in the world can compare with England.

There is also no country comparable to England in the manufacture of very fine things. Among the articles imported into Japan by the Dutch, there have been none more precious than the watches. Some of them are so exquisite that hairs are split to make them. London is thought to produce the finest such workmanship in the world. Next comes Paris in France, and then Amsterdam in Holland. In these three capitals live people virtually without peer in the world, who are the handsomest of men. The houses in their towns and cities, even in the outskirts, are built of stone. They are from two to five stories high and surpassingly beautiful. Why is it that the people of these three cities, who are human beings like everyone else, have attained such excellence? It is because many centuries have elapsed since they were civilized and because their political institutions are founded on the principles of natural government. Their nations are thus so prosperous that even among the commoners one finds many wealthy persons. That is why the Europeans do not begrudge expenses but insist that even the smallest parts of their implements be made with the highest degree of skill.

Since the merit system is practiced in Europe, talented and capable people all flock to these three capitals, and it is because of their efforts that these cities stand unique in the world. It would seem that the inhabitants of these cities must have some special cleverness, but the secret of their supremacy is inseparable from the above considerations. Their prosperity is probably entirely due to the excellence of their political system and the great number of years of experience they have had. This is not an isolated instance, and the excellence of their whole society cannot be conjectured from Japanese and Chinese equivalents.

NOTES

1. By this Honda meant capital, lower-case, italic, etc.

2. There is a confusion here between *furanki,* an old name for firearms, and *Furansu,* the name for France. See Paul Pelliot, "Le Hôja et le Sayyid Husain," *T'oung Pao,* Vol. 38 (1938), 204–205.

3. *Dokujinsen,* literally, "solitary fast ships."

4. Possibly Honda, hearing of the Viceroy of Peru and his court, imagined that the Spanish capital had been moved from Madrid to Lima.

5. Covering the years 1573–1620.

6. A confusion for Pharos? The lantern of Pharos was one of the wonders of the world.

7. This work was actually by Kaempfer, not Feith, and does not contain any account of the imperial palace. Probably a triple confusion, involving Kaempfer's *History of Japan* (Glasgow, 1906).

8. A book of short essays by Kenkō Hōshi (1283–1350), translated into English by Donald Keene under the title *Essays in Idleness* (New York, 1967).

9. Either Honda could not count the number of letters in *hemel* (heaven), or there has been a misprint in the text.

10. *Inkyō* (in Chinese, *Yün-ching*), a late T'ang work on phonetics.

REFERENCE

Dore, R. P. 1972. "Review of Donald Keene's *The Japanese Discovery of Europe, 1720–1830.*" *Journal of the American Oriental Society,* Vol. 92, No. 1 (January–March): 154.

31

From As We Saw Them:
The First Japanese Embassy
to the United States

Masao Miyoshi, 1979

Japan's closed-door policy came to an end in 1853 with the arrival of the American mission led by Commodore Matthew C. Perry. Five years later, a Japanese-American treaty
stipulated that a Japanese envoy would be sent to the United States "for the exchange of
ramifications." Thus, in 1860, the first embassy to the United States, including the chief
ambassador and seventy-eight staff members, left for the United States. Beyond seeking
ratification of the treaty, the Japanese envoy was charged with observing the condition of
the American military, technological advances, and the overall strength of the United
States. The ambassadors arrived in the United States on the eve of the American Civil War,
and during a time of change for Japan as well, though not exactly comparable.

Before the 1860s embassy's departure, most of the leading experts on the world outside
Japan, including those who had directly negotiated the first treaty with Townsend Harris
and other U.S. diplomatic representatives, were removed from the embassy roster during a
period of intrigue. Members of the embassy traveled under the mindful eye of the *metsuke*
watcher. Factional struggles in Japan that led to depositioning senior figures may have made
embassy members particularly self-conscious in front of one another, and these political
machinations influenced the goals of the mission.

Published in 1979, Masao Miyoshi's book on this first diplomatic exchange followed the
notorious uproar provoked by his friend Edward Said's *Orientalism*. The book's title, *As We
Saw Them: The First Japanese Embassy to the United States (1860)*, is ironic, implying the
centrality of *we* and *them*. The excerpts used here, taken from a collection of personal diary
reflections and articles from the American press, are evocative illustrations of cross-cultural
encounters in the wake of centuries of national isolation from the West. The visitors' stay in

Miyoshi, Masao. 2005 [1979]. *As We Saw Them: The First Japanese Embassy to the United States*, Philadelphia: Paul Dry Books. Pp. 32–36, 61–62, 70–74, 79, 84–87, 90–91, 124–125, 131, 185–186. Reprinted
with the permission of Paul Dry Books, Inc., www.PaulDryBooks.com.

1860 was especially jarring for them because of the language barrier. The chapter "Travelers" includes a discussion of discomfort with the American diet, sleeping arrangements, and clothing. On the other hand, the Japanese were not surprised by the sex trade in America, one similar to its counterpart in their own country.

Observations made by the 1860 embassy bear some semblance to those of the Americans who encountered the visitors and who likened the Japanese ambassadors to monkeys and treated them as objects of circuslike entertainment. In turn, the Japanese likened the American congressmen to Nihonbashi fishmongers and the dancing dignitaries at a formal ball to "a number of mice running around and around" (Miyoshi 2005 [1979]:71). At the same time, overlapping forms of racism are present. Both American and Japanese denigrate blacks and identify the superiority of whites. However, the absence in the United States of the ceremony and gestures that the Japanese traditionally employed to designate hierarchical relationships and signs of reverence or respect confounded the Japanese in their encounter with the U.S. president and other high-ranking officials. For example, "the President's ordinary business suit at the reception was a source of wonderment. The Ambassadors— who had a chance to glimpse the Supreme Ruler of Japan before their departure—expected to see in the President a similarly mighty person, elaborately dressed and differentially attended. Since the Shogun was practically a deity, no one dared to look at the divine person; likewise, they expected Americans to lie prostrate before their President, the Shogun of America" (84). The comparison was made without any understanding of the fundamental differences between the political ideologies governing each of the two countries. It was first contact.

Another telling episode is that of the controversial gift exchange. The Americans gave expensive and flamboyant materialistic objects as gifts to the Japanese, whereas the Japanese gave materially humble, largely symbolic gifts. In Japanese culture a gift of material value would constitute a bribe, an insult to an honorable recipient.

Although contemporaries disagreed about what, if anything, this first embassy had accomplished, the travelers took home important knowledge concerning military arms and naval shipyards, useful as a basis for later government policy decisions. Miyoshi's specialty is comparative literature and literacy criticism, not history. His interpretations are included here as an "in-between" commentator. Miyoshi was born in Tokyo in 1928, graduated from the University of Tokyo in 1928, and then, with a Fulbright scholarship, received his PhD at New York University. His later writings focused on relations between Japan and the United States, and until his death in 2009 he held an endowed chair in Japanese language and literature at the University of California, San Diego.

. . .

TRAVELERS

[. . .]

Throughout their trip, the Ambassadors seem to have been quite passive about their plans. The itinerary was set, the transportation arranged, and the entire expense paid by the United States (that is, federal and city governments and volunteer organizations).[1] The only signs of initiative lay in their persistent attempts to refuse invitations to visit officials and cities. The triumvirate composed as many as four letters to the Secretary of State (out of the total of ten they wrote while in America) in which they stubbornly insisted on the need to hurry back as soon as possible. In fact, they were quite reluctant to visit Baltimore, Philadelphia, and New York.[2] But even this resistance was not really a voluntary decision: they had been ordered by the Council of State to avoid everything but the barest essentials and to return home quickly.[3] While in Hawaii, for instance, the Ambassadors were approached by the Foreign Minister of that island kingdom to discuss the possibility of concluding a treaty similar to the one with the United States. The Ambassadors' response was both brief and decisive: greetings (*aisatsu*) would be sent as soon as they returned home.[4] They did initiate a few local visits on their own, but these short trips—for instance, to the Philadelphia Mint for assaying the Japanese coins or to Grace Church in New York City to observe a private wedding—were not frequent; they usually went to places suggested by the protocol officers. Active travel requires at least some understanding of the land and people one visits, and the 1860 Embassy lacked even minimal knowledge of the United States.

It is not easy now to appreciate these men's difficulties in America. Not to speak English was bad enough; not to know what to expect next was worse. [...]

[...]

Such practical hardships being too numerous and tedious to list, let it suffice here to quote from a memoir of Fukuzawa Yukichi as he recalled the experience some forty years later:

> Then we were taken to a hotel. All the floors were covered by carpets—the kind of fabric the richest Japanese splurged on, spending a fortune for square inches so a wallet or pouch could be made. The fabric was spread all over the floor in these huge rooms. And people stepped on them in their street shoes. They didn't change their shoes, so we didn't take off our *zori* either. At once we were served drinks. When a bottle was opened, it exploded with a frightening noise. The strange drink was champagne. There was something floating in our glasses. Of course we didn't know they could have ice in such warm spring weather. Those glasses standing in a row before us, and we trying to drink it up! Some were frightened by the floating objects and spat them out; some were loudly crunching on the cubes. It took us some time before we all realized it was ice. We wanted to smoke. There were no tobacco trays [*tabako bon*], nor ash trays [*hai fuki*]. I lit my pipe from the fire in the stove. I suppose there were matches on the table, but we didn't know what they were. Well, I lit my pipe, but finding no tray to put the ashes in, I pulled out tissue paper from my breast pocket, emptied the ashes into it, and crushing the fire out carefully and twisting the paper into a ball, I put it back into my pocket. I was trying to have another puff, when smoke began to rise from my kimono sleeve. My God! the fire wasn't out, and it was spreading to the pocket![5]

Inexperience, or ignorance, is of course a great incentive for discovery and wonderment. Anything unfamiliar fascinated the men in the Embassy, and practically everything was unfamiliar. Captain Katsu randomly lists his observations in his memoir: the Battery, the city officials, women's clothes, women, ferry boats, gas lights, hospitals, brick buildings, the Mint, printing machines, fire engines, horse carriages, dance parties, theaters, fencing, the naval shipyard, newspapers, and so on.[6] Most records left by the men in the Embassy describe at length the appearance, structure, and operation of such things that happened to catch their eyes.

But even in the gathering of simple data there were serious impediments. The most obvious of these was the unfamiliarity with English. [...]

The strict control of the Embassy members' physical movement was another hindrance to meaningful observation. Before they left Japan, the Ambassadors and Oguri discussed with the office of *metsuke* the method of regimenting their behavior. The envoys' proposal, which was accepted, was to issue to all lower-ranking men a special permit for every outing from their lodgings, and to give oral approval to every higher official's visit out. In accordance with this, the whole entourage was often ordered to stay inside the premises of the hotel. Even when allowed to go out, a curfew of 6:00 P.M. was established, which the Ambassadors themselves were reluctant to break.[7] Furthermore, members were forbidden to wander out alone. This rule was merely an extension of their home habit rather than a specially instituted regulation for foreign travel. No official business was ever transacted by a single individual at home; it naturally followed that the same discipline applied abroad.

Still, some of the younger and lower men were impatient, and several voiced their dissatisfaction. [...]

In fact, Tamamushi, the most articulate of all the diarists in the Embassy, confided his rage to the eighth part of a copy of his *Kō-Bei nichiroku* (The chronicle of the voyage to America). This last section, unlike the preceding seven sections, was clearly marked as "Not to be seen by anybody else."

THE STAY IN WASHINGTON

While in this city, we are prohibited, by the strictest order of our own authorities, from taking even a step outside the hotel. Even when we are allowed to go out for some compelling reason, we are accompanied by our officials. Most officers are wasting their days in the city trying to buy watches and woolen material and velvet, and none are interested in discovering the institutions and conditions of America. People are purchasing things by twos and threes, even by fours and fives, so that they may sell them upon return home. They dash around looking for the cheapest store. How disgraceful it is! Wishing to observe schools and colleges, I asked for permission several times, but I couldn't go since no officer was willing to accompany me there. Needless to say, I couldn't go to charity houses or orphanages, which should be the first on the itinerary if gathering information were the purpose. Among the members of this Mission no one—from the Ambassadors down—is interested in the conditions and customs of the Americans. They [the Americans], on the other hand, are trying to show us everything without any intent of concealment. But no one on our side cares. Some say that the Ambassadors have confined themselves in their rooms never stepping out once and being very cautious. But some people are laughing at them, because they believe that the reason for the Ambassadors' staying home is the fear of the strange American manners, and also the fear that their ignorance and incompetence might lead them into serious trouble. The lower officers, too, decline the Americans' invitations. And only after repeated urgings they consent to go. Apparently they believe that they are so important that they should remain aloof. But actually, their behavior shows that they are merely complying with the Americans' wishes. So how can they be haughty even if they want to be! In buying watches and woolen fabric, some connoisseurs are spending as much as one hundred or even two hundred silver dollars on one item. These are nothing but toys. If the superiors are preoccupied with such things, no one should blame their inferiors for greedily trying to make a profit. Alas, so many things are being done in this voyage that disgrace our country.[8]

[. . .]

VIEWS

[. . .]

How about their reaction to the American racial situation just, as it so happens, on the eve of the Civil War? (Abraham Lincoln was nominated by the Republican party on May 18, while the Embassy was in Washington, D.C.) Did they have any inkling of the enormity of the events that were soon to follow? Do we see anything that might suggest some reaction—however aloof—on the part of the Japanese visitors? For Yanagawa, the racial separation is a simple fact: "The blacks are inferior as human beings and extremely stupid. They are segregated from the whites, and no blacks are wealthy. They work only as servants for the whites, and are forbidden to enter any gathering places for the whites such as our hotel, churches, restaurants, exhibitions, or theatres."[9] Kimura Tetsuta, an attendant for Inspector Oguri, similarly rationalizes the black and white situation: "The laws of the land separate the blacks. They are just like our *eta* caste. But they [the whites] employ the blacks as their servants. The whites are of course intelligent, and the blacks stupid. Thus the seeds of intelligence and unintelligence are not allowed to mix together."[10] Even Sano Kanae, whose diary is packed with unbiased and factual information gleaned from geography textbooks, deviates for once and dismisses the black race, while maintaining his usual matter-of-fact tone.[11]

Most seem unable even to distinguish between the blacks and native Americans. Satō Tsunezō Hidenaga, a servant cook, divides the Americans into whites and blacks, calling the latter "the natives of this land, an imbecile race."[12] Tamamushi, too, makes the same error, although his comments are, unlike most others', moderated by sympathy:

> Of all the people the blacks number one-sixth. Among them there are those who are like blacks but not blacks and like whites but not whites. They come from the mixing of the whites and blacks. All these people are not permitted to participate in the politics of the country. They are employed as servants for the whites or in humble and menial work. But the blacks are the indigenous race of America, and the whites are the English race. It is sad that the guest should usurp the place of the host. Yet the difference between intelligence and idiocy is undeniable. Thus there appears to be something unalterable about the race of a man.[13]

Most men in the Embassy, in short, took the race and slavery question for granted, as though the blacks as a people did not really exist.

There are, however, a few cases where some actual contact seems to have occurred. Morita Kiyoyuki tells a story that is unique among these documents. As the fourth-highest ranking officer on the Mission, he was assigned a personal escort by the State Department when the envoys were received by the President at the White House on May 19. Morita traveled in a carriage with a William Preston, of Louisville, Kentucky, who had been the U.S. Minister to Spain:

> Preston was a big man, around thirty-eight or thirty-nine years of age. He was proud as he pointed out the flags of the Rising Sun to me, saying "very good." As he singled out black women, he said they were the same color as the black wool suit he had on, and sneered at them, calling them ugly. He seemed very pleased with the white people and, whenever he saw white women, said "very good," and pointed them out to me.[14]

Preston's crude remarks on the blacks addressed to a Japanese guest raise a few questions. Does this mean the diplomat felt that the Japanese stood on the white side of the unpassable color line and, further, that his Japanese guest would of course concur with him? Or was he being cynically nonchalant as to the relative racial position of his listener—an attitude that was as contemptuous as that shown toward the blacks? Isn't his boorish behavior itself an expression of supercilious disregard for the Japanese? Morita says nothing about his reaction, but one does suspect that he might not have recorded this episode unless he felt something more tangled and murky underneath.

The same Morita relates yet another experience, this time directly involving a Japanese encounter with a black:

> Ever since our arrival here, all of us had been giving presents (like fans, pictures, and toys) to children, hotel employees, waiters, and waitresses who had been attending us. Almost everyone had been provided with something by now, and those Americans who owned no Japanese gifts looked almost embarrassed. But it seems that those who had received our presents turned out to be mostly white and attractive

people. One day a black woman approached one of our servants who spoke some English, tearfully confiding to him that since Nature had given her a black exterior, she was scorned by everyone and was not lucky enough to be given presents from anybody, and that she hated herself. She also said white people—even children— were getting presents from the Japanese, but she and her people who had such an ugly look received nothing. He felt so sorry for her that he gave her a fan, and she was very grateful. It seems that the whites are beautiful and shrewd and intelligent; and the blacks are ugly and stupid. So the whites always despise the blacks. There are some white-and-black marriages, and their children are between white and black in complexion.[15]

[...]

Most members of the Embassy had seen at least a few Western men before they left Japan. But very few in the Embassy, if any, had seen a Western woman before.[16] [...]

At Secretary Cass's ball in the Embassy's honor, Muragaki had ample opportunity to observe American women:

We arrived at Cass's residence. I wondered about the nature of the ceremony we were going to perform on this occasion, since it was an invitation from the Prime Minister. To our great surprise, however, we found that the hall, passages, and rooms were all packed with hundreds of men and women. Innumerable gas lamps were hanging from the ceilings, and the glass chandeliers decorated with gold and silver were reflected in the mirrors. It was as brilliant and dazzling as day. Though we did not know what was happening, we somehow managed to make our way through the crowd to the room where Cass and his family stood, and were greeted by them. Even his grandchildren and daughters came to shake hands with us. Although we sat on chairs, everyone in the room also came to shake our hands. Since there was no interpreter around, I did not understand at all what was being said. The crowd was extremely dense. DuPont took my hand and led me to an adjoining room, where a large table was laid with gold and silver ware. At the center of the table were the Japanese and American flags to express friendship. We had some drinks and food at the table. Soon we were led away to another large room; its floor was covered with smooth boards. In one corner, there was a band playing something called "music" on instruments that looked like Chinese lutes. Men were in uniform with epaulets and swords, and women with bare shoulders were dressed in thin white clothes. They had those wide skirts around their waists. Men and women moved round the room couple by couple, walking on tiptoe to the tune of the music. It was just like a number of mice running around and around. There was neither taste nor charm. It was quite amusing to watch women's huge skirts spread wider and wider like balloons as they turned. Apparently, high officials and older women, as well as young people, are very fond of this pastime. The men and women went to the table for refreshments, then coming back for another dance. This, we were told, would continue all night. As for myself, I was astonished by the sight, and wondered whether this was a dream or reality. We asked DuPont to say good-night to the host for us, and left for the hotel.

Admittedly, this is a nation with no order or ceremony [*rei*], but it is indeed odd that the Prime Minister should invite an ambassador of another country to an event of this sort! My sense of displeasure is boundless: there is no respect for order and ceremony or obligation [*gi*]. The only way to exonerate them is by recognizing that all this absence of ceremony issues from their feeling of friendship.

> All is strange,
> Appearance and language,
> I must be in a dream-land.

Women are white and beautiful, and they are handsomely dressed with gold and silver decorations. Although I am becoming accustomed to their appearance, I find their reddish hair unattractive, and their eyes look like those of dogs. Now and then, though, I see a black-haired woman who also has black eyes. They must be descendants of some Asian race. Naturally they look very attractive.[17]

One notes in this passage that our Ambassador is not quite so sure of himself as usual. He is visibly tense, not knowing the nature of the occasion. In his own country, a foreign ambassador—or any other high official—would be received with a dignified ceremony undefiled by the presence of women (like, say, the reception of a visiting cardinal at the Vatican). Of course, there might be a banquet later on, and even the company of women might not be altogether unlikely then, but those women would be professionals trained to entertain men. For the warriors and officials of higher ranks and their wives and daughters to mingle together and dance and enjoy themselves in self-abandon is an outrage in decorum that no self-respecting samurai would ever tolerate. Muragaki is indeed distressed by these strange women, but also fascinated, as his detailed observation testifies. But before he admits their attractiveness to himself, his samurai sense of aloofness must intervene. And as is usually the case with him, he writes a *waka* which, again typically, tries to remove his experience as a dream, a remote experience. The poem having cleansed his fears, he is now ready to be a little more honest with himself. So he calls the women "white and beautiful." He is even willing to face the sexual threat he feels vaguely in these women (the "eyes of dogs," or bitches?).[18] Then he re-collects himself with the image of the women of his own kind which was projected on the darkhaired women he saw at the ball.

The dance party was, understandably, a subject for several men of the Embassy. They had been utterly unprepared for such a form of entertainment. Morita Kiyoyuki, who went to the party at Cass's, calls it "indescribably noisy." He too is nervous: "Although there was very little that was licentious or lewd, it was unbearable to watch."[19] Ono Tomogorō, forty-three years old, is not amused either. Although he was quite comfortable with his American hosts at the Mare Island Naval Shipyard and was sufficiently interested in the American women to write about them at fair length, their dance was nothing but a "bore that annoyingly dragged on and on," and their singing reminded him of the "gibberish scream of a bewitched woman."[20] Hidaka Keizaburō Tameyoshi, a twenty-seven-year-old *metsuke* officer, was also present at a party, where "women and maidens were nude from shoulders to arms, and they had various ornaments in their hair. The way men and women, both young and old, mixed in the dance, was simply insufferable to watch."[21] Even the eighteen-year-old Fukushima dismisses the dancing as no more than a lot of "bouncing and leaping," and the ball itself as "noisy and uninteresting."[22] The kindest remark by far on American dancing comes from Muragaki's aide Nonomura, who compares the "dazzling" dancers to "butterflies crazed by the sight of flowers."[23]

Ambassador Muragaki was at his gallant and diplomatic best when he dined at the presidential dinner:

> The President sat at the center, while his niece Lane sat opposite to him, with Shimmi sitting on her right and I on her left.... Including the women and high-ranking officials sitting with us, there were about thirty people at the table. We had two interpreters standing behind us. Soon soup was served, followed by various kinds of meat, and of course champagne, and other drinks. Aware of the President's presence, we were very careful about our manners. It was rather amusing to watch and imitate the table manners of a woman sitting next to me. Lane was behaving like the head of the house, supervising everything during the dinner. Her power and dignity were so impressive that she might have been taken for the Queen, and her uncle, the President, for her Prime Minister. She told us to have more wine, asking in the meantime questions about our country. Most of her questions were posed from the American point of view, and I found them hard to answer. I gave noncommittal replies as best I could to her questions like "how many court ladies does the Shogun keep?" or "what are their manners and customs like?" She also asked which women did I find superior, Japanese or American?—a question I found amusing, since it was, after all, so typically feminine. When I told her the American women are the more beautiful of the two with their fair complexion, she and her companions looked very pleased.[24]
> [...]

[...]

Fukuzawa Yukichi had been the head tutor (*jukuchō*) for several years in the Ogata School in Osaka, noted for its curriculum in Western learning. So he was not at all surprised, according to his reminiscence forty years later, when he saw in San Francisco the telegraph and other signs of advanced technology. But he had difficulty understanding the "social, political, and economical" makeup of the Americans:

> One day I felt curious about the whereabouts of George Washington's descendants, and asked someone about them. His answer was, "There should be a female descendant somewhere who married somebody, but I don't know exactly." He was so indifferent to the question that I was quite taken aback. It struck me as really strange. Of

course, I knew thoroughly well that the United States was a republic with a new president elected every four years, but still I thought Washington's offspring were very important people. After all, I had in mind Lord Minamoto Yoritomo and Shogun Tokugawa Ieyasu. That's why I didn't understand his answer.[25]

Probably he was less familiar with the American social-political structure than this passage suggests; for a few pages later in the same autobiography, he confesses his ignorance more directly. When he went to England a few years later, he didn't even understand the function of Parliament.[26] And if Fukuzawa, one of the best "Western experts" of the time, knew so little, how much did the rest of the Embassy members comprehend?

[...]

More than anything else, the presidency of the United States baffled the Japanese. Before the visit most of them had been under the vague impression that the President was more or less identical with the Shogun. The letters from the Council of State, for instance, were always addressed to "Your Majesty, the President of the United States," as they must have copied from the American letters addressed to "Your Majesty the Tycoon, the Emperor of Japan." Although the books on the West that were largely based on Chinese sources used words like *taiseikan, saijōkan, shutōryō seitōryō, sōtōryō,* and *daitōryō* for "president," Nonomura calls Buchanan *kokuō* (king), as does Yanagawa.[27] James Buchanan, however, did not behave like a monarch. He was incomprehensibly "unassuming and simple."[28] When an entertainment was offered at Willard's in Washington, the President stopped by with his nieces, and, as was the custom in those happy days before the introduction of the Secret Service, he even walked home to the White House alone without a single guard in attendance.[29] The President's ordinary business suit at the reception was itself a source of ceaseless wonderment. The Ambassadors—who had had the chance to glimpse the Supreme Ruler of Japan before their departure—expected to see in the President a similarly mighty person, as elaborately dressed and as deferentially attended. Since the Shogun was practically a deity, no one dared to look at his divine person; likewise, they expected Americans to lie prostrate before their President, the Shogun of America. After the initial shock at the plebeian interview, various attempts were made to comprehend the republican system of kingship. Who becomes the president? How is he chosen? Yanagawa's version is fairly typical:

> At the time of the expiration of a President's term, the Prime Minister and a few other high officials (who have distinguished themselves with their own talents) are considered. If the Prime Minister and these nobles all decline the offer, then they—together with the retired Presidents—hold an "auction" [*nyūsatsu*] and choose the highest bid. According to another theory, the virtuous men are "auctioned" from the entire population, except for the blacks. On public occasions, the officials wear ceremonial attire with splendor and dignity. In private life, however, they are no different from

common people, and they engage in commerce and agriculture in plain clothes. The high officials including the President walk around the city without any attendant, and nobody greets him either by bowing or removing his hat. Once indoors, even the President takes off his hat.[30]

[...]

Muragaki's attitude toward America as a country of barbarians is confirmed at every point by his observations. Notice, for instance, his negative reaction to the burial of two *Roanoke* sailors at sea:

Two sailors, who had fallen ill some time ago, died. Their bodies, each wrapped in canvas and weighted with shot, were brought on deck. The chaplain officiated at the funeral service, attended by the Commodore and other officers on the ship. While the music was being played, the bodies were thrown into the sea, each from either side of the ship. The crew were seriously worried over the many cases of illness among them, caused, as they told us, by staying too long at Aspinwal.

We are told that it is a rule in the United States Navy that the bodies of all officers, up to the captain's rank, are taken to the nearest port for funeral, and that in the case of a commodore or an officer of a higher rank, his body is encased in a glass coffin, and sent back to his home; in the case of sailors, their bodies are buried in the sea. We indeed feel sorry for the unfortunates who died on the high sea.

We were surprised, however, to see the Commodore himself attending the funeral of mere common sailors. [...]

[...]

When he witnessed the Americans respectfully removing their hats as they passed George Washington's grave, he noted that "even in this barbaric country that knows no *rei*, people pay their respects to Washington in accordance with the laws of nature."[31] Secretary Cass's "mild and dignified" manner at their first interview did not satisfy the envoy because Cass treated him cordially as though they had been old friends "without the slightest etiquette [*rei*]."[32] We have already seen his reaction to the ball at Cass's residence. Finally, his response to the presidential reception at the White House runs as follows:

We gathered together and talked of our experience on this memorable day. The President is a silver-haired man of over seventy years of age, and he has a most genial manner without losing noble dignity. He wore a simple black costume of coat and trousers in the same fashion as any merchant, and had no decoration or sword on him. All the high-ranking officials were dressed in the same way as the President, whereas the army and navy officers wore epaulets (the gold tassels attached to the shoulders, of which the length marked the rank), and gold stripes on the sleeves of their costumes (of which the number represented the rank, three stripes signifying the highest); and they carried a sword at their side. It seemed to us a most curious custom to permit the presence of women on such a ceremonious occasion as today. We remembered how we were received at the Sandwich Islands by the women alone—after the main event of our presentation—with somewhat greater formalities; this difference, we attributed, although we were not well acquainted with Western customs and manners, to the fact that the Sandwich Islands constituted a monarchy. The United States is one of the greatest countries in the world, but the President is only a governor voted in [nyūsatsu] every four years. (There will be a changeover on October 1 this year. We heard them suggest a certain man; when we asked how they could tell before the "auction," they answered that this man would be the President, because he was related to the present one. Judging from such remarks, I don't believe that the fundamental laws of this country will last much longer.) The President is thus not a king. Nevertheless, since the Shogun's letter was addressed to him, we adopted such manners of etiquette [rei] as were appropriate to a monarch. It was pointless, however, to put on the formal kariginu robe in his honor, since the Americans attach little importance to hierarchic distinction, and dispense with all ceremony [reigi]. We were, however, exceedingly happy and satisfied to have attained the goal of our mission here, an achievement worthy of any man's ambition, when we learned that the President was highly appreciative and took pride in receiving the first mission from Japan in his country before any other. We were told that he was letting the newspapers show our party dressed in kariginu.[33]

[...]

To Muragaki's traditional hierarchic views, Tamamushi's ideas stand in sharp contrast. Observing the American crew, whom his master dismissed as "disorderly," he makes the following comments:

Their discipline is very strict. But the sailors do not kneel down even before the captain, although they do take off their hats when they meet him. Actually, they make no distinctions between the captain and the other officers, or the officers and the common sailors. The high and low mix freely, and even the common sailors do not especially seem to worship their captain. The captain too does not seem to insist on his high rank, and behaves like their colleague. Their friendship is extremely close, and in case of a crisis they do their best to help each other. When faced with a calamity, they mourn together. These are things so diametrically opposite to what goes on in our country. The moon was brilliant tonight.

In our country the ceremonial rules [reihō] are very strict, and we are not easily granted an audience with the ruler, who is feared like a demonic god. Following his example, anyone with the slightest rank behaves pompously and insultingly to his inferiors. The friendship is so negligible that when a misfortune hits us there is no expression of sympathy. We are greatly different from them. This being the case, who would ever do his best when calamity strikes? Perhaps this is a result of long-lasting peace that has spoiled and softened us dangerously. Deplorable. Should we then prefer a society with no ceremonial rules [reihō usuku] but with intimate personal relations to a society with strict ceremonial rules but no intimate personal relations? I am not necessarily setting a high value on the barbarians' customs, but in view of the recent developments the answer should be obvious.[34]

[...]

Tamamushi was present at the White House reception of the Ambassadors, and was likewise impressed by the unassuming dignity of the President. He was neither upset by the presence of women nor bothered by the absence of elaborate etiquette.[35] His visit to the Capitol, too, was quite differently described from Muragaki's:

> After about 200 yards, we came to the Congress Building called "Captain [Capitol] House." This is the most immense building in Washington and stands three or four storeys high. There is an entrance in every one of the four sides, and the perimeter is almost half a mile long. . . . When they discuss things, the officials and their secretaries sit at the center on the lowest level, and all the people involved in the matters discussed sit on the higher levels. Thus the officials are clearly seen and scrutinized by people, and no one will suspect those in office, who might otherwise secretly mix the public and private [kōshi] interests.[36]

To notice a conflict between the Vice-Ambassador and a menial servant is not to cast the former into the role of an aristocrat of the *ancien regime,* nor to call the latter a bourgeois revolutionary.[37] As we will see later on, Tamamushi's background is as Confucian as anybody else's, and in his later life, too, he leaned toward the feudal Tokugawa rule. At the same time, one notes in Tamamushi's record an articulate challenge to the dominant values.[38] It is even possible to see here a loosening of the vertical ties of loyalty. If it is right that the Meiji Restoration was achieved by lower-ranking samurai seeking effective execution of their program through association of like-minded samurai across the fief lines (thus replacing the feudal loyalty with an inter-fief, "national" fidelity),[39] Tamamushi's feeling is inseparable from such development. However modest his skepticism may be, he is one of the very few who discovered in an utterly different culture something he had seriously missed in his own.

[...]

MINDS

There are two accounts of diplomatic occasions that were very much alike, one by an American and the other by a Japanese. One is Harris's description of his audience with the Shogun in Edo Castle on December 7, 1857, and the other is Muragaki's record of his reception by President Buchanan on May 19, 1860, in the White House. [...]

[...]

And here is Muragaki in the White House:

Intercalary third month 28th [May 19, 1860].
    Cloudy. As the hour for our presentation to the President of the United States was appointed for twelve o'clock, we made all the necessary preparations with the utmost

care. Masaoki (wearing a short sword with silk twined scabbard), I (with a short court sword with gold hilt), and Tadamasa (bearing a sword with scabbard twined in front), were dressed alike in *kariginu* and *eboshi* with light green braided cords, and wore sandals woven of silk threads. Both Morita and Naruse Masanori wore *horoginu*, while the two officers of superintendent's rank put on *su-ō*, and Namura Gorō, our official interpreter, was dressed in *kamishimo*, made of ramie cloth.

We drove off in open carriages-and-four, Masaoki with Captain Du-Pont riding in the first carriage, I with Captain Lee in the second, and Tadamasa with Mr. Ledyard in the third, followed by other members of the Embassy in carriages, and servants on foot. (The First and Second Ambassadors and the Censor each took with them three footmen, one spear-bearer and three retainers, while Morita and Naruse were each accompanied by two retainers, one spear-bearer and one sandal-carrier.) Our procession was headed by a score of men in grey uniform (probably city officials), immediately followed by a band of some thirty musicians, and several mounted cavaliers; then came a group of men, bearing upon their shoulders the dispatch box with a red leather cover, and accompanied by the officer in charge, a foreman and an interpreter; these were followed by a long line of carriages in good order, on either side of which marched the guards to the accompaniment of music played by the band. [...]

[...]

EPILOGUE

[...]

Thousands of travelogues and travelogue fictions have been composed since the mid-nineteenth century by novelists and others who visited America and Europe.[40] In the course of writing this book, I have read scores of those memoirs—for example, by Narushima Ryūhoku, Mori Ōgai, Natsume Sōseki, Nagai Kafū, Arishima Takeo, Shimazaki Tōson, and Tokutomi Roka, as well as more recent ones by Ōoka Shōhei, Yasuoka Shōtarō, Takeyama Michio, Etō Jun, Oda Makoto, and Mori Arimasa. What I have remarked in connection with the 1860 Embassy records stands to be adjusted, of course. And yet here again familiar features are discernible. Few of them make universalist speculative comments about the West. They tend to assemble day-to-day impressions without structuring them into a personal interpretation. Instead of individuals experiencing a place in all its stark immediacy, they refer themselves back to the Japanese idea of it. They are seldom free from the consciousness of being from Japan, their home country unceasingly hovering over them wherever they go. Individuals confronting a foreign culture in their separate ways and finding their own terms for entering into it are not commonplace even among these documents. It is Japan that they inevitably face as they tour in the West. Yokomitsu Riichi's shapeless and sprawling novel *Ryoshū* (Homesickness, 1937) may still be a good specimen of these unresolved cogitations that seem to preoccupy Japanese intellectuals, nearly always torn between the will to discover and reassert the uniquely Japanese and the sighting of the disturbingly, over-whelmingly attractive and/or repulsive West. Agonized people's agonized documents, many are not unlike Tamamushi's *Kō-Bei nichiroku,* book eight.

So seen, today's travelers may yet be found to share much with the 1860 Embassy members. In history's longer terms, a century of contact may still prove to be a very limited one. An intense relationship that culminated in a total war, occupation, and so-called economic cooperation thereafter gives the impression of the two countries mingling and constantly merging in so many aspects. But America and Japan, one might stop to reflect, lie as far apart now as they did a century ago. Before all cultures are made undistinguishable by the ingratiating blight of technology and consumer culture, one might even now recognize and cherish the tenacious difference between the two cultures.[41] It is in this context that the records of the 1860 Embassy seem still fresh and cogent after all that has happened in the intervening century and more.

NOTES

BGKM   *Dai Nihon komonjo, bakumatsu gaikoku kankei monjo*
BIGS   *Bakumatsu ishin gaikō shiryō shūsei*
CJH   *The Complete Journal of Townsend Harris*
KSNS   *Kengai shisetsu nikki sanshū*
SS   *Nichi-Bei Shūkō Tsūshō Hyakunen Kinen Gyōji Uneikai*

1. Congress voted to appropriate $50,000 for the reception of the Embassy. U.S. Congress, Senate, *Bills and Joint Resolutions of the Senate of the United States for the Thirty-Sixth Congress,* April 3, 1860. Various municipal governments, however, seem to have spent far more. According to the San Francisco *Daily Evening Bulletin,* the New York Common Council was presented with bills amounting to $125,000, including the hotel bill for $91,000 (which meant "$137 per day for each guest") that itemized, for instance, 10,000 bottles of champagne. August 2, 1860.

2. These letters are in the *Notes from the Japanese Legation in the United States to the Department of State,* roll 1. The note of urgency is unmistakable in their painfully composed English letters. By the time they wrote the third letter (dated the 9th day of the fourth month of the seventh year of Ansei, i.e., May 28, 1860), they had been advised that the return trip would have to be via the Cape of Good Hope. Their response was: "So we think that as many days will now be lost by the going of the *Niagara* to Panama, we have determined to make the voyage by the Cape of Good Hope, as Dupont mentioned, and to set forth directly from Washington without visiting part of the United States, because we would necessarily give many days to that, and the views of our Government would not be followed out. Therefore we request the Niagara may come to Hampton Roads about the 1st of June, if that be not troublesome to you." In the last letter they wrote on the subject (dated the 16th day of the fourth month of the seventh year of Ansei, i.e., June 4, 1860), they reluctantly accept the invitations to Baltimore, Philadelphia, and New York, but even then they plead, "[the *Niagara* should stop] at such ports only as necessary for providing such articles, as most urgently requested, and in such cases to remain not longer than absolutely necessary for such purposes. They request this for the reason, that their departure has been delayed beyond their calculation and they are much pressed for time; they also think, as the 'Niagara' is a large and strong ship, that sufficient coal, wood, water, and provisions may be put on board of here."

See also Muragaki, *Ken-Bei-shi nikki,* contained in (Ōtsuka Takematsu, ed.) *Kengai shisetsu nikki sanshū* (hereafter referred to as *KSNS*), 1:116–118, 138.

3. A letter from the offices of *ōmetsuke* and *metsuke,* dated the 11th month of the sixth year of Ansei, *BGKM,* 31:35–39.

4. *BIGS,* 5:1–2. The Embassy's first official report to the Council of State, sent from San Francisco, interestingly enough says nothing about this Hawaiian diplomatic approach. The Ambassadors are indeed very timid in the letter, even in mentioning that they had contact with the kingdom, a non-treaty country; they emphasize the absolute need to replenish the ship's supply and apologetically point out that the ship's movement was not up to them, but to its captain. *BGKM,* 37:124–130. It was not until two days after their return to Edo that the Ambassadors reported about the Hawaiian government's approach. They were obviously afraid of a possible censure for even having had a talk with a foreign government outside of the agreed plan. *BIGS,* 5:2–3.

5. *Fukuō jiden,* pp. 112–113.

6. *Kanrin-kan Beikoku tokō, Zenshū,* 12:239–309.

7. *BGKM,* 37:69–71. When the Ambassadors were invited to an evening party by the Hawaiian court, for example, they declined the invitation on the ground that going out at night was against the Japanese customs *(kokufū).* The same expression was used even in Washington to avoid unnecessary exposure to the Americans. See Muragaki's *Ken-Bei-shi nikki, KSNS,* 1:32, 91, 106.

8. *Kō-Bei nichiroku,* pp. 241–242.

9. *Kōkai nikki, KSNS,* 1:288.

10. *Kō-Bei-ki,* p. 157.

11. *Man'en gannen hō-Bei nikki,* p. 128.

12. *Bei-kō nikki, KSNS,* 1:435, 444–445.

13. *Kō-Bei nichiroku,* pp. 156–157.

14. *A-kō nikki, SS,* 1:118.

15. Ibid., 1:156.

16. Commodore Perry was requested to agree that no American women would be brought to Japan. See Hawks, 1:385. There had been very few female Western visitors to Japan before the formal opening: a few in Nagasaki in the earlier nineteenth century; three American women in Shimoda in 1855; the wife of an English consul at Hakodate (C. Pemberton Hodgson, who was in Japan between 1859 and 1860). Yoshida Tsunekichi, *Tōjin Okichi,* pp. 46–53, and Hodgson, *A Residence at Nagasaki and Hakodate;* Kawaji Toshiakira, *Nagasaki nikki, Shimoda nikki,* pp. 209–210.

17. *Ken-Bei-shi nikki, KSNS,* 1:91–93; *Kōkai nikki,* pp. 78–80.

18. The Westerners' eyes were often compared to those of dogs. See, for instance, Amano Shinkei, *Shiojiri zuihitsu* (1782), quoted in Osatake Takeshi, *Meiji ishin,* 1:112.

19. *A-kō nikki, SS,* 1:129.

20. *Kanrin Maru kō-Bei nisshi,* pp. 607, 611.

21. *Beikō nisshi, SS,* 2:16.

22. *Kaki kōkai nisshi, SS,* 3:297.

23. *Kōkai nichiroku, SS,* 3:202.

24. *Ken-Bei-shi nikki, KSNS,* 1:111–112; *Kōkai nikki,* pp. 96–97.

25. *Fukuō jiden,* pp. 115–116.

26. Ibid., pp. 125, 129.

27. *Kōkai nichiroku, SS,* 3:201, 213; Yanagawa, *Kōkai nikki, KSNS,* 1:278. Both Nonomura and Yanagawa, at the same time, also use terms like *daitōryō.* See also Osatake Takeshi, *Ishin zengo ni okeru rikken shisō,* chaps. 1–3.

28. Nonomura, *Kōkai nichiroku, SS,* 3:201.

29. Kimura Tetsuta, *Kō-Bei-ki,* p. 188; Satō Hidenaga, *Bei-kō nikki, KSNS,* 1:456–457.

30. *Kōkai nikki, KSNS,* 1:277–278.

31. *Ken-Bei-shi nikki, KSNS,* 1:79; *Kōkai nikki,* p. 66.
32. *Ken-Bei-shi nikki, KSNS,* 1:84; *Kōkai nikki,* p. 71.
33. *Ken-Bei-shi nikki, KSNS,* 1:88–89; *Kōkai nikki,* pp. 76–77.
34. *Kō-Bei nichiroku,* pp. 63–64. A variant of this entry appears in book eight, pp. 236–237.
35. *Kō-Bei nichiroku,* pp. 94–96.
36. Ibid., pp. 107–108.

37. Sano Kanae, a member of an "outside" fief, who volunteered to serve as a manservant for Masuzu, a Tokugawa vassal, during the voyage, was very much like Tamamushi in his position in the Embassy. He, too, describes the visit to the Capitol, but expresses total bewilderment as to the nature of Congress. *Man 'en gannen hō-Bei nikki,* pp. 64–65.

38. See Bellah, *Tokugawa Religion,* p. 25.
39. Tōyama, *Meiji ishin,* pp. 66–74; Norman, *Origins of the Modern Japanese State.*

40. "Japanese mass tourism has continued the travelogue tradition and has produced a vast quantity of travel literature. There always seems to be a market for travelogues, even those with an amateurish style. According to the *Japanese Publishers Yearbook,* 2,300 travelogues were published in Japan between 1950 and 1970. Most dealt with trips to Europe; only 250 concerned the United States. Thus, even though nearly a third of the passports issued in Japan have been for travel to the United States, the proportion of travelogues about that country has been relatively low." Katō Hidetoshi, "America as Seen by Japanese Travelers," p. 196.

41. The most incisive treatment of change and tradition in modern Japan is Robert N. Bellah's "Continuity and Change in Japanese Society."

REFERENCES

Bellah, Robert N. 1971. "Continuity and Change in Japanese Society," in Bernard Barber and Alex Inkeles, eds., *Stability and Social Change,* Boston: Little, Brown, pp. 377–404.

Blacker, Carmen. 1981. "Review of Masao Miyoshi's *As We Saw Them: The First Japanese Embassy to the United States." Bulletin of the School of Oriental and African Studies, University of London,* Vol. 44, No. 1, pp. 206–207.

Chang, Richard T. 1980. "Review of Masao Miyoshi's *As We Saw Them: The First Japanese Embassy to the United States." American Historical Review,* Vol. 85, No. 4, pp. 983–984.

32

From The Autobiography of Yukichi Fukuzawa

Fukuzawa Yukichi, 1893

A native of Japan, Fukuzawa Yukichi (1835–1901) was influential in the Japan of the Meiji Restoration, which followed the overthrow of the Tokugawa family in 1868. During his lifetime, Japan underwent enormous change, evolving from an isolated country to a modern powerhouse, both economically and militarily. In the latter part of the nineteenth century, the Japanese were able to defeat Chinese and Russian armies and seize control of parts of mainland Asia.

At the age of eighteen, Yukichi was a member of the first Japanese diplomatic mission to the United States in 1860, and a key figure in the modernization of his country. As an educator, he believed in the importance of Western technology to modernity, not necessarily as a strict nationalist but because of a love for his country's well-being. He was born into a poor, low-ranking family, and his father, a Confucian scholar, died young. Yukichi grew up in Osaka, and from an early age his love for learning was said to be greatly influenced by his lifelong teacher, Shozan Shuarshi, a scholar of Confucianism and Han learning. Yukichi turned eleven shortly after Commodore Perry arrived in Japan, a monumental event in modern Japanese history. Later, influenced by the imperial presence of the Dutch, Yukichi entered a school of Dutch studies in Nagasaki, where he became proficient in the Dutch language.

The first Japanese mission to the United States arrived on the *Kanrin Maru*. During a monthlong stay in San Francisco while the ship was being repaired, Yukichi began his study of English. His first publication was an English-Japanese dictionary. In 1862 he joined the first Japanese embassy to Europe. That experience resulted in the publication of his work *Seija Jijo*, translated as *Things Western* or *Conditions in the West*, published in ten volumes

Fukuzawa, Yukichi. 2007. *The Autobiography of Yukichi Fukuzawa*. Eiichi Kiyooka, trans. New York: Columbia University Press. Pp. 117–122. Copyright © 2007 Columbia University Press. Reprinted with the permission of the publisher.

from 1867 to 1870. His works became best sellers, and as a result he was considered the foremost expert in Japan on things Western. It is said that his purpose was to acquaint his countrymen with Western ways in anticipation of increasing European imperialism. His book *All the Countries of the World, for Children Written in Verse* (1869) was used as an official school textbook, with five volumes covering the countries of Asia, Africa, Europe, South America, North America, and Australia, respectively—his introduction to world geography for a people who had been traditionally insulated.

Yukichi had a philosophy that permeated all of his writings about the West: it was translated as "national independence through personal independence." He attributed the power of the West to its high levels of education and promotion of the exchange of ideas. For him, civilization meant the furthering of knowledge and education, with inequality between countries being a result of differences in the attainment of knowledge and education, especially mathematics and science. Yukichi was writing at a time when American and European treaties forced on Japan were widely perceived among the Japanese as violations of national sovereignty. Although he was later criticized as a supporter of Japanese imperialism, his efforts as a reformer and educator helped modernize Japan. Before the Meiji Restoration, these efforts brought attempts on his life, but today he is revered as a key founder of modern Japan. After the restoration, the Japanese government actively sought foreign knowledge, and Yukichi was invited to enter government. He chose, however, to work on the development of an intelligentsia at arm's length from government. He did so by founding schools, writing books, and starting newspapers that were a source of liberal thinking for their readers.

The selection from Yukichi's autobiography is a sample of his comments and observations on what he sees as the weak side of Euro-American culture: the waste and the lack of caring for founding ancestors. Yet he did not think all Westerners "devils," and was concerned about the possible consequences of the antiforeign movement in Japan for his country's international standing. Yukichi was also a popularizer who wrote for ordinary Japanese about issues of home concern: administration of a centralized school system, dormitory rules and regulations, the role of schools and education in a changing society, the relationship between government and education, moral training, and the distrust of men in public office—all issues underlying much of the rest of his work as well.

. . .

As soon as our ship came into the port of San Francisco, we were greeted by many important personages who came on board from all over the country. Along the shores thousands of people were lined up to see the strange newcomers. [. . .]

Our welcome on shore was certainly worthy of a friendly people. They did everything for us, and they could not have done more. The feeling on their part must have been like that of a teacher receiving his old pupil several years after graduation, for it was their Commodore Perry who had effected the opening of our country seven years before, and now here we are on our first visit to America. [. . .]

On our part there were many confusing and embarrassing moments, for we were quite ignorant of the customs of American life. For instance, we were surprised even by the carriages. On seeing a vehicle with horses attached to it, we should easily have guessed what it was. But really we did not identify our mode of conveyance until the door had been opened, [and] we were seated inside. [...]

Our hosts in San Francisco were very considerate in showing us examples of modern industry. There was as yet no railway laid to the city, nor was there any electric light in use. But the telegraph system and also Galvani's electro-plating were already in use. Then we were taken to a sugar refinery and had the principle of the operation explained to us quite minutely. I am sure that our hosts thought they were showing us something entirely new, naturally looking for our surprise at each new device of modern engineering. But on the contrary, there was really nothing new, at least to me. I knew the principle of the telegraphy even if I had not seen the actual machine before; I knew that sugar was bleached by straining the solution with bone-black, and that in boiling down the solution, the vacuum was used to better effect than heat. I had been studying nothing else but such scientific principles ever since I had entered Ogata's school.

Rather, I was surprised by entirely different things in American life. First of all, there seemed to be an enormous waste of iron everywhere. In garbage piles, on the seashores—everywhere—I found lying old oil tins, empty cans, and broken tools. This was remarkable to us, for in Yedo, after a fire, there would appear a swarm of people looking for nails in the ashes. [...]

Things social, political, and economic proved most inexplicable. One day, on a sudden thought, I asked a gentleman where the descendants of George Washington might be. He replied, "I think there is a woman who is directly descended from Washington. I don't know where she is now, but I think I have heard she is married." His answer was so very casual that it shocked me.

Of course, I knew that America was a republic with a new president every four years, but I could not help feeling that the family of Washington would be revered above all other families. My reasoning was based on the reverence in Japan for the founders of the great lines of rulers—like that for Ieyasu of the Tokugawa family of Shōguns, really deified in the popular mind. So I remember the astonishment I felt at receiving this indifferent answer about the Washington family. As for scientific inventions and industrial machinery, there was no great novelty in them for me. It was rather in matters of life and social custom and ways of thinking that I found myself at a loss in America. [...]

Of political situations of that time, I tried to learn as much as I could from various persons that I met in London and Paris, though it was often difficult to understand things clearly as I was yet so unfamiliar with the history of Europe. [...]

While we were in London, a certain member of the Parliament sent us a copy of a bill which he said he had proposed in the House under the name of the party to which he belonged. The bill was a protest against the arrogant attitude of the

British minister to Japan, Alcock, who had at times acted as if Japan were a country conquered by military force. One of the instances mentioned in the bill was that of Alcock's riding his horse into the sacred temple grounds of Shiba, an unpardonable insult to the Japanese.

On reading a copy of this bill, I felt as if a load had been lifted from my chest. After all, the foreigners were not all "devils." I had felt that Japan was enduring some pointed affronts on the part of the foreign ministers who presumed on the ignorance of our government. But now that I had actually come to the minister's native land, I found that there were among them some truly impartial and warmhearted human beings. After this I grew even more determined in my doctrine of free intercourse with the rest of the world.

The country in Europe which gave us the kindest welcome was Holland. This was a natural outcome of the very special relationship which Japan had enjoyed with Holland for the last three hundred years. Moreover all the members of the mission who knew any foreign language at all had studied Dutch before any other language. So it made Holland, so far as the use of language was concerned, seem like our second homeland. There was, I recall, an episode which was rather significant. One day in Amsterdam, during a conversation with some merchants and other gentlemen, our envoy chanced to ask the question: "Is the sale and purchase of land in Amsterdam freely permitted?"

The reply was "Certainly it is free."

"Do you sell land to foreigners also?"

"Yes, as long as a foreigner is willing to pay for the land, we would sell any amount of it to any person."

"Then, suppose a foreigner were to put down a large sum of money to purchase a great tract of land in order to build a fortress, would you allow that too?"

The Hollanders looked puzzled at this, and replied, "We never had occasion to think of such a case. Even though there are many rich men in England and France and other countries, we do not believe any merchant would spend money on such a venture."

Neither side understood the other. We interpreters were much amused by this conversation. It is not to be wondered at that Japan was going through a hard struggle when the control and handling of foreign affairs was in the hands of men who exhibited such reasoning in their contact with the West. [. . .]

While most of the party were feudal retainers of the central government, we three translators belonged to different clans; moreover, we three could read the "strange language written sideways," and we were eager to see and learn everything foreign that we could. These facts were all causes of concern to the high officials.

Every time we wished to go out, one of the *ometsuke* went curiously along. We were not out to smuggle, nor could we possibly impart any national secret. So the "eye fixer" following us was simply a nuisance. But we could put up with this nuisance; the greater inconvenience was that when all the *ometsuke* were occupied elsewhere, we could not go out at all. [...]

Since some time before we had started on our tour, the anti-foreign movement in Japan had been growing worse, and more and more blunders were being made in our foreign diplomacy. [...]

What hope for the future of Japan as long as our people showed this foolish pride, keeping aloof from the actual give-and-take of the rest of the world? The more this movement of Expel-the-Foreigners increased, the more would we lose our national power, to say nothing of prestige. I was mortified when I thought over the possible outcome of national exclusiveness.

REFERENCES

Craig, Albert M. 2009. *Civilization and Enlightenment: The Early Thought of Fukuzawa Yukichi*. Cambridge, MA: Harvard University Press.

Tamaki, Norio. 2001. *Yukichi Fukuzawa, 1835–1901: The Spirit of Enterprise in Modern Japan*. London: Palgrave Macmillan.

Fukuzawa, Yukichi. 1866. 西洋事情 (Things Western). Tokyo: Keio Zohan.

———. 1869. 世界国尽 (All the Countries of the World, for Children Written in Verse). Tokyo: Keio Zohan.

33

Why Security Treaty?

Yuzuru Katagiri, 1961

Yuzuru Katagiri is a poet and translator. He was the leading Japanese translator of the Beat poet Kenneth Rexroth, and also translated Lawrence Ferlinghetti's *Endless Life: Selected Poems* (1981), and is presently a professor emeritus of linguistics at Kyoto Seika University.

Katagiri was a student at Waseda University in Tokyo in 1949. The American scholar S. I. Hayakawa's *Language in Thought and Action* (1949) and his work in semantics inspired Yuzuru Katagiri to think about the "emotive use of words." It was, after all, the magic of words that had led Japan into war, and after World War II staying out of war was of great concern to the Japanese people, most of whom were pacifists.

Under the influence of I. A. Richard's *The Philosophy of Rhetoric* (1936), Katagiri wrote *Introduction to Semantics* (originally published in Japanese in 1965). His interest in linguistics and semantics was further stimulated by his visits to the United States and Canada. In the course of these exchange visits, he developed a critical position on people who are over-specialized and those who tried to be "objective" or "scientific" and who ignored feeling and touch observations. He also referred frequently to the consequences felt by those exposed to nuclear weapons and war. Katagiri was consistent in his opposition to the use of nuclear power, whether for military use or in energy generation.

Of his own work he says: "Some take my work to be so poetic that it is of little value in the theoretical world. Others take it as too scholarly to be of artistic value. I am very unhappy about people being divided in this way" (General Semantics Bulletin 1985).

The U.S. has used Japan for multiple military bases since the Allied occupation at the end of World War II, renewing this military presence through a Security Treaty in 1951 that was extended in 1960. The 1960 treaty met with widespread civil protests that forced the Japanese prime minister to resign. The poem included here protests the 1960 treaty as paternalistic

Katagiri, Yuzuru. 1971 [1961]. "Why Security Treaty?" In *Impact! Asian Views of the West*. Jo Ann White, ed. New York: J. Messner. Pp. 175–178. Reprinted with the permission of Yuzuru Katagiri.

and dangerous. Katagiri's view of where Japan should be headed is in direct opposition to the nationalist position held by Shintaro Ishihara, the author of the following selection, from *The Japan That Can Say No*, a position currently associated with Japanese militarism.

. . .

I live near an airbase
where the noise of jet planes shakes
windowpanes of classrooms
and the children's scores in standard tests
are lower than in other school districts
and scared cows and hens give no milk and no eggs
but there is no escape
Japan is a small country
with poor natural resources
and we don't see why
Japan is in danger of being conquered
by communist countries

I am an Americanized Japanese
who hears Armed Forces Radio Service
which says all men and women are created equal
as the fourth of July is coming near
and we do not see the reason
why we must be the crew of an aircraft carrier
of another country which flies U2's
and I live near an airbase
which might be another Hiroshima
and Japan is a small country
where mountains are tilled to the tops
which seem beautiful to an American eye
who wants to keep Japan as a museum
of old strange cultures
of polite people

I like American people
they are kind and they gave us chocolate
I like American ways of living
they are so comfortable
I like American education in which
boys and girls work and play together and are happy
I wanted Japan to be a state of the United States of America
just after the war

Now I am glad that Japan is not a state of the United States of America
where all young men are taken to be soldiers
and many were killed in Korea without knowing why
where citizens are deceived into believing
their safety in a nuclear air raid if they hide quickly

I am a taxpayer who does not want
to keep such a big army navy airforce
as a result of the Security Treaty
in this age of nuclear weapons
I am a teacher of English
who teach Gettysburg Address
to the third year students of a high school
who are scared by the fear of being taken as soldiers
and sent to another country to defend another country
as Japan is involved automatically in a possible limited war
as a result of the Security Treaty

I am wondering why the government
elected by kind people of America
for the kind people of America, of the kind people of America
which issues 25 cent stamp of Abraham Lincoln
has been helping authoritarian governments
in Korea and Turkey and in Japan
the government of Kishi Brothers & Company
for Kishi Brothers & Company, by Kishi Brothers & Company.
Whenever Kishi went to America and said
Japan and America are good friends
some attempts were made by the Japanese government
to return to the old educational system
to return to the old national religion
to return to the old family system
to return to the old police state
to return to the old militarism
the explosion of which was Pearl Harbor
done by Tōjō and Kishi

REFERENCES

Ferlinghetti, Lawrence. 1981. *Endless Life: Selected Poems*. New York: New Directions.
Hayakawa, Samuel I. 1949. *Language in Thought and Action*. Harcourt, Brace and Company.
Katagiri, Yuzuru. 1965. 意味論入門 (Introduction to Semantics). Japan: Shicho-sha.

———. 1985. "General Semantics Scene in Japan." *General Semantics Bulletin,* Vol. 52, pp. 77–79.

Richard, Ivan A. 1936. *The Philosophy of Rhetoric.* New York: Oxford University Press.

Rimer, J. Thomas, and Van C. Gessel, eds. 2011. "Katagiri Yuzuru." In *The Columbia Anthology of Modern Japanese Literature.* Abridged. New York: Columbia University Press. Pp. 674–676.

34

Japan and the United States:
Partners or Master and Servant?

Shintaro Ishihara, 1991

A pirated version of *The Japan That Can Say No* (1989), by Akio Morita and Shintaro Ishihara, was, without authorization, translated in the United States Pentagon and read into the *Congressional Record* in 1989. Morita was president and founder of the electronics producer Sony Corporation, and Ishihara came to public attention first as a successful writer and then as a prominent member of various conservative parties in Japan. Japanese often write frankly about their concerns *in Japanese,* assuming that their work will not be translated. Thus it is no surprise that the directly translated, unabridged version upset American readers. Americans were especially concerned with the theme of Japanese supremacy in Asia, and with the embarrassing revelation that the Japanese were producing critical military technology for both the Americans and the Soviets. And of course, there were the innuendos and racist comments scattered throughout. But then, the book was written for domestic consumption.

A second version, authored solely by Ishihara and published by Simon and Schuster, was cleaned up with American sensitivities in mind. The "America bashing" was toned down. The book represents a view from the Japanese right, directed to the state and concerned with Japan's position as a world power. There are observations on the perceived foolishness of American business practices, and Japan's at the time new position of economic and technological strength. The Japanese are encouraged to step forth and boldly assume a new role beyond being quiet and passive subordinates.

Ishihara offers a blueprint for reforming Japanese politics on the world stage: how can a country whose military systems depend on Japanese semiconductors refuse to deal with Japan as an equal? As the reviewers comment, Ishihara is of the old Realpolitik school. He wants the power that should come with economic success. Up to now, the United States has called the shots, but it is time for Japan to recognize its own strengths and move toward an "equal partner" role, he exhorts. The tone of the English version is brash and critical, but reviewers of the Japanese version say that the writing is "often taunting, petulant, or boastful" (Hall 1990:661). Ishihara urges his compatriots to "say no" to American imperiousness, as Japan is the older civilization, has advanced technology, and even more important, has a set of assets in its culture and creativity, and has patriotic loyalty that can sustain Japan as a world power.

In his foreword to Ishihara's book Ezra Vogel (1991) points out: "Ishihara's book should not necessarily be read as a guide to how present-day Japanese politicians are likely to behave, but rather as a reflection of deep currents of popular Japanese thinking about the United States. . . . Ishihara is complaining less about the United States than about Japan's obsequious leaders who don't stand tall the way they should. And in that respect, he has his finger on the pulse of a growing segment of the Japanese population" (9). Vogel also comments on Americans' capacity for self-deception, and suggests the need for an Ishihara in the United States, a popular figure who could tell American leaders that they should restructure the economy to promote long-term prosperity and should look in the mirror and see how others perceive the United States' weaknesses.

Ishihara does not come from an elite Japanese family. His father worked his way up to become manager of a shipping company. Ishihara grew up in Kanagawa, graduated from university in 1956, and won a prize for his novel *Season of the Sun*. In the 1960s he wrote plays, novels, and a musical version of *Treasure Island,* and also ran a theater company. He then served more than twenty-five years in the Parliament, was governor of Tokyo from 1999 to 2012, and is still one of Japan's best-known conservative politicians. Some of the policies he introduced, such as restrictions on the operation of diesel-powered vehicles, a cap-and-trade energy tax, and successful bidding for the 2020 Summer Olympics, would not be called far-right in this country. On the other hand, his views on China and on foreigners in Japan are critical. He is known for taking controversial stands about other cultures and being in favor of the Japanese colonization of Korea, nuclear power in Japan, and a stronger defense policy—all of which link him to ideologies of conservative nationalism.

. . .

DOES THE UNITED STATES REGARD JAPAN AS AN EQUAL PARTNER?

When most Japanese say, "The United States is an indispensable partner for Japan," they are expressing admiration and respect for America. But I often have the feeling that when Americans call on Japan to be an "equal partner," they really think that we are inferior, still unworthy of their admiration and respect.

Why do the two peoples have such different feelings about each other? One reason is the legacy of the Pacific War, the victors or losers mentality. Another is that Americans still have a superpower mindset. You can see flashes of this in James Fallows's article "Containing Japan" in *The Atlantic Monthly* of May 1989. Fallows writes: "Unless Japan is contained, therefore, several things that matter to America will be jeopardized: America's own authority to carry out its foreign policy and advance its ideals." He regrets the "sense that the United States is so deep in debt that it can't afford to do many of the things a leading power should do—explore space, improve its schools, maintain its military bases in Japan so that Japan doesn't build its own army, and so on." The comment about U.S. bases shows the U.S.'s motives, I think, namely that the real purpose of U.S. forces in Japan is to keep an eye on our military.

Americans like Fallows consider their "ideals" absolute values, a self-righteousness that blinds them to how annoying their "authority" to "advance" them often is to other countries. Fallows concludes by saying, "We do have the right to defend our interests and our values, and they are not identical to Japan's."

Fallows is correct that the two countries do not share identical interests and values. Yet we do not have to see the world exactly the same way to be partners. We can agree to disagree about many things. Equality is not homogeneity. That is the fallacy in Fallows's argument. He wants to "contain" the Japanese people because we are different. Japan and the United States would want to preserve their own interests and values whether they were allies or not. We have a partnership and should grant each other some leeway. Without nationalism—a strong sense of roots and identity—there cannot be internationalism, only a shallow cosmopolitanism. A country that always says yes to its ally is a vassal state, not an equal.

An American politician whom I know well said to me, "The Japan-U.S. relationship must be preserved. As you say, it's important to both countries and to the rest of the world. We're married to each other." "Well, if we are properly married, okay," I responded. "A wife can talk back to her husband. But a kept woman, afraid the man will kick her out, always has to do what he says. Don't ever think Japan is America's mistress." He was shocked at my metaphor, but we both laughed.

Today, many Americans overreact if Japan has the temerity to act like an independent nation. This happened with the FSX. Using their standard technique of fabricated charges, congressmen attacked the Mitsubishi Group as a way of getting at MHI [Mitsubishi Heavy Industries]. They claimed that Mitsubishi was helping Libya to build a chemical plant to produce poison gas. Later, the allegations were shown to be completely false. Undeterred by truth, these august legislators then demanded that Japan pledge not to help the Libyans build the facility in the future! It was as if a person accused of theft was shown to be innocent, and then the accusers, instead of apologizing, demanded that he promise never to steal again. This is the country that professes to treat Japan as an equal.

Americans will say, "Ishihara, you are the one with a belligerent, uncooperative attitude. You said Japan could change the military balance by selling semiconductors

to the Soviet Union and cutting off the United States." It was a very provocative statement, I admit, but I had good reason to say it. This is what happened.

I was in Washington in 1987, right after Congress passed the resolution on semiconductors. I was at a reception where members of Congress and lobbyists for the
U.S. semiconductor industry were gloating over their victory. There were remarks
like "We got them this time," and "This'll knock the Japanese back a bit." Antipathy
to Japan was thick as an oil spill. Several congressmen made very intemperate
comments to me. One said, "Profound changes are under way in the world that
may fundamentally alter the U.S.-Japan relationship." I had heard the same kind of
remark in Tokyo, so it was not news, but I pretended not to understand and asked
what he meant.

"U.S.-Soviet ties have dramatically improved and it's quite possible that the
partnership between Washington and Tokyo might be dissolved," he said gravely.
"The United States may even abandon Japan." Laughingly I replied, "Do you mean
that Americans and Russians have rediscovered their mutual identity as Caucasians?" He nodded in agreement. I went on, "I will never be a great fan of the
Soviet Union, but if the United States no longer wants Japan as an ally, then we will
have a free hand to look for other friends around the world. By the same token, in
this new situation, when Moscow shops for high technology, it has a choice
between Japan and the United States. If Japan sells certain semiconductors to the
Soviet Union, which only we produce in quantity, wouldn't the United States be in
deep trouble?"

Suddenly the mood became very tense. Our congressional host intervened, "It
is premature to say that the Soviet-U.S. confrontation is over."

Despite the temporary awkwardness, I made some friends there, people with
whom I could speak frankly. One reason I have always respected Americans is that
most of them would not break off a personal relationship just because of a heated
exchange.

But I could not get over that congressman's nod of assent when I asked if the
Russo-American détente was based on both being white. It is perfectly all right for
Americans and Russians to be friendly, of course. But if that means the end of the
Japan-U.S. relationship, what have we been doing for the last forty years?

That congressman would not have said to a German or French politician, "We
may even abandon you." Even if the comment was a childish threat inspired by
frustration over trade imbalances, behind it was prejudice against nonwhite races.
Americans get very upset when I tell them that Caucasians are biased against non-
whites. All human beings have feelings or attitudes they prefer not to talk about.
Bringing up the race problem may violate an American taboo, but I take the risk
because it affects whether the partnership between our countries is equal. Of
course, I'm not suggesting Japanese are without fault. Discrimination is still widespread in Japan. I think Americans and Japanese should admit the obvious.

A Japanese businessman told me of an incident that happened to him and his wife in the United States. One night they went into a restaurant that was virtually empty. A waiter rudely said, "We're full," and turned them away. The executive admires the United States and knows the country well. Unlike me, he is tactful and does not complain about racial prejudice there. Despite this experience, he speaks highly of American society. He adds, however, that it would be an even greater country if it were not for the hostility toward nonwhites.

Perhaps because I have brought up race and been consistently outspoken about other matters that needed airing, an American congressman once said, "You're very direct and provocative for a Japanese. What makes you this way?"

I replied joking, "As a teenager I was struck for no reason by an American soldier."

I told him the whole story. It happened in 1946 when I was a second-year middle-school student. I lived in Zushi, then a quiet seaside resort of about 15,000 people, an hour south of Tokyo by train. Many U.S. troops were stationed in the area because there were former Imperial Navy ammunition dumps nearby.

One day in late August I was walking along the main business street on my way home from school. Three young GIs eating water ices approached from the opposite direction. The war had only been over a year and Japanese in Zushi still timidly moved aside for Americans. The new rulers had the street to themselves and that swaggering trio seemed to glory in the deference. I did not like their attitude, so I walked straight ahead, pretending not to see them. Just as I was about to pass, one GI hit me in the face with his water ice. I guess he did not like my attitude either. I ignored him and continued walking. Other Japanese were watching me, fearful of an incident. I remember feeling proud.

The congressman looked very embarrassed. I felt he was taking it too seriously, so I said, "It's a true story but I meant it as a humorous explanation of my outspokenness. Don't make too much of it. That was a long time ago. It didn't make me anti-American. Later I was crazy about U.S. pop music."

"But you'll never forget it."

"I guess I won't," I replied.

A bit later in the evening, he came up to me. "About your story, were those GIs black?"

Bemused by the question, I said, "No, two were blond and one was a redhead. They still had freckles on their faces."

The congressman, out of friendly concern for what the incident might have meant to me, had inadvertently revealed his own prejudice.

I do not recount this exchange to make fun of racial prejudice among white Americans. There is a certain historical justification for Caucasian attitudes toward other races. Europeans created most of the modern era and they feel superior to Africans and Orientals, who were unable to modernize rapidly and became colonies. Although the Japanese were the only nonwhite people to avoid Western domination, it is not surprising that Europeans and Americans look down on us, too. But as we enter a new era in which Japan and the United States will be the leading players, that attitude imperils trust and cooperation. My point is that Americans ought to face their prejudice toward Japan and overcome it.

Underlying Caucasian racial prejudice is their intense class consciousness, a bias against people of the same race or ethnic group but of different social strata. The European nobility despised commoners and the lower social orders just because they were not of their privileged level, while the hoi polloi both hated the nobility and aspired to their prestige and social standing. Eventually, a democratic fiction that everyone is created equal obscured the obvious hostility between the upper, middle, and lower classes. The nobility prided themselves on a life of ease. Gentlemen did not go into commerce, much less work with their hands. Disregarding the fact that they also benefited from the toil of the masses, the aristocracy viewed the other classes with contempt simply because they worked.

This class consciousness has persisted into the modern era. Western societies still have extraordinary disparities between strata and there is ubiquitous discrimination against the working class. In the United States, for example, fast-track members of the corporate elite will not even type a letter or do secretarial tasks for themselves. To go into the factory and get dirty and sweaty learning how products are made is beneath them.

Class background largely determines the quality of education an American receives. Highly trained U.S. top management do not ask blue-collar personnel for suggestions about how to improve factory operations. Even if they did, the workers probably would have little to say. The situation is quite different in Japan, as the example of the young NEC female employee mentioned earlier illustrates. She used her knowledge and training to discover the cause of defects in semiconductors. In any case, few countries have as egalitarian a class structure as Japan. Lech Walesa, former chairman of Solidarity, visited Japan and toured several factories. After seeing the easy interaction of blue-collar workers, supervisors, and executives, he remarked that Japan was the ideal socialist country. It was a heartfelt and accurate observation, I think.

In Japan, there is no open discrimination on the basis of position, class (everyone knows the word but the postwar generation has no feeling for what it really means), or income. In Europe and the United States, such discrimination is taken for granted. The people I meet in the West are all members of some elite—politics, business, journalism—and when I raise this issue, they do not take it seriously.

Class distinctions reflect the influence of the Catholic Church on Western civilization. Catholic thought celebrated the spirit or intellect and denigrated the body. Consequently, the clergy and nobility disdained labor, especially physical or manual forms, which symbolized the flesh. Although this elite could not have survived without the labor of ordinary people and certainly had their share of carnal desires, an artificial division of society into classes justified their superiority.

Lee Iacocca, chairman of Chrysler Corporation and a cheer-leader of the Japan-bashers with his speeches and TV commercials, typifies that irresponsible breed of American executives who have become fabulously wealthy on the backs of American workers. Instead of being castigated for his price-gouging methods and huge bonuses, he is a kind of folk hero and was even mentioned as a presidential candidate. Iacocca's popularity is not so much incredible as absurd. I agree with Akio Morita's scathing comments about highly paid American executives. Japanese consumers are often said to be naive, and that is true in spades of American workers.

Certain groups in Japan have, in the past, also suffered discrimination for historical or political reasons. But ubiquitous discrimination remains a fixture of Western societies. Class-conscious and racist attitudes are deeply entrenched in the Caucasian psyche. No matter how much non-whites object, Westerners will not soon shed their prejudices.

History gives nations periods of preeminence and decline. These temporary fluctuations in fortunes should not be permanent barriers between people. As a popular Japanese song goes, while you're still crying about one scene, the next has begun. Time marches on.

If the attitude in the United States is that people do not want to hear about all this from a Japanese, then they are hopeless. I believe our partnership will largely shape the next stage of human history. But if Americans say, "Who invited Japan to the party?" then we face a strife-ridden future.

REFERENCES

Hall, Ivan P. 1990. "The Japan That Can Say No: The New U.S.-Japan Relations Card (review)." *Journal of Asian Studies,* Vol. 49, No. 3 (August), pp. 661.

Vogel, Ezra F. 1991. Foreword to *The Japan That Can Say No,* by Shintaro Ishihara. New York: Simon and Schuster. Pp. 7–10.

FOR FURTHER READING

Abu-Lughod, Ibrahim. 1963. *Arab Rediscovery of Europe: A Study in Cultural Encounters.* Princeton, NJ: Princeton University Press.

Adas, Michael. 1989. *Machines as the Measure of Man: Science, Technology and Ideologies of Western Dominance.* Ithaca, NY: Cornell University Press.

Ahmed, Leila. 1982. "Western Ethnocentrism and Perceptions of the Harem." *Feminist Studies,* Vol. 8, no. 3, pp. 521–534.

Alam, Muzaffar, and Sanjay Subrahmanyam. 2007. *Indo-Persian Travels in the Age of Discoveries, 1400–1800.* Cambridge: Cambridge University Press.

Anīs al-Maqdisī. 1963. *Al-Funūn al-Adabiyyah wa A 'lāmuhā.* Beirut: Dār al-Kātib al-ʾArabī.

Asad, Talal, ed. 1973. *Anthropology and the Colonial Encounter.* New York: Humanities Press.

Bellah, Robert Neely. 1996. *Habits of the Heart: Individualism and Commitment in American Life.* Berkeley: University of California Press.

Broadhurst, Roland J. C. 1952. *The Travels of Ibn Jubayr.* London: Camelot Press.

Brockelmann, Carl. 2012. *Geschichte des Arabischen Litteratur.* Leiden, The Netherlands: Brill Academic.

Cachia, Pierre. 1962, 1963, 1966. "An Arab's View of 19th Century Malta," *Maltese Folklore Review,* Vol. 1, No. 1; Vol. 1, No. 2; Vol. 1, No. 3.

Cloake, Margaret M. 1988. *A Persian at the Court of King George (1809–1810).* London: Barrie and Jenkins.

Collins, Michael. 2011. *Empire, Nationalism and the Postcolonial World: Rabindranath Tagore's Writings on History, Politics and Society.* Routledge.

Cremona, Antonio. 1955. "L'antica fondazione della scuola di lingua araba in Malta: Parte Seconda." *Melita Historica: Journal of the Malta Historical Society,* Vol. 1, No. 4, pp. 207–220.

Dirks, Nicholas B. 2008. *The Scandal of Empire: India and the Creation of Imperial Britain.* Cambridge, MA: Belknap Press of Harvard University Press.

Fleet, Kate, Gudrun Krämer, Denis Matringe, John Nawas, and Everett Rowson, eds. 2008. *Encyclopædia of Islam.* 3rd ed. Leiden, The Netherlands: Brill Academic.

Fraser, James B. 1973. *Narrative of the Residence of the Persian Princes in London in 1835 and 1836.* New York: Arno Press.

Gabrieli, Francesco. 1993 [1957]. *Arab Historians of the Crusades.* Barnes and Noble Books.

Gibran, Khalil. 1948. *Nymphs of the Valley.* H.M. Nahmad, transl. London: William Heinemann.

Hay, Stephen N. 1970. *Asian Ideas of East and West: Tagore and His Critics in Japan, China and India.* Cambridge, MA: Harvard University Press.

Hourani, Albert. 1962. *Arabic Thought in the Liberal Age.* Oxford: Oxford University Press.

———. 1980. *Europe and the Middle East.* Berkeley: University of California Press.

Hudson, G. F. 1931. *Europe and China: A Survey of Their Relations from the Earliest Times to 1800.* London: Butler and Tanner.

Iyer, Raghavan, ed. 1965. *The Glass Curtain between Asia and Europe: A Symposium on the Historical Encounters and the Changing Attitudes of the Peoples of the East and West.* London: Oxford University Press.

Jisi, Wang. 2005. "China's Search for Stability with America." *Foreign Affairs,* Vol. 84, No. 5, pp. 39–48.

Kapur, Akash. 2012. "How India Became America." *New York Times,* March 11, 2012. http://www.nytimes.com/2012/03/11/opinion/sunday/how-india-became-america.html . Accessed February 6, 2015.

Kohut, Kader. 2004. "Ethnomasquerade in Ottoman-European Encounters: Reenacting Lady Mary Wortley Montagu." *Criticism,* Vol. 43, No. 3, pp. 393–414.

Lawler, Andrew. 2014. "Sailing Sinbad's Seas." *Science,* Vol. 344, No. 6191, pp. 1440–1460.

Lewis, Reina. 2004. *Rethinking Orientalism: Women, Travel and the Ottoman Harem.* New Brunswick, NJ: Rutgers University Press.

Lewis, Reina, and Nancy Micklewright, eds. 2006. *Gender, Modernity, and Liberty: Middle Eastern and Western Women's Writings.* London: I. B. Tauris.

Maier, John. 1996. *Desert Songs: Western Images of Morocco and Moroccan Images of the West.* Albany: State University of New York Press.

McDougall, Walter. 1998. *Promised Land, Crusader State: The American Encounter with the World since 1776.* Mariner Books.

Melman, Billie. 1992. *Women's Orients: English Women and the Middle East, 1718–1918; Sexuality, Religion and Work.* Ann Arbor: University of Michigan Press.

Mishra, Pankaj. 2012. *From the Ruins of Empire: The Revolt against the West and the Remaking of Asia.* New York: Picador.

Morris, Ian. 2011. *Why the West Rules—For Now: The Patterns of History and What They Reveal about the Future.* New York: Farrar, Straus and Giroux.

Naddaf, Sandra. 1986. "Mirrored Images: Rifaʿah al-Tahtawi and the West." *Alif: Journal of Comparative Poetics,* Vol. 6 (Spring): 73–83.

Nader, Laura. 2009. "What the Rest Think of the West—Legal Dimensions." *Global Jurist,* Vol. 9, No. 1 (March).

Nutting, Anthony. 1964. *The Arabs: A Narrative History from Mohammed to the Present.* New York: Clarkson Potter.

Patterson, Thomas C. 1997. *Inventing Western Civilization.* New York: Monthly Review Press.

Pico, Giandomenico, et al. 2001. *Crossing the Divide: Dialogue among Civilizations.* South Orange, NJ: School of Diplomacy and International Relations, Seton Hall University.

Redhouse, James W. 1995 [1874]. *The Diary of H. M. Shah of Persia during His Tour through Europe in A.D. 1873.* Costa Mesa, CA: Mazda.

Reuters. 2012. "Key Suspect in 9/11 Attacks Calls U.S. the Big Killer." *New York Times,* October 17, 2012. http://www.nytimes.com/2012/10/18/us/accused-9–11-mastermind-calls-us-the-bigger-killer.html. Accessed February 7, 2015.

Rodinson, Maxime. 2002. *Europe and the Mystique of Islam.* Roger Veinus, trans. London: I. B. Tauris.

Rothstein, Edward. 2012. "Jacques Barzun Dies at 104; Cultural Critic Saw the Sun Setting on the West." *New York Times,* October 26, 2012. http://www.nytimes.com/2012/10/26/arts/jacques-barzun-historian-and-scholar-dies-at-104.html. Accessed February 7, 2015.

Said, Edward. 2001. "The Clash of Ignorance." *The Nation,* October 22, 2001, pp. 11–13.

Scott, Joan Wallach, ed. 2008. "Feminism, Democracy, and Empire: Islam and the War on Terror." In *Women's Studies on the Edge: A Differences Book.* Joan Wallach Scott, ed. Durham, NC: Duke University Press. Pp. 81–114.

Sen, Gita. 1984. "Subordination and Social Control: A Comparative View of the Control of Women." *Review of Radical Political Economy,* Vol. 16, No. 1, pp. 133–142.

Siddiqui, Hannana. 1991. "Winning Freedoms." *Feminist Review,* No. 37 (Spring): 78–83.

Spence, Jonathan D. 1991. *The Search for Modern China.* New York: W. W. Norton.

Stephens, Bret. 2007. "Richest Country, Saddest People—Any Coincidence?" *Wall Street Journal,* March 9, 2007.

Tagore, Rabindranâth. 1928. *Letters to a Friend.* London: G. Allen and Unwin.

Wang, Chi. 1990. *History of U.S.-China Relations: A Bibliographical Research Guide.* San Diego, CA: Academic Press.

Wright, Denis. 1985. *The Persians amongst the English: Episodes in Anglo-Persian History.* London: I. B. Tauris.

Yeazell, Ruth Bernard. 2000. *Harems of the Mind: Passages of Western Art and Literature.* New Haven, CT: Yale University Press.

INDEX

churches, 12–13, 36, 289, 292; Franj churches, 22, 26–27; church music, 66, 68

cities, 53, 122, 132, 165, 247; European cities, 48, 55, 73, 287; American cities, 153, 190–91, 220, 243–44, 247–48; Muslim cities, 11; Arab cities, 21

city defense, 16

city-states, 10

civil administration, 149

civil and political rights, 245, 257, 281

civil disobedience, 318

civilian deaths, 108

civilization, xi-xiii, xix-xx, 11, 322–24, 407; American, 185, 416; Arabic, 354; British, 297, 316, 332–33; Chinese, xix, 170, 354; collapse of, xiii; and colonialism, xx; comparison between, 173, 214; critique of, xix-xx, xxiii, 168, 322–42, 333; Egyptian, 28; European, 28, 79, 88, 323, 331–32, 380; ideology of, xii, xix, 53, 55, 104, 260, 285, 311, 322; Indian, xix, 138, 285, 312, 331, 352; Islamic, xviii-xix, 3, 11; Japanese, xix, 416; material civilization, 88, 215; modern civilization, 286, 318–24; non-European civilizations, 349, 352; old civilizations, 235, 352; and positional superiority, xii, xix, xxiii, 214; spiritual civilization, 170, 215; Western, xviii-xix, 215, 302, 310, 319, 420; world civilization, 326

civil rights movement, 204, 245, 252, 282

class, xii; class consciousness, 420–21; class struggle, 209, 329, 339; and colonialism, 281–84, 329, 332; and discrimination, 282, 332, 336, 420–21; and gender, 74, 84; in India, 144–46, 150, 281–84, 308, 332; and race, 282, 420–21; in the U.S., 165, 222

cleanliness, 5, 56, 57, 142, 155, 171. See also ablutions; baths

clothing, 4–7, 37, 49, 53, 75, 272, 287, 322–23; of Asiatic women, 275; of English women, 287; in India, 138, 141–42, 144; in Paris, 54; in the U.S., 221, 223, 390, 395–96, 399

coffee, 45, 48–51, 82, 190, 277; coffee houses, 48–51, 58

college, 250–52, 256, 279, 392. See also education

colonialism, xx-xxii, 207, 232, 349; benefits of colonial presence in India, 295, 297–99; British in India, 295, 335–37, 339; colonialist modernization, 318; and Orientalism, 88, 90, 94; ruler-victim model of colonialism, 319; semi-colonialism, 207, 416–8, 420

Columbia University, 104, 118–19, 211, 220

comic books, 190, 201–2

commerce, 258, 281, 284, 399, 420; in India, 146, 149–150

Commodore Matthew C. Perry, 381, 389, 399, 406–7

communism, 125, 346, 412; in China, 209, 236; Communist party, 208; fight against, 205–7, 336; theory, 182, 216–17

Comnenus, Alexius, 12

comparative consciousness, xvii-xix, xxi. See also reciprocal viewing

comparative method, 173, 193

comparison, xviii-xix, 30, 48, 52, 92, 235; of Americans and Japanese, 390; of gender roles, 272; and pedagogy, 193; similarities, 138, 174, 178, 202; of Westerners and Chinese, 171, 173, 214, 233

configurations of power, 91

conflict: race and class, 329

Confucianism, 137, 172, 206, 292, 385, 401, 406

conquest, 309–10, 349; and the Crusades, 11–12; French conquest of Egypt, 28–46. See also war

Constantinople, 3, 266; Franj attack on, 12–13; Hanoum on, 73, 77, 79, 82. See also Istanbul

consumption, 121, 218, 230, 237, 337, 341, 392; consumer culture, 127–28, 403

contact: four periods, xx

contradictions between capitalist economic system and culture, 229–30

control, 166–67; of capitalism, 179–80; controlling processes, 119, 123, 129, 131; economic, 179–82, 231, 344, 346; governmental, 180, 217, 305, 316, 320, 337; military, 406; political, 178, 409; social, xi-xii, xviii, 122, 130, 195, 201; of youth, 119

Coon, Carleton, xvii

Copernicus, 351

Copts, 18, 29, 36, 39, 43, 57

corporations: corporate America, 120–21, 130, 180–81; corporate executives, xxi; culture, 132; and democratic ideology, 129–30; Morgan Stanley, 236, 240; in China, 235–36; threat of, 166

corruption, 32, 43, 103, 112, 177, 273, 299, 321

cosmopolitanism, xvii, 417

courts of law, 267–68

crime, 73, 96, 267; burglary, 178, 243–44; in China vs. U.S., 177–202.; crime statistics, 177, 202, 243–47, 254; criminality, 201–2, 243; gangs, 178, 205; hate crimes, 254; in India, 147; juvenile crime, 201–2, 211; juvenile delinquency, 200–202, 204, 211; murder, 96, 178,